TRAUMA&
MEMORY

TRAUMA & MEMORY

Linda M. Williams
Victoria L. Banyard

Editors

SAGE Publications
International Educational and Professional Publisher
Thousand Oaks   London   New Delhi

For information:

SAGE Publications, Inc.
2455 Teller Road
Thousand Oaks, California 91320
E-mail: order@sagepub.com

SAGE Publications Ltd.
6 Bonhill Street
London EC2A 4PU
United Kingdom

SAGE Publications India Pvt. Ltd.
M-32 Market
Greater Kailash I
New Delhi 110 048 India

Printed in the United States of America

Library of Congress Cataloging-in-Publication Data

Main entry under title:

Trauma and memory / editors, Linda M. Williams, Victoria L. Banyard.
     p. cm.
    Most of the chapters in this volume were originally presented at a conference held
in Durham, N.H., in June 1996.
    Includes bibliographical references and index.
    ISBN 0-7619-0771-8 (cloth : acid-free paper) ISBN 0-7619-0772-6 (pbk. : acid-free paper)
    1. Psychic trauma. 2. Post-traumatic stress disorder. 3. Memory. 4. Recovered memory.
    RC552.T7 T73 1998
    616.85′21—ddc21   98-25342

00 01 02 03 04 05 10 9 8 7 6 5 4 3 2

Acquiring Editor: C. Terry Hendrix
Editorial Assistant: Fiona Lyon
Production Editor: Sanford Robinson
Production Assistant: Denise Santoyo
Typesetter/Designer: Marion Warren
Indexer: Teri Greenberg

Contents

Part I. Clinical Practice and Legal Issues in Trauma and Memory

Part II. Mental Health and Memories of Traumatic Events

Part III. Cognitive and Physiological Perspectives on Trauma and Memory

Part IV. Evidence and Controversies in Understanding Memories for Traumatic Events

Acknowledgments

There are many people to thank for their contributions to this volume. First, we wish to thank C. Terry Hendrix, senior editor at Sage Publications, for his support of this project, the professionals in the field of child maltreatment and family violence, and everyone involved in Trauma and Memory: An International Research Conference, which brought the authors of the chapters in this book together in Durham, New Hampshire, in June 1996.

Many colleagues helped us to make the conference a reality and to bring some light to an issue that has been fraught with much contentious debate. We thank the conference planning committee members for their assistance in planning the conference and presenting research findings and interpretations in plenary sessions. The committee included Lucy Berliner, John Briere, Doug Bremner, Jon Conte, Matt Friedman, Gail Goodman, Mary Harvey, Ira Hyman, Mary Koss, Elana Newman, and Dan Schacter. We also wish to thank all the conference participants and, especially, the authors who have contributed to this volume.

Siegliende Field and Tara Leary coordinated the Trauma and Memory conference, which resulted in the contributions published in this book; we are appreciative of the dedication and energy they brought to this project. We also wish to acknowledge the contributions of other faculty and staff at the Family Research Laboratory at the University of New Hampshire who assisted with the conference: Doreen Cole, David Finkelhor, Kelly Foster, Glenda Kaufman Kantor, E. Milling Kinard, Murray Straus, and Kaushalia Tailor.

Since the 1996 conference, at the Stone Center we have been fortunate to have the editorial and administrative assistance of Eden Osucha and the support of our colleagues at the Wellesley Centers for Women, Wellesley College.

Work on this volume was partially supported by the National Institute of Mental Health Training Grant 5-T32-MH15161 and by the National Center on Child Abuse and Neglect. Finally, we would like to thank our families and friends for their encouragement and support while we undertook this project.

Introduction

Most of this book's 26 chapters were first presented in 1996 at Trauma and Memory: An International Research Conference. This conference brought to Durham, New Hampshire, more than 300 researchers whose work focuses on this issue. Scholars from a broad array of disciplines and more than 15 nations presented and discussed research on trauma and memory, cognitions and violence, and the social meaning of and societal response to trauma. The conference sessions addressed methodological, theoretical, and ethical issues related to trauma and memory.

The conference was conceived during a time when the controversy about memories of traumatic events was fraught with contentious debate. Conferences, seminars, and meetings that we attended often provided little more than outlets for ad hominem attacks. It was the hope of the conference organizers that this international meeting would provide a platform for careful scientific review and discussion, assist in the integration of research and empirical findings from many disciplines, and contribute to a more useful dialogue about what we already know about trauma and memory, as well as what we need to know. Although many questions still need to be answered and the forward steps we have taken are small, the compilation of selected papers from the conference in this volume is one product of this effort.

Achieving a better understanding of memory for traumatic events—including trauma that is accidental (i.e., natural disasters) and trauma that is inflicted intentionally by others, such as the trauma associated with sexual and physical child abuse and with battering—is crucial both for researchers who study the effects of trauma and for clinicians who work with trauma survivors. Attempts to understand memories for traumatic events have brought together researchers whose work is focused primarily on understanding the effects of trauma and researchers whose focus is on memory and cognition. The contentiousness of the debate about the accuracy of memories of childhood trauma and the problems of false memory may not be solely political or impelled by litigation. Rather, it may in part be the result of communication errors, the different strategies used for clinical and laboratory research, and the application of clinical research methods to the study of forgetting of childhood trauma and of laboratory research designs to the study of implanting false memories. To date there has been little crossover in either direction.

One of the difficulties in understanding the nature of memories of traumatic events is that these are real, not laboratory-derived, events. The characteristics of trauma and its timing cannot be controlled by researchers. Much of the research specifically focused on adults' experiences with forgetting childhood trauma is based on studies of clinical samples of adults in treatment for the consequences of such trauma (war veterans, survivors of child sexual abuse, and so on); such studies often must rely on uncorroborated trauma histories and retrospective reconstruction of memory states. The research focusing on adults' "recall" of fictitious events has occurred in laboratory controlled studies that maximize specificity but draw criticism in regard to ecological validity. It is difficult to construct good analog studies of memories of trauma. Much of the work in this area has focused on suggestibility and problems of source attribution (that is, the memory errors that arise when an individual recalls information that came from some source after the event and when that individual goes on to attribute the information erroneously to the original event).

The studies reported in this book have been conducted by some of the leading researchers in the field, from a variety of disciplines. They represent work with both community and clinical samples made up of individuals who have experienced traumatic events and studies of memory in the controlled setting of the laboratory.

The book is divided into four parts: Part I, "Clinical Practice and Legal Issues in Trauma and Memory"; Part II, "Mental Health and Memories of Traumatic Events"; Part III, "Cognitive and Physiological Perspectives on Trauma and Memory"; and Part IV, "Evidence and Controversies in Understanding Memories for Traumatic Events."

Clinical Practice and Legal Issues in Trauma and Memory

☐ The authors of the chapters in Part I address clinical and legal issues that need to be considered in work related to trauma and memory. Berliner and Briere (Chapter 1) and Harvey (Chapter 2) discuss the debate that has been ongoing among therapists, clients, scientists, and legal professionals. Although Harvey is skeptical of some of the laboratory research, both chapters provide important evidence of a growing middle ground in this debate. Most researchers and practitioners, laboratory-based cognitive scientists, and trauma researchers now agree that both recovered and false memories of prior events are possible. The authors of Chapters 1 and 2, all clinician researchers, suggest that clinical approaches that neither discourage remembering nor discount the importance of memories, but at the same time minimize risks of distorting memory, are in order.

Part I also includes research on the memory functioning of children (Eisen, Goodman, Davis, & Qin, Chapter 3), adult female rape victims (Nishith, Weaver, Resick, & Uhlmansiek, Chapter 4), and incest survivors (Dorado, Chapter 8). These chapters reflect the complexity of memory for traumatic events and the fact that there may be multiple mechanisms that account for the forgetting of trauma. Piers (Chapter 5) discusses a characterological perspective on understanding recollections of trauma. Conte (Chapter 7) examines the intersection of memory research and the law and points to the problems with the science on both sides of this debate. Dorado (Chapter 8) looks at the goodness of fit between the law and the processes of memory recovery as described by incest survivors. Miller (Chapter 6) discusses issues that arise when teaching students about these topics.

Mental Health and Memories of Traumatic Events

☐ Much of the debate in this field has been concerned with the accuracy of recovered memories, situations in which individuals report recalling traumatic events that they previously did not remember. There has been much discussion about the mechanisms for forgetting traumatic events and the implications of the phenomenon for cautious clinical practice. But very little attention has been paid to the mental health consequences associated with problems in memory for traumatic events. Taken together, the chapters in Part II highlight the complex issues involved in trying to answer such questions. Banyard and Williams (Chapter 9) present findings from a study of women sexually abused in childhood that suggest that girls who were older at the time of their victimization and who have memory problems are more symptomatic in several domains. Brewerton, Dansky, Kilpatrick, and O'Neil (Chapter 10) examine the linkages among violent victimization, memory problems, and eating disorders in women from a nationally representative random sample. And Sheiman (Chapter 11) reports that sexual abuse survivors with prior memory loss are more symptomatic than those with no prior memory loss. Warner and Feltey (Chapter 13) describe pathways to recovery for four women survivors with recovered memories of childhood trauma, and Martin, Perrott, Morris, and Romans (Chapter 12) address special issues related to the impacts of research on trauma survivors.

Cognitive and Physiological Perspectives on Trauma and Memory

☐ The contributions in Part III broaden our view of trauma to include events beyond child sexual abuse and also examine the implications of cognitive psychology and cognitive neuroscience for our understanding of the nature of traumatic childhood memories. Hyman and Kleinknecht (Chapter 14) review the laboratory research on the creation of false childhood memories, offer a theoretical explanation of the processes involved in memory creation, and make suggestions concerning how this information may apply in therapy. Schooler and Baum (Chapter 15) examine how intrusive memories occur among survivors of a petrochemical explosion and how cognitive processes affect the experience and frequency of these thoughts. Schooler (Chapter 16) provides a review of the research that in his estimation provides a reasonable foundation for the existence of both recovered and fabricated memories.

New research has focused on the possibility that trauma can have profound physiological

effects on brain structures, such as the hippocampus, that are key components of the memory system. Prolonged stress responses that are created when an individual is traumatized may alter normal physiological stress and memory processes. This can lead to a strengthening of particular memory traces related to traumatic events as well as to gaps in memory, which may be described as amnestic episodes. This research is in its early stages, but it is further supported by several chapters in this volume. Bremner (Chapter 17) reviews the neuroanatomical correlates of the effects of stress on memory. Neuropsychological effects of stress on memory may provide potential explanations for delayed recall of memories of child sexual abuse and other memory problems. Palmer, Frantz, Armsworth, Swank, Copley, and Bush (Chapter 18) examine the developmental impact of chronic stress on children's neurocognitive systems and find negative consequences for children's memory and higher cognitive functions. Drugan (Chapter 19), in a laboratory study of the responses of rats to stress, found that coping with stress interfaces with memory for the event and provides further understanding of the complexities of the relationship between stress and memory. Schacter, Koutstaal, and Norman (Chapter 20) review recent findings from cognitive neuroscience and cognitive psychology that help explain the illusory nature of some recovered memories.

Evidence and Controversies in Understanding Memories for Traumatic Events

☐ Part IV of this volume returns to some of the more fundamental questions about evidence for memory disruption following trauma and factors related to the remembering process. Rooted in many of the initial questions about trauma and memory, the contributors to this section also return to some discussion of the controversies in understanding memories of traumatic events. Several studies document the memory problems of trauma survivors. Koss, Figueredo, Bell, Tharan, and Tromp (Chapter 21) found that rape had a substantial effect on memory. In a comparative study of memories for intense unpleasant and pleasant experiences, rape was associated with memories described as more emotionally intense but less clear and coherent. Romans, Martin, and Morris (Chapter 22) shed light on the defense styles of women who have experienced child sexual abuse. Azarian, Lipsitt, Miller, and Skriptchenko-Gregorian (Chapter 23) describe developmental modifications in children's memories of the 1988 Armenian earthquake. Niles, Newman, Erwin, Fisher, Kaloupek, and Keane (Chapter 24) examine the stability of memories for traumatic events in adulthood and describe fluctuations in veterans' reports of combat exposure. Kluft's chart review of dissociative identity disorder patients (Chapter 25) documents corroboration of memories recovered in therapy as well as inaccuracies in recovered memories. Kristiansen, Gareau, Mittleholt, DeCourville, and Hovdestad (Chapter 26) examine the characteristics of individuals who endorse beliefs in false memory and provide a sociopolitical context for understanding the debate about recovered memories of traumatic events.

Can we reach any definitive conclusions about memories for traumatic abuse? What should our agenda for future research be? How can we enhance the crossover between clinical and cognitive researchers? Undoubtedly, more questions are raised in this volume than are answered. We remain uncertain about the mechanisms for forgetting traumatic events. Clinicians and researchers who have suggested that the findings from studies such as those reported in this volume provide evidence for certain theories about the actual mechanism or mechanisms for forgetting have been harshly criticized. These critics suggest that deliberate nondisclosure, allegations of amnesia for secondary gain, and normal forgetting account for the "lack of recall" of traumatic events. They argue against any specific psychological mechanisms associated with abuse or other forms of traumatic stress. But the chapters in this volume contribute to a growing body of

scientific evidence on the nature of memories for trauma and the psychological effects of such memories that provides support for trauma theory. Together, these findings suggest that forgetting of trauma reflects the use of psychological mechanisms such as cognitive avoidance, dissociation, and repression as coping strategies for the psychological distress associated with prior traumatic events. There is much more that we need to learn about the conditions under which forgetting traumatic events may be adaptive and the conditions under which it may create difficulties.

There is also a profusion of research on suggestibility and memory that shows that memory is reconstructive and imperfect, that memory can be influenced and distorted, that confabulation can occur to fill in memory gaps, and that subjects can be persuaded to believe they heard, saw, or experienced events that they did not. Inaccurate memories can be strongly believed and convincingly described. A number of studies have been conducted to assess directly the implantation of memories for events that would be traumatic had they occurred, to examine types of events that are more likely to be implanted, and to determine the factors associated with successful implantation of memories for events that did not occur. Although most children and adults resist the implantation of such memories, most studies indicate that 15% to 25% of individuals will, after several attempts, report memories for fictitious events. This research suggests that individuals can be made to believe that experiences that did not occur did actually happen to them, but that they are more resistant to the implantation of memories for events for which they have less familiarity.

In bringing together research that speaks to many different facets of this issue, this volume allows a clearer picture of needed future research to emerge. Findings from studies using clinical or community samples of trauma survivors help us to see the need to create new laboratory research designs that are more ecologically valid. Of course, research ethics preclude any experiment that would attempt to implant memories of something as serious as sexual abuse, yet we have begun to see research such as that described by Hyman and Kleinknecht (Chapter 14) that brings actual autobiographical memories into the laboratory for further study and work with both animals and humans that is providing important clues about the psychobiology of trauma and memory.

The work presented in this volume also encourages us to move our research with trauma survivors ahead. Although much of the controversy over trauma and memory has focused on memories of child sexual abuse, there is clearly a much larger range of traumatic events that must be investigated. We need to move beyond documentation of the existence of both false and recovered memories to a more detailed and complex understanding of the perhaps multiple mechanisms involved in producing such phenomena. Furthermore, laboratory work on suggestibility suggests that it would be useful to design research studies that would examine how the dynamics of child sexual abuse, for example, might contribute to the creation of false beliefs of nonabuse. Future research could examine what happens when subjects are encouraged or pressured to forget, as well as the extent to which false memories of true events are influenced by fears and posttraumatic stress disorder or feelings of guilt, shame, or betrayal, or by the reframing of events to fit more socially and personally acceptable scenarios. Just as the social context can distort memory in the direction of the individual's falsely believing that he or she was abused, it seems reasonable that it can distort memory in the direction of dissociation and forgetting.

PART I

CLINICAL PRACTICE AND LEGAL ISSUES IN TRAUMA AND MEMORY

1

Trauma, Memory, and Clinical Practice

Lucy Berliner
John Briere

The prevalence of interpersonal violence and other traumatic events in our culture is now understood to be far greater than previously thought. It is currently estimated that between 40% and 70% of children and adults in the general population will experience at least one major traumatic stressor in their lifetimes (e.g., Breslau, Davis, & Andreski, 1991; Elliott, in press; Finkelhor & Dziuba-Leatherman, 1994; Kilpatrick, Saunders, Veronen, Best, & Von, 1987; MacMillan et al., 1997; Norris, 1992; Richters & Martinez, 1993). Equivalent or higher numbers typically are documented in clinical groups, even when limited to violent victimization rates alone (e.g., Briere, Woo, McRae, Foltz, & Sitzman, 1997; Bryer, Nelson, Miller, & Krol, 1987).

Exposure to traumatic events can be associated with a wide variety of subsequent psychological symptoms and disorders, including posttraumatic and acute stress, dissociation, anxiety, depression, cognitive symptoms such as low self-esteem and guilt, psychosomatic symptoms, sexual difficulties, relationship problems, substance abuse, and suicidality (e.g., Boney-McCoy & Finkelhor, 1995; Briere, 1992; Davidson & Foa, 1993; Herman, 1992; Kulka et al., 1990; Singer, Anglin, Song, & Lunghofer, 1995; Suedfeld, 1990; Weaver & Clum, 1995; Yule & Williams, 1990). These symptoms may persist at significant levels. For example, Kilpatrick and Resnick (1993) report that more than 12% of the victims they studied still had posttraumatic stress disorder (PTSD; American Psychiatric Association, 1994) an average of 15 years after being raped. Some Holocaust survivors report posttraumatic symptoms more than half a century later (Yehuda, Kahana, Schmeidler, & Southwick, 1995). Data on the lasting sequelae of childhood maltreatment in adults suggest similar symptom persistence over even longer periods of time (e.g., Mullen, Martin, Anderson, Romans, & Herbison, 1996; Neumann, Houskamp, Pollock, & Briere, 1996).

Faced with the evidence for acute and long-term trauma-related psychological impact, clinicians have developed therapies that specifi-

3

cally address posttraumatic distress and disorder. Such treatment approaches are predicated on the assumptions that traumatic experiences can cause psychological distress and that therapy is most effective when it addresses explicitly the emotional reactions, maladaptive cognitions, and dysfunctional behaviors resulting from such events (Berliner, 1997; Briere, 1996a, 1996b). Recalling the trauma is thought to be an important ingredient of treatment, and a focus on memories is often (although not inevitably or exclusively) considered necessary to alleviate posttraumatic symptoms.

Although typically a hallmark of trauma-focused treatment, remembering past experiences during therapy is not unique to the treatment of trauma survivors. In fact, recollection and recounting of previous experiences are important components of many forms of psychotherapy with children and adults, whether they be cognitive behavioral (e.g., Meichenbaum, 1993), psychodynamic (e.g., Hamilton, 1988), or interpersonal (e.g., Klerman, Weissman, Rounsaville, & Chevron, 1984). In these therapies, recalling and talking about significant or upsetting events is a primary vehicle for accomplishing important therapeutic activities, such as ventilation of negative affect, understanding the relationship of past experiences to present psychological status, and emotional and cognitive processing of negative life experiences.

Memory-focused interventions are an important aspect of psychological recovery for some traumatized individuals. However, the accuracy of recollections—whether accessed within or outside of treatment—may vary considerably (Briere, 1996b; Enns, McNeilly, Corkery, & Gilbert, 1995). Although the veridicality of a specific memory may or may not be especially important during treatment, it is always an issue in forensic and legal contexts. These two contexts, the therapeutic and the legal, exist simultaneously when therapy clients report being victims of crime or intentional injury, because these psychotherapy consumers are also potential witnesses in legal proceedings. In the latter case, memory may constitute the only evidence that exists regarding the occurrence of a crime. Its relative veracity is thus paramount.

Within this context, a debate is currently raging among therapists, clients, scientists, and legal professionals. This debate concerns, among other things, the accuracy of memories for traumatic events and the particular impact of therapy on these memories. Much of the controversy has been about the phenomenon of *recovered memories,* situations in which individuals report recalling traumatic events that they previously did not remember (Alpert et al., 1996; Enns et al., 1995; Lindsay & Briere, in press; Lindsay & Read, 1994; Loftus, 1994; Pope & Brown, 1996). Early commentators on the issue assumed highly polarized positions, asserting either that recovered memories are technically impossible (and hence "false") and invariably iatrogenic in nature or that memories recovered during treatment are almost always accurate and rarely reflect therapeutic demand characteristics (e.g., Fredrickson, 1992; Ofshe & Watters, 1993). Of late, however, a growing middle ground has emerged, with clinicians and cognitive scientists agreeing that both recovered and false memories of prior events occur, both in and out of therapy (e.g., Briere, 1995; Dalenberg & Carlson, in press; Lindsay & Briere, 1997; Read & Lindsay, 1997; Williams & Banyard, 1997). Yet despite this growing consensus, there is still considerable disagreement between some individuals in the "recovered memory" and "false memory" camps. It is likely that heated debate over the prevalence, etiology, and remediation of false versus recovered memories will continue into the foreseeable future.

Beyond the specific issues associated with recovered memories, the general validity of memories for traumatic events in children and adults has also been the subject of discussion. Memory researchers have long asserted the fallibility of eyewitness memory for events (e.g., Loftus, 1979), and in recent years a large literature has accumulated on the relative suggestibility of young children compared with older children and adults (e.g., Ceci & Bruck, 1993).

We do not intend this chapter to resolve the many extant scientific questions about trauma and memory; rather, we summarize here the available information for the practicing clinician. We acknowledge several seemingly undeniable facts. Clinicians working with children or adults who have experienced trauma must strive to create a therapeutic environment that supports the recollection and psychological processing of the impact and meaning of that trauma. Yet therapy, by virtue of its demand characteristics, and the trust and relative power conferred upon the psychotherapist, can inadvertently confound memory through inadequate attention to its intrinsic suggestive influences. Further, although the literal accuracy of all aspects of memories may not be of singular importance in the consultation room (as opposed to the phenomenological manifestations of the memory and the client's subjective interpretations of it), the majority of therapists agree that it is harmful for patients to have false beliefs that they were abused or maltreated (Walz & Berliner, 1994). In this regard, clinicians should be mindful that there are implications for what patients recall and talk about in therapy. Patient psychological status, family relationships, and legal cases may be affected by what is remembered or believed to be true or false.

Balancing these considerations requires that clinicians be knowledgeable about the memory-related impacts of trauma, the ways that memory works and can be influenced, and the role of remembering in therapy. Clinical approaches that neither discourage remembering nor discount the importance of memories, but at the same time minimize risks of distorting memory, are in order. Fortunately, there is a growing scientific and clinical literature that can inform trauma-specific therapy (e.g., Reviere, 1996; Williams & Banyard, 1997).

Trauma and Memory

☐ Understanding the impact of trauma on memory is complicated by the fact that, in the real world, uncorroborated self-reports often constitute the only possible data regarding specific historical events. In a case of child abuse or adult rape, for example, the only witnesses to the crime in question may be the victim and the perpetrator. As a result, outside individuals may be left to evaluate an uncorroborated report by a psychologically distressed person, sometimes in direct opposition to an equally plausible (and

highly motivated) denial from the only other person present during the event. In contrast, in laboratory settings, where it is possible to create and record events, ethical constraints preclude exposure to experiences that involve real threats of harm or death. Nevertheless, the few non-laboratory studies of trauma survivors where documentation is available provide important information about the persistence and accuracy of memories for traumatic experiences. In addition, investigations with subjects who report histories of trauma can elucidate the characteristics of these memories and the memory-related consequences of the events, even when veridicality cannot be completely established.

Despite the recent focus on reports of lost and recovered memories, it is clear that traumatic events are usually remembered and that the memories are often remarkably accurate (e.g., Koss, Tromp, & Tharan, 1995). Studies of memories for independently verified traumatic events have been conducted with children and adults, and for recent and distant experiences. For example, Jones and Krugman (1986) report a case study of a 3-year-old girl who had been kidnapped and whose assailant subsequently confessed. The child was able to describe the event and correctly identify the defendant. Terr (1988) interviewed a group of children with confirmed histories of trauma occurring before the age of 5 years. Children whose experiences took place when they were slightly older than 2 years could provide accurate, if fragmentary, information about what happened. Very young children seen in emergency departments for injuries provide accounts that are surprisingly accurate both immediately and 6 months later (Howe, Courage, & Peterson, 1994; Peterson, 1996). These researchers noted emotional and behavioral responses in some of the children that appeared to reflect memories of the events, even when the children could not articulate coherent narratives.

In most cases, adults also have good memories for recent and distal trauma. Witnesses to serious, violent crime usually are able to provide detailed and correct information about what happened, the participants, and other relevant details (Cutshall & Yuille, 1992; Yuille & Cutshall, 1986). The majority of adults remember documented childhood physical and sexual abuse experiences from early childhood (Widom & Morris, 1997; Widom & Shepard, 1996; Williams, 1994). Holocaust survivors recall many specific aspects of experiences that took place more than 50 years ago (Wagenaar & Groeneweg, 1990).

However, memories for traumatic events are neither indelible nor error-free. Terr (1983a, 1983b) reports that children and adults can misperceive traumatic events and may be inaccurate about time frames and sequencing of events. Studies of children and adults exposed to sniping incidents have found that, over time, participants' memories regarding their proximity to the shootings change. Those who were closer tend to recall themselves as having been farther away, and the reverse occurs with subjects who were more distant from the violence (Pynoos & Nader, 1988; Schwarz, Kowalski, & McNally, 1993). Some survivors of traumatic events appear to forget significant aspects of their experiences, including being maltreated, seeing mutilated bodies, and witnessing murder (Southwick, Morgan, Nicolaou, & Charney, 1997; Wagenaar & Groeneweg, 1990).

The characteristics of memories for traumatic events seem to differ from those of memories for other events. Tromp, Koss, Figueredo, and Tharan (1995), for example, asked a large sample of women to rate the qualities of their memories for rape and other unpleasant and pleasant events. Rape and unpleasant events were primarily distinguished from pleasant events by the affect associated with the memories. Contrary to prediction, although rape memories had a more negative valance, they were less well remembered, less clear and vivid, and involved less visual detail than memories for other negative events. They were also less likely to be talked and thought about. An additional study with this same sample of women confirmed the differences in memory characteristics between rape memories and memories for other events, pleasant and unpleasant (Koss, Figueredo, Bell, Tharan, & Tromp, 1996; see also Chapter 21, this volume). Appraisal of the experience as rape, per se, and the emotional valence of the experience were correlated with memory characteristics. However, there were

no direct effects of memory factors on psychological or physical symptoms, other than those associated with PTSD.

For trauma survivors, memories of traumatic events are frequently a primary source of distress. PTSD is one of only three diagnoses in the *Diagnostic and Statistical Manual of Mental Disorders* (*DSM-IV;* American Psychiatric Association, 1994) that are specifically associated with traumatic events (the others are acute stress disorder, or ASD, and brief psychotic disorder with marked stressors). Many studies have documented that PTSD occurs at significant rates among children and adults who have experienced, witnessed, or are surviving family members of traumatic events (e.g., Amick-McMullan, Kilpatrick, & Resnick, 1991; Duncan, Saunders, Kilpatrick, Hanson, & Resnick, 1996; Kessler, Sonnega, Bromet, Hughes, & Nelson, 1995; McLeer, Deblinger, Henry, & Orvaschel, 1992; Resnick, Kilpatrick, Dansky, Saunders, & Best, 1993; Saigh, Green, & Korl, 1996). The cardinal symptoms of PTSD are specifically memory related, including intrusive thoughts and recollections of the event, emotional and physiological reactions at reminders of the trauma, and other reexperiencing symptoms such as posttraumatic nightmares and flashbacks. Disturbing memory-related symptoms are commonly present immediately following traumatic events, even though not all victims develop full-blown PTSD (e.g., Briere, 1997; Riggs, Rothbaum, & Foa, 1995; Rothbaum, Foa, Riggs, Murdock, & Walsh, 1992; Yehuda & McFarlane, 1995).

At the other end of the spectrum is the phenomenon of traumatic amnesia. Among the diagnostic criteria for PTSD, ASD, dissociative identity disorder, dissociative fugue, and dissociative amnesia is reference to absence of memory for some or all of a traumatic stressor or other significant life event (American Psychiatric Association, 1994). Numerous studies have found that a significant proportion of adults who report a trauma history also describe a period of time when they did not recall the experience (e.g., Briere & Conte, 1993; Elliott, 1997; Elliott & Briere, 1995; Feldman-Summers & Pope, 1994; Herman & Schatzow, 1987; Loftus, Polonsky, & Fullilove, 1994). The rates of reported forgetting range from approximately 20% to 60%, depending on the study. Three studies of adults with documented childhood sexual and/or physical abuse histories provide confirmation that some survivors appear genuinely not to recall the events (Widom & Morris, 1997; Widom & Shepard, 1996; Williams, 1994). Further, in one of these investigations, 16% of the women who remembered the sexual abuse reported having forgotten and subsequently having recalled the events (Williams, 1995).

Given that several recovered memory studies have involved psychotherapy clients, it is possible that therapy itself could stimulate the development of pseudomemories (Loftus & Ketcham, 1994; Ofshe & Watters, 1993). However, because intentionally suggesting abuse experiences to nonabused subjects would be unethical, the proposition that false memories of sexual abuse or other trauma can be created or implanted has yet to be proven definitively. And several studies describe self-reported recovered memories that occurred in the absence of therapy (e.g., Elliott, in press; Williams, 1995). Nevertheless, based on the fantastical recovered memory reports of some psychotherapy clients, and the apparent suggestibility of some individuals in response to certain interventions, trauma-focused clinicians and researchers generally accept that treatment-related pseudomemories undoubtedly occur in some cases (e.g., Berliner & Williams, 1994; Briere, 1996b; Enns et al., 1995).

Memory Mechanisms

☐ The different ways in which trauma may affect memory can, for the most part, be explained by the established body of knowledge about how memory works. There is a large experimental and naturalistic literature examining the strength of memory, and how and why memory errors and forgetting occur. Memory for trauma is likely to share many properties of memory for other, more mundane autobiographical experiences. And especially, laboratory and field experiments of negative, stressful, or personally significant events provide opportunities to examine the potential impact of trauma on memory.

One of the most important and agreed-upon characteristics of memory is that it is reconstructive; memory is not a faithful reproduction of what was seen, heard, and experienced (Baddely, 1990; Schacter, 1996). Any particular memory is an amalgam of what was encoded at the time of the event, the knowledge base within which the information was integrated, interpretations of the meaning of the information, the adequacy of retrieval strategies, and the context of recall (e.g., Baddely, 1990; Reviere, 1996). Biological, emotional, and cognitive processes act to influence each of the basic components of memory: encoding, consolidation, storage, and retrieval (e.g., Schacter, 1996). Despite the fact that memory is subject to these various influences, it is generally agreed that the gist and central details of autobiographical experiences are usually well remembered for long periods of time by both children and adults (e.g., Fivush, 1993; Usher & Neisser, 1993).

Capacity for autobiographical memory appears to develop with age. There is no evidence that events occurring before the age of 2 years can be recalled in narrative form, although infants and young children do process and retain information (Bauer, 1996). There are various explanations for "infantile amnesia" and its offset, including neurological constraints, the development of an independent sense of self, the acquisition of language, and the role of social interaction (e.g., Howe & Courage, 1993; Nelson, 1993; Pillemer & White, 1989). Self-reported autobiographical memories for traumatic events occurring in the first years of life are unlikely to be the result of true recollection.

Even very young children have been shown to have good memories for experiences and to retain them for relatively long periods (e.g., Fivush, 1993). However, their memories are less complete and less well organized into coherent narratives; young children have less knowledge that can help them understand and make sense of information, and their memories fade more quickly (e.g., Fivush, 1993; Goodman, Quas, Batterman-Faunce, Riddlesberger, & Kuhn, 1994; Pillemer & White, 1989). Young children have more difficulty retrieving detailed episodic memories, and they require more external cuing and prompting to provide accounts of experiences (e.g., Price & Goodman, 1990). It is not surprising that young children's memories for traumatic events are often fragmentary, skeletal, idiosyncratic, and lacking in detail.

Although memory for the central aspects of emotionally significant autobiographical experiences is generally strong, it has been convincingly demonstrated that eyewitness memory in children and adults is susceptible to distortion (e.g., Ceci & Bruck, 1993; Lindsay, 1993). Numerous studies have documented that misinformation introduced during conversations or questioning about an event can be incorporated into subsequent accounts when memory is tested. For example, child and adult subjects sometimes make misattributions for the source of memories and come to believe that they remember information that was suggested in the course of experiments (e.g., Poole & Lindsay, 1995; Weingardt, Loftus, & Lindsay, 1995; Zaragoza & Lane, 1994). There appear to be developmental differences in the tendency to confuse suggested information and actually witnessed experiences, with young children being more vulnerable (Ackil & Zaragoza, 1995).

Not only can recollections of actual events be influenced, memories of entire events that never happened can be successfully suggested to research subjects. Some young children exposed to repeated suggestions about experiences produce elaborate descriptions of these nonevents (Bruck, Hembrooke, & Ceci, 1997; Ceci, Loftus, Leichtman, & Bruck, 1994). A minority of teenagers and adults can also be persuaded that they recall childhood experiences that researchers invented (Hyman, Husband, & Billings, 1995; Loftus & Pickrell, 1995). On the other hand, subjects are quite resistant to adopting false beliefs for highly implausible or unusual events (Pezdek, Finger, & Hodge, 1996).

Memory is more susceptible to influence in young children, in adults who are lax in source monitoring, and under certain other conditions. When memory traces are weak, or considerable time has passed, it is more likely that information from other sources will be incorporated (e.g., Warren, Hulse-Trotter, & Tubbs, 1991).

Studies that have attempted to mislead subjects or implant false memories have found that repeated attempts by authoritarian or presumably knowledgeable interviewers, using leading and suggestive questions, are associated with an increase in errors (e.g., Ceci & Bruck, 1993; Lindsay, 1993). Encouraging child or adult subjects to imagine or repeatedly think about a suggested event can lead to mistakes or false beliefs (Ceci, Huffman, Smith, & Loftus, 1994; Hyman & Pentland, 1996). Individual differences in dissociation and creative imagination are associated with the likelihood of creating false memories in adults (Hyman & Pentland, 1996).

Although it is clear that memory can be distorted and even created, all of the extant research on suggestibility also proves that subjects—even young children—can resist efforts to mislead them much of the time (e.g., Goodman, Rudy, Bottoms, & Aman, 1990). Memory is not so fallible that conversations, thoughts, and questioning invariably lead to significant errors or distortions (e.g., Lindsay, 1993). And it has been shown that mistakes and source confusion in children can be reduced or corrected (e.g., Poole & Lindsay, 1995; Saywitz & Moan-Hardie, 1994).

A particularly important factor in understanding memory for trauma is the impact of stress and the salience of the event in question. Some laboratory studies have shown that anxiety can impair accuracy of reports in children (e.g., Bugental, Blue, Cortez, Fleck, & Rodriguez, 1992; Vandermaas, Hess, & Baker-Ward, 1993). Studies of memories for shocking public events reveal that child and adult subjects are often wrong about the specific details of how they learned about the events (e.g., Neisser & Harsch, 1992; Terr et al., 1996). At the same time, however, there are data showing that emotion improves memory for the central aspects of events (e.g., Burke, Heuer, & Reisberg, 1992).

The ecological validity of studies of stress and memory has been advanced by investigators who have examined children's naturally occurring stressful experiences. Studies have been conducted of children who have received treatment for injuries or have undergone invasive urethral catheterization (Goodman et al., 1994;

Howe et al., 1994; Merritt, Ornstein, & Spicker, 1994; Peterson, 1996). These children evince strong and essentially accurate memories for these events, and there is little evidence of forgetting for the central aspects of the experiences.

In an influential review of emotional stress and eyewitness memory, Christianson (1992) challenges the view that stress has primarily negative effects and concludes that "there is little evidence that stress is bad for memories" (p. 303). Koss et al. (1995) extend the argument explicitly to trauma memories and marshal evidence that the salience and the presence of threat inherent in traumatic experiences makes them especially likely to be well remembered. These commentators suggest that emotional arousal focuses attention and leads to greater encoding of the attended-to aspects of a memory, at the probable cost of accurate recall for more peripheral or less significant elements. Such processes would seem to be evolutionarily adaptive to the extent that enhanced learning would assist with similar dangerous or traumatic situations in the future (LeDoux, 1994).

There may be additional mechanisms operating that are more specific to the nature of traumatic events and that help explain the unusual qualities of memories for trauma. For example, in some cases trauma memories are especially vivid, involve feelings and sensations, are intrusive, and are accompanied by sympathetic nervous system hyperactivation. In other instances, memories of trauma are less often recalled, are hazier in form, and contain fewer sensory components. Sometimes the memory is partially or completely lost, in spite of the fact that recall would be expected based on salience alone. These differences are thought to be the result of biological dynamics and/or coping processes associated with trauma.

One line of research has investigated biological correlates of trauma survivors' memory. Recent reviews have reported various findings regarding the neurophysiological effects of fear and intense emotion (Bremner, Krystal, Southwick, & Charney, 1995; van der Kolk, 1994). Extreme stress appears to exert effects on brain regions that are implicated in memory (e.g., the hippocampus) and may lead to sensitization,

fear conditioning, and failure of extinction. The persistence of intrusive memories and psychophysiological responses to reminders of the trauma that are associated with PTSD are hypothesized to arise, in part, from stress-activated changes in the brain (e.g., involving the beta-adrenergic system) that cause the salience of trauma memories to be especially enhanced (Bremner et al., 1995; Cahill, Prins, Weber, & McGaugh, 1994).

These commentators argue that the general memory deficits and the traumatic amnesia observed in trauma survivors also may be explained by the neurophysiological effects of stress. Memories for traumatic or especially emotion-laden experiences may be encoded differentially (i.e., partially at the somatosensory level, as opposed to more exclusively at verbally mediated levels), the brain structures involved in memory may be altered, or disruptions in the retrieval process may occur. Another biologically based theory argues that traumatic amnesia is a survival mechanism invoked to preserve secure attachment with a parental figure (Freyd, 1994).

As a perusal of modern trauma texts indicates, a primary explanation for psychogenic amnesia rests on the concept of dissociation. In fact, memory loss as a result of trauma is referred to in the *DSM-IV* as *dissociative amnesia* (American Psychiatric Association, 1994). Interestingly, although dissociation may be described phenomenologically (e.g., "a defensive disruption in the normally occurring connections among feelings, thoughts, behavior, and memories, consciously or unconsciously invoked in order to reduce psychological distress"; Briere, 1992, p. 36), the specific mechanism whereby dissociation actually might cause memory loss has not been explained to any significant degree. Writers (including the second author of this chapter) have used this term relatively loosely to refer to any defensive process whereby upsetting material is excluded or blocked from awareness. As our understanding of posttraumatic response increases in sophistication, the notion of dissociation may gain more precision as it relates to memory, or it may become clear that this concept serves primarily as a descriptive heuristic for a variety of different mechanisms and pathways to psychogenic memory loss.

On the other hand, some memory-related impacts of trauma may be the result of more conventional processes. Koss et al. (1995) suggest that cognitive coping strategies may account for findings in a community sample that rape memories are less intrusive and vivid. Similarly, Briere (1996b) argues that cognitive avoidance strategies may become activated semiautonomously, perhaps as a conditioned response to cues for painful memory. At a more voluntary level, intentional forgetting and voluntary thought suppression may be effective ways of decreasing negative associations and aversive memories (Koutstaal & Schacter, 1997). These active efforts at cognitive avoidance may explain some of the subjective reports of forgetting. In addition, depression or a repressive coping style may interfere with capacity to recall negative childhood events (Kuyken & Brewin, 1995; Myers & Brewin, 1994).

Another possible explanation has been advanced by Schooler, Bendiksen, and Ambadar (1997). In a study of corroborated case accounts of recovered memories of trauma, these authors report that not all victims had actually forgotten the experiences, although they believed they had. In most cases, the victims had sudden, intense onsets of remembering. Such events may produce the subjective sense that they were previously unaware of the trauma. Schooler et al. propose that some cases of recovered memory might more aptly be characterized as discovered memory.

Therapy and Memory

Trauma-Specific Therapy

As reviewed in this chapter, memory clearly plays an important role for trauma survivors and therefore is a legitimate focus of therapy. For patients with PTSD, disturbing memories may be the primary presenting complaint. Proven effective treatments for posttraumatic stress typically consist of repeated exposure of the individual to memories of the traumatic event. Exposure-based interventions such as flooding

and prolonged or gradual exposure have been found to reduce posttraumatic stress symptoms in rape victims (e.g., Foa, Rothbaum, Riggs, & Murdock, 1991), veterans (e.g., Keane, Fairbank, Caddell, & Zimering, 1989), and children who have experienced trauma (e.g., Deblinger, Lippmann, & Steer, 1996; Goenjian et al., 1997; Saigh, 1992).

Foa et al. (1991) compared prolonged exposure to a nonspecific supportive treatment that avoided specific discussion of the rape experience. Significant improvements were observed only in the exposure condition. Positive results have been reported in pilot testing of imagery rescripting in which adult survivors of childhood abuse vividly recall the experience and then alter the outcome (Smucker, Dancu, Foa, & Niederee, 1995). Similarly, cognitive processing, in which patients describe, analyze, and correct distortions in trauma memories, appears to be effective in the treatment of rape victims (Resick & Schnicke, 1993). In a randomized trial, this treatment produced significant reductions in PTSD (Resick & Schnicke, 1992). Eye movement desensitization and reprocessing (EMDR), a controversial procedure that involves having patients recall distressing aspects of the trauma memory while engaging in eye movements, has been reported to be successful in clinical trials (Lohr, Kleinknecht, Tolin, & Barrett, 1995).

Memory-specific treatments with children have also been shown to reduce posttraumatic stress symptoms. Children exposed to a massive earthquake who received a treatment that involved remembering and talking about the event and its aftermath were improved compared with children who did not receive treatment (Goenjian et al., 1997). Two controlled trials of abuse-specific treatment with sexually abused children provide preliminary support for the importance of exposure to, and processing of, traumatic memories. Cohen and Mannarino (1996) compared an abuse-specific treatment with a nonspecific supportive intervention for preschoolers and found improvement only in the children receiving the specific treatment. Deblinger et al. (1996) randomly assigned sexually abused children to one of three experimental conditions or to routine community service.

The three conditions varied as to who was the recipient of the treatment: child only, parent only, or parent and child. Children receiving direct treatment that involved gradual exposure to traumatic material had significantly greater reductions in posttraumatic stress symptoms.

These approaches have been tested with trauma survivors who not only recall their experiences, but are disturbed by their memories. No investigations have evaluated the effectiveness of trauma-specific treatment with patients who have no memories, or only vague memories, of the trauma (Lindsay & Briere, 1997). Part of the problem with treating those who have little or no recollection of a trauma, assuming that a trauma actually took place, is that the most effective treatments involve exposure to the traumatic memory—a strategy that obviously would be inapplicable in such cases. However, as Briere (1996a, 1996b) and others have noted, nonsuggestive, generic psychotherapy may gradually reduce the need for avoidance defenses, and sometimes may indirectly cue or trigger remote associations to trauma-related memories. These "new" memories then become available to be addressed through standard exposure or cognitive therapies. This contrasts with approaches in which "memory recovery techniques" or other methods are used specifically to elicit hypothesized unavailable material.

Iatrogenesis

Therapy, therapists, and some therapeutic techniques have been implicated in the creation of illusory memories of abuse experiences (e.g., Lindsay & Read, 1994). It is argued that certain beliefs and practices create the conditions under which vulnerable patients may come to believe, falsely, that they had been sexually abused in childhood. Therapist beliefs that are considered problematic include the following assumptions: that sexual abuse is the source of psychological symptoms, that many victims do not recall their experiences, that remembering is necessary for effective treatment, and that memory is relatively impervious to influence (Lindsay & Read, 1995). Therapist practices of concern include the suggestive use of hypnosis, guided imagery, bibliotherapy, and other therapeutic strategies in which the client is encouraged to think about or imagine possible abuse experiences, or when the therapist quickly forms an opinion that a client has been abused despite the absence of a report of abuse (Lindsay & Read, 1995). To date, however, there are few or no empirical data (in either direction) regarding to what extent such practices actually lead to pseudomemory production.

Several surveys of therapists have investigated the extent to which they hold such beliefs or engage in the presumed "risky practices." One survey of attendees at hypnotherapy conferences revealed alarming levels of endorsement of assertions that memories recalled under hypnosis must be true and that regression to past lives is possible (Yapko, 1994). However, other surveys of licensed mental health professionals indicate that most neither subscribe to the suspect beliefs nor use the identified techniques for the purposes of eliciting memories of abuse (Andrews et al., 1995; Polusny & Follette, 1996; Poole, Lindsay, Memon, & Bull, 1995). Although Poole et al. (1995) acknowledge that such practices are far from universal, they argue that even a nontrivial minority of therapists might affect large numbers of patients.

Many commentators agree that some beliefs and practices are inconsistent with research, are potentially risky under certain conditions, and probably have contributed to illusory memories in some cases (e.g., Berliner & Williams, 1994; Lindsay & Briere, in press). At the same time, it has not been proven that therapy is the primary source of recovered memories, true or false (Elliott, in press; Feldman-Summers & Pope, 1994; Williams, 1995). And therapy may afford the context in which remembering of previous forgotten experiences is a natural result. This may occur because (a) therapy typically involves talking about one's past and thus may trigger associations to otherwise forgotten or avoided events, (b) therapy-induced decreases in distress may reduce the need for defensive avoidance or dissociated memories, and (c) treatment may reestablish relatively rare affective states (e.g., extreme sadness or anger) that may, due to state-dependent memory effects, cue memories of traumatic events that led to similar states (Briere, 1996b; Lindsay & Briere, 1997).

In summary, the extant knowledge about memory and trauma converges on a number of basic propositions. Most traumas are remembered, and with a fair amount of accuracy. The memories are especially strong for the fact of the experience and central details. A significant subset of trauma survivors suffer from psychological distress because their memories are disturbing. Other trauma survivors have vague, hazy memories or memories that are recalled after a period of forgetting. Trauma memories are susceptible to error in many of the ways that memories for more mundane events are. Younger children and adults with certain characteristics are particularly vulnerable under some circumstances. It is likely even possible that false memories or beliefs about trauma can develop. There may also be traumatic impacts on memory that result from stress-related alterations in brain function and from psychological processes such as cognitive avoidance and dissociation. Together, these findings suggest that memory for traumatic events, although often relatively accurate and complete, is susceptible to influences that range from the impact of the event to the context in which the trauma is recounted. In combination with the undetermined possibility of pseudomemory production, such data emphasize the complexity of clinical intervention with those reporting posttraumatic difficulties.

Implications for Clinical Practice

☐ Memories of traumatic events arise in many clinical situations—as does the potential for memory distortion or confabulation. Adult patients may seek therapy or children may be brought for therapy because of the effects of traumatic experiences. Child or adult patients may reveal trauma histories in response to routine inquiry during assessment. Memories for experiences may be cued or evoked as a result of the process of therapy. What patients report or recall may already contain inaccuracies for a variety of reasons, or may be altered because patients are focusing on them or bringing new information or inferences to past experiences. And therapists may inadvertently create the conditions for memory errors or development of false memories.

There are special considerations that must be observed with child patients who reveal physical or sexual abuse experiences. As mandated reporters, therapists are required to notify child protection or criminal justice authorities when child abuse is suspected (Myers, 1992). In cases of previously unreported child abuse, therapists should refrain from detailed inquiry regarding the experiences until official investigative interviews have taken place, because any conversation has the potential to alter memories. In addition, therapists should be prepared to explain the specific questions or context that preceded the report. The legal system, more than therapy, is concerned with the literal accuracy of reports and will evaluate their validity in light of the circumstances of disclosure. Therapy can be supportive and address other concerns in the meantime.

It sometimes happens that children, especially young children, are referred for therapy that is diagnostically focused because of concerns about sexual abuse that persist even though the children have not given statements considered sufficient by the child protection or legal systems. Again, in these cases, it is especially important that therapists be cautious about how the subject of possible abuse is explored. Parents and the authorities may rely on the therapeutic process to reveal whether or not there has been abuse. And if these children eventually do make statements about abuse, there probably will be scrutiny of how the therapists approached the topic and exactly what questions or methods were used to elicit the statements. The weight given the children's statements will depend, in large part, on the perceived adherence of the therapists to investigative standards for interviewing.

Legal interest in the potential for therapy to influence memory may also arise with adults (Bowman & Mertz, 1996). For example, some patients may be victims of recent crimes or recall abuse from the past. Therapists must anticipate that patients will sometimes become involved in prosecution or choose to pursue civil law suits. These patients may have expectations that their therapists will be called as witnesses. This means that therapists should be aware that certain practices may be problematic in the legal arena or may even foreclose legal avenues for their patients. For example, in most jurisdictions, hypnotically "refreshed" memories are excluded as testimony. Therapists should discuss with patients their intentions with regard to legal actions and secure informed consent before embarking on therapeutic approaches that have to the potential to alter memories or lead to decreased credibility in the courtroom. In addition, under certain circumstances therapists may owe a duty to third parties.

Regardless of legal ramifications, therapists would do well to take note of the basic principles for interviewing alleged victims, even during initial exploration of trauma experiences in psychotherapy. First, accurate accounts of events are best elicited by approaches that rely primarily on encouraging free recall and avoid asking many questions or creating an environment that is especially directive or unduly suggestive. Further, just as reporting the facts of a trauma may be subject to influence or distortion by the manner and context of inquiry, so may the client's feelings and interpretations. For example, clients may accommodate to therapists who inform them that certain emotional reactions or beliefs are presumed to be normal or abnormal. They may not feel free to reveal all aspects of the experience or certain reactions to it if therapists communicate expectations or intervene too quickly to correct attributions.

For patients who remember their experiences and have posttraumatic stress symptoms, trauma-specific therapy is usually indicated. In fact, failure to use therapeutic modalities that are known to be effective in such cases may prolong suffering unnecessarily. Trauma-specific treatment may include approaches and techniques designed to promote emotional and cognitive processing of traumatic memories. The nature of the presenting symptoms and the patient's stability and capacity to tolerate restimulated negative affect determines, to some extent, the methods used and level of emphasis on memories (Briere, 1996a).

We want to emphasize, however, that recovering memories of trauma is not a goal of therapy per se, nor are trauma memories the exclusive focus of treatment. Trauma survivors often suffer psychological consequences that are best addressed by therapeutic strategies that decrease immediate distress (including the use of psychotropic medication, when indicated), increase internal stability and affect-regulation capacities, facilitate the development of problem-solving skills, and target beliefs and attributions that interfere with optimal psychological functioning.

An especially cautious approach is indicated when patients are uncertain about their memories, or when memories begin to emerge during the course of therapy. These are the circumstances in which patients may be particularly vulnerable to suggestive influences. They may be disturbed by not being able to remember clearly, and may explicitly seek assistance in enhancing or clarifying trauma memories. The need to relieve anxiety associated with uncertainty or the desire to locate explanations for current distress may cause some patients to "fill in the gaps" or reconstruct memories with material offered by therapists or drawn from other sources.

In recognition of these concerns, professional societies have issued position papers and statements cautioning therapists about the possibility of false memories and urging adherence to basic ethical principles and clinical standards of practice (Alpert et al., 1996; American Medical Association, 1994; American Psychiatric Association, 1993; National Association of Social Workers, 1996). Guidance is now available for safe practice and risk management with adult patients, much of which can also be applied to children (e.g., Courtois, 1997; Knapp & VandeCreek, 1996; Pope & Brown, 1996).

These statements and guidelines contain some general recommendations. Patients who are uncertain of their trauma histories should not be told that certain symptoms are pathognomonic for trauma, should not be encouraged to think about or imagine possible abuse experiences, and should not be placed in group therapy, where they will be exposed to other patients and their histories. In such situations, it is possible that a combination of expectations, source confusion, and social influence might act to create or distort memories, although the specific risk for such outcomes has not been ascertained thus far. It is best to allow patients to control the process of remembering, with minimal therapist intervention. Therapists may need to inform patients that memory is subject to distortion and that in some cases it will not be possible to achieve certainty about exactly what happened or even whether a trauma occurred. Further, to the extent appropriate, therapists should show concern for family relationships and refrain from advocating any particular course of action.

Therapists need not be reticent about routine screening for trauma histories, however, or about encouraging patients to talk about and confront traumatic memories when they are present. In fact, such activities may be of critical importance to eventual recovery from trauma-related distress for some individuals. When therapists avoid suggestive therapeutic approaches there appears to be little danger of significant memory errors or false beliefs as a function of treatment, although patients with serious psychological difficulties may distort memory (and understanding of the therapeutic process) without any input from clinicians. Ultimately, the clinician is faced with a technically challenging task: to facilitate the processing of traumatic memory while not significantly distorting or biasing it in the process. This requires respect not only for the healing aspects of good therapy, but also for the dangers implicit in any powerful treatment technique if inappropriately applied or insufficiently monitored.

References

Ackil, J. K., & Zaragoza, M. S. (1995). Developmental differences in eyewitness suggestibility and memory for source. *Journal of Experimental Child Psychology, 60,* 57-83.

Alpert, J. L., Brown, L. S., Ceci, S. J., Courtois, C. A., Loftus, E. F., & Ornstein, P. A. (Eds.). (1996). *Final report of the Working Group on the Investigation of Memories of Childhood Abuse.* Washington, DC: American Psychological Association.

American Medical Association. (1994). *Report of the Council of Scientific Affairs (1994): Memories of childhood abuse.* Washington, DC: Author.

American Psychiatric Association. (1993). *Statement on memories of sexual abuse.* Washington, DC: Author.

American Psychiatric Association. (1994). *Diagnostic and statistical manual of mental disorders* (4th ed.). Washington, DC: Author.

Amick-McMullan, A., Kilpatrick, D. G., & Resnick, H. S. (1991). Homicide as a risk factor for PTSD among surviving family members. *Behavior Modification, 15,* 545-559.

Andrews, B., Morton, J., Bekeriaan, B. A., Brewin, C. R., Davies, G. M., & Mollon, P. (1995). The recovery of memories in clinical practice: Experiences and beliefs of British Psychological Society practitioners. *Psychologist, 8,* 209-214.

Baddely, A. L. (1990). *Human memory.* Boston: Allyn & Bacon.

Bauer, P. J. (1996). What do infants recall of their lives? Memory for specific events by one- to two-year-olds. *American Psychologist, 51,* 29-41.

Berliner, L. (1997). Trauma-specific therapy for sexually abused children. In D. Wolfe & R. McMahon (Eds.), *Child abuse: New directions in prevention and treatment across the life span* (pp. 157-177). Thousand Oaks, CA: Sage.

Berliner, L., & Williams, L. M. (1994). Memories of child sexual abuse: A response to Lindsay and Read. *Journal of Applied Cognitive Psychology, 8,* 379-387.

Boney-McCoy, S., & Finkelhor, D. (1995). Psychosocial sequelae of violent victimization in a national youth sample. *Journal of Consulting and Clinical Psychology, 63,* 726-736.

Bowman, C. G., & Mertz, E. (1996). A dangerous direction: Legal intervention in sexual abuse survivor therapy. *Harvard Law Review, 109,* 549-639.

Bremner, J. D., Krystal, J. H., Southwick, S. M., & Charney, D. S. (1995). Functional neuroanatomical correlates of the effects of stress on memory. *Journal of Traumatic Stress, 8,* 527-545.

Breslau, N., Davis, G., & Andreski, P. (1991). Traumatic events and post-traumatic stress disorder in an urban population of young adults. *Archives of General Psychiatry, 48,* 216-222.

Briere, J. (1992). *Child abuse trauma: Theory and treatment of the lasting effects.* Newbury Park, CA: Sage.

Briere, J. (1995). Child abuse, memory, and recall: A commentary. *Consciousness and Cognition, 4,* 83-87.

Briere, J. (1996a). A self-trauma model for treating adult survivors of severe child abuse. In J. Briere, L. Berliner, J. A. Bulkley, C. Jenny, & T. Reid (Eds.), *The APSAC handbook on child maltreatment* (pp. 140-157). Thousand Oaks, CA: Sage.

Briere, J. (1996b). *Therapy for adults molested as children: Beyond survival* (2nd ed.). New York: Springer.

Briere, J. (1997). *Psychological assessment of adult posttraumatic states.* Washington, DC: American Psychological Association.

Briere, J., & Conte, J. R. (1993). Self-reported amnesia for abuse in adults molested as children. *Journal of Traumatic Stress, 6,* 21-31.

Briere, J., Woo, R., McRae, B., Foltz, J., & Sitzman, R. (1997). Lifetime victimization history, demographics, and clinical status in female psychiatric emergency room patients. *Journal of Nervous and Mental Disease, 185,* 95-101.

Bruck, M., Hembrooke, H., & Ceci, S. J. (1997). Children's reports of pleasant and unpleasant events. In J. D. Read & D. S. Lindsay (Eds.), *Recollections of trauma: Scientific evidence and clinical practice* (pp. 199-263). New York: Plenum.

Bryer, J. B., Nelson, B. A., Miller, J. B., & Krol, P. A. (1987). Childhood sexual and physical abuse as factors in adult psychiatric illness. *American Journal of Psychiatry, 144,* 1426-1430.

Bugental, D. B., Blue, J., Cortez, V., Fleck, K., & Rodriguez, A. (1992). Influences of witnessed affect on information processing in children. *Child Development, 63,* 774-786.

Burke, A., Heuer, F., & Reisberg, D. (1992). Remembering emotional events. *Memory and Cognition, 20,* 277-290.

Cahill, L., Prins, B., Weber, M., & McGaugh, J. L. (1994). Beta-adrenergic activation and memory for emotional events. *Nature, 371,* 702-704.

Ceci, S. J., & Bruck, M. (1993). Suggestibility of the child witness: A historical review and synthesis. *Psychological Bulletin, 113,* 403-439.

Ceci, S. J., Huffman, M. L. C., Smith, E., & Loftus, E. F. (1994). Repeatedly thinking about a nonevent: Source misattributions among preschoolers. *Consciousness and Cognition, 3,* 388-407.

Ceci, S. J., Loftus, E. F., Leichtman, M. D., & Bruck, M. (1994). The possible role of source misattributions in the creation of false beliefs among preschoolers. *International Journal of Clinical and Experimental Hypnosis, 42,* 304-320.

Christianson, S. A. (1992). Emotional stress and eyewitness memory: A critical review. *Psychological Bulletin, 112,* 284-309.

Cohen, J. A., & Mannarino, A. P. (1996). A treatment outcome study for sexually abused preschool children: Initial findings. *Journal of the American Academy of Child and Adolescent Psychiatry, 35,* 42-50.

Courtois, C. A. (1997). Informed clinical practice and the standard of care: Proposed guidelines for the treatment of adults who report delayed memories of childhood trauma. In J. D. Read & D. S. Lindsay (Eds.), *Recollections of trauma: Scientific evidence and clinical practice* (pp. 337-361). New York: Plenum.

Cutshall, J., & Yuille, J. C. (1992). Field studies of eyewitness memory of actual crimes. In E. Winograd & U. Neisser (Eds.), *Affect and accuracy in recall: Studies of "flashbulb" memories* (pp. 97-124). New York: Cambridge University Press.

Dalenberg, C., & Carlson, E. (in press). Ethical issues in the treatment of recovered memory trauma victims and patients with false memories of trauma. In S. Bucky (Ed.), *The comprehensive textbook of ethics and law in the practice of psychology.* New York: Plenum.

Davidson, J. R. T., & Foa, E. B. (Eds.). (1993). *Posttraumatic stress disorder: DSM-IV and beyond.* Washington, DC: American Psychiatric Press.

Deblinger, E., Lippmann, J. T., & Steer, R. (1996). Sexually abused children suffering post-traumatic stress symptoms: Initial treatment outcome findings. *Child Maltreatment, 1,* 310-321.

Duncan, R. D., Saunders, B. E., Kilpatrick, D. G., Hanson, R. F., & Resnick, H. S. (1996). Childhood physical assault as a risk factor for PTSD, depression, and substance abuse: Findings from a national survey. *American Journal of Orthopsychiatry, 66,* 437-448.

Elliott, D. M. (1997). Traumatic events: Prevalence and delayed recall in the general population. *Journal of Consulting and Clinical Psychology, 65,* 811-820.

Elliott, D. M., & Briere, J. (1995). Posttraumatic stress associated with delayed recall of sexual abuse: A general population study. *Journal of Traumatic Stress, 8,* 629-647.

Enns, C. Z., McNeilly, C. L., Corkery, J. M., & Gilbert, M. S. (1995). The debate about delayed memories of child sexual abuse: A feminist perspective. *Counseling Psychologist, 23,* 181-279.

Feldman-Summers, S., & Pope, K. S. (1994). The experience of "forgetting" childhood abuse: A national survey of psychologists. *Journal of Consulting and Clinical Psychology, 62,* 636-639.

Finkelhor, D., & Dziuba-Leatherman, J. (1994). Children as victims of violence: A national survey. *Pediatrics, 94,* 413-420.

Fivush, R. (1993). Developmental perspectives on autobiographical recall. In G. S. Goodman & B. L. Bottoms (Eds.), *Child victims, child witnesses: Understanding and improving testimony* (pp. 1-24). New York: Guilford.

Foa, E. B., Rothbaum, B. O., Riggs, D. S., & Murdock, T. B. (1991). Treatment of posttraumatic stress disorder in rape victims: A comparison between cognitive-behavioral procedures and counseling. *Journal of Consulting and Clinical Psychology, 59,* 715-723.

Fredrickson, R. (1992). *Repressed memories: A journey to recovery from sexual abuse.* New York: Simon & Schuster.

Freyd, J. J. (1994). Betrayal trauma: Traumatic amnesia as an adaptive response to childhood abuse. *Ethics & Behavior, 4,* 307-329.

Goenjian, A. K., Karayan, I., Pynoos, R. S., Minassian, D., Najarian, L. M., Steinberg, A. M., & Fairbanks, L. A. (1997). Outcome of psychotherapy among early adolescents after trauma. *American Journal of Psychiatry, 154,* 536-542.

Goodman, G. S., Quas, J. A., Batterman-Faunce, J. M., Riddlesberger, M. M., & Kuhn, J. (1994). Predictors of accurate and inaccurate memories of traumatic events experienced in childhood. *Consciousness and Cognition, 3,* 269-294.

Goodman, G. S., Rudy, L., Bottoms, B. L., & Aman, C. (1990). Children's concerns and memory: Ecological issues in the study of children's eyewitness testimony. In R. Fivush & J. A. Hudson (Eds.), *Knowing and remem-*

bering in young children (pp. 249-284). New York: Cambridge University Press.

Hamilton, N. G. (1988). *Self and others: Object relations theory in practice.* Northvale, NJ: Jason Aronson.

Herman, J. L. (1992). *Trauma and recovery: The aftermath of violence—from domestic abuse to political terror.* New York: Basic Books.

Herman, J. L., & Schatzow, E. (1987). Recovery and verification of memories of childhood sexual trauma. *Psychoanalytic Psychology, 4,* 1-14.

Howe, M. L., & Courage, M. L. (1993). On resolving the enigma of infantile amnesia. *Psychological Bulletin, 113,* 305-326.

Howe, M. L., Courage, M. L., & Peterson, C. (1994). How can I remember when "I" wasn't there: Long-term retention of traumatic experiences and emergence of the cognitive self. *Consciousness and Cognition, 3,* 327-355.

Hyman, I. E., Jr., Husband, T. H., & Billings, F. J. (1995). False memories of childhood experiences. *Applied Cognitive Psychology, 9,* 181-197.

Hyman, I. E., Jr., & Pentland, J. (1996). Guided imagery and the creation of false childhood memories. *Journal of Memory and Language, 35,* 101-117.

Jones, D. P. H., & Krugman, R. D. (1986). Can a three-year-old child bear witness to her sexual assault and attempted murder? *Child Abuse & Neglect, 10,* 253-258.

Keane, T. M., Fairbank, J. A., Caddell, J. M., & Zimering, R. T. (1989). Implosive (flooding) therapy reduces symptoms of PTSD in Vietnam combat veterans. *Behavior Therapy, 20,* 245-260.

Kessler, R. C., Sonnega, A., Bromet, E., Hughes, M., & Nelson, C. B. (1995). Posttraumatic stress disorder in the national comorbidity survey. *Archives of General Psychiatry, 52,* 1048-1060.

Kilpatrick, D. G., & Resnick, H. S. (1993). Posttraumatic stress disorder associated with exposure to criminal victimization in clinical and community populations. In J. R. T. Davidson & E. B. Foa (Eds.), *Posttraumatic stress disorder: DSM-IV and beyond* (pp. 113-143). Washington, DC: American Psychiatric Press.

Kilpatrick, D. G., Saunders, B. E., Veronen, L. J., Best, C. L., & Von, J. M. (1987). Criminal victimization: Lifetime prevalence, reporting to police, and psychological impact. *Crime & Delinquency, 33,* 479-489.

Klerman, G., Weissman, M., Rounsaville, B., & Chevron, E. (1984). *Interpersonal psychotherapy of depression.* New York: Guilford.

Knapp, S., & VandeCreek, L. (1996). Risk management for psychologists: Treating patients who recover lost memories of childhood abuse. *Professional Psychology: Research & Practice, 27,* 452-459.

Koss, M. P., Figueredo, A. J., Bell, I., Tharan, M., & Tromp, S. (1996). Traumatic memory characteristics: A cross-validated mediational model of response to rape among employed women. *Journal of Abnormal Psychology, 105,* 421-432.

Koss, M. P., Tromp, S., & Tharan, M. (1995). Traumatic memories: Empirical foundations, clinical and forensic

implications. *Clinical Psychology: Research and Practice, 2,* 111-132.

Koutstaal, W., & Schacter, D. L. (1997). Intentional forgetting and voluntary thought suppression: Two potential methods for coping with childhood trauma. *Review of Psychiatry, 16,* II-79–II-121.

Kulka, R. A., Schlenger, W. E., Fairbank, J. A., Hough, R. L., Jordan, B. K., Marmar, C. R., & Weiss, D. S. (1990). *Trauma and the Vietnam War generation.* New York: Brunner/Mazel.

Kuyken, W., & Brewin, C. R. (1995). Autobiographical memory functioning in depression and reports of early abuse. *Journal of Abnormal Psychology, 104,* 585-591.

LeDoux, J. E. (1994, June). Emotion, memory and the brain. *Scientific American, 270,* 50-57.

Lindsay, D. S. (1993). Eyewitness suggestibility. *Current Directions in Psychological Science, 2,* 86-89.

Lindsay, D. S., & Briere, J. (1997). The controversy regarding recovered memories of childhood sexual abuse: Pitfalls, bridges, and future directions. *Journal of Interpersonal Violence, 12,* 631-647.

Lindsay, D. S., & Read, J. D. (1994). Psychotherapy and memories of childhood sexual abuse: A cognitive perspective. *Journal of Applied Cognitive Psychology, 8,* 281-338.

Lindsay, D. S., & Read, J. D. (1995). "Memory work" and recovered memories of childhood sexual abuse: Scientific evidence and public, professional, and personal issues. *Psychology, Public Policy, and Law, 1,* 846-908.

Loftus, E. F. (1979). *Eyewitness testimony.* Cambridge, MA: Harvard University Press.

Loftus, E. F. (1994). The repressed memory controversy. *American Psychologist, 49,* 443-445.

Loftus, E. F., & Ketcham, K. (1994). *The myth of repressed memory: False memories and allegations of sexual abuse.* New York: St. Martin's.

Loftus, E. F., & Pickrell, J. E. (1995). The formation of false memories. *Psychiatric Annals, 25,* 720-725.

Loftus, E. F., Polonsky, S., & Fullilove, M. T. (1994). Memories of childhood sexual abuse: Remembering and repressing. *Psychology of Women Quarterly, 18,* 67-84.

Lohr, J. M., Kleinknecht, R. A., Tolin, D. F., & Barrett, R. H. (1995). The empirical status of the clinical application of eye movement desensitization and reprocessing. *Journal of Behavioral Therapy and Experimental Psychiatry, 26,* 285-302.

MacMillan, H. L., Fleming, J. E., Trocme, N., Boyle, M. H., Wong, M., Racine, Y. A., Beardslee, W. R., & Offord, D. R. (1997). Prevalence of child physical and sexual abuse in the community. *Journal of the American Medical Association, 278,* 131-135.

McLeer, S. V., Deblinger, E., Henry, D., & Orvaschel, H. (1992). Sexually abused children at high risk for posttraumatic stress disorder. *Journal of the American Academy of Child and Adolescent Psychiatry, 31,* 875-879.

Meichenbaum, D. (1993). Changing conceptions of cognitive behavior modification: Retrospect and prospect. *Journal of Consulting and Clinical Psychology, 61,* 202-204.

Merritt, K. A., Ornstein, P. A., & Spicker, B. (1994). Children's memory for a salient medical procedure: Implications for testimony. *Pediatrics, 94,* 17-23.

Mullen, P. E., Martin, J. L., Anderson, J. C., Romans, S. E., & Herbison, G. P. (1996). The long-term impact of the physical, emotional, and sexual abuse of children: A community study. *Child Abuse & Neglect, 20,* 7-21.

Myers, J. E. B. (1992). *Legal issues in child abuse and neglect.* Newbury Park, CA: Sage.

Myers, L. B., & Brewin, C. R. (1994). Recall of early experience and the repressive coping style. *Journal of Abnormal Psychology, 103,* 288-292.

National Association of Social Workers. (1996). *Evaluation and treatment of adults with the possibility of recovered memories of childhood sexual abuse.* Washington, DC: Author.

Neisser, U., & Harsch, N. (1992). Phantom flashbulbs: False recollection of hearing the news about *Challenger.* In E. Winograd & U. Neisser (Eds.), *Affect and accuracy in recall: Studies of "flashbulb" memories* (pp. 9-31). New York: Cambridge University Press.

Nelson, K. (1993). The psychological and social origins of autobiographical memory. *Psychological Science, 4,* 7-13.

Neumann, D. A., Houskamp, B. M., Pollock, V. E., & Briere, J. (1996). The long-term sequelae of childhood sexual abuse in women: A meta-analytic review. *Child Maltreatment, 1,* 6-16.

Norris, F. H. (1992). Epidemiology of trauma: Frequency and impact of different potentially traumatic events on different demographic groups. *Journal of Consulting and Clinical Psychology, 60,* 409-418.

Ofshe, R. J., & Watters, E. (1993). Making monsters. *Society, 30,* 4-16.

Peterson, C. (1996). The preschool child witness: Errors in accounts of traumatic injury. *Canadian Journal of Behavioural Science, 28,* 36-42.

Pezdek, K., Finger, K., & Hodge, D. (1996, November). *False memories are more likely to be planted if they are familiar.* Paper presented at the annual meeting of the Psychonomic Society, Chicago.

Pillemer, D. B., & White, S. H. (1989). Childhood events recalled by children and adults. *Advances in Child Development and Behavior, 21,* 297-340.

Polusny, M. A., & Follette, V. M. (1996). Remembering childhood sexual abuse: A national survey of psychologists' clinical practices, beliefs, and personal experiences. *Professional Psychology: Research and Practice, 27,* 41-52.

Poole, D. A., & Lindsay, D. S. (1995). Interviewing preschoolers: Effects of nonsuggestive techniques, parental coaching, and leading questions on reports of nonexperienced events. *Journal of Experimental Child Psychology, 60,* 129-154.

Poole, D. A., Lindsay, D. S., Memon, A., & Bull, R. (1995). Psychotherapy and the recovery of memories of childhood sexual abuse: U.S. and British practitioners' beliefs, practices, and experiences. *Journal of Consulting and Clinical Psychology, 63,* 426-437.

Pope, K. S., & Brown, L. S. (1996). *Recovered memories of abuse: Assessment, therapy, forensics.* Washington, DC: American Psychological Association.

Price, D. W., & Goodman, G. S. (1990). Visiting the wizard: Children's memory for a recurring event. *Child Development, 61,* 664-680.

Pynoos, R. S., & Nader, K. (1988). Children's memory and proximity to violence. *Journal of the American Academy of Child and Adolescent Psychiatry, 27,* 567-572.

Read, J. D., & Lindsay, D. S. (Eds.). (1997). *Recollections of trauma: Scientific evidence and clinical practice.* New York: Plenum.

Resick, P. A., & Schnicke, M. K. (1992). Cognitive processing therapy for sexual assault victims. *Journal of Consulting and Clinical Psychology, 60,* 748-756.

Resick, P. A., & Schnicke, M. K. (1993). *Cognitive processing therapy for rape victims: A treatment manual.* Newbury Park, CA: Sage.

Resnick, H. S., Kilpatrick, D. G., Dansky, B. S., Saunders, B. E., & Best, C. L. (1993). Prevalence of civilian trauma and posttraumatic stress disorder in a representative national sample of women. *Journal of Consulting and Clinical Psychology, 61,* 984-991.

Reviere, S. L. (1996). *Memory of childhood trauma: A clinician's guide to the literature.* New York: Guilford.

Richters, J. E., & Martinez, P. (1993). The NIMH Community Violence Project: I. Children as victims of and witnesses to violence. *Psychiatry, 56,* 7-21.

Riggs, D. S., Rothbaum, B. O., & Foa, E. B. (1995). A prospective examination of symptoms of posttraumatic stress disorder in victims of nonsexual assault. *Journal of Interpersonal Violence, 10,* 201-214.

Rothbaum, B. O., Foa, E. B., Riggs, D. S., Murdock, T., & Walsh, W. (1992). A prospective examination of posttraumatic stress disorder in rape victims. *Journal of Traumatic Stress, 5,* 455-475.

Saigh, P. A. (1992). The behavioral treatment of child and adolescent posttraumatic stress disorder. *Advances in Behavior Research and Therapy, 14,* 247-275.

Saigh, P. A., Green, B. L., & Korl, M. (1996). The history and prevalence of posttraumatic stress disorder with special reference to children and adolescents. *Journal of School Psychology, 34,* 107-131.

Saywitz, K. J., & Moan-Hardie, S. (1994). Reducing the potential for distortion of childhood memories. *Consciousness and Cognition, 3,* 408-425.

Schacter, D. L. (1996). *Searching for memory: The brain, the mind, and the past.* New York: Basic Books.

Schooler, J. W., Bendiksen, M., & Ambadar, Z. (1997). Taking the middle line: Can we accommodate both fabricated and recovered memories of sexual abuse? In M. A. Conway (Ed.), *Recovered memories and false memories* (pp. 251-291). New York: Oxford University Press.

Schwarz, E. D., Kowalski, J. M., & McNally, R. J. (1993). Malignant memories: Post-traumatic changes in memory in adults after a school shooting. *Journal of Traumatic Stress, 6,* 545-553.

Singer, M. I., Anglin, T. M., Song, L. Y., & Lunghofer, L. (1995). Adolescents' exposure to violence and associated symptoms of psychological trauma. *Journal of the American Medical Association, 273,* 477-482.

Smucker, M. R., Dancu, C., Foa, E. B., & Niederee, J. L. (1995). Imagery rescripting: A new treatment for survivors of childhood sexual abuse suffering from posttraumatic stress. *Journal of Cognitive Psychotherapy, 9*(1), 3-17.

Southwick, S. M., Morgan, C. A., III, Nicolaou, A. L., & Charney, D. S. (1997). Consistency of memory for combat-related traumatic events in veterans of Operation Desert Storm. *American Journal of Psychiatry, 154,* 173-177.

Suedfeld, P. (1990). *Psychology and torture.* New York: Hemisphere.

Terr, L. C. (1983a). Chowchilla revisited: The effects of psychic trauma four years after a school-bus kidnaping. *American Journal of Psychiatry, 140,* 1543-1550.

Terr, L. C. (1983b). Time sense following psychic trauma: A clinical study of ten adults and twenty children. *American Journal of Orthopsychiatry, 53,* 244-261.

Terr, L. C. (1988). What happens to early memories of trauma? A study of twenty children under age five at the time of documented traumatic events. *Journal of the American Academy of Child and Adolescent Psychiatry, 27,* 96-104.

Terr, L. C., Bloch, D. A., Michel, B. A., Shi, H., Reinhardt, J. A., & Metayer, S. (1996). Children's memories in the wake of *Challenger. American Journal of Psychiatry, 153,* 618-625.

Tromp, S., Koss, M. P., Figueredo, A. J., & Tharan, M. (1995). Are rape memories different? A comparison of rape, other unpleasant, and pleasant memories among employed women. *Journal of Traumatic Stress, 8,* 607-627.

Usher, J. A., & Neisser, U. (1993). Childhood amnesia and the beginnings of memory for four early life events. *Journal of Experimental Psychology: General, 122,* 155-165.

van der Kolk, B. A. (1994). The body keeps the score: Memory and the evolving psychobiology of posttraumatic stress. *Harvard Review of Psychiatry, 1,* 253-265.

Vandermaas, M. O., Hess, T. M., & Baker-Ward, L. (1993). Does anxiety affect children's reports of memory for a stressful event? *Applied Cognitive Psychology, 7,* 109-127.

Wagenaar, W. A., & Groeneweg, J. (1990). The memory of concentration camp survivors. *Applied Cognitive Psychology, 4,* 77-87.

Walz, J., & Berliner, L. (1994, November). *Community survey of therapist approaches to delayed trauma memories.* Paper presented at the annual meeting of the International Society for Traumatic Stress Studies, Chicago.

Warren, A., Hulse-Trotter, K., & Tubbs, E. (1991). Inducing resistance to suggestibility in children. *Law and Human Behavior, 15,* 273-285.

Weaver, T. L., & Clum, G. A. (1995). Psychological distress associated with interpersonal violence: A meta-analysis. *Clinical Psychology Review, 15,* 115-140.

Weingardt, K. R., Loftus, E. F., & Lindsay, D. S. (1995). Misinformation revisited: New evidence on the suggestibility of memory. *Memory and Cognition, 23,* 72-82.

Widom, C. S., & Morris, S. (1997). Accuracy of adult recollections of childhood victimization: Part II. Childhood sexual abuse. *Psychological Assessment, 9,* 34-46.

Widom, C. S., & Shepard, R. L. (1996). Accuracy of adult recollections of childhood victimization: Part I. Childhood physical abuse. *Psychological Assessment, 8,* 412-421.

Williams, L. M. (1994). Recall of childhood trauma: A prospective study of women's memories of child sexual abuse. *Journal of Consulting and Clinical Psychology, 62,* 1167-1176.

Williams, L. M. (1995). Recovered memories of abuse in women with documented child sexual victimization histories. *Journal of Traumatic Stress, 8,* 649-673.

Williams, L. M., & Banyard, V. L. (1997). Perspectives on adult memories of childhood sexual abuse: A research review. In L. J. Dickstein, M. B. Riba, & J. M. Oldham (Eds.), *American Psychiatric Press review of psychiatry* (Vol. 16, pp. II-123–II-151). Washington, DC: American Psychiatric Press.

Yapko, M. D. (1994). Suggestibility and repressed memories of abuse: A survey of psychotherapists' beliefs. *American Journal of Clinical Hypnosis, 36,* 163-171.

Yehuda, R., Kahana, B., Schmeidler, J., & Southwick, S. M. (1995). Impact of cumulative lifetime trauma and recent stress on current posttraumatic stress disorder symptoms in Holocaust survivors. *American Journal of Psychiatry, 152,* 1815-1818.

Yehuda, R., & McFarlane, A. (1995). Conflict between current knowledge about posttraumatic stress disorder and its original conceptual basis. *American Journal of Psychiatry, 152,* 1705-1713.

Yuille, J. C., & Cutshall, J. L. (1986). A case study of eyewitness memory of a crime. *Journal of Applied Psychology, 71,* 291-301.

Yule, W., & Williams, R. (1990). Posttraumatic stress reactions in children. *Journal of Traumatic Stress, 3,* 279-295.

Zaragoza, M. S., & Lane, S. M. (1994). Source misattributions and the suggestibility of eyewitness memory. *Journal of Experimental Psychology: Learning, Memory, and Cognition, 20,* 934-945.

2

Memory Research and Clinical Practice

A Critique of Three Paradigms and a Framework for Psychotherapy With Trauma Survivors

Mary R. Harvey

My goals in this chapter are twofold: first, to comment with a clinician's voice on the research agenda developing around the social phenomenon that has come to be known as the false memory debate; and second, to examine with a skeptical eye at least some of the laboratory research that is proving central to this debate. In addition, I hope to say something about the nature of clinical work with adult survivors whose psychotherapy may entail recall and examination of a traumatic past.

Within any substantive exploration of human memory and the nature of traumatic memory lie complex and compelling questions that should be discussed in an atmosphere of collegial inquiry and respectful disagreement. Unfortunately, the way in which this particular debate is being waged is anything but neutral. With increasing frequency and intensifying venom,

psychotherapy is being misidentified as a probable source of confabulated abuse memories among vulnerable young women who would rather whine about their past than accept responsibility for their present, and clinical observation is disparaged as a useful source of information about human memory.

The problem is exemplified by those authors (e.g., Loftus, 1993; Ofshe & Watters, 1993) who posit a virtual epidemic of false memories and false allegations that they then attribute to widespread psychotherapeutic malpractice and the apparently hypnotic potency of *The Courage to Heal* (Bass & Davis, 1988), a widely circulated self-help book for survivors of sexual trauma. Whatever research may ultimately reveal about the nature of human memory and the accuracy and authenticity of traumatic memory, these generalizations go far beyond the reach of available data and cast a chill on reasoned attempts at serious dialogue.

It is interesting to ask why so many researchers have joined their voices in solid denunciation of *The Courage to Heal*. To the best of my knowledge, there is no empirical evidence whatsoever that demonstrates, nor even a single study that has attempted to demonstrate, that one phrase—that is, "If you think you were abused, then you were"—(or even several phrases) in a self-help book could trigger an "epidemic" of confabulated memories of sexual abuse. Considerable evidence does exist to demonstrate the malleability of human memory and that external conditions can influence the accuracy and reliability of human memory. But one line in one book, however widely read, cannot be considered a singularly potent external influence.

Researchers who caution clinicians about the ethics of clinical practice and the potential for confabulated recall among vulnerable patients have themselves a parallel ethical obligation—namely, to base their warnings on established fact and empirical finding. Outside their own areas of expertise, scientists, like other professionals, are as gullible as any layperson. In bringing their opinions to a public audience, their goal ought always be to guard against exaggeration based on personal bias and/or error based on unexamined stereotypes—in this case, personal biases about types of therapy and stereotypes of psychotherapy patients.

Thus far, neither the science of psychology nor the study of human memory, nor the practice of psychotherapy, has been particularly well served by the so-called false memory debate. Neither has this debate hastened the recovery of trauma survivors or helped to repair painful ruptures between and among family members. Instead, it has developed the potential for actually impeding intellectual inquiry, discrediting and intimidating gifted and committed clinicians, silencing those who ought to be encouraged to speak, and trivializing the physical and sexual violence for which the United States is all too justly known. It is important, therefore, to locate this debate in a social and historical context, and to understand why it has presented itself with such force now.

History

☐ In the past 25 years, we have witnessed a dramatic transformation in public and professional awareness of the high prevalence and psychological harmfulness of child abuse and sexual violence. These same years have also seen significant reforms in the kind and quality of treatment afforded to victims by medical, mental health, and criminal justice practitioners (Harvey & Herman, 1992). Included among these reforms in many states are statutes that extend to victims of childhood trauma the option of filing criminal or civil charges once they have achieved majority age (see *Lofft v. Lofft*, 1989; Washington, 1991) or have acquired new memories or new understandings of abuse experiences located in the distant past (e.g., *Munsey v. Kellett*, 1992; *Riley v. Pressnell*, 1991).

Contrary to popular mythology, victims of violence have not come in droves to seek justice from the courts, nor have they ever as a group fared particularly well in court. Nonetheless, recently secured legal reforms provide new access to legal redress, and some adult survivors have made use of these reforms to seek criminal prosecution of their offenders or to bring civil suits against them. With these litigants have come their stories, and with their stories have come their memories—memories based on clear and continuous recall of childhood events, memories involving painful reassessment of long-remembered events, and memories based on delayed recall following a period of full or partial amnesia (Harvey & Herman, 1994). And with these memories have come the questions: questions concerning the accuracy, authenticity, and credibility of adult memories of childhood trauma; questions concerning the reality of repression; and questions concerning the nature and defining attributes of traumatic memory (see, e.g., Pope & Brown, 1996; Schacter, 1996).

It is, then, in the changing forensic context of newly secured victims' rights that these questions have gained new life and added currency among researchers, clinicians, the media, and the general public. In considering these questions, it is important that memory researchers, clinical investigators, and clinical practitioners begin to draw clear distinctions among three separate sets of issues that are too often merged and confused.

The first of these sets of issues is forensic in nature. It has less to do with what is "true" of a plaintiff's remembered past than it does with considerations of due process and the veracity that jurists and jurors ought to accord evidence brought forward as delayed recall. The particular issues are framed by the following questions: If and when delayed memories of childhood trauma arrive in court as evidence against an accused, should they be considered in the same manner as any other testimony? Ought they be supported by other forms of evidence? How should judges and jurors understand and make use of the research on confabulation, suggestion, and the fallibility of human memory? Lazo (1995) provides a clarifying look at these forensic issues and how they are being debated by the attorneys and adjudicated by the judges who are responsible for resolving them with case law and legal argument.

Associated with the forensic debate are a number of research questions that have yet to be addressed. Among these are questions of prevalence: How often are delayed memories of sexual trauma serving as the sole or even as the primary source of criminal or civil suits? How often do criminal or civil suits arise out of memories accessed in the context of psychotherapy? What is the evidence for the purported epidemic of so-called recovered memory lawsuits? Are there any epidemiological studies of this phenomenon? Are any being planned?

A second set of issues derives from basic research into the nature and reliability of human memory and into the role of strong emotion in the encoding, storage, and retrieval of emotionally laden material: How does traumatic memory differ, if at all, from normal memory? Does the emotional arousal characteristic of traumatic exposure heighten the probability of a deeply engraved memory? Might it instead have a disorganizing effect and actually interfere with memory storage? If traumatic memories are indelibly stored at the point of exposure, then why and how do they get lost? How and under what circumstances are they retrieved?

It is important that clinicians who work with trauma survivors be influenced in their clinical practice by contemporary laboratory research into these questions. Equally important, however, is the obligation of laboratory investigators to be knowledgeable of clinical research and respectful of clinical observation. Ultimately, the starting point of all scientific inquiry is observation and description—repeated observation, reliable description. There is available to the unbiased researcher a plethora of descriptive data, compiled by ethical, observant, and reliable clinicians (see, e.g., Alpert, Brown, & Courtois, 1996; Andrews et al., 1995; Briere & Conte, 1993; Feldman-Summers & Pope, 1994; Harvey & Herman, 1992; Herman & Harvey, 1997). These reports attest to the complexity of human memory as it is revealed and explored in psychotherapy and to the aberrations of memory and consciousness brought to psychotherapy by trauma survivors.

Within a large and growing body of descriptive psychiatric literature, for example, memory disturbances have been reported in many traumatized populations; indeed, aberrations of memory and consciousness are central to the diagnoses of trauma-related dissociative disorders and posttraumatic stress disorder (PTSD; American Psychiatric Association, 1994). Generally recognized symptoms of PTSD include both hypermnesia and amnesia. Like other PTSD symptoms, these disturbances of memory may be apparent immediately following the traumatic event or "after long periods of apparent adjustment."

Retrospective studies conducted with clinical populations suggest that some degree of amnesia is relatively common among adult survivors of childhood trauma, whereas a minority report a period of global amnesia followed by delayed recall. The proportion of patients reporting global amnesia in these studies ranges from 19% to 42% (Andrews et al., 1995; Cameron, 1994; Briere & Conte, 1993; Feldman-Summers & Pope, 1994; Herman & Schatzow, 1987; Loftus, Polonsky, & Fullilove, 1994; Roesler & Wind, 1994). In a prospective community study, Williams (1994) found that among a sample of 129 adult women whose childhood histories of sexual abuse were documented by medical and social service records, 38% failed to recall these events at a follow-up interview 17 years later. Memory researchers cannot ignore and dismiss these data. They must attempt to account for what has been observed repeatedly in clinical conditions, and they must design investigations that have as a goal the kind of ecological validity that makes laboratory investigation relevant to clinical practice.

A final set of issues raised by the false memory debate focuses on the nature of clinical practice with adults who are wondering or reporting about an abusive past. What should psychotherapy with these patients look like? Should clinical practice with patients who have long-remembered histories differ substantially from practice with patients who report newly acquired memories of abuse? How ought the therapist respond to patient speculations about the past? What is a leading question? What is not? How often is psychotherapy the source of delayed recall? How widespread is therapist manipulation of patient recall? How suggestible are trauma patients? Is verification of an abuse history clinically necessary? If so, why? If not, why not?

The literature emerging in response to these questions is one characterized by increasingly polarized and acrimonious debate. At the heart of the debate lie questions about the reliability of human memory, the gullibility and vulnerability of women, and the wizardry of psychotherapy. A point of view emphasized by some (but certainly not by all or even by a majority of) cognitive researchers is that human memory is characteristically inaccurate and unreliable, that adult recall of childhood events is particularly subject to doubt, and that doubt is compounded when recall of these events is not continuous but develops in adulthood, in a state of emotional distress (Loftus, 1993). A long-standing concern among these investigators is the extent to which memory for indexed events may be susceptible to distortion and confabulation, thus falling short of forensic standards (Loftus, 1979; Loftus & Loftus, 1976; Saks & Hastie, 1978).

A competing approach to the study of human memory argues that normal memory, despite its inaccuracies, is a surprisingly valid source of information about the past and a remarkably good guide to behavior (Brewin, Andrews, & Gottlieb, 1993). Supporting this point of view is a body of laboratory research demonstrating that human memory is quite accurate and durable for central events and for events marked by strong emotion (Bower, 1992; Christianson, 1992). Animal studies into the neurological substrates of memory concur, and further suggest that emotional arousal actually enhances memory storage and consolidation (McGaugh, 1990, 1995).

Clinical Implications of Laboratory Research: Another Look at the Data

☐ Two research paradigms are frequently cited as sources of serious doubt regarding the veracity of traumatic memories based on delayed recall, and as evidence of the probable incompetence and malfeasance of clinical practitioners working with trauma survivors. The first is that of the now widely cited "shopping mall" study by Elizabeth Loftus and her students (Loftus & Pickrell, 1995); the second is that of the "child interrogation" studies done by Steven Ceci and his colleagues (e.g., Ceci & Bruck, 1993). A third paradigm, developed by Ira Hyman and his colleagues, attempts, perhaps more successfully than these others, to deal with the issue of ecological validity in laboratory research (Hyman, Husband, & Billings, 1995). These are different paradigms, with quite different implications, and they need to be considered separately.

Loftus's "shopping mall paradigm" examines the susceptibility of adolescent and college-age subjects to the acquisition of false memories of fictitious events that have been described to them in some detail by trusted family members who report having been eyewitnesses to the events recounted. Under these circumstances—and, indeed, in a variety of other highly controlled laboratory conditions—some subjects can be induced to recall and embellish upon events that never happened. Loftus (1993) has suggested that a similar process may occur with patients who remember childhood abuse in the course of psychotherapy.

Generalizing from laboratory research on the fragility of normal memory to the nonlaboratory condition of family violence, Loftus speculates that most if not all delayed memories of childhood trauma are confabulations—that is, fictitious memories inculcated by the suggestive power of self-help literature and the leading questions of naive or unscrupulous psychotherapists.

One thing that can be said about the shopping mall paradigm and the conclusions that Loftus draws from it is that these are not new findings. Laboratory research has long demonstrated that any of several conditions obtaining at the time of memory retrieval—for example, the atmosphere in which questioning occurs, the nature and form of questions posed, subject suggestibility, interrogator expectations, and other demand characteristics of the questioning situation—can influence recall and enhance or minimize the likelihood of recall errors (Marquis, Marshall, & Oskamp, 1972; Muscio, 1915; Saks & Hastie, 1978).

The question that needs answering, however, is not whether human memory is pliable and can be shaped—it is and it can be—but rather whether psychotherapy resembles the conditions under which such shaping is likely to occur. When the question is put this way, the shopping mall study is simply not very informative. Loftus's research paradigm has little if any applicability to a typical psychotherapy encounter. For example, in the shopping mall paradigm, the story of an indexed event—that is, of a child becoming separated from family members while on a shopping excursion—is deliberately planted in scripted detail by a trusted family member. The clinical parallel would require not the naive, inadequately trained, and overzealous therapist suggested by Loftus and others, but rather a highly skilled and malevolent practitioner who is capable of deliberately planting a highly detailed, wholly inaccurate, scripted tale in the suggestible mind of an exceedingly trusting patient. Now, any clinician practicing in this manner ought to stop. It is clearly not good for the patient, and it clearly constitutes unethical practice. How apt an analogue is this to the kind of psychotherapy generally practiced by most clinicians? Absent

compelling evidence to the contrary, the best and most parsimonious answer to this question is simply "Not very apt." Those investigators who, like Loftus, assert that the practice of psychotherapy has great potential to induce confabulated memories of abuse are in need of a more applicable paradigm than that of the shopping mall study.

In the child interrogation paradigm originated by Stephen Ceci and his colleagues, school-aged children are exposed to repeated, misleading questioning by an adult interviewer concerning an actual event that they have indeed witnessed (Ceci & Bruck, 1993; Ceci, Huffman, Smith, & Loftus, 1994). The details of the event are well-known. Under the condition of repeated interrogation by adult interviewers, some of the children report events that never happened and, with increased interrogation, elaborate their reports with increasing detail. The investigators believe that the paradigm mimics the conditions of forensic interrogation that some child witnesses have been subjected to in the context of poorly conducted child sexual abuse investigations, and that these findings establish the potential for memory distortion and confabulation in such circumstances. Ceci and his colleagues (1994) further report that distorted and confabulated recollections of the classroom situation are generally difficult to dislodge, because they appear to replace the original memories.

Now, leaving aside the question of whether the children are in fact producing confabulated memories or simply conforming their reports to the demand characteristics of the recall situation, it does seem that the Ceci paradigm is analogous to the circumstance of improper forensic interrogation of children. Further, Ceci's data and arguments are impressive. Leading and misleading questions posed to children by powerful adults on repeat occasions would seem to entail some risk of confabulation. If you are interviewing children in a forensic context, you must proceed with caution. And if you are a therapist working with children, similar caution is warranted.

However, this caution must be qualified somewhat by another look at the findings produced by these studies. Among them are the following: (a) Absent significant and repeated manipulation by adult authority figures, most children (both younger and older), accurately recalled their experiences; (b) although a very sizable minority of younger children proved vulnerable to memory distortion in the face of significant and repeated manipulative questioning by adult authorities, a majority of children in both age groups continued to recall their experiences accurately despite such pressure; and, most important, (c) "confabulated" recall was not easily produced. According to Ceci, it took a minimum of 11 trials to produce this effect.[1] It is important for clinicians to remember that psychotherapy meets the conditions of repeated trials; it is also important for clinicians to remember that false memory is not easy to produce.

In other words, there is more to Ceci's paradigm than originally meets the eye, and more implications to be drawn from his findings. Although it is true that his data suggest the need for caution in forensic situations, it is not clear that the findings have greater applicability to the condition of psychotherapy than they do to that of child rearing. Indeed, the findings suggest that a risk of memory distortion exists in any circumstance in which a young child is faced with the demands of a powerful adult who has repeated opportunities to influence that child's reported recall. If we generalize from Ceci's findings not to the condition of forensic interrogation and not to the condition of psychotherapy with adult survivors, but instead to conditions obtaining in abusive homes, then we would expect at least some child victims—particularly younger child victims—to conform their reports, their memories, and their interpretations of abuse events to the demands of a perpetrator. And we might further expect these distorted memories and erroneous interpretations to be quite enduring. Indeed, Ceci's findings would lead us to predict exactly the kind of phenomena that clinicians often witness in clinical settings.

A third research paradigm bearing on the false memory debate has been developed by Ira Hyman and his colleagues (Hyman et al., 1995; Hyman & Pentland, 1996). Like Loftus, Hyman has sought in his studies to produce false memories of childhood in college-age students. Like Ceci, Hyman takes the issue of ecological validity quite seriously. The aims of his experiments are to illuminate the process by which confabulated memories might be constructed and to identify the conditions necessary to produce false memory. The paradigm entails these steps: (a) Information about subjects' real-life childhood experiences is gathered from subjects' parents; (b) subjects are then asked to recall three to five real-life events and one "nonevent," which are described by the investigator as having been reported by the parents; (c) repeated interviews are conducted with the subjects about both the real events and the nonevents in an effort to produce false memories of the nonevents; and, finally, (d) researchers suggest to the subjects that with mental practice—that is, by imagining events or just thinking about them—they will begin to remember more and more details about the events (both real and nonreal) they are being asked to recall.

It is important to note, and to emphasize the findings, that under these conditions, no subject falsely remembered a nonevent at an initial recall trial. Moreover, in subsequent trials, 75% of Hyman's subjects continued to recall only true events and never falsely recalled nonevents. Among the 25% who eventually did "falsely recall," half did so clearly (12.5% of the total sample), five subjects (10% of the sample) did so less clearly, and two subjects reported evoking a clear image of the nonevent, but also drew a distinction between "image" and "memory." Repeated inducements to "practice"—to remember the indexed events and, possibly, to visually image these events—apparently led some subjects to produce increased detail concerning both the true and the false events.

Among the most important of Hyman's findings are those concerning the conditions underlying the production of false memories. The single most important factor identified by these studies was that the event remembered be both generally plausible (i.e., a familiar experience to many) and personally plausible (i.e., something that the subject would say might well have happened in his or her family). Also important was the suggestion from a credible source that image generation or continued reflection (i.e., some form of mental practice) would improve recall (Hyman & Pentland, 1996; see also Hyman & Kleinknecht, Chapter 14, this volume). In addition, susceptibility to false recall was increased by the additional suggestion that family members had witnessed and reported the nonevent, by repeated trials of a subject's effort to remember the event, and by idiosyncratic cognitive and personality variables.

With the caveat that virtually all memories contain erroneous as well as factual information, the primary implication of Hyman's findings for clinical practice is that memory for personal events is generally reliable and can be trusted. There is no compelling reason for a therapist to approach the patient who reports childhood sexual abuse with great skepticism. This is especially the case when a patient's memories of abuse existed prior to entering therapy, are largely or completely continuous, did not arise in a context of intense or deliberate suggestion, and are both generally and personally plausible. So long as therapy does not entail the suggestion that specific events or categories of events "probably" or "almost definitely" happened, it is not likely that therapy will generate memories of negative events that are generally and personally implausible.

Overall, studies of memory distortion in both children and adults suggest that errors in recall are most likely to occur in retrieval conditions marked by biased, repeated, and misleading questions posed to particularly suggestible subjects. Such errors are least likely to occur under conditions of freely generated narrative report produced in an atmosphere that permits uncertainty while providing positive support for accurate, clear, and independent recall (Brown, 1995; Ceci & Bruck, 1993; Goodman, Quas, Batterman-Faunce, Riddlesberger, & Kuhn, 1994; Lindsay & Read, 1994; Marquis et al., 1972; Saywitz & Moan-Hardie, 1994). Hopefully, these conditions are analogous to most practices of psychotherapy. As research paradigms achieve ecological validity, research findings appear to pose little challenge to sound clinical practice. Methodological advances in the study of traumatic memory might be realized if clinicians and clinical researchers could

literally be paired with memory researchers to interview traumatized patients jointly; a precondition for such research would be respect for both the clinician and the value of clinical observation.

Psychotherapy and Delayed Recall: The Contribution of Clinical Investigation

☐ Two clinical investigations have undertaken to learn something about the role of psychotherapy in the memory retrieval process. In a study by Feldman-Summers and Pope (1994), 56% of subjects reporting delayed recall of childhood trauma indicated that they had recovered at least some of their memories while in psychotherapy; 44% indicated that memory recovery had occurred in other contexts. A more recent survey of 810 case reports from British psychologists found that most patients with delayed recall of childhood trauma had acquired their memories prior to entering any psychotherapeutic treatment. Approximately one in four practitioners had clients who were currently recovering memories of childhood sexual abuse, and about one in five described patients who had experienced delayed recall of childhood sexual abuse in a prior treatment (Andrews et al., 1995).

To date, there have been relatively few studies on the verifiability of traumatic childhood memories reported during psychotherapy. Herman and Schatzow (1987) found that a majority (74%) of 53 outpatients reporting recall of childhood sexual abuse were able to obtain some confirming evidence from independent sources. In their study of female adolescent patients with borderline personality disorder, Westen, Ludolph, Misle, Ruffins, and Block (1990) obtained independent confirmation in all 14 cases (100%) where childhood sexual abuse was reported. In a retrospective chart review of child and adolescent inpatients with dissociative disorders, Coons (1994) found collateral information confirming patients' accounts of childhood abuse in 20 out of 21 cases (95%). And Silk, Lee, Hill, and Lohr (1995) obtained independent confirmation of patients' reports of childhood sexual abuse from family interviews in 8 of 11 cases (73%). These consistent results indicate that the majority of patients' retrospective reports of childhood trauma are reliable and present no unusual problems with verification.

Some degree of amnesia is not uncommon in the clinical presentation of trauma survivors (including adult survivors of childhood trauma), nor is the phenomenon of "delayed recall" uncommon in this group (Elliott & Briere, 1995; Harvey & Herman, 1994). Though it seems that the retrieval process is triggered by rather idiosyncratic connections between contemporary and earlier events, there is still much we have to learn about the process of delayed recall. However, many researchers suspect that when the abuse has occurred in a relational context, the retrieval cues, or "triggers," may be relational as well. Thus delayed memories of sexual abuse (and delayed interpretations of long-remembered abuse experiences) may first express themselves in the context of a sexual relationship, or when the survivor marries, or gives birth to a child, or when her or his child reaches the age at which the survivor was first abused. Delayed recall may also occur when the victim achieves economic independence from a perpetrator, or when another victim of the same perpetrator discloses the abuse. A recent example of this phenomenon is the case of Father Porter in Massachusetts.

Clinical Encounters With Traumatic Memory

☐ Now, to questions about the clinical work. What does "memory work" with trauma survivors entail? Specifically, what ought we be doing in our 50-minute hours to help patients recover and make meaning of their pasts? How important (and how likely) is "total recall"? How important is accuracy of recall? When do we encourage patients to search actively for images and details of an unremembered past, and when do we discourage it? What does memory work look like over the course of treatment and recovery? What is the therapist's role and what are the limits of that role in the patient's remembering process?

At the Victims of Violence Program, a "stages by dimensions" (Lebowitz, Harvey, & Herman, 1992) view of the recovery process provides a theoretical framework for memory work with adult survivors. Within this framework, a multidimensional definition of trauma recovery (Harvey, in press; Harvey & Harney, 1997; Harvey & Herman, 1994) identifies specific treatment outcome goals and a stages-of-recovery model describes how clinical work with trauma survivors progresses toward these goals through each of three recovery stages (Herman, 1992).

Among the recovery criteria described by this framework are three that consider the role of memory in recovery. The first of these is that the patient acquire new or renewed authority over the remembering process. Traumatic memory assumes control over daily life, so that life for the survivor becomes a barrage of disturbing associations, unbidden intrusions, and amnesic gaps that render these intrusions incomprehensible. The aim of psychotherapy with trauma patients is to change the balance of power between the survivors and their memories: to enable survivors to recall or not recall the events of a distant past, as they choose, and to understand their own agency in selecting particular remembrances for reflection. Partly, the work assures that whatever may have been stored at Time 1 is available for voluntary remembrance at Time 2. Another part of the work is to place once fragmented and incomprehensible images into a narrative and associative context that adds meaning to these remembrances, even as it deprives them of their posttraumatic hold.

A second aim of memory work with trauma survivors is the integration of memory and affect. Often, patients who can recite detailed recollections of horrific events are unable to convey anything in the way of affect about these events. Also common are patients who cannot make sense of their night terrors and dreams, who can relate terrifying fragments of something and yet make no sense of the fragments. The work in therapy is to bring about an integration of these often polar experiences: to place traumatic remembrance in an affective as well as a narrative context. The recovered survivor will feel her or his history. Some of the feelings will mirror those that accompanied the original trauma; terrifying events will be remembered with some remembrance of the fear, violations with some of the anger and rage. Equally important, however, is that these memories will be associated with feelings in the here and now. The survivor who recalls her terror and fear may now feel anger or sadness as well. The combat veteran who banished his fear from awareness will revisit that fear and come to feel sorrow and regret for what then followed from fear. The point of the work is not to relive the past, but to recontextualize it.

A third sign of recovery in this model is that of meaning making. In their recovery process, survivors will come to know not only more of what happened, but also something about why and how it happened. Their review of the past will reveal the kind of context and flow of events that can transform traumatic memory to normal memory. They will be able to acknowledge and grieve at what happened to them, and they will be able to leave it behind. They will be able to approach the future with some kind of self-affirming, life-affirming understanding of their own history. Making meaning of the past is for each survivor deeply personal and psychologically grueling work. The clinician's role in the process is not to shape it or impose upon it his or her own understanding of things, but rather to bear witness to it.

Clinical work toward these outcomes progresses through a series of identifiable stages. Each stage entails a particular kind of work. Early in recovery, the overarching aims are those of safety, stabilization, and self-care. Here, the memory work focuses on the containment of the traumatic material, on establishing distinctions between past and present events, and on fostering skills for managing the symptoms of traumatic memory.

The second stage of treatment begins when safety has been reliably established and when the patient's investment in daily functioning is secure. The therapeutic work turns decidedly inward and may entail an intense exploration of the past. In seeking authority over the remembering process, the survivor will begin to fill in the amnesic gaps and draw connections between things felt and things remembered.

The final stage of recovery involves the safe embrace of a relational existence. The active pursuit and integration of the past gives way to an emphasis on the present. The work may involve a deepening of the survivor's capacity for intimate connectedness, a renegotiation of family relationships that can be repaired and/or final grieving for those that cannot.

Within this framework, the most apt characterization of the adult survivor is that of one who arrives at adulthood with some but not all of her or his memories intact, who at some point in time (often associated with a clear precipitant and typically in a state of considerable distress) begins to confront and rethink the past (blending new memories with earlier ones, new assessments and explanations with alternative ones), and who gradually constructs a meaningful and largely verifiable personal history—a history that is patently "true" though never complete and never wholly accurate in all detail. The process of discovering one's history is not an all-or-none event, does not hang on the accurate and detailed recall of specific events, and is seldom accomplished without a search for confirmation of acts and verification in the remembrances of others.

Psychotherapy With Adult Survivors of Childhood Trauma

☐ Most patients who enter psychotherapy for help in dealing with a traumatic past do so because of what they do remember, and not because of what they do not. This decision is precipitated by years of silence and secrecy, and not by years of amnesia. These patients are hoping to understand more fully the impact of a long-remembered past. Others may find themselves newly preoccupied with long-remembered events and feel stunned by their extreme emotional reactions to new understandings of these events. They enter therapy for help in managing their distress, for assistance in absorbing and "metabolizing" their new understandings, and, sometimes, for help in resolving the issue of family disclosure. Still others have acquired new memories that are deeply troubling. Although these new memories may indeed become a focus of psychotherapy, psycho-therapy is not the source of the memories. When clinicians work with trauma survivors who are experiencing distress as a result of traumatic remembrances, the work typically involves the containment of runaway affect and help with stabilization of functioning, not an archaeologi-cal search for more in the way of traumatic recall. Contrary to the portrait of clinical work with trauma survivors being promulgated by the false memory literature, clinical exploration of the traumatic past does not seek to uncover more and more horror, or to assign blame and responsibility for adult life to others; rather, its goals are to help the adult survivor assign mean-ing and comprehensibility to the past, to facili-tate the integration of traumatic remembrance into an ongoing personal narrative, and to help the patient grieve over the past and ultimately be freed of it.

Note

1. Ceci made this observation at the Invited Symposium on Memory Distortion, Harvard University, 1994.

References

Alpert, J. L., Brown, L. S., & Courtois, C. A. (1996). Symp-tomatic clients and memories of childhood abuse: What the trauma and childhood sexual abuse literature tells us. In J. L. Alpert, L. S. Brown, S. J. Ceci, C. A. Courtois, E. F. Loftus, & P. A. Ornstein (Eds.), *Final report of the Working Group on the Investigation of Memories of Childhood Abuse.* Washington, DC: American Psycho-logical Association.

American Psychiatric Association. (1994). *Diagnostic and statistical manual of mental disorders* (4th ed.). Wash-ington, DC: Author.

Andrews, B., Morton, J., Bekeriaan, D. A., Brewin, C. R., Davies, G. M., & Mollon, P. (1995). The recovery of memories in clinical practice: Experiences and beliefs of British Psychological Society practitioners. *Psy-chologist, 8,* 209-214.

Bass, E., & Davis, L. (1988). *The courage to heal: A guide for women survivors of child sexual abuse.* New York: Harper & Row.

Bower, G. H. (1992). How might emotions affect learning? In S.-A. Christianson (Ed.), *The handbook of emotion and memory: Research and theory* (pp. 3-33). Hillsdale, NJ: Lawrence Erlbaum.

Brewin, C. R., Andrews, B., & Gottlieb, I. H. (1993). Psy-chopathology and early experience: A reappraisal of ret-rospective reports. *Psychological Bulletin, 113,* 82-98.

Briere, J., & Conte, J. R. (1993). Self-reported amnesia for abuse in adults molested as children. *Journal of Trau-matic Stress, 6,* 21-31.

Brown, D. (1995). Pseudomemories, the standard of sci-ence, and the standard of care in trauma treatment. *American Journal of Clinical Hypnosis, 37,* 1-24.

Cameron, C. (1994). Women survivors confronting their abusers: Issues, decisions, and outcomes. *Journal of Child Sexual Abuse, 3,* 7-35.

Ceci, S. J., & Bruck, M. (1993). Suggestibility of the child witness: A historical review and synthesis. *Psychologi-cal Bulletin, 113,* 403-439.

Ceci, S. J., Huffman, M. L. C., Smith, E., & Loftus, E. F. (1994). Repeatedly thinking about a nonevent: Source misattributions among preschoolers. *Consciousness and Cognition, 3,* 388-407.

Christianson, S.-A. (1992). Remembering emotional events: Potential mechanisms. In S.-A. Christianson (Ed.), *The handbook of emotion and memory: Research and theory* (pp. 307-340). Hillsdale, NJ: Lawrence Erlbaum.

Coons, P. M. (1994). Confirmation of childhood abuse in child and adolescent cases of multiple personality dis-order and dissociative disorder not otherwise specified. *Journal of Nervous and Mental Disease, 182,* 461-464.

Elliott, D. M., & Briere, J. (1995). Posttraumatic stress as-sociated with delayed recall of sexual abuse: A general population study. *Journal of Traumatic Stress, 8,* 629-648.

Feldman-Summers, S., & Pope, K. S. (1994). The experi-ence of "forgetting" childhood abuse: A national survey of psychologists. *Journal of Consulting and Clinical Psychology, 62,* 636-639.

Goodman, G. S., Quas, J. A., Batterman-Faunce, J. M., Rid-dlesberger, M. M., & Kuhn, J. (1994). Predictors of ac-curate and inaccurate memories of traumatic events ex-perienced in childhood. *Consciousness and Cognition, 3,* 269-294.

Harvey, M. R. (in press). Principles of practice with remem-bering adults. In A. Tishelman, C. Newberger, & E. Newberger (Eds.), *Trauma and memory.* Cambridge, MA: Harvard University Press.

Harvey, M. R., & Harney, P. (1997). Addressing the after-math of interpersonal violence: The case for long-term care. *Psychoanalytic Inquiry* (Suppl.), 29-44.

Harvey, M. R., & Herman, J. L. (1992). The trauma of sexual victimization: Feminist contributions to theory, re-search, and practice. *PTSD Research Quarterly, 3*(3), 1-7.

Harvey, M. R., & Herman, J. L. (1994). Amnesia, partial amnesia and delayed recall among adult survivors of childhood trauma. *Consciousness and Cognition, 3,* 295-306.

Herman, J. L. (1992). *Trauma and recovery: The aftermath of violence—from domestic abuse to political terror.* New York: Basic Books.

Herman, J. L., & Harvey, M. R. (1997). Adult memories of childhood trauma: A naturalistic clinical study. *Journal of Traumatic Stress, 10,* 557-571.

Herman, J. L., & Schatzow, E. (1987). Recovery and verification of memories of childhood sexual trauma. *Psychoanalytic Psychology, 4,* 1-14.

Hyman, I. E., Jr., Husband, T. H., & Billings, F. J. (1995). False memories of childhood experiences. *Applied Cognitive Psychology, 9,* 181-197.

Hyman, I. E., Jr., & Pentland, J. (1996). Guided imagery and the creation of false childhood memories. *Journal of Memory and Language, 35,* 101-117.

Lazo, J. (1995). True or false: Expert testimony on repressed memory. *Loyola of Los Angeles Law Review, 28,* 1345-1414.

Lebowitz, L., Harvey, M. R., & Herman, J. L. (1992). A stage by dimension model of recovery from sexual trauma. *Journal of Interpersonal Violence, 8,* 378-391.

Lindsay, D. S., & Read, J. D. (1994). Psychotherapy and memories of childhood sexual abuse: A cognitive perspective. *Applied Cognitive Psychology, 8,* 281-338.

Lofft v. Lofft, California Superior Court (1989).

Loftus, E. F. (1979). *Eyewitness testimony.* Cambridge, MA: Harvard University Press.

Loftus, E. F. (1993). The reality of repressed memories. *American Psychologist, 48,* 518-537.

Loftus, E. F., & Pickrell, J. E. (1995). The formation of false memories. *Psychiatric Annals, 25,* 720-725.

Loftus, E. F., Polonsky, S., & Fullilove, M. T. (1994). Memories of childhood sexual abuse: Remembering and repressing. *Psychology of Women Quarterly, 18,* 67-84.

Loftus, G. R., & Loftus, E. F. (1976). *Human memory: The processing of information.* Hillsdale, NJ: Lawrence Erlbaum.

Marquis, K. H., Marshall, J., & Oskamp, S. (1972). Testimony validity as a function of question form, atmosphere, and item difficulty. *Journal of Applied Social Psychology, 2,* 167-186.

McGaugh, J. L. (1990). Significance and remembrance: The role of neuromodulatory systems in the regulation of memory storage. *Annual Review of Neuroscience, 12,* 255-287.

McGaugh, J. L. (1995). Emotional activation, neuromodulatory systems, and memory strength. In D. L. Schacter, J. T. Coyle, G. D. Fischbach, M. M. Mesulam, & L. E. Sullivan (Eds.), *Memory distortion: How minds, brains, and societies reconstruct the past* (pp. 255-273). Cambridge, MA: Harvard University Press.

Munsey v. Kellett, Middlesex (Mass.) Superior Court, Civil Action 91-5984 (1992).

Muscio, B. (1915). The influence of the form of a question. *British Journal of Psychology, 8,* 351-389.

Ofshe, R. J., & Watters, E. (1993). Making monsters. *Society, 30,* 4-16.

Pope, K. S., & Brown, L. S. (1996). *Recovered memories of abuse: Assessment, therapy, forensics.* Washington, DC: American Psychological Association.

Riley v. Pressnell, 409 Mass. 239 (1991).

Roesler, T. A., & Wind, T. W. (1994). Telling the secret: Adult women describe their disclosures of incest. *Journal of Interpersonal Violence, 9,* 327-338.

Saks, M. J., & Hastie, R. (1978). *Social psychology in court.* New York: van Nostrand Reinhold.

Saywitz, K. J., & Moan-Hardie, S. (1994). Reducing the potential for distortion of childhood memories. *Consciousness and Cognition, 3,* 408-425.

Schacter, D. L. (1996). *Searching for memory: The brain, the mind, and the past.* New York: Basic Books.

Silk, K. R., Lee, S., Hill, E. M., & Lohr, N. E. (1995). Borderline personality disorder symptoms and severity of sexual abuse. *American Journal of Psychiatry, 152,* 1059-1064.

Washington Rev. Code Ann. Sec. 4 16.340 (Suppl.) (1989).

Westen, D., Ludolph, P., Misle, B., Ruffins, S., & Block, J. (1990). Physical and sexual abuse in adolescent girls with borderline personality disorder. *American Journal of Orthopsychiatry, 60,* 55-66.

Williams, L. M. (1994). Recall of childhood trauma: A prospective study of women's memories of child sexual abuse. *Journal of Consulting and Clinical Psychology, 62,* 1167-1176.

3

Individual Differences in Maltreated Children's Memory and Suggestibility

Mitchell L. Eisen
Gail S. Goodman
Suzanne L. Davis
Jianjian Qin

In recent years there has been a surge of interest in issues related to children's eyewitness memory. This interest is most evident in heated debates in the scientific literature and popular media on the reliability of memories of sexual abuse. Controversies surrounding false memories of abuse in adults and suggestibility in children have led to increased focus on forensic interviewing techniques, with greater attention paid to the fallibility of memory and the role of suggestibility.

Much of the early laboratory work examining children's memory and suggestibility was used to argue that frequently employed techniques for interviewing children may result in distortions in children's memory reports, yielding invalid information. However, the subject matter of the memory tests in this early work often involved memory for word lists, pictures, stories, or movies, and appeared unrelated to children's ability to recount important events in their lives. Despite this shortcoming, this early

AUTHORS' NOTE: We thank the director, Dr. Richard Macur-Brousil, and the staff of the Under the Rainbow Program at Mt. Sinai Hospital and Medical Center for their assistance. We are also grateful to the Illinois Department of Child and Family Services and Dana Corwin, the guardian of the state of Illinois, for support and approval of our project. A number of research assistants provided valuable help. We would especially like to thank Jason Brown, Ellisa Faye, Clair Henn-Haas, Gary Lee, Jannett Pearson, R.N., Denise Schaeffer, and Ernestine Watts, R.N. Writing of this chapter was facilitated by a grant from the National Center on Child Abuse and Neglect.

work raised suspicions about children's memory abilities and cast doubt on all children's ability to report important details of their personal experiences reliably (Ceci & Bruck, 1993; Goodman, 1984).

In the past few years, research on children's memory and suggestibility has, for the most part, became more ecologically valid. Standard methods for assessing children's memory and resistance to suggestion now involve questioning children about events they witnessed or participated in, or about suggested nonevents. This shift in methodology has resulted in a wave of new research identifying a range of interview factors that influence children's memory reports and resistance to misleading information (e.g., repeated versus single interviews, the types of questions posed, rapport, the language used; for reviews, see Eisen, Goodman, Qin, & Davis, 1998; Goodman, Emery, & Haugaard, 1997). However, child witness studies still vary considerably in their relevance to eyewitness testimony in abuse cases. Typically, these studies pay little or no attention to individual differences in the effects of stress, history of trauma, and the cognitive or emotional functioning of the children studied.

During the most recent period of growth in the area of child witness research, there has been a burgeoning literature aimed at understanding the effects of child abuse and other traumas on memory. However, the trauma memory and child witness literatures have developed largely independent of one another, leaving large gaps in our knowledge of how abuse and trauma may affect children's memory and eyewitness testimony. Most notably, it is important to understand what role individual differences in dissociation, symptoms of posttraumatic stress, depression, and other forms of psychopathology play in children's memory and suggestibility. Additionally, if we are to understand individual differences in the impact of abuse and trauma on children's memory, we must examine variables that may moderate children's responses to abuse and trauma (e.g., coping ability, intellectual ability, and attachment style).

In this chapter, we attempt to bridge the gap between the child witness and trauma memory literatures. We begin with a brief discussion of ecological validity. This is followed by an overview of several interview factors that influence children's memory and suggestibility. We then review the developmental literature on the effects of stress and trauma on memory and examine how individual differences in children's responses to stress and trauma may affect their memory and resistance to misleading information. In the process, we discuss a currently popular model of how dissociation affects memory. Finally, in relation to this model, we present preliminary findings from our recent work examining individual differences in maltreated children's memory for an anogenital examination (Eisen, Goodman, & Qin, 1995).

Ecological Validity

☐ *Ecological validity* refers to how well a research design generalizes from the research context to a real-world context. Ceci (1991) outlines the challenge to researchers interested in children's recollections in a sex abuse case by noting that "in a sex abuse case, the real world analog might be a set of circumstances that includes bodily victimization in the context of high levels of arousal; personal embarrassment; and a web of motives, threats, inducements and suggestions that might tilt the odds one way or another that the victim will tell others what happened and tell them accurately or inaccurately" (p. 5). This assertion presents a formidable challenge to researchers interested in making their studies as generalizable as possible to actual sexual abuse investigations. Although it is by no means presented as a comprehensive list of relevant variables, it does provide a jumping-off point from which to examine factors that affect a child's reporting in a sexual abuse investigation.

The list of relevant factors can be broken down roughly into at least three categories: (a) factors that might influence the child at the time of the interview (e.g., embarrassment, threats, repeated suggestions), (b) factors related to the type of abuse suffered by the child (e.g., bodily victimization in the context of arousal), and (c) individual differences in children's responses to abuse that are likely to influence their memory performance in an interview (e.g., individual differences in the impact of bodily victimization, individual coping responses to threats). We discuss several of these factors in the following section.

Interview Factors

☐ Child witness researchers have identified a number of interview factors that may affect children's eyewitness accuracy and resistance to misinformation. In this section, we briefly discuss several variables identified through scientific research as being particularly relevant to the assessment of eyewitness memory in children, including (a) the type of information about which children are interviewed, (b) the types of questions asked, (c) how often questions are asked, and (d) the interview context. This discussion is not intended to provide an exhaustive review of the numerous factors that influence children's memory reports. Rather, our discussion contains a brief overview of some of the factors identified as particularly relevant to interviewing children in abuse investigations (for expanded reviews, see Ceci & Bruck, 1993; Saywitz & Goodman, 1996; Warren & McGough, 1996).

First, the type of information children are asked to report about a prior experience can have a profound effect on children's memory and suggestibility. Information central or most salient to an experience is generally remembered better by adults and children than is peripheral, nonsalient information (Cassell & Bjorklund, in press; Goodman, Hirschman, Hepps, & Rudy, 1991), and the strength of a person's memory for an event is related to resistance to misleading information for the details of that experience (Loftus, 1979). In this regard, memory for the central details and salient features of an event are often quite robust and resistant to updating even when misinformation techniques are employed, although age differences in memory and suggestibility are to be expected.

Second, the types of questions asked affect children's memory reports. Open-ended questions eliciting free recall typically produce the

least amount of inaccurate information (Dent & Stephenson, 1979; Goodman & Aman, 1991; Hutcheson, Baxter, Telfer, & Warden, 1995; Rudy & Goodman, 1991). However, such open-ended inquiries frequently lead to brief reports in young children that do not reflect the amount of accurate information children are capable of reporting under more structured circumstances. As a result, it is often necessary to elicit information from child witnesses by asking specific questions. Such questions tend to increase the amount of information recalled, but can also lead to greater inaccuracy than open-ended, free-recall questions (Dent & Stephenson, 1979; Goodman & Reed, 1986; Hutcheson et al., 1995). This is particularly relevant when the children being interviewed are very young. A young child may have a detailed memory for an event, but may have difficulty putting it into narrative form. Moreover, young children may lack adequate retrieval cues to access the information at any given moment. Because they lack coherent narratives and adequate retrieval cues, preschool children often depend on adults' questions to cue their recall (Fivush, 1993).

In addition, the developmental appropriateness of questions is an important interview factor. Children have difficulty understanding legal terminology, including such words as *jury* and *court* (Flin, Stevenson, & Davies, 1989; Saywitz, Jaenicke, & Camparo, 1990). Further, children's metacognitive skills are relatively undeveloped compared with those of adults. That is, children are generally unaware when they do not understand a question (Asher, 1976; Markman, 1977; Patterson, Masad, & Cosgrove, 1978; Saywitz & Snyder, 1991), and as a result they answer questions (many times incorrectly) that they do not fully comprehend (Carter, Bottoms, & Levine, 1996; Perry, McAuliff, Tam, Claycomb, Dosal, & Flanagan, 1995). For example, Carter et al. (1996) have reported that children's responses to linguistically complex questions were less accurate than their responses to simple, more developmentally appropriate questions, although the children did not appear to realize that the complex questions were more difficult. When interviewing children, it is important to appreciate that when children are asked complex, multiphrased questions that they do not understand, they may respond as best they can—for example, to the beginning or end part of the entire question. In fact, children with well-developed social skills and good expressive language abilities will often play the role of good conversational partners, responding in a confident and expressive manner to all questions they are asked, despite the fact that the meanings of the questions are well beyond their ability to comprehend. Even when children have clear memories for an event, the types of questions asked play an important role in the accuracy and completeness of their memory reports.

Third, repetition of questions across and within interviews influences children's eyewitness memory performance. A replicated finding is that asking specific or misleading questions repeatedly within an interview can at times result in increased inaccuracies, or at least inconsistencies, for young children (Fivush & Schwarzmueller, 1995; Poole & White, 1995; Siegal, Waters, & Dinwiddie, 1988), presumably because children believe that their first answers were incorrect. However, children can be inoculated against this effect to some degree through warnings that question repetition does not necessarily indicate that their initial responses were incorrect (Saywitz & Moan-Hardie, 1994). Inoculation effects are more difficult to achieve with young children, however.

Repetition across interviews can also influence the accuracy of children's eyewitness memory. Repeatedly asking misleading questions across multiple interviews has an adverse effect on the accuracy of some children's memory reports (see Poole & White, 1995, for a review). In particular, when young children are provided with misinformation in highly suggestive interviews over long periods of time (Bruck, Ceci, Francoeur, & Barr, 1995; Ceci, Loftus, Leichtman, & Bruck, 1994), a subset of children incorporate misinformation into their accounts of prior events. However, repeatedly interviewing children in a less suggestive manner can have a positive effect on children's memory through rehearsal and/or reminiscence (Brainerd & Ornstein, 1991; Dent, 1991; Howe, 1991) or the process of reinstatement (Howe,

Courage, & Bryant-Brown, 1993). In their review of the literature on this topic, Fivush and Schwarzmueller (1995) comment that repeated interviews provide an opportunity for children to rehearse an event, noting that if a memory is not rehearsed, it may remain relatively unorganized and fragmentary, becoming increasingly difficult to retrieve over time. This may be especially relevant to cases of abuse. In such instances, children may choose not to think or talk about particular events because of the painful affect attached to these memories.

Finally, it is important to consider the context of an interview. In actual abuse investigations, children are often removed from their homes and pressured one way or another either to acknowledge abuse or to reveal nothing. An uncomfortable or accusatory interview environment, especially one in which children feel intimidated (Bussey, Lee, & Grimbeek, 1993; Ceci, Ross, & Toglia, 1987; Lepore & Sesco, 1994; Tobey & Goodman, 1992), leads to greater inaccuracies. Social support appears to play an important role in this regard. A lack of social support from others has an adverse effect on children's memory reports (Moston, 1992). In contrast, in more supportive interview environments, in which interviewers spend time building rapport with children, children's accuracy—in particular their resistance to misleading suggestions—is improved relative to control conditions (Carter et al., 1996; Goodman, Bottoms, Schwartz-Kenney, & Rudy, 1991). If a child does not feel comfortable discussing the details of a prior event, perhaps for motivational reasons, he or she may not report even salient details of events that have been adequately stored and are easily accessible (Bottoms, Goodman, Schwartz-Kenney, Sachsenmaier, & Thomas, 1990; Saywitz, Goodman, Nicholas, & Moan (1991). For example, Saywitz et al. (1991) found that older girls who had received a medical examination involving genital touch were less likely than their younger counterparts to disclose freely the details of the examination with an interviewer. These authors argue that there was a motivational factor operating: The older girls, because they were more socially sophisticated, probably realized that talking about the experience could be embarrassing, and as a result withheld information about that experience.

Stress, Traumatic Stress, and Memory

☐ In contrast to the wealth of research on the impact of various interview factors on children's memory, very little work has been done on factors related to the type of abuse suffered by children and individual differences in children's responses to the abuse that are likely to influence their performance in interviews. It is generally accepted that individuals differ in their responses to traumatic experiences and in how such responses affect memory (Shalev, 1996). In his review of the literature on this topic, van der Kolk (1996) notes that the accuracy of memory is influenced by the emotional valence of an experience. He goes on to argue that traumatic stress is qualitatively different from ordinary stress, resulting in unique variants in the way information is stored and retrieved (see also van der Kolk & Fisler, 1995). However, there is considerable debate as to whether traumatic memories are processed in a substantially different manner than ordinary memories and therefore require special explanatory mechanisms (Brown, 1995).

Christianson (1992) hypothesized that increased stress results in a narrowing of attention, which in turn leads to an increased concentration on central information. In times of increased stress and perceived threat, peripheral details are not as strongly encoded or retained, whereas the central details of stressful events are retained especially well in memory. In line with this thinking, several researchers have hypothesized that increased stress may actually enhance memory, through either physiological (Gold, 1987) or psychological means (Bohannon, 1988; Goodman, Hirschman, et al., 1991; Pillemer, 1992). Other studies have indicated that children's memory for stressful or traumatic events is not especially reliable and is particularly malleable (Bugenthal, Blue, Cortez, Fleck, & Rodriguez, 1992; Peters, 1991).

An important trend across several studies and clinical reports is that individual differences exist in children's memories of stressful events. For example, in a study by Steward and Steward (1989), despite a general trend toward increased memory accuracy in distressed children, some highly stressed children showed high error rates. In recent research on a stressful medical procedure involving urethral penetration, Goodman and Quas (in press) found that, when personality and family factors were controlled, stress in and of itself did not impair or strengthen children's memory at 1- to 4-week delays. Mixed results like these demonstrate the likely importance of individual differences in children's memory.

Traumatic Stress

Although we can study individuals' responses to nontraumatic stress in the laboratory, we are clearly more limited in studying individuals' responses to traumatic stress. Therefore, most of the available data on responses to traumatic stress come from case studies. Moreover, much of the relevant theorizing is based on clinical insight and lacks adequate scientific examination.

Several explanations of how traumatic stress might affect memory have been proposed. Bremner, Krystal, Southwick, and Charney (1995) assert that traumatic stress interferes with the processing of information through the creation of abnormalities in the functioning of brain regions and systems involved in memory. Relatedly, van der Kolk (1996) reports evidence from different laboratories all indicating that individuals with posttraumatic stress disorder (PTSD) have decreased hippocampal volume (Bremner et al., 1995; Gurvitz, Shenton, & Pitman, 1995; Stein et al., 1994) and high levels of hippocampal activity (Rauch et al., 1996) that may be related to decrements in memory functioning. In addition, Bremner et al. (1995) found decrements in explicit memory in survivors of childhood abuse and note similar findings for a variety of other traumatized groups, including concentration camp survivors (Helweg-Larsen et al., 1952), prisoners of the Korean War (Stuker, Winstead, Galina, & Allain, 1991), and Vietnam veterans (Bremner, Southwick, Johnson, Yehuda, & Charney, 1993).

Van der Kolk (1996) proposes that the narrowing of attention that accompanies increased stress can often evolve into a complete amnesia for the experience in times of traumatic stress. According to this line of thought, there must logically be a point of watershed where an individual becomes totally overwhelmed and can no longer adequately process the material related to the stressor. It has been proposed that this point is theoretically where stress turns into traumatic stress. This point of watershed differs from person to person and is based on individuals' resilience and pretrauma vulnerabilities (Shalev, 1996).

Van der Kolk and Fisler (1995) argue that traumatic stress overwhelms an individual's coping mechanisms, and that memories from these traumatic events are encoded differently than ordinary events, by virtue of alterations in attentional focus from extreme emotional arousal. Van der Kolk's model of trauma and memory is based on Janet's (1919/1925) pioneering work on dissociation. Janet initially described dissociation as a process in which a person faced with overwhelming emotions is unable to create a narrative memory for the event. The individual therefore compartmentalizes this unintegrated memory, and the fear of facing the overwhelming emotional memory that has been split off keeps him or her from adequately processing the event in a narrative form. Current theories of dissociation propose that these compartmentalized memories consist largely of sensory perceptions and affective states (Nemiah, 1995; van der Kolk & van der Hart, 1989).

Dissociation is increasingly being identified as a key defense mechanism employed by abused children (Briere, 1992; Chu & Dill, 1990; Frischholz, 1985; Hornstein & Tyson, 1991; Lynn & Rue, 1994; Putnam, 1985, 1991; Quimby & Putnam, 1991; Rue, Lynn, Henry, Buhk, & Boyd, 1990). Theoretically, when a child is confronted with the overwhelming stress of abuse or other traumas, he or she is unable to process the information and employs the defense of dissociation. This mode of cognitive avoidance results in the compartmentalization of the traumatic memory, which prohibits the child from adequately processing the event

later. It is hypothesized that the use of this strategy becomes habitual at some point and that the dissociation leads to disturbances in both implicit and explicit memory functioning (Putnam, 1995). It is important to note that there is virtually no empirical research conclusively bearing out the hypotheses generated by this dissociation model.

On the other hand, there is reason to believe that some abused and otherwise traumatized children may possess particularly rich memories for personally experienced stressful events by virtue of their being hypervigilant to the details of threatening situations (Dodge, Bates, & Pettit, 1990). For some children, it is plausible that an increased preparatory or reactive response leads to enhanced attention to the details of situations judged to be threatening. Additionally, the high level of distrust found in many abused children, coupled with this hypervigilance to details in stressful and possibly threatening situations, may lead to better memory and enhanced resistance to misleading information. As noted earlier, there is logically a point of watershed at which some children may become overly stressed and no longer able to process threatening information in an optimal manner, whereas other children remain alert and hypervigilant. This point may vary dramatically from child to child due to differences in such factors as social support, coping skills, resilience, and history of trauma.

Individual Differences and Moderating Variables in Children's Response to Abuse

☐ To understand fully the effects of abuse and trauma on children's memory and suggestibility, we must account for moderating variables that may result in individual differences in children's response to trauma. Cicchetti, Rogosch, Lynch, and Holt (1993) note that some abused children are more resilient than others, and as a result these children show less severe consequences of their maltreatment. Perry (1994) hypothesized that the onset of secondary disorders may be linked to familial dispositions. Other theorists have hypothesized that comorbidity is more dependent on individual predispositions and preexisting psychopathology (for a review, see Pynoos, Steinberg, & Wraith, 1995). It has been found that a history of exposure to extreme stress (such as childhood physical abuse) increases the risk for stress-related symptomatology when individuals are reexposed to traumatic stress later in life (Bremner, Southwick, & Charney, 1994). There is also evidence that when children are sexually abused at a young age, they are more vulnerable to the development of posttraumatic stress symptoms and depression (Wolfe, Gentile, & Wolfe, 1989; Wolfe, Sas, & Wekerle, 1994; for a review, see Cicchetti & Lynch, 1995), which may also affect memory performance.

Two factors have been found to account for a large portion of the variance in children's responses to stress and trauma: the quality of children's attachments and ego resilience (e.g., coping skills; see Cicchetti & Lynch, 1995). The strength and importance of affiliative attachments (Lazarus & Folkman, 1984) plays a critical role in children's vulnerability to extreme stress (Pynoos et al., 1995). Several studies have found that maltreated children are more likely to form insecure attachments with their caretakers than are nonmaltreated children (Crittendon, 1985; Egeland & Srouf, 1981; Lamb, Gaensbaur, Malkin, & Schultz, 1985; Schneider-Rosen, Baunwald, Carlson, & Cicchetti, 1985). Using traditional classification schemes (Ainsworth, Blears, Waters, & Wall, 1978), approximately two thirds of maltreated children show insecure attachments to their mothers (Cicchetti & Lynch, 1995). Using recently updated and revised schemes of attachment (Crittendon, 1992), a review of the literature reveals that an even higher percentage of maltreated children are classified as having insecure or atypical (disorganized/disoriented or avoidant/resistant) attachments (Cicchetti & Lynch, 1995).

These high rates of atypical and insecure attachments found in maltreated children put them at risk for achieving nonadaptive outcomes in interpersonal development (Cicchetti & Lynch, 1993) and are associated with the presence of externalizing and internalizing behavioral problems in high-risk populations

(Lyons-Ruth, 1996). In addition, it has been proposed that the disorganization found in maltreated children's attachment relationships may be related to distortions in affect regulation (Barnett, Ganiban, & Cicchetti, 1992). It is hypothesized that having fear associated with the primary attachment figure early in life may have a profound impact on the individual, leading to long-term psychobiological impairment such as that shown in posttraumatic stress disorder (Cicchetti, Ganiban, & Barnett, 1991). Relatedly, Toth and Cicchetti (1996) have found that the quality of maltreated children's attachments (as indicated by their reported patterns of relatedness) may moderate the effects of maltreated children's perceived competence and depressive symptomatology.

Cicchetti et al. (1993) report that along with the quality of children's attachments, ego resilience is an important variable in moderating the adverse effects of maltreatment. These authors found that ego resilience accounted for a significant share of the variance in adaptive functioning among maltreated children. More data are needed if we are to understand the moderating effects of the quality of children's attachments and ego resilience on the development of trauma-related psychopathology in maltreated children and how this may ultimately affect children's memory and suggestibility.

A Testable Model to Assess Individual Differences in the Impact of Child Abuse on Memory

☐ Not all children are affected equally by the extreme stress that is often associated with physical and sexual abuse. To summarize the above, the quality of children's attachments and their ego resilience (e.g., coping skills) have been found to moderate the impacts of abuse and trauma, resulting in individual differences in children's responses to maltreatment. Also, as noted earlier, dissociation is commonly identified as a defense employed by children when faced with traumatic stress, and it has been implicated in both implicit and explicit memory problems (Putnam, 1995). It is generally believed that children who come to rely on dissociation to deal with traumatic events are also likely to dissociate when confronted with more minor stressful circumstances in everyday life (Bremner et al., 1995; Lynn & Rue, 1994; Spiegel, 1986).

These ideas present us with a testable model that is amenable to empirical investigation. Although to date we have not examined the full model in our research, we describe the general model here, including predictions that await empirical testing. The model would explain that certain children (e.g., children with insecure or disorganized attachments and/or poor coping skills) are more vulnerable than others to developing trauma-related pathology, including dissociative disorders. As a result, a measurable portion of vulnerable children will dissociate when faced with extreme stress. This model would further dictate that stressful experiences that occur subsequent to the traumatic event are likely to activate psychological diatheses for dissociation. As a result, those individuals who experience dissociation at the point of extreme stress are likely to be dissociative during subsequent stressors of significant intensity. Further, the activation of this dissociative state should impair their memory for the events experienced during these subsequent stressful episodes. These formulations are implicit in a number of popular conceptions of dissociation and memory.

One can test this model by addressing a few well-defined questions. Are maltreated children who have insecure or disorganized attachments and/or poor coping skills more likely to be dissociative? Further, if they are more dissociative, will these children respond differently than other maltreated children (psychologically or physiologically) when confronted with significant stressors by employing the defense of dissociation? More specifically, will the "dissociative children" (those children who score high on measures of dissociation) "dissociate" when confronted with stressors, resulting in poorer memory for events occurring in times of elevated stress? Finally, if children who appear to be dissociative show poorer memory for events involving elevated stress, does this translate into increased suggestibility for the details of the stressful events experienced?

In a recent study, we tested the last question and several questions related to it. Of the various predictions raised by the model, we were able to test only hypotheses concerning the impact of dissociation on memory. Unfortunately, we were unable to explore individual differences in attachment and coping and how they moderate vulnerability to trauma-related pathology.

The Initial Under the Rainbow Study

☐ The Under the Rainbow studies were designed to examine individual differences in the influence of stress arousal, dissociation, and other forms of psychopathology on the memory and suggestibility of maltreated children. By studying children who were in the midst of actual abuse investigations, we also hoped to explore these issues in a particularly ecologically valid fashion. A few of our main questions were as follows: (a) Do individual differences in general psychopathology relate to memory and resistance to misleading information? (b) Does level of stress arousal affect maltreated children's memory performance? (c) Do children who score higher on measures of dissociation respond differently to elevated stress? (d) Do individual differences in dissociative tendencies predict maltreated children's memory and suggestibility? In this section we briefly discuss some of the results of a preliminary analysis of the data from our initial study conducted at the Under the Rainbow Program at Mt. Sinai Hospital in Chicago.

Data for this study were collected while children were hospitalized as inpatients in the Under the Rainbow Program. The inpatient assessment program involves the 5-day hospitalization of children who are in the midst of ongoing forensic investigation. All children admitted to the Under the Rainbow Program receive complete medical, psychological, developmental, and social services assessments, and all of the resulting data are made available to the research team. As part of the medical assessment, each child received an anogenital examination, in which a physician examined the child for overt signs of physical and/or sexual abuse. We monitored each child's heart rate during the anogenital examination, and then obtained the doctor's and nurses' ratings of the child's level of stress arousal and discomfort. Within 3 to 5 days after this examination, we conducted with each child a structured interview composed of a series of neutral, leading, and misleading questions, to assess the child's memory and suggestibility for the details of the anogenital exam. Furthermore, at some point during the hospital stay, each child was seen for a psychological consultation. At this time, a clinician interviewed the child, looking for signs and symptoms of trauma and assessing mental status, emotional and cognitive functioning, and affective response to the alleged abuse. Thirty minutes after this consultation, we conducted another structured interview with each child to assess the child's memory and resistance to misleading information for the details of the event.

During this hospitalization, data were also collected on the children's dissociative tendencies using at least one of three measures: the Children's Perceptual Alteration Scale (CPAS; Evers-Szostak & Sanders, 1990), the Dissociative Experiences Scale for Adolescents (A-DES; Armstrong & Carlson, 1993), and the Child Dissociative Checklist (CDC; Putnam, Helmers, & Trickett, 1993). In addition, clinical data on the child's global adaptive functioning (GAF) and diagnosis were provided by the psychology staff of the program. Social service and medical information was made available by the social workers and physicians.

Participants

The study participants were 214 children of low socioeconomic status from the urban areas of Chicago who were referred to the Under the Rainbow Program for assessment of allegations of maltreatment. Referrals to this program come predominantly from the child welfare system. The mean age of the children was 7 years 4 months (range = 3 to 15 years); 92 were males and 122 were females. In terms of ethnic background, 76% of the children were African American, 12% were Hispanic, 9% were Caucasian, and the remaining 3% were of unknown

ethnicity. The children were divided into groups primarily according to type of abuse: (a) children who had been sexually abused (28%), (b) children who had been physically abused (13%), (c) children who had been both physically and sexually abused (11%), (d) children with indicated cases of neglect (including exposure to domestic violence, lack of supervision, and so on) but with no indication of abuse (15%), (e) children with clear documentation of parental drug addiction without neglect or abuse (8%), and (f) children who had no history of abuse or neglect (22%). Some children in all of the groups also had histories of corporal punishment of unspecified duration and magnitude.

Results

Individual Differences in Global Adaptive Functioning

Mean performance on the anogenital examination memory test for each age group is presented in Table 3.1. Preliminary analyses indicated that level of psychopathology as measured by clinicians' estimates of GAF was a statistically significant predictor of performance in the memory interviews, with the higher-scoring children (i.e., those judged to have a higher level of functioning) generally performing better on a test of their memory for the anogenital exam. Specifically, GAF was related to better memory and increased resistance to misleading information (decreased suggestibility), $rs \geq .25$, $ps \leq .025$, with age statistically controlled. GAF was also found to be related to abuse status. Those children who were both sexually and physically abused were rated by the clinicians as being more disturbed than children with no evidence of abuse in their history.

It is important to point out that although GAF was found to be related to abuse, as well as to memory and suggestibility, abuse was not found to be significantly related to memory or suggestibility for events occurring during the anogenital exam. Our data indicate that being abused in and of itself does not necessarily mean that a child is more or less suggestible

Table 3.1 Proportion of Correct, Incorrect, and Don't Know Responses to the Anogenital Examination Memory Test for Each Age Group

	3-5 Years	6-10 Years	11-15 Years	Totals
All questions				
correct[a]	.63	.81	.92	.77
incorrect[a]	.35	.16	.08	.21
don't know	.02	.03	.004	.02
Misleading questions				
correct[b]	.63	.83	.91	.77
incorrect[b]	.36	.14	.08	.21
don't know	.02	.03	.01	.02
Misleading abuse-related questions				
correct[b]	.60	.81	.91	.75
incorrect[b]	.40	.16	.09	.24
don't know[c]	.01	.03	.00	.02

SOURCE: Eisen et al. (in press).

a. Fs (2, 105) > 51.20, ps < .001; planned comparisons revealed that the differences among all three age groups were significant.

b. Fs (2, 105) > 17.31, ps < .001; planned comparisons revealed that the youngest age group differed significantly from the two older groups, but the difference between the two older groups was not significant.

c. The 6- to 10-year-old age group mean was combined with the 11- to 15-year-old age group mean and then compared with the 3- to 5-year-old age group mean. Across question categories, there were no significant differences for "don't know" responses.

than comparable nonabused children (i.e., children in the Under the Rainbow Program who, as judged by hospital staff and social service workers, were unlikely to have suffered abuse). Rather, it appears that individual differences in children's level of psychopathology (GAF) predicted performance in the memory interview. It is not clear whether this effect is related to the children's premorbid functioning or whether children with lower GAF ratings were more disturbed by the abuse (or the situational stress of the abuse evaluation). It is most likely that some combination of these elements is involved.

A preliminary examination of these data indicates that GAF is an important variable to be studied in future research. We will be examining the relation between GAF and suggestibility more closely in our current work and will report these findings in future papers.

Dissociation

In regard to the model of how dissociation might affect memory performance, we found that the relation between the dissociation mea-

sures and memory and/or suggestibility was weak at best and not consistent across the age groups and variables investigated. A preliminary examination of these data indicated that in some instances scores on the CDC were related to a history of abuse. However, these effects were quite variable and not consistent across all age groups examined or across all the measures employed. A-DES and CPAS scores did not predict memory or suggestibility.

The major difficulty we had in examining relations between dissociation and other variables was that some of the dissociation measures appeared to tap different psychological tendencies. A-DES and CPAS scores were positively interrelated (r = .66), but the CDC shared very little variance with either the A-DES (r = .28) or CPAS (r = .14). In addition, the three measures used to assess this construct (CPAS, CDC, and A-DES) performed differently across the age groups studied.

There are several plausible explanations for this pattern of inconsistency in the performance of the dissociation measures. First, it may be that dissociation manifests itself dissimilarly in children as a function of age (e.g., 3- to 5-year-olds versus 6- to 10-year-olds or 11- to 15-year-olds). Or it could be that the three measures are more or less effective in assessing dissociation in these age groups (the CDC relies on a parent checklist, whereas the CPAS relies on self-report). Finally, the lack of consistency in the assessment of dissociation across instruments (within or across age ranges) could very well be a manifestation of poor definition of this construct and a resulting lack of agreement about how dissociation should be measured. The authors of the CPAS had in mind the relation between dissociation and eating disorders when they designed their measure, whereas the A-DES authors had no such conception. The CDC is a parent-report measure, which was administered to caretakers of all children 4 years and above, and is focused on behavioral symptoms. The A-DES and the CPAS are self-report instruments administered only to older children and designed at some level to assess children's and adolescents' internal states of consciousness. These differences between the CDC and the other two measures may account for the relatively high correlation between the CPAS and the A-DES, and also the lack of significant relations between the CDC and the other two instruments. It should also be noted that the sample size in some cells of our study was quite small (e.g., because relatively few adolescents were in the study and because of missing data for some of them, we obtained both the CDC and the A-DES on only 14 adolescents).

The construct of dissociation is fairly ephemeral to start with, and assessing dissociation in children as opposed to adults is even more challenging, due to the lack of available data examining dissociation in children. In addition, developmental differences between adults and children may exist that have not been thoroughly examined and described in the literature. Available retrospective data relating histories of abuse to dissociation in adults is not sufficient to apply to children at this point. This is not to say that the construct of dissociation does not exist in children or cannot be measured. It is reasonable to assume that some children rely on this defense more than others. However, measuring this construct and testing

predictions based on these measures will require further research.

Stress and Memory

We investigated one of the remaining questions implied by popular conceptions of dissociation by examining data related to the anogenital examination. This question concerned whether children who score higher on measures of dissociation respond differently to elevated stress. Preliminary data from the present sample of children indicate that scores on the dissociation measures were not related to heart rate or doctors' and/or nurses' estimates of the children's stress arousal during the anogenital exam.

A potentially important question, one we unfortunately could not examine with our data, concerns whether there was an identifiable dissociative response to stress among a subgroup of children that differentially influenced these children's memory and resistance to misleading information. It should be noted that we had no definitive measure of whether the children were or were not in a "dissociative state" during the anogenital exam (in fact, no such measure exists). However, we were able to examine the relation between scores on the measures of dissociation and memory performance to determine whether the highly dissociative children's memory performance was differentially affected by increasing stress arousal, as would be predicted based on widely accepted notions of dissociation. Dissociation was not related to children's memory or suggestibility for events occurring during the anogenital exam. According to the model, those children who are "dissociative" should "dissociate" in times of elevated stress, and therefore should have poorer memory for the procedures when stress was high. However, no significant interaction was found between the elevation of stress and dissociation in regard to children's memory or suggestibility.

Although at first glance our findings suggest lack of support for the previously mentioned model of dissociation and memory, it is also possible that the levels of stress reached during the anogenital examination generally were not sufficient to cause dissociative responses in the children tested. Although a number of children became quite upset during the medical checkup (e.g., cried, screamed, and had to be restrained) and may have feared bodily harm, still the level of stress needed to precipitate a dissociative response may not have been reached.

In general, preliminary analyses indicated that stress arousal, as measured by heart rate and doctors' and/or nurses' judgments of children's stress, was not related to memory or suggestibility for the anogenital examination in a systematic, linear fashion after the effects of age and base-level heart rate were controlled statistically. In an expanded version of the initial Under the Rainbow study, we are currently examining other testable hypotheses generated by current theories of dissociation.

Future Directions

☐ The study reported above represents an initial step toward integrating the child witness and trauma memory literatures. By applying methods used in the child witness area to clinical samples of maltreated children, we can create new research paradigms that will allow us to examine important individual difference factors that may be especially relevant to the evaluation of allegations of abuse. The challenges involved in conducting such research are great. First and foremost, it is often difficult to gain access to clinical samples of children involved in abuse investigations. Even if such participants are available, child protective services (CPS) officials and workers are likely to be skeptical about research and quite wary of any work that might involve extra effort on their part, such as answering questions, accessing records, and tracking children. Further, some of the procedures used in this type of research (e.g., asking misleading questions of children) tend to raise the eyebrows of CPS officials and clinicians alike. Recent portrayals in the popular media of the deleterious effects of presenting misleading information to children have had a souring effect on CPS officials' willingness to endorse this type of study. In addition, clinical research is often difficult to conduct because of the strain

this type of work puts on physicians, nurses, psychologists, and social workers who assess and treat abused children. Therefore, conducting a project such as the study reported above necessitates a strong alliance among clinicians, researchers, medical and legal professionals, and child welfare agencies. We were exceptionally fortunate to have such support and cooperation.

Even when such alliances are forged and maltreated children are available to be included in studies examining individual difference factors relevant to the assessment of allegations of abuse, conducting this type of research is a tall order. For each additional variable to be examined, large numbers of participants are needed. In addition, for many variables of interest (e.g., dissociation, PTSD, depression) no single instruments are readily acceptable as measures of those constructs, and therefore multiple measures should be employed, creating further methodological challenges. In the case of dissociation, the differences among the measures is marked. The three measures used in the study discussed above differed greatly in regard to their construction and performance.

The study of individual differences in the impact of trauma on children's memory is a newly developing area in which the groundwork is only being laid at this time. Integrating this work with well-established models of memory development presents a wealth of new possibilities.

References

Ainsworth, M. D. S., Blears, M. C., Waters, E., & Wall, S. (1978). *Patterns of attachment: A psychological study of the strange situation.* Hillsdale, NJ: Lawrence Erlbaum.

Armstrong, J., & Carlson, E. (1993). *The Adolescent Dissociative Experiences Scales (A-DES).* Unpublished manuscript.

Asher, S. (1976). Children's ability to appraise their own and other persons' communication performance. *Developmental Psychology, 12,* 24-32.

Barnett, D., Ganiban, J., & Cicchetti, D. (1992, May). *Emotional reactivity regulation and attachment organization in children with Type D attachment: Longitudinal analysis across 12, 18, and 24 months of age.* Paper presented at the biannual meeting of the International Conference on Infant Studies, Miami, FL.

Bohannon, J. N., III. (1988). Flashbulb memories for the space shuttle disaster: A tale of two theories. *Cognition, 29,* 179-196.

Bottoms, B. L., Goodman, G. S., Schwartz-Kenney, B., M., Sachsenmaier, T., & Thomas, S. (1990, March). *Keeping secrets: Implications for children's testimony.* Paper presented at the 99th Annual Meeting of the American Psychology/Law Society, Williamsburg, VA.

Brainerd, C., & Ornstein, P. A. (1991). Children's memory for witnessed events: The developmental backdrop. In J. Doris (Ed.), *The suggestibility of children's recollections: Implications for eyewitness testimony* (pp. 10-20). Washington, DC: American Psychological Association.

Bremner, J. D., Krystal, J. H., Southwick, S. M., & Charney, D. S. (1995). Functional neuroanatomical correlates of the effects of stress on memory. *Journal of Traumatic Stress, 8,* 527-545.

Bremner, J. D., Southwick, S. M., & Charney, D. S. (1994). Etiologic factors in the development of posttraumatic stress disorder. In C. M. Mazure (Ed.), *Stress and psychiatric disorders* (pp. 149-186). Washington, DC: American Psychiatric Press.

Bremner, J. D., Southwick, S. M., Johnson, D. R., Yehuda, R., & Charney, D. S. (1993). Childhood physical abuse in combat-related posttraumatic stress disorder. *American Journal of Psychiatry, 150,* 235-239.

Briere, J. N. (1992). *Child abuse trauma: Theory and treatment of the lasting effects.* Newbury Park, CA: Sage.

Brown, L. S. (1995). Comment. *Consciousness and Cognition, 4,* 130-132.

Bruck, M., Ceci, S. J., Francoeur, E., & Barr, R. (1995). "I hardly cried when I got my shot!": Influencing children's reports about a visit to their pediatrician. *Child Development, 66,* 193-208.

Bugental, D. B., Blue, J., Cortez, V., Fleck, K., & Rodriguez, A. (1992). Influences of witnessed affect on information processing in children. *Child Development, 63,* 774-786.

Bussey, K., Lee, K., & Grimbeek, E. J. (1993). Lies and secrets: Implications for children's reporting of sexual abuse. In G. S. Goodman & B. L. Bottoms (Eds.), *Child victims, child witnesses: Understanding and improving testimony* (pp. 147-168). New York: Guilford.

Carter, C. A., Bottoms, B. L., & Levine, M. (1996). Linguistic and socioemotional influences on the accuracy of children's reports. *Law and Human Behavior, 20,* 335-358.

Cassell, W., & Bjorklund, D. F. (in press). Developmental patterns of eyewitness responses to repeated and increasingly suggestive questions. *Journal of Experimental Child Psychology.*

Ceci, S. J. (1991). Some overarching issues in the children's suggestibility debate. In J. Doris (Ed.), *The suggestibility of children's recollections: Implications for eyewitness testimony* (pp. 1-9). Washington, DC: American Psychological Association.

Ceci, S. J., & Bruck, M. (1993). Suggestibility of the child witness: A historical review and synthesis. *Psychological Bulletin, 3,* 403-439.

Ceci, S. J., Loftus, E. F., Leichtman, M. D., & Bruck, M. (1994). The possible role of source misattributions in the creation of the false beliefs among preschoolers. *International Journal of Clinical and Experimental Hypnosis, 42,* 304-320.

Ceci, S. J., Ross, D. F., & Toglia, M. P. (1987). Suggestibility of children's memory: Psycholegal implications. *Journal of Experimental Psychology, 116,* 38-49.

Christianson, S. A. (1992). Emotional stress and eyewitness memory: A critical review. *Psychological Bulletin, 112,* 284-309.

Chu, J. A., & Dill, D. L. (1990). Dissociative symptoms in relation to childhood physical and sexual abuse. *American Journal of Psychiatry, 147,* 887-892.

Cicchetti, D., Ganiban, J., & Barnett, D. (1991). Contributions from the study of high-risk populations to understanding the development of emotion regulation. In J. Garber & K. Dodge (Eds.), *The development of emotion regulation and disregulation* (pp. 15-48). New York: Cambridge University Press.

Cicchetti, D., & Lynch, M. (1993). Toward an ecological-transactional model of community violence and child maltreatment. *Psychiatry, 56,* 96-118.

Cicchetti, D., & Lynch, M. (1995). Failures in expectable environment and their impact on individual development: The case of child maltreatment. In D. Cicchetti & D. J. Cohen (Eds.), *Developmental psychopathology: Vol. 2. Risk, disorder, and adaptation* (pp. 32-71). New York: John Wiley.

Cicchetti, D., Rogosch, F. A., Lynch, M., & Holt, K. D. (1993). Resilience in maltreated children: Processes leading to adaptive outcome. *Developmental Psychopathology, 5,* 629-647.

Crittendon, P. M. (1985). Social networks, quality of parenting, and child development. *Child Development, 56,* 1299-1313.

Crittendon, P. M. (1992). Quality of attachment in the preschool years. *Development and Psychopathology, 4,* 209-241.

Dent, H. (1991). Experimental studies of interviewing child witnesses. In J. Doris (Ed.), *The suggestibility of children's recollections: Implications for eyewitness testimony* (pp. 138-146). Washington, DC: American Psychological Association.

Dent, H., & Stephenson, G. (1979). An experimental study of the effectiveness of different techniques of questioning child witnesses. *British Journal of Social and Clinical Psychology, 18,* 41-51.

Dodge, K., Bates, J., & Pettit, G. S. (1990). Mechanisms in the cycle of violence. *Science, 250,* 1678-1683.

Egeland, B., & Srouf, L. A. (1981). Developmental sequelae of maltreatment in infancy. *New Directions for Child Development, 11,* 77-92.

Eisen, M. L., Goodman, G. S., & Qin, J. (1995, July). *Eyewitness testimony in victims of child maltreatment: Stress, memory, and suggestibility.* Paper presented at the annual meeting of the Society for Applied Research on Memory and Cognition, Vancouver.

Eisen, M. L., Goodman, G. S., Qin, J., & Davis, S. L. (1998). Memory and suggestibility in maltreated children: New research relevant to evaluating allegations of abuse. In S. J. Lynn (Ed.), *Truth and memory* (pp. 163-189). New York: Guilford.

Evers-Szostak, M., & Sanders, S. (1990, August). *The validity and reliability of the Children's Perceptual Alteration Scale (CPAS): A measure of children's dissociation.* Paper presented at the 99th Annual Meeting of the American Psychological Association, San Francisco.

Fivush, R. (1993). Developmental perspectives on autobiographical recall. In G. S. Goodman & B. L. Bottoms (Eds.), *Child victims, child witnesses: Understanding and improving testimony* (pp. 1-24). New York: Guilford.

Fivush, R., & Schwarzmueller, A. (1995). Say it once again: Effects of repeated questions on children's event recall. *Journal of Traumatic Stress, 8,* 555-580.

Flin, R., Stevenson, Y., & Davies, G. (1989). Children's knowledge of court proceedings. *British Journal of Psychology, 80,* 285-297.

Frischholz, E. J. (1985). The relationship among dissociation, hypnosis, and child abuse in the development of multiple personality disorder. In R. P. Kluft (Ed.), *Childhood antecedents of multiple personality disorder* (pp. 99-126). Washington, DC: American Psychiatric Press.

Gold, P. E. (1987). Sweet memories. *American Scientist, 75,* 151-155.

Goodman, G. S. (1984). Children's testimony in historical perspective. *Journal of Social Issues, 40,* 9-31.

Goodman, G. S., & Aman, C. J. (1991). Children's use of anatomically detailed dolls to recount an event. *Child Development, 61,* 1859-1871.

Goodman, G. S., Bottoms, B. L., Schwartz-Kenney, B. M., & Rudy, L. (1991). Children's testimony about a stressful event: Improving children's reports. *Journal of Narrative and Life History, 1,* 69-99.

Goodman, G. S., Emery, R., & Haugaard, J. (1997). Developmental psychology and law: The cases of divorce, child maltreatment, foster care, and adoption. In I. Sigel & A. Renninger (Eds.), *Handbook of child psychology: Vol. 4. Child psychology in practice* (5th ed.). New York: John Wiley.

Goodman, G. S., Hirschman, J. E., Hepps, D., & Rudy, L. (1991). Children's memory for stressful events. *Merrill Palmer Quarterly, 37,* 109-158.

Goodman, G. S., & Quas, J. (in press). Trauma and memory: Individual differences in children's recounting of a stressful experience. In N. L. Stein, P. A. Ornstein, B. Tversky, & C. Brainerd (Eds.), *Memory for everyday and emotional events.* Mahwah, NJ: Lawrence Erlbaum.

Goodman, G. S., & Reed, R. (1986). Age differences in eyewitness testimony. *Law and Human Behavior, 10,* 317-332.

Gurvitz, T. V., Shenton, M. E., & Pitman, P. K. (1995). *Reduced hippocampal volume on magnetic resonance imaging in chronic post traumatic stress disorder.* Paper presented at the annual meeting of the International Society on Traumatic Stress Studies, Miami, FL.

Helweg-Larsen, Hoffmeyer, Kieler, Thaysen, Thaysen, Thygesen, & Wulff. (1952). Famine disease in German concentration camps: Complications and sequelae. *Acta Psychiatrica et Neurologica Scandinavica* (Suppl. 83), 1-460.

Hornstein, N. L., & Tyson, S. (1991). Inpatient treatment of children with multiple personality disorder/dissociative disorders and their families. *Psychiatric Clinics of North America, 14,* 631-648.

Howe, M. L. (1991). Misleading children's story recall: Forgetting and reminiscence of the facts. *Developmental Psychology, 27,* 746-762.

Howe, M. L., Courage, M. L., & Bryant-Brown, L. (1993). Reinstating preschoolers' memories. *Developmental Psychology, 29,* 854-869.

Hutcheson, G., Baxter, J., Telfer, K., & Warden, D. (1995). Child witness statement quality: Question type and errors of omission. *Law and Human Behavior, 19,* 631-648.

Janet, P. (1925). *Psychological healing* (Vols. 1-2). New York: Macmillan. (Original work published 1919)

Lamb, M., Gaensbaur, T. J., Malkin, C. M., & Schultz, L. A. (1985). The effects of child maltreatment on security of infant-adult attachment. *Infant Behavior and Development, 8,* 35-45.

Lazarus, R. S., & Folkman, S. (1984). *Stress, appraisal, and coping.* New York: Springer.

Lepore, S. J., & Sesco, B. (1994). Distorting children's reports and interpretations of events through suggestion. *Journal of Applied Psychology, 79,* 108-120.

Loftus, E. F. (1979). *Eyewitness testimony.* Cambridge, MA: Harvard University Press.

Lynn, S. J., & Rue, J. W. (Eds.). (1994). *Dissociation: Clinical and theoretical perspectives.* New York: Guilford.

Lyons-Ruth, K. (1996). Attachment relationships among children with aggressive behavior problems: The role of disorganized-early attachment patterns. *Journal of Consulting and Clinical Psychology, 64,* 64-73.

Markman, E. M. (1977). Realizing that you don't understand: A preliminary investigation. *Child Development, 48,* 986-992.

Moston, S. (1992). Social support and children's eyewitness testimony. In H. Dent & R. Flin (Eds.), *Children as witnesses* (pp. 33-46). Chichester, England: John Wiley.

Nemiah, J. C. (1995). Early concepts of trauma, dissociation, and the unconscious: Their history and current implications. In J. D. Bremner & C. R. Marmar (Eds.), *Trauma, memory, and dissociation.* Washington, DC: American Psychiatric Press.

Patterson, C., Masad, C., & Cosgrove, J. (1978). Children's referential communication: Components of plans for effective listening. *Developmental Psychology, 14,* 401-406.

Perry, B. D. (1994). Neurobiological sequelae of childhood trauma. Post-traumatic stress disorders in children. In M. Murberg (Ed.), *Catecholamine function in post-traumatic stress disorder: Emerging concepts* (pp. 233-255). Washington, DC: American Psychiatric Press.

Perry, N., McAuliff, B., Tam, P., Claycomb, L., Dosal, C., & Flanagan, C. (1995). When lawyers question children: Is justice served? *Law and Human Behavior, 19,* 609-630.

Peters, D. P. (1991). The influence of stress and arousal on the child witness. In J. Doris (Ed.), *The suggestibility of children's recollections: Implications for eyewitness testimony* (pp. 60-76). Washington, DC: American Psychological Association.

Pillemer, D. B. (1992). Preschool children's memories of personal circumstances: The fire alarm study. In E. Winograd & U. Neisser (Eds.), *Affect and accuracy in recall: Studies of "flashbulb" memories* (pp. 121-140). New York: Cambridge University Press.

Poole, D. A., & White, L. T. (1995). Tell me again and again: Stability and changes in the repeated testimonies of children and adults. In M. Zaragoza (Ed.), *Memory and testimony in the child witness*. Thousand Oaks, CA: Sage.

Putnam, F. W. (1985). Dissociation as a response to extreme trauma. In R. P. Kluft (Ed.), *Childhood antecedents of multiple personality disorder* (pp. 65-97). Washington, DC: American Psychiatric Press.

Putnam, F. W. (1991). Recent research on multiple personality disorder. *Psychiatric Clinics of North America, 14,* 489-502.

Putnam, F. W. (1995). Development of dissociative disorders. In D. Cicchetti & D. J. Cohen (Eds.), *Developmental psychopathology: Vol. 2. Risk, disorder, and adaptation* (pp. 581-608). New York: John Wiley.

Putnam, F. W., Helmers, K., & Trickett, P. K. (1993). Development, reliability, and validity of a child dissociation scale. *Child Abuse and Neglect, 17,* 731-741.

Pynoos, R. S., Steinberg, A. M., & Wraith, R. (1995). A developmental model of childhood traumatic stress. In D. Cicchetti & D. J. Cohen (Eds.), *Developmental psychopathology: Vol. 2. Risk, disorder, and adaptation* (pp. 72-95). New York: John Wiley.

Quimby, L. G., & Putnam, F. W. (1991). Dissociative symptoms and aggression in a state mental hospital. *Dissociation: Progress in the Dissociative Disorders, 4,* 21-24.

Rauch, S. L., van der Kolk, B. A., Fisler, R. E., Alpert, N. M., Orr, S. P., Savage, C. R., Fischman, A. J., Jenike, M. A., & Pitman, R. K. (1996). A symptom provocation study of posttraumatic stress disorder using positron emission tomography and script driven imagery. *Archives of General Psychiatry, 53,* 380-387.

Rudy, L., & Goodman, G. S. (1991). Effects of participation on children's reports: Implications for children's testimony. *Developmental Psychology, 27,* 1-26.

Rue, J. W., Lynn, S. J., Henry, S., Buhk, K., & Boyd, P. (1990). Child abuse, imagination and hypnotizability. *Imagination, Cognition and Personality, 10,* 53-63.

Saywitz, K. J., & Goodman, G. S. (1996). Interviewing children in and out of court: Current research and practical implications. In J. Briere, L. Berliner, J. A. Bulkley, C. Jenny, & T. Reid (Eds.), *The APSAC handbook on child maltreatment* (pp. 297-318). Thousand Oaks, CA: Sage.

Saywitz, K. J., Goodman, G. S., Nicholas, E., & Moan, S. (1991). Children's memories of physical examination involving genital touch: Implications for reports of child sexual abuse. *Journal of Consulting and Clinical Psychology, 59,* 682-691.

Saywitz, K. J., Jaenicke, C., & Camparo, L. (1990). Children's knowledge of legal terminology. *Law and Human Behavior, 14,* 523-535.

Saywitz, K. J., & Moan-Hardie, S. (1994). Reducing the potential for distortion of childhood memories. *Consciousness and Cognition, 3,* 408-425.

Saywitz, K. J., & Snyder, L. (1991, April). *Preparing child witnesses: The efficacy of comprehension monitoring training.* Paper presented at the biennial meeting of the Society for Research on Child Development, Seattle, WA.

Schneider-Rosen, K., Baunwald, K., Carlson, V., & Cicchetti, D. (1985). Current perspectives in attachment theory: Illustration from the study of maltreated infants. *Monographs of the Society for Research in Child Development, 50*(Serial No. 209), 194-210.

Shalev, A. Y. (1996). Stress vs. traumatic stress: From acute homeostatic reactions to chronic psychopathology. In B. A. van der Kolk, A. C. McFarlane, & L. Weisaeth (Eds.), *Traumatic stress: The effects of overwhelming experience on mind, body, and society* (pp. 77-101). New York: Guilford.

Siegal, M., Waters, L., & Dinwiddie, L. (1988). Misleading children: Causal attributions for inconsistency under repeated questioning. *Journal of Experimental Child Psychology, 45,* 438-456.

Spiegel, D. (1986). Dissociating damage. *American Journal of Clinical Hypnosis, 29,* 122-131.

Stein, M. B., Hannah, C., Koverola, C., Yehuda, R., Torchia, M., & McClarity, B. (1994). *Neuroanotomical and neuroendocrine correlates in adulthood of severe sexual abuse in childhood.* Paper presented at the 33rd Annual Meeting of the American College of Neuropharmacology, San Juan, PR.

Steward, M., & Steward, J. (1989). *The development of a model interview for young child victims of sexual abuse: Comparing the effectiveness of anatomical dolls, drawings, and videographics.* Final report to the National Center on Child Abuse and Neglect, Washington, DC.

Stuker, P. B., Winstead, D. K., Galina, Z. H., & Allain, A. N. (1991). Cognitive deficits and psychopathology among former prisoners of war and combat veterans of the Korean conflict. *American Journal of Psychiatry, 148,* 67-72.

Tobey, A. E., & Goodman, G. S. (1992). Children's eyewitness memory: Effects of participation and forensic context. *Child Abuse and Neglect, 16,* 779-796.

Toth, S. L., & Cicchetti, D. (1996). Patterns of relatedness, depressive symptomatology, and perceived competence in maltreated children. *Journal of Consulting and Clinical Psychology, 64,* 32-41.

van der Kolk, B. A. (1996). Trauma and memory. In B. A. van der Kolk, A. C. McFarlane, & L. Weisaeth (Eds.), *Traumatic stress: The effects of overwhelming experience on mind, body, and society* (pp. 279-302). New York: Guilford.

van der Kolk, B. A., & Fisler, R. E. (1995). Dissociation and the fragmentary nature of traumatic memories: Overview and exploratory study. *Journal of Traumatic Stress, 8,* 505-525.

van der Kolk, B. A., & van der Hart, O. (1989). Pierre Janet
    and the breakdown of adaptation in psychological
    trauma. *American Journal of Psychiatry, 146,* 1530-
    1540.
Warren, A. R., & McGough, L. S. (1996). Research on chil-
    dren's suggestibility: Implications for the investigative
    interview. In B. L. Bottoms & G. S. Goodman (Eds.),
    International perspectives on child abuse and children's

testimony: Psychological research and law. Thousand
    Oaks, CA: Sage.
Wolfe, D. A., Sas, L., & Wekerle, C. (1994). Factors asso-
    ciated with the development of post-traumatic stress dis-
    order among child victims of sexual abuse. *Child Abuse
    and Neglect, 18,* 37-50.
Wolfe, V. V., Gentile, C., & Wolfe, D. A. (1989). The impact
    of sexual abuse on children: A PTSD formulation. *Be-
    havior Therapy, 20,* 215-228.

General Memory Functioning at Pre- and Posttreatment in Female Rape Victims With Posttraumatic Stress Disorder

Pallavi Nishith
Terri L. Weaver
Patricia A. Resick
Mary H. Uhlmansiek

Posttraumatic stress disorder (PTSD) has been conceptualized within the framework of information-processing theories (Chemtob, Roitblat, Hamada, Carlson, & Twentyman, 1988; Foa, Steketee, & Rothbaum, 1989). Traumatic experiences provide an ideal vehicle for examining these processes, because, by definition, the memories for traumatic experiences are (a) hierarchically organized cognitive structures that are (b) easily triggered by trauma-related cues, leading to preferential allocation of attention to threat-related cues (Litz & Keane, 1989; Litz et al., 1996). Based on an information-processing paradigm, research on cognitive processes mediating PTSD has included studies on memory functioning, selective attention, and perceptual distortion.

Studies with varying trauma populations demonstrate an association between symptoms of PTSD and deficits within general memory functioning. Using the verbal (logical) and visual (figural) memory subtests from the Wechsler Memory Scale (Wechsler, 1987), one group of researchers found that Vietnam veterans with

AUTHORS' NOTE: We wish to acknowledge the assistance of Mindy Mechanic, Terese Evans, Gail Pickett, Katie Berezniak, and Dana Cason with conducting diagnostic interviews. We would also like to acknowledge the work of Meg Milstead, Nancy Hansen, Jennifer Boyce, Terri Portell, and Karen Wright for assistance with data entry. Finally, we would like to acknowledge the work of Linda Sharpe-Taylor, Kathleen Chard, and Millie Astin for assistance with implementation of the treatment protocols.

PTSD scored significantly lower on the verbal memory subscales than did comparison subjects who were matched on variables (e.g., age, race, sex, years of education, handedness, socioeconomic status, and alcohol abuse) that could affect memory (Bremner et al., 1993). For verbal memory, PTSD-positive participants' scores were 44% lower on immediate recall and 55% lower on delayed recall, suggesting that there were both immediate and longer-term difficulties with retention of verbally presented stimuli. The groups were not significantly different on their functioning on the visual memory subscale, suggesting that the scale may be a less sensitive measure of altered general memory functioning associated with PTSD. Sutker, Winstead, Galina, and Allain (1991) also used the verbal (logical) memory subscale of the Wechsler Memory Scale and found that a group of Korean veterans who had been prisoners of war (POWs) evidenced significantly poorer functioning on the overall memory scale and on the immediate verbal memory subscale compared with non-POW Korean combat veterans. The two groups did not differ significantly on the task of delayed verbal memory functioning. Of note, this study did not make the group assignments based on the PTSD status of the veterans. Of the veterans within the POW group, 86% were PTSD-positive, and 9% of the comparison group were PTSD-positive. Given that the groups were not distinctive for their PTSD status and that PTSD is hypothesized to play a role in general memory functioning, this methodological limitation could explain the absence of findings for delayed verbal memory recall within the study.

Cognitive processing alterations associated with PTSD have also been demonstrated using the modified version of the Stroop task (Stroop, 1935). Within the original Stroop paradigm, participants were presented with a list of words and were asked to name the color of the ink in which an item was printed, while attempting to ignore the item itself. It has been consistently found that participants evidence longer response latencies (take more time) in naming the colors when the items are competing color names (e.g., the word *yellow* presented in green ink) than when the items are nonrelated stimuli.

Trauma researchers have modified this task to examine the influence of a negative, trauma-related emotional response by including threat-related words and comparing the latency of the color-naming response with neutral words. Studies using the modified Stroop color-naming paradigm with combat veterans found that PTSD-positive veterans evidenced significantly longer response latencies for trauma-related words when compared with non-PTSD veterans (Kaspi, McNally, & Amir, 1995; McNally, English, & Lipke, 1993; McNally, Kaspi, Riemann, & Zeitlin, 1990; Zeitlin & McNally, 1991). Similarly, studies using this paradigm with rape victims also found that rape victims with PTSD demonstrated significantly longer response latencies for rape-related words than did non-PTSD victims (Cassiday, McNally, & Zeitlin, 1992; Foa, Feske, Murdock, Kozak, & McCarthy, 1991). Therefore, these studies suggest that cognitive processing for threat-related words appears to be affected by PTSD. Bryant and Harvey (1995) found that diminished functioning was even robust when trauma victims with PTSD were compared with trauma victims who had another (phobic) anxiety disorder (but no PTSD).

The relationship between altered cognitive processing and PTSD has a number of hypothetical explanations. By definition, the PTSD spectrum includes difficulties with concentration and heightened emotional arousal (American Psychiatric Association, 1987, 1994). Both diminished concentration and heightened emotionality have been connected with memory impairment (Bremner et al., 1993) and disorganization within memory structures (Foa & Kozak, 1986). PTSD also includes hypervigilance for threat or trauma-related cues and exaggerated negative emotional response and flood of trauma-related images following such cues (American Psychiatric Association, 1987, 1994). This heightened emotional arousal for threat-related information and coincident intrusion of trauma-related images may be competing with the cognitive color-naming task required for the Stroop (McNally et al., 1993; Thrasher, Dalgleish, & Yule, 1994). PTSD also includes avoidance of trauma-related stimuli (American Psychiatric Association, 1987,

1994). For example, we have found clinically that rape victims presenting for treatment will often avoid saying the word *rape,* seemingly because the word itself evokes charged and negative emotions. This avoidance component of PTSD could also have a negative impact on participants' performance on the Stroop task.

Because concentration and memory alterations form an integral part of the PTSD spectrum, it follows that most therapies take an information-processing approach in the treatment of PTSD symptomatology. Emotional processing theory is based on information-processing research with rape victims. This theory is currently being applied to the study of rape victim reactions (Foa & Kozak, 1986; Foa et al., 1989). The emotional processing model draws from Lang's (1977) imagery-based information theory of fear. This theory not only treats cognitive attributions and expectations as specific content, it also focuses much of its attention on the structure and process by which information and events are encoded, integrated, and retrieved in memory. Foa et al. (1989) propose that when rape victims' concepts of safety are shattered, they develop an internal fear structure for escape and avoidance behavior, which elicits the symptoms of PTSD. The fear structure consists of trauma memories that are fragmented, disorganized, and disintegrated from the existing schema. Foa and Riggs (1994) propose that repeated reliving of the rape memories during prolonged exposure (PE) treatment (Dancu & Foa, 1992; Rothbaum & Foa, 1992) decreases the anxiety associated with these memories through habituation and enables reevaluation of the meaning representations in the memory. This repeated reliving generates a more organized memory record that can be more readily integrated with the existing schema.

More recently, drawing from the work of McCann, Sakheim, and Abrahamson (1988), Resick and Schnicke (1990, 1992, 1993) have proposed that reactions to a traumatic event represent more than a fear network. Victims report a wide range of affective reactions to traumatic events, not just fear. Resick and Schnicke propose that PTSD results from an inability to integrate the event with prior beliefs and experiences. When new, incompatible events occur, the person either alters (assimilation) the new information to fit prior beliefs or alters the prior beliefs (accommodation) to accept the event. Overaccommodation, or the altering of beliefs in extreme ways, is also possible; victims may make statements like, "No one can be trusted," or "I am never safe." Resick and Schnicke (1992, 1993) have conceptualized the PTSD symptoms of intrusion and avoidance as representing unsuccessful attempts to assimilate or accommodate the event, which they term "stuck points." They have developed cognitive processing therapy (CPT), which tries to help clients process trauma-related affect and identify their stuck points (Calhoun & Resick, 1993; Ellis, Black, & Resick, 1992; Mechanic & Resick, 1994; Resick, 1992, 1994; Resick & Markaway, 1991). These stuck points are then addressed and challenged in therapy in a systematic manner, using education, exposure, and cognitive components, to help clients integrate the trauma and modify their preexisting schemata.

The purpose of the study reported below was to determine if rape victims with PTSD show significantly greater improvement in memory functioning compared with wait-list controls after going through either PE treatment or CPT. Given that participants in both forms of therapy perform the task of processing traumatic memories and the affect related to those memories, this enables them to integrate the traumatic memories and bring about remission in the PTSD symptoms, which include difficulties with concentration and general memory functioning. Therefore, this study represents a first attempt to examine improvement in general memory functioning as the result of two treatments that are based on an information-processing approach. If memory functioning is significantly improved posttreatment, then one could conclude that alterations in cognitive processing are an integral part of the PTSD symptom spectrum. Given that both groups were PTSD-positive at pretreatment, we expected that there would be no initial difference between the treatment and wait-list control groups on immediate and delayed recall on the Wechsler logical memory subscale. We hypothesized that at posttreatment the treatment group would show significantly greater improvement from immediate to delayed recall compared with the wait-list group.

Method

Subjects

The subjects were 90 treatment-seeking rape victims who met diagnosis for PTSD (CAPS-1; Blake et al., 1990). Of these subjects, 68 (75%) also met criteria for either current or lifetime major depression, and 45 (50%) met criteria for comorbid substance use disorders (SCID-III-R; Spitzer, Williams, Gibbon, & First, 1987). The average age of the subjects was 33.13 years (range 18-62 years), and they had an average of 13.5 years of education. The racial distribution of the subjects who were administered the scales described below was as follows: 41 (85%) White, 5 (10%) African American, 1 (2%) Native American, and 1 (2%) Asian American.

Measures

CAPS-1. The CAPS-1 (Blake et al., 1990) is a 30-item scale that uses explicit behavioral anchors as the basis for clinician ratings. It includes items that assess each of the 17 core symptoms that constitute the construct of PTSD as defined by the *Diagnostic and Statistical Manual of Mental Disorders,* third edition, revised (*DSM-III-R;* American Psychiatric Association, 1987). It contains separate frequency and intensity ratings for each symptom. The CAPS-1 has high interrater reliability on frequency and intensity for all three subscales ($rs = .92$ to $.99$ for frequency; $rs > .98$ for intensity). Concurrent validity has been established against the Mississippi Scale for Combat-Related PTSD (Keane, Caddell, & Taylor, 1988), the PTSD subscale of the MMPI (Keane, Malloy, & Fairbank, 1984), and the Combat Exposure Scale (Keane et al., 1989).

SCID-III-R. The SCID-III-R (Spitzer et al., 1987) is a structured diagnostic interview that

assesses 33 of the more frequently diagnosed Axis I *DSM-III-R* disorders in adults. For most of the major categories (bipolar disorder, major depression, schizophrenia, alcohol abuse/dependence), kappas for current and lifetime diagnoses of above .60 have been demonstrated, with a mean kappa of .61 for current and .68 for lifetime diagnoses for the combined samples. In this study, the SCID-III-R was used to assess subjects for mood, panic, and substance use disorders.

Logical Memory I and Logical Memory II, WMS-R. The WMS-R (Wechsler, 1987) comprises a series of brief subtests, each measuring a different facet of general memory, attention, and concentration. The logical memory subscales of the WMS-R are felt to be tests of verbal memory. Logical Memory I comprises two brief stories, which are read to the examinee. After each one, the examinee retells the story from memory. Following a delay of 30 minutes, the examinee is again asked to relate each story, as a measure of delayed recall (Logical Memory II). The median reliability coefficient across age groups for Logical Memory I was .71 after a 4- to 6-week interval. The median reliability coefficient across age groups for Logical Memory II was .75.

Procedures

Subjects who gave informed consent were administered the CAPS-1 and the SCID-III-R to diagnose for PTSD and comorbid substance use disorders. The subjects who met criteria for PTSD were administered the logical memory subscales of the WMS-R at pretreatment, and their total scores on immediate and delayed recall were computed. The subjects were then randomly assigned to the treatment (4.5 to 6 weeks) or the wait-list control (6 weeks) condition. Those in the wait-list control group were telephoned once every 2 weeks to ensure that there were no crises requiring immediate attention. They were then administered the Wechsler memory subscales again after the waiting period, before being assigned to a treatment condition. The subjects initially assigned to the treatment condition were randomly assigned to

Pre

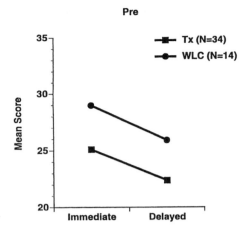

Post

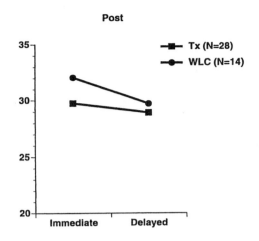

Figure 4.1. Between-Group Comparisons on Immediate and Delayed Recall at Pre- and Posttreatment

NOTE: $F(1, 47) = .15; p < .70.$

Figure 4.2. Within-Group Comparisons on Immediate and Delayed Recall from Pre- to Posttreatment

NOTE: $F(1, 40) = 2.49; p < .10.$

either prolonged exposure therapy (twice a week over 9 sessions, for a total of 13 hours) or cognitive processing therapy (twice a week over 12 sessions, for a total of 13 hours) and were reassessed on the Wechsler memory subscales posttreatment.

Results

Subject and Demographic Characteristics

The treatment and wait-list groups were compared on demographic variables of race, income, mean years of education, mean age, pretreatment level of PTSD, and pretreatment level of depression. Chi-square analyses were conducted for categorical variables (race and income), and *t* tests were conducted for continuous variables (mean years of education, age, PTSD severity, and level of depression). All comparisons were nonsignificant between groups, indicating that the treatment and wait-list comparison groups were comparable for demographic variables and initial level of depressive and PTSD symptomatology. At posttreatment, 86% (N = 24/28) of the treatment

group were no longer meeting criteria for PTSD, whereas 100% of the wait-list controls continued to be PTSD-positive (Nishith, Resick, Weaver, & Uhlmansiek, 1996).

General Memory Functioning

Two sets of 2 × 2 between-within analyses of variance (wait-list control, treatment condition × immediate, delayed recall) were conducted for the pre- and posttreatment assessments. At pretreatment, there was no significant difference between the wait-list control and the treatment subjects on their performance on immediate and delayed recall ($F[1, 47] = .15, p < .70$). At posttreatment, however, the treatment × recall interaction showed a significant trend ($F[1, 40] = .15, p < .70$). with the treatment group showing a greater improvement from immediate to delayed recall compared with the wait-list control group.

A series of *t* tests were also conducted for both the wait-list control and treatment groups to determine their performance on immediate and delayed recall from pre- to posttreatment. The analyses demonstrated that the treatment group improved significantly from pre- to posttreatment on both immediate (t[24] = 4.32, $p <$ .01) and delayed (t[24] = 5.58, $p < .01$) recall. The wait-list control group, on the other hand, did not improve significantly from pre- to post-treatment on immediate recall (t[14] = 2.11, $p =$ ns) and showed a significant improvement on delayed recall (t[13] = 3.17, $p < .007$) only.

Discussion and Implications

☐ The present study was designed to examine changes in general memory functioning following two treatments for rape-related PTSD. These treatments are based on an information-processing model. Toward this end, one treatment group (PE and CPT) and a wait-list comparison group were assessed with the Wechsler logical memory subscales at pre- and posttreatment. These scales assess immediate and delayed (30-minute) recall for verbally presented stimuli.

At pretreatment, there was no difference between the treatment and wait-list comparison groups on immediate and delayed recall. Given the nonsignificant differences for PTSD status for the two groups, it was expected that their memory impairment would be comparable. Similarly, participants were matched on demographic variables and level of initial depression. Taken together, these findings support the contention that there were no a priori differences between the participants assigned to the two groups that could confound the treatment outcome results.

There was preliminary support for the hypothesis that, at posttreatment, the performance of the treatment group from immediate to delayed recall would be significantly improved compared with the performance of the wait-list comparison group. Between-group comparisons using between-within ANOVAs at posttreatment showed a trend ($p < .10$) suggesting that the treatment group showed a greater improvement from immediate to delayed recall compared with the wait-list control group. This finding suggests that the treatment group showed a greater ability to "hold" information following a 30-minute delay from the immediate recall assessment. Given that PTSD was

remitted in the majority of the treatment group sample, this finding provides support for the connection between altered memory functioning and PTSD. It also generalizes the findings from a population of male combat veterans (Bremner et al., 1993; Sutker et al., 1991) to a population of female rape victims using the same instrument. However, these findings are tentative and need to be replicated with larger sample sizes.

Within-group comparisons using paired t tests revealed that both groups showed increases in scores for both immediate (pre- to posttreatment and pre- to post-waiting period for the comparison group) and delayed recall (pre- to posttreatment and pre- to post-waiting period for the comparison group). This finding does suggest that the passage of time alone may lead to improvement in concentration and tracking of verbally presented stimuli. However, as shown by the between-group comparisons, above, the pattern evidenced for the retention (i.e., the memory) of the material showed a greater improvement for the treatment group only, compared with the wait-list control group. This supports the contention that treatment approaches that claim to foster recovery by synthesizing and organizing fragmented trauma memories may be influencing general memory functioning as well. However, this conclusion remains speculative, given that we have not yet been able to examine changes in the trauma-specific memory. Clinically, we have observed patients spontaneously organizing their original memories for traumatic events with continued involvement in either one of the two therapies. As their memories become more organized, we have also observed decreases in trauma-related negative affect. This phenomenon needs to be studied experimentally with more rigorous paradigms. One possibility would be to extend the Stroop paradigm to examine response latencies for trauma stimuli pre- and posttreatment. We would expect there to be a decrease in the response latency if the patient has a more organized memory with less attached negative affect. Taking this approach a step further, future research could also examine the changes in the content of the trauma-specific memory more directly by using content-analytic methodology. The treatment approach of prolonged exposure is particularly amenable to this methodology, given that the primary intervention within this treatment involves having patients repeatedly "relive" or recount their traumatic experiences.

There are a number of limitations within the study reported above. First, the data were collected in the beginning stages of a 5-year treatment study. Therefore, the sample sizes are small, and the power is limited. In addition, the memory-assessment instrument included only one subscale of a more comprehensive assessment measure. Therefore, future research needs to replicate and expand these findings using larger sample sizes and more comprehensive assessment protocols. One possibility is to use the entire Wechsler Memory Scale, which assesses visual memory, verbal memory, and general concentration. This approach would enable the researcher to determine which area of memory impairment is most strongly implicated with PTSD. Future research must also attend to diagnoses that are frequently comorbid with PTSD. For example, depression, which is often comorbid with PTSD, also includes concentration difficulties within its symptom spectrum. We addressed this issue within the study discussed above by assessing for pretreatment level of depression, on which the two groups were found to be comparable. Other overlapping diagnoses that may also have implications for memory alterations and changes in cognitive processing include dissociative disorders and dissociation as part of an acute stress response (American Psychiatric Association, 1994). An association between dissociative symptomatology and PTSD has been reported by several researchers (Bremner et al., 1992; Classen, Koopman, & Spiegel, 1993; Griffin, Resick, & Mechanic, 1994; Marmar et al., 1994; Spiegel, 1984; Waid & Urbanczyk, 1989). It has also been shown that high dissociators with PTSD show significantly lower remission in their PTSD symptoms over time compared with low dissociators (Nishith, Mechanic, Griffin, & Resick, 1995). We therefore recommend that problems with concentration and memory also be studied as functions of other comorbid dissociative disorder diagnoses. Other possibilities

include examining individuals who have marked difficulties with sleep and/or alcohol and drug use, all of which can influence memory and cognitive functioning and are frequently long-term sequelae of trauma.

References

American Psychiatric Association. (1987). *Diagnostic and statistical manual of mental disorders* (3rd ed., rev.). Washington, DC: Author.

American Psychiatric Association. (1994). *Diagnostic and statistical manual of mental disorders* (4th ed.). Washington, DC: Author.

Blake, D. D., Weathers, F. W., Nagy, L. M., Kaloupek, D. G., Klauminzer, G., Charney, D. S., & Keane, T. M. (1990). A clinician rating scale for assessing current and lifetime PTSD: The CAPS-1. *Behavior Therapist, 13,* 187-188.

Bremner, J. D., Scott, T. M., Delaney, R. C., Southwick, S. M., Mason, J. W., Johnson, D. R., Innis, R. B., McCarthy, G., & Charney, D. S. (1993). Deficits in short-term memory in posttraumatic stress disorder. *American Journal of Psychiatry, 150,* 1015-1019.

Bremner, J. D., Southwick, S. M., Brett, E., Fontana, A., Rosenheck, R., & Charney, D. S. (1992). Dissociation and posttraumatic stress disorder in Vietnam combat veterans. *American Journal of Psychiatry, 149,* 328-332.

Bryant, R. A., & Harvey, A. G. (1995). Processing threatening information in posttraumatic stress disorder. *Journal of Abnormal Psychology, 104,* 537-541.

Calhoun, K. S., & Resick, P. A. (1993). Posttraumatic stress disorder. In D. H. Barlow (Ed.), *Clinical handbook of psychological disorders* (pp. 48-98). New York: Guilford.

Cassiday, K. L., McNally, R. J., & Zeitlin, S. B. (1992). Cognitive processing of trauma cues in rape victims with posttraumatic stress disorder. *Cognitive Therapy and Research, 16,* 283-295.

Chemtob, C., Roitblat, H., Hamada, R., Carlson, J., & Twentyman, C. (1988). A cognitive action theory of posttraumatic stress disorder. *Journal of Anxiety Disorders, 2,* 253-275.

Classen, C., Koopman, C., & Spiegel, D. (1993). Trauma and dissociation. *Bulletin of the Menninger Clinic, 57,* 178-194.

Dancu, C. V., & Foa, E. B. (1992). Posttraumatic stress disorder. In A. Freeman & F. M. Dattilio (Eds.), *Comprehensive casebook of cognitive therapy* (pp. 79-88). New York: Plenum.

Ellis, L. F., Black, L. D., & Resick, P. A. (1992). Cognitive-behavioral treatment approaches for victims of crime. In P. A. Keller & S. R. Heyman (Eds.), *Innovations in clinical practice: A source book* (pp. 23-38). Sarasota, FL: Professional Resource Exchange.

Foa, E. B., Feske, U., Murdock, T. B., Kozak, M. J., & McCarthy, P. R. (1991). Processing of threat-related information in rape victims. *Journal of Abnormal Psychology, 100,* 156-162.

Foa, E. B., & Kozak, M. J. (1986). Emotional processing of fear: Exposure to corrective information. *Psychological Bulletin, 99,* 20-35.

Foa, E. B., & Riggs, D. S. (1994). Posttraumatic stress disorder and rape. In R. S. Pynoos (Ed.), *Posttraumatic stress disorder: A clinical review* (pp. 133-158). Lutherville, MD: Sidran.

Foa, E. B., Steketee, G., & Rothbaum, B. O. (1989). Behavioral/cognitive conceptualization of posttraumatic stress disorder. *Behavior Therapy, 20,* 155-176.

Griffin, M. G., Resick, P. A., & Mechanic, M. B. (1994, November). *Psychophysiological and nonverbal assessment of peritraumatic dissociation in rape victims.* Paper presented at the 10th Annual Meeting of the International Society for Traumatic Stress Studies, Chicago.

Kaspi, S. P., McNally, R. J., & Amir, N. (1995). Cognitive processing of emotional information in posttraumatic stress disorder. *Cognitive Therapy and Research, 19,* 319-330.

Keane, T. M., Caddell, J. M., & Taylor, K. L. (1988). Mississippi scale for combat-related posttraumatic stress disorder: Three studies in reliability and validity. *Journal of Consulting and Clinical Psychology, 52,* 888-891.

Keane, T. M., Fairbank, J. A., Caddell, J. M., Zimering, R. T., Taylor, K. L., & Mora, C. A. (1989). Clinical evaluation of a measure to assess combat exposure. *Psychological Assessment, 1,* 53-55.

Keane, T. M., Malloy, P. F., & Fairbank, J. A. (1984). Empirical development of an MMPI subscale for the assessment of combat-related posttraumatic stress disorder. *Journal of Consulting and Clinical Psychology, 52,* 888-891.

Lang, P. J. (1977). Imagery in therapy: An information processing analysis of fear. *Behavior Therapy, 8,* 862-886.

Litz, B. T., & Keane, T. M. (1989). Information processing in anxiety disorders: Application to the understanding of posttraumatic stress disorder. *Clinical Psychology Review, 9,* 243-257.

Litz, B. T., Weathers, F. W., Monaco, V., Herman, D. S., Wulfsohn, M., Marx, B., & Keane, T. M. (1996). Attention, arousal, and memory in posttraumatic stress disorder. *Journal of Traumatic Stress, 9,* 497-519.

Marmar, C. R., Weiss, D. S., Schlenger, W. E., Fairbank, J. A., Jordan, B. K., Kulka, R. A., & Hough, R. L. (1994). Peritraumatic dissociation and posttraumatic stress in male Vietnam theater veterans. *American Journal of Psychiatry, 151,* 902-907.

McCann, I. L., Sakheim, D. K., & Abrahamson, D. J. (1988). Trauma and victimization: A model of psychological adaptation. *Counseling Psychologist, 16,* 531-594.

McNally, R. J., English, G. E., & Lipke, H. J. (1993). Assessment of intrusive cognition in PTSD: Use of modified Stroop paradigm. *Journal of Traumatic Stress, 6,* 33-41.

McNally, R. J., Kaspi, S. P., Riemann, B. C., & Zeitlin, S. B. (1990). Selective processing of threat cues in post-

traumatic stress disorder. *Journal of Abnormal Psychology, 99,* 398-402.

Mechanic, M. B., & Resick, P. A. (1994, July). *An approach to treating posttraumatic stress disorder and depression.* Paper presented at the 20th Annual Meeting of the National Association for Rural Mental Health, Des Moines, IA.

Nishith, P., Mechanic, M. B., Griffin, M. G., & Resick, P. A. (1995, November). *Peritraumatic dissociation and PTSD in rape victims.* Poster presented at the 11th Annual Meeting of the International Society for Traumatic Stress Studies, Boston.

Nishith, P., Resick, P. A., Weaver, T. L., & Uhlmansiek, M. H. (1996, July). *General memory functioning at pre- and post-treatment in female rape victims with posttraumatic stress disorder.* Paper presented at Trauma and Memory: An International Research Conference, Durham, NH.

Resick, P. A. (1992). Cognitive treatment of a crime-related posttraumatic stress disorder. In R. D. Peters, R. J. McMahon, & V. L. Quincey (Eds.), *Aggression and violence throughout the life span* (pp. 171-191). Newbury Park, CA: Sage.

Resick, P. A. (1994). Cognitive processing therapy (CPT) for rape-related PTSD and depression. *National Center for PTSD Clinical Quarterly, 4,* 1-5.

Resick, P. A., & Markaway, B. E. G. (1991). Clinical treatment of adult female victims of sexual assault. In C. R. Hollin & K. Howells (Eds.), *Clinical approaches to sex offenders and their victims* (pp. 261-284). New York: John Wiley.

Resick, P. A., & Schnicke, M. K. (1990). Treating symptoms in adult victims of sexual assault. *Journal of Interpersonal Violence, 5,* 488-506.

Resick, P. A., & Schnicke, M. K. (1992). Cognitive processing therapy for sexual assault victims. *Journal of Consulting and Clinical Psychology, 60,* 748-756.

Resick, P. A., & Schnicke, M. K. (1993). *Cognitive processing therapy for rape victims: A treatment manual.* Newbury Park, CA: Sage.

Rothbaum, B. O., & Foa, E. B. (1992). Exposure therapy for rape victims with post-traumatic stress disorder. *Behavior Therapist, 15,* 219-222.

Spiegel, D. (1984). Multiple personality as a posttraumatic stress disorder. *Psychiatric Clinics of North America, 7,* 101-110.

Spitzer, R. L., Williams, J. B. W., Gibbon, M., & First, M. B. (1987). *Structured clinical interview for DSM-III-R.* Washington, DC: American Psychiatric Press.

Stroop, J. R. (1935). Studies of interference in serial verbal reactions. *Journal of Experimental Psychology, 18,* 643-661.

Sutker, P. B., Winstead, D. K., Galina, Z. H., & Allain, A. N. (1991). Cognitive deficits and psychopathology among former prisoners of war and combat veterans of the Korean conflict. *American Journal of Psychiatry, 148,* 67-72.

Thrasher, S. M., Dalgleish, T., & Yule, W. (1994). Information processing in post-traumatic stress disorder. *Behaviour Research and Therapy, 32,* 247-254.

Waid, L. R., & Urbanczyk, S. A. (1989). *A comparison of high versus low dissociative Vietnam veterans with PTSD.* Paper presented at the 103rd Annual Meeting of the American Psychological Association, New Orleans.

Wechsler, D. (1987). *Wechsler Memory Scale–Revised: Manual.* San Antonio, TX: Psychological Corporation/ Harcourt Brace Jovanovich.

Zeitlin, S. B., & McNally, R. J. (1991). Implicit and explicit memory bias for threat in posttraumatic stress disorder. *Behaviour Research and Therapy, 29,* 451-457.

5

Remembering Trauma

A Characterological Perspective

Craig C. Piers

One can scarcely pick up a professional journal—or a popular publication, for that matter—without some mention of the pathogenic significance of childhood sexual trauma. The gravity and evocative nature of sexual trauma often results in a stereotyping of positions that fuels and obscures the controversy, preventing sober consideration of the issues at hand. In the center of this passionate, often acrimonious dialogue, traumagenic models of psychopathology based on dissociation have reemerged in the clinical literature (Herman, 1992; Hillgard, 1977; Putnam, 1989; Siegel, 1995; Spiegel, 1988; van der Kolk, 1987).

Two interrelated assumptions are embedded in theories of dissociation. One relates to a theory of psychopathology, or an understanding of the patient's problem. The second pertains to an understanding of the task of psychotherapy and the nature of its therapeutic action. In any coherent model of psychopathology and psychotherapy, these assumptions are stated and the second flows logically from the first. That is, the aim and method of treatment depend upon the understanding of the nature of the problem. Dissociation theorists assume that a dissociated trauma—often from childhood—serves as the root and contemporary cause of adult psychopathology, and that retrieval and integration of traumatic memories result in therapeutic change. I will argue that any conception of psychopathology based primarily on past traumatic experience is too narrowly focused, leading clinicians to pay insufficient attention to character.

AUTHOR'S NOTE: I would like to express thanks to Drs. Edward R. Shapiro, James L. Sacksteder, John P. Muller, Eric M. Plakun, J. Christopher Fowler, and Jane G. Tillman of the Austen Riggs Center for their encouragement and thoughtful comments on earlier versions of this chapter. In this regard, I would also like to express my appreciation to Drs. David Shapiro and Andrew Morral. This chapter is an abbreviated version of an article published in *Psychoanalytic Psychology*, vol. 15, pp. 14-33, titled "Contemporary Trauma Theory and Its Relation to Character." Copyright 1998 by the American Psychological Association. Reprinted by permission.

Character is conceived of here as a tension-organizing and anxiety-forestalling dynamic system that constitutes an individual's particular perspective, frame of reference, "mode of existence" (Reich, 1972), or "style" (Shapiro, 1965). Character designates the almost continuous features of the expressive activity of the individual and imposes form and organization on subjective experience. An individual's character style is manifest in the distinctive manner in which he or she perceives, thinks, experiences emotion, speaks, interacts, and remembers. These general and formal consistencies derive from the organizing processes of the individual's mind, processes that are at the same time relatively unarticulated in consciousness. I propose that character, the individual's formal way of organizing subjective experience, greatly influences the contemporary and continued significance of past traumatic experience. In this way, characterological processes—while linked to development and the past—contribute to making and keeping a past experience traumatic.

I shall focus this chapter on patients who report past trauma and enter treatment with serious and long-standing psychological disturbances. They often describe, with much distress, their preoccupation with their traumatic pasts. Thoughts and feelings, as well as vivid memories and nightmares, relating to the trauma dominate their waking and sleeping hours. Their affective expressions are constricted, unregulated, or an alternating mixture of the two. These patients also typically manifest severe instability in their experience of self-worth. Finally, they often demonstrate repetitive interpretations and reactions to people and situations, motivated by their almost continual efforts to manage their own sensitivities and anxieties. This compromises their capacity to form and sustain satisfying interpersonal relationships. These patients typically meet diagnostic criteria for multiple, comorbid Axis I and II disorders. I would include in the group under consideration many of the patients Herman (1992) places under her rubric of "complex posttraumatic stress disorder."

I do not use character pathology here to describe a particular or even a set of personality disorders classified in the fourth edition of the

Diagnostic and Statistical Manual of Mental Disorders (*DSM-IV*; American Psychiatric Association, 1994). *DSM-IV* is "atheoretical" and describes personality disorders as constellations of particular maladaptive traits and features. I am using character pathology to describe a dynamic and restrictive way of organizing conscious experience through which entire aspects of ongoing subjectivity are effectively excluded, leaving the patient estranged from him- or herself. Such dynamic workings of the mind can express themselves in many symptomatic forms, including the personality disorders in *DSM-IV.*

Framing the Point of Divergence

☐ One of Freud's most significant and enduring contributions to our understanding of the mind was his conviction that we have mental content outside of conscious awareness, which, paradoxically, affects our experience. A theory of psychopathology based on unconscious dynamics is a compelling depiction of the patient's problem. Freud's formulation linked his patients' subjective experience with the perplexing nature of symptoms that appeared unrelated to their conscious intentions.

Although there appears to be general agreement about the existence and impact of nonconscious dynamics and how benefit can be derived from their translation into consciousness, clinicians diverge in their understanding of just what is unavailable to consciousness and the processes by which individuals keep painful material out of awareness. This reflects differences in formulating the nature of psychopathology. Freud, for instance, suggested that symptoms derived from ubiquitous unconscious, intrapsychic conflicts from childhood experience, lost through an active act of repression by the ego. Contemporary dissociation theorists, on the other hand, suggest that what is unavailable to consciousness is the detailed remembrance of traumatic experience, accomplished through the passively endured dissociation of the experience (Siegel, 1995; van der Kolk, 1987). I will argue that psychopathology derives from the contemporaneous, restrictive, self-alienating processes of character that keep patients unaware of entire aspects of their ongoing subjective experience, not just past traumatic experiences. These processes go on automatically, without conscious articulation, and mediate the manner in which patients organize (i.e., remember, explore, consider, experience) past events, thereby defining the extent to which they experience past events as traumatic. In short, people perceive, organize, and remember their experiences in their own ways, according to the dimensions of their own conflicted interests, aims, and concerns, regardless of how inaccessible these organizing tendencies are to conscious awareness.

One's view of psychopathology, in turn, informs psychotherapeutic technique (Piers, 1996). For instance, when dissociation theorists link psychopathology to a structural deficit caused by the isolation and encapsulation of a traumagenic pathogen, a historical, reconstructive, and abreactive approach to treatment makes sense. When psychopathology is linked to the ongoing workings of character, the therapeutic attitude and view of change are different. For example, rather than directing the patient to search out and revive dissociated memories of past trauma in hopes of linking current symptomatic behavior to reactions appropriate to these past events, a therapist listens for the trauma's contemporary significance to the patient, heard within the psychological context of a conflicted character. This requires attention to the patient's general style of functioning, which seizes, accentuates, revises, reacts against, dispels, and distorts entire aspects of his or her ongoing subjective experience, including his or her current experience of past traumatic events.

Wilhelm Reich (1972), one of the first psychoanalysts to draw attention to character, conceived of it as a "protective formation that has become chronic, [and] merits the designation armoring" (p. 155). Reich saw character as the single, main resistance to the psychoanalytic cure. He recognized that, although many patients may present with the same "nuclear conflict," they differ in the ways they experience and express the conflict, and in the ways they resist its understanding. These differences derive from each patient's "mode of existence or way of being," and these same processes are involved in perpetuating the patient's conflicted existence. Reich believed that the analysis of character must precede any exploration of early experiences, because a premature interpretive approach to childhood experiences would be deflected or absorbed into the ongoing workings of character without effecting any change.

A modern extension of character analysis is found in the work of David Shapiro (1965, 1981, 1989). Shapiro (1965) uses the term *style* to refer to a "form or mode of functioning—the way or manner of a given area of behavior—that is identifiable, in an individual, through a range of his specific acts" (p. 1). He claims that character serves as the basis of all symptoms. Therefore, psychopathology is always characterological. And Shapiro (1965) contends that "general forms or styles of functioning may be considered a matrix from which the various traits, symptoms and defense mechanisms crystallize" (p. 2). Shapiro sees the persistent and painful nature of conflict as inherent to the restrictive workings of character. The dynamics of character include patients' reflexive, active, and contemporaneous reactions against aspects of their own subjective tendencies, because these aspects run counter to their preferred styles, and thereby stimulate intense discomfort and anxiety. By *preferred,* I am not suggesting that patients choose their particular styles. Rather, patients develop through life experiences ways of binding and forestalling anxiety that feel tolerable, or at least necessary. These characterologically based, yet consciously unrecognized or unarticulated, reactions have the effect of narrowing patients' awareness of themselves. By extension, the restrictive and self-estranging processes of character affect patients' experience and exploration of their pasts, traumatic and otherwise.

Current Trauma Perspective

☐ According to many dissociation theorists, a traumatic experience leaves its mark on the psyche in a different manner from other experiences. Trauma is thought to be split off from the individual's associative and schematic networks. This "dis-association" is due, in part, to the trauma's highly emotional qualities, the nonfocal attention to aspects of the experience during its encoding, and the lack of higher cortical processing of the experience during and after the trauma (Siegel 1995; van der Kolk, 1991). Van der Kolk (1991) proposes that "memories [of traumatic experiences] may form the nucleus of psychopathology and continue to exert their influence on current experience by means of the process of dissociation" (p. 426). Like an abscess, a traumatic experience—including the associated perceptions, sensations, thoughts, feelings, and behaviors— is assumed to lodge itself in the mind. Most dissociation theorists do not conceive of a defensive or motivated forgetting of the trauma, such as repression, but rather a passive encasing and loss of the entire experience.

From this perspective, symptomatic behaviors are thought to be "triggered" by similar auditory, visual, affective, and relational cues (Siegel, 1995; van der Kolk, 1987). When traumatized individuals find themselves in situations reminiscent of the trauma, the dissociated experiences or self-contained, autonomous "mental models" (Siegel, 1995) are set in motion, independent of mediation or control. The lack of higher cortical processing of the trauma results in "broad generalizability and context-independence" of the traumatic response (Siegel, 1995). Past traumatic reactions become transported in whole form to the present, determining symptomatic behavior. From this perspective, the patient is primarily a passive and helpless transmitter of a past traumatic experience.

The method of psychotherapy clearly follows from this conceptualization of psychopathology. Treatment involves detecting, recovering, and integrating dissociated traumatic experiences. As Lewis (1996) writes, "The curative element is recovering dissociated traumatic memories and reintegrating them into normal memory states" (p. 7). The therapy places a premium on abreaction and the integration of the experience into the patient's larger experience of self. "A therapeutic abreaction emphasizes processing—both cognitively and emotionally—of dissociated elements of previously inaccessible or partially inaccessible memory" (Siegel, 1995, p. 117). Through this

process, the dissociated experience of trauma loses its pathological properties, and the patient supposedly can come to live his or her life unencumbered by the past (Chu, 1992).

Herman (1992) writes of the therapeutic action of psychotherapy as resting on the "restorative power of truth-telling" (p. 181). The "truth-telling" process encourages and directs the patient to revive the traumatic experience in vivid detail. A large part of the treatment involves the examination and diminution of the patient's exaggerated experience of responsibility for the event. Such an understanding prevents the patient from unwitting reenactments of the trauma. The misattribution and exaggeration of responsibility often seen in traumatized patients appears to belie a central tenet of dissociation theory: If an experience becomes lost through dissociation, it seems unclear how an individual could simultaneously feel responsible. At the very least, it suggests that there exists a remembrance of the event at some level of awareness, followed by a compensatory, defensive action.

Herman's (1992) method of treatment places a premium on abreaction and the relationship between therapist and patient. She describes a corrective relational experience wherein the therapist provides the patient with an experience of "empowerment and the creation of new connections." The importance of the relationship is linked to the contention that traumatic experiences deform and destroy the basic psychological faculties of trust, initiative, competence, identity, and intimacy. Herman suggests that, inasmuch as these psychological faculties develop in the interactive nature of relationships with others, the therapist attempts to provide the patient with a healthier, growth-promoting relationship in which they can be developed. Although it seems obvious that the maintenance of a respectful, genuine, and empathic attitude toward the patient is a necessary condition for therapeutic change, this does not mean that it is a sufficient condition for therapeutic change.

Finally, psychotherapy, in Herman's view, is also meant to help the patient see the anachronistic and maladaptive nature of his or her symptoms and to see them as solely connected to an experience from the past. Such a view stems from a conception of psychopathology as directly linked to the past, but it makes less sense from a characterological perspective. Rather than seeing symptomatic reactions and behaviors as anachronistic and maladaptive, a characterological view sees them as arising from the here-and-now dynamics of a conflicted character, which provides them with contemporary meaning and significance.

A Critique

☐ Elsewhere, I have critiqued dissociation models of psychopathology and psychotherapy from a number of vantage points (Piers, 1998). In this chapter, I focus exclusively on the formal ways patients remember traumatic experiences, because attention to the ways in which patients take up the content of their pasts reveals the central importance of character.

Ways of Remembering

By most contemporary accounts, remembering is an active and reconstructive process. Research indicates that what we remember is influenced by a number of factors, both at the time of the experience and at the time of recalling it. These influential factors include mood (Eich & Metcalfe, 1989), preexisting knowledge (Bransford, Barclay, & Franks, 1972; Bransford & Johnson, 1972), encoding strategies (Johnson, Raye, Foley, & Foley, 1981; Tulving & Thomson, 1973), contextual cues (Godden & Baddeley, 1975), the quality of retrieval cues (Loftus, 1975; Loftus & Hoffman, 1989; Manier, Piers, Greenstein, & Hirst, 1992), contemporaneous efforts to create a coherent sense of self across time (Barclay & DeCooke, 1988), and character style (Davis & Frank, 1979; Durso, Reardon, & Jolly, 1985; Fowler, 1994; Mayman, 1968; Paul, 1967; Piers, 1992/1995).

Remembering is always an action undertaken by a person. Therefore, it involves a current, self-directed aim or reason. An individual's aim or reason for remembering is independent of the content (event or experience) to be remembered, but may greatly influence what is remembered and how it is remembered. Often there are multiple reasons for remembering, all of which are more or less well articulated in consciousness. The reasons arise from the individual's particular point of view or frame of reference. An individual in a research experiment, for instance, may be interested in being paid, in doing well, in pleasing the experimenter, and (perhaps) in the research study itself. Similarly, a group of old friends, fondly reminiscing about the "good old days," may be interested in invoking an experience of their long-standing connection to one another and in creating a warm and friendly ambience. In these cases, the past is given significance and relevance within the larger context of the individual's current aim or intention. In other words, the past is taken up, interpreted, and made meaningful within a larger and current psychological context.

The same is true of individuals who report past trauma. Clearly, one reason patients have for remembering traumatic experiences is to communicate painful experiences from their lives, sometimes for the first time. But for many patients, the aim of remembering is multifaceted, involving more than a wish to communicate. Patients who are describing past traumatic experiences often appear to be addressing themselves, rather than solely their therapists. That is, they appear to be addressing issues embedded in ongoing workings of their minds, issues that are not fully articulated in consciousness, but affect the way the past is remembered, experienced, and communicated. The manner in which the past is taken up as well as the reasons the past remains significant reveal links to a patient's particular perspective, point of view, or frame of reference: the patient's character.

This phenomenon can be observed in the ways patients speak of their traumatic pasts. For instance, some patients speak of past traumatic experiences carefully and systematically, as if they are building a case, in an effort to prove to themselves the validity and legitimacy of their own experiences. Others speak of traumatic experiences with exaggerated indifference or nonchalance, like they are reading a police report, to convince themselves that they were, and are, unaffected by these experiences. Others continually return to their traumatic pasts in great detail, to remind themselves painfully of their self-conceived debased, damaged, and inferior status. Others take every opportunity to speak out loudly about their abuse, reminding themselves that there remains a score to be settled and that they are no longer going to allow themselves to be pushed around. Others demand verification of their own past experiences, to address their own unarticulated concerns that their feelings are exaggerated, childish, not to be trusted or taken too seriously. Others make only passing and thinly veiled references to past abuse, worried about being too clear, unfair, or blaming. Still others dutifully review their histories, determined to face the facts about the past, concerned that they may prematurely close the subject without first carefully considering and examining, even trying on, every conceivable reaction, thought, and feeling.

In an individual psychotherapy hour, a rather prideful and rigid man forcefully denounces and reproaches his father for the physical abuse that the patient, as a child, sustained from him. He then concludes by saying, as he has many times before:

Patient: I hate my father! I really, really do. I just really hate him.
Therapist: You seem to want to make that point clear.
Patient: [surprised and softer] Well I do hate him. I should. After all, look what he did to me. [Then, more quietly] I don't know why I say it so often.
Therapist: Perhaps you're hoping that it will stick.

The patient then went on to say that he wanted to hate his father. Indeed, he can be seen as trying to convince himself of feelings he did not currently have, or at least to the extent he felt was appropriate or comfortable. Such an effort was motivated by ongoing, more generalized and unarticulated concerns he had about his personal authority, stature, and dignity, or, as he often put it, his "manliness." For him, it was a matter of self-respect. Failing to take and maintain a strong stand against his father felt cowardly, as if he were backing down and admitting defeat. Indeed, he often said with great pride, "I never

took it lying down. I always stood up to him." Even worse for this patient was to allow for a full range of feelings toward his father, especially feelings that he felt reflected "weakness," such as affection, sadness, fear, and loss.

The ways patients take up their life histories is as varied and unique as they are. In understanding a patient's psychology, it is not enough to hear the content of a particular (however traumatic) set of memories; one must also understand the patient's particular frame of reference or the perspective in which his or her memories find significance. The past, in other words, is taken up by an individual according to his or her aims, rather than independently exerting its influence according to its aims.

Conclusion

☐ Dissociation theorists conceive of a whole array of symptomatic behaviors as direct expressions of the patient's traumatic past. Symptomatic behaviors are understood as perceptual, sensory, affective, and behavioral reenactments of the original trauma, passively and automatically set in motion when preserved, but dissociated, memories of the trauma are triggered (Siegel, 1995; van der Kolk, 1987). Past traumatic reactions are transported in whole form to the present and determine behavior relatively independently of the rest of the personality.

Childhood trauma does occur, and its effects are potentially devastating. Providing people with a chance to talk about traumatic experiences is valuable. At issue have been the processes that inhibit self-recognition and self-expression. Dissociation theorists link this inhibition to a structural deformation or partitioning of the mind that bars access to the traumatic memory and leaves in its wake a fragmented psyche. For patients who present with serious character pathology, however, the problem and treatment are more complicated. In these cases, the aspect of psychopathology most deleterious and least amenable to change is located in the patients' consciously unarticulated but continuous mode of functioning. This works to keep patients unaware of entire aspects of their own subjective experience, including their current subjective experience of the past.

Although a patient's problem is most certainly related to historical, childhood experiences, the adult patient's problem cannot be causally reduced to a particular set of childhood events. In fact, whether childhood trauma is a necessary and sufficient cause of dissociation and PTSD, in particular, or adult psychopathology, in general, is in doubt (Hulsey, Sexton, & Nash, 1992; Tillman, Nash, & Lerner, 1994; Yehuda & McFarlane, 1995). It seems more likely that the synthetic workings of the mind intertwine innumerable aspects of life experience into a self-organizing and self-regulating dynamic system, which, in the end, is quite different from its constituents. Trauma no doubt influences a child's experience and the development of character, but its immediate effect will be greatly influenced by the preexisting organizing tendencies of the child and the experiences the child had prior to the trauma, as well as the developmental, familial, and social contexts within which the trauma occurred. Its enduring significance, in turn, will interact with and be influenced by a host of subsequent experiences, and then be subjectively refashioned and modified, given the organizing tendencies of the adult personality. Development is a far more complicated process than the linear causality implied in dissociation theory. The specification of a historical, discrete, and external cause in accounting for adult psychopathology vastly underestimates this complexity. This is supported by the fact that one cannot, with reasonable levels of certainty, predict from childhood experiences the form an adult's problem will take.

One problem that arises from a view of psychopathology based on dissociation is that "recovery and integration" of past experiences become the central focus of treatment, and this is believed to be the avenue of change. Indeed, implicit in this therapeutic stance is a failure to recognize that the very exploration of past trauma—as with the exploration of any other area of conflict—will be affected by the processes of character. Further, the contemporary meaning assigned to a past trauma will be fashioned in ways consistent with the current and ongoing organizing tendencies of the personality.

When a therapist directs the patient's attention to past traumatic experiences, he or she is unnecessarily narrowing the field in which to explore the workings of the adult personality. That is, the patient's character engages the therapeutic work as the patient explores the particulars of the past. This is true if the patient is directed to focus exclusively on the future, the present, or his or her work life, marriage, or relationship with the therapist. In dynamic psychotherapy, the patient is free to explore any area that feels problematic. This will often include past experiences. However, the point here is that any particular set of past experiences is now problematic for the adult who is thinking about those experiences. It is the adult personality that is the focus of therapeutic attention, as the patient feels, thinks about, avoids thinking about, and reacts to aspects of his or her own current subjective experience in reviewing the past. In other words, the focus of treatment is on the way the adult patient takes up the past in the present.

If character can be treated as a by-product of focused exploration of past traumatic experiences, thereby producing therapeutic change, what is the problem? First, placing central focus on traumatic events runs the risk of encouraging patients to organize their identities around victimization, which, in some cases, may interfere with their capacity to assume greater responsibility for their current life circumstances (Haaken & Schlaps, 1991). Second, therapists who hold a prescriptively clear causal relationship between trauma and psychopathology may place unwitting pressure on themselves and their patients to uncover lost traumas. This may ultimately lead to the creation of so-called false memories.

Two recommendations follow. First, therapeutic attention to a patient's descriptions of past traumatic experience should be placed more on that experience's contemporary significance to the patient, rather than on affirming its historical accuracy and directing a detailed review of the trauma. This is because past trauma is experienced by the patient from the current perspective of character and, as such, holds dynamic significance in terms of its continued relevance to the contemporary workings of the mind. Second, the therapist should listen to such material as he or she would to anything the patient says: attending to the ways in which the patient works to remain unaware of aspects of his or her own subjective experience (including thoughts, feelings, reactions, and wishes) in the reporting of these episodes. The content of any communication, including content relating to past experiences, can be more completely understood if the current psychological context of the communication is understood. How a patient takes up his or her past in the present reveals much about that person's continuous mode of functioning and is indispensable to the therapist's understanding of the past's current psychological significance. It informs the therapist not just about what happened, but about the person speaking and the reasons and ways in which the past is problematic for him or her.

This orientation does not diminish the importance of past traumatic material. Rather, it confers equal status to everything patients say and how they say it, with the therapeutic attention remaining the same. Consequently, when a patient is talking about a childhood trauma, it is considered to be one of numerous ways through which the dynamic workings of the patient's mind will be made manifest. This allows the patient, rather than solely what the patient is saying, to become the focus of treatment.

With this in mind, the psychotherapeutic stance changes. The therapist is no longer concerned primarily with uncovering possible developmental roots, be they abusive or otherwise. The main psychotherapeutic task becomes one of enlarging the patient's self-awareness or way of organizing subjective experience, including unarticulated tendencies and reactions against these tendencies. Through this process, the patient becomes more able to explore feelings, thoughts, and reactions to past trauma, as well as to any other area of conflict. This increases the patient's capacity to tell the therapist—and, more important, to tell him- or herself—what he or she has experienced and is currently experiencing, rather than the therapist telling the patient.

References

American Psychiatric Association. (1994). *Diagnostic and statistical manual of mental disorders* (4th ed.). Washington, DC: Author.

Barclay, C. R., & DeCooke, P. A. (1988). Ordinary everyday memory: Some things of which selves are made. In U. Neisser & E. Winograd (Eds.), *Remembering reconsidered: Ecological and traditional approaches to the study of memory* (Vol. 2, pp. 91-125). New York: Cambridge University Press.

Bransford, J. D., Barclay, J. R., & Franks, J. J. (1972). Sentence memory: A constructive versus interpretive approach. *Cognitive Psychology, 3,* 193-209.

Bransford, J. D., & Johnson, M. K. (1972). Contextual prerequisites for understanding: Some investigations of comprehension and recall. *Journal of Verbal Learning and Verbal Behavior, 11,* 717-726.

Chu, J. A. (1992). The therapeutic roller coaster: Dilemma in the treatment of childhood abuse survivors. *Journal of Psychotherapy Practice and Research, 1,* 351-370.

Davis, J. K., & Frank, B. M. (1979). Learning and memory of field independent-dependent individuals. *Journal of Research in Personality, 13,* 469-479.

Durso, F. T., Reardon, R., & Jolly, E. (1985). Self-nonself segregation and reality monitoring. *Journal of Personality and Social Psychology, 48,* 447-455.

Eich, E., & Metcalfe, J. (1989). Mood dependent memory for internal versus external events. *Journal of Experimental Psychology: Learning, Memory, and Cognition, 15,* 443-455.

Fowler, C. (1994). A pragmatic approach to early childhood memories: Shifting the focus from truth to clinical utility. *Psychotherapy, 31,* 676-686.

Godden, D. R., & Baddeley, A. D. (1975). Context-dependent memory in two natural environments: On land and underwater. *British Journal of Psychology, 66,* 325-331.

Haaken, J., & Schlaps, A. (1991). Incest resolution therapy and the objectification of sexual abuse. *Psychotherapy, 28*(1), 39-47.

Herman, J. L. (1992). *Trauma and recovery: The aftermath of violence—from domestic abuse to political terror.* New York: Basic Books.

Hillgard, E. R. (1977). *Divided consciousness: Multiple controls in human thought and action.* New York: John Wiley.

Hulsey, T. L., Sexton, M. C., & Nash, M. R. (1992). Perception of facing treatment and the occurrence of children sexual abuse. *Bulletin of the Menninger Clinic, 56,* 438-450.

Johnson, M. K., Raye, C. L., Foley, H. J., & Foley, M. A. (1981). Cognitive operations and decision bias in reality monitoring. *American Journal of Psychology, 88,* 67-85.

Lewis, J. L. (1996). Two paradigmatic approaches to borderline patients with a history of trauma: The expressive psychotherapy of Otto Kernberg and the trauma model of Judith Lewis Herman. *Journal of Psychotherapy Practice and Research, 5,* 1-19.

Loftus, E. F. (1975). Leading questions and the eyewitness report. *Cognitive Psychology, 7,* 560-572.

Loftus, E. F., & Hoffman, H. G. (1989). Misinformation and memory: The creation of new memories. *Journal of Experimental Psychology: General, 118,* 100-104.

Manier, D., Piers, C. C., Greenstein, M., & Hirst, W. (1992, July). *Implicit knowledge of spatial relationships contributing to false recognition.* Paper presented at the annual meeting of the International Psychological Society, Brussels, Belgium.

Mayman, M. (1968). Early memories and character structure. *Journal of Projective Techniques and Personality Assessment, 32,* 303-316.

Paul, I. H. (1967). *The concept of schema in memory theory: Psychological issues* (Vols. 18-19). New York: International University Press.

Piers, C. C. (1995). Distinguishing among memories of real and imagined events: Source discrimination in the hysterical style (Doctoral dissertation, New School for Social Research, 1992). *UMI Dissertation Abstracts,* 9605983.

Piers, C. C. (1997). Contemporary trauma theory and its relation to character. *Psychoanalytic Psychology, 15*(1), 14-33.

Piers, C. C. (in press). A return to the source: Rereading Freud in the midst of contemporary trauma theory. *Psychotherapy, 33*(4), 539-548.

Putnam, I. W. (1989). *Diagnosis and treatment of multiple personality disorder.* New York: Guilford.

Reich, W. (1972). *Character analysis* (3rd ed.). New York: Simon & Schuster.

Shapiro, D. (1965). *Neurotic styles.* New York: Basic Books.

Shapiro, D. (1981). *Autonomy and rigid character.* New York: Basic Books.

Shapiro, D. (1989). *Psychotherapy of neurotic character.* New York: Basic Books.

Siegel, D. J. (1995). Memory, trauma and psychotherapy: A cognitive science view. *Journal of Psychotherapy Practice and Research, 4,* 94-122.

Spiegel, D. (1988). Dissociation and hypnosis in post-traumatic stress disorder. *Journal of Traumatic Stress, 1,* 17-33.

Tillman, J. G., Nash, M. R., & Lerner, P. M. (1994). Does trauma cause dissociative pathology? In S. J. Lynn & J. W. Rue (Eds.), *Dissociation: Clinical and theoretical perspectives* (pp. 395-414). New York: Guilford.

Tulving, E., & Thomson, D. M. (1973). Encoding specificity and retrieval processes in episodic memory. *Psychological Review, 80,* 352-373.

van der Kolk, B. A. (1987). *Psychological trauma.* Washington, DC: American Psychiatric Press.

van der Kolk, B. A. (1991). The intrusive past: The flexibility of memory and the engraving of trauma. *American Imago, 48,* 425-454.

Yehuda, R., & McFarlane, A. C. (1995). Conflict between current knowledge about posttraumatic stress disorder and its original conceptual basis. *American Journal of Psychiatry, 152,* 1705-1713.

6

Ethical Considerations in the Teaching of Trauma and Dissociation

Student Exposure and Unexpected Memory

Madelyn Miller

Teaching about trauma, dissociation, and treatment is increasing in university settings. Clinical practice departments of graduate programs in social work, psychology, and psychiatry have introduced trauma-related curricula into their course listings. Related departments have integrated traumatic stress perspectives into existing curricula. Even non-academic learning settings—including continuing education classes (Rothman, 1973) for experienced professionals, institute training for psychotherapists, and advanced seminars for practiced clinicians—provide training about traumatic stress and trauma. Courses are designed to help students develop an informed perspective on traumatic stress, empathic clinical skills, and self-awareness about the effects of providing complex and demanding treatment.

As well, they support transformative learning that can occur on intellectual, emotional, and/or philosophical levels.

In these courses, it is a common occurrence for students to disclose previously unrecalled past trauma or abuse experiences, albeit reluctantly and most often in private (Graziano & Miller, 1996; McCammon, 1995; Miller, 1994; Miller, 1995; Miller & Graziano, 1997; Miller, McCammon, Stamm, & Williams, 1995). This unexpected discovery of hidden trauma occurs in each of the aforementioned teaching formats. Instructors may be careful to differentiate the classroom experience from a therapeutic, personal context; nevertheless, these acknowledgments of unforeseen awareness of earlier abuse experience consistently arise.

Faculty in each format for instruction, then, must assume the responsibility of providing a safe frame for learning. This task becomes a real challenge in an academic, clinical practice context, as I will specifically discuss below. Instructors need to find a delicate balance between the encouragement of a deep and collaborative learning process and respect for and protection of students' integrity and basic comfort within the class context (Catherall, 1995; Felman, 1991). Instructors facilitate the continuing development of empathy through a reflective reading of personal internal experience (Muslin & Schlessinger, 1971) while they conscientiously attempt to maintain academic exploration of trauma within a theoretical and clinical treatment framework, rather than within a personal context.

Recent research on forgotten abuse (L. M. Williams, 1994) and delayed recall of childhood trauma, in both community (Williams, 1995) and clinical samples (Briere & Conte, 1993; Herman & Schatzow, 1987), suggests it should not be surprising that we find that students also have prior forgetting of childhood sexual abuse and that their memories are triggered in classes focusing on such trauma (Elliott & Briere, 1995). The broad trauma literature on the processes of remembering and disclosing memories of incest (Courtois, 1988; Davies & Frawley, 1994; Herman, 1992b; Pearlman & Saakvitne, 1995a; van der Kolk, 1987; van der Kolk, McFarlane, & Weisaeth, 1996) also supports the frequent occurrence, throughout the semester, of disclosure upon exposure (van der Kolk, 1994) to material about trauma.

In this chapter, I address the significant ethical issues faced by instructors of trauma-related courses. In particular, I focus on the issues these instructors need to consider regarding student exposure to class material and the potential impact of such material on unexpected discovery of hidden memory during the course of the semester. This discussion is based on my own 6-year experience teaching an intensive graduate social work course on the treatment of adult survivors of incest trauma. At its heart is this dilemma: how to balance an educational learning experience with a personal and safe learning experience for students.

Background on Course Curriculum

☐ A course on treatment of adult survivors provides students with a broad foundation for clinical work with the adult client who is a survivor of incest or other childhood sexual abuse, through a comprehensive understanding of the dimensions of a child's experience of trauma. Such a course is designed to help students identify the pervasiveness of abuse history for clients in a range of settings. Through knowledge of adult presentations and symptoms, students develop and refine their skills of assessment.

This kind of course is designed to help students develop a framework for treatment, and the skills for various intervention approaches, based on particular treatment philosophies, goals, and process. The course encourages students to include the scope of issues related to incest and its significant personal impact in considerations of social policy and service delivery. The therapeutic relationship is understood as central to the treatment setting.

These objectives are framed by a relational perspective regarding the clinical work, which focuses on trauma, attendant dissociation, and abuse-related reenactments, adaptations, and behaviors, as they converge within the treatment setting. The therapeutic relationship, central to the treatment phase, may be as powerful and complex as the abusive interpersonal dyads within the context of earlier traumas. In this context, therapy becomes the setting for articulation, expression, and exploration of these dynamics (Davies & Frawley, 1994; Pearlman & Saakvitne, 1995a).

In such a course, students are able to explore the dynamics of incest after contextualizing incest trauma within the current and evolving trauma literature, exploring the current social climate regarding this and related interpersonal abuses, and then examining incest from within a historical perspective. This occurs through an emphasis on the child's experience of sexual abuse trauma. And just as each adult survivor endures the impact of childhood trauma, so much of clinical work with adult survivors is an expression of childhood.

The actual impacts of abuse of power and betrayal of trust, the experience of invasive boundary violations, and the context of terror, shame, and secrecy are identified. Traumagenic dynamics (Finkelhor & Browne, 1985) and characteristic accommodation behaviors (Summit, 1983) are introduced. Central aspects of a child's experience are addressed, along with complex posttraumatic stress dynamics (Herman, 1992a).

Typically, such a course examines dissociative adaptations to sexual abuse across a continuum, beginning with an identification of characteristic adult presentations and expressions of long-endured trauma. The course contextualizes commonly disguised presentations and interpersonal dynamics and explores the effects of dissociation on memory.

Individual and group treatment principles are identified, the treatment process is explored, and the therapist-client relationship is examined, including transference and countertransference in the context of dissociation and trauma. Self-harming behaviors are explored as responses to the far-reaching impact of disrupted attachments (van der Kolk & Fisler, 1994).

Journal writing is a central aspect of student learning in a typical class on trauma and treatment in this context. Students record their responses to class material and literature. Clear definition is given to the journal as an educational tool to enhance reflection, rather than as a format for unexplored personal expression. Throughout the semester, students' brief journal entries are submitted to the instructor weekly and returned the following week. To encourage students' own processes of internal attunement, rather than a dialogue, the instructor makes minimal comments on the weekly journal entries.

Students use their journals to trace their responses to childhood sexual abuse as it is introduced in class. Also, journal writing encourages students' awareness of their reactions to trauma and, more formally, enables them to assess countertransference, vicarious traumatization, and the development of self-awareness in the clinical role. This important learning tool reinforces developing theoretical and clinical competence, as students periodically review their earlier writing and trace their evolving perceptions and progress. Additionally, the instructor is able to monitor students' experiences with this material.

Student Responses to Childhood Sexual Abuse in the Curriculum

☐ When the curriculum focuses on the atmosphere, texture, and dimensions of childhood, this most powerfully and deeply engages the class in empathic identification. And it is at this stage of learning that some students become aware of or begin their own explorations of earlier traumas.

Using curriculum that first focuses on the dimensions of a child's experience of trauma (e.g., Courtois, 1988; Finkelhor & Browne, 1985; Herman, 1992b; Summit, 1983; van der Kolk & Fisler, 1994) as a foundation for understanding adult experience and adult articulation of childhood (Davies & Frawley, 1994; Pearlman & Saakvitne, 1995a), students experience powerful reactions to the material, significant challenges to earlier conceptualizations, and the development of necessary adaptations. Students may acknowledge the difficulty of the material, mention how they avoid certain readings or feel overwhelmed by them, and express deep reflection and concern about assumptions of children's safety and experience in the world.

Many students revisit their own earlier traumas. Some unexpectedly discover trauma histories, with no preparation and little privacy. An empathic connection to childhood and reactions to class lectures, discussion, literature, and their own clinical fieldwork may result in students' recovery of previously hidden histories of abuse, and may be accompanied by disclosure, dissociation, and/or disorganization.

Students may approach such a course of study with previous knowledge about histories of incest, and may be well established in individual and group treatment. Other students may discover histories of incest during the class, or experience dissociative symptoms without a source. And still other students may have no trauma histories. Yet, regardless of their experiences, most students are intensely affected by the power of the emotional landscape, by the enormity of the issues, and by a changing world perspective. Each of these factors has broad implications for students, including a sense of urgency about becoming active in the field re-

garding traumatic stress issues. When these realities converge with personal histories of childhood abuse, for many students the complexity
of the course work broadens.

Impact of Trauma Study on Students

☐ The impact of trauma study on the student
(Monroe, 1995) must be included formally in
the curriculum, beginning with the first class. It
is equally important that it be introduced as an
aspect of ongoing and active assessment. The
instructor should recognize and identify the
emotional and conceptual challenges presented
by the material to be studied in the class. The
range of powerful reactions to course work in
childhood sexual abuse trauma needs to be nor-
malized. Regardless of students' personal histories, dissociative adaptations and vicarious traumatization, in relation to trauma study, can be
contextualized and presented on a continuum.
From detachment and avoidance to disruptions
in previously held views, students' responses
can be given a conceptual context.

Acknowledgment that such course work
may be unsettling for students—exposing their
vulnerabilities, their own trauma histories, or
related issues—is important. The instructor
should address the class with language that
acknowledges and assumes that male (Lisak,
1993) *and* female students may be survivors
themselves. This expresses respect to male students and male survivors, who are too often
invisible in discussions of this subject matter.
Further, it encourages careful examination of
gender in the literature and in the discourse
regarding trauma.

Role Clarification

☐ Rigorous academic requirements and pressures contextualize the instructor's role and students' experience. In academic course work,
instructors need to differentiate their role as
academic instructors from other clinical teaching functions. And instructors need to understand their role in the classroom as that of
educator, as distinct from clinician. This has

particularly significant implications for how an
instructor responds to disclosures and to the
management of attendant dissociation and disorganization within the academic setting. Instructors must carefully balance their desire for
students to understand the experience of trauma
fully with their awareness that many students
can easily become overwhelmed by abuse material in general, and particularly overwhelmed
if it touches upon their own histories of either
known or hidden abuse.

Attention to Class Affect

☐ Instructors must take care to pace and balance affect within the classroom, so as to avoid
the almost inevitable retraumatization of those
students who are either without access to or very
close to the affect of their histories. Instructors
should further acknowledge this course work's
impact by continuing ongoing assessment of
class members as the material progresses and by
engaging students in assessing the class experience.

Parallels in Learning, Treatment, and Traumatic Stress Response

☐ Instructors' need to pay attention to a safe
environment while dealing with traumatic material illustrates one of several significant parallels that evolve in this particular clinical teaching environment. Here the teaching
environment parallels the treatment context.
The treatment principle of first establishing
safety (Herman, 1992b; M. B. Williams, 1994)
and then balancing exploration with providing
containment is equally important in the learning
process. It allows for evolving awareness and
for the processing of difficult material. The
intensity of this learning and experiencing environment affords deep awareness. It also replicates the original fields of interaction, and thus
requires attention to safety. That is, the intensity
of the class atmosphere in which incest trauma
is introduced, the power distinction between
student and instructor, and student adaptations
to such difficult material by avoidance or de-

tachment parallel the context for the client survivor in the therapeutic setting, who experiences the intensity of past experience regarding trauma, the power of the relationship, and a range of adaptations.

The complexities of the transference within the treatment dyad are reflected within the student-instructor relationship, even though the instructor pays careful attention to the distinction between instructor and clinician. For instance, a student may reflect a survivor's particularly complex transference reactions through expression of anger toward the instructor at having to read such difficult literature and having to rethink concepts of safety, childhood, or dissociation, or having to consider the enormity of implications of traumatic amnesia or the concept of a disguised presentation. This parallels the client's complex transference in relation to the therapist—for example, experiencing the therapist with the intention to harm, abuse, or expose to pain, as in trauma-specific family relationships.

Instruction becomes a model for treatment. The instructor frames the class just as a clinician would frame the treatment context, providing a holding environment (Winnicott, 1965) and a secure base (Bowlby, 1988) for the learning process. Setting clear boundaries for the class through the tone maintained and anticipating students' difficulties as the exploration of course material deepens continue this parallel experience.

The teaching context not only parallels and models the treatment process (Sachs & Shapiro, 1976). Regardless of their own histories, students experience the impact of their study of this topic much as do survivors in treatment (Martin & Henry-Feeney, 1989; Talbot, 1990): with an initial sense of helplessness, the need to avoid or carefully approach the material, and dissociation from it. Much as the client through treatment develops from victim to survivor, the overwhelmed or dissociated student develops (through the semester) a sense of being an active, entitled, and empowered clinician. There are further parallels: A client's conceptualization of the trauma, development of a language to articulate its impact, and experience of becoming an active survivor are comparable to the

student's experience of beginning to apply theory and learning to practice treatment with trauma survivors. The study of trauma and treatment for the student is also similar to the child's exposure to traumatic abuse, with attendant dissociation and complex adaptations that intensify if the student discovers a similar personal history through the course of the semester. Certainly, deeper parallels exist for students with trauma histories.

By introducing the class to each parallel experience and acknowledging the intersection of multiple parallels, the instructor can powerfully illuminate clinical material. Discussion of these parallels gives students a context within which they can understand more deeply traumatic stress dynamics, the client's experiences as an adult and as a child, and their own dynamics and reactions. Such discussion also contributes to students' conceptualization of treatment considerations and helps to guide their intervention and clinical work. The drawing of detailed distinctions between analogous situations, as well as the acknowledgment of intersecting experiences, enables a fuller learning experience.

Dilemmas in Teaching

☐ Complex dilemmas confront instructors in this challenging area of teaching. Philosophical questions remain in regard to providing the context for learning in which some students unexpectedly discover deeply buried traumas, and are thereafter faced with painful awareness. Had they not taken a given course, some students may not have uncovered memories, at least at that particular juncture. Some may have waited until later, perhaps until a safer time, to unfold history and emotion. Nonetheless, many students do begin this difficult process of exploration during or after their class experience.

A related concern is that all students are exposed to trauma in a course on childhood sexual abuse, whether or not the instructor incorporates concerns of safety, validation, and support into the curriculum.

Finally, students inevitably are in the position of trying to integrate and synthesize distinctions between traumatic stress theory and other diagnostic frameworks. They often experience the complexities of doing so, as this study and its conceptual basis is becoming more fully reflected in a wider range of curricula.

Many students express hopefulness in the classroom setting as they observe their clients' responsiveness and resilience and experience their own participation in client empowerment. Students observe clients articulating their traumas in the context of developing therapeutic relationships with them, and observe the beginnings of new forms of relatedness and self-reference. This essential part of learning incorporates practice, theory, and self-awareness, and directly reflects the students' own, often parallel, experiences within the class and in relation to the instructor.

Recommendations

☐ To summarize the discussion thus far, instructors of courses in trauma and dissociation should take care to do the following:

1. Begin the class with discussion of the material's emotional impact and conceptual challenges.
2. Normalize a range of powerful reactions to the study of trauma, specifically child sexual abuse trauma.
3. Acknowledge that the study of trauma may unsettle students' vulnerabilities and related issues, or their trauma histories.
4. Contextualize a range of dissociative reactions to trauma study, regardless of abuse history.
5. Maintain an ongoing assessment of class members as the material progresses, and continually check in with the class.
6. Set clear boundaries of safety for the class in tone, pacing, and balancing of interaction.
7. Have students turn in journal entries weekly, for student assessment of reactions to trauma material.
8. Anticipate students' difficulty as the material deepens.
9. Identify the classroom as a learning environment, with necessary attention to one's own reactions, and clearly distinct from a therapeutic context.
10. Address the class using language that acknowledges and assumes that both male and female students may be survivors.

Disclosures

☐ The classroom setting is not a protected or conducive context for students' personal disclosures of profoundly difficult material. A student may feel vulnerable both among student peers and with an instructor, and may be unprepared for a public expression of emotion or for others' responses. Additionally, the class as a group may not feel safe with disclosures.

It is rare for students to disclose their histories directly during a class. The academic context, expectations of competence, and requirements for achievement make such disclosure unlikely. More often, disclosures are expressed privately: through journal writing, a phone call to the instructor, or in discussion outside of class. Some students will express their experiences indirectly. Others will choose not to share their personal histories.

With the inevitability of a discovery process for some students, it is essential that the instructor provide a safe environment—for both individual students and the collective classroom experience. The instructor must ensure that no expectation is placed on students regarding the sharing of their own histories, whether awareness is long acknowledged, new, or developing. Nor should the instructor directly introduce not sharing one's own history. Instead, the instructor's educational focus, tone, boundaries, and frame for the class can define the parameters of the class discussion and shared expression. This framing can provide students with guidance and an opportunity to develop their own professional boundaries within the class setting. A consistent and active recognition of the course work's deep impact on the student—and, as well, of the even greater demands it places on those students who are themselves survivors of trauma—validates each student's experience. The instructor should encourage students to use other arenas of support to explore any related issues, including their own histories. The instructor's normalizing of students' experiences while providing boundaries for disclosure can ensure safety for both individual students and the class.

From the outset of the course, the instructor must, through instructional language and content choices, acknowledge the assumption that students and clinicians may be survivors of incest (Saakvitne, 1991) or other childhood traumas. Such inclusiveness, combined with an open, accepting atmosphere, will encourage thoughtful analysis of the impact of an individual's history on learning and treatment.

As concepts of countertransference and vicarious traumatization are explored in class, and careful distinctions are made, students may express profound relief and validation. The deep reactions and range of responses evoked by the theoretical and clinical content, and by the emotional demands of the work, both in a personal arena (Danieli, 1994) and in relation to the cumulative effects of this trauma-related material (McCann & Pearlman, 1990; Pearlman & Saakvitne, 1995a), are understood as vital aspects of knowledge, to be explored in supervision, in therapy, among colleagues and peers, and in consultation, and to be given attention with conscientious self-care (Pearlman, 1995; Pearlman & Saakvitne, 1995b).

In responding to student disclosures, the instructor should take care to do the following:

1. Frame the rare public disclosure in the context of the educational format rather than a therapeutic context, while supportively acknowledging the student.
2. Respect students' confidentiality if a private disclosure is made. Respond with a clear sense of the instructor's role as distinct from the therapist's, and with supportive acknowledgment of the disclosure.
3. Respond privately to students who do not disclose a history of trauma but who express particular difficulty with class discussions, assignments, or reading and appear dissociated or disorganized. Engage such students in assessment of their class experience and in establishing safety and finding support.
4. Provide resources and encourage students to find informed student health service clinicians or affordable private therapists, and informed supervisors.

Conclusion

☐ Through lectures, comprehensive reading, clinical material, discussion, journal use, and a careful look at the media and social climate regarding trauma and abuse, students develop assessment and clinical treatment skills. Numerous students finish this course work with a recognition that the study of trauma and treatment of adult incest survivors, beginning with the child's experience, has transformed them deeply, broadening their outlook regarding human behavior. Students may find that their perspectives on psychopathology are completely changed, recontextualized, rethought. Most broadly, many students leave this learning environment with a commitment to include trauma and abuse issues in their work.

Through conscious concern for the safety of the student and deep respect for the self of the student as core principles, developing clinicians are engaged in transformative learning. This can occur in a course with emotionally felt intensity, reflecting the depth and power of trauma experiences. And it can occur with direct acknowledgment of the common reality of trauma histories and their inevitable impacts.

Such course work incorporates an evolving internal awareness that goes beyond the development of clinical competence. The student may emerge with a clearer perspective on the exquisite sensitivity and equal resilience of the individual in the face of often life-threatening abuse and trauma. Teaching that goes beyond content and skill development to acknowledge its process and parallels to the material under study can powerfully and safely engage students in a process of learning.

References

Bowlby, J. (1988). *A secure base: Parent-child attachment and healthy human development.* New York: Basic Books.

Briere, J., & Conte, J. R. (1993). Self-reported amnesia for abuse in adults molested as children. *Journal of Traumatic Stress, 6,* 21-31.

Catherall, D. (1995). Preventing institutional secondary traumatic stress disorder. In C. Figley (Ed.), *Compassion fatigue: Coping with secondary traumatic stress disor-*

der in those who treat the traumatized (pp. 232-247). New York: Brunner/Mazel.

Courtois, C. A. (1988). *Healing the incest wound: Adult survivors in therapy.* New York: W. W. Norton.

Danieli, Y. (1994). Countertransference, trauma, and training. In J. Wilson & J. Lindy (Eds.), *Countertransference in the treatment of PTSD* (pp. 368-388). New York: Guilford.

Davies, J. M., & Frawley, M. G. (1994). *Treating the adult survivor of childhood sexual abuse: A psychoanalytic perspective.* New York: Basic Books.

Elliott, D. M., & Briere, J. (1995). Posttraumatic stress associated with delayed recall of sexual abuse: A general population study. *Journal of Traumatic Stress, 8,* 629-648.

Felman, S. (1991). Education and crisis, or the vicissitudes of teaching. *American Imago, 48,* 13-73.

Finkelhor, D., & Browne, A. (1985). The traumatic impact of child sexual abuse: A conceptualization. *American Journal of Orthopsychiatry, 55,* 530-541.

Graziano, R., & Miller, M. (1996). *Dilemmas in teaching trauma: Concepts, process and responsibilities.* Workshop presented at the annual meeting of the International Society for Traumatic Stress Studies, San Francisco.

Herman, J. L. (1992a). Complex PTSD: A syndrome in survivors of prolonged and repeated trauma. *Journal of Traumatic Stress, 5,* 377-391.

Herman, J. L. (1992b). *Trauma and recovery: The aftermath of violence—from domestic abuse to political terror.* New York: Basic Books.

Herman, J. L., & Schatzow, E. (1987). Recovery and verification of memories of childhood sexual trauma. *Psychoanalytic Psychology, 4,* 1-14.

Lisak, D. (1993). Men as victims: Challenging cultural myths. *Journal of Traumatic Stress, 6,* 577-580.

Martin, M., & Henry-Feeney, J. (1989). Clinical services to persons with AIDS: The parallel nature of the client and worker process. *Clinical Social Work Journal, 17,* 337-349.

McCammon, S. (1995). Painful pedagogy: Teaching about trauma in academic and training settings. In B. H. Stamm (Ed.), *Secondary traumatic stress: Self-care issues for clinicians, researchers, and educators* (pp. 105-120). Lutherville, MD: Sidran.

McCann, I. L., & Pearlman, L. A. (1990). Vicarious traumatization: A framework for understanding the psychological effects of working with victims. *Journal of Traumatic Stress, 3,* 131-149.

Miller, M. (1994). *Particular considerations in teaching about trauma, dissociation and treatment of adult incest survivors in an academic setting.* Paper presented at McCammon et al. workshop, Painful Pedagogy: Trauma Survivors in Academic or Training Classes, at the annual meeting of the International Society for Traumatic Stress Studies, Chicago.

Miller, M. (1995). *Teaching about trauma, dissociation and treatment in an academic setting: Considering student safety.* Paper presented at the annual meeting of the European Society for Traumatic Stress Studies, Paris.

Miller, M., & Graziano, R. (1997). *Teaching trauma: Process and impact.* Workshop presented at the annual meeting of the European Society for Traumatic Stress Studies, Maastricht, Netherlands.

Miller, M., McCammon, S., Stamm, B. H., & Williams, M. B. (1995). *Teaching and training about trauma, dissociation and treatment: Considering student safety.* Poster presented at the annual meeting of the International Society for Traumatic Stress Studies, Boston.

Monroe, J. (1995). Ethical issues associated with secondary trauma in therapists. In B. H. Stamm (Ed.), *Secondary traumatic stress: Self-care issues for clinicians, researchers, and educators* (pp. 211-229). Lutherville, MD: Sidran.

Muslin, H., & Schlessinger, N. (1971). Toward the teaching and learning of empathy. *Bulletin of the Menninger Clinic, 35,* 262-271.

Pearlman, L. (1995). Self-care for trauma therapists: Ameliorating vicarious traumatization. In B. H. Stamm (Ed.), *Secondary traumatic stress: Self-care issues for clinicians, researchers, and educators* (pp. 51-64). Lutherville, MD: Sidran.

Pearlman, L., & Saakvitne, K. (1995a). *Trauma and the therapist: Countertransference and vicarious traumatization in psychotherapy with incest survivors.* New York: W. W. Norton.

Pearlman, L., & Saakvitne, K. (1995b). Treating therapists with vicarious traumatization and secondary traumatic stress disorders. In C. Figley (Ed.), *Compassion fatigue: Coping with secondary traumatic stress disorder in those who treat the traumatized* (pp. 150-177). New York: Brunner/Mazel.

Rothman, B. (1973, Spring). Perspectives on learning and teaching in continuing education. *Education for Social Work,* pp. 39-52.

Saakvitne, K. (1991, August). *Psychoanalytic psychotherapy with incest survivors: When the therapist was abused.* Paper presented at the 99th Annual Meeting of the American Psychological Association, San Francisco.

Sachs, D., & Shapiro, S. (1976). On parallel process in therapy and teaching. *Psychoanalytic Quarterly, 45,* 394-415.

Summit, R. (1983). The child sexual abuse accommodation syndrome. *Child Abuse and Neglect, 7,* 177-192.

Talbot, A. (1990). The importance of parallel process in debriefing crisis counselors. *Journal of Traumatic Stress, 3,* 265-277.

van der Kolk, B. A. (1987). *Psychological trauma.* Washington, DC: American Psychiatric Press.

van der Kolk, B. A. (1994). The body keeps the score: Memory and the evolving psychobiology of posttraumatic stress. *Harvard Review of Psychiatry, 1,* 253-265.

van der Kolk, B. A., & Fisler, R. (1994). Childhood abuse and neglect and loss of self-regulation. *Bulletin of the Menninger Clinic, 58,* 145-168.

van der Kolk, B. A., McFarlane, A. C., & Weisaeth, L. (Eds.). (1996). *Traumatic stress: The effects of overwhelming experience on mind, body, and society.* New York: Guilford.

Williams, L. M. (1994). Recall of childhood trauma: A prospective study of women's memories of child sexual abuse. *Journal of Consulting and Clinical Psychology, 62,* 1167-1176.

Williams, L. M. (1995). Recovered memories of abuse in women with documented child sexual victimization histories. *Journal of Traumatic Stress, 8,* 649-673.

Williams, M. B. (1994). Establishing safety in survivors of severe sexual abuse. In M. B. Williams & J. F. Sommer, Jr. (Eds.), *Handbook of posttraumatic therapy* (pp. 162-178). Westport, CT: Greenwood.

Winnicott, D. W. (1965). *The maturational processes and the facilitating environment.* London: Hogarth.

7

Memory, Research, and the Law

Future Directions

Jon R. Conte

With increasing frequency in courts, psychotherapy offices, and research labs, aspects of the law, psychotherapy, and research are mixed for a wide range of purposes. Not infrequently the observer is left with the impression that the resulting cocktail, like wine and whiskey, does not mix well. This volume, like the conference on trauma and memory held in Durham, New Hampshire, in June 1996, provides an opportunity to look at how these professional areas have been mixed in the past and suggest ways in which integration, if not blending, can take place in the future.

In this chapter I will raise questions about current efforts to mix aspects of the law, psychotherapy, and research as these pertain to contemporary interest in adult traumatic memories and suggest potential areas for future knowledge development. Perhaps I will raise more ques-

tions than I answer; however, I hope to suggest some fruitful topics for research and methods for future investigations in this important area of current professional and legal interest.

My comments originate from a hearing regarding two criminal cases that occurred not far from the site of the 1996 Trauma and Memory conference. These two are among a handful that have received a great deal of national attention due to the fact that they dealt with aspects of current interest in adult memories for childhood trauma (*State of New Hampshire v. Joel Hungerford,* 1995; *State of New Hampshire v. John Morahan,* 1995).

In this chapter, I invite you, the reader, to act as judge and consider part of the evidence that was presented in these cases that involved adult memory for childhood sexual abuse. I invite you to decide if this testimony is consistent with

AUTHOR'S NOTE: I would like to thank Lucy Berliner, William R. Conte, Barbara Jo Levy, and John Weld for commenting on the manuscript, and Rachel K. Conte for her assistance in manuscript preparation.

your understanding of the science and practice that brought conferees together at the conference on trauma and memory and that we must consider virtually every time we work with survivors of trauma.

Assumptions

☐ It is important to establish what I consider to be the foundation or assumptions of our professional work at the Trauma and Memory conference, in our research laboratories, and in our efforts to understand memory for childhood trauma.

Human Memory Is
Malleable and Fallible

Most scholars in the areas of psychotherapy and psychological science will agree that there is no question that human memory, over both short- and long-term periods, is malleable and can be fallible. There is a substantial body of laboratory research and some field research that suggests that human subjects' reports of events can be altered or influenced by factors such as postevent questioning or suggestion (for reviews, see Brown, 1995b; Loftus, 1993; Pope, 1996; Reviere, 1996). We note also that memory can be influenced by the amount of stress or competing events during the time of memory storage and by other factors. Finally, it is common knowledge that human beings do not have perfect recall for every event or thought they experience over periods of a few hours or days and certainly not over years.

Where we appear not always to agree is in the matter of the extent to which human memory can be fallible and under what conditions. Both common experience and some data indicate that human beings can reliably recall and report events, even years after exposure to those events (see Conte, 1997). I will argue below that one of our greatest needs is for data that will help us understand the conditions under which memory can be trusted and those under which it cannot.

Science Is a Demanding
Taskmaster

I assume that most of us would agree, whether we practice it or not when we leave our research labs and offices and move into clinics or courtrooms, that science is a demanding taskmaster. If our goal as professionals and as scientists is reliable knowledge, then we must judge what we know and what we do based on science—not on emotion or politics, but on data. The reliability of scientific knowledge is a direct function of the quality and power of the research design to answer the questions the research is designed to answer. I will outline below a number of research efforts that might improve our understanding of the issues we address today in the law and in clinical practice.

Science progresses through several predictable steps, demonstrating first that phenomena exist. We may hypothesize the existence of phenomena (e.g., subatomic particles), but until we develop measurement technology that can detect and tell us how much of a given phenomenon exists, its existence is an idea, not a fact. This is the problem of measurement that all sciences face. We can only know through science that which it is in our capacity to measure. One of the hallmarks of a mature science is the existence of high-quality, varied methods of measurement available to pursue its questions.

In this regard, it is of considerable interest to me that no memory research I have found has attempted to measure human memory independent of verbal self-report of subjects. The classic memory research paradigm is to expose human subjects to some event (e.g., viewing a film) or to find subjects who witnessed some naturally occurring event (e.g., an injury at a football game or the explosion of the space shuttle *Challenger*) and then ask them questions about that event.

Several methodological problems jump out at us concerning this paradigm. First, it has long been recognized as a threat to scientific study that human subjects tend to tell researchers what they think investigators want to hear. This phenomenon, known as the Hawthorne effect, lies behind the development of scientific research methodologies in which the true purpose of the research is kept from the subjects. The basic memory research paradigm asks subjects to report what they remember. It is rare that memory investigators have attempted to hide the purpose of their questioning from subjects.

Another vexing problem in this area of research is that there is a long history and substantial body of research that demonstrates the dramatic variability of self-report. The reliability of self-report varies according to the behavior being reported, the social valance associated with that behavior, and a host of other factors (see, e.g., Haynes, 1978). What people tell us about their own behavior and experience may or may not be accurate.

It should be noted that a review of the most frequently referenced research in this area provides no estimate of the reliability of self-report. We have no idea how stable (as measured by test-retest reliability) subjects' reports are or the extent to which subjects agree with each other (interreporter reliability). In regard to the stability of subjects' reports, the experience of Loftus and Pickrell (1995) is quite interesting. These researchers report that one of their subjects who first adopted a pseudomemory later reported that the event had not really taken place. Furthermore, it is also interesting to note that memory researchers who compare students' memories with the reports of the students' parents tend to accept the idea that the parents' versions of the students' childhoods are the accurate (reliable) ones, although there is considerable research to support the notion that both parent and child reports are of questionable reliability when both are asked to report the same events at the same time (see, e.g., Humphreys & Ciminero, 1979: Sullaway & Christensen, 1983).

The second task of research is to determine the associations among phenomena. For example, we have been interested in the relationship (association) between child abuse and psychological problems. Associations do not signify causality, only that events co-occur to some degree. Indeed, some factor other than a history of child abuse might be responsible for observed psychological problems. Similarly, it is generally accepted that the existence of particular symptoms (e.g., an eating disorder in adulthood) does not prove the existence of child abuse (i.e., some other factor might be responsible for an eating disorder). It is, however, a task of science to demonstrate cause-and-effect relationships. In the classic paradigm, subjects are randomly assigned to experimental and control groups that differ only in their experience of independent variables. The researcher observes the effects of the independent variables on the dependent variable by noting the effects of exposure of the experimental group to the independent variables.

It is clear that much of the research on memory and trauma has failed to advance beyond the first steps required by science. As I will describe below, some advocates have suggested that their research has, in fact, reached a higher stage of development than it has. But then, in your role as judge in the reading of this chapter, you will decide the veracity of such suggestions.

Today professionals interested in basic memory processes, the impact of trauma on memory, and psychotherapy with traumatized and nontraumatized human beings all have a vested interest in the research on the various subtopics of this area. In assessing the research, we face a host of methodological problems, including the question of the reliability of self-report; the adequacy of research design, especially in dealing with expectancy effects and demand characteristics (i.e., the probability that research subjects will tell us what they think we want to hear); the cross-sectional design or short follow-up period relied upon in most of our research (there have been few studies of human memory over extended time periods comparable to court cases in which witnesses allege that events happened years in the past); and the fact that replication is key to knowledge development.

It is through replication of scientific research that reliable and generalizable knowledge is developed. Results of a single study or even of a few studies may apply appropriately only to the subjects of conditions examined in those studies. There is nothing wrong with a science that discovers potential truths in a laboratory or in a small set of studies, and then extends its initial findings to different subjects or different settings. However, the processes of replication and extension are critical to our knowledge of whether initial findings obtained with one set of subjects or under one set of conditions apply to different subjects, settings, or contexts.

Although memory researchers often argue that they are examining basic memory processes that should apply in all human situations, this, in fact, is little more than a statement of their personal views of their own work. Science demands replication of effects across subjects, settings, and investigations. It is insufficient to assert that effects gained in the laboratory must of necessity apply in the real world. A television commercial of a few years ago asked, "Where's the beef?"; increasingly, in this area of research we must ask those making such claims, "Where are the data?" Replication and extension of laboratory research to subjects or situations more typical to those in the real world are fundamental tasks of scientists who seek to develop generalizable knowledge or to affect social policy or the outcomes of legal cases.

The claim that one is investigating basic memory processes is a critical assumption that must not be viewed as law until demonstrated. For example, it has become quite common in many courts and some clinical practices to blame self-help books for the creation of "false memories." This appears to be based on the cautious scholarship of Lindsay and Read (1994), who have argued, based on extrapolation from laboratory research, that reading *The Courage to Heal* (Bass & Davis, 1988) creates a "substantial risk of leading some readers to create illusory memories or beliefs of childhood sexual abuse" (p. 295). And yet there has never been a study employing *The Courage to Heal*— or any other book for that matter—that has demonstrated that reading produces pseudo-memories. Although I admire the scholarship and note the concerns offered by these memory researchers, the use of their work by others to assert that reading self-help books produces false memories moves far beyond the data. No scientific study has every examined the effects of reading books such as *The Courage to Heal*.

Similarly, several researchers have claimed to demonstrate that some subjects (less than 25%) will adopt pseudomemories in the face of convincing efforts of relatives or investigators. With the exception of Pezdek, Finger, and Hodge (1996), who failed to convince subjects that the subjects had had rectal enemas in childhood, no study has been conducted with individuals directly comparable to the types of subjects seen in psychotherapy practices. No study has yet demonstrated that subjects can be misled to believe that any of their relatives hurt them (e.g., stuck a penis in their mouths).

It is a well-known principle of research that subjects, procedures, and conditions should parallel the real world to which the findings are thought to apply. Knowledge is developed as laboratory or artificial-world efforts (e.g., classroom projects) are replicated and extended to the real world. Memory researchers face a host of methodological and practical problems in their efforts to replicate and extend their findings to the real world. Any investigator who thinks that studying college students' efforts to memorize nonsense syllables is similar to studying the memory of rape and trauma might be well served by spending a few weeks in any emergency room in any community in the United States and observing the effects of sexual assault.

You Be the Judge

☐ The current legal practice in the United States is uniformly not simply to accept mental health or scientific testimony. The law has developed criteria for determining if such testimony can be useful to the trier of fact. The law has long been concerned that novel or untested scientific principles might be employed in courtrooms (or elsewhere in the real world). Although there is some debate over these issues (see, e.g., Cohen, 1996), the U.S. Supreme Court has established a multiple set of factors to be used in determining whether expert testimony will indeed aid the trier of fact (see *Daubert v. Merrell Dow Pharmaceuticals,* 1993). Essentially, it is required that expert opinion be based on scientifically tested and peer-reviewed work, that the methodology or technique used have a known error rate, that standards exist for applying the methodology, and that the methodology be generally accepted in the scientific community (for discussion, see Cohen, 1996; Rotgers & Barrett, 1996). The reader is invited to judge whether the opinions discussed below have in fact been scientifically tested and peer-reviewed, and whether they are generally accepted in the professional community.

Cases

In the hearing that forms the context for this chapter, two cases were joined by a judge in Hillsborough County, New Hampshire. One case involved an adult woman who had recovered memories of sexual abuse by her father. In the second case, a 20-year-old woman recovered memory of vaginal rape by a teacher that occurred while she was in junior high school (*State of New Hampshire v. Joel Hungerford*, 1995; *State of New Hampshire v. John Morahan*, 1995).

Three experts testified for the defense (Drs. Loftus, McHugh, and Hudson) and three for the state (Drs. van der Kolk, Brown, and Conte). Table 7.1 contains illustrative testimony of my University of Washington colleague Elizabeth Loftus. In the pages that follow, I present my understanding of the research on each of Dr. Loftus's points and suggest research that might further our understanding of these points. Again, I urge each reader to evaluate the testimony and argument in terms of his or her own understanding of the research and state of the knowledge in this area.

This commentary is written with a great deal of respect for the pioneering research of Dr. Loftus in eyewitness identification and cognitive science, and in her productive scholarship. My issue is not with her science, but with the ways in which this science is applied to legal matters (e.g., to determine whether a witness may or may not testify). My thesis is that often the application of research about memory (e.g., the misinformation effect) is largely inappropriate, as it extends the science to subjects, settings, or issues (e.g., memory for traumatic events) that have not been the direct focus of the science. In the process, the fundamental research steps of replication and extension are not

undertaken. This misapplication results in legal decisions based on inadequate data or knowledge that is of unknown relevance to the cases before the court. It is my hope that additional research, such as that outlined below, will assist in the creation of knowledge that is more useful to courts and in other applied settings (e.g., the practice of psychotherapy).

Misinformation Effect

☐ There is a large body of research that demonstrates that human beings can be misled or manipulated by postevent interventions (e.g., leading and suggestive questioning). As Brown (1995a) has pointed out, this effect tends to be greater for subjects who are uncertain about the original events, and the research tends to involve memory for trivial events. The rate of error in adults studied tends to be rather low (e.g., less than 20%).

This line of research faces the same methodological problems outlined above and elsewhere by others (e.g., Hyman, Husband, & Billings, 1995). For example, it tends to focus on subjects who have little or no personal investment in the events (e.g., events occurring in a film the subjects are asked to watch).

More critically, current research has failed to provide us with much of an understanding of how the apparent misinformation effect operates. There are many important unanswered questions about this effect. For example, no data are available to help us understand how much of an effort it takes to obtain what level of effect. There are no data that inform us about the permanence of the effect or its resistance to change. Anecdotal information suggests that some subjects do not maintain the effect over the course of a study (see, e.g., Loftus & Pickrell, 1995). More critically, testimony on the misinformation effect seems to suggest that the effect is universal; the implication is that all subjects or witnesses are equally at risk for adopting misinformation. In fact, not all subjects adopt misinformation.

Brown (1995b) has posited suggestibility as a naturally occurring trait that varies across individuals. Thus some individuals might be

Table 7.1 Testimony of Elizabeth Loftus, Ph.D.

1. Misinformation effect

   ". . . And one of the things that I have found over and over in these couple of decades of research is that when people are exposed to misleading information—so in this example they're given the suggestion it was a yield sign instead of a stop sign—their memory is less accurate. They adopt the misinformation and they claim it as their own memory. . . ." (p. 41).

2. Creation of false memory
   (in reference to Loftus's own work and that with her colleagues, and Hyman and colleagues, and Ceci's work with children)

   "So all of these are examples of how you can, through suggestion, get people to create entirely false memories. They're apparently not lying, they have, you know, visualized and adopted this information to succumb to this pressure and created these wholly false memory" (p. 53).

3. Massive repression

   "Well, people try to use other terms that have multiple meanings and I think it's confusing to do that. So sometimes people use the term 'dissociation' or even 'traumatic amnesia,' but these terms have a lot of meanings. And—but if you're just talking about the phenomenon itself that is taking a stream of traumas, supposedly burying them in the unconscious where they are withheld off from the rest of mental life, and then you engage in some activities and can somehow dig these out later and they can be reliable and trusted . . ." (p. 58, also p. 119).

   ". . . no cogent scientific support for it . . ." (p. 59).

4. Ordinary forgetting

   Q: ". . . do you believe that an incident of a sexual attack, rape, two nights before a person's wedding three—uncovered or first recovered two or three years later, or not even two years later, would that be something that you would claim could be ordinary forgetting?" (p. 122).
   A: ". . . I just haven't seen very much evidence that—I mean I am, again, I am looking at the whole package, not just the one incident but the whole package of recollections involved in one of these cases ages five to twenty-three, including violent experiences with guns in the vagina, supposedly unaware of them until a year later when entering therapy and then engaged in a certain set of activities, if this—well, there is just no support of the idea that memory works in the ways as we've talked about . . . so I don't know that you could explain this with the principles of ordinary forgetting and remembering" (p. 123).

5. Case studies of self-reported amnesia

   Q: "If someone retracts and say they had a memory and now says they didn't have a memory and that it was a result of psychotherapy, you accept that as proof, if you, if someone says—it's not someone. If thirty-eight percent of one hundred and twenty . . . some say or a fifty-nine percent of four hundred and fifty-nine say or report that there was a time that they didn't have a memory of abuse, that that's not scientific proof?" (p. 215).
   A: "I didn't say it wasn't scientific, it wasn't just scientific proof for massive repression and reliable recovery later" (p. 215).

more likely to adopt misinformation than would others. Additionally, factors such as IQ, level of stress, emotional state (e.g., level of regression), tendency to believe authority figures, and the plausibility of the misinformation (e.g., being lost as a child versus having a penis inserted in you by a loving adult) may all be associated with the ease with which an individual adopts the misinformation. To date, research has not investigated these or other possible factors associated with variation in the misinformation effect.

Most critically, the provision of testimony that postevent events (e.g., questioning) can negatively affect memory is of little value in determining whether a specific witness suffers the misinformation effect. Testimony that some subjects can be misled or tricked into saying something happened when it did not is virtually useless for finding out whether a specific individual in a specific case was in fact so misled. The only purpose of testimony about this research effect is to attack the credibility of a witness. No expert possesses any special ability

Table 7.1 Continued

6. Therapy as suggestion

"I will tell you about the kind of situation that . . . I and others have worried about. She goes into the therapy. Maybe she's got some symptoms like low self-esteem, depression, any one of a number of symptoms that plague . . . a lot of people. And the therapist begins a series of activities that I and others have been concerned are highly suggestive: questioning about a history of abuse in suggestive and leading ways; taking dreams and nightmares and interpreting them as evidence of childhood sexual abuse memories; breaking through the unconscious; sometimes using hypnosis or sodium amytol to try to dig out these memories in interpreting symptoms as evidence of a history of child sexual abuse" (p. 124).

7. Retractors

Q: "I am asking for the direct scientific evidence that shows that false memories are produced in psychotherapy" (p. 213). A: ". . . The only direct proof that, that we really have is some evidence that comes from the retractors who—it's not perfect evidence but it is . . . at least consistent with the idea that false memories have been produced and that psychotherapy played a major role in that production . . ." (p. 214).

Q: "So let me get this straight, Doctor. You're saying that if you have a few retractors, that that provides scientific proof that false memories are produced?" A: "It provides evidence that's consistent with the idea that what happened to them in psychotherapy played a large role in their problems."

8. Reliability of recovered memory

Q: "Well there's certainly no proof that memory is any more or less reliable than anybody else's memory?" A: "Which one?"

Q: "The recovered memory." A: "Well it depends on whether there's been a lot of suggestion or not. Because if there is a lot of suggestion then I would say it's less reliable"

Q: "There's not proof of that?" A: "There's proof that suggestion has negative consequences on memory."

9. Determining a pseudomemory

"Well, I think they're [sic] probably disagreements about when you have people who are reporting pseudomemories, when you have them reporting things that are, that you know to be false, because when you do experiments you can, you can know that the material is false because you, you know what the original material was, so you can see that the pseudomemory is actually a pseudomemory. Or sometimes you, you know that a pseudomemory is a pseudomemory that is a false memory because what is being remembered is biologically impossible, physiologically impossible, geographically impossible . . ." (p. 81).

". . . independent corroboration . . . which might include . . . medical records, or photographs or videotapes, as occurs in some cases of pornography, or others kinds of external verification . . ." (p. 84).

SOURCE: *State of New Hampshire v. Joel Hungerford, State of New Hampshire v. John Morahan* (1995, Mos. 93-S 1734-1736).

to determine, nor is there any accepted procedure for determining, whether a witness has or has not succumbed to the misinformation effect.

Extension of this line of research toward events that are more similar to abuse and trauma should be encouraged. There are many questions that remain unanswered about the misinformation effect. Are some subjects more and some subjects less resistant to the effect? What parameters of events themselves are associated with misinformation effects? For example, does

the degree of involvement between a subject and the stimulus event affect the ease with which the subject can be misled? Being lost (depending on the level of fear or anxiety associated with the state of being lost) or observing something (e.g., a film) is a more passive experience than being raped. Does the perceived authority of the individual who attempts to persuade a subject have an impact on the ease with which the subject adopts misinformation? Does the natural level of suggestibility in subjects affect ease of adoption of misinformation? Do the level of involvement of the subject with the event, the time period elapsed since the supposed occurrence of the event, and the effort to mislead have any impacts on ease of adoption of misinformation? Even answers to basic questions concerning variations in the effect by gender, age, and intelligence would be useful in helping us to understand this effect.

It is particularly important to extend this line of research away from students as subjects to individuals who are more similar to those for whom this issue is most typically raised. For example, many individuals come to psychotherapy with backgrounds of years of anxiety and angst. It may be that those who are looking for explanations for their anxiety, existential angst, or other vague complaints are more likely than others to adopt misinformation (e.g., they were abused in childhood). Perhaps the believability of the misinformation is associated with the likelihood that a person will adopt it. Additionally, there is some evidence suggesting that individuals' levels of depression have impacts on their recall of childhood events (see, e.g., Gerlsma, Kramer, Scholing, & Emmelkamp, 1994). Perhaps particular levels of depression interact with some types of misinformation and increase the likelihood that individuals will uncritically accept misinformation. For example, a depressed person may be more likely than a nondepressed person to believe that he or she had a negative experience with a parent. Finally, a project well within the scope of current methodologies would be to examine the relationship between locus of control and risk of adopting misinformation. Perhaps individuals with high external locus of control (e.g., those who believe that causes for events lie outside of themselves) are more likely to accept misinformation when it is presented by people in authority. (Attribution of responsibility may be highly correlated with suggestibility; data on this relationship would also be of interest.)

Answers to these and other important questions that can move our understanding of the misinformation effect out of the laboratory and toward more real-world concerns will require that investigators begin to ask more complex questions, employ measurement of phenomena

(e.g., attribution of responsibility, IQ, suggestibility) in samples large enough to allow for statistical analyses that answer more complex questions (e.g., the proportion of variance explained by various factors), and forgo the easier approach of manipulating gross events with crude measures in captive student populations.

Creation of Pseudomemories

☐ There is a novel but relatively small set of studies that some argue demonstrate that false memories for events can easily be created. This line of research is quite interesting, although it should be approached with considerable caution because of the relatively simplistic methodologies employed, which lack scientific rigor. Taken at face value, these studies suggest that it is very difficult to get college students to create pseudomemories. No currently available study has found that more than 25% of subjects adopted pseudomemories (for a good discussion of this line of research, see Williams & Banyard, 1997).

In the first of these studies, Loftus and Pickrell (1995) used university students to recruit subject pairs (usually an adult relative and child who was at least 18 years of age). The researchers interviewed the relative to obtain information about three events that happened to the younger subject when he or she was between 4 and 6 years of age. The relative also provided information about a plausible shopping trip, which the researchers used to construct a false event: information about where the family shopped, which family members usually went shopping, what kinds of stores might have attracted the subject's interest, and verification that the subject had not been lost in a shopping mall around the age of 5. The younger subjects were told that they were participating in a study on childhood memories and were asked to read the booklets completed by their relatives and write what they remembered about the events. After receiving the subjects' completed booklets, the researchers called each subject and scheduled two interviews. Subjects were asked to remember a total of 72 true events and were successful in remembering 68% of the true events. Of 24 subjects, 7 also recalled the false event, either fully or partially. During the first interview, one of the subjects decided she did not remember the false event. A total of 25% of subjects claimed to remember, fully or partially, the false event. This number held for the second interview. When subjects were told at debriefing that one event may have been false, 19 of 24 (79%) correctly chose the "lost in the shopping mall" event as the false one.

In another study, Hyman et al. (1995) conducted two well-designed experiments. In their first study, 20 college students and their parents participated. The parents provided information about the experiences of the students with childhood events: getting lost, going to the hospital, an eventful birthday, loss of a pet, a family vacation, and interaction with a prominent or famous person. The researchers constructed two events, one positive (a party at age 5 during which pizza was served and a clown visited) and one negative (going to the hospital at age 5 with a high fever). Subjects were told that they would be asked to recall and describe a set of childhood events based on information obtained from their parents. At a second interview held 1 to 7 days after the first, subjects were again questioned about the events. At the first interview, subjects recalled 83.8% of true events and no false events. At the second interview, subjects recalled 3 of the 12 events (25%) that had not been remembered at the first interview. Four of the subjects (20%) incorporated false information in event descriptions.

In Hyman et al.'s second experiment, 51 subjects and their parents participated. The parents provided information on the subjects concerning 10 childhood events—the same 6 as in the first experiment, plus winning a contest, car events, weddings, and mischief with a friend. Three false childhood events were constructed: (a) As a child, the subject was running around with other kids at a wedding, which resulted in a punch bowl being spilled on the parents of the bride; (b) a fire extinguisher sprinkler system was activated while the subject was shopping with a parent; and (c) the subject was left in a car while the parent shopped. Subjects were interviewed three times, and the researchers increased the experimental demand for recall by

telling the subjects that more complete recall and accuracy were among the goals of the research. The proportion of recall for true events increased from 88.8% to 95.1% over the three interviews. Each subject was asked about one of the three false events. At the first interview, no subject provided false information; by the third interview, 25.5% did.

In a third study, Pezdek and colleagues (1996) examined two false events (one familiar to subjects, which was getting lost, and one unfamiliar, which was receiving an enema) and found that 3 of 20 subjects adopted the memory for the familiar event and none of the subjects adopted a memory for the unfamiliar event.

Research efforts designed to get subjects to report that they had experiences in childhood that their parents reported they did not are new. These investigations face many methodological problems. As Hyman and his colleagues (1995) point out, there are pressures on human subjects to report results consistent with experimenter expectation. This is a fundamental problem for all research: that the intent of the researcher is known or easily identified by subjects. This issue is at the base of the classic double-blind research paradigm, where the nature of the study is kept from subjects and data collectors, both of whom may report results consistent with the nature of the study and not the real phenomena of interest.

In all studies to date in which attempts were made to "implant memories," the intent is likely to have been clear to subjects, although apparently investigators have not examined this concern. Subjects are asked to pit their "memories" against the memories of people (their parents) whom they presumably hold out as more knowledgeable about their own childhoods. In the case of Loftus and Pickrell (1995), the odds are clearly stacked in favor of getting subjects to report that they experienced the false event, because the event apparently is constructed with some truthful elements about shopping excursions. Additionally, fear of losing parents may well be a universal experience of childhood. Furthermore, it is assumed in these studies that the older relative's version of events is the correct one, although no data are presented on the reliability of parent recall. There is a large body of research on the reliability of parent report of child behavior that indicates that child and parent behaviors are often divergent, and that one parent's report is often unreliable when compared with the report of the other parent (for discussion, see Humphreys & Ciminero, 1979; Sullaway & Christensen, 1983).

Methodological concerns notwithstanding, the results of these three research efforts, albeit in preliminary studies, appear clear. Most subjects fail to report "remembering" false events, and subjects are generally accurate in "remembering" true events. It is extremely difficult to understand how the data from these studies can be viewed as support for the claim that pseudomemories can be implanted easily. On the contrary, such "implantation" appears to be possible in only a minority of subjects.

If a science of memory is really to address the creation of pseudomemories, it will have to advance beyond these initial efforts. Some of the same currently unaddressed questions about the misinformation effect apply equally well here. How much suggestion is necessary to create the effect? What variables explain adoption of the pseudomemory? If it is impossible to get subjects to adopt a memory of an anal enema but it is possible to get them to adopt a memory of being lost in a shopping mall, is there something about the nature of the pseudomemory (e.g., level of pain that might be thought to be associated with it, or the degree of involvement with the subject and the false event) that is associated with adoption of memory of a false event? Can we identify subject variables associated with the adoption of a memory (e.g., level of suggestibility, fantasy proneness, level of depression)?

A potential area of investigation that may further our understanding of trauma and memory would be whether or not it is possible to get an individual who actually had an experience to report that he or she did not have the experience. It would also be helpful to know under what conditions this occurs, how much effort it takes, whether or not there is a relationship between the time elapsed since the event and such reports. In addition, does the level or type of emotion associated with the event increase or decrease the likelihood of subject report that the

event did not take place? From a forensic and clinical perspective, these issues are as interesting as, if not more interesting than, efforts to create pseudomemories. One could argue that the goal of therapy is to help people forget or change the valence associated with memories. Research of this type, in which individuals change the valence or manage to forget experiences, could be very useful in these endeavors.

Massive Repression and Ordinary Forgetting

☐ The argument here is two-pronged. First, it is argued that it is unlikely that an individual can block memories for a series of traumas; second, it is asserted that there is no research that proves the existence of repression.

The first argument is not based on science. It is a conceptual argument based on lay notions about trauma and child abuse and lays a framework that ultimately rejects all possible explanations for memory loss for trauma (or at least nonorganic explanations). It appeals to common stereotypes about the nature of trauma and asserts that, because child abuse is so horrible, it would seem to be impossible to block memory for events that involve so much pain, betrayal, and disgusting behaviors. The argument does little more than state that it would seem impossible not to have memory for something so horrible.

The second prong of this argument is that the lack of memory for trauma is not "normal forgetting." The argument here is that forgetting is a normal process whereby people do not store, or are no longer able to retrieve from storage, memory for relatively insignificant or no longer significant events (e.g., the name of one's second-grade teacher). The argument goes further, noting that traumas are events unlike the events that are often forgotten, hence one cannot say that memory for trauma is forgotten, because such a statement trivializes trauma.

There are few data that directly inform this argument. On the matter of whether it might be possible to block memories of repeated traumas, conceptually it is generally recognized that many mental processes improve with practice.

Hospital nursing staff are familiar with the improved ability of burn patients to dissociate prior to the painful scrubbing that is part of medical treatment for bad burns. It would not be surprising that the ability to block memory for events might also improve with practice.

More critically, the process of "massive repression," as summarized by Ofshe and Singer (1994), is unlikely to be similar to how blocking memory actually works:

> Robust repression is most often claimed to operate immediately following each traumatic event. Commencing as early as a few minutes after the event and continuing until exposed to practitioners' procedures, patients are rendered completely unable to retrieve any information about the traumatic events. (pp. 395-396)

Clinical reports from many victims of trauma indicate that they rarely block memory immediately after the event. Indeed, victims who did would typically go undetected, because they would not have the requisite memory to make disclosures. Victims of all ages report undertaking a large variety of mental processes and activities so as to avoid thinking about and becoming overwhelmed by thinking about the trauma. Some victims describe forcing themselves to think about something else. Others report becoming engaged in activities and projects to focus on anything other than the trauma. Some victims will refuse to talk about the trauma, because talking about it makes it feel more real. Some victims use drugs or alcohol or activity to move their concentration away from the trauma to other events or to mindlessness. It is not completely clear what might be the results of activities and processes such as these, carried on day in and day out for extended periods of time. It may well be that "repressed memory" seen in a victim of trauma years after the trauma may be the result of gradual pushing from awareness of memory through such activities and processes.

There are a number of potential research projects that could be helpful in this area. For example, it would be helpful to track systematically over time the efforts of victims to manage thinking and feeling about the trauma. It would also be useful to understand the ways in which properties of memory for the trauma (e.g., clarity, quantity of details) and of the trauma (e.g., level of physical pain, emotionality associated with the trauma at the time and subsequently as additional events take place) affect memory over time.

Lack of Proof for the Existence of Repression

Experts continue to testify that there is no research support for the existence of repression. Recently, perhaps sensing vulnerability in this testimony, experts have testified that this finding applies equally well to traumatic amnesia and dissociated memory. An important element that makes this testimony more or less honest lies in the use of the term *proof*. As outlined above (and well known by any graduate of a research class), scientific "proof" requires experimental demonstration of the effects of an independent variable on one or more dependent variables.

Indeed, the work often cited to support testimony that repression lacks scientific validation is that of Holmes (1990). Holmes, who examined only a narrow band of possible research, clearly states that his focus of attention is on laboratory research that demonstrates the existence of repression (i.e., selective forgetting that is not under voluntary control and in which the forgotten knowledge is not lost but stored in the unconscious and can return to consciousness; see p. 86). Typical of the laboratory research reviewed by Holmes are experiments in which subjects in a laboratory, some under stress and some not, are later asked to recall lists of words. Holmes also states, "It is important to note that my conclusion that there is no evidence for repression must not be interpreted as suggesting that repression does not exist because, of course, we cannot prove the null hypothesis" (p. 97). He goes on: "Although there is no evidence for repression, it should not be concluded that there is not selectivity in perception and recall. Indeed, there is good evidence that transient and enduring factors such as cognitive sets, emotional states, and the availability of labels can influence what we perceive, store, and recall" (pp. 97-98).

No standard in the law requires that the only testimony that is relevant to the trier of fact is testimony that is experimentally generated. Ironically, often the same experts who cite Holmes (1990) on repression go on to testify about the experiences of "retractors" as support for the idea that memories for trauma can be implanted by psychotherapy (see the section headed "Case Reports" below).

Another problem inherent in both some experts' testimony about repression and recent efforts to extend such arguments to dissociated memory and traumatic amnesia is that the argument confuses the presumed process (repression) whereby memory is lost with its result (memory loss or amnesia). This is refuted by long-standing reports that some victims of trauma claim a period of partial or total amnesia for the trauma. Research on such forgetting has been reviewed extensively elsewhere (see, e.g., Hammond et al., 1995; Williams & Banyard, 1997). However, it is quite true that self-reports by victims of various traumas that they experienced periods of partial or total memory loss for the traumas do not constitute scientific proof.

Future Research

I am unable to conceptualize a way to conduct experimental research that would prove the existence of amnesia. Indeed, as many have pointed out, such research would be unethical. There are, however, a number of potential research efforts that could clarify our understanding of memory loss. For example, it would be interesting to investigate naturally occurring stressful events, especially those where permanent records exist (e.g., videotaped robberies), and how aspects of the trauma (e.g., degree of life threat, amount of interaction between victim and traumatized) affect subsequent memory. It would be interesting to compare the verbal reports of trauma victims with their nonverbal reports of the trauma (e.g., drawings). Seminal work by Professor Mary Koss and her colleagues points to an extremely important research paradigm and area of investigation (see Koss, Figueredo, Bell, Tharan, & Tromp, 1996;

reprinted as Chapter 21, this volume). Using a cross-validation mediational paradigm, Koss et al. examined the effects of rape and other unpleasant versus pleasant events in a large multiethnic sample (N for Study 1 = 2,173; N for Study 2 = 5,411). Subjects responded to a mailed questionnaire. Potential mediational factors included cognitive appraisal of the rape (e.g., "I don't feel I was victimized"), valence (was the experience pleasant or not), and symptoms. The results are complex, but, for our purposes, what is of particular interest is that memory was found to consist of four factors: reexperiencing, nonvisual sensory, clarity, and affect (a factor that comprises valence, magnitude of consequences, and the unexpectedness of the event remembered). Additionally, subjects rated rape memories and, to a lesser extent, other unpleasant memories,

> as less clear and vivid, less visually detailed, less likely to occur in a meaningful order, less well-remembered, less talked about, and less frequently recalled either voluntarily or involuntarily; with less sensory components including sound, smell, touch, and taste; and containing slightly less re-experiencing of the physical sensations, emotions, and thoughts that were present in the original incident. (p. 430)

The research by Koss and her colleagues is extremely important as a model for future work. It is noteworthy in its careful attention to measurement, its cross-validation approach in a very large sample, its search for factors that account for variation in effects (e.g., memory), and its rigorous data analysis. It is important to note that the investigators made no effort to study subjects who were amnesiac or had otherwise blocked memory for rape, and that the study included subjects who reported being raped sometime after their 14th birthdays. Most of the rapes were not recent (more than 90% of each category of rape took place 2 or more years before the study). One of the significant findings of this study is that memory disturbances were found, albeit short of full amnesia, for rape victims. Extension of this methodology to other victim samples (e.g., adults abused in childhood) is likely to have considerable benefit for our understanding of the types and extent of memory disturbances associated with different types of trauma. This is far more important than the name we apply to memory loss (i.e., *amnesia* versus *repressed memory*). Of course, it is also important to note that, as powerful and well executed as Koss et al.'s research is, their work does not "prove" memory disturbance, because it is not of an experimental design nature.

Case Reports

☐ It is an interesting and somewhat curious fact of current memory research that there appears to be some fascination with case reports (see, e.g., Ceci & Loftus, 1994). Often these reports involve presentation of a subset of facts from a legal case, historical anecdote (e.g., Piaget's memory about his false abduction), or reference to testimonials of "retractors." Although reference to "real-world" situations is no doubt a novel writing experience for academics who are used to reporting the results of laboratory investigations of memory, it is of little scientific utility. More critically, reliance upon and reference to testimonials of retractors inherently misrepresents the nature of anecdotal reports. For example, Dr. Loftus has testified that "the only direct proof that, that we really have is some evidence that comes from the retractors who—it's not perfect evidence . . . it provides evidence that's consistent with the idea that what happened to them in psychotherapy played a large role in their problems" (see Table 7.1).

Case Studies

☐ In contrast, case studies do serve an important role in science, especially in early scientific efforts to understand phenomena. Unlike the current use of case reports, case studies are undertaken with careful procedures to assure systematic data collection, control bias, and assure reliability (Feagin, Orum, & Sjoberg, 1991). Data are typically presented completely, and the relationships between the data and the conclusions are outlined. Measurement is systematized and follows established rules. The one-sided presentation of some facts and not others from court cases does not qualify as a case study.

Methodologically well-designed and well-executed case studies could be quite helpful for our understanding of a number of issues of concern here. For example, the experiences of "retractors" and systematic descriptions of their histories, psychology, and other factors might generate hypotheses for more rigorous research on the factors that lead to pseudomemories. The idea often seems to be that it is psychotherapy alone that is the causal agent. It would not be surprising that the production of pseudo-memories is actually the result of a more complex interaction among psychotherapy, the psychology of the individual, and historical events. Case studies detailing the efforts of specific victims to block memory might also be quite useful (see the discussion above).

Therapy as Suggestion

☐ It has become axiomatic for some experts to testify that psychotherapy is suggestive and that certain techniques are suggestive. Further, it is argued that the presence of suggestion destroys believability and hence a witness (e.g., a psychotherapy client) exposed to suggestibility cannot be reliable.

This argument has many problems. It assumes that the effect of psychotherapy is universal and inevitable. It ignores the fact that most things in nature vary, so the suggestive effects of therapy are also likely to vary. It takes Lindsay and Read's 1994 article, which raises concern about the possible suggestive nature of certain therapy techniques (e.g., guided imagery or reading books about child abuse) as a statement of general consensus in the field and as the authoritative summary of research on these techniques. It is important to note that scholars Lindsay and Read themselves state that their article provides a "cognitive perspective" on psychotherapy and memories of childhood sexual abuse. They hope to inform practitioners about relevant research by cognitive psychologists. They argue that many of the factors that cognitive research has shown to increase the likelihood of memory errors are typical of memory recovery therapies. Their well-wrought approach is to review general memory research (much of it from laboratory investigations) and raise questions about certain therapy techniques.

It is not a criticism of Lindsay and Read's obvious scholarship to note that there exist no research data that have documented their concerns that guided imagery, journaling, dream interpretation, and survivors' groups produce the effects they fear. It is a gross misrepresentation of their findings to testify in court that the work "proves" these techniques are problematic.

It is very important for us, and especially important for the trier of fact, to understand how these scholars constructed their argument. For example, in terms of guided imagery, Lindsay and Read mention several concerns: (a) It produces a dissociated state that is similar to a hypnotic state; (b) the effort to build clear memory for events when initially there was little more than feeling or suspicion may lead to the creation of false memory due to increased suggestibility; and (c) Read (1996) has demonstrated that illusionary memories for a non-studied word occurred frequently when subjects mentally rehearsed a set of words closely associated with that word.

There is nothing wrong with academic speculation (hypothesizing) about the effects of guided imagery. It is wrong to take such a conceptual analysis and tell anyone, but especially the trier of fact, that it proves or even suggests that guided imagery is dangerous. Several obvious weaknesses exist in Lindsay and Read's speculation. First, I can locate no research that demonstrates that guided imagery produces a dissociated or hypnotic state. Suggestibility and hypnotizability are naturally occurring states. Some individuals are likely to be resistant to suggestion, whereas others are less resistant.

It is also important for the reader of Lindsay and Read (1994) to understand the nature of the references that these scholars present in their paragraph on guided imagery. It may appear to some readers and some courts that the references are to research directly on the point of

guided imagery. This is not the case. For example, they note:

> In recent years, forensic psychologists (Gudjonsson, 1985; Perry & Nogrady, 1985) have concluded that guided imagery, despite the absence of a hypnotic induction phase, promotes a dissociative state similar to that produced by hypnosis and, as a result, may be equally unreliable as a tool for recovering memories.

Perry and Nogrady (1985) present a conceptual argument, which appeared in the *British Journal of Experimental and Clinical Hypnosis* as a response to an attack on the use of hypnosis by the police, in which they argue that "there is no reason, at present, to exclude hypnosis as an investigative tool, provided that all of the necessary safeguards are applied stringently" (p. 28). They end by stating that "to propose a procedure such as guided imagery, without first verifying empirically its benignness with respect to error in the field situation, may simply return us to the time of Freud who thought, mistakenly, that it was appropriate medically to treat morphine addiction with cocaine" (pp. 29-30).

In the same journal, Gudjonsson (1985) offers a one-page commentary that notes, in part: "It is not clear to me why Perry and Nogrady appear decided to focus on only one of the alternatives, namely guided imagery. . . . A major weakness in the paper is that the authors do not clearly define what they mean by guided imagery and only superficially touch the relevant issues" (p. 37). Finally, the relevance of the unpublished research cited by these scholars (Read, 1994), involving memory for word lists, to understanding memory for human trauma is of considerable question (see Freyd & Gleaves, 1996).

Future Research

☐ The effects of psychotherapy—both intended and unintended—are an area of obvious importance. This is an area where research efforts could add substantially to our understanding about how to help effectively those who have experienced trauma. The effects of each of the techniques criticized by Lindsay and Read (1994) would be a good place to begin. For example, it would be quite interesting to see the effects of reading a book such as *The Courage to Heal* on experimental and control groups in terms of such factors as knowledge about abuse, attitudes toward abuse histories, and therapy.

Basic research on the techniques used in psychotherapy would be quite helpful. Does guided imagery produce a dissociative or hypnotic state? How do variables such as IQ, level of depression, and attitudes toward authority affect willingness to engage in certain therapy techniques or the level of engagement with the techniques? Research on behavior and attitudes in the general public would also be of use for our understanding of the pretreatment baseline of some aspects of this concern. For example, the use of self-help books appears to be quite popular in U.S. culture. As a therapist, I often see individuals who come to therapy having already read one or more books about abuse. I tend to see more individuals who have found these popular books unhelpful. Perhaps individuals who are disposed to gravitate toward self-help books are different in some characteristics from those who do not, and these factors should be evaluated in assessment for treatment and in understanding the effects of therapy techniques.

Conclusions

☐ There seems little doubt that interest in adult memory for trauma has greatly expanded in recent years. It is also apparent that there is an increase in research on various aspects of this topic. Indeed, this volume is part of that trend. In any important academic and applied field, there are always more research questions to be answered, methodologies to be developed, previous work to be critiqued, and new research to replicate or extend that work. This is the nature of science, and it is what draws so many to pursue entire careers as scientists.

The reader of this chapter now has a task quite similar to that of a judge who might be asked to rule on whether testimony such as that

outlined above would be of potential benefit to the trier of fact. A careful review of what is known and not known about the misinformation effect, creation of pseudomemories, massive repression, case reports as proof, and therapy as suggestion, in my opinion, leads to the conclusion that presenting such information as expert opinion should not be allowed in American courts, as such testimony fails to meet the *Daubert* guidelines. Critically, the science on these topics has not yet reached a level of sophistication or a sufficient cumulative mass of work to address critical forensic issues or concerns. Most of the ideas are untested or have been tested only with subjects or under conditions that are dissimilar to those of trauma and abuse. For example, the generalization of research findings developed with one sample of subjects (e.g., college students) to subjects who may differ in critical ways (e.g., alleged victims of trauma) is simply inappropriate absent actual research that extends or replicates the original research in the real world. The testimony discussed above has generally not been the subject of test (e.g., there is no research addressing guided imagery as a suggestive technique), and the concepts that have been subjected to some testing (e.g., the creation of pseudomemories in college students) actually suggest that it is difficult to create memories. Most critically, much of this testimony is not generally accepted in the scientific community. The reader, not unlike the trial judge, is in a position to accept or reject the ideas above. The reader, like the judge, will not bear the direct consequences of making the wrong judgment.

References

Bass, E., & Davis, L. (1988). *The courage to heal: A guide for women survivors of child sexual abuse*. New York: Harper & Row.

Brown, D. (1995a). Pseudomemories: The standard of science and the standard of care in trauma treatment. *American Journal of Clinical Hypnosis, 37*(3), 1-24.

Brown, D. (1995b). Sources of suggestion and their applicability to psychotherapy. In J. L. Alpert (Ed.), *Sexual abuse recalled: Treating trauma in the era of the recovered memory debate* (pp. 61-100). Northvale, NJ: Jason Aronson.

Ceci, S. J., & Loftus, E. F. (1994). "Memory work": A royal road to false memories? *Applied Cognitive Psychology, 8*, 351-364.

Cohen, L. E. (1996). The Daubert decision: Gatekeeper or executioner? *Trial, 32*(8), 53-57.

Conte, J. R. (1997). *Memory, pseudomemory, and psychotherapy.* Manuscript submitted for publication.

Daubert v. Merrell Dow Pharmaceuticals, Inc., 113 S. Ct. 2786 (1993).

Feagin, J. R., Orum, A. M., & Sjoberg, G. (1991). *A case for the case study.* Chapel Hill: University of North Carolina Press.

Freyd, J. J., & Gleaves, D. H. (1996). "Remembering" words not presented in lists: Relevance to the current recovered/false memory controversy. *Journal of Experimental Psychology: Learning, Memory, and Cognition, 22,* 811-813.

Gerlsma, C., Kramer, J. J., Scholing, A., & Emmelkamp, P. M. G. (1994). The influence of mood on memories of parental rearing practices. *British Journal of Clinical Psychology, 33*(2), 159-172.

Gudjonsson, G. H. (1985). The use of hypnosis by the police in the investigation of crime: Is guided imagery a safe substitute? Discussion commentary. *British Journal of Experimental and Clinical Hypnosis, 3*(1), 37.

Hammond, D. C., Garver, R. B., Mutter, C. B., Crasilneck, H. B., Frischholz, E., Gravitz, M. A., Hibler, N. S., Olson, J., Scheflin, A., Spiegel, H., & Wester, W. (1995). *Clinical hypnosis and memory: Guidelines for clinicians and for forensic hypnosis.* Chicago: American Society of Clinical Hypnosis Press.

Haynes, S. N. (1978). *Principles of behavioral assessment.* New York: Gardner.

Holmes, D. S. (1990). The evidence for repression: An examination of sixty years of research. In J. L. Singer (Ed.), *Repression and dissociation: Implications for personality theory, psychopathology, and health* (pp. 85-102). Chicago: University of Chicago Press.

Humphreys, L. E., & Ciminero, A. R. (1979). Parent report measures of child behavior: A review. *Journal of Clinical Child Psychology.*

Hyman, I. E., Jr., Husband, T. H., & Billings, F. J. (1995). False memories of childhood experiences. *Applied Cognitive Psychology, 9,* 181-197.

Koss, M. P., Figueredo, A. J., Bell, I., Tharan, M., & Tromp, S. (1996). Traumatic memory characteristics: A cross-validated mediational model of response to rape among employed women. *Journal of Abnormal Psychology, 105,* 421-432.

Lindsay, D. S., & Read, J. D. (1994). Psychotherapy and memories of childhood sexual abuse: A cognitive perspective. *Applied Cognitive Psychology, 8,* 281-338.

Loftus, E. F. (1993). The reality of repressed memories. *American Psychologist, 48,* 518-537.

Loftus, E. F., & Pickrell, J. E. (1995). The formation of false memories. *Psychiatric Annals, 25,* 720-725.

Ofshe, R. J., & Singer, M. I. (1994). Recovered-memory therapy and robust repression: Influence and pseudomemories. *International Journal of Clinical and Experimental Hypnosis, 42,* 391-410.

Perry, C., & Nogrady, H. (1985). The use of hypnosis by the police in the investigation of crime: Is guided imagery a safe substitute? *British Journal of Experimental and Clinical Hypnosis, 3*(1), 25-31.

Pezdek, K., Finger, K., & Hodge, D. (1996, November). *False memories are more likely to be planted if they are familiar.* Paper presented at the annual meeting of the Psychonomic Society, Chicago.

Pope, K. S. (1996). Memory, abuse, and science: Questioning claims about the false memory syndrome epidemic. *American Psychologist, 51,* 957-974.

Read, J. D. (1996). From a passing thought to a false memory in two minutes. *Psychonomic Bulletin & Review, 3*(1), 105-111.

Reviere, S. L. (1996). *Memory of childhood trauma: A clinician's guide to the literature.* New York: Guilford.

Rotgers, F., & Barrett, D. (1996). *Daubert v. Merrell Dow* and expert testimony by clinical psychologists: Implications and recommendations for practice. *Professional Psychology: Research and Practice, 27,* 467-474.

Sullaway, M., & Christensen, A. (1983). Couples and families as participant observers of their interaction. *Advances in Family Intervention, Assessment and Theory, 3,* 119-160.

Williams, L. M., & Banyard, V. L. (1997). Perspectives on adult memories of childhood sexual abuse: A research review. In L. J. Dickstein, M. B. Riba, & J. M. Oldham (Eds.), *American Psychiatric Press review of psychiatry* (Vol. 16, pp. II-123–II-151). Washington, DC: American Psychiatric Press.

8

Remembering Incest

The Complexities of This Process and Implications for Civil Statutes of Limitations

Joyce Sese Dorado

In recent years, the issue of adults recovering memories of childhood sexual abuse has received national attention and been the focus of heated debate. As adult survivors of childhood incest have begun to attempt to sue their alleged perpetrators in civil court, courts and legislatures have begun to change the manner in which these cases are handled. Statutes of limitations for civil tort actions, typically ranging from 1 to 6 years, normally begin to run from the point in time that the injury occurs. Such statutes are problematic for plaintiffs in cases of incest for a number of reasons. A child, particularly one who is dependent upon and/or lives in the same household as the perpetrator, might not be able to make a complaint until after he or she is out of the perpetrator's control. Further, many incest survivors are unable to remember and/or consciously deal with the meaning, significance, or consequences of sexually abusive acts until sometime in adulthood. If a survivor, for any of these reasons, is unable to disclose the incest to the appropriate professionals or authorities, then filing a civil suit within the bounds of normal statutes of limitations is exceedingly difficult, if not impossible. Changes in statutes of limitations for incest cases that toll statutes (i.e., postpone the point at which a limitations period begins to run) until the plaintiff is 18 years of age or older were originally motivated by such concerns.

Exceptions to normal statutes of limitations applied to incest cases have been based on the legal system's determination of the reasonable

AUTHOR'S NOTE: I would like to thank Margaret Buttenheim and Phoebe Ellsworth. Without their insights, ideas, and support, this study could not have come into being. I am also grateful to Victoria Banyard for her invaluable feedback and encouragement.

amount of time a survivor should be given to file a civil claim after he or she becomes an adult. Such a determination takes into account the concern that evidence on either side of the case will become lost, destroyed, or "stale" if court actions are delayed (Harshaw, 1989). The past several years have seen several changes in judicial decisions and state legislation with regard to both when this period of limitation should begin to run and how long it should be. Although these changes have been a positive step toward providing a legal remedy for adult survivors of childhood incest, many of these changes are not in keeping with what psychologists are beginning to understand about the complicated nature of psychological trauma as experienced by incest survivors.

The purpose of the study discussed in this chapter was to explore the process by which incest survivors remember and come to terms with child sexual abuse. In particular, my goal was to take a look at the remembering process, as experienced by incest survivors themselves, and to examine the goodness of fit of this process with a statute of limitations applied to adult survivors trying to sue their abusers. I conducted this study in Michigan in 1992, when the state was grappling with the issue of providing a legal remedy for incest survivors. Michigan's struggle set the context of the study, and thus the Michigan statute of limitations at that time affected the formulation of the study's questions and the qualitative analysis of the data. Since then, there have been changes to the statute, which I will touch on later in this chapter. In any case, although the state of Michigan provided an initial framework for the current chapter, how to address appropriately cases of adult survivors filing civil suits against their abusers continues to be a controversial legal issue in states across the country. I address this issue more broadly in the discussion section.

A summary of the main findings of this study can be found in a previous article in which I focus on the role of feminist therapists when presented with clients' reported memories of incest (Dorado, 1996). This chapter provides a fuller discussion of the study's findings. I first present psychological approaches to the issue of

remembering sexual abuse, and then touch on Michigan's legal approach to this issue. I later discuss the study's findings, describing the experiences of the research participants to illustrate these findings.

In order to protect the confidentiality of the study's participants, I have changed participants' names and altered identifying details of their cases. Moreover, some of the experiences described in this chapter are composites of the experiences of more than one participant, and no one participant is represented in total. These modifications, however, do not alter the major themes upon which the conceptualization of incest survivors' remembering processes is based.

Psychological Approaches to Traumatic Memory

☐ Clinical experience as well as research shows that incest survivors frequently suffer at least partial amnesia surrounding abusive events (Briere & Conte, 1993). A significant proportion of people who were sexually abused as children do not realize that they were abused until years—and often decades—after the abuse occurred (Russell, 1986). Putting the traumatic event out of one's consciousness is a common defensive mechanism employed by trauma victims of all ages (Russell, 1986). But, unlike some other types of traumas (such as automobile accidents and physical assaults), in the case of incest, the incest itself is typically kept a secret between the perpetrator and the victim. The perpetrator coerces the victim into silence, often through direct or indirect threats of physical violence. This silence can increase the likelihood that such amnesia will occur (Russell, 1986).

What is the nature of amnesia around abusive events that occurs in cases of incest? Some incest survivors do not experience amnesia for the events themselves, but may be amnestic regarding certain aspects of the event. For example, some survivors describe themselves as "not very upset" about their abuse, and yet give accounts of the sexual abuse that indicate they had actually been negatively affected (Russell,

1986). In these cases, survivors are sometimes able to talk about their abuse, yet they use the same neutral tone of voice as they might if they were reading a weather report, with no affective connection to the abusive events or to their significance. In this way, incest survivors often put away from themselves, from their conscious identities, certain elements of the abuse, such as its significance, its connection with current psychological problems, and their feelings of pain or helplessness at the time of the abuse.

Other survivors seem to have pushed the abusive events themselves, the fact that the abuse ever happened, out of their ordinary consciousness. The phenomenon of amnesia for sexually abusive events of childhood has been shown by a number of researchers. For example, Herman and Schatzow (1987) found that 64% of the female outpatients with sexual abuse histories that they studied had experienced at least partial amnesia of their abuse at some point in their lives. These researchers found that the most severe memory deficits were associated with sexual abuse that began in early childhood and terminated before adolescence. They also found a relationship between massive repression and especially violent or sadistic abuse.

Similarly, Briere and Conte (1993) found that 59% of their sample of adults sexually abused as children reported some period before age 18 when they could not remember their first sexual abuse experience. At least partial amnesia for abusive events was related to violent abuse—for example, abuse that involved multiple perpetrators, physical injury, or threat of death. This was in contrast to abuse that might engender psychological conflict, such as abuse in which victims experienced some physical or psychological enjoyment or reward. Finally, an increased likelihood of amnesia was related to early onset of the abuse (mean of 5.8 years) and to a longer duration of the abuse (Briere & Conte, 1993).

In a prospective study of sexual abuse memories, Williams (1994) found that 38% of women in her study with previously documented histories of child sexual abuse did not remember their abuse when asked about it as adults. Women were more likely to have no recollection of their abuse if they were abused at a younger age or by someone they knew.

Research in the area of psychological trauma offers theories that may serve as a framework with which to understand the remembering process of incest survivors. Van der Kolk (1988), providing a definition of trauma, asserts that "the essence of the trauma experience is that it leaves people in a state of 'unspeakable terror.' The experience does not fit into existing conceptual schemata: it overwhelms" (p. 282). Shengold (1989), in his writings on "soul murder" resulting from child abuse, defines a traumatic, abusive experience as "too much too-muchness," an overwhelming, overstimulating, painful, and terrifying event (p. 1).

Janet, in his theory on the psychological processing of traumatic experiences, asserts that under traumatic circumstances (such as child sexual abuse), frightening and novel events may not be able to be fit into existing cognitive schemata (see van der Kolk, Brown, & van der Hart, 1989, for a review of Janet's theory), and thus traumatic experiences can remain unintegrated, split off from voluntary control and conscious awareness. According to Janet (1919/1976), memory is ordinarily "an action: essentially it is the action of telling a story" (p. 661; quoted in van der Kolk et al., 1989, p. 368). He asserts that consciousness is made up of "a unified memory of all psychological facets related to a particular experience: sensations, emotions, thoughts, and actions" (cited in van der Kolk & van der Hart, 1989, p. 1532). Under normal circumstances, people automatically store information in their memories by taking appropriate action, ranging from simple reflexes to carrying out complex and particular skills. In this way, most experiences, habits, values, and skills are integrated into already existing cognitive schemata. Part of taking appropriate action involves being able to make a cognitive assessment and verbally represent or "make a recital of" events (Janet, 1919/1976; cited in van der Kolk et al., 1989), transforming the experiences into a cohesive personal narrative. In this way, the memory system, under conditions of normal functioning, maintains coherence and links the past with the present by perpetually categorizing and organizing new information.

As children mature, they move through different stages in central nervous system development, encoding information using progressively different modes (Piaget, 1973). Developmentally, children move from primarily sensorimotor (motoric action) modes of organizing mental experiences to perceptual representations (iconic), and then to symbolic/linguistic modes (van der Kolk & van der Hart, 1991).

During a traumatic event, a person may become overwhelmed with "speechless terror" (van der Kolk, 1987), and therefore the trauma victim's central nervous system cannot organize the traumatic experience on a linguistic or symbolic level. Instead, the experience may be incorporated on a somatosensory or iconic level which cannot easily be translated into the symbolic language necessary for linguistic retrieval (van der Kolk & van der Hart, 1991). The traumatic experience is assimilated into the unconscious ego without being attached to other memories or to a context that would give it meaning, and thus the memory remains dissociated. Although these dissociated memory fragments may remain unconscious, they continue to affect behavior, perceptions, and emotional states long after they have been split off from ordinary consciousness. Fragments of unintegrated traumatic events may later resurface in a highly disruptive manner as somatic sensations, behavioral reenactments, nightmares, and flashbacks (Brett & Ostroff, 1985), or they may intrude upon normal functioning as inexplicably intense emotional reactions, anxiety attacks, conversion reactions, frightening perceptions, or obsessional preoccupations.

Dissociation as a way of defending against painful intrusions of the unintegrated trauma can follow trauma victims as a way of coping with other stressful events throughout their adult lives. When trauma victims repeatedly and automatically react to stress by allowing events to bypass their ordinary consciousness, they often suffer from a chronic narrowing of consciousness. Their ability to experience a full range of emotions within their personal

consciousness consequently becomes restricted, leading to an enduring feeling of numbness.

Victims of child sexual abuse may be especially susceptible to the psychopathological sequelae of trauma. Janet (1919/1976) argues that "vehement emotions" accompanying a traumatic event further interfere with a person's ability to take appropriate action and thus integrate the event, and the intensity of the vehement emotion is what determines the severity and intensity of the later, posttraumatic reactions (cited in van der Kolk et al., 1989). He also asserts that a person's ability to grasp the totality of his or her experiences determines that person's vulnerability to posttraumatic psychological disorders. This capacity is dependent upon the individual's prior experience, temperament, and physiological state (e.g., illness, intoxication, fatigue, depression), the novelty of the situation, the speed of the events, and the violent emotions caused during the traumatic event. From this list of potential risk factors, it seems clear that children are particularly vulnerable to overwhelming traumas such as child sexual abuse. Furthermore, in the case of incest, the very nature of the trauma is such that the child is told by the perpetrator—directly or indirectly—that he or she must never tell anyone about the abuse. This can only exacerbate the individual's inability to integrate the traumatic abuse into his or her personal narrative.

If incest survivors are contending with these traumatic memory processes, this can present a dilemma for those trying to utilize the legal system to redress the injurious consequences of their abuse. Researchers and clinicians who have studied and treated psychological trauma often cite the above differences between normal memory processes and traumatic memory processes. Do court officials recognize these differences when considering incest survivors' cases? As one example of the legal system's approach to the process of remembering incest, the following section briefly summarizes Michigan's statute of limitations in the early 1990s.

One Legal Approach to Traumatic Memory: Michigan's Statute of Limitations

☐ In Michigan, the normal statute of limitations for personal injury cases in civil court is 3 years after the injurious act. Adult survivors remembering and coming to terms with incest are generally unable to file civil suits under this statute because the injurious acts occurred during their childhoods—years or even decades earlier. However, in a 1988 Michigan case, *Meiers-Post v. Schafer,* the court held that survivors of sexual abuse who have "repressed the memory of the events" of the abuse would be allowed 1 year "after the memory is revived" to pursue their cases in civil court (p. 176). This was provided that the sexual abuse survivors (the plaintiffs) had corroborating evidence that they were actually sexually abused. Without corroborating evidence, adult survivors would not be allowed to seek restitution through the court.

The plaintiff in *Meiers-Post v. Schafer* drew upon an "insanity" exception to the normal 3-year statute of limitations period for personal injury actions. This clause "provides that if a person is insane at the time her claim accrues, she has one year after the disability is removed to bring the action although the applicable period of limitation has run" (p. 178). In this clause, "insane" is defined as "a condition of mental derangement such as to prevent the sufferer from comprehending rights he or she is otherwise bound to know" (pp. 178-179). In *Meiers-Post v. Schafer,* the plaintiff claimed that her memories were triggered by a television show on child sexual abuse. Fortunately for the plaintiff, the defendant had admitted that he had sexually abused her, and this testimony served as corroborating evidence. Consequently, the judges in this case decided that because there was sufficient corroborating evidence that the sexual abuse occurred, allowing the plaintiff to pursue her claim under the insanity clause struck "a fair balance between the risk of stale claims and the unfairness of precluding justifiable causes of action" (p. 183). This was the first case in Michigan to address whether repression and posttraumatic stress syndrome constitute insanity for the purpose of the statute of limitations.

As of January 1995, two other states have applied the insanity exception to the normal personal injury statute to civil suits involving adult incest survivors suing their perpetrators: Colorado and Virginia (Pope & Brown, 1996). Although such laws may begin to address the needs of survivors who have massively dissociated the abusive events themselves, a number of problems with this legal approach are conspicuous. In the first place, these statutes do not provide for any survivors who have dissociated other aspects of their abuse, such as the emotions associated with the abuse or the significance of the abusive events. Additionally, the nature of incest is that it happens in private, and corroborating evidence (as required in Michigan, for example)—such as the confession of the perpetrator or testimony from eyewitnesses—rarely exists. Furthermore, the fact that plaintiffs making use of this statute are required to make their claims under the insanity clause could pose serious problems for incest survivors in terms of their mental health. Typically, part of incest survivors' therapy involves helping them to realize that they are not "crazy" for thinking that something bad happened to them, and moreover that they are not "crazy" for having intense feelings about the abuse so long after it occurred. This therapeutic goal may well be in direct conflict with survivors' having to declare in court that they were insane up until the point when they filed suit. These are some of the more obvious ways in which the insanity exception to the personal injury statute of limitations is not appropriate for incest survivors' experiences and psychological needs.

In the remainder of this chapter, I present the process of remembering sexual abuse as experienced by the incest survivors who participated in the current study, and then discuss how these findings speak to more subtle ways in which the legal system does not adequately take into account the complexity of this remembering process.

Method

☐ Because relatively little research had been conducted on incest survivors' experiences of remembering their abuse, I chose a qualitative approach rather than a quantitative approach. Research on psychological trauma such as that described above informed my thinking on how traumatic memories may be stored and retrieved. In addition, my training as a clinician was useful as I made decisions during the interviews about when and how to probe further particular aspects of the participants' stories.

Formulating a fixed set of hypotheses prior to data collection and then testing these hypotheses through a structured questionnaire would have run the risk of forcing incest survivors' experiences into already existing categories and conceptualizations originating from research on very different populations (e.g., male veterans of the Vietnam War). Instead, the "grounded theory" qualitative approach to research (Glaser & Strauss, 1967; Strauss & Corbin, 1990) indicates that a theory generated from the words and experiences of the survivors themselves ultimately has more construct validity than an a priori theory "proven" through traditional quantitative methods.

Participants

Seven participants were recruited through flyers posted at various mental health agencies at which incest survivors constituted part of the clientele, and through advertisements in a monthly newsletter for incest survivors. Participants were told that they would be participating in a study on "the process of remembering and coming to terms with sexual abuse for women incest survivors." [1]

The study was limited to survivors of intrafamilial sexual abuse as defined by Russell (1983). In her study on the incidence and prevalence of sexual abuse of female children, she defined intrafamilial child sexual abuse as "any kind of exploitative sexual contact that occurred between relatives, no matter how distant the relationship, before the victim turned 18 years old" (pp. 135-136). Experiences involving sexual contact with a relative that were both with a peer and mutually wanted were not regarded as exploitative. A peer relationship was defined as an age difference of fewer than 5 years (Russell, 1983). In the current study, all of the participants reported that they were sexually abused by a parent.

In addition to a definition of incest that involves physical sexual contact, Herman (1981) describes a phenomenon in which the father-daughter relationship is highly sexualized. In these cases, the father is inappropriately "seductive" with his daughter. Within a highly sexualized parent-child relationship, there are psychological sexual boundary violations and the constant implicit threat that these boundary violations could at any moment become physical. Consequently, a highly sexualized parent-child relationship creates a more chronic situation that has many of the characteristics of physical sexual abuse. Although Herman contends that there are similarities between the symptoms caused by physical sexual abuse ("overt incest") and a highly sexualized parent-child relationship ("covert incest"), she maintains the distinction, as do I. All but one of the survivors in this study reported that they experienced overt incest. However, given that Herman does assert that many women who had seductive fathers suffer problems similar to those of overt incest survivors (though milder in degree), the experiences of one survivor of covert incest are also included in this study. The one participant who experienced covert incest will be identified as such throughout this chapter.

About 35 potential participants responded to the flyers and advertisements. Individuals were screened out if they felt they were still in the middle of their remembering process; preference was given to survivors who felt more resolved about their memories (i.e., were not still actively struggling with the impacts of these memories on their lives). I employed this screening criterion to avoid retraumatizing participants and because of concern that retraumatization was a greater risk if survivors discussed their memories while still in the midst of recovering them. Furthermore, because I was particularly interested in the overall course of the remembering process, it was important that I choose participants for whom the process was reasonably complete. In addition, I screened out individuals who had never been in therapy or who no longer had contact with their therapists. This was to ensure that if distressing material arose that could not be resolved during the course of the interviews, the survivors would have resources for dealing with any unresolved difficulties.

I made an attempt to select participants who were diverse in race and ethnic background, socioeconomic status, sexual orientation, and age. Unfortunately, the goal of having racial diversity was not realized; all 7 participants were of European American descent. With regard to socioeconomic status, participants' annual household incomes ranged from approximately $10,000 (a graduate student on stipend) to $41,000 (a combined income with spouse). The mean annual household income was about $22,700. Participants' educational levels ranged from slightly less than 2 years of college to a master's degree. Their ages ranged from 21 to 40 years.

Six of the participants had gone through a period with no conscious memory of the sexually abusive events. Only one participant never dissociated the knowledge of the incestuous behavior, though she had dissociated the significance of this behavior until adulthood. Indeed, the vast majority of calls were from women who had possessed no conscious knowledge of their sexually abusive experiences until they suddenly remembered them in adulthood. This response pattern was both unexpected and unintended in terms of design of the study. In retrospect, it seems likely that it resulted from the advertisement of the study as research "on the remembering process of incest survivors," which may have implied that women *must* have forgotten about their abuse until adulthood in order to participate.

Procedure

Seven incest survivors participated in semi-structured, intensive individual interviews for three sessions of approximately 2 to 3 hours each. One participant was interviewed, at her request, for a fourth session. Ultimately, interviews ranged from 6 to 12 hours per participant,

and were audiotaped and transcribed in full. Notes were also taken during the interviews to record nonverbal cues given by participants and to facilitate follow-up questions.

Throughout the interviews, I tried to create an environment conducive to self-reflection, and attempted to maintain a nonevaluative and reflective demeanor. The main purpose of the interviews was to understand and completely retrace, through the participant's eyes, her experience as a survivor, the process of recognizing and realizing that she was abused, and the ways in which she dealt with this realization. Thus my goal was to follow the direction of the participant so that she could tell her story in her own words, while at the same time ensuring that at some point during the interview the specific research questions were answered.

For the last half hour of the third session, I discussed with the participant my interpretations of what had transpired during the interview, and I answered any questions that she may have had about the study.

Analysis of Data

Methods for data analysis were based on the grounded theory approach to qualitative research (Glaser & Strauss, 1967; McCracken, 1988; Strauss & Corbin, 1990). Transcripts were read through in their entirety as the interview tapes were replayed, and then read through in their entirety at least one more time. Passages relevant to the focus of the study were marked and read through repeatedly. Concepts were drawn from the transcripts and were grouped into categories. Properties of these categories were ascertained, and these properties were dimensionalized (i.e., rated across a qualitative range). The categories were grouped and arranged to illustrate the process over time: the causal conditions for the phenomenon, the phenomenon itself (i.e., remembering, knowing/understanding the significance of remembered abusive events), the intervening conditions that facilitated or hindered action/interactional strategies taken within specific contexts, the actual strategies taken to deal with the phenomenon, the consequences of these strategies, and, in turn, how these consequences set up the

conditions for the next action/interactional sequence (Strauss & Corbin, 1990).

The entire body of results from this analysis
are beyond the scope of this chapter. Here, my
focus is on the early part of the process of the
individual's remembering sexual abuse and integrating these memories into her personal narrative, and on the intervening conditions.

Because this study was exploratory in nature, I expected that the organization of the
themes and categories, and thus the questions
and focus of the interviews, would change and
evolve throughout the course of the study. To
this end, transcripts were preliminarily analyzed as soon as they became available, so that
categories of analysis and hypotheses could
evolve gradually and help guide the following
interview and set of analyses (Glaser & Strauss,
1967).

Throughout this entire process, in order to
diversify the approach to the data, I discussed
my hypotheses with University of Michigan
Department of Psychology faculty members involved in the study. As a result, my experiences
and interpretations of the data did not alone
dictate the theses that emerged from this study.

Results

□ This chapter addresses the following questions: Drawing upon the experiences of survivors themselves, what exactly are the kinds of
factors that constitute and characterize memories of sexual abuse? How do sexual abuse
survivors' experiences of remembering differ
from the common, everyday understanding of
what it means to "remember" an event? Do
statutes of limitations such as those of the state
of Michigan take into account these differences? What are other characteristics of incest
survivors' remembering process that the legal
community should attempt to address? The
findings of this study demonstrate how the process of remembering sexual abuse as experienced by incest survivors is quite different from
ordinary memory processes. This process is
much more intricate than statutes of limitations
such as those in effect in Michigan take into
account.

Remembering for the survivors in this study
consisted of different components. I will focus
on two early phenomena in this process that
emerged from the data: the first recognizable
memory and precursors to the first recognizable
memory.

Definition of Terms

In this discussion, *first recognizable memory*
refers to the first time that a participant remembered something and recognized it as a memory
of sexual abuse, however piecemeal or fragmented the memory. It does not refer to the
remembering of an abusive event in its entirety
from beginning to end. The difference between
these two terms is important. The data from this
study show that after the first recognizable
memory of abuse emerged, it sometimes took
days, weeks, or months before the entire abusive
event was put together or "re-membered," with
all of its sensory and affective components. It
sometimes took years for the context and significance of the event to be integrated into a
survivor's personal narrative, the process
through which, according to trauma theorists
such as Janet, traumatic memory is transformed
into normal memory.

A *precursor* to the first recognizable memory is a traumatic memory fragment that made
no sense to the survivor at the time she experienced it. A precursor was not recognized by the
survivor as being related to the sexual abuse
until later, in retrospect, after she recognized
that she had been abused. This term will be
defined more specifically later in the chapter.

First Recognizable Memories

Although all of this study's participants described flashbacks and related symptoms that
preceded their first recognizable memories,
when asked the question, "When was the first
time you felt somehow, or remembered, that
something happened to you?" most of the participants described a "first memory" that had
enough imagery that the perpetrator was identifiable and the survivor could recognize that
something emotionally or physically painful
was being done to her. The memories also had

enough imagery to locate these events temporally in the survivors' childhoods. More often than not, the first remembering had at least some visual component.

In addition, the first recognizable memory of sexual abuse was generally intrusive, such that the survivor could not shut it out once it had begun. It was also extremely intense, often sending the survivor into a different state of consciousness than her normal, everyday state. It was experienced more as a reexperiencing of the trauma, often with behavioral reenactment, rather than as an ordinary memory.

The experience of one participant, whom I will call Emma, serves as an example of the first recognizable memories of this study's participants. Emma had been talking to her sibling, who, for reasons independent of Emma, was exploring the possibility of having been sexually abused. Many hours later, when Emma was alone and sitting in front of her fireplace, she thought about the earlier conversation with her sibling about sexual abuse, and inexplicably began clenching her mouth shut tightly. As she was wondering why she was doing this, she remembered holding her mouth shut as a child, and heard her father warning her that he would have vaginal intercourse with her if he could not put his penis in her mouth. She then experienced the bodily sensation of her father lifting her and having sexual intercourse with her. Once she began to remember the rape, she did not have control over the traumatic memory or her reactions to it. She was reexperiencing the past rape as though it were happening in the present. Accompanying the visual and auditory components of this memory were intense emotions and physical sensations, as well as a reexperience of her bodily reaction to the rape. She remembered the stinging and burning pain of it, and "the feeling of . . . inside being mushed and mushed." As she was reexperiencing the memory, she was having motoric reactions as though the abuse were taking place in the present day, including bodily contortions such as arching her back as though attempting to get away from the grip of her father. This reexperiencing of the rape so overtook her that the present-day surroundings had temporarily disappeared. She described her reentry into ordinary consciousness:

"And then I was crying and . . . there's this fireplace and I'm like huddled up on the floor screaming into the floor."

Over time, Emma eventually remembered her father forcing oral sex on her and repeatedly vaginally raping her. Before having her first recognizable memory, Emma had believed her abuser to be a good father and a very sweet, upstanding man. She had completely dissociated any of his sexually abusive behavior. In retrospect, she realizes that many of her father's behaviors (some of which she had always remembered) did not fit the perception of him as a "really nice guy." These behaviors included harsh and arbitrary rule setting and disciplining, as well as verbal abuse, such as humiliating her and her siblings, calling them offensive names, and otherwise insulting them many times a day. Her parents used to fight constantly, yelling and screaming at each other. In her "everyday remembering" she always had been conscious of various pieces of evidence indicating physical violence between her father and mother, including bruises on her mother, and her father frequently using physical force (e.g., pulling her hair) to control her. It is very interesting that despite having had conscious access to this knowledge all of her life, she still had an image of her father as "nice" and "sweet." It could be hypothesized that this highly positive image of her father was an unconscious psychological defense, such as reaction formation or vertical splitting (Shengold, 1989). I will discuss such defenses later in the chapter.

There was some variation in the characteristics of traumatic memory present in participants' first memories. For example, the first recognizable memory of abuse experienced by Cynthia began with what she called a "feeling memory." It was a very intense feeling of identification with a woman in an incest survivors' book who was, as Cynthia had been, bulimic. After reading the section describing this bulimic woman, she said: "I looked around, I got very agitated, and panic, complete panic. And then I started to remember being orally sexually abused. But no real pictures."

For many weeks following this "feeling memory," she experienced visual flashes of her father performing oral sex on her. Along with these first visual flashes, she experienced a physical sensation of being "highly aroused" in a way that was "too intense." "It was so stimulating that it was painful," she recounted. She described the flashes as "like puzzle pieces," and as "real intrusive . . . so intrusive, I couldn't stop thinking about this." The pieces usually came with "complete and utter panic," during which time she would lock herself in her bedroom or bathroom. She described how the visual flashes came:

> Flash here, and I deal with this . . . rush of whatever, and then try to sort it all out. And then as soon as I get back on my feet again, and booomm, another one. And they could either be little bits and pieces to one full memory, or they could be another memory that's connected somehow. So I didn't really even know what it was coming at me. I just kinda took it as it came.

Interspersed into Cynthia's memory of oral sex were flashbacks of being vaginally raped by her father. Over time, she eventually remembered that she was sexually abused by her father when they would go to a local site away from their home. Before she remembered the sexual abuse perpetrated by her father, she had known that her father was abusive in other ways (emotionally and physically), but she had "no idea" that he had sexually abused her. A year and a half after her first recognizable memory, subsequent to full realization of the significance and injurious impact of her father's abuse, Cynthia attempted to file a civil suit against him. The 1-year statute of limitations in Michigan, however, prevented her from being able to present her case in court.

Another participant, Debbie, demonstrated other possible characteristics of first memory. Debbie remembered, very suddenly, being sexually abused by her father. She had been going to a counselor for help with inexplicable fear and panic reactions, as well as recurrent, frightening nightmares. This counselor, presumably to help her figure out why she was having these symptoms, had hypnotized her. Debbie woke up from her induced hypnotic state feeling sick, faint, dizzy, in a daze, "completely out of it." The counselor would not tell

Debbie what she had said during the hypnosis.[2] Debbie does not know how she got home from the counselor's office, but once she was home, she lay on her bed, feeling frustrated and wanting to know what she was afraid of.

As she was staring at a shadow of a chair in her room, she realized that she recognized this shadow pattern "from somewhere." She suddenly saw an image of her father choking her. Although she had remembered her father choking her before, the ensuing memories of violent sexual abuse came flooding back for the first time that she was conscious of.

> The minute I remembered I was like, "No, no, no." I started even saying, "No." And I started walking around, saying, "No, nothing like that could ever happen," you know. And I really tried to like talk myself out of it. "This couldn't have happened," you know. And then every time I stopped talking to myself out loud and saying, "This didn't happen" and started thinking about it, I knew that it did. . . . And I didn't feel anything except like I wanted it to go away.

This survivor's first recognizable memory was essentially visual and auditory in form. Though she reported not experiencing the accompanying physical sensations or affect (except feeling like she wanted it to "go away,"), the visual images were very vivid and detailed, and the experience was extremely intense. The memory flashes were quite intrusive. She could not put them out of her consciousness.

Prior to remembering the sexual abuse, Debbie had always known that her father was severely mentally ill and had physically abused her and her siblings. Nevertheless, she had an extremely difficult time believing that her father could have abused her sexually in the way that she was remembering. She actively tried to make the memory and subsequent recognition of violent sexual abuse disappear, but it would not.

She reported that she remembered an entire abusive incident that first day. She remembered details of the moments that led up to her father trying to force an object into her vagina, as well as the moments after, in which her father tried to make her stop bleeding by applying ice to her vagina. Interspersed with this memory were memories of other abusive incidents, some whole, and some piecemeal. Also interspersed were things that she had always remembered from childhood and things that had occurred in her adult life that she had not understood, but in the context of the remembered sexual abuse made a great deal of sense. Nevertheless, the affective and sensory components of the sexual abuse were still dissociated from the rest of the traumatic memory. Debbie described the abuse that she eventually remembered as very violent and painful, perpetrated, from her description, by a very mentally unstable, probably episodically psychotic man.

Remembering the traumatic events put Debbie in a dramatically altered state of consciousness, so much so that when her husband tried to figure out why she was acting so strangely, she was unable to formulate a coherent or communicative answer. She could only say, "My father hurt me. I was looking at a shadow, and I remembered something." She said that in retrospect she was not making any sense, and that she was "hysterical in a way, like not screaming or anything, but just kind of staring."

In summary, the first recognizable memories reported by survivors in this study who had experienced a period of not remembering their abuse had characteristics of traumatic memory processes. The emergence of these memories was not within the survivors' voluntary control. The traumatic memories were intrusive reexperiences of the trauma, often with accompanying visceral sensations and bodily reactions, which propelled survivors into an alternate state of consciousness such that they were unable to function normally. In these ways, these first recognizable memories were unlike ordinary, everyday remembering.

Precursors to the First Recognizable Memory

Most of the participants in this study experienced fragmentary precursors before they gained access to memories recognizable as sexual abuse. For these participants, traumatic memory was composed of many disjointed elements that often did not come together to form

recognizable (much less complete) memories of abuse for a period of time ranging from days to years. All of the participants described experiencing inexplicable occurrences of intrusive thoughts, intrusive affect (i.e., affective memories), bodily sensations or pain (somatic memories), and/or traumatic nightmares (Dorado, 1996). They later identified these occurrences as fragmented reexperiences of their childhood abuse, precursors to their first recognizable memories of sexual abuse.

Examples of intrusive thoughts experienced by this study's participants include one survivor's experience of an overriding feeling of wanting to hold her dress down, even though she was not wearing a dress. She later remembered her parent violently sexually abusing her. Another participant, after stumbling on some cards written to her sister by her father (who died when she was in elementary school), suddenly thought to herself, "Oh, he *isn't* a horrible demon after all." She had no idea why this thought had come to her at the time because it had never in her adult life occurred to her that her father was anything but a wonderful man. She later remembered her father sexually abusing and severely physically abusing her. Some examples of intrusive affect experienced by participants include sudden panic attacks (as though the participant would "start screaming and never stop"), inexplicable fear triggered by smells or tastes, and overwhelming feelings of hopelessness for no apparent reason. Examples of participants' precursor bodily sensations include inexplicable "pain so bad it made the room go white," a feeling of choking and being unable to breathe with no physical precipitant, and an unaccountable sensation of something pushing on the vaginal area.

Cynthia's experience provides further examples of the types of precursors found in the experiences of other participants in this study (Dorado, 1996). Cynthia's first recognizable memory was of her father forcing oral sex on her. Prior to this memory, for as long as Cynthia could recall, about once a month just as she was falling asleep she would have a sensation in her mouth, a feeling that her mouth was full, with an object that was "soft on the outside," but "hard" underneath the soft outside. After she remembered the abuse, she recognized this sensation as a physical reexperiencing of an erect penis inside her mouth, which she believes was her father's penis during sexually abusive incidents.

The following is another component of Cynthia's experience that represents precursors to a first recognizable memory:

> One weekend approximately two years prior to our interview, Cynthia and her children were visiting her parents. During this visit, as she was watching her father walk into the house, she began to stare inexplicably and uncontrollably at his belt and groin area and had a sense that his body was somehow suddenly younger, although when she looked up at him, he appeared once again his older age. Later in the day, she and her father were sitting next to each other on a couch, watching her then two-and-a-half-year-old daughter playing on the floor. Cynthia was resting her head on her father's chest when he said to her daughter, "that's my girl." Cynthia had a sudden and strong emotional reaction to this, and sat up straight. She quickly left her parents' house with her children. Although at the time Cynthia did not understand her intense reaction to her father, this ended up being the last time that she saw him. (Dorado, 1996, p. 120)

This experience is illustrative of fragmentary reexperiences of a past trauma consisting of intrusive thought accompanied by mild visual distortion/hallucination, as well as intrusive, dissociated affect. Although Cynthia did not realize it at the time, it was as though she were suddenly living simultaneously in the present and in the traumatic past.

In summary, for the study participants, prior to the first recognizable memory of abuse, fragments of the unintegrated trauma were reexperienced as precursor symptoms. These symptoms intruded into the survivors' consciousness in the form of intrusive thoughts, inexplicably intense affect, decontextualized bodily sensations, perceptual distortions, and traumatic nightmares. Although the symptoms were distressing, the precursors did not make any sense at the time they were experienced. Only later did these survivors recognize these fragments as

dismembered pieces of their sexual abuse memories.

Exploratory Findings: Further Complexity of the Remembering Process

At least two of the participants reported experiences that suggest that the remembering process may be further complicated by renewed dissociation even after the recognition of possible sexual abuse has emerged. Although this was not the reported experience of a majority of the participants in this study, the phenomenon is sufficiently compelling to warrant some exploration. One participant, whom I will call Anita, was particularly articulate in describing the nonlinear quality of this process.

From early childhood on, Anita experienced a "pervasive lack of boundaries" on her father's part, which resulted in a highly sexualized relationship between them. Her father's behavior toward her fits that of the "seductive father" described by Herman (1981). Although Anita's experience was different from the experiences of the other participants in that, to her knowledge, the sexualized relationship never did manifest itself in physical sexual abuse, she did experience a chronic, ongoing perception of looming, potential danger that the psychological boundaries that were being crossed would become physical. Her father's sexualized relationship with her included his sharing explicit details of his sexual extramarital affairs, telling her that he was "in love" with her, and expressing affection in sexualized ways (e.g., patting her on the buttocks, holding her hand in a romantic, sexualized way). She reported that she never completely forgot all memories of her father's covertly incestuous behavior. She knew of many of the covertly incestuous events themselves, but did not recognize their significance.

Anita's realization of her highly sexualized, insidiously traumatic relationship with her father was composed of very delicate "tips of the balance," both forward and backward. The recognition of her father's seductiveness had a pattern of "rising to the surface, and . . . having . . . momentary clarity, and then just kind of receding" (quoted in Dorado, 1996, p. 99).

In her mid-teens, Anita wrote a letter to a friend (a letter that she never gave her) recognizing her father's seductive behavior and expressing her fear and desperation about it. On the outside of the envelope, she had written words conveying a warning that the contents of the letter contained "dangerous" information. The letter itself described ways in which she felt unsafe with her father, and her fears about the ways in which he treated her as though she were an adult, romantic/sexual partner rather than as his daughter. Very interestingly, Anita has no memory of writing this letter, although she still has it in her possession. She describes the time she wrote it as a "moment of clarity," which then receded again into the darkness of the unconscious.

One year later, Anita told her mother (who had divorced Anita's father many years earlier) about her father's behavior. Taking her seriously, her mother sent her to a therapist. Unfortunately, Anita feels this therapist was not helpful, in part because the therapist treated her as "too capable." He apparently concluded that she no longer needed help and ended her therapy after two sessions. Anita and her mother did not discuss the father's seductive behavior again. Anita only remembered this disclosure recently, and still forgets that she told her mother when she was a teenager. Thus, even though she had told someone who took her disclosure somewhat seriously about the abuse, both the recognition of abuse and the disclosure of the abuse again became split off from consciousness.

It was not until she was in her mid-20s that Anita finally allowed herself to realize fully and dwell on her father's highly sexualized relationship with her. She explained that taking her feelings seriously and actually acting on them by confronting her father "tipped the balance" such that the facts of the sexualized relationship could no longer be kept out of her consciousness. "Just saying the words, I mean just having this word battle—'I believe myself; I don't believe myself'—doesn't get me anywhere. But if I actually act on believing myself, you know, that's that tipping the balance." After she confronted her father, he ultimately admitted that he had perpetrated, in his words, "emotional incest" with her.

Also illustrating the forward and backward movement involved in recognition of abuse is the experience of another participant, Hannah. Unlike Anita, Hannah had experienced a period during which she had no conscious memory of her sexual abuse. The day after she had experienced a particularly distressing somatic flashback (which was sexual but contained no imagery indicating who or what was causing her fear and pain), she told a friend in an affectively dissociated and almost offhand way that she wondered if she might have been somehow sexually abused. Her friend essentially did not react, saying, "Oh," and then changing the subject. Soon after, the friend left. As Hannah described it, after that day, she dissociated both the flashback and the momentary recognition, saying that she "just forgot about it, totally forgot about it." At the time of the interview, she did not even characterize this incident as her "first memory," referring to it only later in the interview. It was another 6 months before she experienced what she calls her "first memory," and, in total, it was more than 2 years after this dissociated disclosure that she attempted to file a civil suit against her father. Michigan's 1-year statute of limitations prevented her from successfully doing so (Dorado, 1996). Strikingly, Hannah still forgets about this early incident of recognition.

Discussion

☐ The findings of this study are consistent with many trauma theorists' views of traumatic memory (e.g., Horowitz, 1990; Janet, 1919/1976, as cited in van der Kolk et al., 1989; Shengold, 1989; van der Kolk, 1987, 1988). Indeed, Janet (1919/1976) notes that the very words we use to describe "traumatic memory" are inaccurate and insufficient, asserting: "It is only for convenience that we speak of it as 'traumatic memory.' The subject is often incapable of making the necessary narrative which we call memory regarding the event" (p. 663; quoted in van der Kolk & van der Hart, 1991, p. 427).

This study's results demonstrate the manner in which adult incest survivors' memories are qualitatively different from ordinary memories. First, recognizable memories for the participants who went through a period of amnesia for the traumatic events were extremely intense, and tended to propel the survivors into an alternate, often dissociative, state of consciousness such that they were unable to perceive their surroundings or function normally. The traumatic first memories of these participants were intrusive, such that the survivors could not voluntarily shut the memories out once they began to emerge. The traumatic memories were not merely visual, but rather were packaged with other sensations—auditory, tactile, and kinesthetic (with bodily reenactment). They were more like reexperiences of the trauma than like ordinary memories, as though the traumatic events were happening to the survivors in the present. The characteristics of these first recognizable memories are consistent with the reexperiencing and hyperarousal symptoms of posttraumatic stress disorder (American Psychiatric Association, 1994; Horowitz, 1990).

The precursor symptoms of the study participants can be seen as fragmentary flashbacks: "a sudden access into consciousness" of dissociated traumatic experiences and related emotions, impulses, and bodily sensations (Blank, 1985). These symptoms were generally unbidden and intrusive, meaning that they had powerful and disturbing emotional effects on the survivors for reasons they did not understand at the time. The precursors experienced were also consistent with trauma theorists' descriptions of traumatic memory processes. For example, van der Kolk (1988) discusses how traumatic experiences stored in a sensorimotor or iconic fashion can be "reactivated" and return as "partial reliving of affective and somatosensory components of traumatic memories, without the symbolic and linguistic representations necessary to place the trauma in its historical context" (p. 283).

The participants experienced these precursors before they consciously remembered the traumatic events engendering the symptoms. Before they had their first recognizable memories of abuse, these survivors had no idea why they were experiencing these symptoms. Only through the eventual narrative memories of their sexual abuse were they ultimately able to make sense of these precursors.

The ways in which incest survivors' remembering processes are different from ordinary memory processes have implications for the statutes of limitations applied to incest survivors' cases. The findings of this study point to problems that many incest survivors may experience if they attempt to seek restitution through the civil courts. As discussed above, a period of limitations (during which a complaint or suit must be filed) such as Michigan's commences at the point at which the "memory" of sexual abuse "is revived." Although what constitutes a "memory" is crucial in determining this beginning point, the statute does not define memory, nor does it clearly specify the necessary characteristics of a first memory (Dorado, 1996). Statutes that rely on the emergence of a memory as the point at which a period of limitations should begin to run appear to assume that the "reviving" of a traumatic memory is a discrete phenomenon. This may be because remembering ordinary events is viewed by the general public as an all-at-once phenomenon. For example, when someone remembers a mildly stressful occurrence (e.g., "I forgot my keys in the house"), this memory comes with cognitive, emotional, and somatosensory elements integrated into a cohesive whole, all of which arises in a singular, "aha" moment of realization. This common view of remembering is consistent with Janet's theory of what constitutes a normal, integrated, and unified memory (see van der Kolk & van der Hart, 1989). However, the experiences of this study's participants clearly demonstrate that, rather than being an all-or-nothing event, remembering sexual abuse is a highly complicated process that can move forward—and sometimes even backward—over a great length of time. The participants' experiences illustrate how a traumatic memory emerges (as one participant expressed it) as "pieces of the puzzle" (Dorado, 1996).

As can be seen from incest survivors' descriptions of their precursor symptoms, precursors are fragments of dissociated traumatic memories intruding into consciousness. This means that survivors' memories of abuse were being "revived" prior to their first recognizable memory (Dorado, 1996). Nevertheless, for the participants in this study, these precursors were so dissociated from the rest of the traumatic memory that there was no way these survivors could reasonably have been expected to see these precursors as a cause for legal action. Thus it is important to make the distinction between the precursors and the "memory" in constructing the start of a period covered by a statute of limitations. Yet statutes such as Michigan's do not make this distinction at all.

The experiences of this study's participants demonstrate how recollecting the trauma of incest is not an easily circumscribed noun (i.e., "a memory"), but rather a fluid verb (i.e., "remembering"), a process unfolding over time. This process has no clear-cut beginning, thus trying to cut this highly complex process at some discrete and definitive time point after which the memory has been "revived" is very difficult, if not impossible. This renders problematic statutes that use the first memory as the beginning point of the limitation period for filing a civil suit. In this way, statutes of limitations such as Michigan's do not take into account the manner in which incest survivors remember their abuse.

Directions for Future Research

☐ The data from this study demonstrate the enormous complexity of traumatic memory as experienced by incest survivors. This research serves as a first step in understanding incest survivors' remembering processes. Although a great deal of information was gathered from each participant to formulate the findings of this study, the small number of participants in the study limits the degree to which these findings can be generalized. Ultimately, rather than providing easy solutions to the legal arena's dilemma of how best to address adult incest survivors' cases, this study raises perplexing issues and creates further questions that should be addressed by future studies. Research with larger samples of participants and with a variety of methods are needed to extend our understanding. The following is an exploration of one of the issues raised by this study.

The Complexity of Integrating the Recognition of Abuse Into Ongoing Consciousness

Further complicating and lengthening the process of remembering and coming to terms with sexual abuse is the manner in which, especially at the beginning of the remembering process, dissociated memories, even once recalled, can move in and out of consciousness. The experiences of at least two of the participants in this study (Anita and Hannah, described above) are examples of this phenomenon. Further examples of this phenomenon can be seen in cases of people who forget prior awareness of abusive events, as discussed by Schooler, Bendiksen, and Ambadar (1997). What is the process by which these participants were able to experience "moments of clarity" in which they recognized that they had been sexually maltreated as children, only to have this recognition recede back out of consciousness?

The work of some trauma theorists may begin to provide further understanding of the difficulty that incest survivors face during the process of integrating the recognition of their abuse into their personal life narratives. For example, Janet's conceptualization of dissociation in the context of trauma refers to a "horizontally layered model of mind: when a subject does not remember a trauma, its 'memory' is contained in an alternate stream of consciousness, which may be subconscious or dominate consciousness, e.g., during traumatic re-enactments" (van der Kolk & van der Hart, 1991, p. 438; see Figure 8.1). In this way, the awareness of a trauma may be pushed out of consciousness altogether for long periods of time, as in the experiences of six of this study's participants, or can potentially slip back and forth between different states of consciousness, as in the experiences of at least two of the participants.

Another approach to understanding the phenomenon of recognition of abuse followed by renewed amnesia is that of trauma theorist Krystal (1988). Discussing posttrauma alexithymia, Krystal asserts that repression entails alienating a memory element from "one's consciously   recognized   self-representation" (p. 132). Simply making unconscious ideas

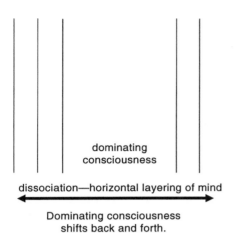

dominating
consciousness

dissociation—horizontal layering of mind

←——————————————————→

Dominating consciousness
shifts back and forth.

Figure 8.1. Janet's Model of Mind and
Consciousness

conscious (i.e., *recognizing* these ideas) does
not necessarily mean that these ideas have become "unrepressed" or reclaimed. Rather, the
ideas or experiences must become "part of the
consciously recognized identity and functionally integrated with oneself" in order to be
"truly reclaimed" (p. 132). Krystal asserts that
coming to terms with "a catastrophic event pro-
ceeds not in a straight line, but more in spiraling
circles of denial and painful recognition as one
descends to the necessary *depth* of grief and
depression. In the process of maintaining the
affective state below the overwhelming level,
one 'doses' oneself gradually with painful
truths" (p. 230). Similarly, the experiences of
some of this study's participants illustrate how
acknowledging and accepting the reality of incest experiences is a complicated, nonlinear
process. It is like a spiral moving generally
upward toward integrating the traumatic memories into ongoing consciousness, but can have
some dips downward toward renewed dissociation of aspects of the abuse.

Shengold's (1989) discussion of the defensive processes employed by many sexual abuse
survivors adds to an understanding of survivors'
processes of remembering. Shengold uses parts
of the phenomenon of "doublethink," a concept
from George Orwell's *1984,* to illustrate this
process. Orwell describes doublethink as follows:

To know and not to know, to be conscious of complete truthfulness while telling carefully constructed lies, to hold simultaneously two opinions
which canceled out, knowing them to be contradictory and believing both . . . to forget whatever
it is necessary to forget, then to draw it back into
the memory again at the moment it was needed,
and then promptly to forget it again, and above all
to apply the same process to the process itself . . .
consciously to induce unconsciousness, and then
once again to become unconscious of the act of
hypnosis you have just performed. (quoted in
Shengold, 1989, p. 76)

This is an extremely powerful description of the
process that incest survivors such as Anita experience, as fragments of the incestuous situ-
ation(s) move in and out of their unconscious.

Doublethink does not simply arise spontaneously out of abusive situations. Rather, the perpetrator of sexual abuse may purposely create doublethink in order to abolish memories of
the abusive events. As Shengold (1989) ex-
plains, the "inhibition of the ego's power to
remember and test reality . . . makes soul murder so effective as a continuing force" (p. 28).
In order to conceal his actions, the abuser acts
as though the abuse never occurred. Alternatively, he tells the child that the abuse is her own
doing, and that he (the parent) is merely being
loving and good. The perpetrator actively hides
the abusive acts by directly or indirectly telling
the child that if she ever tells anyone about what
has happened, something catastrophic will happen to her or to loved ones, and that no one
will believe her even if she does disclose the
abuse.

Because the child depends heavily upon the
very parent who is abusing her, in order to cope
with the abusive situation she must "break with
what has been experienced and out of a desper-
ate need for rescue, must register the parent,
delusionally, as good" (Shengold, 1989, p. 26).
"Bad" must be taken in and remembered as
"good." The child must keep in some compart-
ment in the mind a delusion of good, loving
parents and the delusion that all of the hate,
pain, and horror will turn into love. "This is a
mind-splitting or mind-fragmenting operation"
(p. 26). Shengold calls this compartmentalization "vertical splitting." Employing this isolat-

ing defense allows the traumatized victim to split off and contain overstimulating traumatic experiences. As Shengold (1989) describes, "There is a disconnection between idea and idea, which is one mechanism that can bring about the more defensively fundamental disconnection between thought and affect" (p. 108).

Illustrating this is Anita's continuing experience. The tenuousness of her memories relating to her father's sexualized behavior toward her can be seen in her description of the process by which her psychological defenses "deconstruct" memories related to the emotional sexual abuse: "I had this image of like there being a whole crew in my head of these little people. And they all run in, and they each grab a piece of experience, and they go in opposite directions." Her psyche's old, deeply ingrained defensive mechanism of dissociating and compartmentalizing her memories continues to make it very effortful for her to remember even current-day events that are connected to her abuse.

At this time, the underlying mechanism of traumatic memory processes for incest survivors is not definitively known. Given the extreme complexity of the process of remembering incest, it seems likely that mechanisms differ from case to case, and that some cases employ multiple mechanisms. Further research will be needed to begin to sort out this issue. Regardless of the underlying processes, as can be seen by the experiences of the participants in this study, "re-membering" the trauma of sexual abuse is putting together all of the dismembered pieces that arise, fragment by fragment, throughout the process of coming to terms with incest. As each "piece of the puzzle" falls into place, the memory may begin to carry more and more weight, until this weight is enough to resist the life-old winds of psychological defense that threaten to blow the memories back out of consciousness.

The exploratory findings of this study may have implications for the legal arena. In the first place, the forward and backward movement of the remembering process affects the span of time that transpires before survivors realize the full significance of their sexual abuse and inte-grate the abuse into their personal narratives. It may potentially lengthen the time needed before incest survivors are psychologically able to take any action about their abuse, including filing civil suits against their perpetrators, should they choose to do so.

Furthermore, the back-and-forth movement of the recognition of abuse may also have implications for another legal approach to incest survivors' cases, the use of the delayed discovery rule. As of mid-1995, 22 states had laws applying delayed discovery doctrine to incest cases (Pope & Brown, 1996). Typically, the delayed discovery rule provides that the time limitation for the plaintiff to make her or his claim begins to accrue when the plaintiff "discovers, or through the use of reasonable diligence should have discovered, both that s/he is injured and that the injury was caused by the defendant's misconduct" (Salten, 1984, p. 213). Although delayed discovery may be a more appropriate way to address incest survivors' cases, this study suggests that "discovery," like "remembering," may not necessarily occur at a discrete point in time. Rather, "discovery," or realization of the significance and injurious consequences of sexual abuse, may be a nonlinear process that can unfold over a period of time, in which a survivor may at one point recognize the abuse and its resultant injuries, but may not at another.

Conclusion

□ In conclusion, the process of remembering and coming to terms with sexual abuse as experienced by incest survivors is exceedingly complex, and seems to be qualitatively different from ordinary memory processes. This complexity is not sufficiently addressed by the insanity exception to the normal statute of limitations for civil suits applied to incest survivors suing their perpetrators in some states. It is crucial that future attempts to find legal remedies for adult survivors of childhood incest take into account more fully the intricacies of incest survivors' traumatic memory processes. The evolution of the manner in which Michigan now handles civil suits involving childhood sexual abuse is a case in point. In the mid-1990s, Michigan courts began to apply the delayed discovery rule to cases of incest. In 1993, partially in response to public outcry about the plight of incest survivors, some Michigan legislators attempted to pass a bill that stated that "a victim of sexual abuse may recover damages for injury if the action (i.e., filing the suit) commenced before the victim's 24th birthday or within three years after the victim discovers or should have discovered that the sexual abuse caused the injury, whichever situation is later" (House Bill 4518). This would have constituted some forward progress for incest survivors hoping to sue their perpetrators. However, soon after this bill was proposed, the delayed discovery application to incest survivors' cases was overturned. Currently, Michigan courts have reverted to applying the traditional statute of limitations for personal injury lawsuits to incest survivors' cases.

One factor contributing to this reversal may well be a growing backlash against the believability of incest survivors (Bulkley & Horwitz, 1994). Unfortunately, such a backlash can be inadvertently fueled by well-intentioned but simplistic and prematurely applied solutions to extremely complex problems. In the case of incest survivors trying to sue their perpetrators in Michigan, the changes made before a more complete and in-depth understanding of incest survivors' traumatic memory processes was achieved may have provided temporary and immediate relief for some incest survivors. However, as the complexity of these processes became more apparent and these quick fixes did not satisfy the needs of all sexual abuse cases, those opposed to the changes were able to point an accusing finger at what they asserted (in my belief sometimes justifiably and sometimes spuriously) to be the faults and imprecisions of progressive public policy. It may be that, consequently, many who initially supported progressive legislation became disillusioned and withdrew their support.

Ultimately, jumping to the conclusion that there can be simple answers to this complicated issue can be very damaging. Further investigation into the complexities of traumatic memory as experienced by incest survivors, rather than reductionist rhetoric and polarization, is essential to appropriate treatment of the cases of incest survivors in the courts. This study illustrates how research questions can be extracted from real-world legal dilemmas, as well as ways in which research can begin to inform legal remedies. Clearly, both researchers and practitioners in the psychological and legal communities must work together toward deepening our understanding of the process of remembering sexual abuse for adult incest survivors, approaching the issue with all the caution called for by the complexities of this process.

Notes

1. The study was approved by the Human Subjects Review Board in the Department of Psychology, University of Michigan, in 1992.

2. It should be noted that the counselor who hypnotized Debbie did not accept the idea that Debbie's father had sexually abused her. When Debbie called the counselor for help once her first memories emerged, the counselor told her that what she was remembering could not be true. The counselor's rejection of Debbie's disclosure of the abusive events she was remembering makes improbable the idea that Debbie's memory arose from something that the counselor suggested to her during hypnosis.

References

American Psychiatric Association. (1994). *Diagnostic and statistical manual of mental disorders* (4th ed.). Washington, DC: Author.

Blank, A. S. (1985). The unconscious flashback to the war in Vietnam veterans: Clinical mystery, legal defense, and community problem. In S. M. Sonnenberg, A. S. Blank, & J. A. Talbot (Eds.), *Stress and recovery in Vietnam veterans* (pp. 295-308). Washington, DC: author.

Brett, E. A., & Ostroff, R. (1985). Imagery and posttraumatic stress disorder: An overview. *American Journal of Psychiatry, 142,* 417-424.

Briere, J., & Conte, J. R. (1993). Self-reported amnesia for abuse in adults molested as children. *Journal of Traumatic Stress, 6,* 21-31.

Bulkley, J. A., & Horwitz, M. J. (1994). Adults sexually abused as children: Legal actions and issues. *Behavioral Sciences and the Law, 12,* 65-87.

Dorado, J. S. (1996). Legal and psychological approaches towards adult survivors of childhood incest: Irreconcilable differences? *Women and Therapy, 19*(1), 93-108.

Glasser, B. G., & Strauss, A. L. (1967). *The discovery of grounded theory: Strategies for qualitative research.* Chicago: Aldine.

Harshaw, J. W. (1989). Not enough time? The constitutionality of short statutes of limitations for civil child sexual abuse litigation. *Ohio State Law Journal, 50,* 753-766.

Herman, J. L. (1981). *Father-daughter incest.* Cambridge, MA: Harvard University Press.

Herman, J. L., & Schatzow, E. (1987). Recovery and verification of memories of childhood sexual trauma. *Psychoanalytic Psychology, 4,* 1-14.

Horowitz, M. J. (1990). Posttraumatic stress disorders: Psychosocial aspects of the diagnosis. *International Journal of Mental Health, 19*(1), 21-36.

Janet, P. (1976). *Principles of psychotherapy* (Vol. 2). New York: Arno. (Original work published 1919)

Krystal, H. (1988). *Integration and self-healing: Affect, trauma, alexithymia.* Hillsdale, NJ: Analytic Press.

McCracken, G. (1988). *The long interview.* Newbury Park, CA: Sage.

Meiers-Post v. Schafer, Docket No. 96222, 170 Mich. App. 174-183 (1988).

Piaget, J. (1973). *Structuralism.* New York: Basic Books.

Pope, K. S., & Brown, L. S. (1996). *Recovered memories of abuse: Assessment, therapy, forensics.* Washington, DC: American Psychological Association.

Russell, D. E. H. (1983). The incidence and prevalence of intrafamilial and extrafamilial sexual abuse of female children. *Child Abuse & Neglect, 7,* 133-146.

Russell, D. E. H. (1986). *The secret trauma: Incest in the lives of girls and women.* New York: Basic Books.

Salten, M. G. (1984). Statutes of limitations in civil incest suits: Preserving the victim's remedy. *Harvard Women's Law Journal, 7*(1), 189-220.

Schooler, J. W., Bendiksen, M., & Ambadar, Z. (1997). Taking the middle line: Can we accommodate both fabricated and recovered memories of sexual abuse? In M. A. Conway (Ed.), *Recovered memories and false memories* (pp. 251-291). New York: Oxford University Press.

Shengold, L. (1989). *Soul murder: The effects of childhood abuse and deprivation.* New Haven, CT: Yale University Press.

Strauss, A. L., & Corbin, J. (1990). *Basics of qualitative research: Grounded theory procedures and techniques.* Newbury Park, CA: Sage.

van der Kolk, B. A. (1987). *Psychological trauma.* Washington, DC: American Psychiatric Press.

van der Kolk, B. A. (1988). The trauma spectrum: The interaction of biological and social events in the genesis of the trauma response. *Journal of Traumatic Stress, 1,* 273-290.

van der Kolk, B. A., Brown, P., & van der Hart, O. (1989). Pierre Janet on post-traumatic stress. *Journal of Traumatic Stress, 2,* 365-378.

van der Kolk, B. A., & van der Hart, O. (1989). Pierre Janet and the breakdown of adaptation in psychological trauma. *American Journal of Psychiatry, 146,* 1530-1540.

van der Kolk, B. A., & van der Hart, O. (1991). The intrusive past: The flexibility of memory and the engraving of trauma. *American Imago, 8,* 425-454.

Williams, L. M. (1994). Recall of childhood trauma: A prospective study of women's memories of child sexual abuse. *Journal of Consulting and Clinical Psychology, 62,* 1167-1176.

PART II

MENTAL HEALTH AND MEMORIES OF TRAUMATIC EVENTS

9

Memories for Child Sexual Abuse and Mental Health Functioning

Findings on a Sample of Women and Implications for Future Research

Victoria L. Banyard
Linda M. Williams

There has been much recent attention to adult recollections of child sexual abuse (Williams & Banyard, 1997). Indeed, numerous recent studies have focused both on documenting the numbers of survivors who have some type of memory disruption (Briere & Conte, 1993; Elliott & Briere, 1995; Herman & Schatzow, 1987; Williams, 1994; see also Kluft, Chapter 25, this volume) and on describing the malleability of memories for various life events (Belli & Loftus, in press; Ceci, Caves, & Howe, 1981; Hyman & Pentland, 1996; Loftus, Smith, Klinger, & Fielder, 1992). Although many researchers discuss possible mechanisms for memory problems and hypothesized effects of disruptions in memory, few studies to date have directly examined the consequences of memory

disruptions. In this chapter, we provide some preliminary findings on the effects of memory problems for child sexual abuse from a prospective study of the effects of sexual assault in childhood.

Much of the literature on memories for child sexual abuse has focused on whether substantiated cases of forgetting of sexual abuse exist, under what conditions false memories for abuse may be implanted, and theoretical discussions about why forgetting may occur. Applied discussions of the issue have focused mainly on legal processes, such as investigating the veracity of testimony about child abuse, including the suggestibility of child witnesses (Ceci & Bruck, 1993), with some discussion of the clinical implications of therapy involving adults' memo-

AUTHORS' NOTE: This research was supported by NIMH Training Grant No. 5-T32-MH15161 and NCCAN Grant No. 90-CA-1406. The authors thank Jane Siegel for her valuable assistance.

ries of child sexual abuse (Lindsay & Read, 1995; Poole, Lindsay, Memon, & Bull, 1995). There has been limited empirical attention to the consequences of these memory issues for the functioning of survivors. Two recent studies have directly assessed the impacts of differences in memory on the long-term functioning of child sexual abuse survivors. Briere and Conte (1993) found in their study of a clinical sample that 59% of 450 women and men survivors had some period of their lives during which they had no memory of their abuse. They found that this group also had higher current levels of psychological symptomatology, although they were also more likely to have been abused at an early age and to have experienced more severe abuse. Elliott and Briere (1995) found that 42% of a community sample reported some prior time when they had no memory for the sexual abuse they had experienced. These researchers further divided the group with prior periods of forgetting into those who only recently recalled the abuse (within the past 2 years) and those who had recalled their abuse more than 2 years prior to their participation in the study. They found no significant differences in symptomatology between the remote recall and continuous recall groups. The more distressed group, however, was the recent recall group. For this sample, memory for the abuse per se was not as important in predicting psychological well-being as was the recency of memory recovery. Those with more recent recall were the most distressed. This literature is interesting in its exploration of the clinical effects of different memory processes, yet it does not explain the mechanisms behind the forgetting, and there may indeed be many different reasons people are in the "forgetting" group in any one study.

A review of the literature on memories for child sexual abuse highlights the complexity of issues faced by researchers attempting to formulate hypotheses about the implications of memory problems for the long-term functioning of survivors. There may be vast individual differences in why memories are not available, and these underlying reasons will have differential impacts on mental health. It may not be possible to discover one explanation or one mechanism to explain forgetting, or one clear

implication of memory problems for mental health functioning. Rather, we need to understand the diverse pathways of effects by developing new research designs and measures as well as appreciating and examining individual differences. Three major themes may be seen in current debates about trauma and memory; each has important, particular implications for future research. These include discussions of "normal" or developmental forgetting, adaptive forgetting, and more potentially problematic forgetting. Indeed, a review of recent discussions of memories for child sexual abuse suggests that abuse experienced in childhood may have been forgotten due to developmental changes in memory functioning, ordinary forgetting processes that make large amounts of our lived experience inaccessible to later recollection, or particular defensive or cognitive strategies called upon to facilitate coping in the face of trauma.

Issues related to child development are key to both researchers of memory processes and researchers and other professionals in the field of child sexual abuse. Finkelhor (1995) discusses developmental changes in childhood that may affect both children's risk for being victimized and the effects of traumatic experiences. Kendall-Tackett, Williams, and Finkelhor (1993) and others have called on the field of child maltreatment to pay more attention to a developmental perspective. In terms of memory, the field of child development has long been interested in the ways in which memory—especially autobiographical memory—changes over time. A complete review of this literature is beyond the scope of this chapter, but a few main points are particularly germane to this discussion. In particular, although there is some debate in the field about the existence of "infantile amnesia" as such and about the precise nature of the developmental changes that occur in memory functioning over childhood, there is agreement that autobiographical memory changes to some degree over time. It is fairly common for individuals to have little memory for many life events prior to age 2 or 3. What this suggests is that for survivors of child sexual abuse who were very young at the time of the abuse, absence of memory for the trauma may result from problems encoding or retrieving the memory in a developmentally immature system. Clinically, such forgetting would not necessarily lead to such survivors' exhibiting higher levels of symptoms than other survivors. Indeed, these survivors may even be doing better, as their memories may not be accessible in any way and so the traumatic experiences may not exert influence on their current functioning.

Related to this discussion is the theory of "normal forgetting" that has been discussed by researchers such as Loftus (1995), who assert that if traumatic events such as sexual abuse are forgotten, then it is the result of the same types of forgetting processes that make vast quantities of our lived experiences inaccessible to recall years later. Theories of development and of normal forgetting have similar implications for later mental health functioning. They suggest that a person's having forgotten his or her abuse may have little effect on that individual's functioning. Indeed, the individual may even be doing better because he or she no longer has to think about the event.

A variety of other theories of traumatic memory, however, suggest that memories for traumatic events may be different in some ways from memories for other events. These theories have tended to focus on psychodynamic concepts of defense mechanisms, such as repression and dissociation, or cognitive models of avoidance coping. Enns, McNeilly, Corkery, and Gilbert (1995) discuss the self-protective strategies that children who are abused employ in order to survive and cope with the trauma. One way of understanding the mechanism behind such strategies is through psychodynamic theories of defense mechanisms. Vaillant (1992) discusses the development of these concepts, describing defense mechanisms as strategies used by the ego to deal with conflicts that create uncomfortable negative emotions. Defense mechanisms become important in analytic theory in their relationship to psychopathology. Freud, in his early work with Breuer on the etiology of hysteria, discusses the fact that memories for traumatic events can continue to influence emotions and behaviors long after the events have occurred (Breuer & Freud, 1893/ 1957). In this work, Freud refers to repression

as a process of intentionally forgetting or suppressing from conscious thought something that is distressing. The memory does not go away, however. It and the negative emotions attached to it continue to exert influence on the individual and, according to Freud, are at the root of hysterical symptoms.

Dissociation is another mechanism of defense discussed often in the literature on child sexual abuse. The terms *dissociation* and *repression* have sometimes been used interchangeably; at other times, they are defined as distinctly different phenomena. For example, Bowers and Farvolden (1996) discuss the active, motivated process of forgetting that occurs in repression: "We view repression as motivated forgetting of information that is very threatening to one's self esteem or self concept" (p. 359). Vaillant (1990) describes the ways in which repression is different from more "normal forgetting" processes. Spiegel (1990), on the other hand, discusses dissociation as a process whereby consciousness is divided such that a part of experience is kept out of awareness. Much of the current theory on dissociation derives more from the work of Janet. This literature focuses less on active ongoing suppression of memory and more on problems in encoding information in the first place. During a traumatic event, the person's conscious state is altered so that information is not processed in a way that it is readily available for recall in another state (Bowers & Farvolden, 1996). Spiegel states (1990): "The concept of dissociation implies some kind of divided or parallel access to awareness. Several systems may co-occur, seemingly independently" (p. 127).

There has been much debate about the existence of these mechanisms. Holmes (1990), for example, asserts that there is no empirical evidence for the phenomenon of repression. Bower (1990) cites evidence for conscious motivated forgetting, such as through conscious "motivated nonlearning," in which individuals control whether or not they register events by choosing not to think about them or failure of retrieval cues, but not for unconscious motivated forgetting of the type discussed by psychoanalytic theorists. In a laboratory setting, Wegner, Quillian, and Houston (1996) performed an experiment on the effects of active thought suppression for details of a film. The participants who were instructed to actively suppress thoughts of the film had more problems correctly ordering the film clips later, although there were no group differences on memories for content of the film clips. Erdelyi (1990) discusses "retrieval avoidance," in which, "because of the subject's refusal to access the memory complex, the material remains genuinely outside awareness" (p. 5). Erdelyi asserts that mechanisms such as repression may both "reduce and produce symptoms" (p. 19). Such discussions highlight the fact that the link between forgetting and psychological distress is complex. According to analytic theory, the use of mechanisms such as dissociation and repression are at the root of psychological symptoms. However, discussions by current researchers such as Erdelyi suggest that this may not always be the case.

One other area that has explored links among trauma, memory, and outcome is that of cognitive theories of coping and avoidance. As with the research discussed above, this work raises more questions than it answers and highlights the complex questions confronting researchers who are interested in exploring the mental health consequences of memory problems related to traumatic events. Creamer, Burgess, and Pattison (1992) have examined longitudinal responses to trauma. They found that avoidance reactions, both physical and cognitive, were related to higher symptoms soon after the occurrence of the trauma, but that over time, the relationship between greater use of avoidance and higher symptoms markedly decreased. Their explanation is that avoidance of trauma-related cues or of thinking about the trauma is a strategy that is often used in response to distressing intrusion of images and feelings about the trauma during the time immediately after the trauma occurs: "Over time, however, the avoidance behavior may become entrenched as a coping strategy in its own right and be less dependent on high levels of intrusion. As this occurs, it appears that avoidance becomes a less detrimental strategy, and is less likely to result in high symptom levels" (p. 458). Tromp, Koss, Figueredo, and Tharan (1995) use this idea to help explain their finding that rape memories

are overall less clear than memories for other events. The implications of this research for the current discussion of memory for child sexual abuse is that time since the trauma may be an important variable. Forgetting, as a manifestation of the use of avoidance, may be associated with increased symptoms in the short-term aftermath of the trauma. In terms of long-term effects, however, avoidance or forgetting may have less pathogenic associations as it becomes more of an automatic coping strategy than the kind of intentional or motivated forgetting in response to conflict and anxiety over the intrusion of traumatic material that is suggested by the term *repression* or *dissociation*. This suggests yet another variable to be considered in research on child sexual abuse: whether the abuse is recent or more distal. In samples of adult survivors, where abuse experiences are more distant, lack of memory may have less negative consequences.

A variety of research dilemmas arise when one attempts to untangle the effects of memory problems for survivors of child sexual abuse. Discussions of autobiographical memory suggest that developmental issues are important to consider. Individuals may differ from one another in the mechanisms behind their amnesia for traumatic events based on the age at which the events occurred. This suggests that researchers may need to conduct separate analyses of participants of differing ages: those who were younger at time of abuse and perhaps forgot because of infantile amnesia versus those who should be able to remember. Research on active avoidance suggests that such a strategy may have different consequences depending on how long ago the trauma occurred, therefore attention to the time elapsed since the abuse may be important to investigate. Furthermore, differing theories about the mechanism behind the forgetting of trauma suggest different outcomes: Forgetting as a result of classic repression or dissociation may produce more symptoms, whereas theories of cognitive avoidance suggest that higher levels of distress may not be in evidence. Clearly, designing research to explore this area is complex. First, there are likely to be vast individual differences in the mechanisms behind the forgetting of sexual abuse. In addition, it is not easy to categorize these mechanisms—that is, to predict outcomes that are all good or bad. The implications for adaptation or functioning are complicated. As Creamer et al. (1992) indicate, depending on where an individual is in the recovery process or in dealing with the abuse, various mechanisms may have both survival value and potential costs.

The study reported below sought to build on these findings. Given the possible contradictory hypotheses about the direction of effects of memory disruption suggested by the theoretical literature, the current work is descriptive in nature. This study examined the differences between participants with and without memory disruptions on measures of current psychological symptoms. This study went beyond previous work due to its prospective design. We were able to rely on officially documented histories of child sexual abuse and to reinterview survivors 17 years later. At the time of reinterview, 38% of the women did not report a memory for the index abuse (Williams, 1994). Given the earlier documentation, the current analyses permit examination of a memory disruption group that includes survivors who evidence no recall of their childhood sexual abuse, unlike previous work that has examined only samples of survivors who currently have memories for their abuse but report that at some time in the past they were not aware of these experiences.

Method

Participants

Participants were 129 women from a large U.S. city who were a subset of 206 cases of child sexual abuse examined at a city hospital emergency room in 1973-1975 and interviewed at the time as part of a larger study of the immediate consequences of abuse (McCahill, Meyer, & Fischman, 1979). The girls ranged in age from 10 months to 12 years old and had reported sexual abuse that involved sexual contact by force, threat of force, or misuse of authority, or by a person who was 10 or more years older than the child, even if there was no force. The abuse ranged from genital fondling to sexual intercourse and was perpetrated by a wide range of

Table 9.1 Demographic Characteristics of the Sample ($N = 124$)

Current age (in years)	
M	25.55
SD	3.37
Race (%)	
African American	88
White	12
Education (%)	
High school graduate or GED	46
Current employment (%)	
Working full-time	16
Working part-time	16
Not working in paid-labor market	68
Receiving public assistance (%)	55
Marital status (%)	
Never married	56
Married/common law	32
Divorced/separated	11
Widowed	1

individuals (all male): fathers, stepfathers, other family members, acquaintances, and strangers. Soon after each girl was seen in the hospital the child and caregiver were interviewed. In 1990 and 1991, on average 17 years postabuse, 129 of these girls, who were now adults, were relocated and interviewed. There were no significant differences between interviewed and noninterviewed women on demographic variables or characteristics of the abuse experience that brought them to the attention of the hospital. Table 9.1 lists sample demographics for the 124 women included in the current analyses ($mv = 5$).

Procedures

In 1990 and 1991, after the women were located, they were interviewed individually, face-to-face. Almost all were interviewed in a private office, although a few were interviewed in their own homes. The interviews were conducted by two women trained in building rapport and in conducting interviews on sensitive and potentially upsetting topics. The interviewers were blind to the details of the women's victimization histories, although they knew the purpose of the study. The interview began with questions about more neutral aspects of the woman's life, such as her education and employment status. After sufficient rapport had been established, questions about other topics, such as family of origin relationships, drug and alcohol use, sexual history, psychological functioning, and history of sexual victimization, were asked. If the woman did not recall her sexual victimization, she was not informed of this by the interviewer. The interviews averaged 3 hours in length, and each was followed by a debriefing during which the woman's questions were answered. There was also a discussion of how she was feeling about the interview, and appropriate referrals were made when necessary. The interview was approved by a human subjects review board, and a variety of procedures were used to protect research participants in accordance with research ethics procedures.

Questions About Memory

Memories for the index abuse were assessed using a series of 14 separate and detailed screening questions, following the approach outlined by Russell (1986). The interviewers were blind to the circumstances of the sexual abuse reported in the 1970s. Two raters reviewed each interview to assess whether the woman had or had not recalled the "index event" and to document the differences between the 1970s and 1990s accounts of the event. Usually the woman gave details about the abuse or its disclosure (e.g., where it took place, such as in a movie theater; who was there, such as a cousin visiting from the South; who she told, such as the cashier at a convenience store) that made it quite evident that she was referring to the event found in the records from the 1970s. Frequently, however, there were discrepancies in some details about the abuse experience; these were noted and coded by the rater.

The women who remembered the abuse were asked detailed questions about the sexual molestation, the disclosure, the responses of others, and the impact on their lives. Each was asked to rate how clear her memories were of the incident and was asked, "Was there ever a time when you did not remember that this had happened to you?" The 49 women who did not appear to recall the abuse and the 12 women who reported some prior period of forgetting constitute the "memory problems" group.

Table 9.2 Mean Scores on TSC40 Subscales for Total Sample of Female Child Sexual Abuse Survivors

Subscale	M	SD
Depression	6.04	4.78
Anxiety	5.10	4.17
Sleep problems	5.84	4.24
Sexual problems	3.36	3.93
Sex abuse trauma	3.41	3.36
Dissociation	3.33	3.31
Total TSC40 score	24.70	18.96

Psychological Symptoms

Adult symptoms of emotional distress were assessed in 1990-1991 in the follow-up interviews using the Trauma Symptom Checklist (TSC40; Briere & Runtz, 1987). This is a 40-item measure of emotional difficulties that has been found to distinguish reliably between survivors and nonvictims of childhood sexual abuse (Elliott & Briere, 1992; Gold, Milan, Mayall, & Johnson, 1994). Participants rated on a scale of 0 to 3 how often in the past 2 months they had experienced each of 40 symptoms. Items are summed to form six subscales: anxiety, depression, sleep problems, sexual problems, dissociation, and sexual abuse trauma (Briere & Runtz, 1987). In addition, all 40 items can be summed to create a total score. Table 9.2 provides information on the distribution of scores on the TSC40 for the current sample.

The depression subscale consists of nine items, including questions about insomnia, weight loss, sadness, and uncontrollable crying. For our sample, the Cronbach's alpha was .79. The anxiety subscale is made up of nine items as well. It consists of questions about experiencing anxiety attacks, headaches, stomach problems, fear of men or women, and feeling tense all of the time. Cronbach's alpha was .80 for our sample. Sexual problems are assessed with the use of seven items, including not feeling satisfied with your sex life, having sex you didn't enjoy, bad thoughts or feelings during sex, and sexual problems. Cronbach's alpha was .85. Sleep disturbance is measured using six items, such as trouble getting to sleep, restless sleep, and not feeling rested in the morning. The internal consistency for this scale was .83. Dissociation is measured using six items concerning such things as "spacing out," dizziness, feelings that are "unreal," or that you are not always in your body. For the current sample, this had an alpha of .79. The TSC40 also includes a scale to measure sexual abuse trauma, which includes items such as having flashbacks, sexual problems, fear of men, and memory problems. This scale consists of six items. Cronbach's alpha was .77. These means are similar to those found by Elliott and Briere (1992) in a sample of adult survivors of child sexual abuse.

Table 9.3 Mean Scores (and Standard Deviations) on Outcome Measures for Two Memory Disruption Groups ($N = 124$)

Outcome Measure	Memory Disruption ($n = 61$)	No Memory Disruption ($n = 63$)
TSC total score	24.94 (19.87)	25.56 (18.43)
Depression	6.10 (5.10)	6.25 (4.63)
Anxiety	5.01 (4.22)	5.43 (4.25)
Dissociation	3.66 (3.39)	3.24 (3.33)
Sleep problems	6.04 (4.67)	6.18 (3.95)
Sexual problems	3.20 (4.01)	3.41 (3.73)
Sex abuse trauma	3.94 (3.69)	3.10 (3.13)

NOTE: Ns vary for analyses due to missing cases.

Results

☐ Data analysis proceeded in two steps using analysis of variance. The first was to look at overall differences between participants who reported no memory disruptions and those who had some disruption. The second was to subdivide the sample further by age at time of the abuse, to develop a more complete description of the potential effects of memory disruption on psychological symptoms in adulthood.

We divided the sample of women into two groups: those who reported that they had continuous recall for the index abuse incident (the "no memory problems" group) and those who either did not report any recollections of the index abuse or recalled the index abuse but reported that there was some period of time during which they had forgotten the abuse (the "memory problems" group). (These two categories of memory problems were combined in these analyses because of the small number of participants who had current recall of abuse and reported a prior period of no recall.) A total of 62 women fell into the no memory problems group, and 61 participants had some type of memory disruption (12 women reported some prior period of forgetting, 49 women did not report the index abuse at reinterview).

Bivariate analyses were used to examine descriptively differences between the groups on a number of dimensions. There were no differences on reported experiences of a number of other stressful life events (e.g., number of other

reports of child sexual abuse; being arrested or jailed; death of a spouse, a child, or other close family member; serious illness; poverty; witnessing violence) or on questions related to problems with early caregivers (such as caregivers not showing interest or affection and being unable to talk to them, as well as having caregivers with emotional or substance use problems). Analyses reported elsewhere indicated that there were few differences between the groups in terms of characteristics of the abuse incidents. Women who did not report or remember the index abuse were more likely to be younger at the time of abuse and to have been sexually abused by someone they knew (Williams, 1994).

Analysis of variance was used to investigate whether there were discernible differences between these two groups on current mental health symptoms. Table 9.3 shows mean scores on the TSC for each group. Overall, there were no statistically significant differences between the two groups on measures of mental health symptoms ($F[6, 114] = .09$, ns). Indeed, these analyses raised more questions than they answered, and it remained unclear whether memory status made a difference or not.

Given that the research literature on memory highlighted the potential importance of age in understanding memories for sexual abuse in childhood, a second set of analyses were conducted that sought to take such theories into account. There is evidence that certain aspects of memory develop over time. For this reason there may be multiple mechanisms for forgetting operating within this sample. We decided to divide the sample further into groups by age (a median split was used, dividing groups into those participants who were 9 or younger and those 10 or older at the time of the abuse). The result was four groups.

We hypothesized that there would be no discernible differences between the memory problems and no memory problems groups in the younger age category because of the multiple determinants of their memory status, some of which might predict better adjustment, some worse, some no difference. We further hypothesized, however, that for the older age group, the participants one would expect would recall, those with memory problems would show higher levels of symptomatology.

Table 9.4 presents the range of mental health symptom scores for each group. Next, a series of one-way planned contrasts were performed to examine differences in mean TSC40 scores between the older, memory problems group and each of the three other groups. The results can be seen in Table 9.5. Overall ANOVAs were significant for each of the outcome measures except dissociation. The most marked differences are for age: Women who were older at time of abuse were doing less well on current measures of psychological symptoms. In addition, the means for the older, memory problems group were consistently higher than for any other group. This can be illustrated using the calculation of effect sizes. Effect sizes are used to examine the magnitude of differences between means or how important they are, rather than simply examining statistical significance. They can be used to compare the magnitude of a variety of differences between means—a standardized reference to how big the difference between two means is or the correlation between two variables. Although there are many intricacies to the exact interpretation of effect sizes, Cohen (1969) has cited one scale that finds an effect of .2 to be small, .5 to be moderate, and .8 to be large. For illustrative purposes, we will use that scale here. Effect sizes were computed for each of the comparisons (see Table 9.6). The most significant effects are differences between those who were older at time of abuse and have memory problems and those

Table 9.4 Range of Psychological Symptom Scores for Age × Memory Disruption Groups of Women Sexually Abused in Childhood

Outcome Measure	Group			
	1	2	3	4
TSC total score	0-85	0-46	0-71	1-84
Depression	0-21	0-15	0-15	1-21
Anxiety	0-19	0-9	0-13	0-16
Dissociation	0-14	0-10	0-13	0-14
Sleep problems	0-17	0-15	0-16	1-15
Sexual problems	0-16	0-9	0-16	0-16
Sex abuse trauma	0-14	0-12	0-14	0-14

NOTE: Group 1 = older at time of abuse (> age 9), memory problems ($n = 18$); Group 2 = younger at time of abuse, memory problems ($n = 43$); Group 3 = younger at time of abuse, no memory problems ($n = 24$); Group 4 = older at time of abuse, no memory problems ($n = 38$).

who were younger at the time of abuse and have no memory problems. Effect sizes for comparisons of age groups within the memory problems group, however, were moderate, although only one reached significance. This highlights the importance of age for this sample in analyses of memory status and mental health problems. Again, effect sizes for a comparison of the memory problems versus no memory problems groups among survivors of abuse that occurred at an older age revealed small to moderate findings, with the exception of the sexual abuse trauma scale. There was a significant effect size here, and trends on all outcome measures were in the expected direction. The memory problems group of older survivors reported more of the following types of symptoms: having flashbacks, sexual problems, fear of men, and memory problems.

Discussion

☐ We undertook the current study to add to our understanding of the consequences of memory disruptions for the long-term mental health consequences of child sexual abuse. The findings are somewhat limited in this regard. The first analysis of variance revealed no significant differences in scores on the TSC40 between women who reported continuous recall of their abuse and those who did not. Further dividing

Table 9.5 Mean Scores on Outcome Measures for Four Age × Memory Problem Groups of Women Sexually Abused in Childhood ($N = 122$)

Outcome Measure	Group				F
	1	2	3	4	
TSC total score	37.39	19.10	23.27	27.13	4.44**
	(26.05)	(13.60)	(18.41)	(18.52)	
Depression	9.18	4.73	5.72	6.57	4.05**
	(6.42)	(3.71)	(4.25)	(4.89)	
Anxiety	7.85	3.68	4.63	6.12	5.43**
	(5.65)	(2.69)	(4.38)	(4.12)	
Sleep problems	8.27	4.97	6.03	6.21	2.62*
	(5.15)	(4.09)	(4.22)	(3.88)	
Sex abuse trauma	5.94	2.95	3.27	3.09	3.92**
	(4.75)	(2.75)	(3.19)	(3.12)	
Sexual problems	5.69	2.17	2.69	3.83	4.13**
	(5.90)	(2.33)	(3.68)	(3.79)	
Dissociation	5.34	2.88	3.29	3.24	2.47
	(4.36)	(2.59)	(3.39)	(3.34)	

NOTE: Standard deviations appear in parentheses. Group 1 = older at time of abuse (> age 9), memory problems ($n = 18$); Group 2 = younger at time of abuse, memory problems ($n = 43$); Group 3 = younger at time of abuse, no memory problems ($n = 24$); Group 4 = older at time of abuse, no memory problems ($n = 38$).

*$p < .05$; **$p < .01$.

Table 9.6 Planned One-Way Comparisons Between the Older, Memory Problems Group and the Other Three Groups on Outcome Measures ($N = 122$)

Planned Comparisons	1[a]		2[b]	
	t^c	Effect Size[d]	t	Effect Size
TSC total score	−2.89**	−.78**	−1.50	−.42
Depression	−2.76**	−.76**	−1.53	−.43
Anxiety	−2.99**	−.83**	−1.16	−.33
Sleep problems	−2.42*	−.67**	−1.50	−.42
Sex abuse trauma	−2.51*	−.69**	−2.33*	−.66*
Sexual problems	−2.39*	−.68**	−1.20	−.34
Dissociation	−2.23*	−.62*	−1.81	−.51

a. Compares older (> age 9), memory problems group with younger, memory problems group.
b. Compares older, memory problems group with older, no memory problems group.
c. Effect size measured using corrected d.
d. Separate variance estimates used.
*$p < .05$; **$p < .01$.

the sample by age at time of abuse revealed a different pattern of findings. Those who were older at the time of abuse and had memory problems also reported higher levels of symptoms. These findings are consistent with previous research and suggest important considerations for future work in this area.

In contrast to Briere and Conte's (1993) work, the current study did not find clear differences between the memory problems and no memory problems groups on mental health symptoms. In part, this may be due to differences in the samples. Briere and Conte relied on a clinical sample that may overrepresent symptomatic people with memory issues. Those with memory problems and no symptoms will not be included in such a sample, and yet they are likely part of the sample in the current study.

Furthermore, a large segment of the memory problems group in the current study were those survivors who currently did not report recall for their abuse history. These survivors may be different in many ways from those who have had a prior period of forgetting but currently have the ability to recall their abuse experiences. Indeed, the small sample of women with current recall but some prior period of forgetting prohibited testing specific hypotheses such as those of Elliott and Briere (1995). Indeed, the question remains as to what extent differences between the memory problems and continuous memory groups were driven by high rates of symptoms among those with more recent "recovery" of their memories. Although there were differences among the current study's participants in the recency of their recall, a small sample of such individuals precluded more detailed examination of this phenomenon. Consistent with Elliott and Briere's (1995) work, however, the current study also points to the importance of examining differences within groups of survivors. Interesting differences based on memory were more pronounced in the current sample when age was taken into account.

There are, of course, a number of limitations to these analyses. The first is the relatively small sample size. This interferes with statistical power and makes the achievement of statistical significance difficult. The present study is best seen as preliminary and descriptive in nature. Indeed, there is much future work to be done. In particular, the current memory problems group included both those participants who had no recall for the sexual abuse incident and those who did but who had some period of forgetting, having at some point "recovered" their memories for the incidents. There is some preliminary suggestion that those who are grappling with recently recovered memories are also reporting the highest levels of symptoms, and there is a need to do more to examine this issue (Elliott & Briere, 1995). In addition, future work should consider the issue of grouping participants by age at the time of abuse. This will require the collection of larger samples of abuse survivors and the use of more prospective designs that collect external evidence of abuse so that participants who do not currently recall their abuse can be included in research samples. In addition, there is a great need to use comparison groups of nonabused participants. For example, the current study found no general differences between the continuous and discontinuous memory groups on mental health symptoms. This finding does not indicate how these survivors are doing relative to others who were not abused. Although those with memory problems may not be doing worse than those with continuous recall, they also do not seem to be clearly doing better. This is contrary to some discussions that assert that having no memory for traumatic events may lead individuals to do better than survivors with continuous recall. It is necessary to examine how both groups compare to nonabused women. Those who do not remember the abuse may show effects of abuse at levels comparable to abused women with continuous recall, yet they may have difficulty in obtaining appropriate therapeutic intervention because their abuse is not identified. Furthermore, there is a great need to know more about the mechanisms of forgetting. There may be vast individual differences in why memories are not available, and these underlying reasons may have different impacts on mental health;

ideally, at some point, we would want to be able to examine such differences more closely.

Finally, there is a need to examine a variety of outcome measures. The measure of psychological symptoms used in the current study captures only a small segment of the women's functioning. A more complete understanding of the effects of memory disruption on the long-term functioning of survivors requires that we use multiple measures of outcome to tap functioning in a variety of life roles. This is particularly true in light of discussions that suggest that one mechanism for the forgetting of abuse is that individuals are using dissociation. Dissociation may also lead individuals to be less aware of or less likely to report symptoms of distress. They may minimize or effectively dissociate from awareness of current problems. Future research should go beyond a strict reliance on self-report symptom checklists by perhaps examining other objective descriptions of behaviors or adjustment, such as school performance or risky health behaviors or observational tools. All of these are problems and issues that need to be explored further in future research.

Overall, these results are most significant for the issues they raise for future research, such as the need to consider age when trying to understand issues of memory. There is a need to replicate this with studies of larger samples that would permit examination of the relationship between memory status for traumatic events and long-term psychological adjustment of survivors. Indeed, it would be a misuse of the data presented here to conclude that memory for sexual abuse has no impact on survivors' functioning. Rather, the data indicate what a complex question this is to answer and illustrate the kinds of research dilemmas that we must confront in order to study this topic further.

References

Belli, R. F., & Loftus, E. F. (in press). The pliability of autobiographical memory: Misinformation and the false memory problem. In D. C. Rubin (Ed.), *Constructing our past: An overview of autobiographical memory.* New York: Cambridge University Press.

Bower, G. H. (1990). Awareness, the unconscious, and repression: An experimental psychologist's perspective.

In J. L. Singer (Ed.), *Repression and dissociation: Implications for personality theory, psychopathology, and health* (pp. 209-231). Chicago: University of Chicago Press.

Bowers, K. S., & Farvolden, P. (1996). Revisiting a century-old Freudian slip: From suggestion disavowed to the truth repressed. *Psychological Bulletin, 119,* 355-380.

Breuer, J., & Freud, S. (1957). *Studies on hysteria* (J. Strachey & A. Freud, Eds. & Trans.). New York: Basic Books. (Original work published 1893)

Briere, J., & Conte, J. R. (1993). Self-reported amnesia for abuse in adults molested as children. *Journal of Traumatic Stress, 6,* 21-31.

Briere, J., & Runtz, M. (1987, July). *A brief measure of victimization effects: The Trauma Symptom Checklist (TSC-33).* Paper presented at the Third National Family Violence Research Conference, Durham, NH.

Ceci, S. J., & Bruck, M. (1993). Suggestibility of the child witness: A historical review and synthesis. *Psychological Bulletin, 113,* 403-439.

Ceci, S. J., Caves, R. D., & Howe, M. J. A. (1981). Children's long-term memory for information that is incongruous with their prior knowledge. *British Journal of Psychology, 72,* 443-450.

Cohen, J. (1969). *Statistical powers analysis for the behavioral sciences.* New York: Academic Press.

Creamer, M., Burgess, P., & Pattison, P. (1992). Reaction to trauma: A cognitive processing model. *Journal of Abnormal Psychology, 101,* 452-459.

Elliott, D. M., & Briere, J. (1992). Sexual abuse trauma among professional women: Validating the Trauma Symptom Checklist-40 (TSC-40). *Child Abuse & Neglect, 16,* 391-398.

Elliott, D. M., & Briere, J. (1995). Posttraumatic stress associated with delayed recall of sexual abuse: A general population study. *Journal of Traumatic Stress, 8,* 629-647.

Enns, C. Z., McNeilly, C. L., Corkery, J. M., & Gilbert, M. S. (1995). The debate about delayed memories of child sexual abuse: A feminist perspective. *Counseling Psychologist, 23,* 181-279.

Erdelyi, M. H. (1990). Repression, reconstruction, and defense: History and integration of the psychoanalytic and experimental frameworks. In J. L. Singer (Ed.), *Repression and dissociation: Implications for personality theory, psychopathology, and health* (pp. 1-32). Chicago: University of Chicago Press.

Finkelhor, D. (1995). The victimization of children: A developmental perspective. *American Journal of Orthopsychiatry, 65,* 177-193.

Gold, S. R., Milan, L. D., Mayall, A., & Johnson, A. E. (1994). A cross-validation study of the Trauma Symptom Checklist: The role of mediating variables. *Journal of Interpersonal Violence, 9,* 12-26.

Herman, J. L., & Schatzow, E. (1987). Recovery and verification of memories of childhood sexual trauma. *Psychoanalytic Psychology, 4,* 1-14.

Holmes, D. S. (1990). The evidence for repression: An examination of sixty years of research. In J. L. Singer (Ed.), *Repression and dissociation: Implications for person-* ality theory, psychopathology, and health (pp. 85-102). Chicago: University of Chicago Press.

Hyman, I. E., Jr., & Pentland, J. (1996). Guided imagery and the creation of false childhood memories. *Journal of Memory and Language, 35,* 101-117.

Kendall-Tackett, K., Williams, L. M., & Finkelhor, D. (1993). Impact of sexual abuse on children: A review and synthesis of recent empirical studies. *Psychological Bulletin, 113,* 164-180.

Lindsay, D. S., & Read, J. D. (1995). "Memory work" and recovered memories of childhood sexual abuse: Scientific evidence and public, professional, and personal issues. *Psychology, Public Policy, and Law, 1,* 846-908.

Loftus, E. F. (1995, March-April). Remembering dangerously. *Skeptical Inquirer,* pp. 20-29.

Loftus, E. F., Smith, K. D., Klinger, M. R., & Fielder, J. (1992). Memory and mismemory for health events. In J. M. Tanur (Ed.), *Questions about questions: Inquiries into the cognitive bases of surveys* (pp. 102-137). New York: Russell Sage Foundation.

McCahill, T., Meyer, L. C., & Fischman, A. (1979). *The aftermath of rape.* Lexington, MA: Lexington.

Poole, D. A., Lindsay, D. S., Memon, A., & Bull, R. (1995). Psychotherapy and the recovery of memories of childhood sexual abuse: U.S. and British practitioners' beliefs, practices, and experiences. *Journal of Consulting and Clinical Psychology, 63,* 426-437.

Russell, D. E. H. (1986). *The secret trauma: Incest in the lives of girls and women.* New York: Basic Books.

Spiegel, D. (1990). Hypnosis, dissociation, and trauma: Hidden and overt observers. In J. L. Singer (Ed.), *Repression and dissociation: Implications for personality theory, psychopathology, and health* (pp. 121-142). Chicago: University of Chicago Press.

Tromp, S., Koss, M. P., Figueredo, A. J., & Tharan, M. (1995). Are rape memories different? A comparison of rape, other unpleasant, and pleasant memories among employed women. *Journal of Traumatic Stress, 8,* 607-627.

Vaillant, G. (1990). Repression in college men followed for half a century. In J. L. Singer (Ed.), *Repression and dissociation: Implications for personality theory, psychopathology, and health* (pp. 259-273). Chicago: University of Chicago Press.

Vaillant, G. (1992). *Ego mechanisms of defense: A guide for clinicians and researchers.* Washington, DC: American Psychiatric Press.

Wegner, D. M., Quillian, F., & Houston, C. E. (1996). Memories out of order: Thought suppression and the disturbance of sequence memory. *Journal of Personality and Social Psychology, 71,* 680-691.

Williams, L. M. (1994). Recall of childhood trauma: A prospective study of women's memories of child sexual abuse. *Journal of Consulting and Clinical Psychology, 62,* 1167-1176.

Williams, L. M., & Banyard, V. L. (1997). Perspectives on adult memories of childhood sexual abuse: A research review. In L. J. Dickstein, M. B. Riba, & J. M. Oldham (Eds.), *American Psychiatric Press review of psychiatry* (Vol. 16, pp. II-123–II-151). Washington, DC: American Psychiatric Press.

10

Bulimia Nervosa, PTSD, and Forgetting

Results From the National Women's Study

Timothy D. Brewerton
Bonnie S. Dansky
Dean G. Kilpatrick
Patrick M. O'Neil

The link between victimization experiences and dissociative phenomena has been well described in the literature. Acute dissociative symptoms are commonly associated with severely overwhelming trauma and include derealization, depersonalization, time distortions, cognitive and memory alterations, and somatic sensations. Dissociative disorders (particularly dissociative identity disorder) are disorders of memory and identity that are thought to represent sequelae of unusually severe and chronic violent abuse during childhood. Several authors have reported high frequencies of eating disorders and behaviors in

dissociative identity disorder patients (Goodwin & Attias, 1993; Putnam, Guroff, Silberman, Barban, & Post, 1986; Torem, 1986, 1990, 1993). Conversely, high frequencies of dissociative symptoms have been reported in eating disorder patients, particularly bulimia nervosa (Abraham & Beaumont, 1982; Demitrack, Putnam, Brewerton, Brandt, & Gold, 1990; Everill, Waller, & Macdonald, 1995). There are no studies, however, of both dissociative symptoms, such as psychogenic amnesia, and victimization experiences in a representative group of subjects with and without eating disorders. Data generated as part of the National Women's Study

AUTHORS' NOTE: Preparation of this chapter was supported by NIDA Grant No. R01-DA05520 awarded to Dr. Dean G. Kilpatrick (principal investigator).

(NWS) provided an opportunity for a more controlled examination of this issue.

Using a representative sample of more than 3,000 U.S. women from four stratified geographic regions, we have previously reported significantly higher rates for rape (27% versus 13%), molestation (22% versus 12%), and aggravated assault (27% versus 8%) in respondents with bulimia nervosa (BN) than in nonbulimic respondents (Brewerton & Dansky, 1995; Dansky, Brewerton, O'Neil, & Kilpatrick, 1997). Overall, the rate of direct victimization was significantly higher in BN respondents (54%) compared with nonbulimic respondents (31%). These data strongly contradicted the prevailing belief that there was little evidence that childhood sexual abuse acts as a risk factor for BN (Conners & Morse, 1993; Kinzl, Traweger, Guenther, & Biebl, 1994; Pope & Hudson, 1992; Pope, Mangweith, Negrao, Hudson, & Cordas, 1994; Rorty, Yager, & Rossotto, 1994), though these studies have serious methodological limitations.

More specifically, the major difficulties in interpreting the problems in the extant research may be summarized as follows:

1. Comparison groups have not been used (Kinzl et al., 1994; Pope et al., 1994).

2. Sample sizes have been small (Pope et al., 1994; Rorty et al., 1994).

3. Participants have fallen within a limited age range (Kinzl et al., 1994; Pope et al., 1994; Rorty et al., 1994).

4. Sampling has been nonrandom (Kinzl et al., 1994; Pope et al., 1994; Rorty et al., 1994).

5. Researchers have failed to assess other forms of victimization (e.g., aggravated assault, witnessing a homicide) that occurred in the absence of sexual assault experiences (Rorty et al., 1994).

6. Most samples have consisted either of treatment-seeking individuals or college students (Hall, Tice, Beresford, Wooley, & Klassen, 1989; Root & Fallon, 1988; Steiger & Zanko, 1990). Although the prevalence of disordered eating and sexual abuse in college students has been examined by a number of researchers (Bailey & Gibbons, 1989; Beckman & Burns, 1990; Calam & Slade, 1989; Smolak, Levine, & Sullin, 1990), to date, no one besides our research team had studied the relationship between sexual assault and BN in a national, representative sample of women.

7. How sexual assault and BN have been operationally defined has varied greatly among studies.

8. Prior to this study, scant data existed regarding the relationship between posttraumatic stress disorder (PTSD) and eating disorders. Coinciding with this is that there are no data regarding PA and eating disorders in a representative sample.

The central goals of the present study were (a) to determine the prevalence of forgetting (PA) and its relationship to victimization experiences and BN among women in the United States; (b) to evaluate the nature of any relationships among victimization, PTSD, PA, and BN; and (c) to illuminate any characteristics of disordered eating that may be more highly associated with psychogenic amnesia.

Method

Participants

The data used in this study were obtained from a national household probability sample of 3,006 women who were participants in the third wave of the National Women's Study. Respondents completed structured telephone interviews of approximately 40 minutes' duration, during which time they were screened for (in the following order) sexual harassment, major depression, trauma history, dieting behavior, BN, binge eating disorder (BED), alcohol abuse/dependence, PTSD, and demographics. The mean age (+ SD) for the weighted sample was 46.1 + 17.3 years, and the weighted sample was predominantly Caucasian (86%), with a mostly African American minority group (11%), an accurate reflection of the normal racial composition of the population of women in the United States. The sampling procedures and survey instrument have been described extensively in other publications (Dansky et al., in press; Dansky, Saladin, Brady, Kilpatrick, & Resnick, 1995; Resnick, Kilpatrick, Dansky, Saunders, & Best, 1993).

Procedure

The original sample of 4,009 female adults (Wave 1 sample) was generated by multistage geographic sampling procedures, wherein stratified samples of counties in four regions of the country were generated as primary sampling units during the first of a three-stage sampling procedure. The second and third stages of the sampling procedure involved systematic selection of residential telephone exchanges within the primary sampling units. Random digit dialing was used to target households within each stratum. To ensure random selection within a household, the female adult with the most recent birthday was interviewed (for further details, see Resnick et al., 1993).

Wave 3 interviews were conducted between January and May 1992 by Schulman, Ronca, and Bucuvalas (SRBI), a New York-based survey research firm. Only well-trained, experienced female SRBI interviewers were used. Interviewers were blind to the purpose of the investigation. The consent and completion rate for designated respondents in Wave 1 was 85.2%, and 75% of the Wave 1 participants completed the Wave 3 interview. A majority of the loss of respondents to attrition was due to failure to locate those respondents, rather than their refusal to participate. Because the original sample was identified in 1989, the data were weighted according to estimates of the 1989 U.S. Census figures for age and race. The weighting program was used to ensure that sample data were representative of women in the U.S. population.

Psychiatric Diagnoses

Psychiatric diagnoses were determined by structured interviews based on criteria in the *Diagnostic and Statistical Manual of Mental Disorders,* third edition, revised (*DSM-III-R;* American Psychiatric Association, 1987) and, in the case of BED, in the *DSM-IV Options Book* (American Psychiatric Association, 1991). Binge eating was defined using the following gate question: "Sometimes people will overeat on holidays or special occasions and feel guilty about it afterwards. Not counting

those types of situations, have you ever had an episode where you felt out of control about your eating and ate much more food in one sitting than most people?"

As described in detail elsewhere (Dansky et al., 1997), a diagnosis of BN was assigned to respondents who met the following criteria:

1. The subject had episodes of eating large amounts of food in a brief period of time.
2. During the subject's "worst" period, the episodes occurred at least several times each week.
3. The worst period lasted at least 3 months.
4. The subject engaged in at least two types of binge eating behaviors that are indicators of a loss of control as outlined in the proposed *DSM-IV* criteria for BED.
5. The subject compensated for a binge with excessive exercise, vomiting, laxative use, or diuretic use.

A diagnosis of BED was given to respondents who met all of the criteria for BN but indicated that they did not engage in compensatory behaviors and their "worst period" of bingeing lasted for at least 6 months.

The victimization screening instruments have also been described in detail elsewhere (Dansky et al., 1997). Participants responded to behaviorally specific questions based on legal definitions of rape, molestation, noncontact sexual assault, and aggravated assault, any of which was designated as a "direct assault."

The PTSD screening was completed using the NWS PTSD module (Resnick et al., 1993; Robins, Helzer, Croughan, & Ratcliff, 1981), which was modified from the Diagnostic Interview Schedule used in the National Vietnam Veterans Readjustment Study (Kulka et al., 1990; Robins et al., 1981). Participants were screened for symptoms of PTSD (using *DSM-III-R* criteria), regardless of whether they had experienced an event that met PTSD Criterion A (an event outside of range of usual human experience that would produce marked distress in almost anyone). Respondents were classified as meeting Criterion A, the necessary stressor criterion for PTSD, if they reported the occurrence of at least one traumatic event (e.g., indirect victimization due to witnessing homicide of a significant other, major accidents, natural disasters, direct sexual or physical assault) at some time during their lives. The remaining symptom criteria were obtained via a structured interview schedule designed to assess intrusive symptoms, symptoms of avoidance, and symptoms of increased arousal per *DSM-III-R* criteria. The PTSD measure was prefaced with the following: "People experience a variety of moods and feelings from time to time. In your case, has there ever been a period of a month or more during which . . . ." Statements following this probe were specifically phrased to assess symptom presence, such as "you had repeated bad dreams or nightmares." Lifetime PTSD was assigned if a respondent met the *DSM-III-R* criteria by having the necessary number of Criterion B (one reexperiencing), Criterion C (three avoidance), and Criterion D (two increased arousal) symptoms. Concurrent validity obtained from a slightly modified version of the NWS PTSD module with the SCID-PTSD module administered by trained clinicians was good with a kappa of 0.77 for lifetime PTSD, and the reliability of the PTSD diagnostic interview also was acceptable (Dansky et al., 1995; Resnick et al., 1993).

Psychogenic amnesia screening. As part of the PTSD screening, respondents were asked about a lifetime history of forgetting parts of experiences (psychogenic amnesia; PA) using the following question: "Throughout this interview we've talked about distressing experiences that you have had. Have you EVER felt that there were parts of any experience that you couldn't remember?" Immediately following this question, respondents were asked about recent or current history: "During the last month, have you felt that there were parts of any such experience that you couldn't remember?" Affirmative responses were categorized as "psychogenic amnesia," lifetime or current. One can argue that an affirmative answer to this question ostensibly approximates the first criterion of the *DSM-III-R* definition of psychogenic amnesia, that is, "a sudden inability to recall important personal information that is too extensive to be explained by ordinary forgetfulness." In addition, "the disturbance is not due to an organic mental disorder (e.g., blackouts during alcohol intoxication)." We were unable to assess this criterion specifically, but in order to address this possible effect, we analyzed frequencies of alcohol abuse or dependence and alcohol intoxication, overuse, and tolerance as possible contributors to PA.

Major depression screening. The major depression (MD) screening was based directly on *DSM-III-R* criteria. Respondents were asked about the following items: depressed mood, decreased interest in meaningful activities, weight changes, sleep pattern changes, restlessness, lethargy, feelings of worthlessness or guilt, problems with concentration, and thoughts about hurting themselves. Participants were classified as having lifetime MD if they ever met the criteria, and with current MD if they met the criteria during the previous 6 months.

Alcohol abuse/dependence. The alcohol abuse and dependence (AAD) screening was also based directly on *DSM-III-R* criteria. Respondents were asked questions about frequency, age at onset, and recency of use of alcohol; symptoms of tolerance and dependence; and alcohol-related difficulties at home, work, or in the community. Participants were classified as having lifetime AAD if they ever met the criteria and with current AAD if they met the criteria during the previous 6 months.

Statistical Analyses

The variables measured in this study can be categorized into four groups: (a) victimization variables; (b) PTSD variables, including PA; (c) weight and eating disorder variables; and (d) comorbidity variables, including major depression, PTSD, bulimia nervosa, and alcohol abuse or dependence. Data analyses were conducted to accomplish the following two goals: (a) descriptive analysis of respondents with PA, PTSD, and BN in comparison with respondents without these conditions; and (b) hypothesis testing—that is, that PA would be associated not

Table 10.1 Proportion of Respondents With Psychogenic Amnesia (Lifetime and Current) in Relationship to PTSD Diagnosis (Lifetime and Current) (in percentages)

		Lifetime PTSD	
		+	−
Lifetime psychogenic amnesia	+	41	7
			$p < 0.000001$, chi-square
	−	59	93
			−
Current psychogenic amnesia	+	49	36
			$p < 0.02$, chi-square
	−	51	64

		Current PTSD	
		+	−
Lifetime psychogenic amnesia	+	46	10
			$p < 0.000001$, chi-square
	−	54	90
			−
Current psychogenic amnesia	+	79	33
			$p < 0.000001$, chi-square
	−	21	67

only with criminal victimization and PTSD, but with the prevalence and/or severity of BN and related features as well. Comparisons between respondents with and without PA and BN were performed using chi-square and ANOVA statistics as appropriate.

A hierarchical multiple linear regression was calculated to test the extent to which PA was independently and interactively related to direct victimization variables, PTSD variables, weight and eating disorder variables, and comorbidity variables. All statistical procedures were performed using the SPSS 5.1 software (Norusis, 1992).

Results

□ Overall, 11% of the respondents reported that they had ever had problems remembering parts of traumatic experiences (lifetime PA). Of these respondents, 42% said that they had forgotten parts of experiences during the past month (current PA). Respondents with BN reported lifetime PA significantly more frequently (27%) than did non-BN/non-BED respondents (11%, $p < 0.000033$, chi-square), and there was

a statistical trend for a similar difference between BN and BED respondents (11%, $p < 0.09$).

In order to confirm the relationship between PA and PTSD, we compared their frequencies in a 2×2 table using chi-square analyses (Table 10.1). As expected, the proportions of both current and lifetime reports of PA were significantly higher in respondents with current and lifetime PTSD. Notably, 41% of respondents with lifetime PTSD endorsed lifetime PA, whereas 59% did not. Of those with lifetime PA and PTSD, 49% had current PA.

In order to determine if there were any significant differences between PTSD+ respondents with PA (PA+) versus those without PA (PA−), we compared these groups within the group of respondents with PTSD alone (PTSD+, weighted $n = 381$). Those with PA (PTSD+/ PA+) had significantly higher rates of rape, childhood rape, molestation, aggravated assault, mean number of victimization experiences, and mean number of reexperiencing and avoidance symptoms than did PTSD+/PA− respondents (Table 10.2). They also had more lifetime major depression, bulimia nervosa, laxative abuse, vomiting, diuretic abuse, and greater body mass index (BMI) fluctuations.

Table 10.2 Comparison of PTSD Respondents Alone With and Without Psychogenic Amnesia

	PA+ (n = 160)	PA− (n = 221)
Victimization variables		
rape (%)	49	27****
childhood rape (≤ 17 years old) (%)	37	14****
molestation (%)	43	29**
attempted sexual assault (%)	25	21
aggravated assault (%)	32	21*
any direct victimization (%)	82	63****
witness to homicide (%)	25	22
mean number of victimizations	1.5	1.0****
PTSD variables		
mean number of arousal symptoms	2.2	1.9
mean number of reexperiencing symptoms	1.2	0.9**
mean number of avoidance symptoms	2.4	1.9**
Weight and eating disorder variables		
current BMI	27.3	26.0
maximum BMI	29.3	28.2***
minimum BMI	20.4	20.8
maximum change in BMI	8.9	7.6*
current obesity (%)	40	33
bulimia nervosa diagnosis (%)	10	5
laxative abuse (%)	9	2**
vomiting (%)	16	9*
diuretic abuse (%)	15	8*
Comorbidity variables		
lifetime depression (%)	75	63*
current depression (%)	38	37
alcohol abuse/dependence (%)	15	15
alcohol intoxication (%)	24	35*
overuse of alcohol (%)	16	12
tolerance to alcohol (%)	19	17
total number of comorbid diagnoses	1.8	1.6

*$p < 0.05$; **$p < 0.01$; ***$p < 0.001$; ****$p < 0.0001$.

Significantly, there was no more alcohol abuse/dependence in the PTSD+/PA+ respondents than in the PTSD+/PA− respondents.

We also wanted to determine to what extent PA was related to the same variables irrespective of PTSD. In a comparison of all respondents with PA (weighted $n = 333$, PA+) versus those without PA (weighted $n = 2,622$, PA−), the PA+ respondents had significantly higher rates of rape, childhood rape, molestation, aggravated assault, and any direct victimization, as well as higher mean numbers of victimization experiences and PTSD symptoms and diagnoses than PA− respondents (Table 10.3). They also had more current and lifetime major

depression, bulimia nervosa, laxative abuse, vomiting, diuretic abuse, and higher mean current and maximum BMIs and BMI fluctuations. There was significantly more AAD, alcohol intoxication, overuse, and tolerance in the PA+ respondents than in the PA− respondents. However, when these respondents were eliminated from the analysis, all significant differences described above remained significant.

We next examined potential differences within the group of respondents with PA alone (PA+, weighted $n = 332$) in relationship to the presence of BN. Of those respondents with PA alone, those with BN (PA+/BN+) reported significantly higher rates of lifetime rape, child-

Table 10.3 Comparison of All Respondents With and Without Psychogenic Amnesia

	PA+ (n = 333)	PA– (n = 2,622)
Victimization variables		
rape (%)	36	11****
childhood rape (≤ 17 years old) (%)	27	7****
molestation (%)	33	10****
attempted sexual assault (%)	18	8
aggravated assault (%)	21	7****
any direct victimization (%)	68	27****
witness to homicide (%)	21	13****
mean number of victimizations	1.5	0.3****
PTSD variables		
mean number of arousal symptoms	1.3	0.4****
mean number of reexperiencing symptoms	0.7	0.1****
mean number of avoidance symptoms	1.5	0.3****
lifetime PTSD (%)	46	8****
current PTSD (%)	19	3****
Weight and eating disorder variables		
current BMI	26.4	25.4**
maximum BMI	28.5	27.2***
minimum BMI	20.4	20.5
maximum change in BMI	8.1	6.8****
current obesity (%)	36	27***
bulimia nervosa diagnosis (%)	6	2****
laxative abuse (%)	6	2****
vomiting (%)	11	4****
diuretic abuse (%)	9	3****
Comorbidity variables		
lifetime depression (%)	36	13****
current depression (%)	23	8****
alcohol abuse/dependence (%)	11	5****
alcohol intoxication (%)	23	18*
overuse of alcohol (%)	11	7*
tolerance to alcohol (%)	15	7****
total number of comorbid diagnoses	1.0	0.3****

$*p < 0.05$; $**p < 0.01$; $***p < 0.001$; $****p < 0.0001$.

hood rape, aggravated assault, and any direct victimization, as well as mean numbers of victimization experiences and PTSD symptoms/diagnoses than those without BN (PA+/BN–) (Table 10.4). The PA+/BN+ respondents also had higher mean current and maximum BMIs and higher rates of obesity (defined as BMI > 30) than women in the PA+/BN– group. Importantly, PA+/BN+ respondents had significantly higher rates of lifetime and current major depression, but not alcohol abuse/dependence or alcohol intoxication, overuse, or tolerance, than the PA+/BN– respondents.

Similarly, of those respondents with BN alone (BN+, weighted $n = 69$), the BN+/PA+ respondents had significantly higher rates of lifetime rape, childhood rape, aggravated assault, and any direct victimization, as well as higher mean numbers of victimization experiences and PTSD symptoms/diagnoses than the BN+/PA– respondents (Table 10.5). The BN+/PA+ group also had higher current and maximum mean BMIs and higher rates of current obesity, laxative and diuretic abuse, current and lifetime major depression, and total number of comorbid diagnoses. However, AAD, alcohol

Table 10.4 Comparison of Psychogenic Amnesia Respondents Alone, With and Without Bulimia Nervosa

	BN+ (n = 19)	BN− (n = 313)
Victimization variables		
rape (%)	63	34**
childhood rape (≤ 17 years old) (%)	54	26**
molestation (%)	35	33
attempted sexual assault (%)	15	18
aggravated assault (%)	47	20**
any direct victimization (%)	91	66*
witnessed homicide (%)	21	21
mean number of victimizations	1.6	1.0*
PTSD variables		
mean number of arousal symptoms	2.6	1.2***
mean number of reexperiencing symptoms	1.7	0.6****
mean number of avoidance symptoms	3.3	1.4****
lifetime PTSD (%)	75	44**
current PTSD (%)	49	17***
Weight and eating disorder variables		
current BMI	31.2	26.2***
maximum BMI	36.0	28.0****
minimum BMI	20.8	20.4
maximum change in BMI	15.2	7.6****
current obesity (BMI > 30) (%)	74	36*
Comorbidity variables		
lifetime depression (%)	55	35
current depression (%)	47	22**
alcohol abuse/dependence (%)	19	11
alcohol intoxication (%)	26	23
overuse of alcohol (%)	11	9
tolerance to alcohol (%)	27	14
total number of comorbid diagnoses	2.5	0.9****

$*p < 0.05$; $**p < 0.01$; $***p < 0.001$; $****p < 0.0001$.

intoxication, overuse, and tolerance were not significantly higher in the BN+/PA+ than in the BN+/PA− respondents.

Multiple linear regression using PA as the dependent variable revealed 9 variables of 28 entered that remained in the equation (Table 10.6). Of note was that none of the alcohol abuse variables were related to PA, but the purging variables, laxative abuse and vomiting, were.

In similar analyses for BED respondents, there were no significant differences for any of the measures related to PA, but this was probably a result of the much lower sample sizes for the BED group.

Discussion

☐ This is the first study to assess systematically the relationships among crime victimization, PTSD, PA, and BN in a large, nationally representative sample of women. It has been previously reported that BN respondents had significantly higher prevalence rates of rape, sexual molestation, aggravated assault, direct victimization, and current and lifetime diagnoses of PTSD. We have extended these analyses to the examination of the relationship between forgetting parts of traumatic experiences per se (PA) with several variables, including victimization events, PTSD symptoms and diagnosis,

Table 10.5 Comparison of Bulimia Nervosa Respondents Alone, With and Without Psychogenic Amnesia

	PA+ (n = 19)	PA− (n = 50)
Victimization variables		
rape (%)	63	14****
childhood rape (≤ 17 years old) (%)	54	4****
molestation (%)	35	18
attempted sexual assault (%)	15	10
aggravated assault (%)	47	21*
direct victimization (%)	91%	43***
witnessed homicide (%)	21	12
mean number of victimizations	1.6	0.6****
PTSD variables		
mean number of arousal symptoms	2.5	0.9***
mean number of reexperiencing symptoms	1.7	0.2****
mean number of avoidance symptoms	3.3	1.1****
lifetime PTSD (%)	75	23****
current PTSD (%)	49	12***
Weight and eating disorder variables		
current BMI	31.2	26.4*
maximum BMI	36.0	28.5***
minimum BMI	20.8	21.0
maximum change in BMI	15.2	7.4***
current obesity (%)	74	31***
laxative abuse (%)	46	20*
vomiting (%)	57	36
diuretic abuse (%)	61	27**
Comorbidity variables		
lifetime major depression (%)	55	29*
current major depression (%)	47	23*
alcohol abuse/dependence (%)	19	11
alcohol intoxication (%)	29	27
overuse of alcohol (%)	12	9
tolerance to alcohol (%)	27	20
total number of comorbid diagnoses	2.5	1.6***

$*p < 0.05$; $**p < 0.01$; $***p < 0.001$; $****p < 0.0001$.

weight and eating disorder variables, and other comorbidity, including major depression and alcohol abuse/dependence, intoxication, overuse, and tolerance.

In this chapter we have reported the following major findings:

1. PA was highly associated with PTSD and direct victimization experiences.
2. PA was associated with obesity, weight gain, and weight fluctuations.
3. PA was associated with BN and its related purging behaviors.
4. PA was associated with major depression.
5. Although PA was weakly associated with alcohol abuse/dependence in the total group, when those respondents with AAD ($n = 172$, 5.7% of total sample) were eliminated from the analyses, all of the significant differences persisted. In addition, AAD was not associated with PA in the bulimic group alone, and AAD did not predict PA in the multiple regression analysis.

Because these data are weighted to the 1989 census, these results may have important public

Table 10.6 Multiple Linear Regression Using Psychogenic Amnesia as the Dependent Variable

Variables in the Equation	Beta	t Statistic	Significance (p)
Lifetime PTSD	−0.253	−13.291	0.00001
Childhood rape	−0.108	−5.019	0.00001
Lifetime major depression	−0.068	−3.669	0.0002
Molestation	−0.083	−3.509	0.0005
Emotional problems in family	0.054	3.047	0.0023
Laxative abuse	−0.048	−2.698	0.007
Number of victimization experiences	−0.076	−2.679	0.0074
Age	−0.041	−2.352	0.019
Vomiting	−0.035	−1.975	0.048

NOTE: ANOVA: $n = 2{,}788$; $R = 0.425$; $R^2 = 0.18$; $F = 68.16$; $p = 0.00001$.

health implications for U.S. women. Forgetting parts of traumatic events is not only real, but common, and appears to be related not only to victimization and PTSD, but also to weight and eating disorder-related variables.

Specifically, these data are compatible with the hypothesis that bingeing and purging are maladaptive mechanisms with psychobiological underpinnings that facilitate avoiding, numbing, and forgetting traumatic memories. Several authors have compared the act of bingeing to an altered state of consciousness—much like derealization, depersonalization, or dissociation—that is meant to decrease negative affect (Abraham & Beaumont, 1982; Everill et al., 1995; Heatherton & Baumeister, 1991). According to Heatherton and Baumeister (1991), binge eating may serve as a mechanism for escape from awareness by allowing for a switch from a higher or more conscious level of awareness triggered by anxiety to a lower or less conscious level focused on bodily sensations and the act of bingeing. Negative emotions and the environment are thereby temporarily excluded. These are not the first investigators to identify the phenomenon of using eating disordered behaviors as means of escape from awareness. At the end of the 19th century, in their original and controversial work, Breuer and Freud (1893/1995) proposed that several symptoms—including "persistent vomiting and anorexia even up to the point of refusal of nourishment"—were a result of traumatic experiences. In this study, we did not find a

relationship between PA and minimum lifetime weight or BMI.

To what extent bingeing versus purging contributes to the development of PA is unclear. However, the data suggest that both bingeing and purging behaviors, and perhaps purging alone, are associated with forgetting. Compared with the non-PA group, in the PA group there were higher rates of BN and all major forms of purging (vomiting, laxative, and diuretic abuse), as well as higher current and maximum BMI and maximum change in BMI. The finding that respondents with BN tend to have higher rates of PA than respondents with BED also suggests that purging is a more important contributor to PA than bingeing alone. We have reported elsewhere that the prevalence of sexual assault was almost twice as high among respondents who used two or more methods to compensate for a binge compared with respondents who used one method (Dansky et al., in press). In addition, a higher degree of loss of control over eating was associated with a higher prevalence of sexual assault. To what extent a history of victimization is associated with a particular type of eating behavior or with the severity or chronicity of disordered eating behaviors remains an area that requires future exploration.

Taken together, it is likely that the etiologic contributors to the forgetting phenomena found in the BN respondents are multidetermined, but include victimization history and severity as well as the presence of current and/or lifetime

PTSD, major depression, bulimia nervosa, and related purging behaviors. Although AAD and related variables were higher in the PA+ group compared with the PA– group, the results indicate that AAD did not explain the higher rates of PA reported by the BN respondents alone, the PTSD respondents alone, or the total group of respondents. It is possible that other drugs may have affected these results, but the prevalence of drug abuse or dependence (without alcohol) in the entire sample was very low. Memory alterations, particularly of a state-dependent nature, have been reported not only in association with PTSD, but also in association with major depression, and probably play a role in facilitating PA (Bremner et al., 1995; Reus, 1979; Wolkowitz et al., 1990). Interestingly, many of the same neuroendocrine and neurotransmitter systems reported to be altered in PTSD and major depression are also perturbed in BN, and include cortisol, other stress-related hormones, such as beta-endorphin (Brewerton, Lydiard, Laraia, Shook, & Ballenger, 1992), as well as norepinephrine and serotonin (Brewerton, 1995), all of which have been linked to memory function (Bremner, Krystal, Charney, & Southwick, 1996; Charney, Deutch, Southwick, & Krystal, 1995; Krystal, Bennett, Bremner, Southwick, & Charney, 1995; Wolkowitz et al., 1990).

These results may have important implications for the evaluation and treatment of bulimia nervosa patients in clinical settings. These include, but are not limited to, the following: (a) the realization of the important role of traumatic events in the etiology of BN as well as symptom maintenance; (b) the need to recognize comorbid conditions, including PTSD, PA, major depression, obesity, and substance abuse in individuals with BN; and (c) the likelihood that weight and eating disorder-related behaviors play a role in the avoidance of traumatic memories and the modulation of associated anxiety. Future research directions should include delineating more clearly the nature of the relationship between memory dysfunction and eating disorders as well as the best treatment or combination of treatments for the traumatized bulimic individual.

References

Abraham, S. F., & Beaumont, P. J. V. (1982). How patients describe bulimia or binge eating. *Psychological Medicine, 12,* 625-635.

American Psychiatric Association. (1987). *Diagnostic and statistical manual of mental disorders* (3rd ed., rev.). Washington, DC: Author.

American Psychiatric Association. (1991). *Diagnostic and statistical manual of mental disorders: Options book.* Washington, DC: Author.

Bailey, C. A., & Gibbons, S. J. (1989). Physical victimization and bulimic-like symptoms: Is there a relationship? *Deviant Behavior, 10,* 335-352.

Beckman, K. A., & Burns, G. L. (1990). Relation of sexual abuse and bulimia in college women. *International Journal of Eating Disorders, 9,* 487-492.

Bremner, J. D., Krystal, J. H., Charney, D. S., & Southwick, S. M. (1996). Neural mechanisms in dissociative amnesia for childhood abuse: Relevance to the current controversy surrounding the "false memory syndrome." *American Journal of Psychiatry, 153,* FS71-82.

Bremner, J. D., Randall, P. R., Capelli, S., Scott, T. M., McCarthy, G., & Charney, D. S. (1995). Deficits in short-term memory in adult survivors of childhood abuse. *Psychiatry Research, 59,* 97-107.

Breuer, J., & Freud, S. (1995). *Studies in hysteria* (A. A. Brill, Trans.). New York: Nervous and Mental Disease Publishing. (Original work published 1893)

Brewerton, T. D. (1995). Toward a unified theory of serotonin dysregulation in eating and related disorders. *Psychoneuroendocrinology, 20,* 561-590.

Brewerton, T. D., & Dansky, B. S. (1995). Bulimia nervosa, victimization, and PTSD. *Eating Disorders Review, 3,* 1-2.

Brewerton, T. D., Lydiard, R. B., Laraia, M. T., Shook, J., & Ballenger, J. C. (1992). CSF beta-endorphin and dynorphin in bulimia nervosa. *American Journal of Psychiatry, 149,* 1086-1090.

Calam, R. M., & Slade, P. D. (1989). Sexual experience and eating problems in female undergraduates. *International Journal of Eating Disorders, 8,* 391-397.

Charney, D. S., Deutch, A. Y., Southwick, S. M., & Krystal, J. H. (1995). Neural circuits and mechanisms of posttraumatic stress disorder. In M. J. Friedman, D. S. Charney, & A. Y. Deutch (Eds.), *Neurobiological and clinical consequences of stress: From normal adaptation to PTSD* (pp. 271-287). Philadelphia: Lippincott-Raven.

Conners, M. E., & Morse, W. (1993). Sexual abuse and eating disorders: A review. *International Journal of Eating Disorders, 13,* 1-11.

Dansky, B. S., Brewerton, T. D., O'Neil, P. M., & Kilpatrick, D. G. (1997). The National Women's Study: Relationship of crime victimization and PTSD to bulimia nervosa. *International Journal of Eating Disorders, 21,* 213-228.

Dansky, B. S., Saladin, M. E., Brady, K. T., Kilpatrick, D. G., & Resnick, H. S. (1995). Prevalence of victimization and PTSD among women with substance use disorders: Comparisons of telephone and in-person assessment samples. *International Journal of the Addictions, 30,* 1079-1100.

Demitrack, M. A., Putnam, F. W., Brewerton, T. D., Brandt, H. A., & Gold, P. W. (1990). Dissociative phenomena in eating disorders: Relationship to clinical variables. *American Journal of Psychiatry, 147,* 1184-1188.

Everill, J., Waller, G., & Macdonald, W. (1995). Dissociation in bulimic and non-eating-disordered women. *International Journal of Eating Disorders, 17,* 127-134.

Goodwin, J. M., & Attias, R. (1993). Eating disorders in survivors of multimodal childhood abuse. In R. P. Kluft & C. G. Fine (Eds.), *Clinical perspectives on multiple personality disorder* (pp. 327-341). Washington, DC: American Psychiatric Press.

Hall, R. C., Tice, L., Beresford, T. P., Wooley, B., & Klassen, A. (1989). Sexual abuse in patients with anorexia nervosa and bulimia. *Psychosomatics, 30,* 73-79.

Heatherton, T. F., & Baumeister, R. F. (1991). Binge eating as escape from self-awareness. *Psychological Bulletin, 110,* 86-108.

Kinzl, J. F., Traweger, C., Guenther, V., & Biebl, W. (1994). Family background and sexual abuse associated with eating disorders. *American Journal of Psychiatry, 151,* 1127-1131.

Krystal, J. H., Bennett, A. L., Bremner, J. D., Southwick, S. M., & Charney, D. S. (1995). Toward a cognitive neuroscience of dissociation and altered memory functions in post-traumatic stress disorder. In M. J. Friedman, D. S. Charney, & A. Y. Deutch (Eds.), *Neurobiological and clinical consequences of stress: From normal adaptation to PTSD* (pp. 239-269). Philadelphia: Lippincott-Raven.

Kulka, R. A., Schlenger, W. E., Fairbank, J. A., Hough, R. L., Jordan, B. K., Marmar, C. R., & Weiss, D. S. (1990). *Trauma and the Vietnam war generation.* New York: Brunner/Mazel.

Norusis, M. (1992). *SPSS/PC+ advanced statistics, version 5.0.* Chicago: SPSS.

Pope, H. G., & Hudson, J. I. (1992). Is childhood sexual abuse a risk factor for bulimia nervosa? *American Journal of Psychiatry, 149,* 455-463.

Pope, H. G., Mangweith, B., Negrao, A. B., Hudson, J. I., & Cordas, T. A. (1994). Childhood sexual abuse and bulimia nervosa: A comparison of American, Austrian, and Brazilian women. *American Journal of Psychiatry, 151,* 732-737.

Putnam, F., Guroff, J. J., Silberman, E. K., Barban, L., & Post, R. M. (1986). The clinical phenomenology of multiple personality disorder: A review of 100 cases. *Journal of Clinical Psychiatry, 47,* 285-293.

Resnick, H. S., Kilpatrick, D. G., Dansky, B. S., Saunders, B. E., & Best, C. L. (1993). Prevalence of civilian trauma and posttraumatic stress disorder in a representative national sample of women. *Journal of Consulting and Clinical Psychology, 61,* 984-991.

Reus, V. I. (1979). Clinical implications of state-dependent learning. *American Journal of Psychiatry, 136,* 927-931.

Robins, L. N., Helzer, J. E., Croughan, J., & Ratcliff, K. S. (1981). National Institute of Mental Health Diagnostic Interview Schedule: Its history, characteristics, and validity. *Archives of General Psychiatry, 38,* 381-389.

Root, M. P. P., & Fallon, P. (1988). The incidence of victimization experiences in a bulimic sample. *Journal of Interpersonal Violence, 3,* 161-173.

Rorty, M., Yager, J., & Rossotto, E. (1994). Childhood sexual, physical, and psychological abuse in bulimia nervosa. *American Journal of Psychiatry, 151,* 1122-1126.

Smolak, L., Levine, M., & Sullin, E. (1990). Are child sexual experiences related to eating-disordered attitudes and behaviors in a college sample? *International Journal of Eating Disorders, 9,* 167-178.

Steiger, H., & Zanko, M. (1990). Sexual traumata among eating-disordered, psychiatric, and normal female groups: Comparison of prevalences and defense styles. *Journal of Interpersonal Violence, 5,* 74-86.

Torem, M. S. (1986). Dissociative states presenting as an eating disorder. *American Journal of Clinical Hypnosis, 29,* 137-142.

Torem, M. S. (1990). Covert multiple personality disorder underlying eating disorder. *American Journal of Psychotherapy, 44,* 357-368.

Torem, M. S. (1993). Eating disorders in patients with multiple personality disorder. In R. P. Kluft & C. G. Fine (Eds.), *Clinical perspectives on multiple personality disorder* (pp. 343-353). Washington, DC: American Psychiatric Press.

Wolkowitz, O. M., Reus, V. I., Weingartner, H., Thompson, K., Breier, A., Doran, A., Rubinow, D., & Pickar, D. (1990). Cognitive effects of corticosteroids. *American Journal of Psychiatry, 147,* 1297-1303.

11

Sexual Abuse History With and Without Self-Report of Memory Loss

Differences in Psychopathology, Personality, and Dissociation

Judith A. Sheiman

Much research has been done on adult survivors of childhood sexual abuse. A relatively new area of focus has recently emerged concerning repressed memories of abuse. The controversy over whether recovered memories are accurate or not has been argued by researchers and in the popular press. Although it is not within the scope of this chapter to examine the veracity of these claims, the study described below explored personality and psychological differences between survivors of child sexual abuse who report a period of memory loss and those who do not. Information about these differences can help increase our understanding of the underlying processes.

Although to date there has been little empirical research, the data do suggest some differences in experiences between these two groups. Williams (1994) found that women in her sam-

ple who were age 6 or younger or who knew their abusers were more likely to have no memory of the abuse. Briere and Conte (1993) found that, among their subjects, violence and younger age at the start of the abuse were associated with memory loss. They theorize that this can be explained by the mechanisms of dissociation and denial. The younger children are at the time they are abused, the less able they are to protect themselves. Psychological defense mechanisms such as dissociation, denial, and repression may be a child's only available defenses. Similarly, children of any age have few defenses besides psychological ones against physical violence from adults.

Elliott and Briere (1995) found that participants in their study who reported delayed recall of their abuse were more likely to have experienced threats of harm from their abusers.

However, participants did not differ on age at onset of abuse, on the frequency and duration of abuse, or on the use of actual physical force. Elliott and Briere did find that participants with delayed recall showed a greater number of psychological symptoms on various instruments.

Additionally, the clinical literature suggests some hypotheses based on clinical observations: Individuals who report memory repression are more likely to report having been abused by a parent or stepparent, and to report having the abuse unpredictably interspersed with affection (Briere, 1989). Considering the theoretical defensive function of dissociation and memory loss, this makes sense. The abuser is a significant source of pleasure as well as pain, and amnesia allows the child to accept the affection and "forget" the abuse.

The term *dissociation* has been used to describe mental defense strategies that range from relatively frequent and ordinary experiences, such as "highway hypnosis" (driving a familiar route without awareness), to the more severe symptoms of various mental disorders, such as dissociative identity disorder. As used in this chapter, *dissociation* refers to the exclusion of an experience from conscious awareness. For sexually abused children, dissociation may serve as a primary defense mechanism and method of coping with inescapable trauma (Courtois, 1988). By dissociating, children can protect themselves against overwhelming traumatic feelings and experiences that they are helpless to stop. This gives an immediate, temporary respite from pain. Some children then apparently also forget the traumatic experience. This helps to preserve the original sense of self, and the children are able to continue to develop without having to cope directly with overwhelming experiences. If a child's abuser is a close relative, by "forgetting" about the abuse, the child can enjoy the affection of the relative—often the only affection she or he receives—without distress. However, the cost of this coping strategy often is a sense of self-fragmentation (Spiegel, 1986). The child's experiencing of her or his whole self would mean including the awareness of this split-off "unknown" trauma.

Defense mechanisms such as dissociation may be beneficial in that they help the child deal with immediate, unavoidable, overwhelming trauma. However, although not accessible to conscious awareness, repercussions of the event still exist. The surviving adult comes to feel that the self she or he presents to the world is a "false" self, because there continues to be an awareness, a "sense," that something else is hidden. Amnesiac survivors often fear allowing others to get too close, because they are dimly aware that there is something unknown buried inside of them that others might discover.

Adult survivors who report having periods of time when they were unable to recall their abuse still often show other indirect reactions through symptoms such as depression and low self-esteem (Briere, 1989). There is a sense of fragmentation, of an unauthentic self covering for a damaged, dark self. Some feel numb, unconnected with their bodies. They are sensitive to stimuli that are similar to the original trauma, although not aware of why this is so. Amnesiac survivors may attempt to avoid situations that are similar to the original trauma and, when unable to do so, have exaggerated startle responses. Many have flashbacks to aspects of the original trauma, typically without understanding why (Briere, 1989).

To date, little empirical research has examined the means of memory recovery by those claiming repressed memory. Various triggers—such as environments similar to that of the abuse, sexual experience, and colognes or perfumes originally worn by the abuser—may be likely to cause memories to return. Conversely, those who argue that these memories are false suggest that the memories are "recovered" through therapy and are, intentionally or unintentionally, often induced by therapists.

The study reported below explored the differences in abuse history between participants who said they had had a period of time when they had been unable to remember their abuse, even if someone had asked them about it, and those who reported continuous memories of their abusive past. Those who said their memories had returned after a period of time were asked by what means those memories had returned. It was expected that participants with a period of inability to recall abuse would report more severe abuse experiences, fear of personal harm, earlier ages at onset, and more negative reactions to their abuse.

In addition, individuals who claimed a history of repressed memory (and who now believe they have recovered at least some memories of sexual abuse) were compared with a control group of sexual abuse survivors without such claims and with a control group of nonabused subjects. Because inability to recall abuse may be mediated through dissociation, it was expected that the participants who reported a period when they were unable to remember their abuse would show higher scores on the measures of dissociation.

Overall, it was hypothesized that sexual abuse survivors, regardless of memory loss, would show higher levels of symptoms as measured by the Minnesota Multiphasic Personality Inventory, second edition (MMPI-2; Butcher, Dahlstrom, Graham, Tellegen, & Kaemmer, 1989). The MMPI-2 is designed to provide information about a respondent's personality characteristics and symptomatology (Graham, 1990). It consists of 10 clinical scales as well as supplementary scales and content scales. Scores are considered high and clinically meaningful if they are above 65. High scorers on the Hypochondriasis (Hs) scale endorse large numbers of nonspecific physical problems. They tend to be generally unhappy, angry, and demanding of others. The Depression (D) scale measures endorsement of symptoms of depression, such as sadness and poor self-esteem. High scorers on the Hysteria (Hy) scale are likely to use denial and repression as main defense mechanisms. As with high scorers on Hs, they are likely to endorse physical symptoms. They do not have much insight into the causes of their problems.

The Psychopathic Deviate (Pd) scale measures antisocial behavior. High scorers endorse family problems, trouble with authority, and alcohol or drug abuse. The Masculinity-Femininity (Mf) scale measures stereotypic role endorsement. High scorers on the Paranoia (Pa) scale are suspicious and have trouble trusting others. High scores on the Psychasthenia (Pt) scale show obsessive-compulsive-like symptoms, including rigidity and anxiety. The

Schizophrenia (Sc) scale assesses unusual thinking and beliefs, and at extremely high levels (T > 80) it is often indicative of psychosis. The ninth scale, Mania (Ma), measures energy level and sociability. High scorers are optimistic and have high opinions of themselves. Those who score high on the Social Introversion (Si) scale tend to be introverted and overcontrolled.

The MMPI-2 also includes several supplementary scales. They vary as to the amount of reliability and validity data available. This study employed the supplemental scales of Anxiety, Repression (high scorers are conventional, methodical, and unemotional), Ego Strength (high scorers are stable and self-confident), MacAndrew Alcoholism-Revised, Overcontrolled Hostility (high scorers deny anger even when appropriate and may have occasional aggressive outbursts), and Posttraumatic Stress Disorder-Keane (Graham, 1990).

Previous research has found that sexual abuse survivors show long-term effects of depression, somatic complaints, anxiety, relationship difficulties, low self-esteem, trouble trusting other people, substance abuse, and sexual problems (Beitchman et al., 1992; Finkelhor, 1990; Green, 1993). Both sexually abused groups were expected to have higher elevations than the nonabused group on the scales that assess these symptoms—Hs, D, Hy, Pd, Pa, and Pt. The supplementary scales of Anxiety, MacAndrew Alcoholism-Revised, and Posttraumatic Stress Disorder also are expected to show higher scores in the sexually abused groups than in the control group.

Comparing the two sexually abused groups, participants who were unable to recall their abuse at some time in the past should show greater symptomatology, as measured by the MMPI-2, than those who had continuous recall. It was expected that their use of dissociation as a primary defense mechanism should cause some differences. High levels of dissociation have been found to be associated with high levels of anxiety, anger and hostility, depression, and somatic complaints (Norton, Ross, & Novotny, 1990; Sandberg & Lynn, 1992). It was hypothesized that abuse survivors with a period of memory loss would score higher than the other two groups on the scales of Hs, D, Hy, and Pd.

It was also anticipated that sexually abused subjects would show personality characteristics, as measured by the Revised NEO Personality Inventory (NEO PI-R), different from those of control subjects. The NEO PI-R is a measure of personality traits based on the five-factor model of personality (Costa & McCrae, 1992). The five Domain scores include Neuroticism (N), which measures emotional maladjustment; Extraversion (E), a measure of enjoyment of social activities and groups of other people; Openness (O), which measures interest in and willingness to experience new events; Agreeableness (A), which assesses tendency to be helpful and caring of others; and Conscientiousness (C), which measures self-control and ability to organize. Each Domain scale has six Facet scales that measure the specific characteristics that make up the Domain score. The Neuroticism scale includes Anxiety, Angry Hostility, Depression, Self-Consciousness, Impulsiveness, and Vulnerability. The Extraversion scale has the facets Warmth, Gregariousness, Assertiveness, Activity, Excitement-Seeking, and Positive Emotions. The facets of the Openness scale are Fantasy, Aesthetics, Feelings, Actions, Ideas, and Values. The Agreeableness facets are Trust, Straightforwardness, Altruism, Compliance, Modesty, and Tender-Mindedness. The Conscientiousness scale has the facets Competence, Order, Dutifulness, Achievement, Self-Discipline, and Deliberation.

Both sexual abuse subject groups were expected to have higher scores on several scales than control subjects. It was hypothesized that both would score higher on the Neuroticism Domain scale. Based on the literature reviewed above, both groups were expected to score higher than controls on the facet scales of Anxiety, Angry Hostility, Depression, and Vulnerability. They were expected to score lower on the facet scales of Assertiveness and Trust. Participants with inability to recall were expected to show a greater tendency to use fantasy and daydreams to deal with anxiety and stress, and should therefore have higher scores on Fantasy than either the abuse group without memory loss or the control group.

This study also explored which aspects of abuse experiences were predictive of memory loss. In light of previous research, it was expected that fear for one's life, younger age at time of abuse, and knowing one's abuser well would make memory loss more likely. Because memory loss is theorized to be a result of dissociation, it was also expected that survivors who report a period of memory loss would score higher on the Dissociative Experiences Scale (DES) than nonamnesiac survivors or the control group. The DES was designed to discriminate among clients with degrees of dissociation. It also has been used to quantify dissociative experiences in the general population (Carlson & Putnam, 1993).

Method

Participants

Participants were 174 college students enrolled in an introductory psychology course in a small, midsouthern U.S. university. Participants were placed in the sexual abuse group if they reported a sexual experience before the age of 14 with someone more than 5 years older or with a relative. This group was then divided into two groups: one made up of those who reported having been unable to remember their abuse for some period of time, even if someone had asked them about it, and one made up of those who reported always being able to remember. The total pool of participants contained 31 individuals (17.8%) who were sexually abused and had no periods of inability to remember the abuse and 14 people (8.0%) who were sexually abused and had periods of inability to remember.

A control group was randomly selected from the remainder of the subjects, matched to the sexually abused groups on age and gender. Final participants ranged in age from 18 to 44, with an average age of 21.71 ($SD = 5.36$). There were 90 females and 15 males. Six participants described themselves as African American, and the rest were Caucasian. The majority of members in each group grew up in small towns. Most participants (82) were single; 18 were married and 5 were divorced.

Materials

The questionnaires employed included the MMPI-2 (Butcher et al., 1989), the NEO PI-R (Costa & McCrae, 1992), the DES (Carlson & Putnam, 1993), and a survey questionnaire concerning history of childhood sexual abuse and memory loss and retrieval as well as demographics. The survey questionnaire included a section that asked whether the participant had experienced various events during childhood (see Table 11.1 for the list of experiences). For each experience the participant had had, he or she was asked who the other person was, the participant's age at the time, and the other person's age and gender. Categorical variables were coded 1 = yes; 2 = no. The participant was asked, "Was there ever a time when you were unable to remember the experience or experiences, even if someone had asked you about it?" If the response was yes, the participant was asked to provide the ages during which he or she was unable to remember and how the memories returned. The possible answers to the latter were listed as several options to check (e.g., in therapy, in therapy through hypnosis, triggered by reading material), and a space was also provided in which the participant could write other or additional information. Participants were also asked if they had experienced physical abuse.

Procedure

After filling out the informed consent, participants completed the questionnaires individually, in separate rooms with no one directly observing them. A clinical psychology graduate student was available to answer questions or address concerns.

Results

☐ Results were analyzed in several ways. Demographic and descriptive information was collected and totaled. A stepwise multiple regression was used to find which variables, from the questionnaire surveying history of childhood sexual abuse, best predicted whether a sexual abuse survivor was in the group with or

Table 11.1 Sexual Abuse Experiences

	Abused	Memory Loss
Sexual kissing	38.7	50.0
Abuser exposed self	51.6	57.1
Abuser touched victim's sex organs	67.7	92.9
Abuser's sex organs touched without penetration	22.6	14.3
Oral sex on victim	16.1	14.3
Victim performed oral sex on abuser	19.4	14.3
Penetration by other than sexual organ	22.6	35.7
Vaginal intercourse	16.1	28.6
Anal intercourse	3.2	7.1

Table 11.2 Means of Memory Recovery

	Number
Seeing sexual abuse material on TV or in reading matter	7
Triggered by something	4
Therapy	1
Therapy with hypnosis	1
Other	2

without a time of lost memory. MANOVAs were used to evaluate the MMPI-2 results and the NEO PI-R results.

Participants in both of the sexually abused groups checked off items ranging from "kissing in a sexual way" to "anal intercourse." The percentage of participants in each group who reported having had each experience is shown in Table 11.1.

The participants who reported some time of inability to remember their experience of sexual abuse were asked what caused their memory to return. These data are displayed in Table 11.2. The majority of respondents said that their memories returned after they had seen information about sexual abuse on television or in reading material. The second most frequent response was that memories were triggered by something that reminded them of their experiences, such as having intercourse or being told by an older sister about her abuse experiences.

Average DES score for the participants who reported sexual abuse with no loss of memory was 11.79 ($SD = 9.41$), with a range from 2.14 to 53.93. The participants who had been sexually abused and reported some time when they were unable to remember their abuse experiences had an average DES score of 17.14 ($SD = 8.01$), with a range from 1.79 to 32.14. The control group had an average DES score of 13.80 ($SD = 11.03$), with a range from 1.43 to 59.29.

A stepwise multiple regression was performed to determine the characteristics of the abusive experience that best predicted whether the participant had a period of inability to remember the abuse. The variables for this analysis included DES scores, type of sexual abuse, length of time the abuse continued, age when abuse began, age when abuse ended, how well the victim knew the perpetrator, how strongly the victim liked the perpetrator, use of force, victim's fear for own life, and if the victim told anyone about the abuse at the time it happened. Victim's fear for own life ($p < .001$), physical abuse ($p < .001$), how well the subject knew the abuser ($p < .001$), and average DES score ($p < .008$) were the best predictors of experiencing a period of memory loss. Participants who said they had felt fear for their lives were more likely to have periods of memory loss than were those who did not. Participants who reported no physical abuse also were more likely to report memory loss. The better the subject knew the abuser, the more likely he or she was to experience memory loss. High average DES scores were associated with memory loss. Finally, those reporting the experience of someone touching their sexual organs were more likely also to report a period of time of memory loss. The results are shown in Table 11.3.

A MANOVA was performed on the MMPI-2 basic scales. The overall MANOVA was significant ($F = 2.68$, $p < .001$). The results of the univariate analyses for the individual scales are shown in Table 11.4. Both sexually abused groups scored significantly higher than the control group on the scales of Depression, Psychopathic Deviate, Paranoia, Psychasthenia, and Schizophrenia. Survivors who reported memory loss scored higher than the control group on

Table 11.3 Multiple Regression: Prediction of Group Membership

Variable	T	Significance of T
Fear	−6.64	.000
Physical abuse	4.38	.000
Well-known abuser	−4.01	.000
DES score	2.88	.008
Abuser touching victim's sex organs	−2.23	.035

Table 11.4 Mean Scores on the MMPI-2

Scale	Abused (n = 29)		Memory Loss (n = 14)		Control (n = 53)	
	Mean	SD	Mean	SD	Mean	SD
L	49.21	10.58	48.43	8.06	49.19	8.62
F	57.03[a]	11.70	64.89[b]	14.97	50.36[c]	10.94
K	46.93	9.52	47.07	8.94	47.26	9.95
Hs	54.45	8.63	60.21[a]	11.92	51.02[b]	9.87
D	53.59[a]	10.97	56.29[a]	15.74	48.34[b]	8.56
Hy	49.79[a]	8.63	59.64[b]	11.72	47.64[a]	7.91
Pd	58.90[a]	9.80	61.00[a]	11.96	49.21[b]	6.89
Mf	50.38	9.92	56.79	9.80	56.40	12.46
Pa	56.90[a]	14.03	58.79[a]	11.36	49.13[b]	10.66
Pt	60.28[a]	14.58	64.21[a]	12.81	54.21[b]	11.72
Sc	60.79[a]	14.93	62.43[a]	15.00	51.58[b]	10.76
Ma	57.72	12.15	62.07	12.52	54.98	10.18

NOTE: Means in the same row with different superscripts differ at $p < .05$ with the least-significant difference comparison.

the scale of Hypochondriasis. They scored higher on the scale of Hysteria than either the nonamnesiac group or the control group. Additionally, the percentages of participants in all groups with nonpathological MMPI-2 profiles (no scales with elevations above T = 65) were calculated; these are shown in Figure 11.1. Almost one-half of the control had MMPI-2 profiles with no elevations above T = 65, only 26.9% of the nonamnesiac group and 14.3% of the amnesiac group had no elevations above 65.

A MANOVA was done on the supplemental scales of the MMPI-2 as well. The overall MANOVA was significant ($F = 1.89$, $p < .007$). The univariate results are shown in Table 11.5. Both sexual abuse groups scored significantly higher than the control group on the MacAndrew Al-

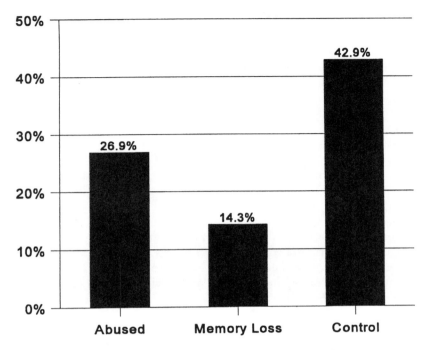

Figure 11.1. Percentage of MMPI-2 Profiles With No Elevations Above T = 65

coholism scale. The memory loss group scored significantly higher than the other groups on the Posttraumatic Stress Disorder scale.

No significant differences were found on the NEO PI-R Domain or facet scales. These analyses included MANOVAs of the NEO PI-R Domain scales Neuroticism ($F = 2.25$, $p < .11$), Extraversion ($F = .50$, $p < .61$), Openness ($F = 2.43$, $p < .09$), Agreeableness ($F = .10$, $p < .90$), and Conscientiousness ($F = 1.20$, $p < .31$), which were not significant. MANOVAs of the Neuroticism facet scales ($F = 1.70$, $p < .07$), Extraversion facet scales ($F = .43$, $p < .95$), Openness facet scales ($F = 1.53$, $p < .12$), Agreeableness facet scales ($F = .93$, $p < .51$), and Conscientiousness facet scales ($F = .81$, $p < .64$) were also not significant.

Discussion

☐ Approximately one-third of the overall sample of sexually abused subjects reported a period of time when they were unable to remember their experience of sexual abuse, even if

someone had asked them about it. Memory return was caused by therapy in only 2 of the 14 cases, and only 1 of these included hypnosis. The majority of subjects reported that their memories were triggered when they saw something about sexual abuse on television or in reading material or heard about it from other people.

The types of abusive experiences differed in several ways between subjects with memory loss and subjects without memory loss. Subjects with memory loss were more likely to know their abusers and have feared for their lives during the abuse. However, similar to Elliott and Briere's (1995) findings, their experiences did not differ in terms of whether or not actual violence occurred. Those without memory loss were also more likely to have reported physical abuse in childhood. Finally, subjects who reported memory loss had higher average DES scores than those who did not report memory loss.

Sexually abused subjects were expected to score higher on the MMPI-2 scales of Hypochondriasis and Hysteria. However, although

Table 11.5 Mean Scores on MMPI-2 Supplemental Scales

Scale	Abused (n = 29)		Memory Loss (n = 14)		Control (n = 53)	
	Mean	SD	Mean	SD	Mean	SD
Anxiety	53.43	11.38	56.00	14.20	52.57	11.49
Repression	46.89	11.08	44.00	8.30	49.63	10.60
Ego Strength	48.75	10.78	44.25	14.11	48.37	9.84
MacAndrew Alcohol	51.61[a]	11.17	52.00[a]	9.64	45.43[b]	8.84
Overcontrolled Hostility	51.64	8.71	56.42	8.57	49.50	10.61
Posttraumatic Stress Disorder-Keane	57.68[ab]	12.13	62.58[a]	13.48	53.82[b]	10.52

NOTE: Means in the same row with different superscripts differ at $p < .05$ with the least-significant difference comparison.

the abused with memory loss group did score significantly higher than the control group, the abused without memory loss group did not differ from the control group. As predicted, both sexually abused groups scored significantly higher on the Depression, Psychopathic Deviate, Paranoia, and Psychasthenia scales. Memory loss subjects tended to show significantly more general symptomatology than those without memory loss on the scales of Hypochondriasis and Hysteria. The hypothesis that they would differ from the sexually abused group without memory loss on the Depression and Psychopathic Deviate scales was not supported.

The high scores on the Hypochondriasis and Hysteria scales suggest a tendency to channel stress through physical symptoms rather than through direct means. These scores also indicate a lack of insight into the cause of symptoms, feelings, and motives. Strong tendencies to dissociate could explain these characteristics. Previous research has not separated abuse survivors with memory loss from those without, thus it is possible that previous results have reflected high proportions of amnesiac survivors in the subject population.

As expected, both sexually abused groups scored significantly higher on the Depression scale than the control group. However, the hypothesis that the group with memory loss would score significantly higher than the group without memory loss was not supported. Yet the memory loss group's average score approached clinical significance. Abused subjects reported depressive symptomatology, including sadness,

pessimism about the future, bad dreams, and lack of self-confidence. A period of time of inability to remember abuse did not affect this. As dissociation is rarely complete, it is possible that although the abused child was unable to recall the abuse, the child did recall the feelings associated with the abuse. Thus the depression may have been present before the memories returned. Another possibility is that survivors with memory loss became depressed after their memories returned.

The two sexually abused groups scored significantly higher on the Psychopathic Deviate scale than the control group. Again, the group with memory loss did not score higher than the group without memory loss, as predicted. High scorers report having bad relationships with family and distrust of authority figures. They tend to blame their families for their problems—in this case, possibly quite accurately. This scale most likely reflects actual family chaos and dysfunction.

Both sexual abuse groups had mild elevations on the Paranoia scale, significantly higher than the control group. This suggests a tendency to see life as a dangerous experience and to have low expectations. Support from others is seen as rarely available. High scorers on this scale worry a great deal about others' opinions of them and feel very suspicious of the motives of other people. Among people scoring in this range, there is commonly a great deal of anger and resentment toward the world.

The scores on the Psychasthenia scale were significantly higher for both abuse groups than for the control group. This indicates a high level of psychological discomfort. High scorers are likely to feel anxious and tense. They have low self-confidence and tend to be very hard on themselves. They are likely to have obsessive-compulsive symptoms.

Both sexually abused groups scored significantly higher on the Schizophrenia scale than the control group. Moderately high scorers report some unusual experiences, which may include flashbacks. They tend to feel isolated and misunderstood by other people. They tend to shy away from others and to fear intimacy. High scorers also feel a great deal of anxiety and resentment.

The hypothesis that both sexually abused groups would score higher on the MacAndrew Alcoholism-Revised scale and the Posttraumatic Stress Disorder scale was supported. Higher scorers on the MacAndrew scale have a greater tendency to abuse alcohol and other substances. Sexually abused subjects who reported memory loss scored significantly higher than controls on the Posttraumatic Stress Disorder scale. The abuse group without memory loss scored in between the two, and did not differ significantly from either. Higher scores show PTSD symptomatology, including emotional distress, sleep problems, fears, unwanted thoughts, and a feeling of being different from and misunderstood by others.

Overall, subjects who were sexually abused showed similar symptomatology, regardless of whether or not they experienced memory loss. Both groups endorsed more symptomatology than the control group. Given that participants in the memory loss group had retrieved their memories by the time of the study, at least in part, this may be an explanation for the similar symptoms. Symptoms of depression and anger toward family may be a result of remembering sexual abuse. The tendency to transform psychological symptoms into physical ones, however, may be associated with the tendency to dissociate. Feelings and conflicts that are dissociated cannot be expressed directly. However, they are still present and may be expressed indirectly, through vague physical symptoms.

Subjects did not differ on any personality characteristics. This is somewhat surprising, especially considering that the NEO PI-R con-

tains subscales such as Fantasy Proneness and Depression. It is possible that these scales measured more than characteristics associated with dissociation and sexual abuse, such as sense of humor and irritability. This might cause an overall lower score.

In summary, sexually abused subjects who reported memory loss shared many of the same experiences and symptoms as sexually abused subjects who did not report memory loss. They also differed in several ways. They were more likely to experience fear for their lives, and abuse by persons well-known to them. They were more likely to dissociate and to report psychological symptomatology. They were not likely to have recovered their memories through therapy or hypnosis; rather, environmental triggers were the most likely cause of memory return. Survivors with memory loss were more likely to experience psychological distress as physical symptoms and to lack insight into the origin of their symptoms. Both sexually abused groups were likely to experience symptoms of depression.

A major limitation of this study is the lack of corroboration for either the sexual abuse histories or the recovery of memories. This is a shortcoming of any study based on self-report. Another possible confounding element is the probable presence in the control group of people who are amnesiac for sexual abuse. The range of DES scores in the control group went to a high of 59.29, which is in the range most often scored by people with dissociative identity disorder (Carlson & Putnam, 1993).

Future research might further explore the lack of differences in personality characteristics among these groups. This may have been due to the presence of amnesiac survivors in the control group or the homogeneity of the various groups in terms of age and life experience. Additional research is also needed on the differential characteristics of the two sexual abuse groups with larger samples.

References

Beitchman, J. H., Zucker, K. J., Hood, J. E., DaCosta, G. A., Akman, D., & Cassavia, E. (1992). A review of the long-term effects of child sexual abuse. *Child Abuse & Neglect, 16,* 101-118.

Briere, J. (1989). *Therapy for adults molested as children: Beyond survival.* New York: Springer.

Briere, J., & Conte, J. R. (1993). Self-reported amnesia for abuse in adults molested as children. *Journal of Traumatic Stress, 6,* 21-31.

Butcher, J. N., Dahlstrom, W. G., Graham, J. R., Tellegen, A., & Kaemmer, B. (1989). *Manual for the Restandardized Minnesota Multiphasic Personality Inventory Guide.* Minneapolis: University of Minnesota Press.

Carlson, E. B., & Putnam, F. W. (1993). An update on the dissociative experiences scale. *Dissociation, 6,* 16-27.

Costa, P. T., & McCrae, R. R. (1992). *Revised NEO Personality Inventory (NEO PI-R) and NEO Five Factor Inventory (NEO-FFI).* Odessa, FL: Psychological Assessment Resources.

Courtois, C. A. (1988). *Healing the incest wound: Adult survivors in therapy.* New York: W. W. Norton.

Elliott, D. M., & Briere, J. (1995). Posttraumatic stress associated with delayed recall of sexual abuse: A general population study. *Journal of Traumatic Stress, 8,* 629-648.

Finkelhor, D. (1990). Early and long-term effects of child sexual abuse: An update. *Professional Psychology: Research and Practice, 21,* 325-330.

Graham, J. R. (1990). *MMPI-2: Assessing personality and psychopathology.* New York: Oxford University Press.

Green, A. H. (1993). Child sexual abuse: Immediate and long-term effects and intervention. *Journal of the American Academy of Child and Adolescent Psychiatry, 32,* 890-902.

Norton, G. R., Ross, C. A., & Novotny, M. F. (1990). Factors that predict scores on the Dissociative Experiences Scale. *Journal of Clinical Psychology, 46,* 273-277.

Sandberg, D. A., & Lynn, S. J. (1992). Dissociative experiences, psychopathology and adjustment, and child and adolescent maltreatment in female college students. *Journal of Abnormal Psychology, 101,* 717-723.

Spiegel, D. (1986). Dissociating damage. *American Journal of Clinical Hypnosis, 29,* 122-131.

Williams, L. M. (1994). Recall of childhood trauma: A prospective study of women's memories of child sexual abuse. *Journal of Consulting and Clinical Psychology, 62,* 1167-1176.

12

Participation in Retrospective Child Sexual Abuse Research

Beneficial or Harmful? What Women Think Six Years Later

Judy L. Martin
Katherine Perrott
Eleanor M. Morris
Sarah E. Romans

The ethical question of possible harm or benefit to women who participate in child sexual abuse research has been overshadowed recently by discussion of the validity of retrospective reporting of child sexual abuse. However, the ethical implications of asking adults to recall and report traumatic experiences are something that every potential researcher in this field must consider. In this chapter we present findings about women's reactions to research focusing on child sexual abuse and mental health that have both ethical and practical im-

plications for researchers interested in pursuing links between trauma and memory.

The ethical difficulties of carrying out research with abused children are particularly problematic, and have been thoroughly reviewed (e.g., Kinard, 1985). Issues such as obtaining consent and coping with distress, as well as situations in which emotional problems or current abuse are revealed, have been discussed, though little research has been available to inform recommendations. Less formal attention has been paid to the ethical implications of

AUTHORS' NOTE: We would like to thank Dr. Jessie Anderson and Dr. Valerie Clifford, interviewers in the 1989 survey, the five interviewers for the 1995 survey, and the women of the Otago Women's Health Survey for their generous input of time and energy. Thanks also to Fiona Robertson for preparing the manuscript. This chapter is based on a presentation given by Judy Martin at Trauma and Memory: An International Research Conference, Durham, New Hampshire, July 1996.

researching trauma in adults, but our communications with other child sexual abuse researchers have assured us of keen interest in this area as well. As a result of comments and queries from other researchers, we have become aware of a number of arguments for particular caution in sexual abuse research, which we list below. Most of these concerns have been raised by reviewing and ethical committees, but we have generated some from discussions with researchers themselves.

1. A random community sample will probably include a large number of potential participants with negative experiences who would not by choice talk about their experiences.

2. Many people cope with abusive experiences through mechanisms involving denial (i.e., choosing not to talk or think about the abuse), and asking them to do so may disrupt this coping strategy (see Himelein & McElrath, 1996).

3. Victimization by child sexual abuse is still regarded by many victims as something to be ashamed of, and there is a general perception that victims are "damaged" in some way, a perception that is reinforced by research that focuses on "pathology."

4. Child sexual abuse victims are often severely traumatized by their experiences, and asking them to recount these experiences again at a time that is not of their choosing may lead to adverse mental health outcomes (see McNulty & Wardle, 1994).

5. Researchers may not have sufficient clinical experience or time to recognize and deal with the mental health sequelae of abuse interviews.

These arguments suggesting possible harm to women from inclusion in such research are at the forefront of ethical questions about retrospective child sexual abuse research, but it is surprising how little published research relating to survey participation directly addresses these issues. It is quite common to monitor reactions to research involvement through direct questioning, but the reactions are reported in an informal fashion, if at all (e.g., Martin, Anderson, Romans-Clarkson, Mullen, & O'Shea, 1993; Russell, 1986, pp. 19-37). Questions

about reactions to an interview are often asked at its end, but this approach has several disadvantages. First, the participant is asked to comment on the interview by the same person who has conducted the interview; this inhibits frankness. Second, the participant can talk only about his or her immediate reactions and not about any delayed reactions, whether positive or negative. It is possible for an initial negative outcome to become positive if the interview process precipitates some form of help seeking or leads the participant to think more closely about his or her experience. A further disadvantage of asking questions about participation at the end of interviews is that the questions are restricted to those people who have actually participated, and do not canvass the opinions of those who have refused to participate.

Most of the published data available on reactions to participation in research on sensitive subjects come from mental health research—in particular from community-based research in Australia (Henderson & Jorm, 1990; Jorm et al., 1994). These reports of a random community sample and a survey of the elderly show that more participants found the interviews beneficial than found them distressing, and the great majority of participants felt that the experience had no effect on them. Distress was found to be related to poorer mental health. Two questions—about whether the questions were distressing and whether they intruded on the participant's privacy—were answered affirmatively by people with lower social desirability scores, suggesting that social desirability may have softened answers in this area, but social desirability was not related to whether the interview changed how subjects coped with problems or felt about life, or made them feel depressed. Henderson and Jorm (1990) note that they did not gather information about the duration of effects, despite their canvassing these reactions at the end of the second wave of interviews.

Turnbull, McLeod, Callahan, and Kessler (1988) also provide information from mental health surveys showing that less than a third of participants exhibited any discomfort in an interview that included questions on both life events and mental health, with more respondents reporting relief for having been able to talk than reporting distress. This study compared clinical and lay interviewers and found that the main difference between them was that the lay interviewers reported more distress themselves at the content of some interviews. Turnbull et al. recommend more intensive interviewer training to overcome such reactions.

A two-stage survey in a community sample of women gave us the opportunity to ask about long-term reactions to involvement in child sexual abuse (CSA) research. As part of this survey, we wanted to record how women remembered and reported their participation after a 6-year interval, to provide more accurate information for those pondering the ethical implications of this research. A particular question we hoped to address was whether significant differences existed between the reactions of CSA reporters and those of non-CSA reporters; we also hoped to gather some information about what might predict negative reactions, to inform recruitment and support procedures.

Method

☐ In 1989, we surveyed 497 women about the prevalence and impact of experiences of childhood sexual abuse. Our results on the prevalence and impact of CSA in this sample have been presented elsewhere (e.g., Anderson, Martin, Mullen, Romans, & Herbison, 1993; Mullen, Martin, Anderson, Romans, & Herbison, 1993, 1994). These women were a stratified subsample of a larger postal sample of 2,250 women whose names were taken at random from the electoral rolls of the city of Dunedin in New Zealand. The electoral rolls include all people over the age of 18 who are eligible to vote in New Zealand, and as such contain records for more than 90% of the population of that age. The interview sample was selected from those less than 65 years old and included all who indicated on their postal responses that they had experienced childhood sexual abuse, along with an equal number of randomly selected women who did not report abuse. The response rate to the postal questionnaire was 73%; to the interview, 80%. Very limited infor-

mation was available on the 27% who did not participate in the postal survey. These women either were not traced or refused to participate by sending back their questionnaires unanswered, or by refusing when contacted by phone. Another group did not return their questionnaires after they had agreed to do so. Comparison of our respondents with nonrespondents on the parameters available from electoral roll data showed no difference in occupational class or whether or not they lived with a partner. Overall, our sample was similar to the demographic composition of the catchment area, except in an underrepresentation of young women below the age of 20. The response rate to the interview was 80%. When contacted for interviews, more "controls" than CSA women refused to be interviewed, but more CSA women were unavailable for other reasons, making response rates equal for both groups. The final interview groups were representative of the postal subsamples from which they were selected.

Interviews were conducted principally by two interviewers, one of whom is an arts graduate with community training in sexual abuse issues; the other is a child psychiatrist. The interviews lasted an average of 1.5 hours, and began with a standardized psychiatric interview commonly used in British and Australasian community mental health surveys—the Present State Examination (PSE; Wing, Nixon, Mann, & Leff, 1977)—and some questions on lifetime psychiatric history. This was followed by a semistructured family interview that collected data on a range of variables about parental and parent-child relations and about the participant's experiences with school, peers, and relationships. Then came an abuse interview that collected data on the participant's experiences of physical assault as an adult, child sexual abuse, and sexual assault as an adult. The questions used to determine the prevalence of CSA have been published elsewhere (Anderson et al., 1993; Martin et al., 1993). From the interview data, women were categorized as CSA cases or non-CSA cases, with six levels of child sexual abuse, ranging from noncontact abuse to intercourse. Less than half of the abused women felt that their childhood sexual abuse experiences had any sort of long-term effects on them

(Mullen et al., 1994). At the end of each interview, the interviewer informally asked the participant how she felt about the interview she had just completed. Many—whether victims of CSA or not—said they had enjoyed the opportunity to talk about themselves, though some said they had found the experience tiring and felt drained. Quite a few women expressed that they thought they had not been very useful to our research because they only had "boring" lives to relate.

Six years after the first interview (1995), we recontacted the women in this interview sample to cover several issues that were not addressed in the early research—particularly health, coping strategies, and dissociation levels—and to reexamine mental health status and stability of sexual abuse reporting. Women who were still residents in the greater Dunedin area were contacted by one of five interviewers and invited to participate in another interview. The first contact was by letter, followed some days later by a telephone call. If a woman indicated at this stage that she did not want to participate, she was asked the following:

1. The reason she did not want to take part
2. How she felt after the last interview
3. Whether the last interview was a positive, neutral, or negative experience, and why
4. What improvements she suggested for interviews of this sort

We gained ethical permission to ask nonparticipants these questions and code their answers because we felt that their feedback was essential for a balanced viewpoint, as they were the most likely to have negative feelings about the research. Refusers were told that their honest views would be particularly useful for the researchers. The women who did participate in the follow-up interviews were presented with an information sheet that made it clear that the current interviewer had no knowledge of the responses they had made last time, and that none of the interviewers from the previous stage were involved in interviewing this time. At the end of each interview, the participant was asked the following questions:

1. How clearly do you remember the last interview? [Likert scale, 1-5] What do you remember about it?
2. How did you feel after the last interview?
3. At the time, did you feel that the interview was a positive, neutral, or negative experience? Why?
4. If you remember, we asked some questions back then about child sexual abuse. How comfortable did you feel talking about the topic? [Likert scale, 1-5] How about later on? Now do you think the interview was a positive, neutral, or negative experience?

Two further questions concerned whether or not the subject had received a mailed report about the survey and whether or not she had seen any publicity about the survey in the media. Finally, the participant was asked how she felt about the interview she had just finished, and whether she had any suggestions for improving such research. Open-ended comments made in response to this and the questions above were written down as close to verbatim as possible, and the transcript was read back to the participant for verification.

The research team content analyzed into broad categories the comments made in response to open-ended questions by the first 120 participants, along with the comments of nonparticipants and all those with negative reactions. Where comparisons are made between CSA reporters and non-CSA reporters, child sexual abuse status is determined on the basis of answers in the first (1989) interviews. A report on the stability of reporting of CSA between the two stages of the survey is in preparation.

Results

☐ The second interview sample comprised 354 women still residing in Dunedin who agreed to participate. Of the eligible women, 48 refused, which gave a 12% refusal rate. A further 66 women had moved out of Dunedin, and 8 had died since the previous interview. Another 21 women could not be traced, despite strenuous efforts to do so. The final return rate for a Dunedin sample could not be determined accurately. In 1995, nonparticipants were younger

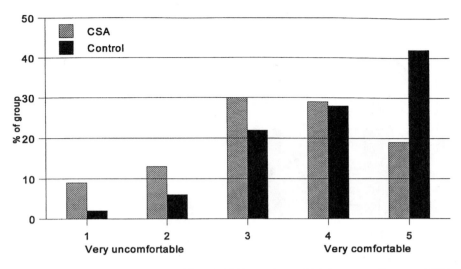

Figure 12.1. Comfort Level Talking About CSA at 1989 Interview—CSA Reporters Compared With Non-CSA Reporters (*N* = 282)

and more likely to be single than participants, which reflects the mobility of the younger women in the sample, many of whom had been students. There were no significant differences between participants and nonparticipants in regard to mental health or abuse histories, measured at the first survey.

Memories of the Last Interview

Participants were asked how clearly they remembered the interviews conducted 6 years before. There was little difference between CSA reporters and non-CSA women, with 21% of the former and 18% of the latter claiming that they did not remember the first interview at all, and only 11% and 8%, respectively, saying that they remembered clearly or very clearly. The mean for the whole sample was 2.35 (*not at all* = 1; *very clearly* = 5). For the CSA reporters, the type of abuse reported was not related to how clearly they remembered the interview. Many of the women who did not remember the last interview did not answer the subsequent questions.

Comfort With CSA Questions

There was a clear distinction between abused and nonabused women in how comfortable they

felt in 1989 talking about child sexual abuse (see Figure 12.1). More of the non-CSA group endorsed the highest comfort level than did any other level (mean 4.0), whereas the CSA group peaked at the moderately comfortable level (mean 3.4, *t* = 24.0, *p* < .001).

Reactions to the Last Interview

Exactly half (177/354) of the participants said that the previous interview had been a positive experience at the time, 109 said it had been a neutral experience, and 21 said it had been a negative experience, leaving 67 (18.9%) who did not rate their reactions. Of the 48 refusers, 36 gave responses: 9 positive, 6 negative, and 21 neutral. Differences in the responses of the abused and nonabused participants were apparent (see Figure 12.2), with abused women more likely to say the interview was a positive experience and nonabused women more likely to say it was a neutral experience. The proportion of refusers who said the last interview was a positive experience was lower than for participants, but the percentage who said it was a negative experience was almost identical. Participants who said the last interview was a positive experience said they remembered it more clearly (mean = 2.6, com-

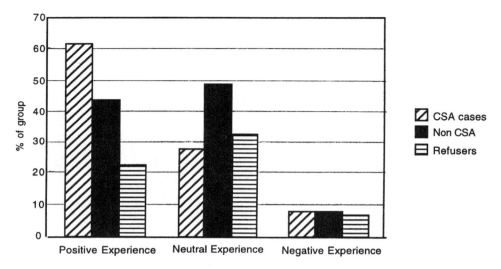

Figure 12.2. Women's Reactions in 1995 to 1989 Interview

pared with 2.3 for the other two groups; $f = 4.7$, $p < .001$). Those who said the last interview was a negative experience felt less comfortable talking about CSA (mean of 2.5, compared with 3.7 for the other groups; $f = 11.65$, $p < .001$).

In response to the question, *"Now* do you think the interview was a positive, neutral, or negative experience?" only 2% still thought it was a negative experience. However, a few of the open-ended comments suggest that some women may have believed that this question referred to the interview just completed, so these data must be treated with caution.

Variables Associated With Reactions to the Interview

Those who evaluated the previous interview positively were more likely to report CSA, whereas controls were more likely to have neutral responses ($\chi^2 = 12.24$, $df = 2$, $p = .002$). Positive reactions to the interview were associated with a higher symptom score on the 1989 PSE mental health interview. Those with negative evaluations also had higher 1989 PSE scores compared with the neutral group ($f = 5.35$, $df = 2$, $p = .005$); this was even more true for 1995, when the mean PSE score for the negative group had increased, whereas the mean had dropped for the other two groups ($f = 9.40$,

$df = 2$, $p < .001$; see Figure 12.3). Negative evaluators were also less likely to have any school qualifications ($\chi^2 = 8.00$, $df = 2$, $p = .02$). The variables that were not associated with the evaluation of the interview included variables about the family of origin, age, and marital status of the woman; who the first interviewer was; and beliefs about child sexual abuse. For CSA victims, reaction to the interview was not related to the type or duration of the abuse, any perpetrator details, or whether the woman had disclosed her abuse before the last interview.

Reasons for Negative Evaluations

A total of 27 women (21 participants and 6 refusers) gave reasons for their negative evaluations. In the previous survey, 14 had reported experiences of childhood sexual abuse. Reasons for negative evaluations seemed to fall into three main areas, and some women expressed more than one reservation.

First, some women had varying degrees of difficulty talking about their negative experiences, particularly sexual abuse experiences ($n = 11$). Some examples of their comments follow:

Refuser: Knocked a lot out of me. Brought back terrible memories. . . . wouldn't like to go through it again.

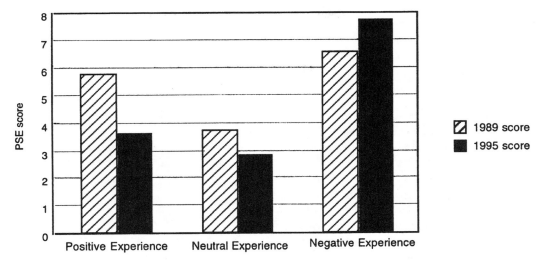

Figure 12.3. Psychiatric Symptom Scores by Reactions to Interview

Participant: It had been a bit more of an ordeal than I had anticipated. . . . it has forced me to remember the assault that I had successfully put out of my mind—did not like admitting it at the time and having to go over again.

Participant who declined to answer child sexual abuse questions at both stages of the survey: I relived the past—I couldn't sleep after it, I started taking tablets.

Second, some had doubts about the value or the relevance of the research ($n = 10$). This reaction included responses from women who did not think the research was relevant to them or did not understand how their replies could help the research. For example:

Participant: I felt I didn't know what use it would be for anyone. I didn't feel I was contributing. They should have talked to people that had more problems.

This group included a few women who were skeptical about the whole basis of the research and thought the researchers were trying to make child sexual abuse seem more prevalent than it actually was, or to exaggerate its effects. None of this group reported child sexual abuse.

Refuser [comments paraphrased by interviewer]: Felt angry after interview. Felt that the results were looking to prove abuse exists at a high rate. . . . Does not believe the results. Does not believe abuse is that high. She put the results in the rubbish when she read them.

Participant: I felt the interviewer was twisting things to get the answers she wanted. I got the impression she thought I should have something bad to say about my father.

Participant: I felt I had probably been sexually abused and didn't recognize it, and I resented it for my father, brother, and my friends.

Third, some women had negative responses to the interview process itself. These took various forms, including dislike of the interviewer's behavior and particular parts of the interview; some commented on their own moods and reactions at the time ($n = 9$).

Participant: This was because of the way the interviewer was, but when I read the results I saw that it did do something positive.

Refuser: Very uncomfortable experience with interviewer. . . . Did not like her manner from the start.

Participant: I'm just pleased to see the back of interviewers in general, I get so many of them.

Participant: I was uncomfortable at not being very honest about how I was feeling.

Participant: I felt a bit cheated that they had got that out of me. A bit angry. I thought it was about women's mental health and I hadn't expected it [i.e., child sexual abuse questions].

Reasons for Positive Evaluations

Common reasons expressed for positive evaluations included finding it helpful to talk about things not usually talked about; these women often specifically mentioned childhood sexual abuse.

Participant: Nobody prompts you to look at yourself in this way, and it's probably quite profitable to do so.

Participant: It puts these things in perspective in your own mind by talking to someone who doesn't know you. It clarifies things for you.

Participant: I felt relieved, it was really nice to be able to talk about things that had been bottled up for many years.

Participant: I talked about things I never talked about—that chap for instance. I used it as a valve.

Some women commented favorably on the interview as something that had changed how they felt and acted about their childhood sexual abuse experiences in particular.

Participant: Let me say that there are a lot of women like me out there. At age 12 I didn't do anything about it or later when raped. In retrospect I feel I handled it badly.

Participant: Probably the first time I have ever acknowledged to anyone anything happening to me in the way of abuse. . . . You have to acknowledge it and know you were not responsible so that you can get on with normal life. . . .

It's a lot easier to deal with now than 5 years ago, it was locked away for me and finally dealing with it in my own mind I know it's no longer affecting my life.

Others commented on feeling they were contributing to useful research as well.

Participant: I felt it was good to talk and get things off my chest. You felt you were helping.

Participant: I've done it to do something that makes me feel pleased that I can give something.

Participant: Anything that gets you thinking is a positive thing—anything that is going to help society and women as a whole is beneficial.

Participant: Made me think about myself quite a bit, and also interested in helping with research if it was going to achieve something worthwhile.

Participant: It's good that people take an interest in females.

A few women said it made them thankful that they had led such uneventful lives.

Participant: Good. I think I felt very lucky to be normal. A lot to be grateful for.

Reasons for Neutral Evaluations

There was a relatively large group of women who had neutral reactions to the interview and who doubted that they were providing useful information.

Participant: Because my experience didn't sound the sort of thing they wanted to hear.

Refuser: I felt that I had little to contribute—I had a very normal upbringing.

Some did not find the topics personally relevant or interesting:

Participant: There wasn't really anything major for me that came up.

Participant: Didn't gain anything out of it personally apart from subsequent discussion with sister, but happy to participate.

Participant: Almost as boring as my answers to this.

Some women's "neutral" evaluations would probably have been better described as mixed, in that they personally found some aspects of the interview uncomfortable, but recognized the importance of the research:

Participant: Someone's got to do it.

Many women cited their lack of clear memories as the reason for their neutral evaluations.

A minority of women suggested improvements to this type of research. Most of the suggestions were directed at shortening the length of the interview and making some questions easier to understand.

Discussion

☐ Our findings about long-term perceptions of research participation have practical and ethical implications for those involved in the design of retrospective research to investigate child sexual abuse and other traumatic events. In discussing the ethical implications of this research, it is important to remember the relative proportions of positive and negative reactions: Exactly 10 times more CSA reporters remembered the interview as positive than remembered it as negative. The number of women who felt positive was twice the number who evaluated the interview either neutrally or negatively. As well, CSA reporters were significantly more likely to evaluate positively than were non-CSA reporters. It is worth noting that most women felt that after 6 years, they retained very incomplete memories of the first interview. A small number of women staunchly maintained that they were sure they had not had an interview at all; a much larger number knew that they had done so but remembered very little about it. It was interesting but unexpected that memories of the interview were not related to the sort of trauma that the participants had experienced. We expected

that women who related the most invasive or chronic abuse would have the clearest memories, probably because those were the interviews that the interviewers themselves remembered, but this was not the case.

One potential ethical criticism of CSA research, as we have noted above, is that a community sample will probably include a large number of potential participants with negative experiences who would not talk about their experiences by choice—the implication being that asking them to do so may be harmful. This is related to another possible criticism, that inviting such participation is going against the suppression or denial that abused women frequently use as a coping strategy. In this research, previous disclosure of CSA was not related to whether women had positive or negative evaluations of the interview. From the responses analyzed, there were many more positive than negative comments about the benefits of talking about CSA. Some women noted that although they found it difficult to talk about the abuse at the first interview, they felt it was much easier the second time around. It is regrettable that questions distinguishing between short- and long-term reactions were ambiguous, so that the drop from 8% to 2% cannot be accepted as confirmation of increased comfort with the subject. The comments from those with negative reactions show that the potential for distress does exist, even though only 3 of the nearly 200 CSA reporters canvassed reported this reaction to a marked degree. The comment of the woman who chose not to answer CSA questions but was distressed by returning memories shows that even the commonly used option of "passing" is not a complete protection.

One view that seems to receive some support from reactions to this survey is the suggestion that CSA research that focuses on pathology reinforces the general perception that victims are damaged in some way. In our 1989 interviews, we were comparing a group of sexually abused women with a group of non-sexually abused women, with the expectation that abused women would be more likely to report negative social and mental health outcomes. Many participants appeared to sense this design. Unfortunately, some made two incorrect assumptions as well: first, that we expected all sexually abused women to be negatively affected, and, second, that participants who had neither abuse nor pathology to report were somehow less valuable to the research. The first belief could inhibit women from disclosing stigmatizing abuse, as some of the comments quoted in the preceding section suggest. The second misconception could conceivably lead women with no trauma to exaggerate insignificant incidents to be helpful, although it is important to add that we never found any example of any woman doing so. Most participants were inclined to minimize rather than maximize their abuse experiences (see Martin et al., 1993).

Possible misconceptions of the purpose of abuse research is a serious concern that does need to be addressed in future research. It might be helpful if any information sheet that includes information about possible negative outcomes of child sexual abuse could also include a statement to the effect that the majority of child sexual abuse victims do not show negative outcomes. Also, it is important to provide a range of material in the schedule, so that all women feel they have something relevant to contribute. Perhaps now that it has been established that childhood sexual abuse and other adverse life events do make some contribution to later problems, for some women it is timely to focus on the majority of abused women who do not show significant negative effects and validate their ways of coping with trauma.

As we mentioned at the outset of this chapter, one fear that is frequently relayed to us is that CSA victims are often severely traumatized by their experiences, and asking them to recount these experiences again at a time not of their choosing may lead to depression or posttraumatic stress disorder. The comments of our participants suggest that this phenomenon does exist, but it was a serious problem for only a tiny proportion of the CSA victims who were interviewed, and we have no clear picture of how long their negative reactions lasted. The negative responses of even this small group show that care must be taken to ensure that women who appear ambivalent or unwilling are not pressured to participate in such research. The finding that women with high psychiatric symptom scores felt either positive or negative reactions to the interview is slightly different from Henderson and Jorm's (1990) finding that negative reaction was associated with psychiatric illness. Our bimodal distribution makes it difficult to make predictions about benefits of research participation for survivors with serious mental health problems. With quantifiable data such as those presented here, it may now be possible for information sheets to express what appears to be the true situation: that although the majority of women with abuse histories find it interesting or helpful to participate in research of this nature, there are a small number who find that such participation brings back memories that are difficult to deal with, and women who are afraid this may happen should think carefully before agreeing to participate. In the end, any judgment balancing the possibility of harm to a few with the positive reactions of the majority of victims and the wider importance of the specific research will need to be made by individual researchers and their ethical advisers. In this equation, the effect of the subject material on women who have not had direct experience of abuse needs to be considered as well, as some comments made by our participants indicate that some of this group found the topic offensive or upsetting, though neutral reactions were most common to this group.

It is interesting, in view of the suggestions that researchers may not have sufficient clinical experience or time to recognize and deal with the mental health sequelae of abuse interviews, that there was no difference in satisfaction ratings for the two principal interviewers: a consultant psychiatrist and a liberal arts graduate with community training in sexual abuse issues. This reinforces a similar finding by Turnbull et al. (1988). It is our experience that very few of our participants have taken up any offer of referral for treatment, and occasionally team members have been concerned about a woman who steadfastly refused any offer of help. Luckily, these situations are very few, but potential researchers need to be aware that even a well-organized support system is not a guarantee of successful intervention. This situation probably parallels the experience of most helping agencies. The interviewers commented that women who said they did address their problems after the interview usually described this decision as something that evolved gradually from their reactions to the interview. This suggests that making participants aware of sources of help available may be useful, and that this could include the research team at any time in the future.

This investigation into the ethical implications of abuse research participation by abused and nonabused women has been only an initial study in an area where reliable information is scarce. In future research, it will be important to distinguish unambiguously between short-term and long-term reactions, and to distinguish more clearly between responses that are neutral or indifferent and those in which positive and negative reactions are mixed. Despite some of these cautions, we believe that our research has shown that participation in well-conducted research on traumatic childhood memories has a much lower potential for harm than has been feared.

References

Anderson, J. C., Martin, J. L., Mullen, P. E., Romans, S. E., & Herbison, P. (1993). Prevalence of childhood sexual abuse experiences in a community sample of women. *Journal of the American Academy of Child and Adolescent Psychiatry, 32,* 911-919.

Henderson, A. S., & Jorm, A. F. (1990). Do mental health surveys disturb? *Psychological Medicine, 20,* 721-724.

Himelein, M. J., & McElrath, J. V. (1996). Resilient child sexual abuse survivors: Cognitive coping and illusion. *Child Abuse & Neglect, 20,* 747-758.

Jorm, A. F., Henderson, A. S., Scott, R., MacKinnon, A. J., Korten, A. E., & Christensen, H. (1994). Do mental health surveys disturb? Further evidence. *Psychological Medicine, 24,* 233-237.

Kinard, E. M. (1985). Ethical issues in research with abused children. *Child Abuse & Neglect, 9,* 301-311.

Martin, J. L., Anderson, J. C., Romans-Clarkson, S. E., Mullen, P., & O'Shea, M. (1993). Asking about child sexual abuse: Methodological implications of a two-stage survey. *Child Abuse & Neglect, 17,* 385-394.

McNulty, C., & Wardle, J. (1994). Adult disclosure of sexual abuse: A primary cause of psychological distress? *Child Abuse & Neglect, 18,* 549-555.

Mullen, P. E., Martin, J. L., Anderson, J. C., Romans, S. E., & Herbison, G. P. (1993). Child sexual abuse and mental health in adult life. *British Journal of Psychiatry, 163,* 721-732.

Mullen, P. E., Martin, J. L., Anderson, J. C., Romans, S. E., & Herbison, G. P. (1994). The effect of child sexual abuse on social, interpersonal and sexual function in adult life. *British Journal of Psychiatry, 165,* 35-47.

Russell, D. E. H. (1986). *The secret trauma: Incest in the lives of girls and women.* New York: Basic Books.

Turnbull, J. E., McLeod, J. D., Callahan, J. M., & Kessler, R. C. (1988). Who should ask? Ethical interviewing in psychiatric epidemiology studies. *American Journal of Orthopsychiatry, 58,* 228-239.

Wing, J. K., Nixon, J. M., Mann, S. A., & Leff, J. P. (1977). Reliability of the PSE (ninth edition) used in a population study. *Psychological Medicine, 7,* 505-516.

13

From Victim to Survivor

Recovered Memories and
Identity Transformation

Susan Warner
Kathryn M. Feltey

The interdisciplinary debate on memory and traumatic childhood experiences in the family has not, for the most part, included sociology. Family violence researchers in sociology have been grappling with how to define violence and abuse, establishing prevalence of the problem in the population, identifying factors that make a family susceptible to abuse, and delineating the outcomes and effects of living with violence in the family (Straus, 1994). To date, we have not questioned the effects of trauma on memory or focused on recovered memories of childhood trauma in our efforts to understand the dynamics of abuse in family life. In fact, few sociologists have addressed the form of abuse most likely to be linked with recovered memory: incest and sexual abuse (Finkelhor, 1984; Russell, 1986).

In this chapter, we are interested in entering the debate from a standpoint that shifts the focus of the question from the validity of memories to the meaning of memories. We are not interested in whether recovered memories are true or false—that is, whether they can be proven or substantiated. Relying on a social constructionist perspective, we assume that if individuals define their memories as real, they have real meaning, and in turn real consequences in their lives (Berger & Luckmann, 1967). Our goal is to understand the process of memory recovery and the meaning of that process to individuals who claim to have recovered memories of childhood abuse. Our theoretical framework is also influenced by the work of identity theorists. Identity is central to the claim of recovered memories; the process of recovery reveals a hidden identity (victim) and often results in the claiming of a new identity (survivor). In this chapter we focus on the experiences of four women who have recovered memories of childhood sexual abuse; we examine the meaning (process) of recovering those memories, as well as the outcome of that process (identity transformation).

Identity Theory

□ Identity theory provides the framework for our analysis. Identity involves various levels of commitment to roles, relationships, and situations (Hewitt, 1989). To self-identify as someone who has experienced childhood trauma, and for this identification to be based on information "stored" over the course of time, suggests a shifting in both perception and interpretation of one's biographical experiences. We are interested in the process of recovering memories, as well as what happens to individual identity as one moves through this process.

There are several identity issues that guide our investigation and interpretation of these data. First, the recovery of memories involves calling formerly accepted definitions of reality into question. As a result, the identity in question becomes an issue for everyone involved (other family members in particular), because the existing situational definitions are challenged as faulty or problematic. According to Hewitt (1989), "As the definition of a situation is first disrupted and then reconstituted, people carve out new roles for themselves, and in locating themselves within these new perspectives they acquire new identities" (p. 162). This process, by definition, implicates and includes other family members in such roles as participants, observers, and bystanders.

Second, assertions of identity are also assertions of motive in that when people tell themselves (and others) who they are, they tell themselves what to do (and they tell others what is to be expected from them). According to Hewitt (1989), an assertion of identity "sharply focuses attention on those situated events that are relevant to that identity" (p. 167). This process is intensified as the individual develops a sustained personal identity "by developing a sense of opposition and resistance, by imagining others who want to limit or restrict one's actions" (p. 189). Thus the identity is produced out of focused attention to relevant events and sustained through an oppositional process. For

someone recovering memories of an abusive history, the focus is on events and circumstances that support that definition, while opposition and resistance from family members (i.e., those claiming that the memories are false) serves to intensify and enhance the process of shifting identity.

Third, opposition can be clearly seen in identity conflict crisis, where, according to Baumeister (1986), the different components of identity are in conflict. One possible outcome of identity conflict crisis is achieved identity, where the individual resolves the crisis through a commitment to specific goals and values, in essence a particular identity direction. According to Baumeister, the subjective experience, the behavior, and the resolution are all stages of the process that one moves through in an identity conflict crisis. Betrayal is a central theme, so that any decision one makes results in one's betraying oneself and one's loyalty to some other persons, an ideology, or an institution (p. 215). This is manifest in the process of recovered memories of child abuse, because the family as primary unit, ideology, and social institution is challenged in fundamental ways. The individual is claiming that, as personal experience, the family was dangerous and failed to provide basic safety and security for life-course development. The ideology of the family as a haven from the perils of public life (Lasch, 1977) is also called into question, as is the family as an institutional source of order and stability.

Fourth, the decision to change is complex and may result from life events (such as childhood abuse) and chronic role strain (such that the individual is unable to perform adequately in social roles; Kiecolt, 1994). According to this model, life events and chronic role strain reduce self-esteem, self-efficacy, and sense of authenticity. As a result, the individual is motivated to change when confronted with contradictions between beliefs or between beliefs and behavior. However, several conditioning factors are necessary to move the individual into an active decision to change: identity relevance, attribution of responsibility, structural supports, belief that change is possible, perceived benefits, and social support. The recovery of memories that redefine one's childhood can be examined using these factors, because the motivation for seeking an alternative definition comes at a later point in life, when conflict arises in managing beliefs, roles, and responsibilities.

Fifth, both structural supports and social support can come in the form of reference groups. Reference groups provide a "standpoint that is used as the frame of reference by the actor" (Shibutani, 1961, p. 257). Significantly, identification with a community and adoption of its perspective provides an important avenue for change. According to Hewitt (1989), this change is about integration and the desire that people have to "be made whole" (p. 186). Thus recovered memories and opposition to them in the form of the idea of a false memory syndrome have developed as social movement and countermovement. With conflicting views about what is possible and real, these two movements provide a frame of reference, along with developed rationales and systematic support, for those who stand on both sides of the debate. Thus the individual seeking to redefine her or his identity in terms of childhood abuse has a significant resource in the existing community of professionals and survivors who can provide perspective and support for the individual's transformation. However, the false memory movement serves the same function for family members seeking to resist redefinition of their family's history and experiences in ways that contradict their definition and understanding.

Finally, in order to participate in the definition of reality, people must see themselves as a social force, rather than as victims of others or circumstances. According to Erickson (1995), this involves a concern with maintaining commitments to the self as an entity in its own right beyond role identities. This shift to the self as a "primary motivating force" allows for an understanding of action on behalf of the self, out of a biographically based perspective. For marginalized groups, such as those identifying as victims of incest, action often requires a choice between self-values and the expectations of "powerful others" (p. 138). Persons claiming memory recovery choose the right to define themselves, as well as their histories, often in direct opposition to "powerful others" in the form of family members. Further, the definitional process is biographically based, and provides the means for understanding the individual as a whole person (with all of the effects and outcomes over time), beyond specific roles held within the family and outside of it. Most important, the process enables the individual to move away from the status of victim to that of survivor, and therefore become the agent of her or his own life and definer of reality.

Method

Participants

In this chapter we report on the first stage of a research project in progress. Because the investigation is exploratory, we are using qualitative methods, interviewing women who claim to have recovered memories of sexual abuse in their childhoods. To date, four women have been interviewed. All four of the women have spoken in public about their identities as survivors of childhood sexual abuse. They were approached about the research as a result of their public statements or activism in relation to these experiences. Despite the willingness of the respondents to be identified (they have self-identified in a variety of public forums), we have protected their confidentiality by changing their names and other identifying information (e.g., names of hometowns, family businesses, schools). All of the respondents were informed about the nature of the research and signed consent forms, in keeping with the human subjects protection requirements for this project. Each was provided with an early draft of this chapter and invited to provide comments and criticisms. Our interpretation and presentation of the data met with their approval.

Procedures

Each interview was conducted in a private conference room at a university in the Midwest. The first author interviewed three women and the second author interviewed one. The interview guide was structured around a sequence of questions concerning the following: the women's lives before the recovery of memories; the process of memory recovery; the role of therapy in memory recovery; the effects of re-covering memories on the women's lives and relationships; and the impact of their experi-ences—especially the process of recovering memories—on their lives overall.

The interviews were tape-recorded, with permission from the respondents and the under-standing that they could decline to answer any question or terminate the interview at any point. All four interviews were successfully com-pleted, with an average interview time of 90 minutes. Upon completion of the interview, the interviewer and respondent chatted informally, "normalizing" the content of the interaction away from the subject of the research to less emotionally charged topics.

The data were analyzed using grounded the-ory procedures as outlined by Strauss and Cor-bin (1990). More specifically, as the study is a work in progress, the majority of the coding was "selective," in that the story line was identified with memory recovery serving as a core cate-gorical concept. Because this is a work in prog-ress, we suggest that our findings are prelimi-nary and anticipate refinement with further data collection.

The first stage of the analysis involved inde-pendent review of the interview data by both authors. We each listened to all four interview tapes, making notes about significant "turning points" in the accounts of the women inter-viewed, using the sequence of the questions as a guide (e.g., What was life like prior to memory recovery?). Then, we both separately tran-scribed each interview within the categories of the sequential process. Finally, we brought the two sets of analyses together and "matched" themes, issues, and events that both of us iden-tified as significant in the data. In this way, we identified patterns in the process of memory recovery and began to build and group catego-ries across story lines.

Descriptions of the Participants

Sally, age 42, was married, the mother of three children, and a full-time student at the time of the interview. She now remembers being

sexually abused from the age of 8 until the age of 15 by her maternal grandfather. Once she began to tell other family members about her recovered memories of childhood abuse, she discovered that there were multiple victimiza-tions in her family, with a total of 27 family members reporting some type of sexual abuse by her grandfather. He was commonly referred to as a "dirty old man" by the women in the family prior to Sally's disclosure and the dis-covery of widespread abuse.

Mary was 28 and in a committed relationship at the time of the interview. She was working two part-time jobs while completing her gradu-ate degree. She remembers being sexually abused by her two older brothers during her childhood.

Kelly was in her 30s, divorced, the mother of two elementary school-aged boys, and a full-time student at the time of the interview. She remembers being sexually abused by her pater-nal uncle when she was 5 years old.

Karen was 38, newly married, and employed full-time in a public service organization at the time of the interview. Her memories suggest to her that she was abused from infancy through her high school years. She remembers being abused by both parents, as well as being the victim of ritual abuse that involved her parents and several members of her extended family.

Findings: The Process and Meaning of Memory Recovery

Life Before the Recovery of Memories

The four women interviewed all had vague senses of discomfort about their childhoods be-fore they recalled specific experiences of abuse. As Sally said, "I was always the best girl, did everything right, but there was always the sense [that] something was wrong." The impression is that life before memory recovery was a "half-life," with something clearly out of place or missing, but not enough to give clear indication of the cause. However, none of the women defined any of their childhood experiences as sexual abuse or incest until they began the pro-cess of recovering memories. In fact, none would have defined their childhoods as abusive or unacceptable until this process began. As Sally explained: "I had some memories of uncomfortable incidences with my grandfather but nothing that I considered at the time [to be] abuse. Now that I look back on it, even what I remembered all along was abusive, but I didn't consider it abusive at the time."

Part of the reason they did not think of their childhoods as abusive is that their memories were sketchy and elusive. Karen's family joked about her inability to remember entire family vacations, and provided explanations for what was missing in her memory. She stated:

> I have a lot of scattered memories of my childhood. One of the biggest family jokes was . . . we'd go on family vacation constantly and that's where a lot of abuse took place, but they would always say that I didn't remember [the vacation] and everyone would joke about it. Because we'd go on a vacation—and I'm talking up until 9, 10, 11 years old [and] I'm still not remembering these family vacations. And what my family did, and I guess a lot of families did, is replace it with stories. The stories all of a sudden become truth. You know, how did I, for example, get a scar on my face. Well, they adapted the story to fit and years later I'm still telling the story and something finally inside of me says, you know what, I don't think that's true, I don't think that's how that happened, but I have been hearing it for so long.

Sally described her memories as "fragments, little pieces that would come back." The blanks in memory were a source of extreme frustration to these women. Mary remembered: "I would awaken in the night with just these horrible feelings. I would have a horrible dream, but then, as usual, you wake up and forget your dream but you've got all the horrible feelings left."

All four of the women recalled episodes of deep depression during their childhoods, especially their teen years, yet were never able to pinpoint the exact causes of that depression. In addition, there were other symptoms of maladjustment, as Kelly described:

> I knew from reading about incest survivors . . . that I had all the symptoms, but I had no history

of sexual abuse so what the hell was going on. I had the depression, the suicide attempts. I had the weight gain. I had the sexual promiscuity. I had the multiple pregnancies. I had all these different common classic [symptoms], screaming out, you know, "sexual abuse survivor," and I did not, I couldn't figure it out.

Although all four described their families as "normal" on the outside, each woman tells of severe dysfunction occurring away from the eyes of the public. "We had the perfect family" was a phrase that appeared in more than one interview. However, the women described their parents as alcoholic, emotionally unavailable, and physically and emotionally abusive. Kelly stated:

> My parents were emotionally unavailable to me. My mother was an alcoholic. My father's a workaholic. There's just a lot of things in the dynamics of my dysfunctional family to where I couldn't go to my parents about anything for help. Couldn't talk to them about [the abuse]. You know I just, I don't think even [then] that I would [have] thought to tell anybody. I didn't know what he did was wrong.

Karen recalled:

> The physical torture I survived [because] after a while [I would] pass out or blank out. It's the emotional abuse [that] terrified me, because one moment she would be loving and supportive and the next moment she would be knocking me down the steps. I didn't know what love was all about and that bonding was just [not there]. I'm talking about from birth until on the way to college so that is something that was probably the most damaging to me.

Two of the women reported that their mothers had also been sexually abused as children, although this was not common knowledge in the family and was not discussed until after these women were adults and had approached their mothers with their own stories and experiences. According to Kelly, her mother remembers being sexually abused: "We talked about it years later and figured out that her aunt sexually abused her." Sally's mother recounted being sexually abused by her father, who went on to abuse Sally and his other grandchildren as well.

> When I told my mother [about the abuse], she told me it had happened to her all the time my grandfather was alive. He had abused her while she was a child, abused her 'til the day he died, too. She would continue to go home with her 4 children and he would follow her around and try to fondle her. As an adult woman she could never tell him no. That was a real shock to me. I'm an adult, but you still think your mother has control.

In sum, the women felt that their parents were ineffective as caregivers and that they had failed to provide them with the proper support and protection. Once they came to perceive their parents as victims, too, the women were able to make sense of their histories.

The Process of Memory Recovery

Memory recovery was a gradual process for all four of the women. It is important to note that none of the women went from having no memories of childhood abuse to having specific memories of abuse. All of the women had some memories of particular relationships that were uncomfortable, embarrassing, fearful, or shameful. Each had told at least one other person that something had happened in a particular relationship that felt inappropriate and had negatively affected them as children. For example, Sally recalled the first time she approached the subject with her soon-to-be husband:

> We were going back to visit my grandmother, and my grandfather had died. We were going back to her house and on the way there, it must have been, now that I look back on it, . . . flashbacks as we were getting closer to the house where it all happened. And I said, there's something that you need to know about my grandfather even though he's dead. And I just told [my husband] that my grandfather had been inappropriate with me, that he had kissed me. That's probably all I ever said was that my grandfather had tried to kiss me and that's why I don't have good feelings about him. That's why I was so devoted to my grandmother because I switched all my affections to my grandmother. . . . He believed me. He got angry and I remember his reaction was anger at my grandfather which made

me feel good because I was angry at him too. Then we put it aside and didn't discuss it anymore.

What constituted a recovery of memory for these women was first identifying a certain behavior or action and then defining it as abusive. Thus the process was more one of memory reconstruction and elaboration than one of total recall. Language was important for understanding what had happened. Meaning is communicated in part through language, and in particular by assigned labels. Without language, the women's experiences were unlabeled and misinterpreted for years, as demonstrated in this exchange between Sally and the interviewer:

Sally: I lived in a very sheltered world and didn't know all this happened to people. I didn't even have terms to explain what happened to me as a child. I had to learn those terms and I had to learn them on my own, by reading. I was so naive about things [and learned by] just stumbling on them.
Interviewer: And what would those words do when you came across them? What would your reaction to them be?
Sally: It would like click, it would be like, yeah, that's what that was. I didn't know that anal sex even happened and when I read it I thought, oh, that's what that was. I didn't know all these things. I was so sheltered from things.

Thus the women did not always know exactly what had happened, but that had less to do with memory lapse than with not understanding what was occurring and not having a conceptual framework for interpreting those events over time.

Obtaining a framework—in the form of language and models of interpretation—was important in their reconstruction of their childhoods as abusive. This information came through a process of self-education, as the symptoms of stress began to interfere in their abilities to function effectively in their adult lives. Three of the women cite reference sources, such as the book *The Courage to Heal* (Bass & Davis, 1988), as instrumental to their memory recovery process. "*The Courage to Heal* really opened my eyes, started me on a journey," said Sally. Others gained understanding through listening to others talk about their life histories and experiencing a recognition or familiarity, as described by Kelly:

> It came up after an Overeaters Anonymous meeting. We were sitting around talking and we happened to be talking about how parents abuse their children and [the] different ways we were abused and how that contributed to our eating disorders, our compulsive eating behavior. And I think somebody else mentioned that they had been sexually abused, incested, and I said oh well I, I, there's no incest in my family, my father never touched me, you know, my father never did. But, then I mentioned what his younger brother had done to me when I was 5. And all the conversation around the table stopped. Everybody looked at me because I was in complete denial or totally unaware that what my uncle had done to me could have had the effect of starting the ball rolling for me [so that I became] a victim over and over again through various offenders.

Some of their memories of childhood were not readily available to them, some were hazy or simply "lost" in that they were not there when they thought about their childhoods. Once they started the process of labeling events in their childhoods as abusive, these "lost" memories came back in the form of flashbacks, body memories, smells, nightmares, and fragments of scenes, such as hands appearing on their bodies or someone walking in the shadows. Often they were triggered by certain events or situations from their pasts. Sally returned to her grandfather's house, where he had abused her.

> I had a lot of confirmation when I went back to the house that was still standing then. By then my grandmother was dead, but one summer I went back and there was a cellar where all of us were abused. I kept remembering that there was a lock on the door. I kept remembering a board that would slide over the inside of the door and no one else remembered it. When I went back, I found out that the door actually did lock from the inside and that was a real important memory to me because why would anybody make this, it was a real crude homemade type of lock that you could lock from inside the cellar. Why would that have been

like that except to be able to lock yourself inside and away from others.

For her, the "evidence" of the cellar lock confirmed her recalled memories. Karen, who remembered ritual abuse in her history, much of it occurring outdoors, found that even a walk in the woods would trigger a memory or a flash of feeling.

Only one of the women was able to obtain independent confirmation of her experiences in the form of corroboration from independent witnesses or others victimized in the same way. None obtained a confession from the accused. In fact, for two of the women there was direct denial that any abuse had taken place. Only Sally was supported, when members of her mother's family began to share their stories of abuse with her.

The Role of Therapy

Much of the work of memory recovery was accomplished alone. As Karen said, "All of my recovery I've done, like a lot of survivors, on my own, recovering memories and then going to therapy and finding support for what I already know is true." All four of the women sought professional help as they began to realize that there was a history of abuse in their lives. They were often frightened and confused, sometimes questioning their own sanity, as Karen describes:

> I was going to seek therapy for something and I was putting names to things that really they were just starting to write books about. [It was] scary at first. Probably a couple of times in my recovery in the last 6 years I have questioned my sanity. The first was when the memories of ritual abuse came. The incest was why I [felt] crazy. The ritual abuse was . . . I remember telling my friend who I was on the trip with, I am going off the side of the earth and I'm not coming back. I remember laying on the ground and pounding my head, not hard, but pounding my head on the ground and saying I feel like I am in between heaven and hell and hell is winning.

Therapy was not always helpful. For example, at times therapists were unwilling to deal with the issue of incest, or were not sensitive enough in the approach taken with these women. Sally's initial experience in therapy generated a sense of powerlessness, as she described:

> I got involved with a therapist that was a real crackpot. It was a really bad experience. . . . I went in saying I was a victim of sexual abuse and I haven't dealt with it. She climbs up on her desk and sits cross-legged on her desk and the first thing she started doing was berating my parents for not having seen this in my life because I related to her that I had been depressed as a teenager and a lot of other things. She started on my parents which I wasn't ready to accept at that point. . . . I went back to her again and her tone was not what I was looking for. Her tone was really aggressive and she continued to sit on her desk which really bugged me because it was a power thing, you know. She's sitting cross-legged up on her desk and here I am down in a chair and now that I look back on it, that was the major thing that bothered me, although it sounds funny. I never put myself in positions where I was powerless because I learned a long time ago not to do that and I felt very powerless in that situation.

Mary recalled her first experience in therapy:

> I remember trying to deal with it when I was seeing a therapist and she didn't want to deal with it. . . . I brought it up and I initiated the questions and she just didn't want to deal with it and it was almost 10 years later when I started dealing with it again.

Three of the women attended group sessions that focused specifically on incest and found this to be immensely satisfying. It was only through the support of either a good therapist or other women who had similar experiences that these women felt they were able to face their pasts. "Therapy allowed me to be realistic about what was going on . . . call my family dysfunctional," Sally said. Kelly noted:

> In therapy, later, when I went over that with my counselor, and she took me back in an age regression to that moment, I had a body flashback. And I felt the physical feelings that maybe I couldn't have, couldn't feel as a child or couldn't allow myself to feel. It was horrible. 'Cause what happened

when I was going over what he did, when I was telling about it in therapy, was that my genitals started throbbing and I got this flushed horrible, it was a sexual feeling but it was horrible because I was a child and you know that's when I finally, it finally came—became real for me that what he did to me was wrong and really fucked me up.

Effects of Recovered Memories on Relationships

Confrontation was also a part of the memory recovery process for these women. Karen confronted both her mother and father in person, whereas Mary chose to write a letter to her mother, followed by a newsletter sent to every member of her family. Sally found that breaking the silence in her family opened the door to memories shared with 26 other family members who were also victimized. Other families, like Kelly's, had trouble accepting the recovered memories: "My mother was like, 'Oh we don't have to talk about it. You don't have to tell everybody.'" The interviewer asked her, "But they believed you? Or were they doubtful?" She answered:

> Um, they were . . . they minimized. My parents . . . I had to drill into their heads what I had learned, of what the significance was, of what he did and what other things had happened to me. But see, my parents didn't want to look at it because that would mean they would have to admit their guilt and not being there for me and not protecting me and not being aware that something was wrong.

For others, the confrontation meant the end of any relationship with their parents when their parents would not accept what they were claiming. Karen said, "[I had a] confrontation with my mother and I remember thinking, it doesn't get any worse than this, I mean, I am completely alone and I feel crazy half the time, I mean, the memories are coming and I just don't know what to do."

They felt a need to tell their stories once they had memories of their childhoods that they defined as abusive. It was important to "break the silence." Sally said: "As I tell my story, it gets easier every time. I find it freeing to talk about it. If [people] are not able to accept it, that's their problem. I tell pretty much everybody. This needs to be understood as a real problem for women." Often this was uncomfortable for their families. Kelly stated: "I knew [my mother] didn't want me to tell anybody. But I was fucking tired of keeping it to myself. It was important to me that the people in my life that I loved, understand me." Telling is not only part of recovery, it is about establishing and supporting an identity as survivor. Mary, for example, drew a parallel between being gay and talking about that in public forums with the goal of educating and enlightening and being an incest survivor and writing and performing a play about that.

Another critical step in the recovery process included forgiveness of themselves and their perpetrators. Kelly stated:

> I'm not saying you have to do it right away, but when I don't forgive my perpetrators, I bash people in my life today and I want them to be perfect because I want them to make up for everything that my mother and my father didn't do for me. And I'm like 4 years old, sitting there whining about something and it's like, a lot of bad things happen to people. There are no guarantees.

Often, this forgiveness included a spiritual dimension. Each survivor recounted the importance of developing reliance on a source of power beyond this world. Sally said: "My Christianity has allowed me to forgive, to just put it behind me. I'm finished with this and I'm no longer going to allow it to control my life." Karen, a devout Christian at this point in her life, said: "I want to go through life every day, to the best of my ability, [as] . . . a testimony to God and to healing, to grace, and to the fact of the power of unconditional love that we have, despite how many times we've been abused and by whom. Spiritually, forgiveness allows a release, allows God to do his thing."

However, forgiveness was not an easy answer. For these women, forgiveness did not offer excuses for the abuse they had suffered, nor did it mean that the former relationships could continue. Sally described her frustration with her pastor's encouragement for her to forgive, which to him meant putting it in the past

and forgetting about what had happened. Forgiveness is not absolution; although Karen told her perpetrators that she forgave them, she still found it necessary to break off all contact with her family in order to feel "normal" in her life:

> The denial [in the family] is so thick. It's just like toxin in my bloodstream you know. Today I choose to have people in my life who are supportive and if I feel like somebody is not supportive I'll just say I'm going to spend less time with that person. So, to me, my family, complete denial is really toxic to me. Kinda like avoiding liquor stores, I just avoid it.

Impact of Memory Recovery Overall

The process of recovery has moved these women from the half-lives they experienced before their reclaimed memories to lives full with peace and purpose. They have a commitment to share their stories with others who are still struggling; in a sense, their understanding has given new meaning to their lives. Mary and Karen coauthored a play, using their journal entries as the dialogue, which they perform before a variety of audiences detailing the process of their recovery.

All four of the women claimed that their relationships with others have improved and that they are better able to make wiser choices about the priorities in their lives. They have a realistic outlook on what life has to offer them now, as Karen described:

> I guess I had that pink cloud thing where once I thought I had the memories recovered, a lot of them, that life would be grand. I forgot the fact that living is a big problem. It's tough and recovery has taught me how to handle those problems. Not so much that every day is going to be blissful but for me I've learned that it can be even and despite what is happening. I can have a serenity inside myself.

As might be expected, the women are deeply concerned about what they consider to be the backlash toward memory recovery. Sally offered her view on why family members might deny that this has occurred, deny that it is even a possibility in their family: "Maybe abusers don't believe it themselves. Maybe, to live with themselves, *they* have to repress it." So the false memories, according to this perspective, may reside within the abusive adult and the other family members who share in the denial, rather than within the victim who tries to share her or his "truth." Karen stated that she can understand why someone would recant recovered memories:

> I can understand why the backlash is there. It's very painful. When somebody recants a story, I have no trouble believing somebody would recant. You start going through memories and you realize that your mother or father or somebody you really care about has done this to you and you have two choices. You can move forward and say okay, I'm going to take it or I'm going to turn around and say I'll take what I can get now and I'll recant.

None doubted the stories of women who have claimed to recover memories. As Kelly stated:

> I really have a hard time [with] this issue of people saying that therapists put false memories into the patient's head. I watched the other women in my group, when it was their turn to talk. And you can see the pain when it's the real stuff. You can see it on their faces in the way they hold their bodies, their tears, the pain, the, you can see it. And I suppose what I would say is don't presume to counsel someone about this issue unless you are also a survivor yourself.

Ultimately, the goal was to incorporate the reconstruction of their biographies into their current and future lives—to use their new identities as survivors as a springboard into a future that includes this reality. Karen said:

> For the past 6 years it's been, I'm a survivor, I'm a survivor. Now that's part of who I am, I mean I think we are all survivors of something, but I want to try to . . . close that chapter in my life and take all this stuff and focus the recovery stuff and survivor agency and focus more on living today and working with survivors of all different types of trauma and really bringing that message out, especially with children.

Discussion

☐ The women interviewed shared their understanding of the process of memory recovery, based on their experiences. They described similar trajectories: a vague sense of "something wrong"; exposure to someone else's story or information about abuse that "triggered" something for them in terms of their own experiences; reading and research into the subject matter of family abuse; redefining and reconstructing their life experiences as abusive and as causing or contributing to the stress-related symptoms (depression, suicidal feelings) in their adult lives; work with a professional therapist to gain understanding and direction; developing an identity as a survivor (rather than victim); and a sense of acceptance and improvement in their symptoms and life circumstances.

As suggested by identity theory, chronic role strain can provide motivation for change (Kiecolt, 1994). In our study, all of the women reported a sense of discomfort and disease in their lives prior to their recovery of memories. They all had a vague sense of "something wrong," without a discernible cause. They all knew that pieces of their lives were missing in terms of specific memories (e.g., family vacations, time spent with a particular relative). They all suffered from various manifestations of stress: depression, suicide ideation, overeating, alcohol abuse, multiple pregnancies. The chronic role strain experienced as a result of the dysfunction in their lives became increasingly troublesome and disruptive. They were highly motivated to understand and find explanations for the problems in their lives.

Calling into question their childhood experiences, these women challenged the existing definitions of their families' lives (Hewitt, 1989). In making the claim that they were abused as children, and that the abuse had shaped outcomes in their adult lives, they asserted a new identity as well as motive (Hewitt, 1989). As a result, for the time period of memory recovery, their identities were centered on their reconstructed histories. In addition, opposition to their claims of abuse in the form of family denial and the larger false memory movement served to sustain the formation of their new identities as survivors (Hewitt, 1989). Another source of conflict in the process was their own internal struggles over destroying the image of their family life as "normal." In affirming their identities as survivors, they betrayed their families (Baumeister, 1986), resulting in lost relationships. The resolution of the conflict was the achieved identity of survivor, with a high degree of commitment to this role and to the dissemination of information about abuse and recovered memories in the larger community (Baumeister, 1986).

Structural supports for redefining and reconstructing their lives (Kiecolt, 1994) were available in the form of an emerging literature on the experience and effects of early abuse, for example, *The Courage to Heal* (Bass & Davis, 1988). Other sources of information included support groups (e.g., for specific disorders, such as overeating) and popular culture. Something would "click" and the women would research further, developing a framework that "explained" their situations, their feelings, their experiences. This reference to and identification with therapeutic models of recovery provided a community perspective, a reference group, an avenue for change (Shibutani, 1961). The process was one of "naming and claiming." At this point the women were able to identify experiences that they remembered with the labels and information provided by these sources. Other experiences were not readily available to them, but came in the form of feelings, sensations, physical symptoms, and fleeting images or impressions. This led them to believe that there was more to their histories than they had previously thought, and to seek further assistance with the recovery process.

Therapy provided social support and reinforced the belief that change was possible (Kiecolt, 1994). Therapy was seen as a safe setting in which to explore the memories that the women were beginning to identify and label. For some, this happened on a weekly or biweekly basis, and for one it was a 30-day treatment program; another experienced a combination of treatment models. One important activity in therapy was the linking of memory with feelings, because the women were detached emotionally from their experiences of abuse. Another was support for the women's version of reality. That is, the women felt supported and believed by their therapists. None of the women felt that a therapist had been coercive or suggestive in the process of memory recovery. In fact, the women would question their own memories, suggesting that if something so horrible had happened, surely they would have remembered it more immediately and vividly. The therapists' responses provided support and validation. The therapists acted as guides, but, in the experiences of these women, did not contribute hypothetical scenarios or explanations for their situations or conditions.

All of the women felt that their lives are better, fuller, richer, and healthier since they have recovered these memories and their histories of abuse. In other words, there were very real benefits (Kiecolt, 1994) attached to the process of recovering memories and claiming a history of sexual abuse. Contrary to much of what is written in the popular press about the negative effects of recovered memories, the women we interviewed claimed to have better lives as a result of this process. And it was a process—the women did not move from prememory to postmemory without a transition that was often experienced as terrifying, agonizing, and crisis-filled. However, all four of the women indicated that this transition was worth the final results, and that living with their memories is preferable to the half-lives they had before.

The process of memory recovery for these women ended with their forging new identities as survivors, rather than victims. They were reconstituted as "whole" selves, based on self-definition supported by a new set of references from the recovery movement. They see themselves as a social force (Erickson, 1995), as demonstrated by their public activism around the issues of remembering abuse, speaking out, and moving beyond victimization to survival. The transition, although costly, gave each of these women a sense of personal power as she defined the conditions and terms of her own history and life.

Limitations

☐ There are a number of limitations to this research project. First, because this is research in progress, the findings are tentative and preliminary. Further investigation with adults who have recovered memories may contribute other themes and patterns not discerned in this early effort. Related to this is the size of the sample. At this point, four women have been interviewed. Although case studies can allow for great insights (see, e.g., Russell, 1995), our goal is to identify commonalities across cases. Therefore, a larger, more heterogeneous sample (e.g., diversified in terms of race, class, sexuality) would be beneficial to our ongoing research. Also, we did not explore the influence of these identities on the memory recovery process; this limits our conclusions. Despite these limitations, this study makes an important contribution in shifting the focus away from the validity of recovered memories to the meaning of those memories for those who have recovered them.

Conclusion

☐ Identity formation, development, and change constitute a vehicle for exploring the recovery of memories of childhood abuse. The debate has revolved around the truth or validity of such claims and the ways that memory functions over time. This work represents another way of conceptualizing this phenomenon, another way of "getting at" the way that memory functions in adult identity. We have identified the ways in which memory recovery has influenced and shaped the adult identities of four women. The findings of this research suggest that memories of abuse, although traumatic in the process of recovery, can bring about positive changes in the lives of individuals. This warrants further investigation, especially in light of the claim that lives are being destroyed by "false" claims of recovered memories. Clearly,

the lives of these women—in terms of their own perceptions of personal wholeness, integration, and meaning—have been enhanced. These findings also suggest that there is a process involved in the recovery of memories, with stages of transition that are dependent upon a number of factors. Further study of this process, with specific attention to the relationships among factors, is called for. Not only will this bring the experiences of those with recovered memories to the center of the debate, which we have attempted to do, but it will contribute to our understanding of how identities are developed, maintained, and changed over time.

References

Bass, E., & Davis, L. (1988). *The courage to heal: A guide for women survivors of child sexual abuse.* New York: Harper & Row.

Baumeister, R. F. (1986). *Identity: Cultural change and the struggle for self.* New York: Oxford University Press.

Berger, P. L., & Luckmann, T. (1967). *The social construction of reality: A treatise in the sociology of knowledge.* Garden City, NY: Doubleday.

Erickson, R. J. (1995). The importance of authenticity for self and society. *Symbolic Interaction, 18,* 121-214.

Finkelhor, D. (1984). *Child sexual abuse: New theory and research.* New York: Free Press.

Hewitt, J. P. (1989). *Dilemmas of the American self.* Philadelphia: Temple University Press.

Kiecolt, J. K. (1994). Stress and the decision to change oneself: A theoretical model. *Social Psychology Quarterly, 57,* 49-63.

Lasch, C. (1977). *Haven in a heartless world.* New York: Basic Books.

Russell, D. E. H. (1986). *The secret trauma: Incest in the lives of girls and women.* New York: Basic Books.

Russell, D. E. H. (1995). "I didn't remember for 33 years": An incest survivor tells her story. *Journal of Psychohistory, 23,* 149-190.

Shibutani, T. (1961). *Society and personality.* Englewood Cliffs, NJ: Prentice Hall.

Straus, M. A. (1994). *Beating the devil out of them: Corporal punishment in American families.* New York: Macmillan.

Strauss, A. L., & Corbin, J. (1990). *Basics of qualitative research: Grounded theory procedures and techniques.* Newbury Park, CA: Sage.

PART III

COGNITIVE AND PHYSIOLOGICAL PERSPECTIVES ON TRAUMA AND MEMORY

14

False Childhood Memories

Research, Theory, and Applications

Ira E. Hyman, Jr.
Erica E. Kleinknecht

A few years ago, memory researchers (e.g., Lindsay & Read, 1994; Loftus, 1993) and others (e.g., Ofshe & Watters, 1993) began questioning the validity of some recovered memories of childhood sexual abuse and other trauma. The issue was raised in response to legal cases and numerous other cases portrayed in the mass media. In the instances that first drew attention, people (usually women) with no previous histories of abuse recovered memories of abuse over the course of therapy. In these cases, individuals (usually therapists) had repeatedly suggested abuse as the cause of the clients' problems. In light of an extensive history of memory experiments documenting that people make memory errors, memory researchers argued that some recovered memories were likely to be false. Making the argument concerning false childhood memories, memory researchers cited evidence accrued from research on the misinformation effect (Lindsay & Read, 1994; Loftus, 1993). The misinformation effect is a common and easily demonstrated memory error. In misinformation effect studies, participants (usually college students) are shown videotapes or slide shows of crimes or accidents. Later, misleading information about the events (commonly referred to as misinformation) is given to the students. Typical misinformation might be the suggestion that the participant viewed a stop sign instead of a yield sign, a hammer instead of a screwdriver, or a man with a mustache instead of a clean-shaven man. Upon further questioning, participants often unintentionally incorporate the suggestions into their recollections of the original events. These studies demonstrate that suggestions can modify pieces of memory for observed events. The misinformation effect research has been applied to therapy situations in which suggestions about the past are made. For example, consider a person who has experienced a benign childhood (the original event). Several years later, someone suggests that abuse may have been a part of that childhood (the misinformation). Eventually, after several such suggestions,

175

the person includes abuse as a part of the story of childhood.

It seems reasonable, however, to wonder whether the misinformation research tapped a cognitive process that would lead one to accept a whole, emotional, yet false memory. The misinformation studies do not directly imply that a false memory of a complete event can be created by suggestion, because several differences between the misinformation experiments and therapy situations make generalization risky. For example, in the experiments, aspects of an event are changed in response to misleading suggestions, whereas in therapy, entire life events are supposedly created in response to misleading suggestions. Further, in the lab, the event does not relate to the self, nor is the self involved in the event, whereas in therapy the self is intricately involved with the created events. Finally, in the lab the participant has little or no emotional involvement with the event, whereas in therapy the event being suggested may be highly emotional or traumatic for the client. Given these striking differences, the direct generalization of misinformation experiments to the creation of false childhood memories was premature. Nonetheless, the comparison raised an important question: Can people be led to create false memories of entire events if the event includes the self and is emotional? In other words, if the research paradigm more closely mirrored the therapy situation, what would happen?

In response to that question, over the past 5 years several researchers have investigated whether people will create memories of complete, self-involving, emotional events. In this chapter, we will first describe the research on false memory creation, then discuss a theoretical explanation of the processes involved in memory creation, and finally offer some suggestions for how such information may pertain to the therapy situation.

In undertaking this task, we believe it is important to be clear about what we are not saying. We are not arguing that abuse does not exist—abuse happens far too often and is a cause of many child and adult problems. We are not claiming that people are not able to remember childhood abuse and other trauma—people

do remember such trauma for years. Nor are we arguing that people cannot forget trauma and later recover memories of the trauma—this question, which the media have often placed in an either/or relationship with memory creation, is actually an unrelated empirical question, and recent research has demonstrated that people do forget and recover memories of abuse and trauma (e.g., Schooler, 1995; Williams, 1995). Instead, we will be discussing how people can create memories of things that never happened.

The Creation of False Childhood Memories

☐ Most researchers who have investigated the creation of false memories have used similar methodologies (Ceci, Huffman, Smith, & Loftus, 1994; Ceci, Loftus, Leichtman, & Bruck, 1994; Hyman & Billings, in press; Hyman, Husband, & Billings, 1995; Hyman & Pentland, 1996; Loftus & Pickrell, 1995; Pezdek, 1995). In general, the researchers obtain some information about real events that happened to the participant during childhood. The participant is then asked to describe these true events and in the midst of remembering true events is asked to remember a false event—an event that the researchers are fairly sure did not happen to the participant. The participant is usually repeatedly interviewed about the true and false events, and led to believe that he or she will remember more over time. The most important outcome is how the participant responds to the false events—does the participant not only come to believe that the event occurred but also describe the event as a personal memory?

As a concrete example of false memory research, we will describe Experiment 2 from Hyman et al. (1995). In that experiment, the researchers obtained information about some true childhood events by writing to the parents of college students. The researchers then sent the parents a survey that asked them to describe events that happened to their child when the child was between the ages of 2 and 10. The survey provided parents with 10 categories of experiences within which they could describe events: getting lost, going to the hospital, an

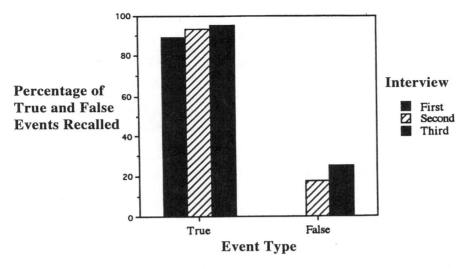

Figure 14.1. Percentage of True and False Events Recalled in Hyman et al. (1995), Experiment 2

eventful birthday, the loss of a pet, a family vacation, interaction with a famous person, winning a contest, car events, weddings, and mischief with a friend. Generally, the parents described events in some but not all categories. When the questionnaires were returned, the researchers asked the students to participate in a series of interviews investigating their memories for early childhood experiences. The researchers told the students that the questions were based on information from their parents, that their responses would be compared with those of their parents, and that they were expected to remember more over time. In each of three interviews (separated by one day between interviews), the students were asked to remember three to five true events plus one false event. For all events, the interviewer provided the students with a basic description (the description included age, event, a few actions, other people involved, and often a location) and asked what they remembered about the event. Three different false events were used in this study. One was the punch bowl event: "When you were 6 years old, you were at the wedding of a friend of the family; you were running around with some other kids when you bumped into the table the punch bowl was sitting on and spilled punch on the parents of the bride." The second false event was the sprinkler event: "When you were 6

years old you were shopping at a grocery store with a parent when the fire extinguisher sprinkler system came on; the store was evacuated, but there was no fire." The third was the car event: "When you were 6 years old, one of your parents left you in the car while he or she ran into a store for a minute; you managed to release the parking brake and the car rolled into something." The researchers randomly varied the false event and the age of suggestion (2, 6, or 10). A total of 51 students participated in all three interviews.

As Figure 14.1 shows, the participants generally recalled the true events and remembered more of the true events over time. There are two ways to explain the increased recall of the true events. One possibility is that by thinking about events, the students provided themselves with additional memory cues that led to the recollection of previously unretrieved memories—a form of hypermnesia (see Erdelyi, 1990). Another possibility is that the participants created, rather than recalled, memories that matched the cues provided. Whether this recovery of memory for the true experiences represents actual memories or the creation of memories, we cannot say.

Figure 14.1 also shows that no participants remembered the false event during the first interview and that 13 (25%) did by the third interview. Six of these were very clear and included the critical information (such as turning over the punch bowl) and consistent elaborations (such as parents being upset). Five were less clear, in that the students may have included little of the critical suggested information although they would elaborate in a consistent fashion. Two of the students created clear images of the interviewer's suggestions yet were not sure whether they were remembering or simply imagining the events. (Further descriptions of these categories and examples are provided in Hyman et al., 1995.)

Hyman et al. (1995) found that how the students responded to the false event in the first two interviews predicted who would eventually create false memories. They classified participants based on whether or not they provided any related self-knowledge in response to the false events—such as talking about whose wedding it could have been, which other kids would have been there, or where the wedding would have been held. Significantly more individuals who talked about related self-knowledge created false memories than did individuals who did not describe self-knowledge. The creation of false memories may involve combining false suggestions with some true information in a constructive process. At the very least, a constructed memory that involves false suggestions and the addition of self-related knowledge makes the discrimination of a false memory more difficult.

That false childhood memories can be created was clearly demonstrated in the Hyman et al. (1995) study. Therefore, the next step was to develop an understanding of the factors that make memory creation more or less likely to occur. Thus Hyman and Pentland (1996) used the same basic methodology in an experiment investigating whether mental imagery would influence the creation of false memories. Similar to Hyman et al. (1995), Hyman and Pentland received information about real childhood events from the parents of college students. The students were repeatedly interviewed about true events and one false event (the false event for all students was the spilled punch bowl at the wedding). How the interviewer responded when a student failed to recall an event (whether a true event or the false event) served as the

manipulation in this experiment. The interviewer asked those in the imagery group to form a mental image of the event and describe the image. In contrast, the interviewer asked those in the control group to sit and think about the event for one minute. The interviewer told both groups that their activity would help them remember the experience. As in the Hyman et al. (1995) study, the students remembered the majority of the true events and remembered more of them over the course of the three interviews.

Interestingly, the imagery group recovered more true memories than did the control group. The imagery manipulation either aided in the recovery of memories or aided in creating memories that matched the true suggestions; it is difficult to discern which took place, and we suspect that some of each occurred. With respect to the false event, students in the imagery group created more false memories than did the students in the control group (37.5% versus 12.1%). Finally, Hyman and Pentland had the students rate their memories on amount of emotion, clarity of mental imagery, and their confidence in the memory. The researchers found no difference between created false memories and recovered true memories.

The creation of false memories appears to be a reliable phenomenon. It occurs with a variety of events and populations. Using methodology similar to Hyman et al. (1995), several researchers have included a variety of false events. In addition to spilling a punch bowl at a wedding, Hyman and his colleagues have used the following: overnight hospital visits for earaches, clowns at birthday parties, minor car accidents, and sprinkler systems going on in grocery stores. Loftus and Pickrell (1995) used being lost in a shopping mall. Pezdek (1995; Pezdek, Finger, & Hodge, 1996) has also used being lost in a mall and events associated with different religious activities. On the other hand, Pezdek has been unable to have participants create memories of receiving an enema, suggesting that there may be limits on the types of events that people will create. It ought to be noted, however, that Pezdek used an interview format that may have been less demanding than that used in other studies. Under heavier demands, people may create memories of receiving an enema—in other words, the limits of memory creation have not yet been drawn. This caveat seems reasonable given some of the real-world false memories that some individuals apparently have created: memories of past lives, alien abduction, and satanic ritual abuse. What Pezdek and her colleagues have shown is that events that are more similar to experiences a person has had, or plausible, are easier to suggest than events about which a person knows little.

In much the way that false memory researchers have used a variety of events, they have also used more than just one population (i.e., college students). Loftus and Pickrell (1995) and Pezdek and her colleagues (Pezdek, 1995; Pezdek et al., 1996) have used adults of different ages in their studies. Ceci and his colleagues (Ceci, Huffman, et al., 1994; Ceci, Loftus, et al., 1994) have used preschool-aged children in studies of false memory creation. They have found that some young children will create a variety of false memories and that the younger the child, the more likely the child will create a false memory.

The studies described thus far all share one methodology that may limit generalizability: Family members generated the true events, and the false event was presented as being drawn from the same information. However, Kelley, Amodio, and Lindsay (1996) have developed a new methodology that relies on false feedback rather than family members as the source of the false event suggestion (see also Loftus, 1996). In this methodology the participants take a test and receive feedback supposedly based on the test. They are then told that people like themselves often have had experiences of a certain type and are asked to try to remember such experiences; they are given a few days to do this. For example, Kelley et al. gave participants a test to measure their innate handedness (i.e., whether they were born to prefer their left or right hand). All of the participants were right-handed, and the test did not really measure natural handedness. The researchers told the participants that the test was still being worked on and that they were not sure if it was reliable. Nonetheless, half of the participants were told that the test indicated that they were born left-

handed (the others were told that they were always right-handed). The researchers asked all participants to try to think of instances in which their hand use had been shaped. Many more of the participants who were told they were left-handed came up with hand-shaping instances. Similarly, Loftus and her colleagues (Loftus, Garry, DuBreuil, & Spanos, described by Loftus, 1996) gave participants a test of visual acuity and told some participants that their results indicated that they might have been exposed to an exceptionally colorful mobile at birth. Those participants were very likely to come up with memories of gazing at such a mobile while they were in the hospital immediately after birth. Admittedly, the events on hand-shaping supplied by Kelley et al.'s participants may have been events that actually occurred that have been reinterpreted to fit the information supplied to the participants. This view of memory reinterpretation as opposed to memory creation does not, however, fit well with the memories of mobiles at birth described by Loftus.

From this sampling of the research on false memory creation, it is clear that memories for entire events that are self-involving and emotional can be created. Further, the variations in methodology, suggested events, and populations studied offer convergent validity that this is a robust phenomenon.

Theoretical Explanation of False Memory Creation

☐ Before we can apply the research to the problem of the possible creation of false abuse memories, it is important that we have an understanding of the processes involved in memory creation. There are three conditions necessary for the creation of a false memory: event acceptance, memory construction, and a source-monitoring error of claiming the constructed narrative as a personal memory.

Event Acceptance

In order for a person to create a false memory, the suggested event needs to be plausible. That is, the event needs to be something that the person believes could have happened. For example, some participants in our experiments (Hyman & Billings, in press; Hyman et al., 1995; Hyman & Pentland, 1996) did not create memories of spilling a punch bowl at a wedding because they believed that they had never attended a wedding as a child. They refused to accept the event as a plausible personal experience.

Several factors may influence whether a person sees an event as plausible. For example, the source of the suggestion will affect plausibility assessments. In the typical false memory experiment, the suggested event is presented by an experimenter and the information is based on information supposedly from the participant's parents; these are two generally reliable sources of information (although students would occasionally suggest that their parents must have them confused with a sibling again). Not only will the source affect whether a person views an event as plausible, but the event itself will matter—whether the person views the event as something that happens. For example, for most people suggestions that they have been abducted by extraterrestrials may not be considered plausible, whereas others may consider such events to be common. Spanos, Cross, Dickson, and DuBreuil (1993) found that belief in alien visitations was the primary variable that differentiated people who claimed memories of UFO experiences from individuals who did not claim such experiences. In addition, implications that the experience is not only generally likely but also personally likely will increase willingness to believe an event may have occurred. In this fashion, studies using false feedback (e.g., Kelley et al., 1996) are effective in part because the researchers provide reasons for the participants to believe that they had particular experiences.

Group membership may affect plausibility, and thus the creation of false memories, if two conditions are involved. If the new people are introduced to a group that "is similar to themselves" and if all of the other members of the group share common memories of an experience that the new members lack, the new members may be at risk of constructing similar memories. In this example, the group members' memories of a similar experience act as the feedback, such that people who share a common characteristic are likely to have had such a class of experiences.

The point here is that we can affect people's impressions of the likelihood of suggested events having occurred (Garry, Manning, Loftus, & Sherman, 1996). For example, consider again those students who doubted they attended a wedding and thus refused to see their spilling a punch bowl as likely. In such cases, the experimenter could manipulate the participant's judgment of the event plausibility by suggesting some reasons for this erroneous belief—perhaps the student repressed memories of weddings, or perhaps the parents were embarrassed and thus never talked about it.

Memory Construction

A person can believe that an event is likely, or even that the event occurred, but must still construct a memory—an image with a narrative. Since the time of Bartlett (1932), researchers have studied memory construction. Memory is not like videotape—a person does not simply retrieve a memory and replay the experience. Instead, an individual constructs a memory by combining schematic knowledge from various sources with personal experiences, suggestions, and current demands. Memory researchers have demonstrated construction in material from word lists (Roediger & McDermott, 1995), to songs (Hyman & Rubin, 1990), stories (Bartlett, 1932), and autobiographical memories (Barclay & DeCooke, 1988; Ross, 1989). All memories are constructions.

Several activities may make false memory construction more likely. For example, tying a false event to self-knowledge will encourage false memory creation (Hyman et al., 1995). In this situation, when the person thinks again about the false event, he or she will have actual self-knowledge come to mind. The image a person constructs will likely involve some true information as well. In addition, encouraging a person to construct and describe an image of a false event also leads to memory construction

(Hyman & Pentland, 1996). In fact, probably any activity that encourages people to think about, imagine, and talk about events will lead to the construction of an image and narrative. Thus activities like journaling and dream interpretation may lead to memory creation if the focus is on trying to remember events.

Source-Monitoring Errors

Even if a person believes an event is plausible and constructs an image of the event, he or she still may not think that the event is a memory. All of the participants in the imagery condition in Hyman and Pentland's (1996) study constructed an image of spilling the punch bowl at a wedding. Many, however, did not claim the image as a memory; instead, they correctly noted that this was just an image they had created. In this fashion they had correctly monitored the source of the image. In order to have a false memory, an individual must make a source-monitoring error—he or she must claim the image as a personal memory. Many studies have shown that people experience difficulties in remembering the sources of information they have learned (see Johnson, Hastroudi, & Lindsay, 1993). In addition, source misattributions have been suggested as a primary cause of the misinformation effect: People remember the misleading postevent information and incorrectly claim that the information was part of the original event (e.g., Zaragoza & Lane, 1994). The error for a false memory is claiming the suggestion and/or constructed image as a personal memory.

Situational demands may affect whether or not a source-monitoring error occurs. For example, if a person shares an image and notes that he or she is not sure if it is a memory, others (an experimenter, members of a group) may tell the person that the image is a memory. Time elapsed since a false suggestion may also affect source-monitoring errors. Memory for the source of information fades more rapidly than memory for the content. Thus people may remember the false suggestion, forget the source, and attribute the source to their own memory. Zaragoza and Mitchell (1996) recently found that repetition

of false suggestions also increases the likelihood of source-monitoring failures.

In writing this theoretical section with the order of event acceptance, memory construction, and source-monitoring error, we imply that these processes occur in a linear fashion, and that each is dependent on the preceding step. However, we actually suspect that the processes are somewhat interactive. For example, constructing a clear image may influence one's assessment of the plausibility of an event's having occurred (Garry et al., 1996). It is more correct to state that all three processes are necessary for false memory creation and that they are somewhat independent in the sense that different factors influence each process. In addition, recently researchers have found that individual differences contribute to memory creation (Hyman & Billings, in press; Winograd, Glover, & Peluso, 1996). At this point, we do not know if individual differences affect event acceptance, memory construction, or reality monitoring. Various cognitive and personality characteristics may differentially affect each process.

Applications to Normal Social Settings

☐ Before we delve into our discussion of how to apply our theory of false memory creation to therapy situations, we need to make an important point: The process described here is a normal memory process. In other words, remembering is always a creative process. People construct recollections out of the contents of the mind to meet the needs of the current context. Constructed recollections are generally accurate. That is, the gist of what happened generally will be the base of the memory, although some erroneous details may be embedded within the memory as well. Large-scale errors should be more rare—people who make large memory errors on a frequent basis would experience some difficulties in their day-to-day functioning.

Nonetheless, both small and large errors often are the result of social interaction. People do much of their remembering in social inter-actions where events are described, questions are asked, and people hear others' recollections of the same or similar events (Hyman & Faries, 1992). Often, other participants within a social interaction are family members and friends. In such storytelling interactions, people may adopt information from others. This adoption leads to changes in aspects of the memories, such as changing who was at the event. Further, when considering a conversation partner's perspec-tive, an individual may also inadvertently change his or her own attitude toward or inter-pretation of the memory.

People may consciously manipulate the con-tent of shared memories as well. Sometimes an individual will alter the telling of a story simply to avoid conflict with another person. For exam-ple, you may not be convinced that another person was really present at a given event, but rather than fight about it you simply continue the story. Over time, you may recollect the changed information (that the person was pre-sent) without recalling the source of the infor-mation—that you modified your story to avoid conflict.

In more extreme cases, it is also possible for people to adopt completely others' descriptions of events as personal recollections. This seems particularly likely in family settings. To illus-trate, children may hear their parents repeatedly tell stories about things all of the children have done. At first, the children may have no recollection of these events. However, listening to the stories may eventually lead the children to imagine the experiences as if they actually did happen and accept the stories as personal memories. At various stages of this process people may be uncertain as to whether they actually remember the event or simply know the event occurred. Most people have memo-ries like this (Hyman, Gilstrap, Decker, & Wilkin-son, 1996). In this way, through social inter-actions, errors may creep into a person's memories.

Generally in families and other social set-tings, the malleability of memory is a good thing. One goal of remembering is the strength-ening of social bonds. Social groups (whether families, friends, corporations, ethnic groups, or countries) have shared narratives. In fact, such shared narratives have been used as a defi-nition of the concept of culture. To a certain extent, these shared narratives are creations of group remembering, in which individuals share versions of the past and perhaps adopt the group's story (Edwards & Middleton, 1986a, 1986b; Edwards, Potter, & Middleton, 1992; Hyman, 1994). The development of common stories thus helps maintain social bonds.

Memory's susceptibility to social influence is not always positive, however. First, if all memories are constructed, then differentiating true from false memories may become difficult. All autobiographical memories likely contain some information from the original event, some general information, and some suggestions. Therefore, memories contain only some truth (sometimes more, other times less). False events generated in the research described (such as spilling a punch bowl at a wedding; Hyman et al., 1995; Hyman & Pentland, 1996) probably contain some true information as well, however: images from real weddings or weddings seen in the media, knowledge of personal attributes, and/or real experiences of parental responses to embarrassing accidents. Therefore, some truth exists within both real and false memory con-structions.

Second, in an extreme case, the malleability of memory could contribute to the denial, rein-terpretation, and forgetting of child abuse. If the abuser is a person who has open access to the child (such as a family member), that person can make suggestions to the child regarding the abuse. For example, the abuser might label the activities differently or even deny that the events occurred, causing the child to doubt his or her memory. The validity of this generalization re-mains an empirical question. We need research on how people come to disbelieve, doubt, and forget personal experiences in response to so-cial suggestion. In some cases, researchers have found that directions to forget an item will decrease remembering (Erdelyi, 1990), but at other times, such directions lead to an increase in attention to the item (Wegner, 1989). We suspect that in this case, the nature of an event makes a difference in how one responds to social pressure to forget it.

Applications to Therapy

☐ The type of research that we have described in this chapter more closely mirrors the potential creation of memories of abuse and other trauma than earlier research on memory errors. People will create memories of complete, emotional, self-involving events. Nonetheless, there exist some important differences between the psychology lab and the therapy session. These differences, however, do not mean that we should not generalize, because failing to consider generalizations is problematic. If laboratory research implies that there are risks attached to some therapies, we need to consider the possible harm clients might experience. However, generalizing without considering these differences can lead to overgeneralizations, which can cause harm as well. Thus we turn to a consideration of the major differences between the lab context and the context of a therapy session.

The clearest difference lies in the nature of the events to be discussed. In the research lab, suggestions of single, emotional events have been made. No one has attempted to cause subjects to create memories of extremely painful events or memories of repeated painful experiences. For obvious ethical reasons, researchers cannot create false memories of traumatic events. This naturally limits generalization. We also know that the nature of the suggested event will influence memory creation: Pezdek (1995) found that less familiar suggested events (an enema compared to being lost) were less likely to result in the creation of false memories. In light of the theory we have discussed, however, these findings are not surprising: An event must be plausible before someone can accept it as a memory. Therefore, one can assume that presenting a suggestion in a plausible manner may increase the likelihood that the suggestion will lead to a false memory. The point here is that we need further research on how the nature and presentation of an event

affect the creation of memories. If, however, one were to dismiss the current research findings because the events tested have not been traumatic ones, then one would forever dismiss research on memory creation, because creating traumatic memories is unethical. Instead, we recommend considering the existing research and carefully generalizing to therapy contexts.

The nature of social interaction differs between the lab and a therapy session as well. There is not one social context in therapy. Rather, there are many different social settings. In some therapy settings, there is almost no focus on remembering, little suggestive pressure, and limited social demands, especially in comparison to the memory creation experiments. In other therapy settings, there is an extensive focus on remembering, abundant use of suggestion, and extreme demands for the client to remember; this is a situation much more intense and often longer lasting than any memory experiment to date. Therefore, all we can say is the following: Certain conditions are likely to lead to the creation of false memories. These conditions, based on the research reviewed, include interactions where the focus is memory, where false suggestions are made, that involve some social demands, that are of relatively short duration (a few hours over 2 or 3 days), and that include participants with limited internal motivation. In such settings, somewhere between 15% and 40% of traditional college students will create false childhood memories. Whether less pressure leads to memory creation, whether more pressure leads to more people creating memories, whether people who have a personal need to remember are more at risk, and how individual differences are related to memory creation remain to be clarified—all need to be studied. Again, however, our theory guides our thinking when we consider contexts beyond those studied thus far: Situations that increase the plausibility of an event for an individual, that cause a person to engage in constructive activities (such as forming images, creating stories, interpreting dreams; see Lindsay & Read, 1994), or that lead people to confuse the source of information will more likely lead to memory creation.

Keeping in mind the limitations for generalizing memory creation experiments, we would like to consider clients that a therapist is likely to encounter. In so doing, our classification will focus only on the status of the client's recollections concerning abuse and trauma history. As such, a therapist might see three types of clients: clients who enter therapy with memories of abuse or trauma (these people may recover more memories over time), clients who enter therapy with no memories of abuse or trauma, and clients who initially claim no memories but later report memories of abuse or other trauma.

Clients With Memories

When clients enter therapy with memories, these memories are likely to be generally accurate. The therapist should keep in mind two issues, however: First, that these memories may include errors of various sorts, and, second, that it is difficult to know if the person has ever previously experienced any pressure to retrieve memories of abuse. That is, the person may have seen other therapists who have made suggestions of abuse. Indeed, recent surveys of therapists indicate that some do use leading techniques with memory recovery as the goal (Polusny & Follette, 1996; Poole, Lindsay, Memon, & Bull, 1995). In addition, the client may have read books that clearly state that a relationship exists between a variety of symptoms and abuse, followed by various memory recovery techniques (e.g., Bass & Davis, 1988; Fredrickson, 1992). Thus one should always be concerned about the accuracy of memories, be they about abuse or any other topic. On a positive note, however, in contexts in which a person has not been exposed to suggestive pressures, one can probably assume that the person's memory is generally accurate.

In the case where a client presents with memories of abuse or trauma, and if those memories become a topic of therapy conversations, the therapist should expect the client to recover more memories. When a person is presented with more cues, he or she will remember more—cognitive psychologists refer to this as encoding specificity (Tulving & Thomson,

1973). This means that memories are encoded in particular contexts, and more information will be retrieved if the specific contexts are reinstated. For example, if you visit a place you have not lived in or visited in a number of years, recollections from that time period are likely to come flooding back. This does not mean that the memories were repressed; rather, there was nothing to bring the memories back to mind during the intervening time. Therefore, once a client focuses on the childhood experiences and starts thinking about such topics, related experiences are likely to come to mind. Talking about abuse, however, may result in the reconstruction of false or erroneous memories as well, particularly if the discussions occur in a demanding and leading social context. The errors could be small (e.g., when something happened) or large (e.g., who the perpetrator was, or that satanic ritual abuse occurred).

Given the risk of creating memory errors from talking about abuse experiences, should therapists talk about abuse with clients who fall into this first group? We think that this depends on the goals of the therapy. If dealing with the memories is one goal of therapy, then of course the therapist should address the memories as part of therapy. Briere (1996) states that in trauma therapy, exposure through talking about traumatic experiences is a crucial component of therapy. Silver, Boon, and Stones (1983) found that many women who were abused continued to think about and search for an understanding of the abuse for years. In addition, Harber and Pennebaker (1992) have found that communicating about painful experiences may have mental and physical health benefits. Thus for clients who present with memories and for whom addressing issues related to those memories is a goal of therapy, the therapist should facilitate discussion, while always keeping in mind the problems of memory accuracy. Indeed, Spence (1982) argues that one goal of therapy is the creation of a reasonable narrative truth for a client, such as one that allows the person to move forward with his or her life. Spence also notes that narrative truth, the story that a person develops, is not necessarily "historical truth," or what actually occurred.

Clients With No Memories

For the second type of client, who reports no history of abuse or other trauma, memory accuracy is still an issue—some reports of no abuse are erroneous. For example, some clients will remember abuse but choose not to report it. Although acknowledging abuse has become more socially acceptable, it may still be something that people do not choose to disclose early in a therapy relationship. Other clients may have forgotten their abuse, which is somewhat more likely if the abuse occurred at a young age (Williams, 1994). Still other abused clients may experience memory difficulties related to suggestive pressures—the perpetrator may have labeled the abuse as something else or may have convinced the person that the abuse never happened.

In spite of the fact that some clients reporting no memories may have been abused, it is of paramount importance that therapists avoid suggestions that abuse, or any other trauma, occurred. Such clients may be looking for an explanation for their problems and may take any suggestion that the therapist makes very seriously. In particular, we urge therapists to avoid anything that makes abuse appear plausible—such as claiming that people with certain symptoms were necessarily abused. Therapists should not use activities that encourage memory creation—such as using mental imagery, journaling, dream interpretation, or hypnosis—when memory recovery is the goal. These techniques have value in other settings, but when used to recover memories they will likely lead, instead, to memory construction. Therapists should also avoid activities and suggestions that lead people to claim any images and thoughts as memories. Cognitive psychologists have focused on how therapists treat clients who enter therapy without memories (Lindsay & Read, 1994; Loftus, 1993). If therapists (or anyone else) use suggestive, leading, demanding techniques with such clients, false memory creation may result, and the false memories may actually cause great harm. A client may develop a painful narrative truth, may come to dislike or disown certain family members, or may fail to address or recognize the actual problems that

led him or her to therapy in the first place (Loftus & Ketcham, 1994, have made this argument based on some individuals they describe).

Thus clear statements of advice can be made with respect to clients who do not report abuse memories. There is no clear evidence that the recovery of memories is necessary for therapy. Therapy focused on memory recovery runs the risk of memory creation, therefore therapy focused on memory recovery should be avoided.

Clients Who Recover Memories

For those clients who originally claim no memories but who eventually recover memories during therapy, the issue of memory accuracy becomes critical. Memory recovery may occur during a therapy session or outside of therapy but during the life period in which the client is participating in therapy. Should we automatically assume that the memory recovered is a false memory? No. This may simply be an instance in which a person chose not to disclose at the start of therapy and has since chosen differently. In this situation, the person may have had access to the memory all along, but waited to share the experience with the therapist. Another possibility is that the person has had a genuine memory recovery experience. This could be due to a number of things, such as encoding specificity, in that the client was provided with the appropriate cues to regain access to the memory. For example, if the person has been addressing other childhood experiences, thinking of those experiences may have brought additional events to mind. Still a third possibility is that the person has developed a new interpretation of some well-remembered experience. The client may have known about the experience, but not previously labeled it as abuse or as traumatic. Thus there are several ways in which a memory recovered in therapy could be at least as accurate as any other autobiographical recollection.

Therefore, should a therapist assume that the memory recovered is true? Again, the answer is no. It is possible that the client could have created a false memory. Even if a therapist is confident that he or she did not use overtly suggestive pressures regarding memories of abuse, this still does not eliminate the possibility of memory creation. As Lindsay and Read (1994) argue, people are not adept at evaluating when they are being suggestive, nor are they expert at remembering the contents of conversations that have taken place over several months. Admittedly, suggestive pressures that therapists have difficulty recognizing are unlikely to be grossly leading techniqes (such as hypnotizing a client and then asking him or her to remember the abuse he or she experienced at age 2). Thus we cannot argue strongly that such mild suggestive pressure will lead to memory creation, but there is at least some risk. Even if one believes there has been little or no suggestive pressure on the part of a therapist, however, one still cannot assume that the recovered memories are true. A therapist is only one influence on a person's life. Further, a client sees a therapist for only an hour or a few hours per week. There are many opportunities for other suggestions and pressures to influence a client: TV programs, books, friends, lectures. Unlessa therapist is aware of all these possible influences, the conclusion that a recovered memory is not the result of suggestion would be premature.

Having pointed out that a recovered memory could be either true or false, we want to reiterate a point we made earlier: There is no way to determine truth based on the content of the memories (Hyman & Pentland, 1996; Leichtman & Ceci, 1995). Even very vivid memories can be erroneous (Neisser & Harsch, 1992). Schacter, Koutstaal, and Norman (Chapter 20, this volume) have suggested that the location of brain activity may differentiate true from false memories. This suggestion stems from research examining one type of error that occurs when people are remembering a word list. Unfortunately, how such work applies to discerning false autobiographical memories, which people construct from both false suggestions and true information, is unclear. Basically, there is still no way to determine if a recovered memory is true without corroborating evidence.

This leaves therapists in a serious ethical bind. If the recovered memories are accurate, or at least mostly accurate, then addressing the memories may be an important concern for therapy. In addition, if the perpetrator is someone who still has access to children, there is a need to ensure that this person is no longer abusing children. If the memories are false, or even mostly false (e.g., the client was abused, but has accused the wrong person), then the false memories may lead the progression of therapy in the wrong direction. This may thereby create new problems rather than heal old ones. Additionally, the memories may disrupt a family or may result in a responsible person's having his or her access to children interrupted. Our current state of knowledge is such that we believe both recovered memories and false memories can occur, but we do not know (and have no means to estimate) the relative likelihood of either occurring. There is no easy way out of this dilemma.

Our best advice to therapists in this situation is to acknowledge the dilemma with recognition that recovered memories could be either true or false. Therapists may need to share information about memory accuracy with clients who recover memories. We all—researchers, therapists, and clients—need to learn to accept ambiguity with respect to memories.

Conclusion

☐ People can create false memories of entire personal, emotional experiences. The creation of a false memory involves accepting a suggested event as plausible, constructing an image and narrative of the event, and failing to monitor accurately the source of the constructed narrative. Although there are several differences between the research and the possible creation of memories in therapy, we feel that, given the risks associated with memory creation, generalization is justified.

Further, it is difficult, if not impossible, to detect differences between true and false memories. Perhaps this is due to the fact that our memory processes operate in much the same way whether the memories we construct are essentially true or false. Therefore, clinicians and clients must be aware of the fact that memories always contain a bit of uncertainty. If a client recovers a memory, it may be false or it may be true. In such a case those involved must approach the memory with caution, keeping in mind the consequences of either accepting a false (and perhaps traumatic) memory or disregarding a true one.

References

Barclay, C. R., & DeCooke, P. A. (1988). Ordinary everyday memories: Some of the things of which selves are made. In U. Neisser & E. Winograd (Eds.), *Remembering reconsidered: Ecological and traditional approaches to the study of memory* (pp. 91-125). Cambridge: Cambridge University Press.

Bartlett, F. C. (1932). *Remembering: A study in experimental and social psychology.* Cambridge: Cambridge University Press.

Bass, E., & Davis, L. (1988). *The courage to heal: A guide for women survivors of child sexual abuse.* New York: Harper & Row.

Briere, J. (1996, June). *An integrated clinical approach to self-reported recovered memories of abuse.* Paper presented at the NATO Advanced Study Institute "Recollections of Trauma: Scientific Research and Clinical Practice," Port de Bourgenay, France.

Ceci, S. J., Huffman, M. L. C., Smith, E., & Loftus, E. F. (1994). Repeatedly thinking about a nonevent: Source misattributions among preschoolers. *Consciousness and Cognition, 3,* 388-407.

Ceci, S. J., Loftus, E. F., Leichtman, M. D., & Bruck, M. (1994). The possible role of source misattributions in the creation of false beliefs among preschoolers. *International Journal of Clinical and Experimental Hypnosis, 42,* 304-320.

Edwards, D., & Middleton, D. (1986a). Joint remembering: Constructing an account of shared experience through conversational discourse. *Discourse Processes, 9,* 423-459.

Edwards, D., & Middleton, D. (1986b). Text for memory: Joint recall with a scribe. *Human Learning, 5,* 125-138.

Edwards, D., Potter, J., & Middleton, D. (1992). Toward a discursive psychology of remembering. *Psychologist, 5,* 441-446.

Erdelyi, M. H. (1990). Repression, reconstruction, and defense: History and integration of the psychoanalytic and experimental frameworks. In J. L. Singer (Ed.), *Repression and dissociation: Implications for personality theory, psychopathology, and health* (pp. 1-32). Chicago: University of Chicago Press.

Fredrickson, R. (1992). *Repressed memories: A journey to recovery from sexual abuse.* New York: Simon & Schuster.

Garry, M., Manning, C. G., Loftus, E. F., & Sherman, S. J. (1996). Imagination inflation: Imaging a childhood event inflates confidence that it occurred. *Psychonomic Bulletin & Review, 3,* 208-214.

Harber, K. D., & Pennebaker, J. W. (1992). Overcoming traumatic memories. In S.-A. Christianson (Ed.), *The handbook of emotion and memory: Research and theory* (pp. 359-388). Hillsdale, NJ: Lawrence Erlbaum.

Hyman, I. E., Jr. (1994). Conversational remembering: Story recall with a peer versus for an experimenter. *Applied Cognitive Psychology, 8,* 49-66.

Hyman, I. E., Jr., & Billings, F. J. (in press). Individual differences and the creation of false childhood memories. *Memory.*

Hyman, I. E., Jr., & Faries, J. M. (1992). The functions of autobiographical memories. In M. A. Conway, D. C. Rubin, H. Spinnler, & W. A. Wagenaar (Eds.), *Theoretical perspectives on autobiographical memory* (pp. 207-221). Dordrecht, The Netherlands: Kluwer.

Hyman, I. E., Jr., Gilstrap, L. L., Decker, K., & Wilkinson, C. (1996, April). *Manipulating remember versus know judgments in autobiographical memories.* Poster presented at the annual meeting of the Western Psychological Association, San Jose, CA.

Hyman, I. E., Jr., Husband, T. H., & Billings, J. F. (1995). False memories of childhood experiences. *Applied Cognitive Psychology, 9,* 181-197.

Hyman, I. E., Jr., & Pentland, J. (1996). Guided imagery and the creation of false childhood memories. *Journal of Memory and Language, 35,* 101-117.

Hyman, I. E., Jr., & Rubin, D. C. (1990). Memorabeatlia: A naturalistic study of long-term memory. *Memory and Cognition, 18,* 205-214.

Johnson, M. K., Hastroudi, S., & Lindsay, D. S. (1993). Source monitoring. *Psychological Bulletin, 114,* 3-28.

Kelley, C., Amodio, D., & Lindsay, D. S. (1996, July). *The effects of "diagnosis" and memory work on memories of handedness shaping.* Paper presented at the International Conference on Memory, Padua, Italy.

Leichtman, M. D., & Ceci, S. J. (1995). The effects of stereotypes and suggestions on preschoolers' reports. *Developmental Psychology, 31,* 568-578.

Lindsay, D. S., & Read, J. D. (1994). Psychotherapy and memories of childhood sexual abuse: A cognitive perspective. *Applied Cognitive Psychology, 8,* 281-338.

Loftus, E. F. (1993). The reality of repressed memories. *American Psychologist, 48,* 518-537.

Loftus, E. F. (1996). *Imaginary memories.* Paper presented at the International Conference on Memory, Padua, Italy.

Loftus, E. F., & Ketcham, K. (1994). *The myth of repressed memory: False memories and allegations of sexual abuse.* New York: St. Martin's.

Loftus, E. F., & Pickrell, J. E. (1995). The formation of false memories. *Psychiatric Annals, 25,* 720-725.

Neisser, U., & Harsch, N. (1992). Phantom flashbulbs: False recollection of hearing the news about *Challenger.* In E. Winograd & U. Neisser (Eds.), *Affect and accuracy in recall: Studies of "flashbulb" memories* (pp. 9-31). New York: Cambridge University Press.

Ofshe, R. J., & Watters, E. (1993). Making monsters. *Society, 30,* 4-16.

Pezdek, K. (1995, July). *Childhood memories: What types of false memories can be suggestively planted?* Paper presented at the annual meeting of the Society for Applied Research in Memory and Cognition, Vancouver.

Pezdek, K., Finger, K., & Hodge, D. (1996, November). *False memories are more likely to be planted if they are familiar.* Paper presented at the annual meeting of the Psychonomic Society, Chicago.

Polusny, M. A., & Follette, V. M. (1996). Remembering childhood sexual abuse: A national survey of psychologists' clinical practices, beliefs, and personal experiences. *Professional Psychology: Research and Practice, 27,* 41-52.

Poole, D. A., Lindsay, D. S., Memon, A., & Bull, R. (1995). Psychotherapy and the recovery of memories of childhood sexual abuse: U.S. and British practitioners' beliefs, practices, and experiences. *Journal of Consulting and Clinical Psychology, 63,* 426-437.

Roediger, H. L., III, & McDermott, K. B. (1995). Creating false memories: Remembering words not presented in lists. *Journal of Experimental Psychology: Learning, Memory, and Cognition, 21,* 803-814.

Ross, M. (1989). The relation of implicit theories to the construction of personal histories. *Psychological Review, 96,* 341-357.

Schooler, J. W. (1995, June). *A cognitive corroborative case study approach for investigating alleged recovered memories of abuse.* Paper presented at the NATO Advanced Study Institute "Recollections of Trauma: Scientific Research and Clinical Practice," Port de Bourgenay, France.

Silver, R. L., Boon, C., & Stones, M. H. (1983). Searching for meaning in misfortune: Making sense of incest. *Journal of Social Issues, 39,* 81-102.

Spanos, N. P., Cross, P. A., Dickson, K., & DuBreuil, S. C. (1993). Close encounters: An examination of UFO experiences. *Journal of Abnormal Psychology, 102,* 624-632.

Spence, D. P. (1982). *Narrative truth and historical truth: Meaning and interpretation in psychoanalysis.* New York: W. W. Norton.

Tulving, E., & Thomson, D. M. (1973). Encoding specificity and retrieval processes in episodic memory. *Psychological Review, 80,* 352-373.

Wegner, D. M. (1989). *White bears and other unwanted thoughts: Suppression, obsession, and the psychology of mental control.* New York: Guilford.

Williams, L. M. (1994). Recall of childhood trauma: A prospective study of women's memories of child sexual abuse. *Journal of Consulting and Clinical Psychology, 62,* 1167-1176.

Williams, L. M. (1995). Recovered memories of abuse in women with documented child sexual victimization histories. *Journal of Traumatic Stress, 8,* 649-673.

Winograd, G., Glover, T. A., & Peluso, J. (1996, November). *Individual differences in susceptibility to memory illusions.* Paper presented at the annual meeting of the Psychonomic Society, Chicago.

Zaragoza, M. S., & Lane, S. M. (1994). Source misattributions and the suggestibility of eyewitness memory. *Journal of Experimental Psychology: Learning, Memory, and Cognition, 20,* 934-945.

Zaragoza, M. S., & Mitchell, K. J. (1996). Repeated exposure to suggestion and the creation of false memories. *Psychological Science, 7,* 294-300.

15

Memories of a Petrochemical Explosion

A Cognitive-Phenomenological Study of Intrusive Thoughts

Tonya Y. Schooler
Andrew Baum

Memories of traumatic events, including repetitive, uncontrollable, intrusive thoughts or images, appear to be involved in perpetuating the stress response well beyond the life of the stressor. Research has clearly shown that events lasting only a few minutes or hours can induce persistent chronic stress, and suggests that this is due to activation and involuntary experience of memories of the stressor (Baum, 1990; Baum, O'Keeffe, & Davidson, 1990). These intrusive thoughts, along with the feeling of reexperiencing the traumatic event, are central elements of acute stress disorder and posttraumatic stress disorder (PTSD; American Psychiatric Association, 1994). However, relatively little is known about how intrusive memories occur or how cognitive processes affect the experience and frequency of these thoughts. These cognitive processes may involve how

people characterize and contend with memories of the traumatic event.

Intrusive memories are very common in individuals who have experienced severe stressors, and may persist for years. As time passes, both the frequency of intrusive thoughts and the magnitude of distress typically decrease (e.g., Foa & Riggs, 1995; Horowitz, 1986). However, some victims continue to experience frequent and distressing intrusions over time, and these intrusive thoughts have been implicated in both the experience and the maintenance of chronic stress (e.g., Baum, Cohen, & Hall, 1993). After a trauma, they may function as acute stressors, with each unbidden memory initiating or evoking stress responding (Baum et al., 1993). People may be bothered and aroused by these involuntary and unpleasant memories. Further, the distress stemming from these thoughts does not appear to be adaptive; habituation and extinction would seemingly produce better mental and physical health outcomes. They are common symptoms of PTSD following cataclysmic events such as a hurricane or cancer diagnosis, combat exposure, abuse, and HIV-status notification, but are also important elements in daily life (Antoni, 1990; Berntsen, 1996; Ironson et al., 1997; Kent, 1989; Niler, 1989; Palmer, 1993; Wolfe, 1991; Zimering, Caddell, Fairbank, & Keane, 1993). Consequently, intrusive thoughts can be considered both a cause and a symptom of distress, with the content of these thoughts varying with the stressor.

Although we have learned a good deal about the occurrence of intrusive thoughts and memories, we know little about what they feel like, how they affect distress, and how they are produced. Intrusive thoughts have been defined in several ways, for example, as "any thought that implies non-volitional entry into awareness, requires suppressive effort or is hard to dispel, occurs perseveratively, or is experienced as something to be avoided" (Horowitz, 1975, p. 1458). These conceptions tend to be very broad and do not describe the experience of such thoughts or why they occur. Most investigations are concerned with negative and unwanted thoughts, though study of a broader class of intrusions suggests that many are neutral or mood congruent (Berntsen, 1996). Most assume that memory for the trauma *feels* negative, but there have been few attempts at cataloging the phenomenal experience of traumatic memory and the resulting intrusions (although see Tromp, Koss, Figueredo, & Tharan, 1995).

Another unresolved characteristic of traumatic memory is its selective impact. Whereas intrusive thoughts about a stressor are broadly experienced immediately after it occurs, some victims continue to have high levels of intrusions that persist for months and even years after a traumatic event (Davidson & Baum, 1986; Horowitz & Reidbord, 1992). Examining the experience of memory intrusions may reveal strategies that people use to cope with the intrusions *as they occur* and may reveal differences between the memory qualities of victims who

show a decline in intrusions and distress and those of victims who do not.

Our research focused on the memories of petrochemical workers who experienced an explosion at their workplace. To appreciate the nature of the impact of petrochemical disasters, one should consider several important characteristics of such events. First, petrochemical accidents usually involve human-made elements, human error, or breakdown of human-made systems. The human role in these accidents is a key factor differentiating natural and technological disasters (Baum, 1987), and it may be one reason stress responding appears to persist longer among victims of human-caused disasters (see also Smith & North, 1993). Petrochemical explosions are intense events that involve considerable life threat, and they are sudden and dramatic in nature. Loss of control over what was once assumed to be under control also contributes to chronic stress, as do the presence of toxic gases and the lack of a clear point where the worst of the disaster is over (Baum, Fleming, & Davidson, 1983). These events can completely disfigure or destroy a familiar environment, seemingly in an instant. Workers must also adopt roles as emergency workers, and must salvage the plant in the days following the disaster. There is often a financial impact as well; jobs may be threatened if the plant must shut down.

Characterization of Intrusive Thoughts

☐ The relationships among qualities and contents of participants' memories for a petrochemical explosion were examined. The goal was to explore the phenomenology of intrusive thoughts and to identify qualitative differences in these memories within subjects over time. This prospective analysis included comparisons between groups of workers who experienced repeated memories of the trauma within 3 weeks of the accident and workers who did not experience such memories. The contents of these memory descriptions elicited soon after an event may be predictive of future levels of intrusive thoughts and of prolonged stress. In addition, how victims react when they think about the accident may have implications for later distress and frequency of intrusive thoughts. For example, reliance on distraction or more intensive attempts not to think about traumatic events may contribute to intrusive memories through a cognitive thought suppression mechanism (e.g., Wegner, 1994). Furthermore, people having repeated memories of the accident soon afterward may react differently to these memories and may vary in the extent to which they reexperience the trauma. To address these issues, we asked participants to describe their memories after the accident, and we then examined how they characterized their memories as well as whether cognitive coping strategies such as distraction were related to frequency or persistence of intrusive thoughts. We also evaluated the degree to which memory qualities or contents predicted intrusive thoughts and distress at later time points.

Method

Design and Subjects

This study of memories of workplace explosions is part of a multisite, prospective, longitudinal study of stress responding in petrochemical workers. The focus of the study was an explosion at an oil processing plant that killed four workers. Participants were 47 workers at the damaged plant, and data were collected 3 weeks, 3 months, and 6 months after the explosion.

A total of 70 oil workers were contacted, of whom 47 agreed to participate; 6 discontinued participation over the course of the study, leaving 41 participants, 40 males (2 of whom were African American) and 1 female. This is representative of the population of oil processing workers at the site where the explosion took place. The mean age was 42 years, and the median income was $50,000. The majority of participants had graduated from high school and had some college education (79%); 84% of participants were married. No significant differ-

ences were found for these variables between those who agreed to participate and those who refused. Participants were paid $25.00 for each of six sessions over a 2-year period.

Measures

To measure frequency of intrusive thoughts, the Impact of Event Scale (IES; Horowitz, Wilner, & Alvarez, 1979) was administered at each assessment. Participants also rated characteristics of their memories on 7-point scales, including the clarity and lifelike qualities of these memories and their dynamic qualities (e.g., whether the images seem more like snapshots or a rolling film). We also assessed reactions to thinking about the accident—that is, what people thought or did when memories of the accident were activated. For example, participants were asked to respond to the statement "When I think about the accident, I . . ." with one of the following: (a) "actively try to think about something else"; (b) "think about my reaction at the time of the accident"; (c) "am concerned that the memory keeps coming back"; or (d) "feel like I am reexperiencing the accident." Scales ranging from 1 (*none of my thoughts are related to this*) to 7 (*most of my thoughts concern this*) followed each item.

Participants also provided descriptions of their memories for the accident, guided by the following set of instructions:

> Describe your memory of the accident in as much detail as possible, including what you remember happened before and after the accident. Even if you did not witness the explosion yourself, you may have thoughts related to the explosion, or where you were when it happened. Please describe these thoughts in as much detail as possible. If you have no memory of the event, please indicate in the space below.

Following the memory description, these instructions were given:

> Please look again at your description of the accident. If there are any memories or thoughts that seem to come back to you again and again, either list them below or underline them in your descrip-

tion above. If no memories or thoughts about the accident come back to you again and again, please write "none" below.

Duration of memory experience was also assessed with this statement:

If you have memories of the accident, please try to make an estimate of how long your typical memory of the event stays in your mind. Please try to estimate how long the image or images of the event stay in your mind rather than the amount of time you spend thinking about the accident after the images come to your mind.

The duration options ranged from between 1 and 5 seconds to more than 10 minutes, with a total of eight alternatives.

Procedure

Informed consent was obtained at the first assessment, 3 weeks after the explosion. Subjects were seen individually or in small groups before or after their shifts at the refinery, or during their lunch break. The questionnaires were administered in a local government building across the street from the plant. Subjects returned the questionnaires the following day. All items were presented in written form, and the same procedure was used at each time point.

To test hypotheses about differences between victims who experienced repeated memories of the event and those who did not, participants were classified at Time 1 as RM (Repeated Memory) and No-RM (No Repeated Memory). This division was based on whether or not subjects indicated that they had memories of the explosion that came back again and again. Data presented in this chapter are based on this classification at Time 1, allowing the examination of the predictive value of such a distinction for responses in later assessments. Of the 41 participants, 21 were classified as RM. The remaining 20 participants reported that they did not have repeated memories of the accident.

Repeated-measures analyses of variance (ANOVAs) were conducted on characteristics of participants' memories crossing group (RM/ No-RM) and time of assessment (3 weeks/3 months/6 months).

Results

Clarity

Significant effects of group and a group by time interaction were found for self-rated clarity and lifelike qualities of participants' memories of the accident, $F(1, 38) = 6.41$, $p = .016$, and $F(2, 37) = 3.28$, $p = .05$. Participants reporting that they had repeated memories rated their memories as clearer and more lifelike than did people who were not having repeated memories of the accident (see Figure 15.1). Differences in clarity declined over time, due primarily to a decrease in clarity in the RM group, but it is notable that in the 6-month period following the accident, significant decreases in self-rated memory clarity were not observed.

Dynamic Quality

Subjects were asked about the extent to which their memorial images seem more like snapshots (still pictures of the event) or a rolling film (progressing images of the event). Based on the fragmentary nature of accounts of traumatic memory found in the PTSD literature (e.g., Laub & Auerhahn, 1993; van der Kolk & Fisler, 1995; Wegner, Quillian, & Houston, 1996), we expected to find that workers with repeated memories would rate their memories as having a more splintered, snapshot-like quality. Contrary to these predictions, the No-RM group's memories were rated as being more like snapshots than were the RM group's memories, $F(1, 38) = 9.05$, $p = .005$ (see Figure 15.2). A main effect of time was found, $F(2, 37) = 3.42$, $p < .04$, but the interaction between group and time was not significant.

Duration of Memory

It was predicted that subjects with repeated memories would show briefer, more fleeting memories of the event than would subjects without repeated memories. However, no dif-

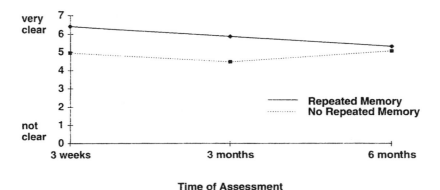

Figure 15.1. Subjects' Mean Ratings of Memory Clarity and Vividness

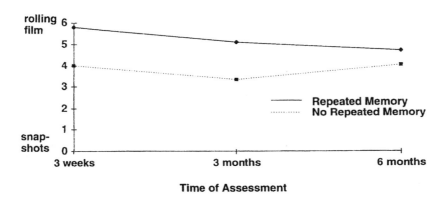

Figure 15.2. Dynamic Quality of Subjects' Memories

ferences were found for participants' estimates of how long a typical memory of the accident remained in mind. Subjects in both groups estimated that their memories of the accident lasted about 10 to 30 seconds, and this estimation did not change significantly over time.

Distraction

Consistent with hypotheses, differences were found for the degree to which participants actively tried to think of something else when they remembered the accident. The Repeated Memory group showed a greater propensity for actively searching for something other than the accident to think about than did the No-RM group, $F(1, 38) = 5.57, p < .023$. No main effect or interactions with time were found (see Figure 15.3).

Reaction at the Time of the Accident

Individuals with repeating memories tended to think more about their reactions at the time of the accident than those who were not having repeated memories, $F(1, 38) = 4.17, p = .05$. As can be seen in Figure 15.4, this difference did not change over time.

Concern that memory keeps coming back. When they thought about the accident, the Repeated Memory group reported greater concern about the fact that memories keep coming back to them than the No-RM group, $F(1,$

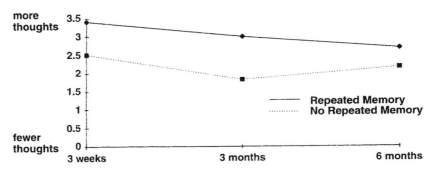

Figure 15.3. Degree to Which Subjects' Thoughts Concern Actively Trying to Think of Something Else

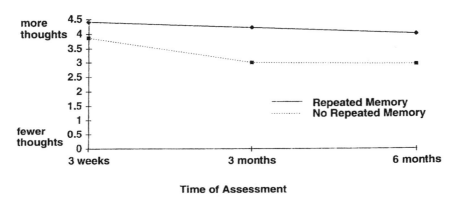

Figure 15.4. Degree to Which Subjects' Thoughts Concern Their Reactions at the Time of the Accident

39) $= 12.45$, $p < .001$. This result can be viewed as a manipulation check of sorts. The group that experiences the repeated memories should be more concerned that they keep coming back. No main effect of time was found, nor was there any interaction between group and time (see Figure 15.5).

Feelings of Reexperiencing the Accident

When participants with repeated memories thought about the accident, they had more feelings of reexperiencing the event than people who did not have repeated memories of the accident, $F(1, 37) = 9.38$, $p = .004$. No main effect or interaction with time was found (all Fs < 1; see Figure 15.6).

Correlational Analyses

We examined the predictive value of memory characteristics by correlating memory characteristics 3 weeks after the accident with IES scores 6 months after the accident. Table 15.1 summarizes responses to these items correlated with each other at or below the $p < .01$ level of significance. All variables in Table 15.1 were associated with higher IES scores at Time 3. However, in a simultaneous regression (exclud-

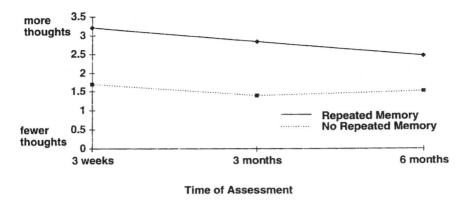

Figure 15.5. Degree to Which Subjects' Thoughts Reflect Concern That the Memory Keeps Coming Back

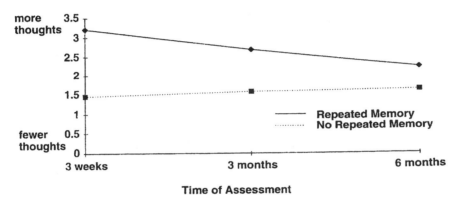

Figure 15.6. Degree to Which Subjects' Thoughts Concern Feeling Like They Are Reexperiencing the Event

ing IES Time 1), only the variable "thinking about another topic" explained a significant portion of the variance in IES scores 6 months after the explosion, $\beta = .40$, $F(1, 26) = 4.41$, $p < .05$. The other memory variables did not explain significant portions of the variance (all βs $< .31$, all ps $> .12$). The full model $R^2 = .43$.

Content Analysis

Two raters content analyzed subjects' memory descriptions at each of the three time points. Interrater reliability was $r = .90$. Participants' descriptions were coded for the following features: number of words; number of mentions of sight and sound; use of the pronoun *I;* cognitive

metastatements such as remembering, thinking, wondering; number of emotion-laden words, such as *shock, terror,* and *anger;* and amount of detail.

No significant differences between the RM and No-RM groups were found for any of these variables, except for number of words used in the memory descriptions. A main effect of group was found, $F(1, 36) = 6.45$, $p < .02$, with members of the RM group using a greater number of words in their memory descriptions than those in the No-RM group. A main effect of time was also found, $F(2, 35) = 11.66$, $p < .001$, but the interaction between group and time did not reach significance (all Fs < 1). As can be seen in Figure 15.7, members of the RM group used

Table 15.1 Correlations Among Time 1 Memory Variables and Impact of Event Scale Scores at Times 1 and 3

	Actively Trying to Think of Something Else	Concern That Memories Keep Coming Back	Feelings of Reexperiencing the Event	IES (Time 1)	IES (Time 3)
Actively trying to think of something else		.54	.52	.56	.48
Concern that memories keep coming back			.74	.57	.53
Feelings of reexperiencing the event				.50	.42
IES (Time 1)					.56

an average of approximately 100 more words in their descriptions at Times 1 and 2, and approximately 60 more words at Time 3 than those in the No-RM group.

The Characterization of Traumatic Memory

□ After witnessing a petrochemical explosion at their workplace, some workers experienced repeated memories of the event and some did not. Having repeated memories 3 weeks after the explosion was associated with more vivid and lifelike memories. These memories had dynamic qualities resembling rolling film rather than snapshots. When thinking about the accident, workers with repeating memories showed a greater propensity to try to distract themselves from their memories. Those with repeating memories also reexperienced the event more often, expressed more concern about the memory coming back, and reported more thoughts about their reactions at the time of the accident. Participants who were not having repeated memories showed a different pattern of response. Moreover, the differences between the two groups were stable over time. That is, the experience of repeated memories 3 weeks after the accident set a clear division between these two groups that remained 6 months later. Aside from number of words used, no differences between the groups were found with respect to the contents of their event descriptions, nor did

the contents yield significant relationships with frequency of intrusive thoughts. However, some memory characteristics at the first assessment were related to IES scores 6 months later.

Experiencing repeated memories 3 weeks after the accident was associated with memories that were more vivid and lifelike. Although our data do not permit evaluation of causal direction of observed relationships, it is tempting to speculate that vivid memories of the event cause a higher level of distress that is then reflected in the experience of repeated memories of the explosion. Alternatively, having repeated memories may provide rehearsal for the explosion memories, keeping them lifelike and vivid. Continued measurement of these phenomena may help. If distress and frequency of intrusions decrease while vividness ratings remain stable, then the latter rehearsal hypothesis may become less attractive. The same would be true if vividness ratings decrease while distress and frequency of intrusions remain stable. However, if vividness and intrusions continue to either remain stable or decrease in parallel, no conclusions could be drawn concerning whether the vivid quality of the memory contributes to intrusions or whether intrusions contribute to the lifelike quality of the memories. This relationship will be investigated in the ensuing assessment periods.

With respect to dynamic quality, members of the RM group reported that their memories for the accident were more like rolling film than snapshots of the event. This result ran counter

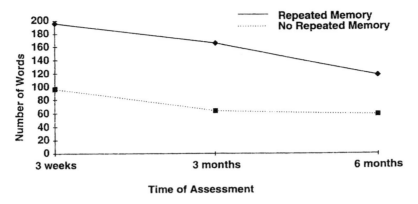

Figure 15.7. Mean Number of Words in Memory Descriptions

to expectations. According to descriptions elicited from individuals with PTSD, fragmentary
memories are common, and we expected that
participants showing other signs of PTSD (i.e.,
repeating memories and higher levels of intrusive thoughts) would rate their memorial experience as having a more snapshot-like quality.
However, those in the No-RM group were significantly more likely to rate their memories as
snapshot-like than were those having repeated
memories. It is interesting to note that, despite
this difference in dynamic quality, the groups
did not differ in their estimation of how long a
typical memory of the event stayed in mind.
Again, the duration was brief for both groups:
10 to 30 seconds. So, regardless of whether the
memory experience resembled moving pictures
or still snapshots, the estimated duration was
rather fleeting for both groups.

When probed about their reactions to thinking about the accident, workers with repeating
memories reported a greater propensity to try to
think about something other than that event.
This result may reflect both how aversive thinking about the accident is to the members of this
group and how these individuals may be using
a counterproductive strategy to dispel their intrusions. According to research on thought suppression and distraction (e.g., Gold & Wegner,
1995), trying not to think about an event sets up
a cognitive environment in which the to-be-sup-
pressed items attain activation. However, the
correlational nature of these data do not permit
causal inferences, and we cannot know whether

this was in fact what happened or whether use
of distraction or avoidance was simply more
common for those with repeated memories.

Participants who reported repeating memories also reexperienced the event more than
other subjects, which is consistent with symptoms of PTSD. This finding indicates that the
memory experience or reaction to the event may
have been either qualitatively different or more
intense in those with repeated memories than in
workers whose memories did not seem to repeat. Though this result was expected, it accentuates the puzzling finding that no significant
differences were found in the contents of the
groups' memory descriptions. At Time 1, there
were no encoding differences between the groups
that could be reflected in the descriptions. In
addition, the lack of content differences 3 and 6
months after the explosion indicates that memory intrusions and feelings of reexperiencing
were not reflected in the memory descriptions.
We would have expected that subjects having
repeated memories and feelings of reexperiencing might mention these feelings within their
descriptions and would mention more sensory
events or use more emotion-laden wording.

The observation that members of the RM
group were more concerned that the memory
keeps coming back could be interpreted as a
manipulation check for the occurrence of repeated memories. However, this result also suggests something about how these memories
were appraised. These items were prefaced by
the statement, "When I think about the accident,

I . . . ." From their memory descriptions, it was clear that those in the No-RM group remembered the accident, and though they may have thought about the event from time to time, they simply did not have repeated memories of the event. Concern over the memory coming back could apply to these subjects' nonrepeating memories, but they were not appraised as aversive.

The finding that members of the RM group had more thoughts about their reactions at the time of the accident is provocative. We do not know, however, whether those in this group had more self-reflective encoding at the time of the accident or whether their reactions were so salient or unusual that they really stood out to the participants. Unfortunately, no information concerning this issue could be gleaned from memory description contents. There were no differences in use of the pronoun I, nor were there differences in use of emotion-laden words.

Correlational analyses revealed significant relationships between the reactions workers had when they thought about the accident and the frequency of intrusive and avoidant thought and behavior as measured on the IES. With regard to intrusive thoughts, the most important finding involved the predictive value of distraction at Time 1 on the frequency of intrusive thoughts at Time 3. The more individuals actively sought to think about something other than the accident, the more frequent were their experiences of intrusive thoughts at Time 3. Actively trying to think about something else may fuel the activation of trauma memory through the mechanism of thought suppression, and distraction has also been viewed as thought suppression through auxiliary concentration (e.g., trying to think of something else; Wegner, 1989). The present data support Wegner's (1989) hypothesis that trying not to think about something actually increases the probability that the suppressed item will be activated, especially when the subject is under cognitive load or stress. However, the high correlations between IES scores at the two time points and between IES and distraction at each time point make it impossible to determine causal direction.

The lack of relationships between the contents of participants' memory descriptions and other variables was surprising. No differences were found between those with and without repeated memories in terms of contents of memory descriptions. The only significant difference between these groups was the number of words used in descriptions. Those having repeated memories used an average of 100 more words per description than those without repeating memories. Both groups showed a 40% loss of words between the 3-week and the 6-month assessment. However, the pattern of decline was different. The RM group lost 15% of words between Time 1 and Time 2 (3 months postaccident), whereas the No-RM group lost double that amount in the same time period (33%). In contrast, the remaining percentage of words lost between Times 2 and 3 for the RM group was twice that lost in this time period by participants in the No-RM group. If the omission of words is even remotely related to underlying memory (Anderson & Schooler, 1991), then, taking into account motivation decrements, this result may reflect different forgetting slopes for the two groups. Though this idea is speculative, the occurrence of repeated memories may serve as a form of rehearsal, which, as has been demonstrated in many laboratory studies, delays forgetting and alters the function of forgetting curves in recall paradigms (see Anderson, 1995, pp. 198-235). Even if this result is due to decreases in motivation or to fatigue, it still is striking that the two groups differed so much in their rates of word loss.

We coded the workers' free recall descriptions for variables that were similar to probes given in studies asking trauma victims about what they saw, heard, smelled, and felt (e.g., the Traumatic Memory Inventory [van der Kolk & Fisler, 1995] and the Memory Qualities Inventory [Suengas & Johnson, 1988]). It is not yet clear whether providing categories such as sound and smell can change the way subjects' memories are coded. One could imagine that introducing sensory categories to victims may focus them toward those very items in their memories, perhaps strengthening these factors in their representations. Though we avoided this problem by eliciting free recall, we may have missed information that subjects could have reported on inventory measures.

Another finding, or lack thereof, in the content analysis was the striking absence of emotion-laden words. Even within narratives comprising 250 words, an average of 2 emotion words were found. Perhaps this predominantly male population of petrochemical workers viewed the task as more descriptive of events than an outlet for emotional expression, or perhaps they inhibited expression of emotional responses for other reasons. It is difficult to conclude that memories of this fatal accident are exclusively emotion-free and descriptive.

It is important to note, however, that it *was* possible for these workers to form narratives of their experiences. In an analysis of traumatic and nontraumatic memory in individuals with PTSD, van der Kolk and Fisler (1995) had participants respond to various inquiries, including sensory, affective, and narrative ratings of their memory qualities. These researchers argue that memory for traumatic events is initially stored as fragments, without a coherent semantic component. As a victim becomes aware of more and more elements of the traumatic experience, he or she may be able to construct a narrative that can serve as a socially communicable story. Thus, although trauma memory may have indelible sensory and affective elements, once these enter semantic memory they are subject to distortion and reappraisal. According to van der Kolk and van der Hart (1991), it is the failure to integrate the traumatic event into narrative form that results in the experience of memory intrusions. However, it was clear from our data that memory intrusions were experienced by people who could form narratives of their experience.

There are other mechanisms that may explain why victims of trauma have intrusive thoughts. For example, emotional processing perspectives emphasize the possibility that memories of a traumatic event come back to the individual in fragments because the person would be unable to cope with the entire traumatic event memory at once. Fragmentary memory intrusions allow for "working through" a trauma and integrating the experience into a schema or worldview. Schemata in long-term memory are activated after a trau-

matic event, and intrusive thoughts are a product of trying to integrate memories of the traumatic event into a schema of the world as a benign and controllable place.

It should be noted, however, that the cognitive system does not need to activate inconsistent information repeatedly in order to integrate the discrepant information. Nor does the information necessarily need to be integrated. Individuals may create new substructures through subtyping and branching (e.g., Weber & Crocker, 1983), or they may refute, dismiss, or do some other cognitive work on information in order to make it consistent with an existing schema (e.g., Hastie & Kumar, 1979). Moreover, the strength and pervasiveness of the drive to integrate schema-inconsistent events may be overestimated. Extrapolating from cognitive consistency theory (e.g., Cooper & Fazio, 1984), the "drive" for consistency—that is, to make sense out of a cataclysmic event by integrating the trauma into a preexisting worldview—may not be as strong as once thought. It turns out that people vary widely in their capacity for tolerating inconsistent information (see Budner, 1962; Kruglanski, 1989).

Though these theories borrow the cognitive concept of schema activation, several problems arise when they are examined from a more traditional cognitive perspective. First, as Greenberg (1995) and Litz and Keane (1989) have observed, there is no evidence for the assumption that schema-discrepant information is repeatedly activated and accessed until integration occurs. Nor is there evidence that memory fragments are repeatedly activated in short-term memory until "consolidated" into long-term memory, as proponents of emotional processing theories claim (e.g., Horowitz, 1990). In fact, many of these emotional processing theories of intrusive thoughts are incompatible with aspects of information-processing theory (for a discussion, see Greenberg, 1995). A potential source of confusion involves clinical accounts of traumatic event integration being referred to as "cognitive processing," whereas a very different set of mechanisms stemming from memory research in the domain of cognitive psychology would account for the phenomenon in a different way. More care in explicitly defining what *processing* means is in order.

Another issue in need of attention involves the difference between having an intrusive thought and the actual contents of that intrusive thought. It has been shown that when intrusive thoughts are themselves appraised as harmful, anxiety is produced that motivates the individual to reduce this discomfort (Salkovskis, 1989). As discussed earlier, how the individual reacts to having unbidden thoughts about the event could have important implications for the likelihood that the thought will recur. At the risk of entering an infinite regress, the appraisal of having the intrusive thought may be what leads to strategies such as thought suppression. It is assumed that thoughts or memories that come to mind involuntarily feel intrusive. However, the extent to which the involuntary nature of the memories contributes to distress, above and beyond their content, is not known.

Finally, the prospective nature of the current study, combined with the timing of the first assessment, allowed us to examine *relatively untainted* memories of this destructive event. The majority of studies of traumatic memory examine memories for events that happened years before the time of assessment. Though our data come from a period when the event presumably is fresh in the workers' minds, the next year and a half may prove to be even more interesting with respect to divergent patterns of memory characteristics, as well as to reactions to having memory intrusions.

References

American Psychiatric Association. (1994). *Diagnostic and statistical manual of mental disorders* (4th ed.). Washington, DC: Author.

Anderson, J. R. (1995). *Cognitive psychology and its implications.* New York: W. H. Freeman.

Anderson, J. R., & Schooler, L. J. (1991). Reflections of the environment in memory. *Psychological Science, 2,* 396-408.

Antoni, M. H. (1990). Psychological and neuroendocrine measures related to functional immune changes in anticipation of HIV-1 serostatus notification. *Psychosomatic Medicine, 52,* 496-510.

Baum, A. (1987). Toxins, technology, and natural disasters. In G. R. VandenBos & B. K. Bryant (Eds.), *Cataclysms,*

crises, and catastrophes: Psychology in action. Washington, DC: American Psychological Association.

Baum, A. (1990). Stress, intrusive imagery, and chronic distress. *Health Psychology, 9,* 653-675.

Baum, A., Cohen, L., & Hall, M. (1993). Control and intrusive memories as possible determinants of chronic stress. *Psychosomatic Medicine, 55,* 274-286.

Baum, A., Fleming, R., & Davidson, L. M. (1983). Natural disaster and technological catastrophe. *Environment and Behavior, 15,* 333-335.

Baum, A., O'Keeffe, M. K., & Davidson, L. M. (1990). Acute stressors and chronic response: The case of traumatic stress. *Journal of Applied Social Psychology, 20,* 1643-1754.

Berntsen, D. (1996). Involuntary autobiographical memories. *Applied Cognitive Psychology, 10*(5), 435-454.

Budner, S. (1962). Intolerance of ambiguity as a personality variable. *Journal of Personality, 30,* 29-50.

Cooper, J., & Fazio, R. H. (1984). A new look at dissonance theory. In L. Berkowitz (Ed.), *Advances in experimental social psychology* (Vol. 17). Orlando, FL: Academic Press.

Davidson, L. M., & Baum, A. (1986). Posttraumatic stress as a function of chronic stress and toxic exposure. In C. P. Figley (Ed.), *Trauma and its wake* (pp. 55-77). New York: Brunner/Mazel.

Foa, E. B., & Riggs, D. S. (1995). Posttraumatic stress disorder following assaults: Theoretical considerations and empirical findings. *Current Directions in Psychological Science, 4,* 61-65.

Gold, D. B., & Wegner, D. M. (1995). Origins of ruminative thought: Trauma, incompleteness, nondisclosure, and suppression. *Journal of Applied Social Psychology, 25,* 1245-1261.

Greenberg, M. A. (1995). Cognitive processing of traumas: The role of intrusive thoughts and reappraisals. *Journal of Applied Social Psychology, 25,* 1262-1296.

Hastie, R., & Kumar, P. A. (1979). Person memory: Personality traits as organizing principles in memory for behavior. *Journal of Personality and Social Psychology, 37,* 25-38.

Horowitz, M. J. (1975). Intrusive and repetitive thought after experimental stress. *Archives of General Psychiatry, 32,* 1457-1463.

Horowitz, M. J. (1986). *Stress response syndromes.* Northvale, NJ: Jason Aronson.

Horowitz, M. J. (1990). Posttraumatic stress disorders: Psychosocial aspects of the diagnosis. *International Journal of Mental Health, 19*(1), 21-36.

Horowitz, M. J., & Reidbord, S. P. (1992). Memory, emotion, and response to trauma. In S.-A. Christianson (Ed.), *The handbook of emotion and memory: Research and theory* (pp. 343-357). Hillsdale, NJ: Lawrence Erlbaum.

Horowitz, M. J., Wilner, N., & Alvarez, W. (1979). Impact of Event Scale: A measure of subjective stress. *Psychosomatic Medicine, 41,* 209-308.

Ironson, G., Wynings, C., Schneiderman, N., Baum, A., Rodriguez, M., Greenwood, D., Benight, C., Antoni, M., LaPerriere, A., Huang, H., Klimas, N., & Fletcher, M. A. (1997). Posttraumatic stress syndromes, intrusive thoughts, loss and immune function after Hurricane Andrew. *Psychosomatic Medicine, 59*(2), 128-141.

Kent, G. (1989). A longitudinal study of the intrusiveness of cognitions in test anxiety. *Behaviour Research and Therapy, 27,* 43-50.

Kruglanski, A. (1989). Individual differences in need for closure. *Journal of Personality and Social Psychology, 67,* 1049-1062.

Laub, D., & Auerhahn, N. C. (1993). Knowing and not knowing massive psychic trauma: Forms of traumatic memory. *International Journal of Psycho-analysis, 74,* 287-302.

Litz, B. T., & Keane, T. M. (1989). Information processing in anxiety disorders: Application to the understanding of post-traumatic stress disorder. *Clinical Psychology Review, 9,* 243-257.

Niler, E. R. (1989). The relationship among guilt, dysphoria, anxiety and obsessions in a normal population. *Behaviour Research and Therapy, 27,* 213-220.

Palmer, A. G. (1993). Understanding women's responses to treatment for cervical intra-epithelial neoplasia. *British Journal of Clinical Psychology, 32*(1), 101-112.

Salkovskis, P. M. (1989). Cognitive-behavioral factors and the persistence of intrusive thoughts in obsessional problems. *Behaviour Research and Therapy, 27,* 677-682.

Smith, E. M., & North, C. S. (1993). Posttraumatic stress disorders in natural disasters and technological accidents. In J. P. Wilson & B. Raphael (Eds.), *International handbook of traumatic stress syndromes* (pp. 405-419). New York: Plenum.

Suengas, A. G., & Johnson, M. K. (1988). Qualitative effects of rehearsal on memories for perceived and imagined complex events. *Journal of Experimental Psychology: General, 117,* 377-389.

Tromp, S., Koss, M. P., Figueredo, A. J., & Tharan, M. (1995). Are rape memories different? A comparison of rape, other unpleasant, and pleasant memories among employed women. *Journal of Traumatic Stress, 8,* 607-627.

van der Kolk, B. A., & Fisler, R. (1995). Dissociation and the fragmentary nature of traumatic memory: Overview and exploratory study. *Journal of Traumatic Stress, 8,* 505-525.

van der Kolk, B. A., & van der Hart, O. (1991). The intrusive past: The flexibility of memory and the engraving of trauma. *American Imago, 48,* 425-454.

Weber, R., & Crocker, J. (1983). Cognitive processes in the revision of stereotypic beliefs. *Journal of Personality and Social Psychology, 45,* 961-977.

Wegner, D. M. (1989). *White bears and other unwanted thoughts: Suppression, obsession, and the psychology of mental control.* New York: Guilford.

Wegner, D. M. (1994). Ironic processes of mental control. *Psychological Review, 101,* 34-52.

Wegner, D. M., Quillian, F., & Houston, C. (1996). Memories out of order: Thought suppression and the disassembly of remembered experience. *Journal of Personality and Social Psychology, 71*(4), 680-691.

Wolfe, J. (1991). The children's Impact of Event Scale: A measure of post sexual abuse PTSD symptoms. *Behavioral Assessment, 13,* 354-383.

Zimering, R. T., Caddell, J. M., Fairbank, J. A., & Keane, T. M. (1993). Posttraumatic stress disorder in Vietnam veterans: An experimental validation of the *DSM-III* diagnostic criteria. *Journal of Traumatic Stress, 6,* 327-342.

16

Seeking the Core

The Issues and Evidence Surrounding Recovered Accounts of Sexual Trauma

Jonathan W. Schooler

Forming conclusions about the issues surrounding recovered accounts of sexual abuse is much like peeling an onion: The removal of each layer leaves another to reckon with, and it seems as if one could continue the process indefinitely without revealing a final incontrovertible core. The many levels and complexities of the issue, together with its great emotional weight, have combined to polarize the field. Some vehemently assert that the recovery of long-forgotten episodes of sexual abuse should generally be considered valid (e.g., Herman & Schatzow, 1987; Williams, 1994), while others suggest that such accounts should be viewed with marked skepticism (e.g., Loftus, 1993; Ofshe, 1992). Although we can hope for a time when the unpeeling of this issue leads to a solid core of evidence, at present it is not even entirely clear what such a "core" of evidence would have to look like. Consequently, individuals unsatisfied with the conclusions revealed at any one layer may reasonably argue that we have not yet gotten to the bottom of the question. While we may never be able to agree about what evidence lies below, we can nevertheless make headway by attempting to classify and keep track of the layers that have been exposed. Indeed, some (although certainly not all) of the disagreements may result from disparities between the levels of analysis at which individuals are considering the issue. In an effort to bring some clarity to the issue, I will attempt to demarcate some of the layers that I have encountered in weighing the evidence on this complex and emotional topic.

AUTHOR'S NOTE: The writing of this chapter was supported by a grant to the author from the National Institute of Mental Health. I thank Marte Fallshore, Steve Fiore, Elizabeth Loftus, Joe Melcher, Tonya Schooler, and Carmi Schooler for comments on earlier drafts. This chapter appeared originally in *Consciousness and Cognition,* vol. 3, pp. 452-469. Copyright 1994 by Academic Press. Reprinted by permission.

The Nature of Evidence

☐ Both sides of the debate frequently argue that there is little or no direct evidence for the claims of the opposing view. For example, in a recent *U.S. News & World Report* interview, Ofshe, a major advocate of the notion that recovered accounts of trauma are likely to be the product of suggestion, observed, "No one has ever shown that the memory of repeated abuses can be uncontrollably and completely stripped from a person's consciousness" (quoted in Horn, 1993, p. 55). On the other side, Harvey and Herman (1994), who emphasize the veridicality of recovered memories, assert that "there is no evidence to suggest that psychotherapists have the degree of power and influence that would be required to produce this [fabricated memories] effect" (p. 4). In considering claims of "no evidence," it may be useful to distinguish between two different possible meanings of the phrase. The absence of evidence for a claim may result from the failure of appropriately designed research to reveal the phenomenon in question. This type of a positive failure can be a compelling argument that the concept in question is either invalid or at least in need of revision. Alternatively, the absence of evidence can result because no research has been able to address the question directly, one way or the other. In this latter case, a lack of evidence should not necessarily be used as an argument against the concept.

In the absence of direct research, we must be cautious in drawing conclusions of "no evidence," just as we would be cautious in using an untested drug simply because there is no direct evidence that it might be harmful. Rather, we should consider the converging implications of the available indirect sources of evidence. While such evidence may not provide the proof of direct experimental demonstration, the confluence of indirect sources of evidence can be informative. Exactly how we use such indirect sources of evidence, however, again returns us to the level at which we are addressing the question. Different decisions require different degrees of evidence. If we are concerned about the use of a procedure that may have possible ill effects, then we would be well-advised to con-

sider all sources of indirect evidence. Such reasoning is involved in using the indirect evidence of animal studies as the basis for decisions regarding the safety of products for humans. Legal decisions require far greater degrees of evidence, but even there the amount of evidence depends on the type of case: A preponderance of evidence is necessary for civil suits, whereas certainty beyond a reasonable doubt is required for criminal cases. A similar argument can be made in considering the evidence on recovered and fabricated memories of abuse. The amount of evidence necessary to inform a treatment decision may be markedly less than that required to convict an individual of child abuse. Perhaps some of the heat of this debate has been due to the difference between the criteria for evidence required for different types of judgments. Thus, in reviewing the literature it may be helpful to refrain from making absolute judgments on the topic and instead attempt to assess the degree of evidence associated with each issue.

As several contributors to this volume have noted, the issues of recovered and fabricated memories of abuse are often made out to be an either/or debate. Nevertheless, it is quite possible that some recovered memory reports may reflect real trauma, while others may be merely the product of suggestion. In short, there are two distinct questions at issue: (a) Can memories be recovered? and (b) Can memories be suggested? Both draw on distinct bodies of evidence, and both deserve separate consideration. In an effort to keep these two issues as distinct as possible, I will first review the issues surrounding recovered memories and then turn to memory fabrication.

Recovered Memory Reports

☐ The issue of reports of recovered memories of long-forgotten traumatic events subsumes many difficult layers. For example, it begs the question of what mechanisms might be involved. Discussions of recovered memories often vacillate between considering the evidence for psychodynamic repression mechanisms versus the evidence that individuals can have recovery experiences in which they retrieve memories of trauma that they do not recall being aware of. While the mechanisms underlying reports of recovered memories of traumatic events are of great interest, the issue of mechanism can and should be differentiated from the question of whether this class of experience occurs at all. Even when we try to limit the question to whether individuals can recover memories for trauma, we can run into difficulties because of the issue of what it means to "recover" a memory. An individual who reports recovering a memory for trauma is really indicating two sentiments: (a) that abuse occurred and (b) that there was a period of time in which the memory was not accessible.

Memory for the Abuse

Considerations of individuals' memory for abuse again require a distinction between memory for the occurrence and the details of the abuse. While certain details of an abuse event may be critical, for example, in making a determination between whether an adult was fondling a child or simply cleaning her, in many other cases the full specifics are really secondary. In short, one can have a valid memory for an abuse occurrence—that is, that an impropriety occurred—without necessarily maintaining a flawless recollection of that abuse.

The Prior Unavailability of the Memory

A central component of the memory recovery experience is the report that prior to recovery, the memory was unavailable. However, this issue itself breaks down into multiple levels. At one extreme is the possibility that an individual might claim unavailability when in fact he or she is fully aware that his or her memory had been intact. Such strategic enactment has been suggested as an explanation for alleged memory lapses and other symptoms reported with multiple personality disorder (e.g., Spanos, 1989). At the other extreme is the possibility that the individual had a period in which he or she was completely incapable of recalling the event. Between these two extremes is a full continuum of possible prior memory states. As Tulving and

Pearlstone (1966) observed many years ago, available memories require the appropriate retrieval conditions in order to be accessed. This distinction highlights the fact that a prolonged period in which a memory was not accessed does not necessarily indicate that memory was not available; it may simply reflect the previous absence of appropriate retrieval conditions. Thus, the retrospective determination that a memory was unavailable requires remembering instances in which one was exposed to the appropriate retrieval conditions yet nevertheless failed to recall the memory. Otherwise, such assessments must be based on the rather dubious task of estimating what one *would* have remembered had the appropriate retrieval conditions occurred.

To make matters worse, there is substantial evidence from other domains documenting the marked difficulty of reconstructing a prior knowledge state from the vantage of a new state. For example, individuals who are told facts about a topic tend to misremember that they previously knew those facts, even when independent evidence suggests that they did not (Fischoff, 1982). Similarly, individuals whose attitudes change as a result of persuasion tend to misremember their prior attitudes as being consistent with their newly acquired ones (Bem, 1972). Admittedly, these studies illustrate memory errors of *minimizing* differences between present and past knowledge states, whereas recovered memory errors may involve *exaggerating* such differences. Nevertheless, at another level, both types of errors could reflect the well-documented tendency to maintain consistency (e.g., Festinger, 1980). Accordingly, individuals who have recovered memory experiences may misconstrue their prior knowledge state as being more different than it actually was, thereby maintaining the consistency of their attitude toward that knowledge (i.e., My memories of abuse must have been unavailable, because otherwise I would have been as upset then as I am now).

Because of the many layers associated with the issue of recovery, it may be helpful to begin to review the evidence with a rudimentary question: Can reported recoveries of abuse correspond to real incidents? This bare-bones question leaves out many important issues, including the mechanism of the recovery, the completeness of the recollection, and the actual prior unavailability of the memory. However, it addresses an issue that is of tantamount importance to individuals who believe that they have had recovered memory experiences: whether their recollection of abuse may have some bearing in reality.

Corroborating the Abuse Associated With Recovered Memory Reports

In reviewing the evidence documenting the abuse implicated in recovered memory reports, one observation seems clear: There simply is not a lot of research on which to base conclusions one way or the other. Some might argue that the absence of documentation reflects the absence of a phenomenon. However, because of the sensitivity of the issue, the difficulties of corroboration, and the dearth of systematic investigation, the relative lack of corroborated evidence for the contents of recovered memory reports may reflect nothing more than an absence of research. Indeed, given the current state of the field, it is not at all clear that we could reasonably expect greater evidence of corroborated recovered memory reports even if such reports commonly reflected actual experiences. As a case in point, until recently we had little idea of the frequency of childhood abuse simply because systematic investigation had not been conducted. Furthermore, consideration of the little direct evidence that does exist is at least consistent with the notion that recovered memory reports can correspond to actual abuse. Thus, while the existing corroboration for recovered memory reports may be scant, it is nevertheless sufficiently compelling to support the strong likelihood that such reports can correspond to actual incidents of abuse.

Herman and Schatzow (1987) describe the only published systematic effort to corroborate the memories of a sample of patients who reported recovered accounts of childhood trauma. Of 53 patients participating in group therapy for childhood abuse, they found that 64% reported severe or moderate forgetting of childhood abuse and 74% claimed to have what the authors

viewed as strong corroboration (e.g., pornographic photos, diaries, confessions from the perpetrator). While this study provides suggestive evidence in support of memory recoveries, it is not as well documented as it might be. For example, the authors do not provide an independent analysis of the group of greatest interest, the 26% who reported completely forgetting the incident. On the basis of the published article it could be speculated that the corroborated memories were limited to the 74% of the patient population who had full or partial recall. However, in a personal communication, Herman (June 1994) indicated that there was no relationship in this study between patients' reports of forgetting and their likelihood of providing corroborating evidence. It is also conceivable that individuals who reported complete forgetting may have made up their evidence of corroboration. However, if we make the reasonable assumption that there was no widespread and deliberate attempt to mislead, then this study provides at least suggestive evidence that recovered memory reports can correspond to actual instances of abuse.

In addition to the Herman and Schatzow (1987) study, there are also a number of published cases of recovered memories of abuse for which there was corroborating evidence associating the alleged abuser with other instances of abuse (see Horn, 1993). Here I briefly review a new case for which I was personally able to acquire some indirect corroborative evidence. This case was introduced to me by ND, a clinical psychology faculty member and productive researcher at a major state university who had treated the individual in question, JR, for a totally unrelated problem approximately 9 years before his recovered memory report. Subsequent to the treatment, ND and JR became good friends, and ND was thus privy to the unfolding of JR's recovered memory report and subsequent corroboration efforts. In a telephone interview, JR described how, at the age of 30, he had experienced marked agitation while watching a movie in which the main character grapples with memories of sexual molestation. Several hours after the movie, while lying in bed, JR remembered an incident in which his parish priest had sexually molested him on a camping trip when he was 11 years old. Subsequently, JR reported recovering additional memories of abuse that he estimates spanned over the next several years.

There are multiple sources of indirect corroboration of this case. First, there is JR's description of his attempts to corroborate the abuse. According to JR, upon confrontation, the priest acknowledged the molestation and tried to assuage JR by indicating that he had sought treatment for sexually abusive clergy following an incident with another individual. Three of JR's brothers also indicated that they had been approached by the priest. In addition to JR's report of corroboration, there are also indirect corroborating accounts of other individuals. Although ND learned of the events of this case only indirectly, he maintained regular contact with JR throughout this ordeal. Thus, ND can at a minimum corroborate the temporal order in which the reported corroborating events took place. ND also knows JR quite well, and it is therefore of some interest that ND strongly discounts the possibility that JR could have invented all of the corroborating evidence that he reported in their numerous conversations. In addition, subsequent to JR's memory recovery and attempted lawsuit, another individual reported that he too had been sexually approached by the priest. In a separate telephone interview, this individual described how at age 18 he went to the priest for counseling about homosexuality, whereupon the priest made sexual advances toward him. This individual indicated that he had maintained an intact memory for the priest's sexual improprieties, but had been reluctant to disclose the memory due to his embarrassment.

There are a number of observations worth extracting from the above case. First, the evidence was indirect; that is, there were no actual witnesses or direct physical evidence of the reported abuse. Thus, this case does not speak to the precision of individuals' memories of abuse. Furthermore, there was no independent verification of JR's memory gap prior to the report of recovery, so we cannot determine to what degree the memories were previously unavailable.[1] While there are aspects of this case that cannot be validated, other elements strongly suggest that it did correspond to actual

incidents of abuse. First, it involved a recovery that occurred outside the context of therapy, thereby reducing the likelihood that it was the product of a therapist's suggestion. Second, there was another individual who indicated that he had been involved in abusive behavior by the alleged perpetrator. While this corroborating report was elicited after the initial recovered memory, and was therefore potentially vulnerable to suggestion, it is worth noting that it was produced by an individual who claimed never to have forgotten the abusive incident. Even skeptics of recovered memories are reluctant to question the memories of an individual who "suffered silently her whole life with memories of abuse" (Loftus, 1994, p. 443). Thus, taken together with other published cases, the present case provides converging evidence that recovered memory reports can, at least sometimes, be corroborated to the degree that they can implicate individuals who are prone to engage in abusive behaviors.

Additional Aspects of the Question of Recovery

So far I have argued only for the most bare-bones claim that some reports of recovered memories seem likely to have some correspondence to actual incidents of abuse. In paring the question down to this basic issue, I sloughed off many important layers. I now return to consider three of these other aspects of the recovered memory experience: (a) Do individuals actually forget memory for trauma? (b) Can memory for trauma fluctuate in availability? (c) What mechanisms might lead to the forgetting and recovery of trauma?

Evidence that individuals can actually forget trauma. Much of the research examining the incidence of forgetting childhood abuse has involved the retrospective reports of patients currently seeking treatment for sexual abuse (e.g., Briere & Conte, 1993; Gold, Hughes, & Hohnecker, 1994; Herman & Schatzow, 1987; Loftus, Polonsky, & Fullilove, 1994). Aside from the potential difficulties in corroborating the abuse and determining how patients interpreted the questions used to elicit their reports (see Ceci, Huffman, Smith, & Loftus, 1994), such studies are constrained by the intrinsic difficulties associated with (a) distinguishing a prolonged period in which a memory was not accessed from the claim that a memory was actually unavailable during that period and (b) assessing a prior knowledge state from the vantage of an altered knowledge state (see earlier discussion). Given the problems inherent in retrospective claims of unavailability, we should be cautious in using patients' retrospective reports as a source for conclusions about the actual prior state of their memories. Rather, the primary value of patients' retrospective analyses lies in documenting the frequency with which victims of sexual abuse *believe* that their memories were previously unavailable.

A more direct method of documenting actual forgetting of trauma is to identify individuals on the basis of their experience of trauma and then query them to determine whether they currently remember it. This approach can thereby document forgetting while it is still intact. Along these lines, Williams (1994) identified women who had been taken to a sex abuse clinic as children 17 years earlier. Of the 129 women who were interviewed in the study, 38% did not recall the abuse for which they had been treated. Williams conducted a variety of analyses to rule out explanations other than forgetting. For example, contrary to the suggestion that these results might reflect a failure to disclose abuse, she found that patients who failed to recall the abuse were just as likely to reveal other intimate facts as individuals who recalled the abuse. Against the suggestion that these results were due to infantile amnesia, Williams found that nearly one-third of those abused between the ages of 7 and 10 and over one-quarter of those abused between 11 and 12 reported no recollection of the abuse. Although Williams's study takes important steps toward documenting forgetting of incidents of sexual trauma, it does have some limitations. First, the study addresses only memory for individual instances of abuse and does not bear on the more general claim that individuals can forget repeated episodes of abuse. Second, many (68%) of the individuals who did not recall the particular incident for

which they were treated nevertheless recalled other sexual assaults. It is thus possible that some of these individuals may have confused their recollections of abuse rather than totally forgetting them. However, even when individuals who recalled other instances of abuse are removed, there still remains 12% of this population who reported that they were never sexually abused, when in fact they had been treated for such abuse. It would be nice to know the demographics (e.g., age distribution) of this particular subset of Williams's population. Nevertheless, at a minimum Williams's study suggests that individuals can forget individual episodes of abuse and at least some may forget that they were the victims of abuse altogether.

Another potential difficulty for the claim, implied by Williams's study, that forgetting of childhood sexual traumas can be common is the frequent demonstration that children typically maintain intact memories for a variety of nonsexual traumatic experiences, including kidnapping (Terr, 1979), sniper attack (Pynoos & Nader, 1988), lightning strike (Dollinger, 1985), emergency room treatments (Howe, Courage, & Peterson, 1994), and even urinary tract catheterization (Goodman, Quas, Batterman-Faunce, Riddlesberger, & Kuhn, 1994). One important consideration in assessing the implications of reports of children's intact memories for trauma is that these studies involve children's rather than adults' memories for childhood trauma. It is therefore quite possible, indeed likely, that greater forgetting would occur with further passage of time. It is also worth noting that there may be important differences between the traumatic events mentioned above and sexual abuse. The above traumas corresponded to single events that could be discussed with others and that would not entail profound degrees of embarrassment. The one exception to this generalization is the Goodman et al. (1994) study involving urinary tract catheterization, which at least hints at the possibility that some of these factors may be important. In many respects Goodman et al.'s study comes the closest to approximating the trauma associated with sexual abuse. The procedure was painful and embarrassing (entailing genital penetration and public urination), and at least some parents were reluctant to talk about the procedure with their children. If there is some validity to the notion of forgetting childhood sexual abuse, then given the similarities between the procedure involved in Goodman et al.'s study and sexual abuse, one would expect to see greater hints of precursors to forgetting of trauma in this study than in the other studies. And in fact, there are such hints. For one, a few children (the authors do not give the precise number) out of a sample of 46 denied that they experienced the medical test altogether. Although it is not possible to determine the reason for these denials, this is certainly the type of precursor to actual forgetting that one might expect. Second, Goodman et al. found that a number of factors that seem likely to be associated with sexual abuse were predictive of poor memory performance in their study. Specifically, embarrassment, lack of discussion of the procedure with parents, and PTSD symptoms were all negatively correlated with memory performance. If we extrapolate the trends observed in Goodman et al.'s studies to adult recollection of childhood sexual abuse, in which the delay is much greater, the embarrassment potentially more pronounced, the discussion of the trauma typically a nonoccurrence (with secrecy frequently ensured by threats of violence), and the incidence of PTSD symptoms frequent (Terr, 1991), then it is not unreasonable to expect that some individuals might in fact forget the abuse.

Examination of adult memory for nonsexual trauma also provides somewhat of a mixed picture, but one that is again not inconsistent with the possibility that individuals can forget memory for trauma. A number of studies have documented general memory disturbances with adults following a variety of nonsexual traumatic events, including tornado (Madakasira & O'Brien, 1987), fire (McFarlane, 1986, 1988), airplane crash (Sloan, 1988), and the Hyatt Regency Hotel disaster (Wilkinson, 1983). Unfortunately, these studies do not specify the precise nature of the memory deficits. Thus, while such studies suggest a general relationship between traumatic experience and forgetting, they cannot be used to provide direct evidence for specific forgetting of traumatic experiences. Although more scant, there have been a number of

reports of specific forgetting of traumatic experiences, particularly wartime experiences (e.g., Parson, 1988; Silver & Kelly, 1985; van Devanter, 1985; Wilson, 1988). The reported forgetting of wartime memories is of particular relevance to the claim of forgetting of sexual abuse because of certain similarities between these two types of trauma. Specifically, in both cases individuals may have been involved in activities that they are especially reluctant to discuss. Indeed, many of the reported instances of forgetting of wartime trauma involved particularly troubling events, such as the killing of women or children (Parson, 1988; Silver & Kelly, 1985; Wilson, 1988).

The suggestion that reported forgetting of trauma may be particularly associated with events involving embarrassment or shame (see Lewis, 1990) leads readily to the possibility that such reports do not entail forgetting at all, but rather reflect an unwillingness to disclose the events in question. As mentioned already, there is some evidence arguing against a failure-to-disclose explanation for traumatic forgetting, such as Williams's (1994) finding that predisposition to disclose intimate information was not associated with forgetting. However, even if we grant the possibility that an unwillingness to disclose may sometimes be involved in reports of forgetting, there is still good reason to believe that individuals may go for periods in which the traumatic event is relatively less accessible and then becomes much more so.

Fluctuations in the accessibility of trauma. The notion of fluctuation in access to traumatic events is strongly suggested by veterans' delayed reactivations of traumatic experiences. Reactivation of traumatic experiences can occur after durations in which individuals experience relatively few symptoms (Christenson, Walker, Ross, & Maltbie, 1981; Defazio, Rustin, & Diamond, 1975; Grinker, 1945; McGee, 1984; Williams, 1983). For example, Christenson et al. (1981) describe the case of Mr. A, which they characterize as a typical example of a delayed reactivation of traumatic conflict. Following a brief treatment for "nerves" after World War II, Mr. A experienced a long period of good adjustment.

Then, one day while working in an emergency room, he was asked to clean up a 9-year-old boy whom he did not know was already dead. The discovery that the boy was dead horrified Mr. A and was immediately followed by the onset of anxiety, depression, and nightmares about his wartime experiences. Mr. A was admitted to a hospital, where he revealed the following information that he had not discussed for 35 years. Apparently, during a particularly traumatic period in the war, Mr. A had shot a 10-year-old boy who had been suspected of being wired as a human bomb. Although the above-cited report does not make any claims with regard to whether Mr. A ever completely forgot about this incident, it clearly suggests that the traumatic and troubling experience became much more accessible following the triggering event.

There are a number of important observations that may be gleaned from consideration of veterans' delayed reactivation episodes. First, while we cannot know the precision of their memories, the fact that these individuals were involved in wartime events supports the strong likelihood that the reactivations are associated with some type of actual traumatic activity. At a minimum, veterans' reactivation episodes illustrate a situation in which individual experience increased accessibility to the fact that they were previously exposed to actual trauma. Thus, such experiences provide a useful comparison to reports of recovered memories of sexual abuse, for which the participation in actual trauma is less clear. And when we make the comparison the similarities are striking. First, as the above example illustrates, both delayed veteran reactivations and childhood sexual abuse can correspond to particularly troubling events for which the individual would understandably feel embarrassed or ashamed. Second, in both cases individuals can go for periods in which they do not discuss the event or show direct evidence of being troubled by it. Third, in both cases a triggering event that shares some similarity with the alleged traumatic event (e.g., seeing a dead child, watching a movie about sex abuse) produces an onrush of emotion associated with the reported traumatic event. Fourth, after the triggering event, the

individual begins discussing the traumatic experience. The striking parallels between recovered memory reports and veterans' delayed reactivations suggest that recovered accounts of sexual abuse may result from increased access to the fact that one was previously exposed to trauma. With this in mind, I now turn to a discussion of what mechanisms might drive such a process.

Mechanisms of recovered memory reports. In considering the mechanisms that might lead to recovered memory experiences, it may be useful to consider what processes might produce the various attributes of both delayed veteran reactivations (see McGee, 1984) and recovered memories outlined above. First, the fact that these experiences correspond to situations that may cause embarrassment or shame suggests that individuals may be reluctant to talk about these experiences. Considerable research suggests that talking about experiences helps to integrate those experiences into one's life narrative, thereby increasing their potential accessibility (Nelson, 1993). The absence of such discussion may thus reduce the accessibility of these experiences (Johnson, 1988b; Tessler & Nelson, 1994). In addition, embarrassment/shame may particularly predispose individuals to actively avoid (suppress) thinking about these experiences, which may result in their temporarily reduced accessibility (Kihlstrom & Hoyt, 1990). Other mechanisms, including general forgetting as well as processes more specific to trauma, such as dissociation (Spiegel & Cardena, 1991), physiological processes (Southwick et al., 1993), and perhaps even repression (Erdelyi, 1990), might also contribute to the decreased accessibility of traumatic memories. As a result of this decreased accessibility, individuals may go for some time without showing obvious extrinsic evidence of possessing these memories. However, when they encounter a situation that shares some fundamental similarity with the original traumatic experience, with respect to either context (Tulving & Thomson, 1973) or affective/physiological state (Clark & Teasdale, 1982; Goodwin, Powell, Bremer, Hoine, & Stern, 1969), the accessibility of the traumatic memory may increase, along with its associated powerful emotions. Therapy situations may also increase accessibility of traumatic memories by eliciting emotional states corresponding to the trauma or by inducing relevant associative chaining that helps to cue the memory (Bower, 1990). Once access to the memory is increased, to the degree that suppression processes were involved in the initial reduction in accessibility to the memory, rebound effects may be experienced in which there is a flooding of the previously suppressed thoughts (Wegner, 1994). The resulting prevalence of thoughts about the trauma may powerfully contrast with the prior relative absence of such thoughts. From the perspective of this current flooding of thoughts about the trauma, the previous relatively reduced accessibility of the memory may be construed as complete unavailability. The above account provides a highly feasible characterization of the recovered memory process without having to draw on the notion that traumatic memories are ever completely unavailable. This is not to say that traumatic memories may not be completely unavailable for some period of time, but merely that we do not need to postulate such a memory state in order to account for sincere reports of recovered memory experiences corresponding to actual incidents of trauma. At a minimum, we cannot argue against the possibility of recovered memory experiences on the basis that there is no existing way to explain them.

Fabricated Memories

☐ The suggestion that recovered memory experiences can be associated with the increased accessibility to memories of actual abuse should not preclude the likelihood that recovered accounts of abuse might also be generated in response to suggestion. As with recovered memories, at present it is difficult to provide incontrovertible direct evidence for the premise of fabricated memories of abuse. Nevertheless, consideration of the indirect evidence at hand strongly supports the contention that recollec-

tions of abuse can result from suggestion.[2] In assessing the question of fabricated memories it may be useful to consider three questions: (a) Can suggestion lead to the production of images/impressions that are sufficiently vivid to enable them to be confused with reality? (b) If such images/impressions were produced in regard to childhood abuse, could individuals be persuaded to believe in them? (c) Is there any case evidence suggesting that individuals may have been persuaded to believe in false memories of abuse? I discuss each of these questions in turn.

Confusing Suggestions With Reality

There have now been innumerable demonstrations that individuals can come to remember vividly things that they never in fact experienced. This evidence comes from many different research traditions. Neurocognitive evidence of individuals with frontal lobe damage indicates that patients can readily fabricate and believe elaborate memories that are confabulated in order to tie together the real bits of memory that they retrieve (e.g., Moscovitch, 1989). Research on reality monitoring has shown that individuals can confuse self-generated thoughts with perceived thoughts, such that they remember experiencing stimuli that they in fact only imagined (e.g., Johnson, 1988a; Johnson & Raye, 1981). Research on the effects of postevent information has demonstrated that people can integrate the contents of misleading suggestions into their memories (for a brief review, see Loftus, Garry, & Brown, 1994). The resulting memories can be held with as much confidence as real memories (Loftus, Donders, Hoffman, & Schooler, 1989), can be described in marked detail (Schooler, Clark, & Loftus, 1988; Schooler, Gerhard, & Loftus, 1986), and are as likely as real memories to be maintained in the face of contradictory information (Loftus, Korf, & Schooler, 1989).

One criticism about applying the research on both reality monitoring and misleading postevent suggestion to the present topic is that these research traditions frequently involve details about events rather than events themselves (e.g., Pezdek & Roe, 1994). However, all of the above-mentioned lines of research have demonstrated that individuals can be led to misrecollect entire events that never happened. The neurocognitive evidence reveals remarkably detailed and complex confabulations of entire events. Research in reality monitoring has shown that people can come to remember having had dreams that were in fact only told to them by others (Johnson, Kahan, & Raye, 1984). Research on the effects of misleading postevent suggestion has demonstrated that individuals can, as a result of suggestion, come to remember entire events, such as being lost in a shopping mall (Loftus & Ketcham, 1994) or getting one's finger caught in a mouse trap (Ceci, Huffman, et al., 1994; Ceci, Loftus, Leichtman, & Bruck, 1994). These fabricated accounts of entire events can also be described in great detail and maintained in the face of contradiction (Ceci, Huffman, et al., 1994). In short, it seems that the mind is quite capable of remembering vivid accounts of things that never actually happened.

Accepting False Accounts of Abuse

If the mind is capable of producing vivid accounts of events that never in fact took place, then there is no principled reason why such accounts could not be fabricated with respect to childhood abuse. What is of question is whether, once generated, individuals could come to believe that such events actually occurred. There could be some scenarios that are simply too inconceivable to be confused with reality, no matter how vividly they are produced in one's mind.

In considering whether individuals can be persuaded to believe in fabricated memories of abuse, it is important to remember the many painful lessons, ranging from Nazi-era Germany to Milgram's (1963) classic studies of obedience, demonstrating the remarkable degree to which individuals can be led to accept preposterous suggestions when they are exposed to persuasive individuals in positions of authority. Thus, in assessing the possibility of fabricated memories of abuse, we must be ever vigilant not to make the same mistake we have made time and time before: underestimating

just how persuadable people can be. There is, in fact, every reason to believe that people's propensity for persuasion extends to accepting memories for the seemingly preposterous. As a poignant example, in response to suggestions by leaders of religious groups, individuals have been known to report recovering memories of having been visited or abducted by space aliens (Persinger, 1992). Furthermore, both recovered accounts of sexual abuse and alien abduction can be (a) elicited following the suggestions of the leader of a group, (b) "remembered" suddenly, (c) associated with a reduction of anxiety and panic attacks, and (d) accompanied by subsequent recollections of additional "memories" (Persinger, 1992). If individuals can recover (presumably false) childhood memories of being abducted or visited by space aliens, then certainly they should be capable of falsely remembering being abused as children. Moreover, the striking parallels (with respect to both the suggestion and the recovery) between the situations surrounding at least some recovered accounts of sexual abuse and alien abductions suggest that similar dysfunctional mechanisms might be involved in the fabrication of both types of memories.

Retractions of Recovered Memories

If individuals could be persuaded to believe in memories of abuse that did not in fact occur, then one would expect that at least sometimes people would realize that they had been misled and retract their accounts. While such retractions would not necessarily prove that the memories were fabricated, they would at least be consistent with such a view. In a recent edited volume, Goldstein and Farmer (1993) provide a number of examples of such retractors including the account of Pasley (1993), who sought treatment for bulimia. Pasley's therapist told her that bulimia was commonly caused by sexual abuse and suggested that she had been abused. Following repeated suggestions by her therapist, often while under hypnosis, Pasley began having bizarre dreams and flashbacks including group sexual abuse and being sexually abused by animals—all of which Pasley's therapist insisted really happened. After 4 years in therapy,

Pasley came to the conclusion that these alleged memories were in fact fictitious, the product of her imagination's collaboration with her therapist's suggestion.

One can of course interpret the above case in a manner that does not implicate the therapist's suggestions. Pasley could have reforgotten the memories or simply found it more palatable to reframe them as suggestions. However, there are compelling reasons to suspect that suggestions may have played a role. First, the recovery did not occur spontaneously, as in the cases described earlier, but only following the suggestion of a therapist that the reported symptoms were a likely product of sexual abuse. Second, the recovery occurred during hypnosis, which is known to increase individuals' susceptibility to misleading memory suggestions (e.g., Putnam, 1979; suggestibility is, after all, one of the hallmarks of the hypnotic state). Third, despite all of her therapy, Pasley ultimately concluded that her memories had no basis. In fact, her belief in the falseness of her memories was sufficient to convince a jury that her memories had been planted and to award her a six-figure settlement on that basis.

Pasley's case is not an isolated instance, but rather reflects the sentiment of a growing number of individuals who have become disenfranchised with their recovered memories of abuse. It is of course possible that such retractions merely reflect individuals returning to denial stage (e.g., Gleaves, 1994). However, there is a certain irony to believing individuals when they recover memories but disbelieving them when they recant such memories (or vice versa, for that matter). The fact that individuals can shift between believing and disbelieving in their recovered memories demonstrates the fundamental ontological uncertainty of such memories. It thus seems most appropriate that we be extremely cautious in assessing individuals' claims regarding either the veracity or the falseness of their recovered memories.

Conclusion

☐ In sum, although the available evidence remains primarily indirect, there is nevertheless a reasonable foundation for the existence of both recovered and fabricated memories. Even a skeptical view about the frequency with which one or the other of these phenomena actually occurs should be tempered by the importance of their probable existence. For example, even if the forgetting/recovery is an extremely rare reaction to trauma, given current estimates of the incidence of childhood sexual abuse (some studies estimate as many as one in three women, e.g., McCann, Sakheim, & Abrahamson, 1988), the absolute frequency of recovered memories could still be quite substantial. Similarly, even if fabricated memories occur only in highly suggestive circumstances, the documented, and perhaps even frequent, use of hypnosis, truth serum, and persistent suggestion by practitioners convinced that such abuse must have occurred (see Loftus, 1993) implies that whatever it takes to create a fabricated memory of abuse is likely to be occurring.

While there is certainly great controversy surrounding the topic of recovered accounts of sexual abuse, there is one point on which everyone is likely to agree: More research is needed. In closing, it may be helpful to identify briefly some of the research topics that the present analysis suggests are worthy of pursuit. With respect to recovered memories, two general lines of research seem especially important. First, extensive and thorough research is warranted to determine just how often the sexual abuse associated with recovered memory reports can be corroborated. Second, longitudinal assessments of documented victims of various types of traumas may help to identify the specific situations, personality factors, and mechanisms that may mediate forgetting, remembering, and fluctuations in access to memories for trauma. (It should be noted of course that repeated interviewing of individuals regarding their trauma is likely to have an impact on their memories.) With respect to the issue of fabricated memories of trauma, extensive surveys of therapy practices are needed (see Poole, Lindsay, Memon, & Bull, 1995) to assess the frequency with which individuals may be subjected to therapeutic techniques that risk introducing fabricated memories. It would be especially interesting to know the relationship between the use of suggestive therapeutic techniques and the relative likelihoods of both the occurrence and the possibility of corroborating recovered memory reports. If the recovered memory reports elicited in suggestive therapy situations are more common and less readily corroborated than those elicited by less suggestive practices, this would provide rather compelling evidence that suggestion may create memories of abuse.

The above-recommended research would clearly help to clarify some of the difficult issues that surround recovered accounts of childhood abuse. However, in the meantime we must rely on the evidence at hand. Although it is conceivable that in the unrevealed layers lies a core of definitive evidence in favor of one or the other extreme position, at present it seems appropriate that we take the probable existence of both recovered and fabricated memories very seriously.

Notes

1. It might be noted that although ND never discussed sex abuse with JR, they did discuss many intimate aspects of JR's life that ND believes were on par with the embarrassment one might feel at being sexually involved with a priest. The fact that JR discussed these other events but not his memories of the priest leads ND, at least, to believe that JR was truly unaware of possessing the memories of abuse.

2. The difference in the relative amount of discussion dedicated here to recovered and fabricated memories should not be taken as a reflection of the degree of evidence for these two constructs. It simply reflects the greater complexity of issues surrounding the topic of recovered memories and the preexistence of an excellent review of the evidence for fabricated memories by Loftus (1993).

References

Bem, D. J. (1972). Self-perception theory. In L. Berkowitz (Ed.), *Advances in experimental social psychology.* New York: Academic Press.

Bower, G. H. (1990). Awareness, the unconscious, and repression: An experimental psychologist's perspective. In J. L. Singer (Ed.), *Repression and dissociation: Implications for personality theory, psychopathology, and health* (pp. 209-231). Chicago: University of Chicago Press.

Briere, J., & Conte, J. R. (1993). Self-reported amnesia for abuse in adults molested as children. *Journal of Traumatic Stress, 6,* 21-31.

Ceci, S. J., Huffman, M. L. C., Smith, E., & Loftus, E. F. (1994). Repeatedly thinking about a nonevent: Source misattributions among preschoolers. *Consciousness and Cognition, 3,* 388-407.

Ceci, S. J., Loftus, E. F., Leichtman, M. D., & Bruck, M. (1994). The possible role of source misattributions in the creation of false beliefs among preschoolers. *International Journal of Clinical and Experimental Hypnosis, 42,* 304-320.

Christenson, R. M., Walker, J. I., Ross, D. R., & Maltbie, A. (1981). Reactivation of traumatic conflicts. *American Journal of Psychiatry, 138,* 984-985.

Clark, D. M., & Teasdale, J. D. (1982). Diurnal variation in clinical depression and accessibility of memories of positive and negative experiences. *Journal of Abnormal Psychology, 91,* 87-95.

Defazio, V., Rustin, S., & Diamond, A. (1975). Symptom development in Vietnam era veterans. *American Journal of Orthopsychiatry, 45,* 158-163.

Dollinger, S. J. (1985). Lightning-strike disaster among children. *British Journal of Medical Psychology, 58,* 375-383.

Erdelyi, M. H. (1990). Repression, reconstruction, and defense: History and integration of the psychoanalytic and experimental frameworks. In J. L. Singer (Ed.), *Repression and dissociation: Implications for personality theory, psychopathology, and health* (pp. 1-32). Chicago: University of Chicago Press.

Festinger, L. (1980). Looking backward. In L. Festinger (Ed.), *Retrospections on social psychology.* New York: Oxford University Press.

Fischoff, B. (1982). For those condemned to study the past: Heuristics and biases in hindsight. In D. Kahneman, P. Slovic, & A. Tversky (Eds.), *Judgment under uncertainty: Heuristics and biases* (pp. 335-351). New York: Cambridge University Press.

Gleaves, D. H. (1994). On "The reality of repressed memories." *American Psychologist, 49,* 440-441.

Gold, S. N., Hughes, D., & Hohnecker, L. (1994). Degrees of repression of sexual abuse memories. *American Psychologist, 49,* 441-442.

Goldstein, E., & Farmer, K. (Eds.). (1993). *True stories of false memories.* Boca Raton, FL: Sirs.

Goodman, G. S., Quas, J. A., Batterman-Faunce, J. M., Riddlesberger, M. M., & Kuhn, J. (1994). Predictors of accurate and inaccurate memories of traumatic events experienced in childhood. *Consciousness and Cognition, 3,* 269-294.

Goodwin, D. W., Powell, B., Bremer, D., Hoine, H., & Stern, J. (1969). Alcohol and recall: State dependent effects in man. *Science, 163,* 1358-1360.

Grinker, R. R. (1945). Psychiatric disorders in combat crews overseas and returnees. *Medical Clinics of North America, 29,* 729-739.

Harvey, M. R., & Herman, J. L. (1994). Amnesia, partial amnesia and delayed recall among adult survivors of childhood trauma. *Consciousness and Cognition, 3,* 295-306.

Herman, J. L., & Schatzow, E. (1987). Recovery and verification of memories of childhood sexual trauma. *Psychoanalytic Psychology, 4,* 1-14.

Horn, M. (1993, November 29). Memories lost and found. *U.S. News & World Report,* pp. 53-63.

Howe, M. L., Courage, M. L., & Peterson, C. (1994). How can I remember when "I" wasn't there: Long-term retention of traumatic experiences and emergence of the cognitive self. *Consciousness and Cognition, 3,* 327-355.

Johnson, M. K. (1988a). Discriminating the origin of information. In T. F. Oltmanns & B. A. Maher (Eds.), *Delusional beliefs: Interdisciplinary perspectives* (pp. 34-65). New York: John Wiley.

Johnson, M. K. (1988b). Reality monitoring: An experimental phenomenological approach. *Journal of Experimental Psychology: General, 117,* 390-394.

Johnson, M. K., Kahan, T. L., & Raye, C. L. (1984). Dreams and reality monitoring. *Journal of Experimental Psychology: General, 113,* 329-344.

Johnson, M. K., & Raye, C. L. (1981). Reality monitoring. *Psychological Review, 88,* 67-85.

Kihlstrom, J. F., & Hoyt, I. P. (1990). Repression, dissociation, and hypnosis. In J. L. Singer (Ed.), *Repression and dissociation: Implications for personality theory, psychopathology, and health.* Chicago: University of Chicago Press.

Lewis, H. B. (1990). Shame, repression, field dependence, and psychopathology. In J. L. Singer (Ed.), *Repression and dissociation: Implications for personality theory, psychopathology, and health.* Chicago: University of Chicago Press.

Loftus, E. F. (1993). The reality of repressed memories. *American Psychologist, 48,* 518-537.

Loftus, E. F. (1994). The repressed memory controversy. *American Psychologist, 49,* 443-445.

Loftus, E. F., Donders, K., Hoffman, H. G., & Schooler, J. W. (1989). Creating new memories that are quickly accessed and confidently held. *Memory and Cognition, 17,* 607-616.

Loftus, E. F., Garry, M., & Brown, S. W. (1994). Memory: A river runs through it. *Consciousness and Cognition, 3,* 438-451.

Loftus, E. F., & Ketcham, K. (1994). *The myth of repressed memory: False memories and allegations of sexual abuse.* New York: St. Martin's.

Loftus, E. F., Korf, N., & Schooler, J. W. (1989). Misguided memories: Sincere distortions of reality. In J. Yuille (Ed.), *Credibility assessment: A theoretical and research perspective* (pp. 155-174). Boston: Kluwer.

Loftus, E. F., Polonsky, S., & Fullilove, M. T. (1994). Memories of childhood sexual abuse: Remembering and repressing. *Psychology of Women Quarterly, 18,* 67-84.

Madakasira, S., & O'Brien, K. (1987). Acute posttraumatic stress disorder in victims of a natural disaster. *Journal of Nervous and Mental Disease, 175,* 286-290.

McCann, I. L., Sakheim, D. K., & Abrahamson, D. J. (1988). Trauma and victimization: A model of psychological adaptation. *Counseling Psychologist, 16,* 531-594.

McFarlane, A. C. (1986). Posttraumatic morbidity of a disaster. *Journal of Nervous and Mental Disease, 174,* 4-14.

McFarlane, A. C. (1988). The longitudinal course of posttraumatic morbidity. *Journal of Nervous and Mental Disease, 176,* 30-39.

McGee, R. (1984). Flashbacks and memory phenomena. *Journal of Nervous and Mental Disease, 172,* 273-278.

Milgram, S. (1963). Behavioral study of obedience. *Journal of Abnormal and Social Psychology, 67,* 371-378.

Moscovitch, M. (1989). Confabulation and the frontal systems: Strategic versus associative retrieval in neuropsychological theories of memory. In H. L. Roediger III & F. I. M. Craik (Eds.), *Varieties of memory and consciousness: Essays in honor of Endel Tulving.* Hillsdale. NJ: Lawrence Erlbaum.

Nelson, K. (1993). The psychological and social origins of autobiographical memory. *Psychological Science, 4,* 1-8.

Ofshe, R. J. (1992). Inadvertent hypnosis during interrogation: False confession due to dissociative state; misidentified multiple personality and the satanic cult hypothesis. *Internal Journal of Clinical and Experimental Hypnosis, 40,* 125-156.

Parson, E. R. (1988). Post-traumatic self disorders. In J. P. Wilson, Z. Harel, & B. Kahana (Eds.), *Human adaptation to extreme stress: From the holocaust to Vietnam.* New York: Plenum.

Pasley, L. E. (1993). Misplaced trust. In E. Goldstein & K. Farmer (Eds.), *True stories of false memories* (pp. 347-365). Boca Raton. FL: Sirs.

Persinger, M. A. (1992). Neuropsychological profiles of adults who report "sudden remembering" of early childhood memories: Implications for claims of sex abuse and alien visitation/abduction experiences. *Perceptual and Motor Skills, 75,* 259-266.

Pezdek, K., & Roe, C. (1994). Memory for childhood events: How suggestible is it? *Consciousness and Cognition, 3,* 374-387.

Poole, D. A., Lindsay, D. S., Memon, A., & Bull, R. (1995). Psychotherapy and the recovery of memories of childhood sexual abuse: U.S. and British practitioners' beliefs, practices, and experiences. *Journal of Consulting and Clinical Psychology, 3,* 426-437.

Putnam, B. (1979). Hypnosis and distortion in eyewitness memory. *International Journal of Clinical and Experimental Hypnosis, 4,* 437-448.

Pynoos, R. S., & Nader, K. (1988). Children's memory and proximity to violence. *Journal of the American Academy of Child and Adolescent Psychiatry, 27,* 567-572.

Schooler, J. W., Clark, C. A., & Loftus, E. F. (1988). Knowing when memory is real. In M. Gruneberg, P. Morris, & R. N. Sykes (Eds.), *Practical aspects of memory* (pp. 83-88). New York: John Wiley.

Schooler, J. W., Gerhard, D., & Loftus, E. F. (1986). Qualities of the unreal. *Journal of Experimental Psychology: Learning, Memory, and Cognition, 12,* 171-181.

Silver, S. M., & Kelly, W. E. (1985). Hypnotherapy of posttraumatic stress disorder in combat veterans from WW II and Vietnam. In W. E. Kelly (Ed.), *Post-traumatic stress disorder and the war veteran patient.* New York: Brunner/Mazel.

Sloan, P. (1988). Post-traumatic stress in survivors of an airplane crash landing: A clinical and exploratory research intervention. *Journal of Traumatic Stress, 1,* 211-299.

Southwick, S. M., Krystal, J. H., Morgan, C. A., Johnson, D. R., Nagy, L. M., Nicolaou, A., Heninger, G. R., & Charney, D. S. (1993). Abnormal nonadrenergic function in posttraumatic stress disorder. *Archives of General Psychiatry, 50,* 266-274.

Spanos, N. P. (1989). Hypnosis, demonic possession, and multiple personality: Strategic enactments and disavowals of responsibility for actions. In C. E. Ward (Ed.), *Altered states of consciousness and mental health* (pp. 96-124). Newbury Park, CA: Sage.

Spiegel, D., & Cardena, E. (1991). Disintegrated experience: The dissociative disorders revisited. *Journal of Abnormal Psychology, 100,* 366-378.

Terr, L. C. (1979). Children of Chowchilla: A study of psychic trauma. In A. J. Solnit, R. Eissler, M. Freud, M. Kriss, & P. B. Neubauer (Eds.), *The psychoanalytic study of the child* (pp. 1543-1550). New Haven, CT: Yale University Press.

Terr, L. C. (1991). Childhood traumas: An outline and overview. *American Journal of Psychiatry, 148,* 10-20.

Tessler, M., & Nelson, K. (1994). Making memories: The influence of joint encoding on later recall by young children. *Consciousness and Cognition, 3,* 307-326.

Tulving, E., & Pearlstone, Z. (1966). Availability versus accessibility of information in memory for words. *Journal of Verbal Learning and Verbal Behavior, 5,* 381-391.

Tulving, E., & Thomson, D. M. (1973). Encoding specificity and retrieval processes in episodic memory. *Psychological Review, 80,* 352-373.

van Devanter, L. M. (1985). The unknown warriors: Implications of the experiences of women in Vietnam. In W. E. Kelly (Ed.), *Post-traumatic stress disorder and the war veteran patient.* New York: Brunner/Mazel.

Wegner, D. M. (1994). Ironic processes of mental control. *Psychological Review, 101,* 34-52.

Wilkinson, C. B. (1983). Aftermath of a disaster: The collapse of the Hyatt Regency Hotel skywalks. *American Journal of Psychiatry, 150,* 1134-1139.

Williams, C. C. (1983). The mental foxhole: The Vietnam veteran's search for meaning. *American Journal of Orthopsychiatry, 53,* 4-17.

Williams, L. M. (1994). Recall of childhood trauma: A prospective study of women's memories of child sexual abuse. *Journal of Consulting and Clinical Psychology, 62,* 1167-1176.

Wilson, J. P. (1988). Treating the Vietnam veteran. In F. M. Ochberg (Ed.), *Post-traumatic therapy and victims of violence.* New York: Brunner/Mazel.

17

Traumatic Memories Lost and Found

Can Lost Memories of Abuse Be Found in the Brain?

J. Douglas Bremner

Inscribed over the door of the Jewish Holocaust Museum in New York City is the motto "Never Forget." This is the credo of many witnesses and survivors of traumatic events, which reflects the feeling that the sufferings and loss of others who were victims of traumatic experiences should not be allowed to lapse into the shadows of lost remembrance. This credo is paradoxical, and perhaps even tragic, in the face of the reality of the fate of many traumatic memories. These memories are subject to fragmentation and to a loss of the sense of context of the memories in space and time. In many cases, memories can be just outside of conscious awareness for many years, before specific cues or triggers bring them back into consciousness in full force, with all of the negative thoughts and emotions associated with the original events. Some of these memories, on the other hand, may be permanently sealed from resurrection by the conscious mind.

There is, in fact, considerable controversy now about the validity of delayed recall of traumatic events, such as childhood abuse (Loftus, Garry, & Feldman, 1994; Loftus, Polonsky, & Fullilove, 1994; Williams, 1994a, 1994b). Until recently, there has been little solid evidence upon which to base an opinion about this issue. Most studies have been performed by cognitive psychologists in populations of normal human subjects. These studies have provided evidence for the idea that memory is subject to distortion or postencoding modification. For example, in a typical study, subjects were shown a series of slides that told a story involving a stop sign. These slides were followed by the reading of a similar verbal narrative in which the reference to the stop sign was replaced by a reference to a yield sign. When subjects were tested on recall of material related to the slides, they were more likely to report (incorrectly) having seen a yield sign than did subjects who did not receive the misleading information. The researchers who conducted this study concluded that misleading information led to "overwriting" of the original memory trace (Loftus, Miller, & Burns, 1978). These findings have been quoted in support of the idea that delayed recall of episodes of childhood abuse is often due to "false memory," or suggestibility effects, propagated by overzealous psychotherapists.

Other studies have suggested that this phenomenon is due to a source amnesia effect—that is, subjects do not have an overwriting of the memory; rather, they do not remember where they obtained the information (Lindsay & Johnson, 1989). For instance, in one study, subjects were assessed with a test in which they saw slides that included a hammer, followed by misleading verbal information involving a screwdriver, and then a forced-choice test of what they had seen in the slides between a hammer and an item to which they had previously not been exposed (a wrench). The researchers argue that if there is a true overwriting phenomenon with misleading verbal material, then subjects exposed to misleading information should have a decrement in recall in comparison with subjects who have not previously been exposed to such information (McCloskey & Zaragoza, 1985). They found no decrement in recall in this paradigm in subjects for whom the misleading item was not one of the possible choices in the forced-choice test of recall.

The studies described above, as well as other studies, have raised doubts about the degree to which traumatic memories are susceptible to distortion due to misleading and suggestive statements (as may occur during psychotherapy). Recent findings also suggest that stress itself can lead to modifications in memory traces.

The Effects of Stress on Memory in Normal Human Subjects

☐ Stress exposure results in alterations in the laying down of memory in normal human subjects. The assassination of President Kennedy raised the observation that most people have an enhanced awareness of where they were and what they were doing at the time they received news of this event. This led to the "flashbulb" hypothesis, formulated by Brown and Kulik (1977): Certain events that are surprising and consequential (emotionally charged) lead to an enhancement of memory for personal circumstances surrounding the event. These include such facts as what the person was wearing and what he or she was doing at the time (Bohannon, 1988; Bohannon & Symons, 1992). Studies involving exposure of subjects to traumatic slides involving injury or threat have found enhanced recall of central details of the slides, and reduced recall of peripheral details, in comparison with neutral slides (Christianson & Loftus, 1987, 1991). In children, the stress of inoculation has also been associated with relative enhancement of memory for central details related to the procedure (Goodman, Hirschman, Hepps, & Rudy, 1991). In summary, the findings are consistent with an enhancing effect of stress on memory, especially recall for central details.

Neuroanatomical Correlates of Memory

☐ Studies in normal human subjects may not be applicable to victims of extreme trauma, such as childhood abuse. In order to understand this population better, it is useful to look at findings related to the long-term effects of extreme stress on memory function (Bremner, Krystal, Charney, & Southwick, 1996a, 1996b; Bremner, Krystal, Southwick, & Charney, 1995). Memory formation involves encoding (the initial laying down of the memory trace), storage (or consolidation), and retrieval. Consolidation occurs over several weeks or more, during which time the memory trace is susceptible to modification. Explicit (or declarative) memory includes free recall of facts and lists, and working memory. In contrast, implicit memory is demonstrated only through tasks or skills in which the knowledge is embedded, or through phenomena such as conditioning.

Memory is mediated by several connected subcortical and cortical brain regions (reviewed in Schacter & Tulving, 1994). The hippocampus plays an important role in explicit memory. Studies showed deficits in explicit memory following lesions of the hippocampal formation (dentate gyrus, hippocampus proper, subicular complex, and entorhinal cortex), amygdala, and surrounding perirhinal and parahippocampal cortices (Mishkin, 1978; Murray & Mishkin, 1986; Zola-Morgan, Squire, & Amaral, 1989; Zola-Morgan, Squire, Amaral, & Suzuki, 1989). These findings have been confirmed in human subjects, as in the case of H.M., who suffered from a bilateral stroke involving these structures (Scoville & Milner, 1957). The hippocampus also plays a role in the fear responding to the context of a situation. In animals, exposure to a testing box from which electric shock was previously administered will result in a "freezing" response (which is characteristic of fear), even in the absence of the shock. Lesions of the hippocampus interfere with acquisition of conditioned emotional responses to the context in which the shock took place (Kim & Fanselow, 1992; Phillips & LeDoux, 1992). The thalamus, in addition to being a gateway for sensory information to be relayed to cortex and other regions, is involved in explicit memory. Dorsolateral prefrontal cortex (middle frontal gyrus) is involved in working memory (Goldman-Rakic, 1988). *Working memory* refers to the ability to store information in a visual or verbal buffer while performing a particular operation utilizing that information.

The anteromedial (or ventromesial) prefrontal cortex includes the anterior cingulate gyrus and is functionally and anatomically distinct from the dorsolateral prefrontal cortex. In the late 19th century, the famous patient Phineas Gage had a projectile metal spike pass through his frontal cortex, with damage specifically to the anterior cingulate, anteromedial prefrontal cortex, and parts of the orbitofrontal cortex. Following the accident, the patient had normal memory recall and cognitive function, but his behavior deteriorated to irresponsibility, profanity, and lack of social conventions, which indicated a deficit in the planning and execution of socially suitable behavior, suggesting a role for the anteromedial frontal cortex (including anterior cingulate) in these behaviors (Damasio, Grabowski, Frank, Galaburda, & Damasio,

1994). The orbitofrontal cortex is the primary sensory cortical area for smell, and it plays a role in the fear response, extinction to fear (Morgan & LeDoux, 1994), and certain types of memory. Parietal cortex is involved in spatial memory and attention.

The amygdala is an important mediator of emotional memory. The paradigm of conditioned fear has been utilized as an animal model for stress-induced abnormalities of emotional memory (Davis, 1992). In the fear-potentiated startle paradigm, a normally neutral stimulus (something that typically has no effect on the animal), such as a bright light, is paired with an aversive stimulus, such as electric shock. With repetitive pairing of the light and the shock, a learning process occurs (conditioning) in which the light alone eventually causes an increase in the startle response (referred to as *fear-potentiated startle*). The shock in this example is termed the *unconditioned* stimulus, because no training was required for it to have the effect of potentiating startle, whereas the light is referred to as the *conditioned* stimulus, as the training trials pairing it with the shock were required for it to develop the capacity for potentiating the startle response. Lesions of the central nucleus of the amygdala eliminate the conditioned fear response (Hitchcock & Davis, 1986; Hitchcock, Sananes, & Davis, 1989), whereas electrical stimulation of the central nucleus increases acoustic startle (Rosen & Davis, 1988), confirming the important role that this structure plays in this phenomenon.

Explicit memory formation is not instantaneous. After the laying down of the original memory trace, consolidation—a process that lasts from weeks to months—occurs, during which the stored memory is subject to modification or deletion (Squire, Slater, & Chace, 1975). Although the hippocampus and adjacent structures are important in encoding and retrieval, they do not play a major role in the long-term storage of explicit memory (Zola-Morgan & Squire, 1990). The evidence is consistent with the fact that memories are stored in the primary neocortical sensory and motor areas and later evoked in those same cortical areas. It has been hypothesized that the role of the hippocampus is to bring together memory elements from diverse neocortical areas at the time of retrieval of explicit memory (Zola-Morgan & Squire, 1990).

Neuroanatomical Correlates of the Effects of Stress on Memory: Relevance to a Model for Delayed Recall of Childhood Abuse

☐ Brain regions involved in memory also play a prominent role in the execution of the stress response. In the early part of the 20th century, the observation was made that with the removal of the cerebral cortex, a hyperexcitability of anger termed *shame rage* developed (Cannon, 1931). Animals in the shame rage state were quick to attack and behaved as if they were experiencing a profoundly threatening situation. Papez (1937) proposed that hypothalamus, thalamus, hippocampus, and cingulate are responsible for the behaviors of the decorticate cat. Kluver and Bucy (1937) noted that removal of the temporal lobe (including hippocampus and amygdala) resulted in the absence of anger and fear. These observations led to the development of the concept of the limbi...

possible test Q)

...studies suggested that hippocampal damage is associated with direct exposure of glucocorticoids to the hippocampus (Sapolsky, Uno, Rebert, & Finch, 1990). Studies in a variety of animal species have shown that direct

glucocorticoid exposure results in a loss of pyramidal neurons (Sapolsky, Krey, & McEwen, 1985) and dendritic branching (Wooley, Gould, & McEwen, 1990) that are steroid and tissue specific (Packan & Sapolsky, 1990). Glucocorticoids appear to exert their effect by increasing the vulnerability of hippocampal neurons to endogenously released excitatory amino acids (Sapolsky & Pulsinelli, 1985). These effects of cortisol on hippocampal neurons are associated with deficits in memory function (Luine, Villages, Martinex, & McEwen, 1994).

Traumatic stress has long-term effects on memory function in human populations as well as in animals. These effects may provide a rationale for delayed recall of abuse in traumatized individuals suffering from neuropsychiatric disorders such as posttraumatic stress disorder (PTSD). Empirical studies using reliable and valid instruments have documented that the symptom of dissociative amnesia is strongly related to the diagnosis of PTSD in highly traumatized populations, such as Vietnam combat veterans (Bremner, Steinberg, Southwick, Johnson, & Charney, 1993). Amnesia involves gaps in memory lasting from minutes to hours or days. These episodes can include such things as driving on the highway and suddenly noticing that 3 hours have passed or suddenly finding oneself in a new city and having no idea how one got there. Dissociative amnesia may also include absent recall of episodes of childhood sexual abuse. Evidence is also consistent with abnormalities of verbal memory as measured with standardized neuropsychological testing. We have measured explicit memory function with the Wechsler Memory Scale (WMS)-Logical (verbal memory) and -Figural (visual memory) components in Vietnam combat veterans with PTSD ($N = 26$) and controls matched for factors that could affect memory function ($N = 15$). PTSD patients had a significant decrease in free verbal recall (explicit memory) as measured by the WMS-Logical component, without deficits in IQ, as measured by the Wechsler Adult Intelligence Scale-Revised (Bremner, Scott, et al., 1993). PTSD patients also had deficits in explicit recall, as measured with the Selective Reminding Test, for both verbal and

Table 17.1 Neural Mechanisms and Brain Regions Involved in Delayed Recall of Childhood Abuse

Neural Mechanism	Brain Region	Mechanism in Delayed Recall
Retrieval deficits	hippocampus	inability to retrieve traumatic memories
Fragmented recall	hippocampus, neocortex	distortion of traumatic memories; inability to localize memories to actual abuse events
Conditioned fear	amygdala	avoidance of traumatic cues leads to decreased recall
Failure of extinction	orbitofrontal cortex	increased fear responding due to failure of extinction leads to avoidance of traumatic cues, decreased recall
Sensitization	hippocampus locus coeruleus	increased responsiveness to stressors leads to avoidance of stimuli, decreased recall
Neuromodulation of memory	multiple	long-term changes in neuromodulators with chronic stress lead to altered encoding and retrieval
State-dependent memory	multiple	"excessive" emotions required for retrieval of memories encoded in exceptional circumstances

visual components. We have subsequently found deficits in explicit memory tasks of free verbal recall measured by the WMS-Logical component in adult survivors of childhood abuse seeking treatment for psychiatric disorders (Bremner, Randall, et al., 1995). Studies have found deficits in explicit short-term memory as assessed with the Auditory Verbal Learning Test in Vietnam combat veterans with PTSD in comparison with National Guard veterans without PTSD (Uddo, Vasterling, Brailey, & Sutker, 1993) and the California New Learning Test in Vietnam veterans with combat-related PTSD in comparison with controls (Yehuda et al., 1995).

These verbal memory deficits were associated with reductions in volume of the hippocampus. As reviewed above, increased circulating glucocorticoids appear to be toxic to the hippocampus. We compared hippocampal volume measured with MRI in Vietnam combat veterans with PTSD ($N = 26$) and healthy subjects ($N = 22$) matched for factors that may affect hippocampal volume, including age, sex, race, years of education, height, weight, handedness, and years of alcohol abuse. Patients with combat-related PTSD had an 8% decrease in right hippocampal volume in comparison with controls ($p < .05$), but there was no significant decrease in volume of comparison structures, including temporal lobe and caudate. Deficits in free verbal recall (explicit memory) as measured by the WMS-Logical component, percentage retention, were associated with decreased right hippocampal volume in the PTSD patients ($r = 0.64$; $p < .05$). There was no significant difference between PTSD patients and controls in left hippocampal volume, or in volume of the comparison regions measured in this study, left or right caudate and temporal lobe volume (minus hippocampus) (141). Patients with severe childhood physical and/or sexual abuse-related PTSD ($N = 17$) had a statistically significant 12% decrease in left hippocampal volume in relation to 17 controls matched on a case-by-case basis with the patients (Bremner, Randall, et al., 1997). These studies support preclinical findings of stress-induced damage to the hippocampus with associated memory deficits.

Deficits in hippocampal function may lead to alterations in recall of events of childhood abuse in patients with PTSD. The hippocampus has been hypothesized to play a role in the integration of memory elements at the time of recall, and in placing events in space and time (Nadel & Willner, 1980). We have hypothesized that hippocampal dysfunction in trauma survivors with PTSD may lead to the following: a fragmentation of traumatic memories, an inability to place these memories in space and time, and deficits in retrieval that lead to delayed recall (Bremner, Krystal, et al., 1995). For instance, if a woman was locked in a closet as a child for many hours, she may recall the sound of a clock (outside the closet) and the subjective sense of fear, but she may have no other recall related to the event. Or she may recall only the smell of clothes (on the floor of the closet). Smelling something similar may later trigger a flooded recall of the entire event, with all of its negative emotionality. Facilitating associations in a comfortable and "safe" environment may also facilitate recall, leading to the appearance that delayed recall occurs only during psychotherapy. Stress-induced hippocampal dysfunction may also be involved in the phenomenon of dissociative amnesia, which essentially involves a loss of the normal context of space and time for specific memory traces.

The amygdala places the emotional valence on a memory trace, a crucial aspect of memories for childhood traumatic events. The paradigm of conditioned fear has been used to study function of the amygdala and emotional memory. Conditioned fear reactions characterize many of the abnormalities in responsiveness of PTSD patients, and may explain delayed recall of events of childhood abuse. Due to the conditioned fear effect, exposure to cues related to the original traumatic event is associated with intense negative emotional responding. The lives of particular patients may become highly irregular as these individuals attempt to develop patterns of behavior that are most likely to avoid traumatic cues. For instance, some PTSD patients refuse to answer the telephone, giving the rationale that (because bad news is usually communicated by telephone) if you don't answer the phone, you won't receive any bad news. It is also common for PTSD patients to exhibit behaviors such as not leaving the house, in order to avoid cues to recall, which may include relatively innocuous events. The purpose of such

behaviors may not be within the individual's conscious awareness. Avoidance of traumatic cues also has the effect of decreasing associations to traumatic events. This leads to the traumatic memory becoming, in effect, "walled off" from other normal memories. Traumatic events of childhood are also not a part of normal life; many individuals may never have verbalized their experiences at any time in their lives. This adds to the paucity of associations between these events and ordinary cues to recall. It may take an unusual situation to cue recall of a traumatic childhood event that has been subject to these types of influences.

Other neural mechanisms, such as stress sensitization, may explain delayed recall of childhood abuse. *Stress sensitization* refers to the phenomenon in which repeated exposure to a stressor results in an amplification of responsiveness to subsequent stressors. For example, acute stress results in an increased release of norepinephrine in the hippocampus as well as other brain regions. Animals with histories of exposure to prior stressors become sensitized to exposure to subsequent stressors, so that there is an accentuation of norepinephrine release in the hippocampus with a subsequent stressor (Abercrombie, Keller, & Zigmond, 1988), which may modulate memory formation and retrieval. This raises the possibility that stress sensitization, acting through neuromodulators such as norepinephrine, may be associated with alteration in memory encoding and retrieval, which, as discussed above, may have implications for our understanding of the mechanisms of delayed recall in PTSD.

Stress sensitization has clinical applications for PTSD. We have found that exposure to the stressor of childhood physical abuse increases the risk for development of combat-related PTSD (Bremner, Southwick, et al., 1993). Israeli veterans with histories of previous combat-related acute stress reactions have been found to be at increased risk for reactivation of combat-related stress reactions in comparison with combat veterans without histories of stress reactions in response to combat (Solomon, Garb, Bleich, & Grupper, 1987). There are also other examples of how a history of exposure to prior stress increases the risk for stress-related symptomatology upon reexposure to stressors (reviewed in Bremner, Southwick, & Charney, 1994).

Other brain regions, such as the orbitofrontal cortex, are also involved in emotional memory, and probably play a role in phenomena such as delayed recall of childhood abuse. Studies of human patients with brain lesions have shown that lesions of the orbitofrontal cortex result in symptoms of intense fear during seizures. In addition, some patients have been observed to experience visual hallucinations during seizures (Goldensohn, 1992). Some case reports have described a relationship between damage to the orbitofrontal cortex and visual hallucinations that appear to be similar to the flashbacks that are characteristic of PTSD (Fornazzari, Farcnik, Smith, Heasman, & Ichise, 1992). Yohimbine is an alpha-2 noradrenergic antagonist that causes an increase in brain norepinephrine release and increased symptoms of PTSD (Southwick et al., 1993). We have found a differential response of cerebral metabolism in PTSD patients and controls following administration of yohimbine as assessed by PET [^{18}F]2-fluoro-2-deoxyglucose (FDG). Patients showed a relative decrease with yohimbine, in comparison with controls (Bremner, Innis, et al., 1997). The greatest magnitude of difference was seen in the orbitofrontal cortex: Patients showed slight decreases in metabolism with yohimbine, and controls showed significant increases. Differences were also seen in prefrontal, temporal, and parietal cortex. PTSD is hypothesized to be associated with an increase in noradrenergic activity (reviewed in Bremner, Krystal, Charney, & Southwick, 1996; Bremner, Krystal, Southwick, & Charney, 1996b), and norepinephrine has a dose-dependent effect on neocortical metabolism, with high levels resulting in a decrease in metabolism and low levels resulting in increased metabolism. Our PET findings are therefore consistent with increased noradrenergic activity in PTSD. We also used PET H$_2$[^{15}O] (radiolabeled water) to compare brain blood flow response to combat-related slides and sounds and neutral slides and sounds in Vietnam combat veterans with PTSD ($N = 10$) and combat veterans without PTSD ($N = 10$). The data were analyzed using statistical parametric mapping (SPM95). We found relatively greater increases in blood flow in PTSD patients in comparison with controls with combat slides and sounds in left parietal cortex, left motor cortex, dorsal pons, right lingual gyrus (posterior parahippocampus), and mid-cingulate ($z >$ 3.00, $p < .001$). These regions are involved in spatial and motor memory and emotion. Non-PTSD veterans (but not PTSD veterans) activated orbitofrontal cortex with traumatic cues (Bremner et al., unpublished data, 1998). Other PET H$_2$[^{15}O] studies using trauma-related scripts in PTSD patients found increased blood flow in right temporal lobe and insula, visual association cortex, orbitofrontal cortex, and anterior cingulate, with decreased blood flow in left inferior frontal and middle temporal cortex, although this study did not include a control group (Rauch et al., 1996).

In our studies, the failure of orbitofrontal cortex activation in PTSD patients, seen in the cognitive and pharmacological stress challenges, suggests a possible neuroanatomical correlate of the failure of extinction to fear, a typical manifestation of PTSD. In the conditioned fear paradigm, repeated pairing of a light (conditioned stimulus) with a shock (unconditioned stimulus) leads to an increase in fear responding to the light alone. With repeated presentation of the light alone, however, the fear responding gradually diminishes over time, a phenomenon known as extinction. The mechanism of extinction involves orbitofrontal inhibition of amygdala function. This has led us to hypothesize that a failure in orbitofrontal function in PTSD may lead to the failure of extinction, which is a prominent part of these patients' clinical presentation (Bremner, Krystal, et al., 1995), a hypothesis supported by our PET studies. Victims of childhood abuse clinically exhibit a failure of extinction to trauma-related stimuli. For instance, an individual who was locked in a closet may continue to show anxiety reactions when he is in a close space, even when there is no real threat of danger. A failure of extinction may act in a similar fashion to conditioned fear responses in PTSD, to modulate patient behavior to avoid cues to recall of the original traumatic childhood event. This often subconscious behavior is in the service of avoiding recall of traumatic events associated with extremely negative emotionality, in part due to the failure of extinction to fear in these patients.

Neurotransmitters and neuropeptides released during stress have a modulatory effect on memory function. Several neurotransmitters and neuropeptides that have effects on learning and memory are released during stress, including norepinephrine, epinephrine, adrenocorticotropic hormone, glucocorticoids, corticotropin releasing factor (CRF), opioid peptides, endogenous benzodiazepines, dopamine, vasopressin, and oxytocin (De Wied & Croiset, 1991). Brain regions involved in memory, including hippocampus and adjacent cortex, amygdala, and prefrontal cortex, are richly innervated by these neurotransmitters and neuropeptides. These neuromodulators act at the level of the hippocampus, amygdala, and other brain regions involved in memory. Chronic abnormalities in the function of these neurotransmitter and neuropeptide systems in PTSD may contribute to the abnormalities in memory seen in these patients. For example, vasopressin has been shown to facilitate traumatic recall in patients with PTSD (Pitman, Orr, & Lasko, 1993). We have found elevated levels of CRF in the cerebrospinal fluid of patients with PTSD relative to healthy controls (Bremner, Licinio, et al., 1997). Exposure to subsequent stressors could also be associated with altered release of neuromodulators, resulting in altered memory recall in PTSD patients. Dysfunction in neuromodulators of memory in PTSD patients may lead to altered encoding—or retrieval—of traumatic childhood memories, leading to phenomena such as delayed recall of episodes of childhood abuse.

Mechanisms involving state-dependent recall may also be applicable to delayed recall of abuse (Bower, 1981). *State-dependent recall* refers to the phenomenon in which a similar affective state to the time of encoding leads to facilitation of memory retrieval. For instance, memories that were encoded during a state of sadness will have facilitated retrieval during similar states of sadness. Similar situations can occur for other emotional states. To extend this concept to victims of abuse, it can be seen that

particular emotions tend to predominate at the time of the original abuse, such as extreme fear or sadness. These emotional states occur infrequently during routine adult lives, which are typically free of traumatic stressors. The recurrence of the state of extreme fear or sadness that occurred during the original abuse during psychotherapy or with exposure to a subsequent stressor may lead to delayed recall of the original abuse experiences. A clinical example of this would be the victim of sexual abuse who has no recall of her sexual abuse experiences until subsequent victimization by rape as an adult, leading to a recall of the original trauma.

Conclusion

☐ In this chapter I have attempted to address the paradox of "Never Forget" in trauma survivors in the face of the loss of memories of childhood abuse in patients with PTSD. I have asked whether memories of childhood trauma not easily available to consciousness can be found in the brain. It is clear that memory function and the brain regions that mediate memory differ between the chronically stressed individual and the normal individual. These differences may be invoked to provide a rationale for delayed recall of childhood abuse. There are also several phenomena and mechanisms that may explain delayed recall of abuse. For instance, there is mounting evidence for deficits in hippocampal function and structure in PTSD. Because the hippocampus is thought to be involved in memory recall and the placing of memories in space and time, it has been hypothesized that hippocampal dysfunction is involved in memory fragmentation and delayed or impaired recall in PTSD patients. There is a wealth of evidence in animal studies for abnormalities in conditioned fear responding and amygdala function with stress. Conditioned fear may lead PTSD patients to avoid traumatic cues (unconsciously), in order to avoid the extreme negative emotionality associated with such cues. In a similar fashion, failure of extinction and sensitization may lead to negative emotionality with cue exposure, which leads to avoidance behaviors. This may "wall off" traumatic memories, creating few associations to the event and making cues for recall rare.

Other concepts also provide potential explanations for delayed recall of memories of childhood abuse. These include state-dependent memory and modulation of memory traces during and after encoding by neurotransmitters and neuropeptides, which are released in high levels during stress. These mechanisms are probably applicable only to patients with disorders such as PTSD secondary to abuse. They probably are not pertinent to the entire range of individuals who are exposed to childhood abuse, including those who do not develop abuse-related psychiatric disorders.

This review has not provided a comprehensive analysis that can set to rest the controversy over delayed recall of childhood abuse. Rather, I have attempted to outline neural mechanisms that are known to be operative in situations of extreme stress and that may provide explanations for delayed recall of childhood abuse. Hopefully, future research work in this area will provide answers to some of the questions this controversy has raised.

References

Abercrombie, E. D., Keller, R. W., Jr., & Zigmond, M. J. (1988). Characterization of hippocampal norepinephrine release as measured by microdialysis perfusion: Pharmacological and behavioral studies. *Neuroscience, 27,* 897-904.

Bohannon, J. N., III. (1988). Flashbulb memories for the space shuttle disaster: A tale of two theories. *Cognition, 29,* 179-196.

Bohannon, J. N., III, & Symons, V. L. (1992). Flashbulb memories: Confidence, consistency and quantity. In E. Winograd & U. Neisser (Eds.), *Affect and accuracy in recall: Studies of "flashbulb" memories* (pp. 65-94). New York: Cambridge University Press.

Bower, G. H. (1981). Mood and memory. *American Psychologist, 36,* 129-148.

Bremner, J. D., Innis, R. B., Ng, C. K., Staib, L., Duncan, J., Bronen, R. A., Zubal, G., Rich, D., Krystal, J. H., Dey, H., Soufer, R., & Charney, D. S. (1997). PET measurement of central metabolic correlates of yohimbine administration in posttraumatic stress disorder. *Archives of General Psychiatry, 54,* 246-256.

Bremner, J. D., Krystal, J. H., Charney, D. S., & Southwick, S. M. (1996). Neural mechanisms in dissociative amnesia for childhood abuse: Relevance to the current controversy surrounding the "false memory syndrome." *American Journal of Psychiatry, 153,* FS71-82.

Bremner, J. D., Krystal, J. H., Southwick, S. M., & Charney, D. S. (1995). Functional neuroanatomical correlates of the effects of stress on memory. *Journal of Traumatic Stress, 8,* 527-545.

Bremner, J. D., Krystal, J. H., Southwick, S. M., & Charney, D. S. (1996a). Noradrenergic mechanisms in stress and anxiety: I. Preclinical studies. *Synapse, 23,* 28-38.

Bremner, J. D., Krystal, J. H., Southwick, S. M., & Charney, D. S. (1996b). Noradrenergic mechanisms in stress and anxiety: II. Clinical studies. *Synapse, 23,* 39-51.

Bremner, J. D., Licinio, J., Darnell, A., Krystal, J. H., Owens, M., Southwick, S. M., Nemeroff, C. B., & Charney, D. S. (1997). Elevated CSF corticotropin-releasing factor concentrations in posttraumatic stress disorder. *American Journal of Psychiatry, 154,* 624-629.

Bremner, J. D., Randall, P. R., Capelli, S., Scott, T. M., McCarthy, G., & Charney, D. S. (1995). Deficits in short-term memory in adult survivors of childhood abuse. *Psychiatry Research, 59,* 97-107.

Bremner, J. D., Randall, P. R., Vermetten, E., Staib, L., Bronen, R. A., Mazure, C. M., Capelli, S., McCarthy, G., Innis, R. B., & Charney, D. S. (1997). MRI-based measurement of hippocampal volume in posttraumatic stress disorder related to childhood physical and sexual abuse: A preliminary report. *Biological Psychiatry, 41,* 23-32.

Bremner, J. D., Scott, T. M., Delaney, R. C., Southwick, S. M., Mason, J. W., Johnson, D. R., Innis, R. B., McCarthy, G., & Charney, D. S. (1993). Deficits in short-term memory in post-traumatic stress disorder. *American Journal of Psychiatry, 150,* 1015-1019.

Bremner, J. D., Southwick, S. M., & Charney, D. S. (1994). Etiologic factors in the development of posttraumatic stress disorder. In C. M. Mazure (Ed.), *Stress and psychiatric disorders* (pp. 149-186). Washington, DC: American Psychiatric Press.

Bremner, J. D., Southwick, S. M., Johnson, D. R., Yehuda, R., & Charney, D. S. (1993). Childhood physical abuse in combat-related posttraumatic stress disorder. *American Journal of Psychiatry, 150,* 235-239.

Bremner, J. D., Steinberg, M., Southwick, S. M., Johnson, D. R., & Charney, D. S. (1993). Use of the Structured Clinical Interview for DSM-IV dissociative disorders for systematic assessment of dissociative symptoms in posttraumatic stress disorder. *American Journal of Psychiatry, 150,* 1011-1014.

Brown, R., & Kulik, J. (1977). Flashbulb memories. *Cognition, 5,* 73-99.

Cannon, W. B. (1931). Again the James-Lange and the thalamic theories of emotion. *Psychological Review, 38,* 281-295.

Christianson, S. A., & Loftus, E. F. (1987). Memory for traumatic events. *Applied Cognitive Psychology, 1,* 225-239.

Christianson, S. A., & Loftus, E. F. (1991). Remembering emotional events: The fate of detailed information. *Emotion and Cognition, 5,* 81-108.

Damasio, H., Grabowski, T., Frank, R., Galaburda, A. M., & Damasio, A. R. (1994). The return of Phineas Gage:

Clues about the brain from the skull of a famous patient. *Science, 264,* 1102-1105.

Davis, M. (1992). The role of the amygdala in fear and anxiety. *Annual Reviews of Neuroscience, 15,* 353-375.

De Wied, D., & Croiset, G. (1991). Stress modulation of learning and memory processes. *Methods of Achievement in Experimental Pathology, 15,* 167-199.

Fornazzari, L., Farcnik, K., Smith, I., Heasman, G. A., & Ichise, M. (1992). Violent visual hallucinations in frontal lobe dysfunction: Clinical manifestations of deep orbitofrontal foci. *Journal of Neuropsychiatry and Clinical Neurosciences, 4,* 42-44.

Goldensohn, E. (1992). Structural lesions of the frontal lobe: Manifestations, classification, and prognosis. In P. Chauvel, A. V. Delgado-Escueta, et al. (Eds.), *Advances in neurology.* New York: Raven.

Goldman-Rakic, P. S. (1988). Topography of cognition: Parallel distributed networks in primate association cortex. *Annual Reviews of Neuroscience, 11,* 137-156.

Goodman, G. S., Hirschman, J. E., Hepps, J. E., & Rudy, L. (1991). Children's memory for stressful events. *Merrill-Palmer Quarterly, 37,* 109-158.

Hitchcock, J. M., & Davis, M. (1986). Lesions of the amygdala, but not of the cerebellum or red nucleus, block conditioned fear as measured with the potentiated startle paradigm. *Behavioral Neurosciences, 100,* 11-22.

Hitchcock, J. M., Sananes, C. B., & Davis, M. (1989). Sensitization of the startle reflex by footshock: Blockade by lesions of the central nucleus of the amygdala or its efferent pathway to the brainstem. *Behavioral Neurosciences, 103,* 509-518.

Kim, J. J., & Fanselow, M. S. (1992). Modality-specific retrograde amnesia of fear. *Science, 256,* 675-677.

Kluver, H., & Bucy, P. C. (1937). "Psychic blindness" and other symptoms following bilateral temporal lobectomy in rhesus monkeys. *American Journal of Physiology, 119,* 352-353.

Lindsay, D. S., & Johnson, M. K. (1989). The eyewitness suggestibility effect and memory for source. *Memory and Cognition, 17,* 349-358.

Loftus, E. F., Garry, M., & Feldman, J. (1994). Forgetting sexual trauma: What does it mean when 38% forget? *Journal of Consulting and Clinical Psychology, 62,* 1177-1181.

Loftus, E. F., Miller, D. G., & Burns, H. J. (1978). Semantic integration of verbal information into a visual memory. *Journal of Experimental Psychology: Human Learning and Memory, 4,* 19-31.

Loftus, E. F., Polonsky, S., & Fullilove, M. T. (1994). Memories of childhood sexual abuse: Remembering and repressing. *Psychology of Women Quarterly, 18,* 67-84.

Luine, V., Villages, M., Martinex, C., & McEwen, B. S. (1994). Repeated stress causes reversible impairments of spatial memory performance. *Brain Research, 639,* 167-170.

MacLean, P. D. (1949). Psychosomatic disease and the visceral brain: Recent developments bearing on the Papez theory of emotion. *Psychosomatic Medicine, 11,* 338-353.

McCloskey, M., & Zaragoza, M. (1985). Misleading postevent information and memory for events: Arguments and evidence against memory impairment hypotheses. *Journal of Experimental Psychology: General, 114,* 1-16.

Mishkin, M. (1978). Memory in monkeys severely impaired by combined but not separate removal of amygdala and hippocampus. *Nature, 173,* 297-298.

Morgan, M. A., & LeDoux, J. E. (1994). Medial orbital lesions increase resistance to extinction but do not affect acquisition of fear conditioning. *Proceedings of the Society for Neuroscience, 2,* 1006.

Murray, E. A., & Mishkin, M. (1986). Visual recognition in monkeys following rhinal cortical ablations combined with either amygdalectomy or hippocampectomy. *Journal of Neuroscience, 6,* 1991-2003.

Nadel, L., & Willner, J. (1980). Context and conditioning: A place for space. *Physiological Psychology, 8,* 218-228.

Packan, D. R., & Sapolsky, R. M. (1990). Glucocorticoid endangerment of the hippocampus: Tissue, steroid and receptor specificity. *Neuroendocrinology, 51,* 613-618.

Papez, J. W. (1937). A proposed mechanism of emotion. *American Medical Association Archives of Neurology and Psychiatry, 38,* 725-743.

Phillips, R. G., & LeDoux, J. E. (1992). Differential contribution of amygdala and hippocampus to cued and contextual fear conditioning. *Behavioral Neuroscience, 106,* 274-285.

Pitman, R. K. (1989). Posttraumatic stress disorder, hormones, and memory. *Biological Psychiatry, 26,* 221-223.

Pitman, R. K., Orr, S. P., & Lasko, N. B. (1993). Effects of intranasal vasopressin and oxytocin on physiologic responding during personal combat imagery in Vietnam veterans with posttraumatic stress disorder. *Psychiatry Research, 48,* 107-117.

Rauch, S. L., van der Kolk, B. A., Fisler, R. E., Alpert, N. M., Orr, S. P., Savage, C. R., Fischman, A. J., Jenike, M. A., & Pitman, R. K. (1996). A symptom provocation study of posttraumatic stress disorder using positron emission tomography and script driven imagery. *Archives of General Psychiatry, 53,* 380-387.

Rosen, J. B., & Davis, M. (1988). Enhancement of acoustic startle by electrical stimulation of the amygdala. *Behavioral Neurosciences, 102,* 195-202.

Sapolsky, R. M., Krey, L. C., & McEwen, B. S. (1985). Prolonged glucocorticoid exposure reduces hippocampal neuron number: Implications for aging. *Journal of Neuroscience, 5,* 1221-1226.

Sapolsky, R. M., & Pulsinelli, W. (1985). Glucocorticoids potentiate ischemic injury to neurons: Therapeutic implications. *Science, 229,* 1397-1400.

Sapolsky, R. M., Uno, H., Rebert, C. S., & Finch, C. E. (1990). Hippocampal damage associated with prolonged glucocorticoid exposure in primates. *Journal of Neuroscience, 10,* 2897-2902.

Schacter, D. L., & Tulving, E. (Eds.). (1994). *Memory systems.* Cambridge: MIT Press.

Scoville, W. B., & Milner, B. (1957). Loss of recent memory after bilateral hippocampal lesions. *Journal of Neurology and Psychiatry, 20,* 11-21.

Solomon, Z., Garb, R., Bleich, A., & Grupper, D. (1987). Reactivation of combat-related posttraumatic stress disorder. *American Journal of Psychiatry, 144,* 51-55.

Southwick, S. M., Krystal, J. H., Morgan, C. A., Johnson, D. R., Nagy, L. M., Nicolaou, A., Heninger, G. R., & Charney, D. S. (1993). Abnormal noradrenergic function in posttraumatic stress disorder. *Archives of General Psychiatry, 50,* 266-274.

Squire, L. R., Slater, P. C., & Chace, P. M. (1975). Retrograde amnesia: Temporal gradient in very long term memory following electroconvulsive therapy. *Science, 187,* 77-79.

Uddo, M., Vasterling, J. T., Brailey, K., & Sutker, P. B. (1993). Memory and attention in posttraumatic stress disorder. *Journal of Psychopathology and Behavioral Assessment, 15,* 43-52.

Uno, H., Tarara, R., Else, J. G., Suleman, M. A., & Sapolsky, R. M. (1989). Hippocampal damage associated with prolonged and fatal stress in primates. *Journal of Neuroscience, 9,* 1705-1711.

Williams, L. M. (1994a). Recall of childhood trauma: A prospective study of women's memories of child sexual abuse. *Journal of Clinical and Consulting Psychology, 62,* 1167-1176.

Williams, L. M. (1994b). What does it mean to forget child sexual abuse? A reply to Loftus, Garry, and Feldman (1994). *Journal of Clinical and Consulting Psychology, 62,* 1182-1186.

Wooley, C. S., Gould, E., & McEwen, B. S. (1990). Exposure to excess glucocorticoids alters dendritic morphology of adult hippocampal pyramidal neurons. *Brain Research, 531,* 225-231.

Yehuda, R., Keefer, R. S. E., Harvey, P. D., Levengood, R. A., Gerber, D. K., Geni, J., & Siever, L. J. (1995). Learning and memory in combat veterans with posttraumatic stress disorder. *American Journal of Psychiatry, 152,* 137-139.

Zola-Morgan, S. M., & Squire, L. R. (1990). The primate hippocampal formation: Evidence for a time-limited role in memory storage. *Science, 250,* 288-290.

Zola-Morgan, S. M., Squire, L. R., & Amaral, D. G. (1989). Lesions of the amygdala that spare adjacent cortical regions do not impair memory or exacerbate the impairment following lesions of the hippocampal formation. *Journal of Neuroscience, 9,* 1922-1936.

Zola-Morgan, S. M., Squire, L. R., Amaral, D. G., & Suzuki, W. A. (1989). Lesions of perirhinal and parahippocampal cortex that spare the amygdala and hippocampal formation produce severe memory impairment. *Journal of Neuroscience, 9,* 4355-4370.

18

Neuropsychological Sequelae of Chronically Psychologically Traumatized Children

Specific Findings in Memory and Higher Cognitive Functions

Laura K. Palmer
Corinne E. Frantz
Mary W. Armsworth
Paul Swank
Juanita V. Copley
Gordon A. Bush

Traumatized children often exhibit a spectrum of psychological consequences defined as posttraumatic stress disorder (PTSD). This spectrum may include the following: altered attention processes, deficient explicit memory system, inefficient cognitive systems necessary for learning, inefficient affective responsiveness, and an altered sense of self in relation to others (Cicchetti, 1984; Cicchetti & Rizley, 1981; Terr, 1983; van der Kolk, 1987). These psychological features have cortical bases; specifically, the functions of the frontal lobe and limbic systems of the brain would predictably be involved in the human experience of psychological trauma. Additionally, critical periods of neurophysiological development represent a process that is interdependent with other aspects of development and is susceptible to injury, insult, or delays that may result from emotional and physical trauma. Thus delays in neurophysiological development, specifically in the frontolimbic systems, would likely result in various neuropsychological difficulties for the school-aged child.

Interest in the association between trauma and its psychological sequelae has been well documented since the 19th century. Pierre Janet (1919/1925) believed that the individual's sense of being traumatized by an event resulted from his or her failing to take effective action against a potential threat. However, there are many situations in which the individual has not developed the necessary skills, resources, or strength to take adaptive action to ward off potential threats, as with child abuse and neglect.

Incidence and Prevalence of Child Abuse

☐ More than 2 million children are annually reported as abused or neglected. The actual prevalence of sexual abuse is more difficult to document accurately, because few victims disclose such abuse for various reasons, including fear, guilt, repression, and shame (Finkelhor, 1979; Russell, 1983; Schultz, 1973). A working estimate of prevalence suggests that at least 20% of American women and 5% to 10% of American men have experienced some form of sexual abuse as children. Approximately 150,000 confirmed cases of child sexual abuse were reported to child welfare authorities in 1993 (Finkelhor, 1994).

Emotional, Physical, and Cognitive Sequelae of Psychological Trauma

☐ Many studies have shown that early life trauma, including incest, can result in various psychological consequences: delayed development in physically abused children (Oates, 1984), posttraumatic stress disorders (Terr, 1985), and attachment disturbances (Bowlby, 1984). Herman, Russell, and Trocki (1986) found that one-half of their survey population of women who were sexually abused as children perceived that their experiences of incest had enduring negative effects, which included anxiety, distrust, and difficulty in forming and maintaining intimate relationships. Blake-White and Kline (1985) also suggest that sexual abuse can interrupt psychosocial development, and, de-

pending on the child's age at the onset of incest and the duration of the abuse, the victim may experience unsatisfactory developmental task resolution. Williams (1993) has published research findings indicating that the impact of traumatic events may vary regarding personal outcomes, depending on "how the events are processed, perceived, and appraised" (p. 53). Williams concludes that the major contributory factors of an event that results in more negative psychological outcomes include an appraisal of more severe impact, the relationship between the perpetrator and victim, maximum intrusiveness of abuse with force, multiple perpetrators, bizarre abuse, and sexual abuse accompanied by physical abuse.

Posttraumatic stress disorder has been identified by van der Kolk (1987) as a process that results in an interruption of cognitive and psychosocial development. Goodwin's (1988) research supports this thesis; Goodwin notes that "abuse in children initiates a syndrome that includes: fears and anxiety, re-enactment of the abuse, nightmares and depressive symptoms, ego constriction, and disturbed discharge of aggression" (p. 481).

In a study that addressed the issue of the actual occurrence of PTSD in sexually abused children, Famularo, Fenton, and Kinscherff (1993) documented that children who had experienced sexual abuse were more likely to develop PTSD than were those in a comparison group of the maltreated sample who had no history of sexual abuse.

A neuropsychological framework suggests that symptoms of PTSD have cortical bases and correlates. Of particular interest is the correlation of PTSD syndrome in childhood and cognitive developmental delays. Kempe (1985) found that a majority of a small sample ($N = 13$) of abused preschool children experienced scores below 100 on the Stanford Binet and developmental delays. Four of these children had clear (although unspecified) neurological symptoms. In most of the children, speech was delayed, and they lacked organization of behavior when engaged in planned or structured activity. Cicchetti (1984; Cicchetti & Rizley, 1981) found several indicators that suggest neurocognitive developmental consequences of abuse and neglect: lags in motor development in maltreated infants, delays in flexible and systematic use of cognitive operations in preoperational and operational abused children, and delayed verbal abilities in (physically) abused children. Similarly, Terr (1983) has documented the following sequelae among the children involved in the Chowchilla bus incident: distorted time concepts, selective encoding of memories, transfer of perceptual memories to other modalities, verbal restrictions, visual and auditory perceptual distortions, and visual hallucinations. Van der Kolk (1987) has conducted research focused on the functions, operations, and structures within cognitive domains affected by trauma, and has identified the following affected domains: knowledge of self and other, the capacity to self-correct, encoding of memories of the abuse, flexibility of organized schemata in all domains, and increased occurrence of attention deficit disorder in abused children.

Neurocognitive Sequelae in Adults With PTSD

☐ A few studies have reviewed neuropsychological sequelae in traumatized adult populations, providing some possible areas of focus for investigation of traumatized children. Kolb (1987) has suggested that neuropsychological impairment be included in the PTSD-associated features based on his research, which indicates that adrenergic hypersensitivity within the locus coerulus and its projections into the limbic and neocortical regions may serve as the physiological and anatomical substrate of PTSD. Specifically, Kolb presents a review of neurochemical, synaptic, and associated structural changes that occur because of excessive emotional stimulation. Sapolsky, Krey, and McEwen (1984) initially reported hippocampal cell death in neurons with high glucocorticoid receptors. This has recently been supported by Bremner, Randall, Scott, et al.'s (1995) finding of reduced right-hippocampal volume in veterans who suffer from PTSD. Everly and Horton (1989) explain this physiological process, suggesting that "high intensity neural stimulation . . . lead[s] to a subsequent hypersensitivity for excitation in

the limbic system. This hypersensitivity is postulated to cause a wide variety of psychological disturbance" (p. 807). These authors suggest that this position is consistent with the presence of dysfunction that can have an impact on memory (i.e., hippocampus cell death). Everly and Horton's pilot study included 14 patients diagnosed as having PTSD who were found to have impairment of short-term memory significant at a clinical level, although no impairment of long-term memory was found.

Wolfe and Charney (1991) note that "reports from [adult] patients with PTSD include frequent complaints about a variety of cognitive disturbances, including memory, learning, attention, and concentration difficulties. Deficits in planning, organization, and judgment have also been noted during clinical evaluation" (p. 573). These authors further delineate the effects of psychological trauma upon the function of memory in PTSD by looking at explicit versus implicit memory. They suggest that in PTSD adult patients, implicit memory, which represents an individual's ability to recall information without being consciously aware of doing so, appears to be quite preserved, whereas explicit memory (the ability to consciously recall earlier experience) is deficient.

Impact of Psychological Stress Upon the Developing Cortical Systems

☐ The complexity of the neuropsychological systems theorized as involved in the PTSD syndrome generates many questions about pediatric populations, given the process of neurodevelopment. One study we reviewed involved assessment of PTSD symptoms in children who had witnessed a sniper attack on their peers at a playground. Nader, Pynoos, Fairbanks, and Frederick (1990) found that children directly exposed to the violence demonstrated selective recovery, detachment, increased activity, and interference with learning. It is important to note that this single incident of traumatic experience resulted in 28.3% (n = 45) of the children experiencing interference with learning and concentration 1 month after the incident. After a 14-month period, 7% of the reinterviewed traumatized children ($n = 7$) continued to report interference with learning, and 10% ($n = 10$) reported difficulty concentrating. This study documents long-term effects from acute danger. Garbarino, Kostelny, and Dubrow (1991) suggest that "chronic danger imposes a requirement for developmental adjustment—accommodations that are likely to include persistent PTSD, alterations of personality, and major changes in patterns of behavior or articulations of ideological interpretations of the world that provide a framework for making sense of ongoing danger, particularly when the danger comes from violent overthrow of day-to-day social reality" (p. 377).

Teicher, Glod, Surrey, and Swett (1993) hypothesized that early traumatic experiences could lead to altered limbic system maturation, and consequently lead to many possible long-term neurobiological consequences, such as dissociation, memory impairment, and episodic aggression. This was supported by Ito et al. (1993), who conducted a retrospective study of children who had been hospitalized at a psychiatric facility and found concurrent EEG or brain electrical activity mapping abnormalities in 54.5% of the children who had physical or sexual abuse histories. Comparatively, only 26.9% of the nonabused sample demonstrated similar findings. Previous research by Davies (1978-1979) found EEG abnormalities in 76% of a clinical sample of adults who had incest histories ($n = 22$).

Brain Morphology, Developmental Processes, Lateralization, and Asymmetry

□ The adult PTSD studies that have implicated sequelae in the central nervous system, though important, are not directly applicable to children because of the nature of development, critical and sensitive periods, and the notion of plasticity. The child's neurological development is postnatally continuous at various rates ranging from the first few months until late adolescence. Although the brain reaches 90% of its adult size by age 5, cognitive development and physical maturation continue throughout childhood and adolescence and into young adulthood.

Fischer and Rose (1994) have outlined a framework for understanding the dynamic development of the human brain as it occurs in coordination with behavior. Brain development is a dynamic process involving myelination, synaptic density, dendritic branching, brain mass, pruning of neurons and synapses, and brain electrical activity that changes systematically with age throughout childhood and into young adulthood. It has been proposed that the neural networks develop through an ongoing, dynamic process of coordination and competition. This theory suggests that neurons that are active are sustained and those receiving minimal input are "pruned," influenced by various environmental demands and experiences (Fischer & Rose, 1994). Huttenlocher (1994) provides a review of a related concept: synaptogenesis. This term refers to reduction of the number of synapses and modification of connectivity of cortical structures as a result of environmental demands and experience. This process appears to occur at varying rates in different cortical regions throughout infancy and childhood. In summary, the developing neurophysiological system appears to have critical or sensitive periods of growth and development. These various critical or sensitive periods may be linked to susceptibility to injury and disruption resulting from environmental stressors.

Yehuda, Giller, Southwick, Lowy, and Mason (1991) have suggested that prolonged exposure to stress during the neonatal period can have profound effects of subsequent hypothalamic-pituitary-adrenal (HPA) response to stress, possibly altering the response of the HPA axis to subsequent stress, and may involve an altered sensitivity of the hippocampal glucocorticoid receptors. There have been similar demonstrations on the effects of brain injury during critical periods of language acquisition and brain lateralization (Spreen, Tupper, Risser, Tuokko, & Edgell, 1984). Additionally, the level of environmental enrichment or deprivation during critical periods has been shown to have significant effects on the level of brain density in laboratory-reared animals (Hebb, 1949).

Cortical Structures Critical to Effective Stress Response

☐ The interaction of two cortical systems is pertinent to the subject of this research: the limbic and frontal systems. The term *limbic* describes the interconnected system involving the hypothalamus, the anterior thalamus, cingulate gyrus, and hippocampus with the amygdala, septum, and association cortex (Schefft, Moses, & Schmidt, 1985). McLean (1949) has suggested that one primary function of the limbic system is to modulate effective quality of stimuli and controlled autonomic responses. Luria (1973) asserts that the prefrontal cortex actually serves as association cortex for the limbic system, and together the two are involved in the modulation, interpretation, and provision of meaning to emotional stimuli. The major structures of the limbic system—the amygdala, septum, and hippocampus—are critical in the storage and retrieval of memories, and are essential functions to learning and behavior.

The other relevant neurocognitive structure is the frontal cortex, a complex system responsible for modulation of motor responses, involved in the regulation of complex purposive and affective behavior and in the evaluation of ongoing responses on the basis of changing environmental demands, and, as reviewed earlier, reciprocally involved with limbic structures in the control of arousal and emotional responses (Malloy, Webster, & Russell, 1985). Affective responsiveness, timing of responses, and the strength of affective response appear to be mediated by the anterior frontal regions (Stuss, Gow, & Hetherington, 1992).

Stuss (1992) delineates the functions of the frontal lobes as occurring across a three-stage, progressive developmental process. The first stage is characterized by simple planning and an organized visual search by 6 years of age; the second stage includes set maintenance, hypothesis testing, and impulse control by age 10;

and the third involves complex planning, sequencing, and verbal fluency during adolescence. Stuss suggests that temporal ordering follows a developmental pattern from age 6 to 12. Related to frontal cortex development is the concept of self or self-awareness. Stuss and Benson (1986) assert that self-reflectiveness is the highest of frontal functions. The executive control functions of goal formation, planning, executing goal-directed plans, self-monitoring, self-regulation, and effective performance (Lezak, 1983) are functions of the frontal cortex, but are also dependent on subcortical structures, the limbic systems, and some right-hemisphere structures.

That these two neurocognitive systems are critically important to learning is quickly apparent. It has also been noted that overstimulation of the neurochemical processes of the limbic system can result in altered patterns of responsiveness to situations (Charney, Deutch, Krystal, Southwick, & Davis, 1993; Thatcher, 1994; Yehuda, Lowy, Southwick, Shaffer, & Geller, 1991). It is suggested that chronic alteration of the limbic-frontal loop may alter the effective functioning of the respective systems. One hypothesized consequence of altered functioning would be decreased capacity in some of the skills that form the foundation for academic success in school-aged children. These skills are represented by memory, higher cognitive functions, the executive functions, and the ability for sustained attention (Denckla, 1996).

Developmental Implications for the Frontal and Limbic Structures

☐ Regarding the developmental implications of both the limbic structures and the frontal and prefrontal cortices, knowing the course of development and potentially sensitive periods is important. Stuss (1992) suggests that development of the frontal cortex is incomplete at birth. Although morphological maturation is reached around puberty, quantitative and qualitative changes may continue into later years (Orzhekhovskaya, 1981; Yakovlev, 1962). Neurocognitive development appears largely hierarchical; tertiary association areas (including frontal) mature last, reaching maturity by puberty (Stuss, 1992).

Summary

☐ The skills necessary for learning include short- and long-term memory, attention, perceptual and visual organization, language acquisition, impulse control, sensory discrimination, and the ability to regulate, plan, and initiate responses. In the preceding review, there have been indications that various cognitive structures necessary for the acquisition of learning may be affected by psychological trauma. Most samples in the reviewed studies were limited to small numbers of adult subjects, and they had other complicating variables that were not controlled for (e.g., history of substance abuse, genetic factors, head injuries, illness). Additionally, few studies included comparison samples. Continued research in the form of well-controlled, descriptive studies with pediatric populations is imperative if we are to anticipate appropriate academic, therapeutic, and neuropsychological interventions for traumatized children, as these areas are not systematically addressed in clinical interventions with this population.

Hypothesis

☐ The preceding literature review formed the basis of the following hypothesis: Group membership (i.e., abused/nonabused) can be differentiated based on neuropsychological sequelae in the discrete areas of memory and higher cognitive functions. (Other areas of neurocognitive functions were also investigated; we will address these in future papers.)

Method

Sample

The subjects were 20 sexually abused girls and 20 nonabused girls. The abused subjects ranged in age from 7 years through 12 years, 11 months, with a mean age of 9 years, 10 months. These children were recruited through the Rapid Intervention Team and the Children of Rape Trauma Syndrome Clinic, two programs administered by the Children's Hospital of Newark, New Jersey. Both programs provide medical and psychological assessments to children who are suspected to be victims of child sexual abuse. The comparative nonabused sample was recruited through the Continuity Clinic, a well-child pediatric service, and through referrals by employees of Children's Hospital. The mean age of the comparison sample was 10 years, 8 months, with a range from 6 years, 9 months, through 14 years, 6 months.

The two groups were equivalent for age, handedness, socioeconomic status (SES), and approximate environmental factors, factors documented using the Neuropsychological History Form. Due to the nature of the independent variable, sexual abuse, using a matched comparison sample was not possible. Briere (1992) suggests that although matched controls represents the optimal comparison group, it is not always clear what variables should be matched. As an alternative, he advises drawing representative abused and nonabused subjects from the same population of a geographic area rather than attempting to approximate equivalence. Judd, Smith, and Kidder (1991) support this position; they see the attempt to match samples in nonrandomly assigned groups as representing a threat to internal validity, specifically, resulting in regression to the mean. Thus the comparative sample was not a true matched sample, but was selected from a similar geographic location and compared on the variables of sex, age, and SES, along with the criterion variables. To ensure protection of subjects, the research was reviewed and approved by the institutional review boards of Children's Hospital and the University of Houston.

Children were excluded from this study if there was documented evidence of prenatal insult, severe physical abuse, a known neurological disorder or developmental delay, preexisting educational classification (MR, NI, PI), or current use of psychotropic medication. To control for asymmetrical development between male and female brains, we used only female subjects in this study. Both samples were prescreened for the exclusion criteria.

Subjects in the clinical sample had confirmed histories of child sexual abuse verified by psychological and/or medical evaluation. The level of severity of trauma (Trauma Score) was coded using Wolfe's History of Victimization Form Coding Scheme (Wolfe, Gentile, & Bourdeau, 1986). The Trauma Score was coded as a cumulative score based on the following information: type of sexual abuse (1-5, with a higher score for more intrusive forms of abuse), type of force or coercion used (1-4, again with the highest being the most severe), relationship to the perpetrator (1-4, with increasing degrees of relatedness), frequency of abuse (1-4, where 1 = 1-3 incidents, 2 = 4-8 incidents, 3 = 9-12 incidents, 4 > 13 incidents), and number of perpetrators (exact number entered).

Procedures and Instruments

The specific procedures employed were as follows:

1. Parents completed the Achenbach Child Behavior Checklist (Achenbach & Edelbrock, 1983) and Neuropsychological History Form (Greenberg, 1990).

2. The clinical subject's clinician completed the History of Victimization Questionnaire (Wolfe et al., 1986).

3. Both samples of children completed the following battery of neuropsychological tests: the Test of Memory and Learning (eight subtests that comprise the Verbal Memory Index [VMI], the Nonverbal Memory Index [NMI], and the Delayed Memory Index [DMI], used in the analyses; Reynolds & Bigler, 1994); Rey-Osterrieth Complex Figure (Rey, 1941); the Test of Variables of Attention (Greenberg, 1991); the Wisconsin Card Sorting Test, computerized version (Grant & Berg, 1948; Heaton & PAR Staff, 1993); and the Wechsler Intelligence Scale for Children, third edition (WISC-III; Wechsler, 1991). (The battery utilized the following 11 subtests of the WISC-III: Comprehension, Arithmetic, Similarities, Vocabulary, Digit Span, Picture Arrangement, Picture Completion, Object Assembly, Block Design, Coding, and Symbol Search. The scoring procedures produced

the Verbal Intelligence Quotient [VIQ], the Performance Intelligence Quotient [PIQ], and the Full Scale Intelligence Quotient [FSIQ], which were used in the analyses.) All subjects and parents were given an overview of the test results upon request.

Data Analyses and Results

☐ For purposes of analysis, subjects were divided into two groups: sexually abused (child sexual abuse, or CSA) and nontraumatized. Analyses of variance (ANOVAs) indicated there were no statistically significant differences between the two groups concerning age (F ratio = 1.61, p = .21) and SES (F ratio = 2.2, p = .14). Using a chi-square test for homogeneity of proportions, we determined that handedness was equal for both groups, with 90% of

Three of the children had experienced sexual abuse by multiple perpetrators. Most (75%; n = 15) had experienced repeated sexual abuse, whereas only 25% (n = 5) experienced sexual abuse that involved one incident. Only two subjects experienced the use of physical violence or force during their molestation. Seven of the children complied because they experienced various forms of threat (e.g., the perpetrator threatened to kill the child, kill the child's sibling, or kill himself). Although other sources of trauma were not consistently documented for this sample, 50% of the CSA children had ex-

Table 18.1 Types of Abuse and Relationships of Abused to Perpetrators

	Number	Percentage
Type of abuse		
vaginal/anal intercourse	17	68.0
digital penetration	2	8.0
exposure to pornography	1	4.0
fondling	2	8.0
multiple forms of abuse	3	12.0
Relationship to perpetrator		
stepfather	4	17.4
grandfather	4	17.4
adolescent relative	4	17.4
father	3	13.0
acquaintance	3	13.0
stepbrother	2	8.7
grandmother	1	4.3
stranger	1	4.3

perienced multiple forms of trauma, including removal from their homes following disclosure, multiple out-of-home placements, homelessness, death of a parent, and the witnessing of domestic violence.

Regarding the multiple analyses of variance (MANOVAs), the dependent variables were not preordered for entry into the analyses. There were no univariate or multivariate within-cell outliers at alpha = .001. Evaluation of assumptions of normality, homogeneity of variance-covariance matrices, linearity, and multicollinearity were satisfactory.

Sample sizes of the two cells of this analysis were CSA ($n = 20$) and nonabused children ($n = 20$). The measures used to assess memory were the VMI, NMI, and DMI. Pearson correlations among these three outcome variables were all significant at the $p < .03$ level: VMI-DMI ($r = .59$), NMI-VMI ($r = .56$), and DMI-NMI ($r = .45$). Even though these variables are highly correlated, conceptually they contribute different information about the child's memory functioning. Thus we decided to assess the relationship of trauma to these discrete memory functions. Using Wilks's criterion, we found the combined dependent variables for memory not to vary significantly as a function of trauma; approximate $F(1, 36) = .96$, $p > .05$. The univariate tests for the three memory subtests by CSA were examined to test the a priori hypothe-

sis that traumatized children would do less well on measures of memory functions than would children without histories of psychological trauma. Contrary to the prediction, the results for these three variables were not significant: DMI, $F(1, 38) = .48$, $p > .05$; NMI, $F(1, 38) = 1.09$, $p > .05$; and VMI, $F(1, 38) = 1.15$, $p > .05$. This finding suggests that CSA is not necessarily associated with decreased memory functioning in children.

The dependent variables used to assess higher cognitive functioning were the composite VIQ and PIQ scores. Pearson correlations between these two outcome variables were significant at the $p > .000$ level; VIQ-PIQ ($r = .67$). Although these variables are highly correlated, conceptually they contribute different information about the child's cognitive functioning. Thus we decided to assess the impact of trauma upon these discrete cognitive domains. Using Wilks's criterion, we found the combined dependent variables to vary significantly as a function of trauma; approximate $F(2, 37) = 4.18$, $p = .023$. The univariate tests of the two higher cognitive variables by trauma were examined to test the a priori hypothesis that traumatized children would demonstrate higher cognitive deficit than children without histories of psychological trauma. In support of the prediction, the results for one of these variables was significant: VIQ, $F(1, 38) = 7.09$, $p = .01$. However,

Table 18.2 Main Effects, Mean Scores, and Standard Deviations of Higher Cognitive Functions in Children as a Function of Those Who Have Experienced Childhood Sexual Abuse

	CSA (n = 20)		Nonabused (n = 20)	
	Mean	*SD*	*Mean*	*SD*
VIQ	89.25	14.91	101.90	15.13
PIQ	88.55	14.77	92.80	14.75
Significance Tests	*df*	*F*	*Significance of F*	
Multivariate	2, 37	4.18	.02	
Univariate				
VIQ	1, 38	7.09	.01	
PIQ	1, 38	.82	.36	

SOURCE: Multivariate effect size and observed power at .0500 level; independent univariate .9500 confidence intervals and two-tailed observed power taken at .0500 level.

the results for PIQ were not significant: $F(1, 38) = .82$, $p > .05$. The mean FSIQ of the WISC-III for the clinical and comparison groups was 87.8 + 14.18 and 97.2 + 15.49, respectively.

This finding, with the results from the overall analysis, suggests that trauma is associated with decreased higher cognitive functioning in children in the verbal domain but not in the performance domain. The results of this analysis are shown in Table 18.2.

Current level of anxiety/depression as measured by the Achenbach Child Behavior Checklist did differ significantly between the two groups; $F(1, 34) = 10.8$, $p = .002$. The amount of anxiety/depression a child is currently experiencing predicted the greatest amount of unique variance across all outcome measures. This suggests that there is a high degree of overlap in the effect of trauma coupled with the concomitant effect of anxiety and depression upon the neuropsychological functioning in children, specifically in the area of verbal IQ.

Discussion

☐ The study reported here is an exploratory one, employing a small sample. It was designed to identify whether neuropsychological deficits in the areas of memory and higher cognitive functioning are associated with a history of childhood sexual abuse. Based on a review of

the literature, it was predicted that psychological trauma would increase the chances of children's demonstrating neuropsychological deficits. Specifically, such children would be expected to show deficient performance on tests of memory and higher cognitive functioning.

To control for gender-specific developmental differences in neurocognitive functioning, we limited our sample exclusively to female subjects. Because of this, the ability to generalize the present findings to a larger population of children who have sustained some form of psychological trauma must be viewed with caution.

Memory and Child Sexual Abuse

Concerning the relation between memory functioning and CSA, there were no significant differences on any of the composite scores between the two groups. This finding is contrary to recent findings in studies of adult victims of child sexual abuse. Bremner and his colleagues (unpublished data) have found deficits in explicit recall for verbal information in adult survivors of child abuse. It is interesting to note that Bremner, Randall, Capelli, et al. (1995) found that abused subjects demonstrated a tendency, although not a significant difference, to score higher on a visual memory task than did their comparison subjects. These findings also may be a factor of a small sample size. Uddo, Vasterling, Brailey, and Sutker (1993) found deficits in short-term verbal memory as assessed by the Rey Auditory Verbal Learning Test in Vietnam combat veterans. In a related study, Sutker, Winstead, Galina, and Allain (1991) report findings of impairment in verbal recall as measured by the Logical Memory Component of the Wechsler Memory Scale in adults who had been prisoners of war during the Korean conflict. However, Sutker et al. found that the degree of starvation and body waste experienced by veterans who had been prisoners of war was highly correlated with level of memory impairment (Sutker, Galina, West, & Allain, 1990; Sutker, Vasterling, Brailey, & Allain, 1995). It should be noted that these studies all involve small samples of adults who have experienced traumatizing events. In this regard, it is important to consider a central premise of this study—specifically, adult neuropsychological functioning is not an explanatory model for pediatric neurocognitive functions. Nor can it be assumed that PTSD resulting from child sexual abuse is equivalent to that resulting from combat stress and experience. Additionally, the studies that involved veterans who developed PTSD did not appear to factor in that these individuals were often exposed to toxins, head injuries, malnutrition, and other factors associated with deficient neuropsychological functioning.

Higher Cognitive Functions and Child Sexual Abuse

Concerning the relation between higher cognitive functioning and history of CSA, the study reported here documented that there was a difference between the two groups on VIQ in the direction of the hypothesis. That is, the VIQ scores of children with histories of CSA were lower than those of children in the comparison group. One aspect of the data that has to be discussed is the impact of anxiety/depression upon performance on the tests. Neuropsychological research indicates that the presence of anxiety and depression will negatively alter the performance of subjects on neuropsychological measures (Miller, 1975; Newman & Sweet, 1986). It has been determined that depression can generally be detected in neurocog-

nitive measures by reduced scores on performance measures (Dalton, Pederson, & Ryan, 1989). In adults, scores on the subtests Digit Span and Digit Symbol, the adult equivalent of Coding, tend to be sensitive to anxiety (Golden, 1979). It is interesting to return to this study, in which there were no significant differences between these two groups on the PIQ, Coding, or Digit Span scores. It may be that depression is a related and contributing factor to a coexisting neurophysiological accommodation to the level of psychological trauma, and not merely a masking variable. Researchers will have to explore this in future studies by including children with histories of CSA who either are not exhibiting any level of depression or anxiety or are being treated psychopharmacologically for depression.

As with the memory domains, the higher cognitive domain subtests were subjected to univariate tests both with and without covarying for the anxious/depressed covariate. Several subtests were significantly affected by the presence of a history of CSA. These included Comprehension, Information, Similarities, and Vocabulary. Collectively, these subtests represent several cognitive functions, including abstract verbal reasoning, social knowledgeability and judgment, and acquired factual information. These are significant skills necessary for everyday emotional and interpersonal functioning, and clinically known to be very deficient in many traumatized children. There were no significant differences demonstrated on the subtests of PIQ, but there was a significant difference between groups with regard to the FSIQ, again in the direction of the hypothesis.

Concerning previous research, other studies cite variable results regarding the impact of psychological trauma on higher cognitive functioning in adults. Bremner, Randall, Capelli, et al. (1995) found no significant difference in Wechsler Adult Intelligent Scale scores between adult survivors of severe childhood physical and sexual abuse and controls, although there was a tendency for the abused subjects to have slightly lower FSIQ scores. Klonoff, McDougall, Clark, Kramer, and Horgan (1976) found significant differences on IQ scores between samples of prisoner of war survivors who had either a highly stressful internment in a Japanese prison camp or a less stressful imprisonment in Europe during World War II. Those prisoners held in the highly stressful condition demonstrated lower overall FSIQ than did those in the less stressful condition. Perry (1995) documents depressed VIQ scores in a sample of 200 traumatized children, which supports the findings of the current study.

Given the impact of the anxious/depressed variable, the particular items endorsed by the CSA sample parents were reviewed. It is interesting that many of the items frequently endorsed on the Achenbach Child Behavior Checklist for the CSA sample (e.g., nervous, self-conscious, fears others are out to get her, fearful) are very consistently reported in clinical presentations of traumatized children. Given the level of descriptive overlap of this variable with those that are the generally accepted manifestations of the emotional sequelae of traumatizing events in children (Briere & Elliott, 1994; Browne & Finkelhor, 1986; James, 1989), it is also reasonable that the anxious/depressed variable is actually a collateral of the trauma variable and not a masking or a confounding variable.

Taken together, there was modest support for the hypothesis concerning the higher cognitive domain. These results may have been even more robust given a larger sample size. Concerning memory and higher cognitive function, it was not possible, given the size of the sample, to evaluate the difference in memory functioning within the traumatized group as a function of severity of trauma. This may partially explain the difference between the findings of the current study and the documented memory deficits in adults with histories of psychological trauma. It may also be the case that there is a longitudinal decrement in memory functioning, given the repeated neurochemical assaults on the integrity of the neural structures that facilitate memory. If so, it is unclear what role the effective intervention of trauma may then play in ameliorating such a process.

There is also another way to consider the findings. The results on the memory tests may actually reflect the clinical subjects' ability to acquire and recall new information given a highly structured environment. In contrast, the lower VIQ scores demonstrated by the clinical sample may actually reflect the traumatized children's difficulty with acquisition, encoding, and recall of verbally mediated information presented in a less structured, more distractible environment, such as the classroom.

The observed difference between VIQ-PIQ in the abused sample may be best explained by Perry's (1995) premise that the brain develops in a "use-dependent" process in that the "undifferentiated neural systems are critically dependent upon sets of environmental and microenvironmental cues (e.g., neurotransmitters, cellular adhesion molecules, neurohormones, amino acids, ions) to appropriately organize from their undifferentiated, immature forms" (p. 7). The brain also develops in a sequential and hierarchical fashion. Research by Fox, Bell, and Jones (1992) suggests support for individual differences in hemispheric responses to stress. What does this mean for traumatized children? Where one may view a child's becoming distressed when his or her caretaker leaves the room as an adaptive response, Perry (1995) would suggest that, for infants and children who live in violent environments, this could potentially be maladaptive and even fatal. An alternate explanation might be that the children who demonstrate higher levels of deficit on measures of left-hemisphere neurocognitive functions may have had preexisting right-hemispheric baseline specialization, and thus experience more pronounced responses to traumatic events. We will review the relevance of this perspective to the study at hand in future papers.

The present results are consistent with what Briere (1988) terms the "first wave" of prospective research on the sequelae of sexually abused children. Given that this is an exploratory study, the findings are as important for what they do not tell us as they are for what they do.

Although it is not indicated that these findings can be generalized in any way, it is nevertheless interesting that we found no significant differences in the memory functions. This point is contrary to what is currently being reported in the adult neuroanatomical and neuropsychological research. It is also relevant given the controversy about children's specific recall of information as it relates to their credibility. A child's explicit recall of nonrelevant information cannot necessarily predict his or her recall of a highly emotionally charged memory of being sexually assaulted. However, this study does not support the assertion that sexually abused children's overall explicit memory is significantly different from that of children in a comparison group. It could also be argued that the deficits in VIQ are actually a measure of long-term verbal memory, and thus represent deficiencies in several areas: sustained attention to verbally mediated information, efficient encoding and storage of verbal material, and correct recall and organization of verbal information. Relatedly, the scores on the Test of Memory and Learning may reflect the traumatized child's ability for incidental learning of both verbally and visually mediated information within a highly structured environment. Thus the findings potentially have great significance regarding traumatized children's academic potential and should be evaluated in future studies.

Limitations

☐ The study reported above presents several methodological challenges and limitations found in the research on sexually abused children: the issues of definition, sample selection, and the use of "matched" controls and analysis. Briere (1992) addresses each of these concerns. Briefly, there continue to be discrepancies in the definitions used in the literature for what actions constitute sexual abuse. For purposes of this chapter, we defined child sexual abuse using the definitions of incestuous and extrafamilial abuse found in Russell's (1986) work, as this is a well-respected and definitive study in the field of sexual abuse.

Another limitation is the assessment of the impact of trauma, and of multiple forms of trauma. It was not possible to control for all forms of secondary trauma or concomitant traumas experienced by sexually abused children.

We screened for known physical abuse, and children with histories of severe physical abuse (e.g., shaken baby syndrome or head injury) were excluded, as the possibility of head trauma resulting from physical abuse would confound the results. In a related issue, it is also necessary to address the fact that a portion of the comparative sample of nonabused children may have experienced some form of trauma that has not been disclosed.

Due to the nature of the legal and sociocultural aspects of child sexual victimization, it is difficult to infer that sexual abuse is the only source of trauma experienced by the subjects. Relatedly, a child's experience of an event as traumatizing is mediated by many familial factors, such as parental reaction to and support of the disclosure, current relationship and attachment to the caregiver, and parental responsiveness to the need for intervention. Positive and appropriate parental responsiveness was inferred from both the parents' participation in the project and their follow-through with clinical recommendations as evidenced by their consistency with clinic and evaluation appointments.

A related issue involves the definition of how a child experiences sexual abuse and how to determine the acuity or chronicity of the experience. It is understood that several factors may influence the subjective experience of trauma: the child's relationship to the perpetrator, the use of violence or amount of pain involved, the number of perpetrators, and the type of sexual abuse (Russell, 1983; Williams, 1993). Additionally, the child's ability to process the experience cognitively and give it a meaning that subserves his or her sense of safety varies according to the level of neurocognitive maturation. It would be advisable for future studies to include a self-report measure for children with PTSD symptoms. This would increase the researchers' ability to partition effects of trauma based on severity of symptoms.

An additional limitation of this study is related to neuropsychological assessment of children, which is a complex process. An initial challenge was how to account for developmental changes of cognitive structures and processes, and then accommodate this in the assessment protocol. Insult or injury to developing brain tissue results in more diffuse consequences in children than does similar injury in adults (Reitan & Davidson, 1974). Dean and Gray (1990) also suggest that another problem exists in the limited availability of data on neuropsychological tests regarding normal developmental trends for children.

A complication in the measurement of this theory is the role of depression, a concomitant feature of PTSD, and a depressant of neuropsychological function. Depression is a prominent feature in traumatized children (Oates, O'Toole, Lynch, Stern, & Cooney, 1994; Terr, 1985; van der Kolk, 1987), and it has also been found to result in performance deficits on neuropsychological tests (Newman & Sweet, 1986). However, the findings suggest qualitative differences in response patterns of depressed patients when compared with neurologically impaired individuals in that depressed patients are inconsistent in responses, whereas impaired patients make consistent errors in areas of deficits. Although a formal pattern analysis was not conducted in the current study, an inconsistent response pattern was not discerned in the CSA protocols.

A final limitation may exist in the measures of neuropsychological functioning and the assessment of premorbid functioning (prior to the trauma). The actual levels of premorbid functioning had to be inferred from the neurophysiological and developmental histories.

Conclusions and Direction for Future Research

☐ The area of neuropsychological sequelae of psychological trauma in a pediatric population is one of great relevance to current research. A primary task of the latency-age child is to achieve to optimal academic ability. For the sexually abused child, there may exist critical impediments in the form of neurocognitive deficiencies that have to be accommodated. This study does not indicate that children with histories of sexual abuse have impaired abilities to learn and retain new information in highly structured environments. It does, however, present the possibility that sexually abused girls may have more difficulty in higher cognitive functions in the verbal domain.

This study raises many questions to be addressed in future studies. First, given the findings of modest association in a small sample of girls between history of sexual abuse and mild neurocognitive deficits, would these findings be more robustly represented in a larger sample? Also, would there be similar findings given a sample that included multiple forms of trauma, such as witnessing domestic violence, loss of a family member, or surviving a disaster or terrorist activity? Future studies should include a subjective measure of anxiety, depression, and trauma. Additionally, the issue of chronicity and severity of trauma will need to be measured more rigorously. The inclusion in future research of a sample of boys would also be important to determine if there are relevant gender differences. Further, it would be useful to include a measure of academic achievement to address the actual deficit of acquired learning or recall of previous learning. Additionally, a cross-sectional study of children who have experienced trauma at different critical periods in neurocognitive development would be important to determine developmental impacts in a more precise manner. Finally, a cross-sectional, longitudinal study would be important to determine if neurocognitive deficits appear after a certain amount of time has lapsed without adequate intervention. We will address many of these questions, in addition to the specific impacts of trauma on the executive functions and attention, in forthcoming papers.

References

Achenbach, T., & Edelbrock, C. (1983). *Manual for the Child Behavior Checklist and Revised Child Behavior Profile.* Burlington: University of Vermont.

Blake-White, J., & Kline, C. (1985). Treating the dissociative process in adult victims of childhood incest. *Journal of Contemporary Social Work, 9,* 394-402.

Bowlby, J. (1984). Violence in the family as a disorder of the attachment and caregiving systems. *American Journal of Psychoanalysis, 44,* 9-27.

Bremner, J. D., Randall, P. R., Capelli, S., Scott, T. M., McCarthy, G., & Charney, D. S. (1995). Deficits in short-term memory in adult survivors of childhood abuse. *Psychiatry Research, 59,* 97-107.

Bremner, J. D., Randall, P. R., Scott, T. M., Bronen, R. A., Seibyl, J. P., Southwick, S. M., Delaney, R. C., McCarthy, G., Charney, D. S., & Innis, R. B. (1995). MRI-based measurement of hippocampal volume in patients with combat-related posttraumatic stress disorder. *American Journal of Psychiatry, 152,* 973-981.

Briere, J. (1988). Controlling for family variables in abuse effects research: A critique of the "partialling" approach. *Journal of Interpersonal Violence, 3,* 80-89.

Briere, J. (1992). Methodological issues in the study of sexual abuse effects. *Journal of Consulting and Clinical Psychology, 60,* 196-203.

Briere, J., & Elliott, D. (1994). Immediate and long-term impacts of child sexual abuse. *The Future of Children: Sexual Abuse of Children, 4,* 54-69.

Browne, A., & Finkelhor, D. (1986). Impact of child sexual abuse: A review of the research. *Psychological Bulletin, 99,* 66-77.

Charney, D. S., Deutch, A. Y., Krystal, J. H., Southwick, S. M., & Davis, M. (1993). Psychobiologic mechanisms of posttraumatic stress disorder. *Archives of General Psychiatry, 50,* 294-299.

Cicchetti, D. (1984). The emergence of developmental psychopathology. *Child Development, 55,* 1-7.

Cicchetti, D., & Rizley, A. (1981). Developmental perspectives on the etiology, intergenerational transmission and sequelae of child maltreatment. *New Directions for Child Development, 11,* 31-55.

Dalton, J. E., Pederson, S. L., & Ryan, J. J. (1989). Effects of posttraumatic stress disorder on neuropsychological test performance. *International Journal of Clinical Neuropsychology, 11,* 121-123.

Davies, R. K. (1978-1979). Incest: Some neuropsychiatric findings. *International Journal of Psychiatric Medicine, 9,* 117-121.

Dean, R. S., & Gray, J. W. (1990). Traditional approaches to neuropsychological assessment. In C. R. Reynolds & R. W. Kamphus (Eds.), *Handbook of psychological and educational assessment of children: Intelligence and achievement* (pp. 372-388). New York: Guilford.

Denckla, M. (1996). Research on executive functions in a neurodevelopmental context: Applications for clinical measures. *Developmental Neuropsychology, 12,* 5-16.

Everly, G. S., & Horton, A. M. (1989). Neuropsychology of post-traumatic stress disorder: A pilot study. *Perceptual and Motor Skills, 68,* 807-810.

Famularo, R., Fenton, T., & Kinscherff, R. (1993). Child maltreatment and the development of posttraumatic stress disorder. *American Journal of the Developing Child, 147,* 755-760.

Finkelhor, D. (1979). *Sexually victimized children.* New York: Free Press.

Finkelhor, D. (1994). Current information of the scope and nature of child sexual abuse. *The Future of Children: Sexual Abuse of Children, 4,* 31-53.

Fischer, K. W., & Rose, S. P. (1994). Dynamic development of coordination of components in brain and behavior: A framework for theory and research. In G. Dawson & K. W. Fischer (Eds.), *Human behavior and the developing brain* (pp. 3-66). New York: Guilford.

Fox, N. A., Bell, M. A., & Jones, N. A. (1992). Individual differences in response to stress and cerebral asymmetry. *Developmental Neuropsychology, 8,* 161-184.

Garbarino, J., Kostelny, K., & Dubrow, N. (1991). What children can tell us about living in danger. *American Psychologist, 46,* 376-383.

Golden, C. J. (1979). *Clinical interpretation of objective psychological tests.* Englewood Cliffs, NJ: Prentice Hall.

Goodwin, J. (1988). Posttraumatic symptoms in abused children. *Journal of Traumatic Stress, 1,* 475-488.

Grant, D. A., & Berg, E. A. (1948). A behavioral analysis of degree of impairment and ease of shifting to new responses in a Weigl-type card sorting problem. *Journal of Experimental Psychology, 39,* 404-411.

Greenberg, G. D. (1990). *Child neuropsychological history.* Worthington, OH: International Diagnostic Systems.

Greenberg, L. M. (1991). *T.O.V.A. interpretation manual: Test of Variables of Attention computer program version 5.01, 5.0A.* Minneapolis: University of Minnesota Press.

Heaton, R. K., & PAR Staff. (1993). *Wisconsin Card Sorting Test: Computer version-2.* Odessa, FL: Psychological Assessment Resources.

Hebb, D. O. (1949). *The organization of behavior: A neuropsychological theory.* New York: John Wiley.

Herman, J., Russell, D., & Trocki, K. (1986). Long-term effects of incestuous abuse in childhood. *American Journal of Psychiatry, 143,* 1293-1296.

Huttenlocher, P. R. (1994). Synaptogenesis in human cerebral cortex. In G. Dawson & K. W. Fischer (Eds.), *Human behavior and the developing brain* (pp. 137-152). New York: Guilford.

Ito, Y., Teicher, M. H., Glod, C. A., Harper, D., Magnus, E., & Gelbard, H. A. (1993). EEG abnormalities in abused children. *Journal of Neuropsychiatry, 5,* 401-408.

James, B. (1989). *Treating the traumatized child.* Lexington, MA: Lexington.

Janet, P. (1925). *Psychological healing* (Vols. 1-2). New York: Macmillan. (Original work published 1919)

Judd, C., Smith, E., & Kidder, L. (1991). *Research methods in social relations* (6th ed.). Orlando, FL: Holt, Rinehart & Winston.

Kempe, C. (1985). *The battered child.* Chicago: University of Chicago Press.

Klonoff, H., McDougall, G., Clark, C., Kramer, P., & Horgan, J. (1976). The neuropsychological, psychiatric, and physical effects of prolonged and severe stress: 30 years later. *Journal of Nervous and Mental Disease, 163,* 246-252.

Kolb, L. C. (1987). A neuropsychological hypothesis explaining post-traumatic stress disorders. *American Journal of Psychiatry, 144,* 989-995.

Lezak, M. D. (1983). *Neuropsychological assessment* (2nd ed.). New York: Oxford University Press.

Luria, A. R. (1973). *The working brain: An introduction to neuropsychology.* New York: Basic Books.

Malloy, P. F., Webster, J. S., & Russell, W. (1985). Luria's frontal lobe syndromes. *International Journal of Clinical Neuropsychology, 7,* 88-95.

McLean, P. D. (1949). Psychosomatic disease and the "visceral brain." *Psychosomatic Medicine, 11,* 338-353.

Miller, W. (1975). Psychological deficit in depression. *Psychological Bulletin, 82,* 238-260.

Nader, K., Pynoos, R. S., Fairbanks, L. A., & Frederick, C. (1990). Children's PTSD reactions one year after a sniper attack at their school. *American Journal of Psychiatry, 147,* 1526-1530.

Newman, P. J., & Sweet, J. J. (1986). The effects of clinical depression on the Luria-Nebraska Neuropsychological Battery. *International Journal of Clinical Neuropsychology, 8,* 109-114.

Oates, K. (1984). The development of abused children. *Developmental Medicine and Child Neurology, 26,* 649-656.

Oates, R. K., O'Toole, B. I., Lynch, D. L., Stern, A., & Cooney, G. (1994). Stability and change in outcomes for sexually abused children. *Journal of the American Academy of Child and Adolescent Psychiatry, 33,* 945-953.

Orzhekhovskaya, N. S. (1981). Fronto-striatal relationships in primate ontogeny. *Neuroscience and Behavioral Physiology, 11,* 379-385.

Perry, B. (1995). *Neurodevelopmental adaptations to severe maltreatment: Dissociation and hyperarousal.* Paper presented at the Third Annual Colloquium of the American Professional Society on the Abuse of Children, Tucson, AZ.

Reitan, R. M., & Davidson, L. A. (1974). *Clinical neuropsychology: Current status and clinical applications.* New York: V. H. Winston.

Rey, A. (1941). L'examen psychologique dan les cas d'encephalopathie traumatique. *Archives de Psychologie, 28,* 286-340.

Reynolds, C. R., & Bigler, E. D. (1994). *Test of Memory and Learning: Examiner's manual.* Austin, TX: Pro-Ed.

Russell, D. E. H. (1983). The incidence and relevance of intrafamilial and extrafamilial sexual abuse of female children. *Child Abuse & Neglect, 7,* 133-149.

Russell, D. E. H. (1986). *The secret trauma: Incest in the lives of girls and women.* New York: Basic Books.

Sapolsky, R. M., Krey, L. C., & McEwen, B. S. (1984). Glucocorticoid-sensitive hippocampal neurons are involved in terminating the adrenocortical stress response. *Procedures From the National Academy of Science USA, 81,* 6174-6171.

Schefft, B., Moses, J., & Schmidt, G. (1985). Neuropsychology and emotion: A self-regulatory model. *International Journal of Clinical Neuropsychology, 7,* 201-213.

Schultz, L. G. (1973). The child sex victim: Social, psychological and legal perspectives. *Child Welfare, 52,* 147-148.

Spreen, O., Tupper, D., Risser, A., Tuokko, H., & Edgell, D. (1984). *Human developmental neuropsychology.* New York: Oxford University Press.

Stuss, D. T. (1992). Biological and psychological development of executive functions. *Brain and Cognition, 20,* 8-23.

Stuss, D. T., & Benson, D. F. (1986). *The frontal lobes.* New York: Raven.

Stuss, D. T., Gow, C. A., & Hetherington, C. R. (1992). "No longer Gage": Frontal lobe dysfunction and emotional changes. *Journal of Consulting and Clinical Psychology, 60,* 349-359.

Sutker, P. B., Galina, Z. H., West, J. A., & Allain, A. N. (1990). Trauma-induced weight loss and cognitive deficits among former prisoners of war. *American Journal of Psychiatry, 147,* 323-328.

Sutker, P. B., Vasterling, J. J., Brailey, K., & Allain, A. N. (1995). Memory, attention, and executive deficits in POW survivors: Contributing biological and psychological factors. *Neuropsychology, 9,* 118-125.

Sutker, P. B., Winstead, D. K., Galina, Z. H., & Allain, A. N. (1991). Cognitive deficits and psychopathology among former prisoners of war and combat veterans of the Korean conflict. *American Journal of Psychiatry, 148,* 67-72.

Teicher, M. H., Glod, C. A., Surrey, J., & Swett, C., Jr. (1993). Early childhood abuse and limbic system ratings in adult psychiatric outpatients. *Journal of Neuropsychiatry, 5,* 301-306.

Terr, L. C. (1983). Chowchilla revisited: The effects of psychic trauma four years after a school-bus kidnapping. *American Journal of Psychiatry, 140,* 1543-1550.

Terr, L. C. (1985). Psychic trauma in children and adolescents. *Psychiatric Clinics of North America, 8,* 815-835.

Thatcher, R. W. (1994). Cyclic cortical reorganization: Origins of human cognitive development. In G. Dawson & K. W. Fischer (Eds.), *Human behavior and the developing brain* (pp. 232-268). New York: Guilford.

Uddo, M., Vasterling, J. T., Brailey, K., & Sutker, P. B. (1993). Memory and attention in posttraumatic stress disorder. *Journal of Psychopathology and Behavioral Assessment, 15,* 43-52.

van der Kolk, B. A. (1987). *Psychological trauma.* Washington, DC: American Psychiatric Press.

Wechsler, D. (1991). *Manual for the WISC* (3rd ed.). San Antonio, TX: Psychological Corporation/Harcourt Brace Jovanovich.

Williams, M. B. (1993). Assessing the traumatic impact of child sexual abuse: What makes it more severe? *Journal of Child Sexual Abuse, 2,* 41-61.

Wolfe, J., & Charney, D. S. (1991). Use of neuropsychological assessment in post traumatic stress disorder. *Psychological Assessment, 3,* 573-580.

Wolfe, V. V., Gentile, C., & Bourdeau, P. (1986). *History of Victimization Questionnaire.* (Available from Vicky Veitch Wolfe, Ph.D., Department of Psychology, Children's Hospital of Western Ontario, 800 Commissioners Rd., London, ON N6A 4G5, Canada)

Yakovlev, P. I. (1962). Morphological criteria of growth and maturation of the nervous system in man. *Research Publication Association for Research in Nervous and Mental Diseases, 39,* 3-46.

Yehuda, R., Giller, E., Southwick, S. M., Lowy, M., & Mason, J. (1991). Hypothalamic-pituitary-adrenal dysfunction in post traumatic stress disorder. *Biological Psychiatry, 30,* 1031-1048.

Yehuda, R., Lowy, M., Southwick, S. M., Shaffer, D., & Geller, E. (1991). Lymphocyte gluticorticoid receptor number in posttraumatic stress disorder. *American Journal of Psychiatry, 148,* 499-504.

19

Coping With Traumatic Stress Interferes With Memory of the Event

A New Conceptual Mechanism for the Protective Effects of Stress Control

Robert C. Drugan

The marked impact of stress on the biology of an organism has been appreciated since the pioneering work of Cannon (1928) and Selye (1936), often referred to as the "fathers of stress research." In their early studies, Cannon and Selye noted that prolonged exposure to uncontrollable stress led to a breakdown in bodily functions and hypersecretion of hormones such as norepinephrine and corticosterone. Present-day studies have verified and extended these initial observations by characterizing the various hormonal systems associated with stress, including the sympathetic nervous system (Kvetnansky & Mikulaj, 1970; Stone & McCarty,

1983; Weiss et al., 1981), hypothalamic-pituitary-adrenal axis (DeSouza & Van Loon, 1985; Guillemin et al., 1977; Young & Akil, 1985), and endogenous opiates (Drugan, Grau, Maier, Madden, & Barchas, 1981; Guillemin et al., 1977; Lewis, Cannon, & Liebeskind, 1980; Madden, Akil, Patrick, & Barchas, 1977; Maier et al., 1980). Remarkably, the psychological dynamics of a stress experience (e.g., predictability, controllability) are very influential regarding physiological reactivity and pathological outcome. In fact, psychological aspects of stress may be as critical to the organism as the nature, type, and severity of the physical

AUTHOR'S NOTE: The research presented in this chapter was supported by NIMH Grant No. 45475. All behavioral procedures were reviewed and approved by the Brown University Institutional Animal Care and Use Committee. The significant empirical and conceptual contributions of Denis Healy are greatly appreciated. This chapter was originally presented as a paper at Trauma and Memory: An International Research Conference, Durham, New Hampshire, July 26-28, 1996.

stress itself. In this chapter, I describe several ways in which actively coping with stress in animals may afford resilience, and how this may map onto clinical observations. Similarly, when coping behavior is neither available nor effective, this may set into motion changes in the brain that may set the stage for vulnerability to disorders such as depression and posttraumatic stress disorder (PTSD). Several etiological mechanisms appear compelling, particularly altered emotional hedonics during the stressor and memory alterations for the stress event. Finally, the consequences of these stress changes on sites in the brain where certain classes of drugs of abuse have their actions suggest important links between stress and coping, memory, self-medication, and the potential for drug abuse.

Controllability of Stress and Bodily Changes: Implications for a Critical Role of Anxiety

☐ During the past three decades, much research has focused on the behavioral, biochemical, and pathological sequelae of inescapable stress exposure in both animal models and humans. The debilitating effects of uncontrollable stress exposure include interference with subsequent learning (Anisman & Sklar, 1979; Maier & Seligman, 1976; Seligman & Maier, 1967), opiate stress-induced analgesia (Drugan, Ader, & Maier, 1985; Jackson, Maier, & Coon, 1979; Lewis et al., 1980; Madden et al., 1977; Maier et al., 1980), immunosuppression (Kusnecov & Rabin, 1993; Laudenslager, Ryan, Drugan, Hyson, & Maier, 1983; Seiber et al., 1992; Weiss, Sundar, & Becker, 1989), and gastric ulceration (Weiss, 1971). Virtually every neurotransmitter system is altered as a result of prolonged inescapable stress exposure, including dopamine (Anisman & Zacharko, 1990; Fadda et al., 1978; Fekete, Szentendrei, Kanyicska, & Palkovits, 1981), norepinephrine (Weiss et al., 1981; Weiss, Stone, & Harrell, 1970), acetylcholine (Anisman, Remington, & Sklar, 1979), serotonin (Dunn, 1988; Petty, Kramer, & Wilson, 1992; Sherman & Petty, 1982), and GABA (Drugan, McIntyre, Alpern, &

Maier, 1985; Petty & Sherman, 1981). Interestingly, equal amounts of escapable or controllable stress result in few to none of the above effects.

The biological concomitants of intense anxiety have been postulated as a critical condition for the above stress effects, because the administration of antianxiety agents prior to inescapable stress blocks the majority of these changes. Injections of benzodiazepines, such as chlordiazepoxide or diazepam, prior to inescapable shock block the learning deficits (Drugan, Ryan, Minor, & Maier, 1984; Sherman, Allers, Petty, & Henn, 1979), opioid stress-induced analgesia (Drugan et al., 1984; Maier, 1990), gastric ulceration (File & Pearce, 1981), and stress-induced secretion of corticosterone (LeFur, Guillox, Mitrani, Mizoule, & Uzan, 1979). Benzodiazepines also block the neurochemical sequelae of stress mentioned above. These data suggest that intense anxiety may be both a necessary and a sufficient condition for producing this wide array of stress pathologies.

Many of the pathological effects of stress are also reduced—if not eliminated—when the subject is allowed to make an active behavioral response to alter the pattern, onset, duration, or intensity of stress (Maier & Seligman, 1976; Weiss, 1971; Weiss et al., 1970). The similarity between the protective effects of active escape behavior (i.e., "coping") and those of prestress administration of benzodiazepines led to the proposal that active coping may release an antianxiety compound in brain (Drugan, McIntyre, et al., 1985).

This hypothesis has received recent support from both behavioral and neurochemical studies. Escapably shocked rats show a reduced fear response when reexposed to context cues associated with the stressor (Desiderato & Newman, 1971; Mineka, Cook, & Miller, 1984) and show no change in social interaction poststress (Short & Maier, 1993). Many neurotransmitters have been implicated in the pathophysiology of anxiety or stress: norepinephrine (Redmond & Huang, 1979; Weiss et al., 1970), serotonin (Dunn, 1988; Tye, Everett, & Iverson, 1977), dopamine (Antelman & Eicher, 1979; MacLennan & Maier, 1983), and the benzodiazepine/

GABA receptor (Dorow, Horowski, Paschelke, Amin, & Braestrup, 1983; Drugan et al., 1989; Paul, Marangos, & Skolnick, 1981). However, until recently, the nature of this antianxiety compound associated with stress control has remained elusive.

Endogenous Systems That May Modulate Stress Resilience in Coping Subjects

□ There are several reports of neurotransmitter systems that are differentially changed as a function of the stress control versus lack of control: norepinephrine (NE), dopamine (DA), serotonin (5-HT), and gamma-aminobutyric acid (GABA).

Norepinephrine

The work of Weiss and colleagues (1970) illustrates that stress control (e.g., the ability to escape or avoid shock) is associated with an increase in whole brain NE in comparison with yoked inescapable shock and nonshock controls in both a mild and more severe stress situation. This "coping-induced" increase in brain NE would prevent NE depletion, which is associated with the behavioral depression observed following inescapable shock exposure.

Dopamine

Cabib and Puglisi-Allegra (1994) report an increase in mesolimbic dopamine systems (e.g., 3-methoxytyramine) in the nucleus accumbens septi following escapable but not inescapable shock in mice in comparison with nonshock controls. The summary of their findings supports the view that exposure to controllable shock elicits an increase of mesolimbic DA release, whereas exposure to uncontrollable shock induces a decrease of DA release in this brain area. Environmental conditions that afford an organism behavioral coping opportunities in the face of stress prevent the inhibition of mesolimbic DA release.

Serotonin

Petty and colleagues (1992) found that either behavioral or pharmacological treatments that prevent stress-induced behavioral depression—including behavioral control/coping, prestress benzodiazepine administration, and tricyclic antidepressant administration—are associated with a normal level of serotonin in frontal cortex. This level of serotonergic function in frontal cortex was determined by potassium (K+)-stimulated release and measured by microdialysis. In stress-vulnerable subjects, frontal cortex 5-HT levels are depleted.

Gamma-aminobutyric Acid

Our laboratory has evaluated the impact of stress control on GABAergic tone in rats. We originally found that stress control is associated with a release of an endogenous compound that protects the organism from the convulsant action of the GABA antagonist, bicuculline (Drugan, McIntyre, et al., 1985), as well as the chloride channel antagonist, picrotoxinin (Drugan, Basile, Ha, & Ferland, 1994). In addition, we found that rats that are able to cope with stress, or are stress resilient, have changes in certain binding domains at the benzodiazepine/GABA receptor complex that indicate the release of an endogenous valium-like substance (e.g., increases [3H]muscimol binding and decreased [35S]t-butylbicyclophosphorothionate [TBPS] binding; Drugan et al., 1994; Drugan, Paul, & Crawley, 1993). Controllable stress is associated with the release of a substance in brain that competes with radioactive diazepam at the benzodiazepine receptor as determined by chlorobutane extraction and subsequent in vitro receptor binding competition analysis. More specifically, active behavioral coping is associated with a two- to threefold increase in the whole brain of a benzodiazepine-like agonist (Drugan et al., 1994). These data complement the findings of Petty and colleagues that indicate a paucity of GABA in certain brain structures, including hippocampus concomitant with behavioral depression. Conversely, microinjections of GABA into this site protect against this syndrome (Petty & Sherman, 1981). Although several neurotransmitter systems do show changes in the coping subject above and beyond the naive control, the benzodiazepine/ GABA evidence most closely approximates the exogenous valium prophylaxis. Therefore, we have focused on the BDZ/GABA system because it appears to represent a final common pathway for both behavioral and pharmacological immunization against stress effects.

Molecular Pharmacology of the Benzodiazepine/GABA-Chloride Ionophore Receptor Complex

☐ The benzodiazepine/GABA-chloride ionophore receptor complex (BGRC) is a prototypical ligand-gated ion channel found in central nervous system tissue. The binding of compounds at this receptor complex have their actions by the opening or closing of a chloride ion channel. This "supramolecular receptor complex" is the site of minor tranquilizer action in the brain (Paul et al., 1981), with binding sites for benzodiazepines (e.g., valium), barbiturates, and ethanol, as well as the cell surface actions of certain neuroactive and brain-derived neurosteroids (e.g., deoxycorticosterone and allopregnenolone; Gee, Bolger, Brinton, Coirini, & McEwen, 1988; McEwen, 1991; Olsen, 1982; Ticku & Ramanjaneyulu, 1984). All of these minor tranquilizers have the common action of increasing chloride flow into the cell producing hyperpolarization, neural inhibition, muscle relaxation, and sedation in a dose-dependent fashion. The BGRC has also been implicated in the pathophysiology of anxiety in that another class of compounds that act at this receptor complex, the B-carbolines, produce opposite effects, including depolarization, anxiety, and seizures (Dorow et al., 1983; Schweri, Cain, Cook, Paul, & Skolnick, 1982).

Coping With Stress May Protect Against Pathology by Altered Memory of the Stress Experience

☐ If active behavioral control over stress, or "coping," is associated with the release of a GABA-enhancing substance in the brain simi-

lar to the minor tranquilizers mentioned above, then we might expect to see an interference in memory, because many of these anti-anxiety compounds also have an amnestic profile (File & Pellow, 1988; Izquierdo & Medina, 1991; Katz & Liebler, 1978; Lister, 1985; Lucki, Rickels, Giesecke, & Geller, 1987; McNamara & Skelton, 1992; McNaughton & Morris, 1987; Theibot, 1985; Venault et al., 1986). Our hypothesis was that stress resilience afforded to the coping subjects may be due, in part, to an interference in the memory of the initial stress experience. This "emotional memory" deficit may prove to be beneficial by reducing proactive interference of the initial stress experience on subsequent learning and physiology.

We chose to evaluate the above hypothesis by testing the impact of escapable, inescapable, and no shock exposure on the subsequent acquisition and retention of spatial memory using the Morris water maze. We selected this place-learning task because it is highly sensitive to changes in hippocampal function (Morris, 1981), a brain area known to have changes in GABA function in response to stress (Foy, Foy, Levine, & Thompson, 1990; Foy, Stanton, Levine, & Thompson, 1987; Petty & Sherman, 1981; Sherman et al., 1979) as well as in stress-resilient or coping subjects (Drugan et al., 1993, 1994). Therefore, if active behavioral coping or stress control causes the release of an endogenous BDZ-like compound, then these subjects should show poorer retention of the location of a platform that they had learned just following escapable stress exposure in comparison to yoked-inescapable shock and nonshock controls.

Rats in this study were exposed to one of the following: 80 unsignaled escapable shocks, yoked-inescapable shocks, or no shock. Immediately thereafter, they were trained to find a submerged platform in a circular water maze (Morris, 1981) in a procedure modeled after that employed by Warren, Castro, Rudy, and Maier (1991). Training consisted of 18 trials presented in 9 blocks of 2 trials each. If the subject failed to find the platform within 60 seconds, the animal was placed on the platform and a latency of 60 seconds was recorded. Retention probes were conducted in a between-group design at 2 hours, 4 hours, and 24 hours postshock.

There were no differences in acquisition among all groups. However, the rats exposed to escapable stress exhibited poor retention of the platform location in comparison with both yoked-inescapable shock and nonshock controls, which did not differ from one another. We determined this impairment by scoring the subjects' searching behavior without the platform 24 hours later as determined by time spent swimming in the critical quadrant (i.e., where the platform stood on training day) during a 60-second probe trial. The experimenter scoring the latency was blind to group membership. In summary, stress control is associated with impaired memory for events that occurred around the time of the stress on the previous day (Healy & Drugan, 1996). We were interested in determining the nature of this amnestic compound released in the brain as a function of stress control.

Role of Neurosteroids as Mediators of Coping-Induced Memory Interference

☐ Many of the effects of stress controllability take several hours to develop. Stress control-induced protection against GABA-antagonist convulsions is observed after 2 hours but is not apparent immediately poststress (Drugan et al., 1994; Drugan, McIntyre, et al., 1985). There is no difference in stress-induced analgesia or shuttlebox escape performance between escape and yoked subjects immediately postshock. However, a divergence is seen several hours later (Drugan & Maier, 1986; Glazer & Weiss, 1976). A significant increase in levels of a BDZ-like agonist in the brains of coping subjects is detected 2 hours poststress (Drugan et al., 1994).

The time-dependent nature of stress control facilitation of GABAergic tone suggests that the endogenous factor(s) responsible for this effect may be the A-ring reduced metabolites of certain steroids ($3\alpha,5\alpha$-tetrahydrodeoxycorticosterone [THDOC], and $3\alpha,5\alpha$-dihydroprogesterone [OH-DHP]). The pharmacologic actions of these steroid metabolites are reminiscent of behavioral "coping": (a) They have an anxiolytic (Crawley, Glowa, Majewska, & Paul, 1986) as well as an anticonvulsant profile

(Belelli, Bolger, & Gee, 1989; Belelli, Lan, & Gee, 1990; Kokate, Svensson, & Rogawski, 1994); (b) they inhibit the binding of [35S]TBPS at or near the chloride channel (Gee, Chang, Britton, & McEwen, 1987; Majewska, Harrison, Schwartz, Barker, & Paul, 1986); and (c) they disrupt memory (Mayo et al., 1993). The 2-hour delay of the stress controllability effects may represent the optimal time for the accumulation of these metabolites in brain. There are reports of stress-induced release of GABAa receptor-positive modulatory steroids in rat brain (Purdy, Morrow, Moore, & Paul, 1991).

We tested the possibility that these GABAa receptor-positive neurosteroid metabolites are responsible for the stress control-induced amnesia by administering a drug that inhibits the formation of these neuroactive steroids in the brain and peripheral nervous system. N,N-diethyl-4-methyl-3-oxo-4-aza-5 alpha androstane-17 beta-carboxamide (4-MA) is a potent inhibitor of the 5-alpha reductase enzyme responsible for cleaving the parent steroid hormones into the bioactive GABAa receptor modulators, allopregnenolone, and THDOC (Toomey, Goode, Petrow, & Neubauer, 1991). If the escapable shock-induced memory deficit is mediated by an endogenous GABAa receptor-active steroid, we can expect to see a reversal of this deficit with the administration of the steroid synthesis inhibitor, 4-MA.

The results of the experiment were clear. Administration of the steroid synthesis inhibitor blocked the memory deficit seen in the escapable stress subjects and brought them back to control levels (Healy & Drugan, 1996). Conversely, 4-MA produced a learning deficit in the inescapably stressed subjects that was not observed in the vehicle treated group. This suggests that lack of coping causes the release of a negative GABAa receptor neurosteroid that acts like B-carbolines in these subjects to maintain the memory of the event. In summary, the coping-induced alterations in memory and the sustained level of recall in the inescapable stress group appear dependent upon neuroactive steroids. However, whether these compounds originate in the brain or the peripheral nervous system remains unknown. This issue is the focus of current research.

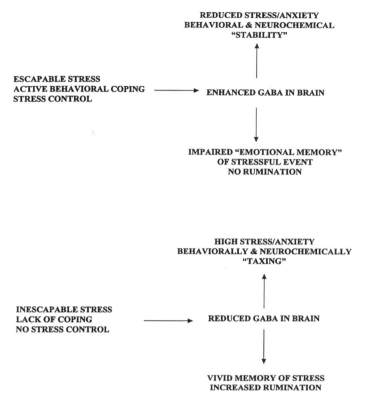

Figure 19.1. Alterations in GABAergic Transmission Following Either Coping or Lack of Coping With Stress, and How They May Affect Anxiety Levels, Neurochemistry, and Memory

The above results inspired a model to illustrate how stress control-induced GABAergic facilitation may have stress-protective effects. The two major contributions deal with alterations in the severity of anxiety during and after the initial stress exposure and with alterations in the subsequent memory of the event. Figure 19.1 shows the possible mechanisms that underlie the protective effects of active behavioral coping versus the pathological effects associated with lack of coping.

As the figure indicates, coping behavior causes the release of a valium-like substance in the brain that facilitates the actions of the major inhibitory neurotransmitter, GABA. Because GABAergic neurons tonically inhibit the actions of a variety of neurotransmitter systems in the brain that are involved in anxiety (e.g., NE, DA, and 5-HT; Iverson, 1983), this would re-

duce the emotional and neurochemical demands on the organism. Similarly, because the release of such an antianxiety compound may interfere with memory of the event, subsequent behavior will not be as influenced by this prior stress experience. Conversely, lack of control over stress or poor coping is known to produce intense anxiety-like behavior (Mineka et al., 1984; Short & Maier, 1993). This places heavy emotional and neurochemical demands on the organism. The interference with or reduction in GABAergic tone may facilitate memory for the stress event and potentiate carryover effects of this stressful experience on subsequent learning and physiology. There is abundant empirical support in the animal literature for the memory-enhancing effects of anxiety-producing compounds (File & Pellow, 1988; Holmes & Drugan, 1991; Venault et al., 1986).

Possible Interrelationships Among Stress, Coping, Memory, and Potential for Drug Use/Abuse/Addiction

☐ The facilitation of GABAergic neurotransmission by the release of this BDZ-like neurosteroid may have additional benefits to the organism above and beyond reduced anxiety and memory of the stressor. These two factors may prevent actively coping subjects from falling prey to drug abuse, unlike their non-coping counterparts. It is well established in the clinical literature that heightened memory for an event is a necessary condition for rumination, and this results in poor prognosis. Rholes (1989) found that ruminating subjects are more at risk for depression than those who use an action-oriented coping strategy. Rumination may compel the subject to self-medicate with drugs of abuse as a way of coping with this recurrent stress. Clinical reports support this notion in that self-administration in both adolescent and adult populations is increased in the face of life-, battle-, and job-related stress (Bruns & Geist, 1984; McAuliffe, Rohman, & Wechsler, 1984; Yager, Laufer, & Gallops, 1984). So the initial step in the progression from recurrent stress via rumination to drug use and potential drug abuse is demonstrated in certain clinical populations that choose palliative coping strategies, such as the use of drugs, to reduce the aversiveness of life stress (Lazarus, 1977).

An additional predisposing factor might be an altered or exaggerated reaction to the drug when it is taken. A number of studies in the animal literature have reported an impact of stress on subsequent reactivity to pharmaceutical compounds. More specifically, exposure to uncontrollable stress but not to controllable stress potentiates the organism's reactivity to several drugs of abuse, including morphine (Grau, Hyson, Maier, Madden, & Barchas, 1981), cocaine and amphetamines (MacLennan & Maier, 1983), alcohol (Drugan, Coyle, Healy, & Chen, 1996; Drugan et al., 1992), benzodiazepines (Drugan et al., 1996), and tetrahydrocanabinol analogues (Drugan, unpublished observations).

In all of the examples listed above, uncontrollable stress prior to drug exposure results in exaggerated reactivity to these pharmaceutical agents in comparison with controllable-shock and nonshock controls. This enhanced behavioral pharmacological reactivity may also hold true for clinical populations by enhancing the reinforcing properties (i.e., greater anxiety relief, greater euphoria, amnesia, or forgetting of one's problems) and thereby hastening the addiction process in individuals who resort to self-medication as a coping response to rumination.

Similar to the human data on self-administration, rats exposed to uncontrollable stress exhibit greater self-administration of opiates (Shaham, 1993; Shaham, Alvares, Nespor, & Grunberg, 1992), cocaine (Goeders & Guerin, 1994; Miczek, Vivian, & Valentine, 1994; Ramsey & van Ree, 1993), amphetamine (Antelman & Eicher, 1979; Piazza, Deminiere, LeMoal, & Simon, 1990), and alcohol (Blanchard, Yudko, & Blanchard, 1993; Mollenauer, Bryson, Robison, & Sardo, 1993). In a select clinical population (certain depressed or PTSD patients with poor or ineffective coping skills), rumination or reliving of the stressful event may be the catalyst to propel these subjects into a setting of drug use and subsequent abuse. Pharmacological "coping"—coupled with the enhanced reactivity to these compounds mentioned above—may hasten the addiction process. Figure 19.2 presents a conceptual model that illustrates the possible interrelationships among stress controllability, brain neurochemical changes in certain systems, and heightened reactivity to certain drugs of abuse that may render poorly coping subjects more vulnerable to drug dependence and addiction. The differential memory of the stress event in coping (poorer memory) versus noncoping (vivid memory and rumination) subjects may be the critical determining factor in the divergence of these two groups, in terms of their prognoses.

The model in Figure 19.2 represents work from animal data showing enhanced reactivity to certain drugs of abuse. This may have implications for clinical populations exposed to uncontrollable stress where there is a lack of cop-

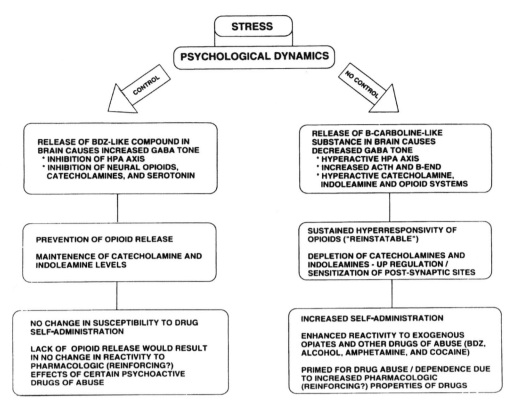

Figure 19.2. Impact of Psychological Dynamics of Stress on GABAergic Transmission in the Brain

NOTE: The opposite effects on GABA either inhibit or enhance the reactivity of other neurotransmitters to stress, which prevents or hastens neurochemical depletion, respectively. These actions may influence self-administration behavior, change organismic reactivity to several classes of drugs of abuse, and thereby modulate vulnerability to drug abuse.

ing or poor coping responses utilized (e.g., depression, PTSD). This model is presented as a heuristic, suggesting that more effective coping strategies for individuals exposed to traumatic stress may "pay double dividends" by (a) changing coping strategies (e.g., problem solving rather than self-medication) and (b) reducing the risk of heightened drug reactivity that may hasten the addiction process.

For the non-coping group, the mechanism responsible for heightened self-administration may involve the release of endogenous opioids during the stress. Uncontrollable stress (but not controllable stress) is associated with the release of endogenous opioids in animals (Drugan, Ader, & Maier, 1985; Grau et al., 1981; Maier et al., 1980). Blockade of the endogenous opioid system by naltrexone reduces ethanol

consumption during chronic drinking in rhesus monkeys (Kornet, Goosen, & van Ree, 1991).

In summary, the alterations of memory in coping versus noncoping subjects may have significant consequences for several interrelated aspects of a patient's life: frequency of rumination, anxiety levels, and vulnerability to drug abuse.

References

Anisman, H., Remington, G., & Sklar, L. S. (1979). Effects of inescapable shock on subsequent escape performance: Catecholaminergic and cholinergic mediation of response initiation and maintenance. *Psychopharmacology, 61,* 107-124.

Anisman, H., & Sklar, L. S. (1979). Catecholamine depletion upon re-exposure to stress: Mediation of the escape deficits produced by inescapable shock. *Journal of Comparative and Physiological Psychology, 93,* 610-625.

Anisman, H., & Zacharko, R. M. (1990). Multiple neurochemical and behavioral consequences of stressors: Implications for depression. *Pharmacological Therapeutics, 46,* 119-136.

Antelman, S. M., & Eicher, A. J. (1979). Persistent effects of stress on dopamine-related behaviors: Clinical implications. In E. Usdin, I. J. Kopin, & J. D. Barchas (Eds.), *Catecholamines: Basic and clinical frontiers* (pp. 1759-1761). New York: Pergamon.

Belelli, D., Bolger, M. B., & Gee, K. W. (1989). Anticonvulsant profile of the progesterone metabolite 5-pregnan-3-ol-20-one. *European Journal of Pharmacology, 166,* 325-329.

Belelli, D., Lan, N. C., & Gee, K. W. (1990). Anticonvulsant steroids and the GABA/benzodiazepine receptor-chloride ionophore complex. *Neuroscience and Biobehavioral Reviews, 14,* 315-322.

Blanchard, R. J., Yudko, E. B., & Blanchard, D. C. (1993). Alcohol, aggression and the stress of subordination. *Journal of Studies on Alcohol* (Suppl. 11), 146-155.

Bruns, C., & Geist, C. S. (1984). Stressful life events and drug use among adolescents. *Journal of Human Stress, 10,* 135-139.

Cabib, S., & Puglisi-Allegra, S. (1994). Opposite responses of mesolimbic system to controllable and uncontrollable aversive experiences. *Journal of Neuroscience, 14,* 3333-3340.

Cannon, W. B. (1928). The mechanism of emotional disturbance of bodily functions. *New England Journal of Medicine, 198,* 877-884.

Crawley, J. N., Glowa, J. R., Majewska, M. D., & Paul, S. M. (1986). Anxiolytic activity of an endogenous adrenal steroid. *Brain Research, 398,* 382-385.

Desiderato, O., & Newman, A. (1971). Conditioned suppression produced in rats by tones paired with escapable and inescapable shock. *Journal of Comparative and Physiological Psychology, 77,* 427-431.

DeSouza, E. B., & van Loon, G. R. (1985). Differential plasma B-endorphin, B-lipotropin and adrenocorticotropin responses to stress in rats. *Endocrinology, 116,* 1577-1586.

Dorow, R., Horowski, R., Paschelke, G., Amin, M., & Braestrup, C. (1983). Severe anxiety induced by FG-7142, a B-carboline ligand for benzodiazepine receptors. *Lancet, 9,* 98-99.

Drugan, R. C., Ader, D. N., & Maier, S. F. (1985). Shock controllability and the nature of stress-induced analgesia. *Behavioral Neuroscience, 99,* 791-801.

Drugan, R. C., Basile, A. S., Ha, J. H., & Ferland, R. J. (1994). The protective effects of stress control may be mediated by increased brain levels of benzodiazepine receptor agonists. *Brain Research, 661,* 127-136.

Drugan, R. C., Coyle, T. S., Healy, D. J., & Chen, S. (1996). Stress controllability influences the ataxic properties of both ethanol and midazolam in the rat. *Behavioral Neuroscience, 110,* 360-367.

Drugan, R. C., Deutsch, S. I., Weizman, A., Weizman, R., Vocci, F. J., Crawley, J. N., Skolnick, P., & Paul, S. M. (1989). Molecular mechanisms of stress and anxiety: Alteration in the benzodiazepine/GABA receptor complex. In H. Weiner, I. Florin, R. Murison, & D. Hellhammer (Eds.), *Frontiers of stress research* (pp. 148-159). Toronto: Hans Huber.

Drugan, R. C., Grau, J. W., Maier, S. F., Madden, J., & Barchas, J. D. (1981). Cross tolerance between morphine and the long-term analgesic reaction to inescapable shock. *Pharmacology, Biochemistry and Behavior, 14,* 677-682.

Drugan, R. C., & Maier, S. F. (1986). Control versus lack of control over aversive stimuli: Nonopioid-opioid analgesic consequences [Monograph]. *Neurobiology of Behavioral Control in Drug Abuse, 74,* 71-89.

Drugan, R. C., McIntyre, T. D., Alpern, H. P., & Maier, S. F. (1985). Coping and seizure susceptibility: Control over shock protects against bicuculline-induced seizures. *Brain Research, 342,* 9-17.

Drugan, R. C., Paul, S. M., & Crawley, J. N. (1993). Decreased forebrain [35S]TBPS binding and increased [3H]muscimol binding in rats that do not develop stress-induced behavioral depression. *Brain Research, 631,* 270-276.

Drugan, R. C., Ryan, S. M., Minor, T. R., & Maier, S. F. (1984). Librium prevents the analgesia and shuttlebox escape deficit typically observed following inescapable shock. *Pharmacology, Biochemistry and Behavior, 21,* 749-754.

Drugan, R. C., Scher, D. M., Sarabanchong, V., Guglielmi, A., Meng, I. D., Chang, J. K., Bloom, K., Sylvia, S., & Holmes, P. V. (1992). Controllability and duration of stress alter central nervous system depressant-induced sleeptime in rats. *Behavioral Neuroscience, 106,* 682-689.

Dunn, A. J. (1988). Changes in plasma and brain tryptophan and serotonin and 5-hydroxyindoleacetic acid after footshock stress. *Life Sciences, 42,* 1847-1853.

Fadda, F., Argiolas, A., Melis, M. R., Tissari, A. H., Onali, P. L., & Gessa, G. L. (1978). Stress-induced increase in 3,4-dihydroxyphenylacetic acid (DOPAC) levels in the cerebral cortex and nucleus accumbens: Reversal by diazepam. *Life Sciences, 23,* 2219-2224.

Fekete, M. I., Szentendrei, T., Kanyicska, B., & Palkovits, M. (1981). Effects of anxiolytic drugs on the catecholamine and DOPAC (3,4-dihydroxyphenacetic acid) levels in brain cortical areas and on corticosterone and prolactin secretion in rats subjected to stress. *Psychoneuroendocrinology, 6,* 113-120.

File, S. E., & Pearce, J. B. (1981). Benzodiazepines reduce gastric ulcers induced in rats by stress. *British Journal of Pharmacology, 74,* 593-599.

File, S. E., & Pellow, S. (1988). Low and high doses of benzodiazepine inverse agonists respectively improve and impair performance in passive avoidance but do not effect habituation. *Behavioral Brain Research, 30,* 31-36.

Foy, M. R., Foy, J. G., Levine, S., & Thompson, R. F. (1990). Manipulation of pituitary-adrenal activity affects neural plasticity in the hippocampus. *Psychological Science, 1,* 201-204.

Foy, M. R., Stanton, M. E., Levine, S., & Thompson, R. F. (1987). Behavioral stress impairs long-term potentiation in rodent hippocampus. *Behavioral and Neural Biology, 48,* 138-149.

Gee, K. W., Bolger, M. B., Brinton, R. E., Coirini, H., & McEwen, B. S. (1988). Steroid modulation of the chloride ionophore in rat brain: Structure-activity requirements, regional dependents and mechanism of action. *Journal of Pharmacology and Experimental Therapeutics, 246,* 803-812.

Gee, K. W., Chang, W. C., Britton, R. E., & McEwen, B. S. (1987). GABA-dependent modulation of the Cl-ionophore by steroids in rat brain. *European Journal of Pharmacology, 136,* 419-423.

Glazer, H. I., & Weiss, J. M. (1976). Long-term and transitory interference effects. *Journal of Experimental Psychology: Animal Behavior Processes, 2,* 505-517.

Goeders, N. E., & Guerin, G. F. (1994). Non-contingent electric footshock facilitates the acquisition of intravenous cocaine self-administration in rats. *Psychopharmacology, 114,* 63-70.

Grau, J. W., Hyson, R. L., Maier, S. F., Madden, J., & Barchas, J. D. (1981). Long-term stress-induced analgesia and activation of the opiate system. *Science, 213,* 1409-1411.

Guillemin, R., Vargo, T., Rossier, J., Minick, S., Ling, N., Rivier, C., Vale, W., & Bloom, F. E. (1977). B-endorphin and adrenocorticotropin are secreted concomitantly by the pituitary gland. *Science, 197,* 1367-1369.

Healy, D. J., & Drugan, R. C. (1996). Escapable stress modulates retention of spatial learning in rats: Preliminary evidence for involvement of neurosteroids. *Psychobiology, 24,* 110-117.

Holmes, P. V., & Drugan, R. C. (1991). Differential effects of anxiogenic central and peripheral benzodiazepine receptor ligands on learning and memory. *Psychopharmacology, 104,* 249-254.

Iverson, S. D. (1983). Where in the brain do the benzodiazepines act? In M. R. Trimble (Ed.), *Benzodiazepines divided* (pp. 167-186). New York: John Wiley.

Izquierdo, I., & Medina, J. (1991). GABAa receptor modulation of memory: The role of endogenous benzodiazepines. *Trends in Pharmacological Science, 12,* 260-265.

Jackson, R. L., Maier, S. F., & Coon, D. J. (1979). Long-term analgesic effects of inescapable shock and learned helplessness. *Science, 206,* 91-94.

Katz, R. J., & Liebler, L. (1978). GABA involvement in memory consolidation: evidence from post-trial amino-oxyacetic acid. *Psychopharmacology, 56,* 191-193.

Kokate, T. G., Svensson, B. E., & Rogawski, M. A. (1994). Anticonvulsant activity of neurosteroids: Correlation with gamma aminobutyric acid-evoked chloride current potentiation. *Journal of Pharmacology and Experimental Therapeutics, 270,* 1223-1229.

Kornet, M., Goosen, C., & van Ree, J. M. (1991). Effect of naltrexone on alcohol consumption during chronic alcohol drinking and after a period of imposed abstinence in free-choice drinking rhesus monkeys. *Psychopharmacology, 104,* 367-376.

Kusnecov, A. W., & Rabin, B. S. (1993). Inescapable footshock exposure differentially alters antigen- and mitogen-stimulated spleen cell proliferation in rats. *Journal of Neuroimmunology, 44,* 33-42.

Kvetnansky, R., & Mikulaj, L. (1970). Adrenal and urinary catecholamines in rats during adaptation to repeated immobilization stress. *Endocrinology, 87,* 738-743.

Laudenslager, M. L., Ryan, S. M., Drugan, R. C., Hyson, R. L., & Maier, S. F. (1983). Coping and immunosuppression: Inescapable but not escapable shock suppresses lymphocyte proliferation. *Science, 221,* 568-571.

Lazarus, R. S. (1977). Psychological stress and coping in adaptation and illness. In Z. J. Lipowski, D. R. Lipsitt, & P. C. Whybrow (Eds.), *Psychosomatic medicine: Current trends in clinical applications* (pp. 14-26). New York: Oxford University Press.

LeFur, G., Guillox, F., Mitrani, N., Mizoule, J., & Uzan, A. (1979). Relationships between plasma corticosterone and benzodiazepines in stress. *Journal of Pharmacology and Experimental Therapeutics, 211,* 305-308.

Lewis, J. W., Cannon, J. T., & Liebeskind, J. C. (1980). Opioid and nonopioid mechanisms of stress analgesia. *Science, 208,* 623-625.

Lister, R. G. (1985). The amnestic action of benzodiazepines in man. *Neuroscience and Biobehavioral Reviews, 9,* 87-94.

Lucki, I., Rickels, K., Giesecke, A., & Geller, A. (1987). Differential effects of anxiolytic drugs, diazepam and buspirone, on memory function. *British Journal of Clinical Pharmacology, 23,* 207-211.

MacLennan, A. J., & Maier, S. F. (1983). Coping and the stress-induced potentiation of stimulant stereotypy in the rat. *Science, 219,* 1091-1093.

Madden, J., Akil, H., Patrick, R. L., & Barchas, J. D. (1977). Stress-induced parallel changes in central opioid levels and pain responsiveness in the rat. *Nature, 265,* 358-360.

Maier, S. F. (1990). Diazepam modulation of stress-induced analgesia depends on the type of analgesia. *Behavioral Neuroscience, 104,* 339-347.

Maier, S. F., Davies, S., Grau, J. W., Jackson, R. L., Morrison, D. H., Moye, T. B., Madden, J., & Barchas, J. D. (1980). Opiate antagonists and the long-term analgesic reaction induced by inescapable shock. *Journal of Comparative and Physiological Psychology, 94,* 1172-1183.

Maier, S. F., & Seligman, M. E. P. (1976). Learned helplessness: Theory and evidence. *Journal of Experimental Psychology: General, 105,* 3-46.

Majewska, M. D., Harrison, N. L., Schwartz, R. D., Barker, J. L., & Paul, S. M. (1986). Steroid hormone metabolites are barbiturate-like modulators of the GABAa receptor. *Science, 232,* 1004-1007.

Mayo, W., Dellu, F., Robel, P., Cherkaoui, J., LeMoal, M., Balieu, E. E., & Simon, H. (1993). Infusions of pregnenolone sulfate into the nucleus basalis magnocellularis affects cognitive processes in the rat. *Brain Research, 607,* 324-328.

McAuliffe, W. E., Rohman, M., & Wechsler, H. (1984). Alcohol, substance abuse and other risk factors of impairment in a sample of physicians-in-training. *Advances in Substance Abuse, 4,* 67-87.

McEwen, B. S. (1991). Non-genomic and genomic effects of steroids on neural activity. *Trends in Pharmacological Sciences, 12,* 141-147.

McNamara, R. K., & Skelton, R. W. (1992). Assessment of cholinergic contribution to chlordiazepoxide-induced deficits of place learning in the Morris water maze. *Pharmacology, Biochemistry and Behavior, 41,* 529-538.

McNaughton, N., & Morris, R. G. M. (1987). Chlordiazepoxide, an anxiolytic benzodiazepine, impairs place navigation in rats. *Behavioral Brain Research, 24,* 39-46.

Miczek, K. A., Vivian, J. A., & Valentine, J. O. (1994). Social stress: Cocaine reinforcing and stimulus effects. *Society for Neuroscience Abstracts, 20,* 593.

Mineka, S., Cook, M., & Miller, S. (1984). Fear conditioned with escapable and inescapable shock: The effects of a feedback stimulus. *Journal of Experimental Psychology: Animal Behavior Processes, 10,* 307-323.

Mollenauer, S., Bryson, R., Robison, M., & Sardo, J. (1993). ETOH self-administration in anticipation of noise stress in C57BL/6J mice. *Pharmacology, Biochemistry and Behavior, 46,* 35-38.

Morris, R. G. M. (1981). Spatial localization does not require the presence of local cues. *Learning and Motivation, 12,* 239-260.

Olsen, R. W. (1982). Drug interactions at the GABA receptor ionophore complex. *Annual Review of Pharmacology and Toxicology, 22,* 245-277.

Paul, S. M., Marangos, P. J., & Skolnick, P. (1981). The benzodiazepine/GABA receptor chloride ionophore receptor complex: Site of minor tranquilizer action. *Biological Psychiatry, 16,* 213-229.

Petty, F., Kramer, G., & Wilson, L. (1992). Prevention of learned helplessness: In vivo correlation with cortical serotonin. *Pharmacology, Biochemistry and Behavior, 43,* 361-367.

Petty, F., & Sherman, A. D. (1981). GABAergic modulation of learned helplessness. *Pharmacology, Biochemistry and Behavior, 15,* 453-457.

Piazza, P. V., Deminiere, J. M., LeMoal, M., & Simon, H. (1990). Stress and pharmacologically-induced behavioral sensitization increases vulnerability to acquisition of amphetamine self-administration. *Brain Research, 514*(Suppl.), 22-26.

Purdy, R. H., Morrow, A. L., Moore, P. H., & Paul, S. M. (1991). Stress-induced elevations of gamma-aminobutyric acid type A receptor active steroids in the rat brain. *Proceedings of the National Academy of Sciences, 88,* 4553-4557.

Ramsey, N. F., & van Ree, J. M. (1993). Emotional but not physical stress enhances intravenous cocaine self-administration in drug naive rats. *Brain Research, 608,* 216-222.

Redmond, D. E., & Huang, Y. H. (1979). New evidence for a locus coeruleus-norepinephrine connection with anxiety. *Life Sciences, 25,* 2149-2162.

Rholes, W. S. (1989). Action control as a vulnerability factor in depressed mood. *Cognitive Therapy and Research, 13,* 263-274.

Schweri, M., Cain, M., Cook, J., Paul, S. M., & Skolnick, P. (1982). Blockade of 3-carbomethoxy-B-carboline induced seizures by diazepam and the benzodiazepine antagonists Ro15-1788 and CGS 8216. *Pharmacology, Biochemistry and Behavior, 17,* 457-460.

Seiber, W. J., Rodin, J., Larson, L., Ortega, S., Cummings, N., Levy, S., Whiteside, T., & Herberman, R. (1992). Modulation of human natural killer cell activity by exposure to uncontrollable stress. *Brain, Behavior and Immunity, 6,* 141-156.

Seligman, M. E. P., & Maier, S. F. (1967). Failure to escape traumatic shock. *Journal of Experimental Psychology, 74,* 1-9.

Selye, H. (1936). A syndrome produced by diverse nocuous agents. *Nature, 138,* 32-34.

Shaham, Y. (1993). Immobilization stress-induced oral opioid self-administration and withdrawal in rats: Role of conditioning factors and the effect of stress on "relapse" to opioid drugs. *Psychopharmacology, 111,* 477-485.

Shaham, Y., Alvares, K., Nespor, S. M., & Grunberg, N. E. (1992). Effect of stress on oral morphine and fentanyl self-administration in rats. *Pharmacology, Biochemistry and Behavior, 41,* 615-619.

Sherman, A. D., Allers, G. L., Petty, F., & Henn, F. A. (1979). A neuropharmacologically-relevant animal model of depression. *Neuropharmacology, 18,* 891-893.

Sherman, A. D., & Petty, F. (1982). Additivity of neurochemical changes in learned helplessness and imipramine. *Behavioral and Neural Biology, 35,* 344-353.

Short, K. R., & Maier, S. F. (1993). Stress controllability, social interaction and benzodiazepine systems. *Pharmacology, Biochemistry and Behavior, 45,* 827-835.

Stone, E. A., & McCarty, R. (1983). Adaptation to stress: Tyrosine hydroxylase activity and catecholamine release. *Neuroscience and Biobehavioral Reviews, 7,* 29-34.

Theibot, M. (1985). Some evidence for amnestic-like effects of benzodiazepines in animals. *Neuroscience and Biobehavioral Reviews, 9,* 95-100.

Ticku, M. K., & Ramanjaneyulu, R. (1984). Differential interactions of GABA agonists, depressant and convulsant drugs with [35S]t-butylbicyclophosphorothionate binding sites in cortex and cerebellum. *Pharmacology, Biochemistry and Behavior, 21,* 151-158.

Toomey, R. E., Goode, R. L., Petrow, V., & Neubauer, B. L. (1991). In vivo assay for conversion of testosterone to dihydrotestosterone by rat prostatic steroid 5-alpha reductase and comparison of 2 inhibitors. *Prostate, 19,* 63-72.

Tye, N. C., Everett, B. J., & Iverson, S. D. (1977). 5-hydroxytryptamine and punsihment. *Nature, 268,* 741-743.

Venault, P., Chapouthier, G., Prado De Carvalho, L., Simiand, J., Morre, M., Dodd, R. H., & Rossier, J. (1986). Benzodiazepine impairs and b-carboline enhances performance in learning and memory tasks. *Nature, 321,* 864-866.

Warren, D. A., Castro, C. A., Rudy, J. W., & Maier, S. F. (1991). No spatial learning impairment following exposure to inescapable shock. *Psychobiology, 19,* 127-134.

Weiss, J. M. (1971). Effects of punishing the coping response (conflict) on stress pathology in rats. *Journal of Comparative and Physiological Psychology, 77,* 14-21.

Weiss, J. M., Goodman, P. A., Losito, B. G., Corrigan, S., Charry, J. M., & Bailey, W. H. (1981). Behavioral depression produced by an uncontrollable stressor: Relationship to norepinephrine, dopamine and serotonin levels in various regions of rat brain. *Brain Research Reviews, 3,* 167-205.

Weiss, J. M., Stone, E. A., & Harrell, N. (1970). Coping behavior and brain norepinephrine levels in rats. *Journal of Comparative and Physiological Psychology, 72,* 153-160.

Weiss, J. M., Sundar, S. K., & Becker, K. J. (1989). Stress-induced immunosuppression and immunoenhancement: Cellular immune changes and mechanisms. In E. J. Goetz & N. H. Spector (Eds.), *Neuroimmune networks: Physiology and diseases* (pp. 193-206). New York: Alan R. Liss.

Yager, T., Laufer, R., & Gallops, M. (1984). Some problems associated with war experience in men of the Vietnam generation. *Archives of General Psychiatry, 41,* 327-333.

Young, E. A., & Akil, H. (1985). Corticotropin-releasing factor stimulation of adrenocorticotropin and B-endorphin release: Effects of acute and chronic stress. *Endocrinology, 117,* 23-30.

20

Can Cognitive Neuroscience Illuminate the Nature of Traumatic Childhood Memories?

Daniel L. Schacter
Wilma Koutstaal
Kenneth A. Norman

Cognitive neuroscience studies of memory have many important implications for everyday life. Such implications are nowhere more evident than in the recent explosion of cases in which adult women and men, usually in the context of psychotherapy, claim to have recovered long-forgotten memories of childhood abuse suffered at the hands of parents, friends, or other adults. The memories range from single incidents of inappropriate fondling to years of rape and even ritualistic abuse. People who recover such memories are often certain that they reflect actual past events. This conviction is shared by some psychotherapists, who have argued that memories of sexual abuse can

be repressed and later recovered (e.g., Fredrickson, 1992; Terr, 1994; Whitfield, 1995). Yet those who are accused of perpetrating the abuse frequently deny that the incidents ever occurred. A variety of psychologists, psychiatrists, and others have argued that recovered memories are frequently illusory and are attributable to suggestive practices used in psychotherapy (see Lindsay & Read, 1994; Loftus, 1993; Loftus & Ketcham, 1994; Ofshe & Watters, 1994; Pendergrast, 1995).

The recovered memories debate raises issues that are relevant to cognitive neuroscience. How accurate is memory and under what conditions is it subject to distortion? Can traumatic events

AUTHORS' NOTE: We thank Eric Kandel and Larry Squire for helpful comments on an earlier draft of this chapter. Preparation of this chapter was supported by National Institute of Neurological Disorders and Stroke Grant PO1 NS27950 and National Institute on Aging Grant AG08441-06. This chapter appeared originally, in slightly different form, in *Current Opinion in Neurobiology,* vol. 6, pp. 207-214. Copyright 1996 by Current Biology Ltd. Reprinted by permission of Rapid Science Publishers.

be forgotten, and if so, can they be later recovered? We first consider evidence that pertains to claims of recovered memories of trauma. We then consider the relevant memory phenomena in the context of concepts and findings from the contemporary cognitive neuroscience of memory.

The Recovered Memories Debate: What Do We Know?

☐ The controversy over recovered memories is a complex affair that involves several intertwined psychological and social issues (for elaboration of this point, see Baars & McGovern, 1995; Pendergrast, 1995; Schacter, 1995a, 1995b, 1996; Schooler, 1994). Here, we consider four critical questions. First, can memories of abuse be forgotten? Second, does the evidence warrant the postulation of a special mechanism of repression? Third, can memories of childhood trauma, if forgotten, later be remembered accurately? And, finally, is there evidence that false memories of abuse can occur?

Can Memories of Abuse Be Forgotten?

In several studies, patients who reported that they were sexually abused as children also said there were periods of time in the past when they had forgotten about the abuse (Briere & Conte, 1993; Elliott & Briere, 1995; Herman & Schatzow, 1987; Loftus, Polonsky, & Fullilove, 1994). However, these studies provide only weak evidence that abuse can be forgotten, because, first, none of them contained corroborating evidence that the reported abuse had actually occurred, and second, all of them relied on retrospective estimates of forgetting, which are of questionable validity (for discussion, see Kihlstrom, 1995; Loftus, 1993; Pendergrast, 1995; Pope & Hudson, 1995). Stronger evidence for forgetting has been provided by Williams (1994), who found that 38% of women who had been brought to a hospital emergency room as children for treatment of abuse failed to report the incident when interviewed two decades later. Most remembered other episodes

of abuse, but 12% reported no memory of any abuse. Likewise, several individual cases have been reported in which incidents of corroborated abuse were temporarily forgotten (e.g., Nash, 1994; Schooler, 1994). Thus, although the evidence indicates that most adults who were abused during childhood always remember their abuse, it also shows that some abusive episodes can be forgotten.

Does the Evidence Warrant Postulation of a Special Mechanism of Repression?

Although it is apparent that forgetting of abusive events can occur, ordinary mechanisms of forgetting, such as decay, interference, or infantile and childhood amnesia, are probably sufficient to explain inaccessibility of some traumatic incidents (Hembrooke & Ceci, 1995; Loftus, Garry, & Feldman, 1994). For example, when people fail to remember single incidents of sexual abuse that occurred when they were children (e.g., Nash, 1994; Williams, 1994), forgetting may be caused by the same ordinary mechanisms that are responsible for forgetting of nontraumatic experiences.

In contrast, when people claim to have forgotten about extended periods of repeated and horrific abuse, something more than ordinary forgetting is probably involved. Although there is little firm evidence for such extraordinary forgetting, some researchers have invoked the concept of repression to account for it (e.g., Fredrickson, 1992; Whitfield, 1995). The notion of repression has a long and controversial history, dating to Freud's early contributions (see Singer, 1990), and the strength of the evidence for it depends on how the concept is defined.

On the one hand, repression may be defined as a process of conscious avoidance, in which a person fails to think about, talk about, or otherwise rehearse an unpleasant experience. Cognitive research has shown that such motivated or "directed" forgetting can lead to a reduced likelihood of recalling an event (for a review, see Johnson, 1994). On the other hand, repression may be defined as an automatic defensive process that functions to exclude threatening material from awareness. However, little or no experimental evidence for this latter kind of repression exists (Holmes, 1990; Pope & Hudson, 1995). With respect to the recovered memories debate, the consciously motivated form of repression that results in failure to rehearse or think about traumatic events could account for gradual forgetting of an abusive episode or episodes over time (see, for example, Williams, 1995). However, this form of repression does not seem powerful enough to produce severe amnesia for repeated, horrific events soon after they occur.

Can Memories of Childhood Trauma, If Forgotten, Later Be Remembered Accurately?

The fact that some episodes of abuse can be forgotten need not mean that they can be recalled again years later. However, several cases have been reported in which people who have recovered previously forgotten memories of abuse have obtained corroboration that the abuse occurred (e.g., Nash, 1994; Schooler, 1994; Williams, 1995; for discussion of corroborated cases, see Pendergrast, 1995; Schacter, 1996). Recovery of such memories may simply reflect the well-established fact that appropriate retrieval cues can produce recall of aspects of seemingly forgotten experiences (e.g., Feldman-Summers & Pope, 1994; Koutstaal & Schacter, 1997).

Is There Evidence That False Memories of Abuse Can Occur?

There is no direct experimental evidence that illusory memories of sexual abuse can be created, and such a demonstration is precluded for ethical reasons. Nevertheless, several lines of evidence support the conclusion that illusory memories of abuse do indeed occur. First, some techniques used by therapists to recover forgotten memories, such as hypnosis (see Poole, Lindsay, Memon, & Bull, 1995), are known to produce subjectively compelling pseudomemories in suggestible subjects

(Kihlstrom, 1997; Lynn & Nash, 1994), including memories for having been abused in a "past life" (Spanos, Menary, Gabora, DuBreuil, & Dewhirst, 1991). Second, some people claim to have recovered memories of previously forgotten ritualistic abuse in satanic cults, yet no evidence for any such abuse has ever been uncovered, despite extensive investigations by law enforcement agencies (Nathan & Snedeker, 1995; Ofshe & Watters, 1994; Wright, 1994). Finally, a growing number of people have disavowed or "retracted" their recovered memories, and recent evidence indicates that many of these individuals were treated by therapists who used suggestive techniques to recover memories (Nelson & Simpson, 1994).

Our brief overview of recovered memories reveals, therefore, that some may be accurate and others illusory. We now examine insights and evidence from cognitive neuroscience that are relevant to both sides of the issue.

Illusory Memories: Cognitive and Neurobiological Perspectives

☐ Memory usually preserves a reasonably accurate representation of the past. Nonetheless, most researchers acknowledge that memory does not preserve an exact or "photographic" representation of all aspects of past experiences. Instead, memory is a fundamentally constructive process. Cognitive psychologists have argued that memories of past experiences are constructed from several sources: stored fragments of an event; preexisting knowledge, beliefs, and expectations that the remerember brings to an experience; and properties of the environment in which the experience is retrieved (see Bartlett, 1932; Jacoby, Kelley, & Dywan, 1989; Johnson, Hastroudi, & Lindsay, 1993; Neisser, 1967; Schacter, 1989, 1996; Tulving, 1983). Likewise, neuroscientists have argued that memories are constructed on the basis of stored fragments of experiences that are distributed throughout a variety of cortical regions and are bound together by systems that work cooperatively with cortical storage areas during encoding and retrieval (see Damasio,

1989; McClelland, McNaughton, & O'Reilly, 1995; Squire, 1987, 1992). From both the cognitive and neurobiological perspectives, memory distortions are a natural by-product of the fundamentally constructive nature of the memory process (Schacter, 1996).

Recent research has begun to illuminate the cognitive and neurobiological factors that contribute to illusory memories. One important phenomenon is known as source memory or source monitoring—remembering when, where, and how a memory was acquired (Johnson et al., 1993). Numerous studies with college students have shown that recollections of external events and internal imaginings can be confused, thereby producing distorted memories (e.g., Suengas & Johnson, 1988). Failures of source memory also play a key role in memory distortions that occur when people are exposed to misleading postevent suggestions, as observed initially in studies by Loftus and colleagues (e.g., Loftus, Miller, & Burns, 1978). When people witness a particular event (e.g., a car stopped at a stop sign) and are later given misleading information about it (e.g., the car stopped at a yield sign), they often fail to remember whether the critical information was part of the original event or was only suggested to them later (e.g., Belli, Lindsay, Gales, & McCarthy, 1994; Lindsay, 1990; Zaragoza & Lane, 1994).

Source memory has also been implicated in recent studies showing that some young adults can be induced to create false memories of childhood experiences in response to repeated questioning (Hyman, Husband, & Billings, 1995; Loftus & Pickrell, 1995). For instance, Hyman et al. (1995) asked college students about unusual events from their pasts that, according to their parents, had never occurred (e.g., an overnight stay at a hospital for an ear infection at age 5, or a birthday party with pizza and a clown). In two separate experiments, no students initially remembered any such event. However, after being repeatedly questioned about the event, 4 of 20 subjects (20%) in Experiment 1, and 13 of 51 subjects (26%) in Experiment 2 developed elaborate illusory memories. Hyman et al. suggest that with repeated questioning, subjects may recall isolated fragments of actual childhood events and then misattribute them to the fabricated target event.

Source memory also plays a role in another recently described form of memory distortion. Roediger and McDermott (1995), using a procedure originally introduced by Deese (1959), showed that people who study a list of words in which each is associated to a nonpresented theme word subsequently often incorrectly "remember" having encountered the nonpresented theme word (e.g., subjects who study *drowsy, bed, tired, pillow, rest, pajamas,* and other related words later claim with high confidence to remember having been exposed to the theme word *sleep,* even though it was not presented). Schacter, Verfaellie, and Pradere (1996) showed that amnesic patients are less susceptible than normal subjects to this memory distortion, and argued that the illusion is based on recollection of the semantic gist of the studied lists, together with inadequate monitoring of the source of the memory.

Source memory appears to depend critically on the functioning of frontal lobe systems that are involved in strategic retrieval and monitoring of past experiences (Janowsky, Shimamura, & Squire, 1989; Schacter, Harbluk, & McLachlan, 1984; Schacter, Kagan, & Leichtman, 1995; Shimamura & Squire, 1987; Squire, 1995). Indeed, patients with frontal lobe damage exhibit a variety of memory illusions and distortions (DeLuca & Cicerone, 1991; Johnson, 1991; Moscovitch, 1995; Schacter & Curran, 1995; Schacter, Curran, Galluccio, Milberg, & Bates, 1996).

It is not yet known whether source memory failures play a role in illusory memories of abuse. However, some false memories may be created when elements of actual experiences are recalled and their source is forgotten, with the result that something that was said, suggested, or imagined is mistaken as an actual event from one's past. Recent neuroimaging research indicates that some of the same posterior brain regions involved in perceiving are also involved in imagining (Kosslyn et al., 1993; Kosslyn, Thompson, Kim, & Alpert, 1995), which may be one reason why experiences that are only imagined can nonetheless be experienced as real.

Forgetting and Recovery of Memories of Abuse: What Can Cognitive Neuroscience Offer?

☐ In this section, we consider several lines of evidence that are potentially relevant to forgetting and recovery of traumatic experience. As stated earlier, however, it remains unclear whether explanations above and beyond ordinary forgetting and conscious avoidance are required to account for documented cases of forgetting and recovery (e.g., Nash, 1994; Schooler, 1994; Williams, 1995).

Brain Systems in Victims of Sexual Abuse

A recent study of abused women (M. B. Stein et al., personal communication) revealed abnormalities in the hippocampal region, which is known to be critically important for explicit or declarative memory (Cohen, & Eichenbaum, 1993; Moscovitch, 1994; Schacter, Alpert, Savage, Rauch, & Albert, 1996; Schacter, Reiman, et al., 1995; Squire et al., 1992). Stein et al. (personal communication) used structural magnetic resonance imaging (MRI) to examine the brains of 22 women with histories of prolonged and severe sexual abuse. They found a significant reduction (5%) of left hippocampal volume in abused women compared with nonabused women. Although alternative interpretations of the observed hippocampal volume reductions are possible (see Bremner et al., 1995), decreased hippocampal volume might be related to toxic effects of glucocorticoids that are released in response to prolonged stress (DeBellis et al., 1994; Sapolsky, 1992; Sapolsky, Uno, Rebert, & Finch, 1990) and can produce memory deficits (Keenan, Jacobson, Soleymani, & Newcomer, 1995; Newcomer, Craft, Hershey, Askins, & Bardgett, 1994; Wolkowitz et al., 1990). However, none of the women in Stein et al.'s study were amnesic for their abuse, and, as a group, they showed normal performance on laboratory tests of explicit memory for recently studied information.

Studies of women with reported histories of sexual abuse have revealed some deficits in recalling autobiographical incidents (Kuyken & Brewin, 1995; Parks & Balon, 1995). However,

these deficits—involving the failure to retrieve specific episodic childhood memories in response to single word cues or the tendency to retrieve "overgeneral" memories that do not refer to a single episode—may not be specifically linked to hippocampal function, and may reflect a combination of deficient encoding and retrieval strategies (Williams, 1992). Moreover, even if hippocampal volume reductions in abuse survivors do produce memory deficits, they would not readily explain recovery of forgotten traumas. Thus, there is currently no evidence that hippocampal volume reductions in survivors of sexual abuse are related to forgetting of traumatic experiences.

Retrograde Amnesia: A Model for Forgotten Trauma?

Retrograde amnesia refers to impaired memory for experiences that occurred before brain injury or psychological trauma. In psychogenic or functional retrograde amnesias, people can temporarily forget large portions of their pasts and/or identities after various kinds of disturbing events (for reviews, see Kihlstrom & Schacter, 1995; Schacter, 1996; Schacter & Kihlstrom, 1989). Appropriate cuing and other factors often lead to recovery of memory in such cases, but it is unknown how such amnesias are related to forgetting of sexual abuse.

Patients with amnesic syndromes that result from damage to the hippocampus and related medial temporal lobe/diencephalic structures show a form of temporally graded retrograde loss, such that relatively recent memories are most affected and more remote experiences, particularly childhood memories, are less affected or entirely unaffected (Squire, 1992). This well-known pattern, commonly referred to as Ribot's Law, is usually permanent and typically accompanied by significant anterograde amnesia for ongoing events; it therefore differs from the kind of amnesia purported to be operative in cases of recovered memories, which primarily involves childhood events. Other patients with damage extending into cortical association areas, the likely sites of long-term memory storage, show more extensive retrograde amnesias, sometimes covering virtually the entire personal past (see, e.g., Kapur, 1993; Lucchelli, Muggia, & Spinnler, 1995; O'Connor, Butters, Miliotis, Eslinger, & Cermak, 1992; Tulving, Schacter, McLachlan, & Moscovitch, 1988). Amnesia is usually permanent, although sudden recovery has been reported (Lucchelli et al., 1995). Although the mechanisms of such recovery remain poorly understood, such extensive retrograde amnesias do not appear to provide a promising model for the kind of forgetting at issue in the recovered memories controversy.

Stress, Encoding, and Repression

In retrograde amnesia, experiences that were normally encoded and stored become inaccessible as a result of subsequent events. However, traumatic experiences may not be encoded and stored normally in the first place. Indeed, it has been suggested that traumatic experiences may be encoded differently from nontraumatic ones (Krystal, Bennett, Bremner, Southwick, & Charney, 1995; Spiegel, 1995).

The most common outcome of emotionally traumatic experiences is intrusive and repetitive recollection of the traumatic event (for recent reviews, see Schacter, 1996; Spiegel, 1995). Laboratory studies of both rats and people suggest that enhanced memory for traumatic events is mediated by stress-related hormones such as epinephrine (Cahill, Prins, Weber, & McGaugh, 1994); other substances released by the brain in stressful situations, such as opioid peptides, have inhibitory effects on memory retention (for a review, see McGaugh, 1995). Many of these influences on memory act via the "final common pathway" of increasing or decreasing the release of the adrenergic neuromodulator norepinephrine in the amygdala. For example, epinephrine boosts release of norepinephrine, and opiates inhibit norepinephrine release (McGaugh et al., 1993).

In order for the effects of stress-related hormones to be relevant to the recovery of traumatic memories, these hormones must result in a trace that is available in memory, but rendered temporarily inaccessible by traumatic stress (as opposed to a very weak and permanently unavailable trace). This would be the case if neurochemicals that are released in response to extreme stress made memories state dependent. Kandel and Kandel (1994) have speculated that the release of opioid peptides during a stressful experience might lead to a temporary inability to remember the trauma; later, another arousing experience could trigger the release of neurochemicals that (if accompanied by other appropriate retrieval cues) activate the formerly inaccessible memory. Evidence pertaining to state-dependent explanations of opiate effects on memory is equivocal (see Castellano & McGaugh, 1989; Izquierdo, 1984).

Another approach to explaining how memories for trauma might come to be "available but inaccessible" focuses on the link between trauma and dissociation. Many clinicians and researchers have argued that traumatic experiences can produce a dissociative state in some individuals; in this state, mechanisms that normally lead to integrated perceptual experience and memory traces are disrupted, resulting in fragmentary engrams that are difficult to retrieve (Krystal, Bennett, et al., 1995; Krystal, Southwick, & Charney, 1995; Terr, 1994; van der Kolk, 1994; van der Kolk & Fisler, 1995). Experimental analogues of dissociative states have been produced in human subjects using the N-methyl-D-aspartate receptor antagonist ketamine, which disrupts glutamatergic transmission and produces impairments in thinking, problem solving, and memory that resemble deficits observed after frontal lobe lesions (Ghoneim, Hinrichs, Mewaldt, & Petersen, 1985; Krystal, Karper, Bennett, et al., 1994; Krystal, Karper, Seibyl, et al., 1994). The frontal lobes play an important integrative role in memory, both by promoting elaborative encodings in which new experiences become integrated with preexisting knowledge (Demb et al., 1995; Kapur et al., 1994) and by allowing effortful, strategic search of memory (Kapur et al., 1995; Moscovitch, 1994, 1995; Schacter, Alpert, et al., 1996). However, it is not known whether the effects of ketamine mimic the effects of stress during a traumatic experience, nor is there any evidence that disrupted frontal lobe functioning could produce dense amnesia for repeated traumatic experiences, as has been reported in some alleged cases of recovered memories.

Finally, we note recent observations by Ramachandran (1995) that may bear on the issue of defensive repression. A patient who sustained a right parietal stroke and had lost the use of her left arm denied that it was paralyzed (the phenomenon of anosognosia; for reviews, see McGlynn & Schacter, 1991; Prigatano & Schacter, 1991). Both immediately and 30 minutes after irrigation of her left ear with cold water, the patient acknowledged that her left arm was paralyzed and had been for several days (similar effects have been reported in other patients, although the mechanism is poorly understood; see Bisiach, Rusconi, & Vallar, 1992; Cappa, Sterzi, Vallar, & Bisiach, 1987). Eight hours later, when the effects of the cold water irrigation had worn off, she once again denied her paralysis. Asked about what the two doctors had done to her that morning, she remembered correctly that her ear had been irrigated. But the patient had apparently forgotten her earlier admission of paralysis, and she incorrectly recalled that she had stated earlier that her arm was fine. Ramachandran suggests that the patient had selectively "repressed" the part of her memory that was inconsistent with her present beliefs. Although this is an intriguing idea, more data concerning what the patient did and did not remember from the irrigation episode are needed before it can be interpreted confidently. Although observations from brain-damaged patients cannot speak directly to the question of whether non-brain-damaged people are capable of a kind of repression that would create amnesia for overwhelming traumas, they can provide clues concerning possibly relevant processes and mechanisms.

Concluding Comments

□ The possible links we have considered between cognitive neuroscience research and recovered memories of childhood sexual abuse are no more than suggestive. One major limitation is that so few systematic studies have ex-amined illusory memories of abuse or accurate recovered memories. Before we can confidently apply evidence and ideas from basic cognitive neuroscience, the phenomena that we are attempting to explain must be characterized more fully. Unless, and until, more reliable information becomes available, we urge researchers to be cautious when extrapolating from cognitive neuroscience to the complex and important issues at stake in debates about recovered memories.

References and Recommended Reading

Note: Entries marked with asterisks are works of particular interest published within the annual period of review: *of special interest; **of outstanding interest.

Baars, B. J., & McGovern, K. (1995). Steps toward healing: False memories and traumagenic amnesia may co-exist in vulnerable populations. *Consciousness and Cognition, 4,* 68-74.

Bartlett, F. C. (1932). *Remembering: A study in experimental and social psychology.* Cambridge, UK: Cambridge University Press.

Belli, R. F., Lindsay, D. S., Gales, M. S., & McCarthy, T. S. L. (1994). Memory impairment and source misattribution in postevent misinformation experiments with short retention intervals. *Memory and Cognition, 22,* 40-54.

Bisiach, E., Rusconi, M. L., & Vallar, G. (1992). Remission of somatophrenic delusion through vestibular stimulation. *Neuropsychologia, 29,* 1029-1031.

*Bremner, J. D., Randall, P. R., Scott, T. M., Bronen, R. A., Seibyl, J. P., Southwick, S. M., Delaney, R. C., McCarthy, G., Charney, D. S., & Innis, R. B. (1995). MRI-based measurement of hippocampal volume in patients with combat-related posttraumatic stress disorder. *American Journal of Psychiatry, 152,* 973-981.

Used magnetic resonance imaging to measure the hippocampal volume of 26 Vietnam combat veterans with combat-related posttraumatic stress disorder (PTSD) and 22 comparison subjects without combat exposure. Veterans with PTSD had significantly reduced right hippocampal volume (reduction of 8%) and a nonsignificant reduction in left hippocampal volume (reduction of 3.8%). Veterans with PTSD also showed impaired immediate and delayed verbal recall on the Wechsler Memory Scale (Revised). Developmental risk factors and/or trauma-related release of glucocorticoids, excitatory amino acids, serotonin, and other neurotransmitters and neuropeptides may have led to the reduced hippocampal volume.

Briere, J., & Conte, J. R. (1993). Self-reported amnesia for abuse in adults molested as children. *Journal of Traumatic Stress, 6,* 21-31.

**Cahill, L., Prins, B., Weber, M., & McGaugh, J. L. (1994). Beta-adrenergic activation and memory for emotional events. *Nature, 371,* 702-704.

Subjects watched a series of slides depicting a neutral story or an emotional story after receiving either placebo or the beta-adrenergic receptor antagonist propranolol hydrochloride. Propranolol significantly impaired memory for the emotionally arousing story but did not impair memory for the neutral story. These results were not attributable to differences in emotional responsiveness or to nonspecific attentional or sedative effects and suggest that enhanced memory for emotionally arousing events involves activation of the beta-adrenergic system. This important study provides a bridge from the extensive animal literature on memory and adrenergic chemicals to human memory.

Cappa, S., Sterzi, R., Vallar, G., & Bisiach, E. (1987). Remission of hemineglect and anosognosia after vestibular stimulation. *Neuropsychologia, 25,* 755-782.

Castellano, C., & McGaugh, J. L. (1989). Effect of morphine on one-trial inhibitory avoidance in mice: Lack of state-dependency. *Psychobiology, 17,* 89-92.

Cohen, N. J., & Eichenbaum, H. (1993). *Memory, amnesia and the hippocampus.* Cambridge: MIT Press.

Damasio, A. R. (1989). Time-locked multiregional retroactivation: A systems-level proposal for the neural substrates of recall and recognition. *Cognition, 33,* 25-62.

*DeBellis, M. D., Chrousos, G. P., Dorn, L. D., Burke, L., Helmers, K., Kling, M. A., Trickett, P. K., & Putnam, F. W. (1994). Hypothalamic-pituitary-adrenal axis dysregulation in sexually abused girls. *Journal of Clinical Endocrinology and Metabolism, 78,* 249-255.

Measured plasma adrenocorticotropic hormone (ACTH), and total and free cortisol responses to ovine corticotropin-releasing hormone (CRH) stimulation in a self-selected sample of sexually abused and control girls (aged 7-15 years). Relative to controls, sexually abused girls showed lower basal and net ovine CRH-stimulated plasma ACTH levels and reduced total ACTH responses, but their total and free basal and CRH-stimulated plasma cortisol levels did not differ. It is hypothesized that chronic and/or intermittent endogenous CRH hypersecretion due to previous emotional and physical stress associated with the sexual trauma led to hypersensitivity of the adrenal cortices, which release cortisol in response to ACTH. Downregulation of ACTH release is viewed as a compensatory response aimed at maintaining normal levels of cortisol secretion. Insofar as excessive exposure to glucocorticoids can result in hippocampal damage, the hypothalamic-pituitary-adrenal axis dysfunction discussed here is relevant to explaining poor memory in sexual abuse victims.

Deese, J. (1959). On the prediction of occurrence of particular verbal intrusions in immediate recall. *Journal of Experimental Psychology, 58,* 17-22.

DeLuca, J., & Cicerone, K. D. (1991). Confabulation following aneurysm of the anterio communicating artery. *Cortex, 27,* 417-423.

Demb, J., Desmond, J. E., Wagner, A. D., Vaidya, C. J., Glover, G. H., & Gabrieli, J. D. E. (1995). Semantic encoding and retrieval in the left inferior prefrontal cortex: A functional MRI study of task difficulty and process specificity. *Journal of Neuroscience, 15,* 5870-5878.

Elliott, D. M., & Briere, J. (1995). Posttraumatic stress associated with delayed recall of sexual abuse: A general population study. *Journal of Traumatic Stress, 8,* 629-647.

Feldman-Summers, S., & Pope, K. S. (1994). The experience of "forgetting" childhood abuse: A national survey of psychologists. *Journal of Consulting and Clinical Psychology, 62,* 636-639.

Fredrickson, R. (1992). *Repressed memories: A journey to recovery from sexual abuse.* New York: Simon & Schuster.

Ghoneim, M. M., Hinrichs, J. V., Mewaldt, S. P., & Petersen, R. C. (1985). Ketamine: Behavioral effects of subanesthetic doses. *Journal of Clinical Psychopharmacology, 5,* 70-77.

Hembrooke, H., & Ceci, S. J. (1995). Traumatic memories: Do we need to invoke special mechanisms? *Consciousness and Cognition, 4,* 75-82.

Herman, J. L., & Schatzow, E. (1987). Recovery and verification of memories of childhood sexual trauma. *Psychoanalytic Psychology, 4,* 1-14.

Holmes, D. S. (1990). The evidence for repression: An examination of sixty years of research. In J. L. Singer (Ed.), *Repression and dissociation: Implications for personality theory, psychopathology, and health* (pp. 85-102). Chicago: University of Chicago Press.

Hyman, I. E., Jr., Husband, T. H., & Billings, F. J. (1995). False memories of childhood experiences. *Applied Cognitive Psychology, 9,* 181-197.

Izquierdo, I. (1984). Endogenous state dependency: Memory depends on the relation between the neurohumoral and hormonal states present after training and at the time of testing. In G. Lynch, J. L. McGaugh, & N. M. Weinberger (Eds.), *Neurobiology of learning and memory* (pp. 333-350). New York: Guilford.

Jacoby, J. L., Kelley, C. M., & Dywan, J. (1989). Memory attributions. In H. L. Roediger III & F. I. M. Craik (Eds.), *Varieties of memory and consciousness: Essays in honor of Endel Tulving* (pp. 391-422). Hillsdale, NJ: Lawrence Erlbaum.

Janowsky, J. S., Shimamura, A. P., & Squire, L. R. (1989). Source memory impairment in patients with frontal lobe lesions. *Neuropsychologia, 27,* 1043-1056.

Johnson, H. M. (1994). Processes of intentional forgetting. *Psychological Bulletin, 116,* 274-292.

Johnson, M. K. (1991). Reality monitoring: Evidence from confabulation in organic brain disease patients. In G. Prigatano & D. L. Schacter (Eds.), *Awareness of defi-*

cit after brain injury (pp. 176-197). New York: Oxford University Press.

Johnson, M. K., Hastroudi, S., & Lindsay, D. S. (1993). Source monitoring. *Psychological Bulletin, 114,* 3-28.

Kandel, M., & Kandel, E. (1994). Flights of memory. *Discover, 15,* 32-36.

Kapur, N. (1993). Focal retrograde amnesia in neurological disease: A critical review. *Cortex, 29,* 217-234.

*Kapur, S., Craik, F. I. M., Jones, C., Brown, G. M., Houle, S., & Tulving, E. (1995). Functional role of prefrontal cortex in retrieval of memories: A PET study. *Neuroreport, 6,* 1880-1884.

Provides evidence from positron emission tomography that right prefrontal cortex, which had been implicated previously in explicit or episodic memory retrieval, is primarily involved in retrieval attempt or effort, as opposed to successful recall. The right prefrontal region showed increased blood flow when subjects attempted to determine whether a word had appeared on a recent study list compared with a condition in which they read the word but did not perform any retrieval operations. However, the same regions did not show further increases in conditions in which successful recognition increased significantly.

*Kapur, S., Craik, F. I. M., Tulving, E., Wilson, A. A., Houle, S., & Brown, G. (1994). Neuroanatomical correlates of encoding in episodic memory: Levels of processing effect. *Proceedings of the National Academy of Sciences, USA, 91,* 2008-2011.

Provides evidence from positron emission tomography that the left inferior prefrontal region is associated with elaborative encoding of semantic information. During separate scans, subjects performed encoding tasks that involved either extensive semantic elaboration or limited perceptual processing. When estimates of regional cerebral blood flow in the latter condition were subtracted from the blood flow estimates in the former condition, a significant difference was observed in the left inferior frontal lobe.

*Keenan, P. A., Jacobson, M. W., Soleymani, R. M., & Newcomer, J. W. (1995). Commonly used therapeutic doses of glucocorticoids impair explicit memory. *Annals of the New York Academy of Science, 761,* 400-402.

Evaluated memory and cognitive performance of 25 patients receiving long-term prednisone treatment for systemic disease without central nervous system involvement, in comparison to 25 control medical patients matched for age, gender, IQ, and diagnosis. Patients receiving long-term prednisone treatment (duration of at least 1 year) were significantly impaired at delayed paragraph recall and showed a trend toward impaired delayed recall of word lists (both tests of explicit memory), but were not impaired on an implicit task (word stem priming) or a vigilance task, thereby supporting the notion that glucocorticoid exposure may selectively impair hippocampal function.

Kihlstrom, J. F. (1995). The trauma-memory argument. *Consciousness and Cognition, 4,* 63-67.

Kihlstrom, J. F. (1997). Hypnosis, memory, and amnesia. In L. R. Squire & D. L. Schacter (Eds.), Biological and psychological perspectives on memory and memory disorders [Special issue]. *Philosophical Transactions of the Royal Society of London, Series B, 352,* 1727-1732.

Kihlstrom, J. F., & Schacter, D. L. (1995). Functional disorders of autobiographical memory. In A. D. Baddeley, B. A. Wilson, & F. N. Watts (Eds.), *Handbook of memory disorders* (pp. 337-364). New York: John Wiley.

Kosslyn, S. M., Alpert, N. M., Thompson, W. L., Maljkovic, V., Weise, S. B., Chabris, C. F., Hamilton, S. E., Rauch, S. L., & Buonanno, F. S. (1993). Visual mental imagery activates topographically organized visual cortex: PET investigations. *Journal of Cognitive Neuroscience, 5,* 263-287.

Kosslyn, S. M., Thompson, W. L., Kim, U., & Alpert, N. M. (1995). Topographical representations of mental images in primary visual cortex. *Nature, 378,* 496-498.

Koutstaal, W., & Schacter, D. L. (1997). Inaccuracy and inaccessibility in memory retrieval: Contributions from cognitive psychology and cognitive neuropsychology. In P. S. Appelbaum, L. Uyehara, & M. Elin (Eds.), *Trauma and memory: Clinical and legal issues.* New York: Oxford University Press.

*Krystal, J. H., Bennett, A. L., Bremner, J. D., Southwick, S. M., & Charney, D. S. (1995). Toward a cognitive neuroscience of dissociation and altered memory functions in post-traumatic stress disorder. In M. J. Friedman, D. S. Charney, & A. Y. Deutch (Eds.), *Neurobiological and clinical consequences of stress: From normal adaptation to PTSD* (pp. 239-269). Philadelphia: Lippincott-Raven.

A very useful integrative review of brain mechanisms/ systems that are potentially relevant to understanding dissociation and memory dysfunction in patients with posttraumatic stress disorder.

Krystal, J. H., Karper, L. P., Bennett, A., Abi-Dargham, A., D'Souza, D. C., Gil, R., & Charney, D. S. (1994). Modulation of frontal cortical function by glutamate and dopamine antagonists in healthy subjects and schizophrenic patients: A neuropsychological perspective. *Neuropsychopharmacology, 10*(Suppl. 43-198), 230S.

*Krystal, J. H., Karper, L. P., Seibyl, J. P., Freeman, G. K., Delaney, R., Bremner, J. D., Heninger, G. R., Bowers, M. B., Jr., & Charney, D. S. (1994). Subanesthetic effects of the NMDA antagonist, ketamine, in humans: Psychotomimetic, perceptual, cognitive, and neuroendocrine effects. *Archives of General Psychiatry, 51,* 199-214.

The behavioral, cognitive, physiological, and neuroendocrine effects of ketamine were examined in healthy subjects in a randomized, double-blind, placebo-controlled study. On one of three test days, subjects received 40 minutes of intravenous placebo, low dose (0.1 mg kg^{-1}) or high dose (0.5 mg kg^{-1}) ketamine hydrochloride. Ketamine resulted in impaired performance on tests sensitive to frontal lobe function (the Wisconsin Card Sorting Test, verbal fluency, and a continuous performance vigilance task) and selectively impaired delayed recall (10 minutes poststudy) of word triplets, but not immediate recall or postdistraction recall of these triplets. Ketamine administration also led to alterations in perception and an increase in behaviors resembling the positive and negative symptoms of schizophrenia.

Krystal, J. H., Southwick, S. M., & Charney, D. S. (1995). Posttraumatic stress disorder: Psychological mechanisms in traumatic remembrance. In D. L. Schacter, J. T. Coyle, G. D. Fischbach, M. M. Mesulam, & L. E. Sullivan (Eds.), *Memory distortion: How minds, brains, and societies reconstruct the past* (pp. 150-172). Cambridge, MA: Harvard University Press.

*Kuyken, W., & Brewin, C. R. (1995). Autobiographical memory functioning in depression and reports of early abuse. *Journal of Abnormal Psychology, 104,* 585-591.

The authors examined autobiographical memory functioning in depressed women patients with, versus without, a reported history of childhood physical and/or sexual abuse. Patients were asked to retrieve a specific personal memory in response to cue words describing positive and negative emotions (e.g., happy and angry). Patients with a reported history of sexual abuse or a history of both physical and sexual abuse retrieved more "overgeneral" (nonspecific) autobiographical memories to both positive and negative cue words than did either patients without a history of abuse or patients with a history of physical abuse alone. Overgeneral memories may arise from high levels of avoidance of abuse-related memories, or incorporation of events into general schematic representations of positive and negative experiences.

Lindsay, D. S. (1990). Misleading suggestions can impair eyewitnesses' ability to remember event details. *Journal of Experimental Psychology: Learning, Memory, and Cognition, 16,* 1077-1083.

*Lindsay, D. S., & Read, J. D. (1994). Psychotherapy and memories of childhood sexual abuse: A cognitive perspective. *Journal of Applied Cognitive Psychology, 8,* 281-338.

An extremely thorough, nuanced, and fair review of ideas and findings from cognitive psychology that sheds light on how true and false recovered memories of sexual abuse might arise.

Loftus, E. F. (1993). The reality of repressed memories. *American Psychologist, 48,* 518-537.

Loftus, E. F., Garry, M., & Feldman, J. (1994). Forgetting sexual trauma: What does it mean when 38% forget? *Journal of Consulting and Clinical Psychology, 62,* 1177-1181.

Loftus, E. F., & Ketcham, K. (1994). *The myth of repressed memory: False memories and allegations of sexual abuse.* New York: St. Martin's.

Loftus, E. F., Miller, D. G., & Burns, H. J. (1978). Semantic integration of verbal information into a visual memory. *Journal of Experimental Psychology: Human Learning and Memory, 4,* 19-31.

Loftus, E. F., & Pickrell, J. E. (1995). The formation of false memories. *Psychiatric Annals, 25,* 720-725.

Loftus, E. F., Polonsky, S., & Fullilove, M. T. (1994). Memories of childhood sexual abuse: Remembering and repressing. *Psychology of Women Quarterly, 18,* 67-84.

**Lucchelli, F., Muggia, S., & Spinnler, H. (1995). The "petites madeleines" phenomenon in two amnesic patients: Sudden recovery of forgotten memories. *Brain, 118,* 167-183.

Reports two cases of sudden, full, and permanent recovery from retrograde amnesia, one involving left thalamic infarction and a persistent anterograde deficit; the second involving mild head trauma and no anterograde deficit. In both cases, recovery from the retrograde amnesia was initiated by the involuntary recall of a unique autobiographical event that was highly similar to the patients' current situation. Although psychogenic factors cannot be conclusively ruled out, there was little reason to suspect secondary gain. The authors attribute these reversible retrograde deficits to temporary distortion of the neural matrices subserving memory representations.

Lynn, S. J., & Nash, M. R. (1994). Truth in memory: Ramifications for psychotherapy and hypnotherapy. *American Journal of Clinical Hypnosis, 36,* 194-208.

McClelland, J. L., McNaughton, B. L., & O'Reilly, R. C. (1995). Why there are complementary learning systems in the hippocampus and neocortex: Insights from the successes and failures of connectionist models of learning and memory. *Psychological Review, 102,* 419-437.

McGaugh, J. L. (1995). Emotional activation, neuromodulatory systems, and memory strength. In D. L. Schacter, J. T. Coyle, G. D. Fischbach, M. M. Mesulam, & L. E. Sullivan (Eds.), *Memory distortion: How minds, brains, and societies reconstruct the past* (pp. 255-273). Cambridge, MA: Harvard University Press.

McGaugh, J. L., Introini-Collison, I. B., Cahill, L. F., Castellano, C., Dalmaz, C., Parent, M. B., & Williams, D. L. (1993). Neuromodulatory systems and memory storage: Role of the amygdala. *Behavioral Brain Research, 58,* 81-90.

McGlynn, S. M., & Schacter, D. L. (1989). Unawareness of deficits in neuropsychological syndromes. *Journal of Clinical and Experimental Neuropsychology, 11,* 143-205.

Moscovitch, M. (1994). Memory and working with memory: Evaluation of a component process model and comparisons with other models. In D. L. Schacter & E. Tulving (Eds.), *Memory systems* (pp. 269-310). Cambridge: MIT Press.

Moscovitch, M. (1995). Confabulation. In D. L. Schacter, J. T. Coyle, G. D. Fischbach, M. M. Mesulam, & L. E. Sullivan (Eds.), *Memory distortion: How minds, brains, and societies reconstruct the past* (pp. 226-254). Cambridge, MA: Harvard University Press.

Nash, M. R. (1994). Memory distortion and sexual trauma: The problem of false negatives and false positives. *International Journal of Clinical and Experimental Hypnosis, 42,* 346-362.

Nathan, D., & Snedeker, M. (1995). *Satan's silence: Ritual abuse and the making of a modern American witch hunt.* New York: Basic Books.

Neisser, U. (1967). *Cognitive psychology.* New York: Appleton-Century-Crofts.

Nelson, E. L., & Simpson, P. (1994). First glimpse: An initial examination of subjects who have rejected their recovered visualizations as false memories. *Issues in Child Abuse Accusations, 6,* 123-133.

*Newcomer, J. W., Craft, S., Hershey, T., Askins, K., & Bardgett, M. E. (1994). Glucocorticoid-induced impairment in declarative memory performance in adult humans. *Journal of Neuroscience, 14,* 2047-2053.

Reports a double-blind, placebo-controlled study of the cognitive consequences of brief glucocorticoid exposure in normal adults. Subjects who received dexamethasone for 4 consecutive days (0.5 mg, 1.0 mg, 1.0 mg, 1.0 mg, respectively) showed impaired immediate and delayed recall of paragraphs at both 4 days and 11 days compared with placebo controls. Other cognitive measures were not affected by dexamethasone treatment, thereby arguing against a nonspecific effect of glucocorticoids on arousal or attention.

O'Connor, M., Butters, N., Miliotis, P., Eslinger, P., & Cermak, L. S. (1992). The dissociation of anterograde and retrograde amnesia in a patient with Herpes encephalitis. *Journal of Clinical and Experimental Neuropsychology, 14,* 159-178.

Ofshe, R. J., & Watters, E. (1994). *Making monsters: False memory, psychotherapy, and sexual hysteria.* New York: Scribner's.

*Parks, E. D., & Balon, R. (1995). Autobiographical memory for childhood events: Pattern of recall in psychiatric patients with a history of alleged trauma. *Psychiatry, 58,* 199-208.

Psychiatric outpatients with a reported history of childhood sexual and/or physical abuse, psychiatric outpatients without a history of abuse, and nonpatient controls were tested using an autobiographical word cuing technique requiring the generation of a specific personal memory from before 16 years of age. Patients reporting childhood abuse more often failed to generate memories to affective cue words than did either control group, and retrieved fewer early memories than nonpatient controls; the groups did not differ on nonautobiographical memory function as measured by the Wechsler Memory Scale (Revised).

Pendergrast, M. (1995). *Victims of memory: Incest accusations and shattered lives.* Hinesburg, VT: Upper Access.

Poole, D. A., Lindsay, D. S., Memon, A., & Bull, R. (1995). Psychotherapy and the recovery of memories of childhood sexual abuse: U.S. and British practitioners' beliefs, practices, and experiences. *Journal of Consulting and Clinical Psychology, 63,* 426-437.

Pope, H. G., Jr., & Hudson, J. I. (1995). Can memories of childhood sexual abuse be repressed? *Psychological Medicine, 25,* 121-126.

Prigatano, G., & Schacter, D. L. (Eds.). (1991). *Awareness of deficit after brain injury.* New York: Oxford University Press.

Ramachandran, V. S. (1995). Anosognosia in parietal lobe syndrome. *Consciousness and Cognition, 4,* 22-51.

*Roediger, H. L., III, & McDermott, K. B. (1995). Creating false memories: Remembering words not presented in lists. *Journal of Experimental Psychology: Learning, Memory, and Cognition, 21,* 803-814.

Documents a memory illusion whereby subjects exposed to a list of associates to a nonpresented "theme word" later claim (with high confidence) to remember having studied the theme word; the false alarm rate for nonstudied theme words approaches, and in some cases exceeds, the hit rate. Furthermore, when subjects are asked whether they consciously recollect encountering the theme word at study, or whether they just "know" it was presented, subjects tend to choose the former alternative. The ease with which false memories can be generated in young subjects using the paradigm, and the vividness of these memories, makes this a very promising tool for probing memory distortion.

Sapolsky, R. M. (1992). *Stress, the aging brain, and the mechanisms of neuronal death.* Cambridge: MIT Press.

Sapolsky, R. M., Uno, H., Rebert, C. S., & Finch, C. E. (1990). Hippocampal damage associated with prolonged glucocorticoid exposure in primates. *Journal of Neuroscience, 10,* 2897-2902.

Schacter, D. L. (1989). Memory. In M. I. Posner (Ed.), *Foundations of cognitive science* (pp. 683-725). Cambridge: MIT Press.

Schacter, D. L. (1995a). Memory distortion: History and current status. In D. L. Schacter, J. T. Coyle, G. D. Fischbach, M. M. Mesulam, & L. E. Sullivan (Eds.), *Memory distortion: How minds, brains, and societies reconstruct the past* (pp. 1-46). Cambridge, MA: Harvard University Press.

Schacter, D. L. (1995b). Memory wars. *Scientific American, 272,* 135-139.

Schacter, D. L. (1996). *Searching for memory: The brain, the mind, and the past.* New York: Basic Books.

**Schacter, D. L., Alpert, N. M., Savage, C., Rauch, S., & Albert, M. S. (1996). Conscious recollection and the human hippocampal formation: Evidence from positron emission tomography. *Proceedings of the National Academy of Sciences, USA, 93,* 321-325.

Analysis of positron emission tomography (PET) scan images was used to separate out two aspects of memory retrieval: the effort involved in attempting to retrieve a past event and the actual recollection of the event. Subjects studied some words several times with an elaborative encoding task (high recall condition) and studied other words just once with a perceptual encoding task (low recall condition). Subjects were later asked to remember high recall words and low recall words in response to three-letter word cues during separate PET scans. Hippocampal activation was observed in the high recall condition, in which subjects easily recollected many words, but not in the low recall condition. Conversely, prefrontal activations were observed in the low recall condition, where subjects made extensive efforts to remember words but recollected few of them, but not in the high recall condition.

Schacter, D. L., & Curran, T. (1995). The cognitive neuroscience of false memories. *Psychiatric Annals, 25,* 726-730.

Schacter, D. L., Curran, T., Galluccio, L. D., Milberg, W. P., & Bates, J. (1996). False recognition and the right frontal lobe: A case study. *Neuropsychologia, 34,* 793-808.

Schacter, D. L., Harbluk, J. L., & McLachlan, D. R. (1984). Retrieval without recollection: An experimental analysis of source amnesia. *Journal of Verbal Learning and Verbal Behavior, 23,* 593-611.

Schacter, D. L., Kagan, J., & Leichtman, M. D. (1995). True and false memories in children and adults: A cognitive neuroscience perspective. *Psychology, Public Policy, and Law, 1,* 411-428.

Schacter, D. L., & Kihlstrom, F. J. (1989). Functional amnesia. In F. Boller & J. Grafman (Eds.), *Handbook of neuropsychology* (Vol. 3, pp. 209-231). New York: Elsevier Science.

Schacter, D. L., Reiman, E., Uecker, A., Polster, M. R., Uyn, L. S., & Cooper, L. A. (1995). Brain regions associated with retrieval of structurally coherent visual information. *Nature, 376,* 587-590.

Schacter, D. L., Verfaellie, M., & Pradere, D. (1996). The neuropsychology of memory illusions: False recall and recognition in amnesic patients. *Journal of Memory and Language, 35,* 319-334.

Schooler, J. W. (1994). Seeking the core: The issues and evidence surrounding recovered accounts of sexual trauma. *Consciousness and Cognition, 3,* 452-469.

Shimamura, A. P., & Squire, L. R. (1987). A neuropsychological study of fact memory and source amnesia. *Journal of Experimental Psychology: Learning, Memory, and Cognition, 13,* 464-473.

Singer, J. L. (Ed.). (1990). *Repression and dissociation: Implications for personality theory, psychopathology, and health.* Chicago: University of Chicago Press.

Spanos, N. P., Menary, E., Gabora, N. J., DuBreuil, S. C., & Dewhirst, B. (1991). Secondary identity enactments during hypnotic past-life regression: A sociocognitive perspective. *Journal of Personality and Social Psychology, 61,* 308-320.

Spiegel, D. (1995). Hypnosis and suggestion. In D. L. Schacter, J. T. Coyle, G. D. Fischbach, M. M. Mesulam, & L. E. Sullivan (Eds.), *Memory distortion: How minds, brains, and societies reconstruct the past* (pp. 129-149). Cambridge, MA: Harvard University Press.

Squire, L. R. (1987). *Memory and brain.* New York: Oxford University Press.

Squire, L. R. (1992). Memory and the hippocampus: A synthesis of findings with rats, monkeys, and humans. *Psychological Review, 99,* 195-231.

Squire, L. R. (1995). Biological foundations of accuracy and inaccuracy in memory. In D. L. Schacter, J. T. Coyle, G. D. Fischbach, M. M. Mesulam, & L. E. Sullivan (Eds.), *Memory distortion: How minds, brains, and societies reconstruct the past* (pp. 197-225). Cambridge, MA: Harvard University Press.

Squire, L. R., Ojemann, J. G., Miesin, F. M., Petersen, S. E., Videen, T. O., & Raichle, M. E. (1992). Activation of the hippocampus in normal humans: A functional anatomical study of memory. *Proceedings of the National Academy of Sciences, USA, 89,* 1837-1841.

Suengas, A. G., & Johnson, M. K. (1988). Qualitative effects of rehearsal on memories for perceived and imagined complex events. *Journal of Experimental Psychology: General, 117,* 377-389.

Terr, L. C. (1994). *Unchained memories: True stories of traumatic memories lost and found.* New York: Basic Books.

Tulving, E. (1983). *Elements of episodic memory.* New York: Oxford University Press.

Tulving, E., Schacter, D. L., McLachlan, D. R., & Moscovitch, M. (1988). Priming of semantic autobiographical knowledge: A case study of retrograde amnesia. *Brain and Cognition, 8,* 3-20.

van der Kolk, B. A. (1994). The body keeps the score: Memory and the evolving psychobiology of posttraumatic stress. *Harvard Review of Psychiatry, 1,* 253-265.

van der Kolk, B. A., & Fisler, R. E. (1995). Dissociation and the fragmentary nature of traumatic memories: Overview and exploratory study. *Journal of Traumatic Stress, 8,* 505-525.

Whitfield, C. L. (1995). The forgotten difference: Ordinary memory versus traumatic memory. *Consciousness and Cognition, 4,* 88-94.

Williams, J. M. G. (1992). Autobiographical memory and emotional disorders. In S.-A. Christianson (Ed.), *The handbook of emotion and memory: Research and theory* (pp. 451-477). Hillsdale, NJ: Lawrence Erlbaum.

**Williams, L. M. (1994). Recall of childhood trauma: A prospective study of women's memories of child sexual abuse. *Journal of Consulting and Clinical Psychology, 62,* 1167-1176.

Reports the results of detailed interviews with 129 women who, some 17 years earlier and when aged between 10 months and 12 years of age, had been brought to a hospital emergency room for treatment of sexual abuse. A total of 38% of the women did not recall the incident of abuse for which they were taken to hospital. Many of these women (68%) did remember other incidents of abuse, but 32% of those without recall (12% of the total sample) reported that they were never sexually abused in childhood. Although no follow-up clarification interviews were performed to determine whether failure to report abuse reflects memory loss or report withholding associated with social factors, memory loss is a plausible explanation of the results. Additional factors associated with recall or recall failure (e.g., age at time of abuse) are explored.

Williams, L. M. (1995). Recovered memories of abuse in women with documented child sexual victimization histories. *Journal of Traumatic Stress, 8,* 649-673.

Wolkowitz, O. M., Reus, V. I., Weingartner, H., Thompson, K., Breier, A., Doran, A., Rubinow, D., &

Pickar, D. (1990). Cognitive effects of corticosteroids. *American Journal of Psychiatry, 147,* 1297-1303.

Wright, L. (1994). *Remembering Satan.* New York: Knopf.

Zaragoza, M. S., & Lane, S. M. (1994). Source misattributions and the suggestibility of eyewitness memory. *Journal of Experimental Psychology: Learning, Memory, and Cognition, 20,* 934-945.

PART IV

EVIDENCE AND CONTROVERSIES IN UNDERSTANDING MEMORIES FOR TRAUMATIC EVENTS

21

Traumatic Memory Characteristics

A Cross-Validated Mediational Model of Response to Rape Among Employed Women

Mary P. Koss
Aurelio José Figueredo
Iris Bell
Melinda Tharan
Shannon Tromp

Emotional arousal stemming from shock-ing, personally consequential experiences has been shown to etch long-lasting, detailed memories compared to memories for neutral personal experiences (for reviews, see Chris-tianson, 1992; Koss, Tromp, & Tharan, 1995). The detail and persistence of emotional memo-ries are multiply determined. Emotional arousal triggers neurohormonal changes that influence the strength of encoding (e.g., LeDoux, 1994), directs attentional resources to the event (Chris-tianson, Loftus, Hoffman, & Loftus, 1991), en-gages greater elaborative processing of the stimulus because of its consequentiality and un-usualness (e.g., Christianson & Loftus, 1991), and influences how and how much the memories are talked about (e.g., Bohannon & Symons, 1992).

AUTHORS' NOTE: This study was supported by a Research Career Development Award from the National Institute of Mental Health (NIMH) and research funding from the Violence and Traumatic Stress Studies Branch of NIMH and from the Women's Health Office of the National Institutes of Health. We gratefully acknowledge John Kihlstrom's contributions to the theory and methodology of this study. Correspondence concerning this article should be addressed to Mary P. Koss, Arizona Prevention Center, Department of Family and Community Medicine, University of Arizona, 2223 East Speedway Boulevard, Tucson, Arizona 85719. This chapter appeared originally in the *Journal of Abnormal Psychology,* vol. 105, pp. 421-432. Copyright 1996 by the American Psychological Association. Reprinted by permission.

Viewed from a clinical perspective, past research on emotional memories is particularly thin in some areas. First, very few studies involved actual as opposed to simulated events, and even fewer studies involved targeted victims as opposed to eyewitnesses to the event (Cutshall & Yuille, 1992; Wagenaar & Groeneweg, 1990). Second, the neural mechanisms underlying emotional memory suggest that any event that evokes intense arousal, positive or negative, could result in vivid and persistent memories (Cahill, Prins, Weber, & McGaugh, 1994). However, researchers have concentrated mainly on negative emotional events (Christianson, 1992). Third, most studies limited examination of memory characteristics to issues of detail, persistence, and sometimes frequency of discussing the memory. These foci represent only a subset of the phenomena that characterize autobiographical memories (Suengas & Johnson, 1988). In the present study we contribute to these understudied areas by examining women's recollections of rape, other unpleasant experiences, and pleasant experiences using a multifactor memory characteristics questionnaire. A cross-validated mediational model is described that tested hypothesized relationships among intense experiences, cognitive appraisal and valence, memory characteristics, and physical health outcomes.

On the basis of prior studies demonstrating that the perceived threat inherent in a rape attack is a more powerful predictor of later symptoms than the actual violence, we reasoned that how rape is cognitively construed may predict the qualities of the reconstructed memory (Girelli, Resick, Marhoefer-Dvorak, & Hutter, 1986; Kilpatrick, Saunders, Veronen, Best, & Von, 1987; Norris & Kaniasty, 1991; Sales, Baum, & Shore, 1984). Charges aired in the public media have suggested that researchers err in considering as rape victims women who sustained sexual assaults that meet legal standards for rape but who do not cognitively appraise themselves as rape victims (Gilbert, 1991, 1994). The question of whether the deleterious effects of rape stem from the coerced, unwanted sexual intercourse itself, from one's self-appraisal as a vic-

tim, or from both is empirically tested in our model.

Like many trauma victims, rape survivors experience deleterious effects of victimization on their physical health (Golding, 1994; Kimerling & Calhoun, 1994; Koss, Koss, & Woodruff, 1991; Wolfe, Schnurr, Brown, & Furey, 1994; for reviews, see Dunn & Gilchrist, 1993; Hendricks-Mathews, 1993; Koss & Heslet, 1992). Unfortunately, none of these studies illuminates the causal pathways by which victimization influences health. In our model, we considered frequent remembering as a mediator through which disease might be created. The following indirect sequence of causation was hypothesized regarding the relationships among rape, memory for rape, and symptoms: (a) The level of rape, as legally defined, directly influenced both the cognitive appraisal and the emotional valence related to the incident; (b) both cognitive appraisal and valence directly influenced the memories related to the incident; and, finally, (c) memory characteristics directly influenced physical symptoms. This sequence assigned causal priority according to the following theoretical principles: first, to the formal characteristics of rape, as defined by the law; second, to the cognitive and affective construals of the rape, as retrospectively defined by the respondent; and third, to the detailed representation of the rape, as reconstructed from memory.

The conceptual model of the cognitive and symptomatic sequelae of rape is illustrated in Figure 21.1. The focus of the model is on a range of memory phenomena broader than but partially overlapping with the diagnostic entity of posttraumatic stress disorder (PTSD), the hallmark of which is intrusive memory. Our assumption was that memory phenomena occur on a continuum of severity, which at some point become diagnosable. Some of the memory processes examined in the present study could occur among people who do not meet diagnostic criteria for PTSD but who still experience dysfunction to some degree. We used community samples to examine this continuum and to avoid limiting the range of severity to clinically significant intensity.

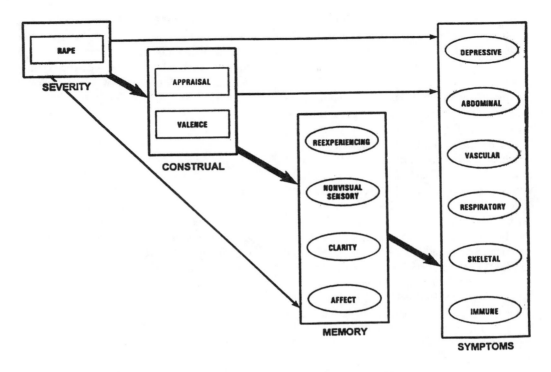

Figure 21.1. Conceptual Model of the Cognitive and Symptomatic Sequelae of Rape

Method

□ The data were collected by a short mail survey using the total design method (Dillman, 1978). This method involved design criteria including survey length requiring less than 10 minutes of respondent's time, a presurvey publicity campaign, a preliminary first-class letter sent to the members of the sample set 2 weeks prior to the survey being mailed, the main survey mailing, and a follow-up mailing 2 weeks later. Women whose first-class letters were returned as undeliverable were removed from the sample frame. A phone number and instructions in Spanish were given on the cover for respondents who preferred to complete the survey in Spanish.

Participants

Sample 1 consisted of 2,173 surveys mailed to medical center employees, from which re-

sponses were received from 1,037 women (48% response rate). Their demographic characteristics were as follows: mean age 36.6 years, range 18-67 years; 84% non-Hispanic White, 13% Hispanic, and 1% each of African American, Asian-Pacific Islander, and Native American; 65% married or cohabiting, 19% single, 16% separated, divorced, or widowed; 2% high school education or less, 36% business, technical, or some college training, and 62% college graduates; 13% with family incomes less than $15,000, 36% between $15,501 and $35,000, and 51% over $35,000. The medical center workforce is an average of 38.3 years old and 76% White, 18% Hispanic, 3% African American, 2% Asian, and 1% Native American. Compared with the population, our sample was on average 1.7 years younger ($d = -.19$, $t[992] = -6.074$, $p < .05$) and contained 8% more Whites, 5% fewer Hispanics, and 3% fewer members of other ethnic groups, $\chi^2(4, N = 1,004) = 33.43$, $p < .05$.

Sample 2 consisted of 5,411 surveys mailed to university employees, from which responses were received from 2,142 women (40% response rate; the slightly lower rate was due to a financially based decision to omit the follow-up mailing in this sample). The demographic characteristics of the respondents were as follows: mean age 40.5 years, range 17-75 years; 88% White, 8% Hispanic, 1% African American, 2% Asian, and 1% Native American; 63% married or cohabiting, 17% single, 20% separated, divorced, or widowed; 6% high school education or less, 27% business, technical, or some college, and 67% college graduates; 12% with family incomes less than $15,000, 37% between $15,501 and $35,000, and 51% over $35,000. The female university workforce was an average of 39.9 years old and consisted of 79% non-Hispanic Whites, 12% Hispanics, 5% Asians, and 2% each African Americans and Native Americans. Compared with the workforce, respondents were 0.6 years older ($d = .06$, $t[2,014] = 2.642$, $p < .05$) and contained 9% more non-Hispanic Whites, 4% fewer Hispanics, 3% fewer Asians, and 1% fewer each African Americans and Native Americans, $\chi^2(4, N = 2,047) = 90.008, p < .05$. Demographic differences between the two samples were not of concern to us because all data analyses were conducted in one sample and cross-validated in the other. However, we were concerned about the slight departures from representativeness, which suggest caution in generalizing the results and raise questions about the potential effects of demographic characteristics on the study variables. We address these problems statistically and fully describe our procedures in the analyses section.

Survey Contents

Respondents first answered health questions. Then they turned a page and found questions that screened for attempted and completed rape. If they checked yes to one of these items, they were asked to recall their most recent or most significant experience and indicate their cognitive appraisal of the incident. If respondents had not experienced a sexual assault, they were asked to pick another intense life experi-

ence and to check whether its emotional valence was pleasant or unpleasant. All respondents then described their memory of the target experience on standard items that measure memory characteristics. A measure of social desirability and demographic questions completed the survey.

Rape

Five items based on the Sexual Experiences Survey as previously modified for use with women workers (see Koss, Woodruff, & Koss, 1991) were used to screen for rape and attempted rape. The recall period for the five items was bounded by the participant's 14th birthday. This cutoff represented the statutory age for rape (the age below which sexual penetration is automatically rape). Only two states set a statutory age below 14 years (Searles & Berger, 1987). The questions operationalized rape, which was legally defined as vaginal, oral, or anal penetration against consent, by force, threat of force, or when the victim was intoxicated and incapable of giving consent. Penetration, no matter how slight, was sufficient to complete rape. Attempted rape included overt attempts to achieve intercourse, where for various reasons penetration did not occur. An example of a typical item is the following: "Has a man made you have sex by using force or threatening to harm you? When we use the word 'sex' we mean a man putting his penis in your vagina even if he didn't ejaculate (come)." The word *rape* was not used in these questions, allowing a woman to endorse a "rape" item without considering herself a "rape victim." The rape and attempted rape items had the following internal consistency reliabilities: Sample 1, .74; Sample 2, .72. Significant correlations have been reported in similar samples of working women between the level of victimization on the basis of anonymous self-report and the level as related to an interviewer (Koss, Woodruff, & Koss, 1991; $\kappa = .51, p < .001$). Consistent with existing cross-sectional studies, most of the rapes reported on the surveys were nonrecent: 92% of forcible vaginal rapes, 93% of forcible oral and anal rapes, and 93% of nonforcible rapes when intoxicated occurred 2 or more years prior to the study.

The study variable *rape* was scored ordinally according to the level of severity reported. Women who responded no to all the items were scored zero for nonvictims. The remaining respondents were scored as 1 (attempted rape victims) or 2 (rape victims), depending on the highest level of victimization they endorsed. In Sample 1, 8% of the respondents reported the most severe victimization they had encountered was an attempted rape, and 30% reported at least one completed rape. In Sample 2, the figures for attempted rape and rape were 8% and 29%, respectively. The rape figure is slightly higher than reported in earlier work with a similar sample of working women (Koss, Woodruff, & Koss, 1991).

Appraisal

The appraisal question was addressed exclusively to rape victimization. Victimizations other than rape and nonrape memories were scored zero. Women who had been raped or experienced attempts were asked to select the expression that best captured their cognitive appraisal: (a) I don't feel I was victimized, (b) I believe I was a victim of a serious miscommunication, (c) I believe I was a victim of a crime other than rape, (d) I believe I was a victim of rape. In Sample 1, 41% of respondents saw themselves as rape victims, 16% believed they were victims of some crime other than rape, 33% believed they were victims of a serious miscommunication, and only 10% said they did not feel victimized. The figures for Sample 2 were virtually identical, with 55% of the women classified as rape victims appraising their experience as rape. These figures are higher than previously reported for college student rape victims (Koss, 1985). The differences may be explained by heightened consciousness about what constitutes rape facilitated by media coverage of the topic that has occurred over the past 10 years or by developmental changes in the differentiation of consensual versus coercive sex.

According to statutes, the crime of rape includes attempts, so cognitive appraisal as a rape victim was equally applicable. However, the data showed the differences between legal definitions and personal labels in that only 5% of the attempted rape victims appraised their experience as rape, 37% believed they were victims of a crime other than rape, 38% believed they were victims of a serious miscommunication, and 21% did not feel victimized. The figures for Sample 2 were very similar, with 5% of the attempted rape victims appraising their experience as rape.

Valence

Valence was a dichotomous item. Respondents with a rape memory were assumed to be rating an unpleasant memory. No empirical evidence suggests that rape is potentially pleasant. Respondents without a rape experience rated their intense life experience as pleasant or unpleasant. In Sample 1, 35% checked that their memory was pleasant and 65% described it as unpleasant; the figures for Sample 2 were 30% and 70%, respectively. This procedure ascribes a single level of negative intensity to all unpleasant experiences. However, many would argue that the rape could differ in severity from other unpleasant experiences. The inclusion of a multi-item measure of memory affect (see the section on the measurement model, below) allowed us to test the performance of the dichotomous valence measure.

Memory

Most of the memory items were taken from the first factor of the Memory Characteristics Questionnaire, developed by Suengas and Johnson (1988). This questionnaire assesses characteristics of memory that have proven useful for distinguishing real from imagined experiences. Imagined as opposed to real memories differ on dimensions that include clarity, visual detail, vividness, event detail, comprehensibility of the order of events, and the frequency the memory is recalled. The instructions read, "Please answer the following questions about the memory . . . ." All items were rated on a 7-point scale. The instructions do not indicate a reference period, because the ratings are intended to reflect the memory as it is currently reconstructed for purposes of responding to the survey. These 17 items were supplemented by 6 items relating to flashbulb memory qualities (J. F. Kihlstrom, personal communication, July 15, 1991). *Flashbulb memory* is a descriptive term for memories of highly surprising and consequential events (for a review, see Winograd & Neisser, 1992, pp. 162-170).

Symptoms

Because past literature has reported relatively low prevalence of somatization disorder among sexual assault victims (Burnam et al., 1988) and elevated prevalence of both medically explained and medically unexplained symptoms (Golding, 1994), we sought a symptom checklist that addressed the psychophysiological spectrum of symptoms. We selected the Psychosomatic Symptom Checklist (Attansio, Andraski, Blanchard, & Arena, 1984), which requires respondents to indicate which of 17 symptoms (e.g., joint pain, indigestion) or diseases (e.g., diabetes, irritable bowel) they have had within the past 30 days. The reported test-retest correlation is .90 for 1 week (Attansio et al., 1984). We added 22 items to supplement the breadth of assessment while remaining faithful to the conceptual underpinnings of the instrument.

Data Analyses

Univariate Analyses

Several univariate analyses addressed internal and external validity.

Test for social desirability. To address concerns that participant responses may have been motivated by a desire to appear socially appropriate, 11 items from the Marlowe-Crowne Social Desirability scale (Crowne & Marlowe, 1960) were included and aggregated into an index following the method developed by Schwartz (G. Schwartz, personal communication, May 15, 1991). The Marlowe-Crowne has been used extensively over the past 30 years and consists of true-false items

pertaining to culturally approved behaviors that have a low incidence of occurrence. Using general linear models, this single index for social desirability was used to predict each of the 65 individual items in the survey (not including demographics). Of the 130 regressions (65 items times 2 samples), only 9 were significant using a Bonferonni significance level of $p < .0007$. In Sample 1, the social desirability index predicted about 3% of the variance in the PSC item "anxiety," and less than 1% of the variance in two memory items. In Sample 2, all the significant effects accounted for 1% or less of the variance. Thus, we deemed the influence of social desirability to be negligible for practical purposes.

Test for missing data bias. About 18% of Sample 1 and 17% of Sample 2 respondents were dropped because of missing data. Although this still left us with a more than adequate sample size, the question of whether dropped respondents differed systematically from those with complete data remained. To test for systematic "missingness bias" (Cohen & Cohen, 1983), a dichotomous dummy variable was constructed to distinguish all the respondents to be dropped from those to be retained. These two groups were compared by chi-square tests on six demographic variables (age, marital status, ethnicity, religion, income, and education), victimization level, cognitive appraisal, and valence. Of the 16 comparisons, 3 reached the Bonferonni corrected significance level of $p < .006$ in Sample 1, and the same 3 did in Sample 2. Because of the power resulting from large sample sizes, we computed effect sizes (Cohen's d) to determine the practical magnitude of these significant differences (Cohen, 1990). According to Cohen (1988; Cohen & Cohen, 1983), an effect size of .10 indicates a small effect, .30 indicates a medium effect, and .50 or higher indicates a large effect. The results of the chi-square comparisons can be found in Table 21.1. There were small to moderate effects for age (those with missing data were slightly older), for education (those with missing data were slightly less educated), and for ethnicity (those with missing data were somewhat more

Table 21.1 Missing Data Effect Size Comparisons

Variable	Sample 1				Sample 2			
	Cohen's d	χ^2	df	p	Cohen's d	χ^2	df	p
Age	.18	16.59	4	.0023***	.24	28.74	5	.0000***
Marital status	.11	7.28	4	.1219	.002	2.65	4	.6173
Ethnicity	−.23	14.78	4	.0052***	−.16	14.68	4	.0054***
Religion	−.11	1.70	6	.9453	.24	15.91	6	.0142
Income	−.19	4.65	5	.4594	−.10	5.53	5	.3546
Education	−.36	24.92	6	.0004***	−.21	16.98	5	.0045***
Cognitive appraisal	.05	1.29	3	.7303	.07	9.85	3	.0199
Valence	.11	3.51	1	.0611	.07	4.32	1	.0376
Rape	.10	1.53	2	.4651	.16	10.12	2	.0064

***$p < .0055$ (Bonferroni significance level).

likely to be non-White). The significant demographics were the same variables in both samples and similar in both magnitude and direction, which suggests that they were not merely Type 1 errors. The pattern of missingness is fairly typical of the types of people who generally respond and do not respond more favorably to surveys. The next section describes the procedures implemented for the statistical control of demographic biases.

Residualization on demographics. Some demographic variables might have been correlated with some of the variables used in the model. To determine the amount of variance in the study variables accounted for by demographics, we entered them into regression equations to predict each of the 65 variables to be included in our multivariate model. In Sample 1, 10/65 regressions resulted in R^2s significant at the Bonferonni corrected probability of $p < .0007$. The range of variance accounted for was 4% to 11%, with an average of 3%. We chose to residualize the variables prior to multivariate analysis. Residualization subtracts any deviation systematically predicted by demographic variables from each score (Cohen & Cohen, 1983). This procedure statistically controlled for the influence of demographics by removing any spurious covariances between study variables attributable to them, without explicitly including demographics in the multivariate model (P. M. Bentler, personal communication, October 1989).

The adjusted scores, or regression residuals, were then used for multivariate modeling.

Multivariate Analyses

A factor-analytic structural equations model consists of two major components: a measurement model and a structural model.

Measurement model. The measurement model was a confirmatory factor analysis accomplished using Bentler's (1989) structural equations modeling program. A number of directly measured items (called *manifest variables* or *indicators*) were related to a smaller set of hypothetical constructs (called *latent variables* or *common factors*) presumed to be underlying the correlations between them. The development of the measurement model was based on an initial exploratory factor analysis in Sample 1 using a principal axis extraction and a varimax (orthogonal) followed by a promax (oblique) rotation, some empirical respecification and post hoc theoretical "trimming" of the model on that sample, followed by a confirmatory cross-validation of the cleaned-up model in Sample 2 with no further respecification. Only the results of the confirmatory factor analysis are reported in this chapter.

Structural model. The structural component of the model is essentially a path analysis between the latent constructs that were produced by the factor analysis. Path analysis, or structural equations modeling, consists of imposing a restricted set of causal pathways, also specified a priori, and testing them against the correlations between the constructs. A saturated structural model is one that freely estimates the direct correlations among all of the common factors. However, any structural model that can adequately reproduce that pattern of intercorrelations with a reduced set of hypothesized causal pathways is judged superior by the principle of parsimony. Three analyses were performed. First, a saturated structural equations model was constructed for Sample 1. Second, a restricted structural model was tested for this sample in which all of the nonsignificant effects were eliminated. The nonsignificance of each of the parameters eliminated was initially determined by the examination of individual critical ratios but was tested afterward in an omnibus null hypothesis by nested model comparisons between the saturated and restricted models. Third, the restricted model obtained from Sample 1 was directly cross-validated on Sample 2. The saturated structural model was also retested in Sample 2 to determine how much of the loss in goodness of fit to the data of the restricted structural model was due to the added structural restrictions of that model as opposed to the prior measurement restrictions that were imposed in the confirmatory factor analysis. Because a saturated model imposes no structural restrictions whatsoever, any lack of goodness of fit to the data must be entirely attributable to that of the measurement model, and the comparison can therefore be used to assess separately the performance of the structural model. Because no post hoc respecification of model parameters was done, the confirmatory nature of this analysis was not compromised. As with the measurement model, only the results of the confirmatory structural equations model are reported here.

Structural equations models were evaluated by use of chi-square, the Bentler-Bonnett Comparative Fit Index (CFI), the Bentler-Bonnett Normed Fit Index (NFI), and the Bentler-Bonnett NonNormed Fit Index (NNFI; Bentler, 1989; Bentler & Bonnett, 1980). Chi-square

measures the statistical goodness of fit of the covariance matrix observed to that reproduced by the model. A significant chi-square is therefore grounds for rejection of the model specified. The Bentler-Bonnett indices are measures of practical goodness of fit for large sample sizes, because a small effect often results in a statistically significant lack of fit. Index values greater than 0.90 are considered satisfactory levels of practical goodness of fit, even if significant chi-square values are obtained (Bentler, 1989; Bentler & Bonnett, 1980). Differences between hierarchically nested (e.g., progressively more restricted) models in either statistical or practical indices of fit indicate the relative loss of fit of the model to the data entailed by the additional model restrictions, such as the elimination of selected causal pathways. Where the results of such difference tests are found to be either statistically nonsignificant or negligible for practical purposes, they indicate that a restricted model performs as well as a more saturated model in predicting the observed covariances (see Widaman, 1985, for a discussion of hierarchically nested covariance structure models). Because we anticipated substantial inhomogeneities of variance in the natural distributions of study variables, all structural equation models were estimated by generalized least squares (GLS), which has very similar properties and assumptions to maximum likelihood, but with the added virtue of producing the best linear unbiased estimators under conditions of either heteroskedasticity or autocorrelation (Berry & Feldman, 1985).

Results

Measurement Model

Memories

The items that composed the first factor of Suengas and Johnson's (1988) Memory Characteristics Questionnaire did not prove to be unifactorial in our analyses, which was not surprising given the differences between the present samples and the derivation sample of college students. Instead, we were able to

Table 21.2 Memory Factors: Item Content and Standardized Regression Coefficients

	Memory Factors			
Item Description	Reexperiencing	Nonvisual Sensory	Clarity	Affect
Intensity now	.661*			
Reexperiencing physical sensations	.709*			
Reexperiencing emotions–feelings	.828*			
Reexperiencing thoughts	.732*			
Frequency, thought about it	.168*		.491*	
Memory involves				
sound		.688*		
smell		.623*		
touch		.563*		
taste		.519*		
Memory for event			.884*	
Visual detail			.740*	
Black and white or color			.519*	
Vividness overall			.902*	
Order of events			−.382*	
Overall, I remember experiences			.905*	
Intensity, feelings at time			.377*	
Frequency, talked about it			.548*	
Affect, feelings at time				.879*
Affect now				.862*
Unexpected				.529*
Affect, consequences				.616*
Point of view				
Consequences, amount				

*$p < .05$.

discriminate four distinct but correlated factors and assign the six flashbulb items among them. These factors were confirmed in Sample 2, and all items loaded significantly on the same factors identified in Sample 1. A summary of the item content and the factor loadings is found in Table 21.2. Because confirmatory factor analysis is essentially a structural equations model, the matrix of factor loadings produced is equivalent to a traditional factor pattern rather than a factor structure (Bentler, 1989). The difference is simply that the elements of a factor pattern are expressed as standardized regression coefficients, or *beta* weights, rather than bivariate correlations (see Gorsuch, 1983). This distinction is important because the factors were oblique (intercorrelated), and this necessarily created indirect bivariate correlations between items that loaded uniquely on one particular factor and any other factors that happened to be correlated with it. Thus, reporting a factor structure of bivariate corrections for a set of intercor-

related factors might present the appearance of factorial complexity where there was none. A factor pattern distinguishes between cases of real factorial complexity and cases of indirect relationships attributable to nonzero off-diagonal elements in the matrix of factor intercorrelations between a set of oblique factors. For example, it can be seen in Table 21.2 that the frequency of recalling the memory was an item that truly loaded on two different factors.

The first factor, named *Reexperiencing* ($\alpha =$ .84), contained 5 items, including ratings of the emotional intensity experienced as the memory is recalled; the extent to which the remember feels like she is reexperiencing the physical sensations, emotions, and thoughts that characterized the original experience; and the frequency the memory has been recalled. The second factor, called *Nonvisual Sensory* ($\alpha = .68$), represented all the sensory modalities except vision. Therefore, it described the extent to which the memory involved sound, smell,

Table 21.3 Means and Standard Deviations for Memory Factors

| | Unpleasant | | | | Pleasant | |
| | Not Raped | | Raped | | | |
Factor	M	SD	M	SD	M	SD
Clarity						
Sample 1	48.7	8.6	42.3	9.7	51.3	5.8
Sample 2	48.3	8.0	41.2	9.0	51.1	5.9
Affect						
Sample 1	21.2	4.8	23.4	3.5	7.3	4.2
Sample 2	21.2	4.8	23.0	4.0	7.4	3.5
Reexperiencing						
Sample 1	22.7	6.8	20.7	7.0	24.0	5.4
Sample 2	22.3	6.6	20.4	6.8	23.3	
Nonvisual Sensory						
Sample 1	12.4	5.2	13.5	6.0	15.4	5.3
Sample 2	12.0	5.3	12.8	5.7	14.7	5.1

touch, and taste. The visual imagery of the memory loaded on the third factor, called *Clarity* ($\alpha = .78$). In addition to visual detail, it contained 8 items, including ratings of memory sharpness, color, vividness, emotional intensity of the feelings at the time of the event, meaningfulness of the order of events, and frequency the memory is thought and talked about. The final factor was labeled *Affect* ($\alpha = .84$) and contained 4 items, including ratings of the valence (positivity or negativity) of feelings at the time, the valence of the feelings now, the magnitude of consequences engendered as a result of the experience, and the unexpectedness of the event remembered. Only 2 items did not load significantly on any factor: whether the rememberer was an actor in the memory or a spectator and whether the consequences of the event remembered were positive or negative. The means and standard deviations of scores on the memory factors are presented in Table 21.3.

Symptoms

Investigators using clinical populations as opposed to college students have not replicated the single-factor solution for the Psychosomatic Symptom Checklist, and they were not unidimensional in our data (Attansio et al., 1984; Chibnall & Tait, 1989). Therefore, one of us

(Iris Bell), who is a medical doctor with extensive experience in behavioral medicine, sorted the checklist items into six theoretically based categories aggregating symptoms and diseases that share underlying mechanisms. The following symptom spectrums were specified: depression, cardiovascular spasm-stress, gastrointestinal stress, smooth muscle spasm-stress, skeletal muscle-joint, and immune dysfunction. After the factor structure was developed for the checklist items, the additional items we added were theoretically assigned among the factors. The factor structure obtained in Sample 1 was then confirmed in Sample 2. The factors were renamed on the basis of the item content that cross-validated with shorthand labels intended to signify the theoretical basis for symptom aggregation. The first factor was labeled *Depressive Symptoms* ($\alpha = .72$) and contained 13 items that reflected vegetative symptoms of the depression spectrum, including difficulty sleeping, fatigue, general stiffness, difficulty concentrating, weakness, grogginess, constipation, depression, and anxiety. The second factor was named *Vascular* ($\alpha = .52$), to reflect symptoms in the cardiovascular spasm-stress spectrum. Examples of the 9 items on this factor include migraine headache, headaches, dizziness, ringing in the ears, heart palpitations, joint pains, and nausea. The third factor was labeled *Respi-*

rator ($\alpha = .44$), to reflect the item content of the only items in the smooth muscle spasm spectrum that cross-validated—asthma and difficulty breathing. The fourth factor was labeled *Abdominal* ($\alpha = .53$) and included 9 gastrointestinal and pelvic symptoms, including ulcers, irritable bowel, stomach pain, indigestion, diarrhea, nausea, chronic pelvic pain, menstrual cramps, and burning in pelvic organs. The fifth factor, named *Skeletal* ($\alpha = .52$), contained 6 items, including arthritis, osteoporosis, backaches, general stiffness, joint pain, and clumsiness. The last factor was called *Immune* ($\alpha = .44$); it contained 6 items, including hay fever, allergies, asthma, itching, food or chemical reaction, and arthritis. All of the symptom items loaded significantly on at least one factor.

These alpha reliabilities must be viewed as minimal estimates because the symptom items were dichotomous, which attenuated correlations and resulted in underestimates using the traditional validity coefficients. The formulas for disattenuation were inappropriate here because they assume normality, and our symptom data were skewed. In practical terms, the use of confirmatory factor analysis made high internal consistency among the items unnecessary for two reasons. First, common factors use only the common variance between items, and, therefore, have a much higher reliability and validity than any single item. Also, the factors created by confirmatory factor analysis were no longer dichotomous once the composite was made, thus transcending limitations of measurement at the item level. Second, formal significance tests for the factor loadings of individual items were performed (see Table 21.4), so we did not need to rely on a composite index of item agreement. The item content, endorsement percentage, and factor loadings of the symptoms can be found in Table 21.4.

Structural Model

Figure 21.2 shows the final results of the restricted structural equations model. The path coefficients are standardized regression weights obtained by GLS estimation. Only the cross-validated path coefficients are shown. The correlated residuals among endogenous factors are not represented graphically in Figure 21.2 to avoid visual clutter, but they are presented later. Table 21.5 displays the statistical and practical goodness-of-fit indices for both the saturated and restricted structural equations models. Although the chi-square values for both models were statistically significant ($p < .01$), indicating that the models did not perfectly predict the covariances between the constructs, all three of the practical indices of fit were highly acceptable. The differences between the saturated and restricted structural models was statistically significant ($p < .05$) according to the chi-square criterion but virtually negligible for practical purposes according to all three Bentler-Bonnett fit indices. Thus, the restricted structural model performed almost as well as the saturated structural model in predicting the observed covariance and should be preferred as the more parsimonious of the two.

What follows is a description of the results of this model, considering the effects on each endogenous construct in the order of hypothesized causal priority. The nonsignificant causal pathways that were deleted from the restricted model were the following: (a) all 24 possible direct effects of the 4 Memory factors on the 6 Symptom factors, (b) 4 out of the 6 possible direct effects of Appraisal on the Symptom factors (two significant pathways remained), (c) all 6 possible direct effects of Valence on the Symptom factors, (d) the direct effect of Valence on the Reexperiencing factor (significant effects on the 3 other Memory factors remained), and (e) the direct effect of Rape on the Affect factor (significant effects on the 3 other Memory factors again remained).

Appraisal and Valence

Rape had direct effects on both Appraisal and Valence. Both effects were positive in direction, but the effect on Appraisal was much larger in magnitude than that on Valence. The effect on Appraisal justified our assumption that rape experiences predict, but are not identical with, cognitive appraisal of oneself as a rape victim. The smaller effect on Valence reflected the fact that most of the nonrape memories reported in our study were also unpleasant.

Table 21.4 Symptom Factors: Item Content, Endorsement Percentages, and Standardized Regression
Coefficients

Item Description	Symptom (%)	Health Factors					
		Depressive	Vascular	Respiratory	Abdominal	Skeletal	Immune
Difficulty concentrating	17.5	.496*					
Weakness	07.1	.483*					
Depression	22.7	.480*					−.036
Anxiety	31.3	.449*	.036				
Fatigue	52.5	.416*	.020				
Daytime grogginess	19.6	.406*					
Difficulty sleeping	39.6	.398*					
Clumsiness	06.9	.374*			−.066	−.088*	
Constipation	15.3	.270*	.028				
Dizziness	10.1	.222*	.209*				
General stiffness	20.2	.208*	−.003			.406*	
Eye pain with reading	04.5	.207*					
High blood pressure	09.1	.072*					
Migraine headache	14.2	−.155	.355*				
Heart palpitations	07.3		.298*				
Ringing in the ears	08.4		.294*				
Headaches	60.9		.280*				
Low thyroid	08.1		.132*				
Nausea	09.6		.132*		.287*		
Joint pain	21.5		.107*			.651*	
Diabetes	01.7		.068*				
Difficulty breathing	05.8			1.00*			
Asthma	08.8			.261*			.376*
Menstrual cramps	34.9			−.041	.157*		
Chronic pelvic pain	01.5			−.018	.090*		
Diarrhea	15.1			−.011	.379*		
Irritable bowel	11.2			−.007	.380*		
Stomach pain	19.5				.483*		
Indigestion	21.1				.419*		
Ulcers	05.6				.303*		
Burning sensation in pelvic organs	03.6				.262*		
Arthritis	11.8					.528*	.094*
Backaches	40.7					.348*	
Osteoporosis	01.8					.102*	
Hay fever	18.4			.029		−.016	.428*
Allergies	41.2						
Food or chemical reactions	04.7					.244*	
Itching skin or hives	11.8						.179*
Cancer	04.0						.024

*$p < .05$.

Memories

Appraisal had direct effects on all four Memory factors. These effects were all positive in direction, although not very large in magnitude. This finding supported the literature on memory reconstruction in that the retrospective cogni-tive construal of rape influenced, to some extent, *all* of the memory characteristics measured. However, the relatively modest magnitude of these effects on memory cautioned against overestimating the importance of construal of victimization in relation to what was actually experienced. Valence also had direct

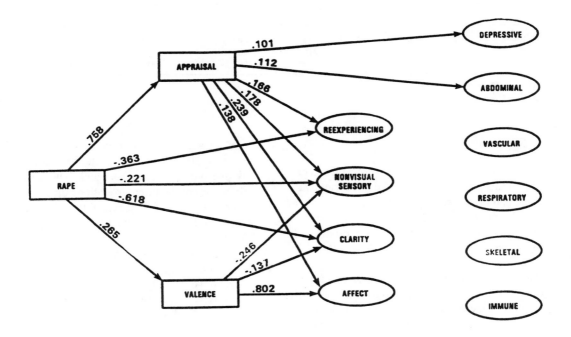

Figure 21.2. Memory Mediators of Rape

effects on three out of the four Memory factors. These effects, however, were inconsistent in both direction and magnitude: They were positive and large on the Affect factor but negative and somewhat smaller on both Clarity and Sensory. The large effect of Valence on memory Affect (.802) supported the adequacy of our dichotomous item differentiating pleasant from unpleasant experiences (the means on the Affect factors were 21 and 23, respectively, for those rating rape and other unpleasant experiences versus 7 for those rating pleasant experiences on the 28-point Affect factor). In addition, the finding affirmed our assumption that rape is almost universally perceived as an unpleasant experience and rejected the hypothesis that rape is affectively similar to any other unpleasant experience. Rape had indirect effects on the Memory factors that were mediated through Appraisal and Valence, respectively. The directions and magnitudes of these indirect effects can be obtained by simple multiplication of the successive direct effects.

In addition, Rape had direct effects on three out of four Memory factors that were not mediated through either Appraisal or Valence. These effects were on the Clarity, Reexperiencing, and Nonvisual Sensory Memory factors. All three effects were negative and large in magnitude, with the effect on the Clarity Memory factor being by far the largest. These findings indicated that the rape, as defined by legal-descriptive criteria, possessed an independent causal agency beyond that of the subjective cognitive construals. Thus, rape can directly influence memory without being rated by the individual as a perceived victimization. Furthermore, the magnitude of the direct effects of Rape also indicated that it contributed to the characteristics of memory over and above the effects typically created by unpleasant events in general. Rape memories, compared with other unpleasant memories, were less clear and vivid, were less likely to occur in a meaningful order, were less well remembered, and were less thought and talked about.

Table 21.5 Nested Factor-Analytic Structural Equation Models

Model	df	χ^2	NFI	NNFI	CFI
Restricted	1,832	4,150.313**	.983	.990	.991
Saturated	1,796	4,096.214	.984	.990	.991
Difference	36	54.099*	−.001	.000	.000

NOTE: For all models, $N = 1,757$.
*$p < .05$; **$p < .01$.

Symptoms

The Memory factors had no direct effects on Symptoms. Therefore, Rape, Appraisal, and Valence had no indirect effects on Symptoms that were mediated through Memories. Nevertheless, Appraisal did have direct effects on Symptoms that were not mediated through memories. These direct effects were on Depressive and Abdominal symptoms. Both effects were in the positive direction but rather weak in magnitude. Valence had no direct or indirect effects on either these or any other Symptoms. Therefore, Rape had indirect effects on these two Symptoms that were mediated through Appraisal but were not mediated through either Valence or the Memory factors.

Factor Intercorrelations

Because women who were raped may have been overrepresented in our sample of respondents (compared with the prevalence of rape in the general population), the unresidualized bivariate correlations among the Memory and Symptom factors were somewhat inflated by the spurious components attributable to the common rape experience. Residualized correlations represent those portions of the correlations between variables that remain unexplained by the model because they are not attributable to any specified causal influences. Thus, they are interrelationships between the endogenous constructs that are unrelated to any effects of the model predictors. For example, those between physical symptoms could be interpreted as the natural comorbidities of certain organic disorders for which purely biomedical explanations might exist. Residual correlations probably represent more generalizable estimates of the

"natural" correlations that might exist between these constructs independent of the particulars of any one type of experience, and they most closely represent the intercorrelations other investigators will find if they extend this work to populations other than rape victims. Tables 21.6 and 21.7 present the residual correlations between our two sets of endogenous constructs below the diagonal and the unresidualized correlations above the diagonal. No other residual correlations were specified in any of the models tested.

Overview of Effect Sizes

Using only the significant predictors, the coefficients of determination (R^2) for the Memory factors ranged in magnitude from very large, to substantial but moderate, to relatively small: .706 for the Affect factor, .267 for the Clarity factor, .068 for the Reexperiencing factor, .092 for the Sensory factor. On the other hand, the two direct effects of Appraisal on the Symptom factors were quite weak: .008 for the Depressive factor and .011 for the Abdominal factor. By multiplication of successive causal pathways, the indirect effects of Rape on these two Symptoms were weaker still. Because of the lack of significant predictors in the model, the coefficients of determination (R^2) for the other four Symptom factors were reduced statistically to zero. The direct and indirect effects of Valence and the four Memory factors that were tested on the Symptoms were also statistically nonsignificant.

Summing across all direct and indirect effects, the total effects of Rape on each of the memory factors were as follows: −.473 for Clarity, .317 for Affect, −.237 for Reexperiencing, and −.151 for Sensory. Because Rape had no

Table 21.6 Memory Factor Intercorrelation Matrix

Memory factor	1	2	3	4
1. Clarity	—	-.094*	.603*	.727*
2. Affect	.042	—	.073*	-.126*
3. Reexperiencing	.494*	.175*	—	.568*
4. Nonvisual Sensory	.724*	-.014	.521*	—

NOTE: The numbers above the diagonal are unresidualized correlations; those below the diagonal are residualized. See text for discussion of each type of correlation.

*p < .05.

Table 21.7 Physical Symptom Factor Intercorrelation Matrix

Physical Symptom Factor	1	2	3	4	5	6
1. Depressive	—	.780*	.248*	.608*	.314*	.373*
2. Vascular	.745*	—	.307*	.656*	.476*	.423*
3. Respiratory	.253*	.350*	—	.250*	.086*	.334*
4. Abdominal	.577*	.632*	.252*	—	.387*	.439*
5. Skeletal	.193*	.379*	.055	.322*	—	.251*
6. Immune	.323*	.309*	.307*	.363*	.159*	—

NOTE: The numbers above the diagonal are unresidualized correlations; those below the diagonal are residualized. See text for discussion of each type of correlation.

*p < .05.

significant direct effects on Symptoms, the total effects were reduced to the indirect effects of Rape that were mediated through Appraisal: .081 for Depressive and .085 for Abdominal.

Discussion

☐ Respondents described either rape or another memory under instructions to select "an intense life experience." Neurohormonal theories of the affect-memory relationship predict more clear and detailed memories under high levels of arousal, regardless of whether the emotions experienced were positive or negative. However, the rape memories reconstructed for the purpose of responding to the survey, and to a lesser extent the unpleasant memories in general, compared with memories for pleasant experiences, were rated as less clear and vivid, less visually detailed, less likely to occur in a meaningful order, less well remembered, less talked about, and less frequently recalled either voluntarily or involuntarily; with fewer sensory com-

ponents, including sound, smell, touch, and taste; and containing slightly less reexperiencing of the physical sensations, emotions, and thoughts that were present in the original incident. Thus, memories of events that were unexpected and highly negative both in their emotional valence and in their consequences were differentiated from memories of pleasant life events. The present data cannot reveal whether traumatized respondents possessed more detailed memories than they described, levels that might have been accessed by clinical treatments such as exposure (e.g., Foa, Rothbaum, Riggs, & Murdock, 1991) or by cognitive interviewing procedures (e.g., Fisher, McCauley, & Geiselman, 1994).

Rape victims often face a disclosure environment that holds them accountable for their assault, which could explain the reduced tendency to talk about their memories. The lower clarity and likelihood that the memory is thought about could be a demonstration that highly traumatized respondents were using cognitive avoidance, damping down some characteristics while remembering their trauma. However, any cognitive avoidance that was taking place was not very effective in reducing negative affect. These findings are consistent with a recent factor-analytic study of the PTSD symptom scale, which revealed that avoidance formed a factor with arousal and not with numbing (Foa, Riggs, & Gershyny, 1995). Thus, numbing of emotion might function independent of avoidance of thoughts about the trauma. The present results could be explained without avoidance and numbing through models of memory that emphasize multiple representations of the same experience (e.g., dual coding—Paivio, 1990; or fuzzy trace theory—Reyna & Brainerd, 1995). These theoretical perspectives all emphasize the potential for formation of multiple memories from a single incident, memories that may differ in accessibility to later recall and that functionally separate emotion from other components of the experience.

The results demonstrated that rape had direct effects on memory beyond what could be accounted for by its status as an unpleasant event and independent of how a woman cognitively appraised her experience as a victim. Existing literature establishes the primacy of subjectively felt threat over objectively rated severity in predicting rape aftereffects. However, memory characteristics were better predicted by the event itself as opposed to the cognitive appraisal of victimization. It was simply *not* the case that those who merely denied sexual victimization were identical in memory characteristics to those who never experienced rape. On the other hand, the findings suggest that the affective component of construal exerted major effects on the qualities of recall.

The depth of measurement in the present study was limited by the necessity to keep the survey short to maximize response rate. There are a number of other pieces of information that would have contributed to the interpretation of the findings. For example, the lower intensity of the rape memories could relate to the fact that some victims were probably intoxicated at the time of their rape. Police files reveal the high frequency with which victims of and witnesses to *all* crimes are under the influence of alcohol (Yuille & Tollestrup, 1990). However, alcohol-

memory studies designed for forensic relevance do not explain the vague and hazy memories for intense unpleasant events in the present study. Witnesses of staged crimes who were under the influence of alcohol provided somewhat less scorable detail than nondrinking controls, but their level of accuracy or clarity was similar (Yuille & Tollestrup, 1990). Other potential influences on our results include possible differences between the age at which the rape occurred versus the other unpleasant incidents and differences in the amount of time that had elapsed since the experience. Unfortunately, we cannot characterize any further the content of the nonrape memories, nor can we substantiate that the types of memories were equivalent in developmental stage or recency. Furthermore, the influence of demographic variables was not modeled in the present study. A final limitation is the lack of effects on physical symptoms, which could be related to the choice of measurement instrument. Our ongoing research involves in-depth face-to-face interviews and multioperationalized assessment of physical, social, and psychological health in both a cross-sectional and a prospective sample. Therefore, we will have many additional variables that will allow us to test a number of relevant effects within the current model of memory, evaluate some competing explanations for our findings, and examine a broader range of outcome phenomena. The contributions of the present study include the exploration of the responses of real victims describing events they actually experienced, the use of large community samples, the inclusion of intense pleasant memories along with unpleasant ones, the assessment of a range of memory phenomena, and the relevance of the results to theories of emotional memory, cognitive avoidance, and numbing.

It is commonly assumed that one's strongest memories are those central to self-identity (Neisser & Fivush, 1994). If so, then rape memories, although long-lasting, would be predicted on the basis of their lower clarity to be less important than nonrape unpleasant memories and pleasant memories for self-concept, attributions, beliefs, and role constructs. This assertion is contrary to clinical experience with sexual assault survivors, which clearly reveals the severe crisis in meaning for the victim that is triggered. Thus, the present results argue for an expanded agenda of research on the inter-relationships between social cognitions and traumatic memories and the role of both sets of variables as mediators between trauma and outcomes.

References

Attansio, V., Andraski, F., Blanchard, E. B., & Arena, J. G. (1984). Psychometric properties of the SUNYA Revision of the Psychosomatic Symptom Checklist. *Journal of Behavioral Medicine, 7,* 247-257.

Bentler, P. M. (1989). *EQS: Structural equations program manual.* Los Angeles: BMDP Statistical Software.

Bentler, P. M., & Bonnett, D. G. (1980). Significance tests and goodness of fit in the analysis of covariance structures. *Psychological Bulletin, 88,* 588-606.

Berry, W. D., & Feldman, S. (1985). *Multiple regression in practice.* Beverly Hills, CA: Sage.

Bohannon, J. N., & Symons, V. L. (1992). Flashbulb memories: Confidence, consistency, and quantity. In E. Winograd & U. Neisser (Eds.), *Affect and accuracy in recall: Studies of "flashbulb" memories* (pp. 65-91). New York: Cambridge University Press.

Burnam, M. A., Stein, J. A., Golding, J., Siegel, J. M., Sorenson, S. B., Forsythe, A. B., & Telles, C. A. (1988). Sexual assault and mental disorders in a community sample. *Journal of Consulting and Clinical Psychology, 56,* 843-850.

Cahill, L., Prins, B., Weber, M., & McGaugh, J. L. (1994). Beta-adrenergic activation and memory for emotional events. *Nature, 371,* 702-704.

Chibnall, J. T., & Tait, R. C. (1989). The Psychosomatic Symptom Checklist revisited: Reliability and validity in a chronic pain population. *Journal of Behavioral Medicine, 12,* 297-307.

Christianson, S. A. (1992). Emotional stress and eyewitness memory: A critical review. *Psychological Bulletin, 112,* 284-309.

Christianson, S. A., & Loftus, E. F. (1991). Remembering emotional events: The fate of detailed information. *Cognition and Emotion, 5,* 81-108.

Christianson, S. A., Loftus, E. F., Hoffman, H., & Loftus, G. R. (1991). Eye fixations and memory for emotional events. *Journal of Experimental Psychology: Learning, Memory, and Cognition, 17,* 693-701.

Cohen, J. (1988). *Statistical power analysis for the behavioral sciences* (2nd ed). Hillsdale, NJ: Lawrence Erlbaum.

Cohen, J. (1990). Things I have learned (so far). *American Psychologist, 45,* 1304-1312.

Cohen, J., & Cohen, P. (1983). *Applied multiple regression/ correlation analysis for the behavioral sciences.* Hillsdale, NJ: Lawrence Erlbaum.

Crowne, D. P., & Marlowe, D. A. (1960). A new scale of social desirability independent of psychopathology. *Journal of Consulting and Clinical Psychology, 24,* 349-354.

Cutshall, J., & Yuille, J. C. (1992). Field studies of eyewitness memory of actual crimes. In E. Winograd & U. Neisser (Eds.), *Affect and accuracy in recall: Studies of "flashbulb" memories* (pp. 97-124). New York: Cambridge University Press.

Dillman, D. A. (1978). *Mail and telephone surveys: The total design method.* New York: Wiley-Interscience.

Dunn, S. F., & Gilchrist, V. J. (1993). Sexual assault. *Primary Care, 20,* 3184-3189.

Fisher, R. P., McCauley, M. R., & Geiselman, R. E. (1994). Improving eyewitness testimony with the cognitive interview. In D. F. Ross, J. D. Read, & M. P. Toglia (Eds.), *Adult eyewitness testimony: Current trends and developments* (pp. 245-269). New York: Cambridge University Press.

Foa, E. B., Riggs, D. S., & Gershyny, B. S. (1995). Arousal, numbing, and intrusion: Symptom structure of PTSD following assault. *American Journal of Psychiatry, 152,* 116-120.

Foa, E. B., Rothbaum, B. O., Riggs, D. S., & Murdock, T. B. (1991). Treatment of posttraumatic stress disorder in rape victims: A comparison between cognitive-behavioral procedures and counseling. *Journal of Consulting and Clinical Psychology, 59,* 715-723.

Gilbert, N. (1991, June 27). The campus rape scare. *Wall Street Journal,* p. A10.

Gilbert, N. (1994, June 29). The wrong response to rape. *Wall Street Journal,* p. A18.

Girelli, S. A., Resick, P. A., Marhoefer-Dvorak, S., & Hutter, C. K. (1986). Subjective distress and violence during rape: Their effects on long-term fear. *Violence and Victims, 1,* 35-45.

Golding, J. M. (1994). Sexual assault history and physical health in randomly selected Los Angeles women. *Health Psychology, 13,* 130-138.

Gorsuch, R. L. (1983). *Factor analysis.* Hillsdale, NJ: Lawrence Erlbaum.

Hendricks-Mathews, M. K. (1993). Survivors of abuse: Health care issues. *Primary Care, 20,* 391-406.

Kilpatrick, D. G., Saunders, B. E., Veronen, L. J., Best, C. L., & Von, J. M. (1987). Criminal victimization: Lifetime prevalence, reporting to police, and psychological impact. *Crime & Delinquency, 33,* 470-489.

Kimerling, R., & Calhoun, K. S. (1994). Somatic symptoms, social support, and treatment seeking among sexual assault victims. *Journal of Consulting and Clinical Psychology, 62,* 333-340.

Koss, M. P. (1985). The hidden rape victim: Personality, attitudinal, and situational characteristics. *Psychology of Women Quarterly, 9,* 193-212.

Koss, M. P., & Heslet, L. (1992). Somatic consequences of violence against women. *Archives of Family Medicine, 1,* 53-59.

Koss, M. P., Koss, P. G., & Woodruff, W. J. (1991). Deleterious effects of criminal victimization on women's health and medical utilization. *Archives of Internal Medicine, 151,* 342-347.

Koss, M. P., Tromp, S., & Tharan, M. (1995). Traumatic memories: Empirical findings, clinical and forensic implications. *Clinical Psychology: Research and Practice, 2,* 111-132.

Koss, M. P., Woodruff, W. J., & Koss, P. G. (1991). Relation of criminal victimization to health perceptions among women medical patients. *Journal of Consulting and Clinical Psychology, 58,* 147-152.

LeDoux, J. E. (1994, June). Emotion, memory and the brain. *Scientific American, 270,* 50-57.

Neisser, U., & Fivush, R. (Eds.). (1994). *The remembering self: Construction and accuracy in the self-narrative.* New York: Cambridge University Press.

Norris, F. H., & Kaniasty, K. (1991). The psychological experience of crime: A test of the mediating role of beliefs in explaining the distress of victims. *Journal of Social and Clinical Psychology, 10,* 239-261.

Paivio, A. (1990). *Mental representations: A dual coding approach.* New York: Oxford University Press.

Reyna, V. F., & Brainerd, C. J. (1995). Fuzzy-trace theory: An interim synthesis. *Learning and Individual Differences, 7,* 1-75.

Sales, E., Baum, M., & Shore, B. (1984). Victim readjustment following assault. *Journal of Social Issues, 37,* 5-27.

Searles, P., & Berger, R. J. (1987). The current status of rape reform legislation: An examination of state statutes. *Women's Rights Law Reporter, 10,* 25-43.

Suengas, A. G., & Johnson, M. K. (1988). Qualitative effects of rehearsal on memories for perceived and imagined complex events. *Journal of Experimental Psychology: General, 117,* 377-389.

Wagenaar, W. A., & Groeneweg, J. (1990). The memory of concentration camp survivors. *Applied Cognitive Psychology, 4,* 77-87.

Widaman, K. F. (1985). Hierarchically nested covariance structure models for multitrait-multimethod data. *Applied Psychological Measurement, 9,* 1-26.

Winograd, E., & Neisser, U. (Eds.). (1992). *Affect and accuracy in recall: Studies of "flashbulb" memories.* New York: Cambridge University Press.

Wolfe, J., Schnurr, P. P., Brown, P. J., & Furey, J. (1994). Posttraumatic stress disorder and war-zone exposure as correlates of perceived health in female Vietnam War veterans. *Journal of Consulting and Clinical Psychology, 62,* 1091-1095.

Yuille, J. C., & Tollestrup, P. A. (1990). Some effects of alcohol on eyewitness memory. *Journal of Applied Psychology, 75,* 268-273.

22

Defense Styles of Women Who Have Experienced Child Sexual Abuse

A Comparative Community Study

Sarah E. Romans
Judy L. Martin
Eleanor M. Morris

Intense research over the past 10 years has brought substantial progress in our understanding of the phenomenon of child sexual abuse (CSA) and its variable impacts on those involved. We now have a consensus about its prevalence, with a firm understanding that it occurs in most societies that have been studied (Finkelhor, 1994). It is clear that child sexual abuse is often followed by adverse psychological and social effects (Beitchman et al., 1992; Finkelhor & Dziuba-Leatherman, 1994; Green, 1993; Mullen, Martin, Anderson, Romans, & Herbison, 1993, 1994, 1995). Attention from clinicians, researchers, and policymakers is now turning to learning about the ways in which victims of child sexual abuse cope with its impacts. Adult consequences are shaped by the coping strategies employed by individuals both during the trauma and subsequently. Individuals generate coping thoughts and actions to deal with stress; these thoughts and actions include how people appraise given situations and judge their resources for dealing with stressors.

There is more to the accurate recall of a past event than having an intact neuropsychological system for the encoding and retrieval of long-term memories. There is currently much interest in exploring the hypothesis that active forgetting may be adaptive in certain situations for certain individuals. Theories about coping and defense styles have evolved over the years, but there is still no agreement on how these mental mechanisms can best be assessed. Recently, researchers, particularly in North America, have focused a great deal of attention on dissociation, one postulated defensive mechanism, and its link to child sexual abuse (Chu & Dill, 1990; Coons, 1994; Herman, Russell, & Trocki, 1986; Irwin, 1994; Kirby, Chu, & Dill, 1993; Roesler & McKenzie, 1994; Saxe et al., 1993; van der Kolk & Perry, 1991; Zlotnick et al., 1994, 1995). These researchers have used as their subjects patients from hospital wards and out-patient clinics, thus their studies are subject to uncertain bias arising from the treatment referral process.

Dissociation has been defined as the temporary, drastic modification of one's character or sense of personal identity to avoid emotional distress (Vaillant, 1971). When used excessively, dissociation impairs memory for the traumatic event. However, dissociation is only one of a number of defense or coping mechanisms that may impair the encoding of a memory, preventing its accurate later recall. Others that may also act to impair memory are suppression, denial, and autistic fantasy.

The concept of a hierarchy of defenses or coping strategies first elaborated by Anna Freud was subsequently developed empirically by George Vaillant and his coworkers on the Harvard men's study (Freud, 1937; Vaillant, 1971). In a series of papers, this group showed that maturity of defense style is linked to better physical and psychological health, career success, higher quality of intimate relationships, and even the ability to relax fully and take a vacation. These researchers have also shown that defenses mature as individuals age. They used a method of indirectly assessing defenses from vignettes collected during the semistructured part of their research interviews. Although they took care to ensure satisfactory interrater reliability, the assessments were made by the interviewing research team alone. This method is time-consuming and therefore expensive for use in large-scale research projects.

Recently, a new self-rated questionnaire has been developed that purports to document an individual's coping style. This instrument, the Defense Style Questionnaire (DSQ), was developed by Bond and colleagues and has subsequently been modified both by Vaillant's group and by others (Andrews, Pollock, &

Stewart, 1989; Andrews, Singh, & Bond, 1993; Bond, Gardner, Christian, & Sigal, 1983; Vaillant, Bond, & Vaillant, 1986). Although it has not yet been widely used, some normative data have been published (Andrews et al., 1989). Also, evidence has been produced showing that patients with anxiety disorders have less mature styles than the general population and family practice attenders, that maturity of defense style varies with severity of neurotic and personality disorder, and that recovery from depression is associated with a decrease in immature styles (Akkerman, Carr, & Lewin, 1992; Andrews et al., 1989; Sammallahti, Aalberg, & Pentinsaari, 1994). These early results look promising, and suggest that the instrument may be valuable in the assessment of coping in a range of nonclinical groups.

The Otago Women's Health Survey study group has been examining coping styles in a group of women who reported child sexual abuse and a control group of women without such experiences. As part of this investigation, the DSQ was administered in the follow-up wave. The project aimed to quantify the frequency of defenses likely to impair accurate memory for trauma in these two groups.

Method

☐ The follow-up Otago study reinterviewed, in 1995, as many subjects as possible who were first studied 6 years earlier. In the original 1989 Otago Women's Health Survey CSA study, two groups of women, one made up of women who reported child sexual abuse before the age of 16 and a control group of women who did not report such abuse, were assessed by postal questionnaire and personal interview on a wide range of developmental and psychosocial variables (Anderson, Martin, Mullen, Romans, & Herbison, 1993; Mullen et al., 1993). Both groups had been randomly selected from the electoral rolls. Women who had participated in the first project were recontacted by mail and telephone and reinterviewed by a team of five interviewers who were selected for their ability to handle sensitive material. The main focus of this project was to find out how women cope with child sexual abuse and other adverse developmental events. The data reported here all come from the 1995 interview set. The child sexual abuse was subtyped into three groups, according to the most severe or intrusive events the subject recalled experiencing: (a) nongenital CSA, which included noncontact abuse; (b) genital CSA, but excluding intercourse; and (c) attempted and completed intercourse.

The Defense Style Questionnaire was used to assess psychological coping strategies habitually used by the research subjects (Andrews et al., 1993). In its current form, the DSQ consists of 40 items arranged in 20 pairs, each pair purporting to assess one defense. The subject is presented with statements with which he or she is asked to agree or disagree, using a 9-point Likert scale. The scoring was rearranged so that a higher score indicated stronger agreement and therefore greater use of that particular defense. The 20 defenses are sorted into one of three maturity categories as follows:

- 4 *mature* defenses (humor, suppression, sublimation, anticipation)

- 4 *neurotic* defenses (reaction formation, idealization, pseudoaltruism, undoing) (These intermediate-level mental mechanisms are considered common in healthy adults when under stress.)

- 12 *immature* defenses (rationalization, fantasy, displacement, dissociation, isolation, devaluation, splitting, denial, passive aggression, somatization, acting out, projection)

A combination score was calculated by summing all items for each of the three defense categories: mature, neurotic, and immature.

Statistical Analyses

The strength of endorsement for individual DSQ items by the CSA and control groups of subjects was compared using Student's *t* test; one-way ANOVAs, with Duncan's multiple-range post hoc test, were used to compare the mean scores of subjects subdivided by CSA type.

Results

□ A reasonable response rate of 71.2% of those previously interviewed was again achieved. A total of 354 women were interviewed in the follow-up phase; complete data were obtained for 173 from the group reporting child sexual abuse and 178 from the non-CSA control group. Of the women in the CSA group, 40 reported nongenital CSA, 80 reported genital contact, and 53 reported intercourse CSA (24 attempted and 29 completed).

Individual DSQ Items

Of the 40 DSQ individual items, 10 were scored differently by the CSA and non-CSA groups. All except one came from the Immature category and all of these were endorsed more frequently by CSA subjects. The final item was a Mature item (sublimation) and was endorsed more often by the non-CSA control women. Table 22.1 provides a list of the items that differed between the two subject groups.

Of those likely to affect memory for distant traumatic events, both autistic fantasy items were found more frequently in the CSA group of subjects. There were no differences for denial, suppression or, more importantly, for dissociation. The mean scores for the dissociation items were as follows:

1. "I ignore all danger as if I were Superman." For the CSA subjects, $M = 2.50$, $SD = 1.77$; for the non-CSA group, $M = 2.65$, $SD = 1.96$; $1- < 0.01$ *ns*.

2. "I have special talents . . ." For the CSA subjects, $M = 3.71$, $SD = 1.94$; for the non-CSA group, $M = 3.39$, $SD - 1.95$.

Mean Scores for DSQ Maturity Category

Comparing the whole group of CSA subjects with the non-CSA control subjects, there were no differences in mean scores for the mature or immature categories of defenses. There was a trend at the 10% level for a higher mean score for neurotic defenses for the CSA group: Neu-

Table 22.1 Individual DSQ Items With Mean Endorsement Scores That Differ Between CSA and Control Subjects

Item	Defense	Type	Non-CSA Controls n = 178		CSA n = 171		t	p
			Mean	(SD)	Mean	(SD)		
I work out my anxiety through doing something constructive and creative like painting or woodwork.	sublimation	mature	5.7	(2.2)	5.1	(2.5)	2.5	0.012
People tend to mistreat me.	projection	immature	2.2	(1.5)	2.9	(1.1)	-3.7	<0.001
I'm a very inhibited person.	devaluation	immature	3.3	(2.0)	3.8	(2.1)	-2.0	0.05
I get more satisfaction from my fantasies than from my real life.	autistic fantasy	immature	2.1	(1.7)	2.6	(2.0)	-2.4	0.02
I work more things out in my daydreams than in my real life.	autistic fantasy	immature	2.7	(1.8)	3.1	(2.1)	-2.1	0.03
I get openly aggressive when I feel hurt.	acting out	immature	3.1	(2.0)	3.9	(2.5)	-3.2	0.002
I am sure I get a raw deal from life.	projection	immature	2.5	(2.0)	3.3	(2.3)	-3.2	0.001
Doctors never really understand what is wrong with me.	displacement	immature	2.6	(2.0)	3.1	(2.2)	-2.3	0.02
When I'm depressed or anxious, eating makes me feel better	displacement	immature	4.1	(2.6)	4.7	(2.7)	-2.2	0.03
No matter how much I complain, I never get a satisfactory response.	passive aggression	immature	3.3	(1.8)	3.8	(2.3)	-2.6	0.01

NOTE: A higher score indicates greater use of that defense.

Table 22.2 Mean DSQ Category Score by CSA Subtype

CSA	n	Mature	Neurotic	Immature
No CSA	178	5.3, SD 1.3	4.3, SD 1.1	3.2, SD 0.9
Nongenital CSA	39	5.5, SD 1.2	4.4, SD 1.3	3.3, SD 0.9
Genital CSA	80	5.2, SD 1.2	4.4, SD 1.2	3.4, SD 0.9
Intercourse	54	5.2, SD 1.4	4.6, SD 1.3	3.6, SD 1.2
Test statistic		ns	ns	T = 2.18, df 350, p = 0.09

rotic CSA 4.46 ± 1.23, non-CSA 4.30 ± 1.14, 1 – 1.31, df 348n, $p = 0.09$."

Comparing the CSA group by CSA subtype and the control group, the results of the one-way ANOVA revealed that only the immature category showed differences when analyzed by type of CSA (see Table 22.2). Women reporting the most intrusive CSA—that is, attempted or completed intercourse—showed a trend at the 0.10 level of significance toward a higher use of immature defenses than the rest of the subjects. The mean immature DSQ score for intercourse CSA (both attempted and completed) was 3.6 ± 1.2, greater than the other two types of CSA (non-genital and genital-non-intercourse) and the control group mean. When the ANOVA was repeated with six types of CSA, and attempted intercourse CSA entered separately from completed intercourse CSA, the F ratio was 2.69, $p = 0.015$, with completed CSA differing significantly from the other CSA types.

Age and Maturity of Defenses

The women were divided into decades by age. For both the CSA subjects and the control women, immature defenses became less frequent with age ($F = 2.54$, $p = 0.04$, and $F = 2.62$, $p = 0.04$, respectively). For the CSA women, those up to the age of 30 had higher immature defense scores than women aged either 30 to 39 or 50 to 59 years old. For the control women, those from 25 to 39 years old and from 40 to 49 had a higher use of immature defenses than did women over the age of 60. There was no association between age and the mean score for mature or neurotic defenses.

Finally, there were no differences in DSQ scores, either total or subcategory, for those

women who gave consistent accounts of their experiences of childhood sexual abuse and those few who altered their accounts.

Discussion

☐ The validity of these findings depends to a large extent on the adequacy of the DSQ: how good it is at detecting what are postulated to be usually unconscious processes outside of the individual's awareness. Can an individual accurately report on her or his own habitual coping strategies? In justification of the self-report structure of this instrument, it can be said that when people's defenses fail, they become aware of their habitual ways of handling conflict (Andrews et al., 1989). Often, people who know an individual well will comment on how she or he is dealing with a conflict, drawing attention to what they have noticed about the individual's usual mental mechanisms. Finally, in a study such as this, which attempts to shed light on childhood events from an adult perspective, what are the relationships between the coping strategies used in childhood and those activated in adult life?

Some of the DSQ items seem relatively slight in importance and lacking in the detail needed to lead to a considered judgment about the maturity of coping. For example, if a woman who has experienced childhood sexual abuse agrees that people tend to mistreat her, this can be viewed as an accurate comparison of her past experience to that of others, rather than the immature defense of projection. Coping theories have been criticized for paying inadequate attention to the relative powerlessness of women in society and the ways in which sex discrimination may limit the coping strategies available to women (Banyard & Graham-Bermann, 1993). The DSQ, arising as it does in part from a psychodynamic therapy tradition that many find pejorative, may not be free of the accusation of gender insensitivity. The DSQ can best be viewed as a broad but superficial screen for coping style that has the advantage of being free of the therapist subjectivity of information collected in the clinic. Future studies might profitably combine both self- and clinician sources of information.

Assuming acceptable DSQ validity, the characteristic difference between the defense style profiles of the two groups was increased use by the CSA subjects of the immature defenses of autistic fantasy, displacement, projection, passive aggressiveness, acting out, and devaluation. For only the first two of these did both of the pair of items depicting that defense show statistical differences; for the remaining immature defenses, only one of the pair was used more frequently by CSA subjects. This suggests a patchy rather than a global increase in immature defenses. In addition, one mature defense differed, but sublimation was seen more frequently in the control subjects. No differences were found for the neurotic defenses.

Only one of the defenses thought likely to impair memory was more frequent in the CSA group. These included both autistic fantasy items. It is noteworthy that the mean scores for dissociation and for the mature defense of suppression failed to differ between the two subject groups. It appears that although CSA is followed by a greater use of immature defenses in adult life in women randomly selected from the general community, these are not the defenses that particularly affect memory. In attempting to understand what this means, it should be noted that the women in this random community sample were selected on their affirmation of childhood sexual abuse at the interview. Any woman who had experienced childhood sexual abuse but had no recollection of it would not appear in the CSA group. However, this aspect of the methodology is unlikely to explain fully the failure to find more dissociation and suppression among the CSA group than among the nonabused.

Autistic fantasy, sometimes called *schizoid fantasy,* refers to the tendency to use fantasy for the purpose of conflict resolution and gratification, and has been described as "serving to obliterate the overt expression of aggressive or sexual impulses towards others" (Vaillant, 1971). In that it involves an active turning away of conscious attention from the events occurring at the time, it shares a number of common features with dissociation. Being less dramatic, it may more frequently differentiate between traumatized and nontraumatized subjects. Given that it has emerged in this study as important when dissociation failed to be significant, further study is warranted. Does the choice of fantasy protect the trauma victim against subsequent anxiety, and what is the likely outcome of its increased use? What is the exact effect on memory for past events? This latter question, too, will need to be examined scientifically. The research preoccupation with dissociation needs to be balanced by focus on other cognitive coping strategies. Certainly, many CSA subjects report clinically that they developed strategies early for blocking out of awareness what was happening to them; this has often been interpreted as dissociation, but more accurately refers to the defensive use of fantasy. Dissociation may be more handicapping in adult life and likely to be found in those referred for specialist treatment and who feature in the clinical studies cited earlier in this chapter.

These results also suggest an impact of severe childhood sexual abuse on the maturity of defense habitually used by adult women. This conclusion applies only for those who had reported the most intrusive experiences of child sexual abuse: completed intercourse. These women used more immature defenses. However, they were not less likely to use mature defenses. Mature and immature defenses are orthogonally related, confirmed by a lack of correlation ($r = -0.016$, *ns*). As with the control non-CSA subjects, their use of immature defenses decreased with increasing age.

There are major difficulties in studying the accuracy of memory for significant life trauma many years after the events. Only indirect evidence can be gathered that can complement information accruing from the simulated memory studies in the laboratory. The strength of the study reported here comes from the nonclinical nature of its subjects with all severities of abuse, including a significant minority of the subjects who had experienced severe childhood sexual abuse. The results show that the increased rate of dissociation reported by studies using inpatient and outpatient samples did not pertain in this community study. Dissociation may be linked to problems in adult life that lead to referral to specialist services, rather than to the trauma itself. More study of abused subjects who do not choose to seek treatment may shed light on adaptive ways of coping with childhood trauma such as child sexual abuse. An increased use of fantasy as a coping strategy may be significant. These insights could then inform treatment efforts.

References

Akkerman, K., Carr, V., & Lewin, T. (1992). Changes in ego defenses with recovery from depression. *Journal of Nervous and Mental Disease, 180,* 634-638.

Anderson, J. C., Martin, J. L., Mullen, P. E., Romans, S. E., & Herbison, P. (1993). Prevalence of childhood sexual abuse experiences in a community sample of women. *Journal of the American Academy of Child and Adolescent Psychiatry, 32,* 911-919.

Andrews, G., Pollock, C., & Stewart, G. (1989). The determination of defense style by questionnaire. *Archives of General Psychiatry, 46,* 455-460.

Andrews, G., Singh, M., & Bond, M. (1993). The Defense Style Questionnaire. *Journal of Nervous and Mental Disease, 181,* 246-256.

Banyard, V. L., & Graham-Bermann, S. A. (1993). Can women cope? A gender analysis of theories of coping with stress. *Psychology of Women Quarterly, 17,* 303-318.

Beitchman, J. H., Zucker, K. J., Hood, J. E., da Costa, G. A., Akman, D., & Cassavia, E. (1992). A review of the long-term effects of child sexual abuse. *Child Abuse & Neglect, 16,* 101-118.

Bond, M., Gardner, S., Christian, J., & Sigal, J. J. (1983). Empirical study of self-rated defense styles. *Archives of General Psychiatry, 40,* 333-338.

Chu, J. A., & Dill, D. L. (1990). Dissociative symptoms in relation to childhood physical and sexual abuse. *American Journal of Psychiatry, 147,* 887-892.

Coons, P. M. (1994). Confirmation of childhood abuse in child and adolescent cases of multiple personality disorder and dissociative disorder not otherwise specified. *Journal of Nervous and Mental Disease, 182,* 461-464.

Finkelhor, D. (1994). The international epidemiology of child sexual abuse. *Child Abuse & Neglect, 18,* 409-417.

Finkelhor, D., & Dziuba-Leatherman, J. (1994). Children as victims of violence: A national survey. *Pediatrics, 94,* 413-420.

Freud, A. (1937). *Ego and the mechanisms of defense.* London: Hogarth.

Green, A. H. (1993). Child sexual abuse: Immediate and long-term effects and intervention. *Journal of the American Academy of Child and Adolescent Psychiatry, 32,* 890-902.

Herman, J., Russell, D., & Trocki, K. (1986). Long-term effects of incestuous abuse in childhood. *American Journal of Psychiatry, 143,* 1293-1296.

Irwin, H. (1994). Proneness to dissociation and traumatic childhood events. *Journal of Nervous and Mental Disease, 182,* 456-460.

Kirby, J. S., Chu, J. A., & Dill, D. L. (1993). Correlates of dissociative symptomatology in patients with physical and sexual abuse histories. *Comprehensive Psychiatry, 34,* 258-263.

Mullen, P. E., Martin, J. L., Anderson, J. C., Romans, S. E., & Herbison, G. P. (1993). Child sexual abuse and mental health in adult life. *British Journal of Psychiatry, 163,* 721-732.

Mullen, P. E., Martin, J. L., Anderson, J. C., Romans, S. E., & Herbison, G. P. (1994). The effect of child sexual abuse on social, interpersonal and sexual function in adult life. *British Journal of Psychiatry, 165,* 35-47.

Mullen, P. E., Martin, J. L., Anderson, J. C., Romans, S. E., & Herbison, G. P. (1995). The long-term impact of the physical, emotional, and sexual abuse of children: A community study. *Child Abuse & Neglect, 20,* 7-21.

Roesler, T., & McKenzie, C. D. (1994). Effects of childhood trauma on psychological adjustment in adults sexually abused as children. *Journal of Nervous and Mental Disease, 182,* 145-150.

Sammallahti, P., Aalberg, V., & Pentinsaari, J.-P. (1994). Does defense style vary with severity of mental disorder? *Acta Psychiatrica Scandinavica, 90,* 290-294.

Saxe, G. N., van der Kolk, B. A., Berkowitz, R., Chinman, G., Hall, K., Lieberg, G., & Schwartz, J. (1993). Dissociative disorders in psychiatric inpatients. *American Journal of Psychiatry, 150,* 1037-1042.

Vaillant, G. E. (1971). Theoretical hierarchy of adaptive ego mechanisms: A thirty year follow-up of 30 men selected for psychological health. *Archives of General Psychiatry, 24,* 107-118.

Vaillant, G. E., Bond, M., & Vaillant, C. (1986). An empirically validated hierarchy of defense mechanisms. *Archives of General Psychiatry, 43,* 786-794.

van der Kolk, B. A., & Perry, J. C. (1991). Childhood origins of self-destructive behavior. *American Journal of Psychiatry, 148,* 1665-1671.

Zlotnick, C., Bergin, A., Shea, T., Pearlstein, T., Simpson, E., & Costello, E. (1994). The relationship between characteristics of sexual abuse and dissociative experiences. *Comprehensive Psychiatry, 35,* 465-470.

Zlotnick, C., Shea, T., Zakriski, A., Costello, E., Pearlstein, T., & Simpson, E. (1995). Stressors and close relationships during childhood and dissociative experiences in survivors of sexual abuse among psychiatric inpatient women. *Comprehensive Psychiatry, 36,* 207-212.

23

Toddlers Remember Quake Trauma

Anait G. Azarian
Lewis P. Lipsitt
Thomas W. Miller
Vitali G. Skriptchenko-Gregorian

There is currently a tremendous amount of interest regarding young children's ability to remember traumatic experiences. This issue has come under public scrutiny as a result of the rapidly increasing number of cases in which children are called to testify as witnesses to violence, or in which adults testify about abuse in childhood (Ceci & Bruck, 1995; Goldstein & Farmer, 1993; Goodman & Helgelson, 1985). Many professionals, clinicians, and academicians have addressed the controversy concerning the reliability of retrieved traumatic childhood memories after the passage of time (e.g., Loftus, 1991, 1993; Terr, 1990, 1994). There have been many attempts to verify the clinical findings on early childhood memories through the use of controlled laboratory experiments with groups of children and adults (Fivush & Hamond, 1990; Kihlstrom & Haraskiewicz, 1982; Myers, Clifton, & Clarkson, 1987; Pillemer & White, 1989; Winograd & Killinger, 1983). Unfortunately, even very similar studies have produced disparities in results (Sheingold & Tenney, 1982; Usher & Neisser, 1993).

One question that contributes to the difficulty of interpreting experimental laboratory findings, data, and clinical cases is whether memories are retained in unchanged form or undergo developmental modifications that reflect children's maturation, including changes in brain structure, memory reconstruction, and adults' interventions. Furthermore, the traumatic event itself may also influence the manner in which a child perceives and understands that event (Pynoos & Eth, 1984). Many clinicians note that experimental research that is reliant on children and students in psychology labs is unable to simulate real instances of trauma. Being lost in a big shopping mall, listening to reports of JFK's assassination, or watching reportage of the *Challenger* space shuttle explosion cannot replicate such profound personal traumas as abuse, kidnapping, or experiencing a plane crash or a natural disaster.

In this chapter, we report and discuss data on toddlers' traumatic memories. These data were fortuitously obtained after the devastating 1988 Armenian earthquake. To our knowledge, no research focused on memory for traumatic events has examined memory in young survivors of natural disasters. Traumatic memories observed in young survivors of a large-scale disaster may in fact provide valuable information that may help us to understand the manner in which children remember profound events.

Two of the authors of the present study are very well acquainted with the Armenian quake, having personally lived through the disaster. As a result of the immense need in the affected community, they founded and directed the Children's Psychotherapy Center, located within the disaster zone in Kirovakan, Armenia (Heusser-Markun, 1992; Watts, 1989). This center, the first of its kind in the former Soviet Union, provided professional help for more than 2,500 children and adolescents traumatized by the quake. In the process, it provided an opportunity for the authors to collect data relative to the manner in which young survivors of a large-scale disaster remember the traumatic experience (Azarian, Miller, & Skriptchenko-Gregorian, 1994, 1996).

On December 7, 1988, at 11:41 a.m., a devastating earthquake (6.9 on the Richter scale) struck over 40% of the territory of Armenia, killing more than 100,000 people within 41 seconds (Verluise, 1995). More than 40,000 people were saved from burial under the ruins, and at least 53,000 families were left homeless (Grigorova, Gasparian, & Manukian, 1990; Noji, 1989). Arguably, the children suffered more than the adults, because at the time of the earthquake they were in schools that were inadequately designed and constructed (Pomonis, 1990). In all, 83 schools and 90 kindergartens were destroyed (Grigorova et al., 1990).

Many Armenian children experienced severe physical and psychological trauma as a result of the mass devastation. They suffered from numerous postquake emotional, behavioral, and psychosomatic disturbances (Azarian et al.,

1994; Pynoos, Goenjian, Tashjian, et al., 1993). This provided the authors the opportunity to study children's memory directly in the field of trauma. The subjects, from a rather homogeneous environment and background, were young patients with real, profound, and naturally caused traumas who experienced the same type of traumatic event with (of course) diverse vulnerabilities and consequences.

It should be mentioned that, in routinely gathering data at that time, the Armenian authors did not do so with any particular preconceptions about research on early childhood memory. They were preoccupied with the center's daily problems of organization and administration, and with providing immediate services for children. They were quite unaware of the existing bitter debates about early childhood memory that have, in recent times, been of great concern to Western psychologists. One may regard this circumstance, then, as an additional criterion of and contribution to objectivity of the authors. On the other hand, these circumstances also explain inevitable omissions in the data collected via the child interview protocol used at that time.

Method

Subjects

The subjects were 90 toddlers, survivors of the 1988 Armenian earthquake, who attended the Children's Psychotherapy Center for diagnostic evaluation and subsequent psychological treatment. The age of the subjects at the time of evaluation ranged from 15 to 48 months (average 36.7 months) and from 10 to 44 months at the time of disaster (average 30.7 months). The subject pool included 47 girls (52.2%) and 43 boys (47.8%).

Each child was interviewed using a structured clinical interview addressing diagnostic symptomatology and personal experience associated with traumatization in the quake. Nobody asked the children and their guardians to participate in interviews; they voluntarily came to the center for professional help due to the children's symptoms of postquake stress disturbances.

There was always a steady volume of parents, grandparents, and adult relatives presenting themselves at the clinic, seeking assistance for traumatized children. On average, the children were interviewed 6 months after the earthquake.

Interviewing

Each interview lasted approximately 60 minutes. The portion of the interview devoted to the child's disaster experience usually was of 20 minutes' duration—if there was a story and the child was able and wanted to talk about it.

Reflecting regard for the very young age of the children, the interviews took place in the presence of their guardians. This preferred mode of interviewing fostered feelings of safety and trust in these little, frightened survivors, and it provided an opportunity to facilitate their recollections with the help of close family members. During the interviews, the first responses always came from the children; adults participated in confirming and verifying the children's stories, in defining details, and in providing necessary information related to recent changes in the children's behavioral, emotional, and somatic states following the disaster. There were toys and dolls, crayons, and paper on the table, and the children were encouraged to express their experiences through drawing and play.

All of the interviews were conducted by Anait Azarian. After each interview, she constructed a narrative based on the child's answers and on the adults' remarks. She also noted her own observations of the children's behavioral and emotional reactions.

The children were given the opportunity to report the details of the trauma spontaneously. Interview questions were not designed to elicit specific assessment of completeness or inaccuracies in memory. A few varied and neutral questions were used to initiate the children's spontaneous recall of their personal quake experiences, and to keep them remembering for a while: "Do you remember the earthquake?" "Where were you at that time?" "What happened with you?" "What did you see on the streets?" "What did your mother/father/sibling do at that time?" and so on. Some subjects needed very little cuing to elicit recall. It was enough if they were asked about certain events or places related to the quake: "How did you injure your hand?" "Why did your family leave your house?" "Where is your brother/father/grandma now?" "Are you afraid of something?"

The children and the accompanying adults also were asked to describe the spontaneous play activity, drawings, dreams, fears, phobias, and any unusual behaviors or reactions of the children following the quake.

Assessment

This is a descriptive study based on the open-ended questions posed to the young survivors during the interviews. The interviewer's focus was first to evaluate these children for PTSD symptoms (which were quite likely to be present, due to the profound impact of the quake stressors) and, accordingly, to examine how these young survivors reexperienced the disaster. It is for this reason that the early evaluations assessed different memory forms (thoughts, behaviors, reactions, and so on) that constituted the children's personal quake experiences.

We did not return to these interviews 6 years later to assess somehow the fullness of the toddlers' memories, for example, by rating their abilities to tell complete quake stories or their abilities to recall only some part of their experiences. The naturalistic, descriptive flow of the interviews did not permit such analyses. Our goal was simply to assess the presence of quake memory for the children at the time of evaluation.

Verbal Memory Forms

We concluded that a subject had a verbal memory of the quake if the child could spontaneously or with only little cuing recall his or her personal quake experience, verified by an adult as true or quite possible. The memory could consist of a very short story, even just a few phrases, but it had to include what the young survivor felt, saw, heard, smelled, or how he or she acted, and of what he or she was scared.

Incoherent or meaningless, trivial statements about the earthquake, lacking any self-experienced contents, were not counted as verbal memory. We counted the absence of verbal memory in a child if he or she could recall nothing; that is, no matter if the child tried to do so, the result was that he or she could not retrieve and verbalize any memory of what happened nearby during the disaster. For some of the children, it was impossible to assess whether they did or did not have verbal memory. These children constitute a third group. Some of these children bluntly refused to discuss their disaster experiences, whereas others presented stories that were complete reiterations of the stories of others, seemingly appropriated by these children, from their parents, siblings, or relatives.

Nonverbal Memory Forms

Terr (1988) has pointed out that traumatic memory can be recovered from other than verbal sources and that these other memory forms have not been sufficiently examined. Terr assessed children's behavioral memories, including play, fears, and personality changes, after traumatic events. She observed the posttraumatic play or reenactment as the most consistent and prevalent index of behavioral memory. Play can indeed provide very accurate representations of a traumatic event experienced in reality (Saylor, Swenson, & Powell, 1992; Sugar, 1992); the same representations have been found in postdisaster children's repetitive drawings (Skriptchenko-Gregorian, Azarian, & DeMaria, 1996).

In the present study, we restricted our observations of the subjects' behavioral representations by considering postquake personality changes (e.g., avoidance, detachment, withdrawal), fearful and aggressive behaviors, and attitudes and subsequent acts directly related to their quake experiences. For example, we did not count general aggressive or avoidant behavior as behavioral memory of the quake trauma. We counted such behavior only when the child's aggression or avoidance was directed toward an individual who, for example, was with the child and somehow unintentionally hurt or frightened him or her during the quake. We also included repetitive postquake play and repetitive drawing of the disaster scenes as ex-

pressive forms of children's memories. Finally, we included the contents of children's dreams and nightmares as well as any unusual reactions (e.g., sweating and palpitations, head- and stomachaches, nausea and vomiting, confusion and agitation, stupor and freezing) to physical stimuli that could serve as reminders of the psychosensory influence of the quake or their particular disaster circumstances.

Results

Verbal Memory

Of the 90 toddlers, more than half (53.3%) produced verbal memories of what they personally experienced during the quake (see Table 23.1). This is about twice the proportion of toddlers (27.8%) who exhibited no verbal memories about the experienced disaster. About one-fifth (18.9%) of the toddlers refused to talk about the disaster issues or repeated the stories of others.

Many young survivors of the quake were able to give vivid verbal descriptions of their personal disaster experiences and sometimes recounted details of the tragic day that adults had not even noticed. For example, toddlers were more likely to recall unusual behaviors or actions by significant adults, as well as the physical impact of the quake.

One boy, age 30 months at the time of the disaster and 38 months at the time of the evaluation, told the interviewer:

> The house broke in pieces. At first, the glass in windows broke. . . . Dz-z-z-z . . . all glass, then stones fell down from the roof. The roof also fell down, the roof fell down directly on our little apple tree. The tree broke and the house sat on the ground. . . . I hate this house. I want my toys and collection of little cars from the house.

A girl (age 33/37 months) related:

> My mother kept me in her hands and did not let me go by myself or stand near her. We were watching what our neighbors were dragging out from the building. Aunt Rosa rescued a big bowl with

Table 23.1 Distribution of the Toddlers With and Without Verbal Memory and With Repetition/Refusal Reactions

	Number	Percentage
With verbal memory	48	53.3
Without verbal memory	25	27.8
With repetition/refusal reactions	17	18.9
Total	90	100

Table 23.2 Distribution of the Toddlers With Different Nonverbal Forms of Disaster Memory ($N = 90$)

	Number	Percentage
With one or more		
nonverbal form of memory	81	90.0
physical-stimulus memory	57	63.3
behavioral memory	53	58.9
expressive memory	31	34.4
dreams of quake trauma	17	18.9
Without any form of the quake memory	9	10.0

NOTE: Columns total more than 90 subjects and more than 100% because children evidenced multiple nonverbal forms of memory.

food. Why did she do that? Do you know? We stayed in our yard a very long time, but our father did not come. Mother cried, I didn't, I knew he would come. Also, I remember that people shouted at each other—"Cut the light! Cut the gas!" [To prevent fire.] Why they did say that? Do you know? I can tell you that our cat was in the yard with us, near us. Then she disappeared. I wanted to take her, but my mother did not listen to me. So we now have no cat; I do not know where she could be. Then my father came, he was very dirty. He said: "I am so glad you are safe and sound!"

Nonverbal Memory

The overwhelming majority of the toddlers (90.0%) evidenced nonverbal memory of the experienced disaster (see Table 23.2). Many of these children simultaneously exhibited one or more of the examined forms of nonverbal memory. Most (63.3%) evidenced their memory of the quake through new and unusual reactions to different physical stimuli that reminded them of their psychosensory experience of the quake (loud noises, vibrations, the smell of fire and/or dust, darkness, closeness, and so on). Also, many young survivors (58.9%) began manifesting strong avoidant behavior toward places and people.

One young boy (age 12/20 months) was asleep when the quake began; he was awakened by the terrible underground noise ("growling") of the quake, people's shouts and screams, and the sounds of things falling and breaking in the apartment. After that, he shuddered in response to even "usual" noises or sounds: his parents talking loudly, car sounds on the streets, the sound of the vacuum cleaner, and so on. Simi-

larly, one girl (age 22/28 months) began to react even to so small a noise as a buzzing fly.

One girl (age 42/46 months) spent more than 4 hours after the quake under the body of her father, who had shielded her against falling concrete debris. After her rescue, she began to exhibit sharp sensitivity to darkness and hot temperatures. She was afraid to enter a darkened room and suddenly felt stifled and suffocated when she was exposed to regular oven heat or covered by a blanket. The girl was also extremely sensitive to her father's scent: She would seek out his old shirts and peak caps, and bring these things to her face and smell them. She persistently wanted to keep these old clothes and became very angry if her grandmother removed them.

One small boy (age 26/30 months) was carried by his mother during the quake as they escaped a shaking, multistoried building. While the strong vibrations continued, his mother fell twice with him on the stairs. After that, the boy was markedly impaired in his attitude toward his mother, refusing to approach her or to play with her. He became very cold toward her.

One father wrapped his daughter (age 18/26 months) in a blanket and ran out of a collapsing building. After that, the girl did not want to be with him. She cried when he took her in his arms, pushing him away with her feet if he did so. The parents also noticed that their daughter was afraid to be covered with a blanket when she was prepared for sleep.

Age

In order to analyze the possible role of age in the children's memories of disaster, we divided the overall sample into three age groups: 10 to 24 months ($n = 21$), 25 to 36 months ($n = 39$), and 37 to 44 months ($n = 30$) at the time of the earthquake. We then considered the results of the toddlers' interviews separately within these age groups (see Table 23.3).

The toddlers' ages had considerable influence on their verbal memory abilities. Only 14.3% of subjects who were 2 years of age and younger could remember, 6 months later, something that had happened to them during the quake. Many more (61.5%) of those who were 2-3 years old at the time of the disaster could remember. This difference in verbal memory ability was statistically significant ($p = 0.0004$). When we compare the youngest and middle age groups, the difference in verbal memory is marked. In the youngest group, the overwhelming majority of the subjects (85.7%) could not remember what they had experienced during the quake. Many fewer subjects in the middle age group (12.8%) remembered nothing about the quake ($p = 0.00005$).

However, age was associated with verbal memory when we compared only the middle age group (25-36 months). On verbal memory ability, there were no significant differences between the middle age group and the eldest examined age group (37-44 months). In these groups, about the same proportions of toddlers—61.5% and 70.0%—had verbal memories of the quake. Similarly, we found no significant difference between the proportions of toddlers in these age groups—12.8% and 6.7%, respectively—who did not have verbal memories of the quake.

The subjects from the youngest age group did not demonstrate repetition or refusal reactions during the interviews. Occurrence of subjects with such reactions in the two older groups was about equal—25.7% and 23.3%.

Nonverbal forms of disaster memory occurred about equally among the three age groups of toddlers: 85.7%, 94.9%, and 86.7%. The toddlers' ages, therefore, did not play a significant role in their ability to exhibit behav-

ioral and physical-stimulus memory, which, as Table 23.2 shows, were their major forms of nonverbal memory. Age universality of behavioral memories was vividly demonstrated in cases of siblings who experienced the same quake impact.

One girl (age 37/41 months) and her younger brother (age 22/26 months) were playing peacefully together on a carpet when the quake struck. At the time of the evaluation, the sister could describe that the floor started to "move" violently. Books and crockery poured down on the terrorized children. The brother was unable to provide any verbal account of the quake trauma. However, shortly after this traumatic experience, he developed a phobia toward the carpet. He never again played on the carpet, refusing to sit or even stand on it; he preferred to be on a couch or in an adult's arms. His sister, too, began to show personality and behavior changes, such as anger toward her little brother (who was with her during the quake). She frequently kicked, pushed, and pinched him, and she never played with him again.

One set of triplets (age 36/40 months)—two brothers and a sister—recalled the quake day and exhibited identical behavioral changes, postquake play and drawing, and physical stimuli reactions. They began to avoid their mother, who was with them during the quake, and they evidenced great confusion and disorganized panic actions. The children's attitudes and relations with their father—who, during the quake's aftermath, had arrived to help—had not changed. The triplets' younger brother (age 11/15 months) exhibited intense startle reactions to any loud sounds and vibrations.

It is also interesting to examine the earliest age at which the children are able to recall the quake. Usher and Neisser (1993) have classically defined such a threshold as the youngest age at which at least half the subjects recall something about an important event. In our entire sample of toddlers who experienced the quake, we found that 53.3% (i.e., a little more than half) remembered and verbally recalled something about their personal experiences of the earthquake (see Table 23.1). However, the age boundaries of the entire sample are wide—from 10 to 44 months (average 30.7

Table 23.3 Distribution Memory (With and Without Verbal Memory, With Repetition/Refusal Reactions, and With Nonverbal Form of Disaster Memory) for Toddlers by Three Age Groups at Time of Quake

	10-24 Months (n = 12)		25-36 Months (n = 11)		37-44 Months (n = 16)	
	No.	%	No.	%	No.	%
With verbal memory	3	14.3	24	61.5	21	70.0
Without verbal memory	18	85.7	5	12.8	2	6.7
Repetition/refusal reactions	0	0.0	10	25.7	7	23.3
With nonverbal form of memory	18	85.7	37	94.9	26	86.7

months)—and an average range is needed to establish an age threshold for remembering the natural disaster.

To obtain a more precise value of the age threshold, we narrowed the age boundaries of the examined sample. The criterion we used was applied separately to the three age groups that together made up the entire sample (Table 23.3). At this point, the age threshold of recalling the quake became the middle age group (from 25 to 36 months; average age 31.1 months). In this age group 61.5% of the toddlers—much more than 50%—were able to recall the traumatic event. Toddlers in this age group showed significantly greater recall than did toddlers in the younger group ($p = 0.0004$).

To assess the age threshold more carefully, we divided the middle age group into three smaller age subgroups: 25-28 months, 29-32 months, and 33-36 months. The results are shown in Table 23.4. The narrowest or most precise age group that contains the threshold of recalling the quake trauma is 29-32 months (average age 30.4 months). In this age subgroup, 72.7% of the toddlers verbally recalled their quake experience, whereas only 41.7% of the toddlers from the younger age subgroup (25-28 months) were able to do the same.

Discussion

☐ This study of trauma memory in 90 toddlers who survived a devastating earthquake produced the following findings:

1. Most toddlers remembered what they personally experienced during the profound natural

disaster, which had happened about 6 months earlier.

2. An overwhelming number of the subjects were able to remember the disaster in nonverbal forms of memory, and this ability was not associated with age at the time of the quake.

3. The toddlers' verbal memories depended greatly on their age: Those who were 2½ years old at the time of the quake were most likely to recall.

The results show that most of the toddlers in the sample (90.0%) remembered the quake, either verbally or nonverbally. Even in the youngest age group (10-24 months at the time of the quake), 85.7% of the children appeared to remember (mostly as measured through behavioral representations and physical reactions) 6 months after the event. Three children in this age group provided some verbal recollections. These data demonstrate that toddlers indeed have the ability to remember profoundly traumatic events that happen to them. However, the individual observations show that there are limits to children's registering and storing these memories. The children in this study remembered very selectively, mostly recalling only events that had some personal meaning for them. During the quake, they noticed mostly what was most important to them and directly affected their interests. This suggests that their stories were true and not recollections of what others had told them about the event. As a matter of fact, young quake survivors remembered not the natural disaster, but rather what had personally happened to them, their favorite belongings, and the people important to their welfare. A child could notice and then recall the loss of

Table 23.4 Distribution of the Toddlers by Age at Time of the Disaster With Verbal Memory of the Quake (Three Age Subgroups)

	25-28 Months (n = 21)		29-32 Months (n = 39)		33-36 Months (n = 30)	
	No.	%	No.	%	No.	%
With verbal memory	5	41.7	8	72.7	11	68.8

his stuffed toy bear, and yet could pay no attention to a multistoried building that had collapsed on his street. Also, the children often expressed irritation or anger with their memories of dead parents, because, due to the parents' absence, they had begun to experience certain inconveniences. These small egoists would remember, for example, how their totally confused and panicked mothers or grandmothers behaved and sometimes unintentionally frightened them at the very moment of the terrible disaster. The children often exhibited behavioral memories revealed by their anger, hatred, and avoidance reactions as a sort of behavioral memory toward adults who had accidentally hurt them while rescuing them from dangerous places.

Such egocentricity of young children should be considered among other important mechanisms of trauma memory impairment. It has already been shown that young children's traumatic memory impairment may be a result of their own perceptual errors and distortions (Terr, 1988, 1990), the distorting influence of the profound traumatic event (Pynoos & Eth, 1984), or later implantation of memories made by adults (Loftus, 1993). Also, Williams (1994b) suggests that negative psychosocial consequences of devastating trauma may have significant negative effects on a victim's traumatic memory across the life span. Williams (1994a) has reported evidence that women can forget childhood trauma, even such intense trauma as sexual abuse. The evidence presented here suggests that toddlers' memory limitations may be caused by their selective memorizing of aspects of the event that are most relevant to them at the time of trauma. This should be taken into consideration by researchers addressing issues of young children's memory, accuracy, and

reliability in research, forensic, and psychotherapy fields.

The second finding of this study corresponds well with the observations made by Gaensbauer, Chatoor, Drell, Siegel, and Zeanah (1995), Scheeringa, Zeanah, Drell, and Larrieu (1995), Terr (1988, 1990), and others. These researchers have noted that representations of trauma in the memory of young children are usually encoded in nonverbal forms—behavioral, sensory, affective, and physiological. Thus, in Terr's well-known study, 18 of 20 young subjects demonstrated the presence of behavioral (nonverbal) memories of trauma. In our study, 81 of 90 examined toddlers, regardless of their ages, showed nonverbal memories of the quake.

Discussing the universality of behavioral memory in children, Terr (1988) concludes that behavioral memory appears to operate by different rules than verbal recollections: Behavioral memory does not rely on conscious awareness. The marked prevalence of nonverbal forms of quake memory—especially behavioral and physical-stimulus memory (Table 23.2)—that do not require verbal skills and conscious awareness and do not depend on the examined toddlers' ages may be accounted for by the mechanism of stress conditioning (Azarian, Lipsitt, & Skriptchenko-Gregorian, 1996). There now is no doubt that even very young children are quite efficient learning organisms (Lipsitt, 1967). For learning to occur, children must be sensitive to environmental events. Under certain conditions, environmental events can function as reinforcing stimuli that shape or selectively strengthen responses in the behavioral repertoire of the young child. At this time, the final effect of the stimulus depends on the external background or milieu against which the stimulus is applied, as well as on the current internal state of the organism (Wyrwicka, 1972). Thus, a new and "surprising" stimulus of very high intensity (e.g., during the quake, the mother grabs the child from his bed), applied against the external background of profound stress (the mother presses the child to her chest, runs from the collapsing building, and falls on the stairs while holding the child) and the child's specific internal state (the child was sleeping in his bed), may at once evoke very persistent and aversive reactions in the child when the mother attempts, later, to take him in her arms.

Young children's learning mechanisms and related behavioral memories are psychobiologically adapted for warning, avoiding, freezing, or fight/flight reactions, but not for comparatively long, time-consuming, conscious processes. Very young humans lacking verbal and analysis skills need such mechanisms and memories to survive in a hostile environment in spite of their developmental disadvantages. Verbal coping mechanisms for dealing with past experiences, and the presence of mediating corresponding verbal memories, are characteristic of older children and adults.

The earliest age at which a salient event can be verbally remembered is one of the most intriguing topics in the study of childhood memory. Sheingold and Tenney (1982) examined 42 college students and pointed to the period between 3 and 4 years of age as critical to their subjects' ability to recall a sibling birth. Usher and Neisser (1993) also examined college students ($N = 222$) and found that their earliest age of recall was 2 years for such past events as hospitalization and sibling birth. In their study, 2 years was defined as 24 to 35.99 months. Terr (1988) points to the approximate age of 28-36 months as the "cutoff point" in ability to recall traumatic events. She argues that at this age, children begin constructing grammatically ordered phrases and are able to express some inner feelings verbally. Sugar (1992) observed a 26-month-old girl spontaneously verbalize a clear description of her trauma in a plane crash, which she had experienced at the age of 16 months. He also observed a 27-month-old boy who was able to recall in detail the trauma of a car accident experienced 3 months before. Sugar indicates that the age at which traumatic memories can be verbalized depends on the age of onset of speech phrases and the young victim's cognitive ability. Some studies in nonpatient adult populations with nontraumatic memories have shown availability of earliest verbal memories between the ages of 3 and 4 years (Kihlstrom & Haraskiewicz, 1982; Pillemer & White, 1989).

Efforts to establish an exact earliest age of verbal memory (age threshold) that might be generally acceptable have thus far not proved successful. The age threshold of recalling the quake in our examined toddlers was found to be about $2\frac{1}{2}$ years (29-32 months). The findings in our study are consistent with the findings of researchers who have dealt with traumatized patients. However, the results obtained in different populations must be compared cautiously; the variances may be due not only to differences in degree of subjects' traumatization, their current age, and delays in asking to recall, but also to the nature of the traumatic event. Terr (1988, 1990, 1994) emphasizes the idea that different traumatic events can result in different memories in terms of completeness and stability. In her 1988 study, repeated events (child sexual abuse) were remembered more poorly than single events (e.g., a plane crash). The same was found for long events versus short events, with memory for short events being more complete. We have been unable to find in the literature any studies of comparable traumas to compare with our toddlers' memories of the quake. Studies of children's traumatic memories have focused mainly on sexual abuse, which represents a long-lasting, repeated, "secret" trauma. Disaster trauma, on the other hand, has a sudden impact of multiple psychophysiological, emotional, and information stressors occurring simultaneously. Postdisaster stress occurs along all sensory channels, and it may contribute to the development of distinctive forms of memory, such as strong physical-stimulus memory and behavioral memory.

Limitations of the current study's comparability with other data can be overcome only through further investigation of a variety of stressful and traumatic life events. Memories of young survivors who have experienced natural and human-made disasters, transportation accidents, and some forms of domestic violence have not been sufficiently studied. The implications of this study for further research are that it is necessary to explore (a) whether gender differences influence subjects' traumatic memories, (b) how delay in asking young children to recall the traumatic event may affect their verbal memory ability, (c) whether it is possible that different degrees of traumatization—even during the same mass traumatic event—can produce different qualities of remembering, and (d) what constitute the major personal/ environmental dimensions of the space within which the child selectively memorizes.

References

Azarian, A. G., Lipsitt, L. P., & Skriptchenko-Gregorian, V. G. (1996, April). *Behavioral psychopathology in infants of disaster.* Paper presented at the 10th Biennial International Conference on Infant Studies, Providence, RI.

Azarian, A. G., Miller, T. W., & Skriptchenko-Gregorian, V. G. (1994). Childhood trauma in victims of the Armenian earthquake. *Journal of Contemporary Psychotherapy, 24*(2), 77-85.

Azarian, A. G., Miller, T. W., & Skriptchenko-Gregorian, V. G. (1996). Baseline assessment of children traumatized by the Armenian earthquake. *Child Psychiatry and Human Development, 27*(1), 29-41.

Ceci, S. J., & Bruck, M. (1995). *Jeopardy in the courtroom: A scientific analysis of children's testimony.* Washington, DC: American Psychological Association.

Fivush, R., & Hamond, N. (1990). Autobiographical memory across the preschool years: Toward reconceptualizing childhood amnesia. In R. Fivush & J. A. Hudson (Eds.), *Knowing and remembering in young children* (pp. 223-248). New York: Cambridge University Press.

Gaensbauer, T. J., Chatoor, I., Drell, M. J., Siegel, D., & Zeanah, C. H. (1995). Traumatic loss in a one-year-old girl. *Journal of the American Academy of Child and Adolescent Psychiatry, 34*, 520-528.

Goldstein, E., & Farmer, K. (Eds.). (1993). *True stories of false memories.* Boca Raton, FL: Sirs.

Goodman, G., & Helgelson, V. (1985). Child sexual assault: Children's memory and the law. *University of Miami Law Review, 40*, 181-208.

Grigorova, L. F., Gasparian, A. A., & Manukian, L. H. (1990). *Armenia, December, 1988.* Yerevan, Armenia: Haiastan.

Heusser-Markun, R. (1992). Anahid Azarian—Hilfe für Kinder mit Erdbebentrauma. *Neue Zurcher Zeitung, 21*, 15.

Kihlstrom, J. F., & Haraskiewicz, J. M. (1982). The earliest recollection: A new survey. *Journal of Personality, 50*, 134-148.

Lipsitt, L. P. (1967). Learning in the human infant. In H. W. Stevenson, E. H. Hess, & H. L. Rheingold (Eds.), *Early behavior* (pp. 225-248). New York: John Wiley.

Loftus, E. F. (1991). *Witness for the defense: The accused, the eyewitness, and the expert who puts memory on trial.* New York: St. Martin's.

Loftus, E. F. (1993). The reality of repressed memories. *American Psychologist, 48*, 518-537.

Myers, N., Clifton, R., & Clarkson, M. (1987). When they were very young: Almost threes remember two years ago. *Infant Behavior and Development, 10*, 123-132.

Noji, E. K. (1989). The 1988 earthquake in Soviet Armenia: Implications for earthquake preparedness. *Disasters, 13*, 255-262.

Pillemer, D. B., & White, S. H. (1989). Childhood events recalled by children and adults. In H. W. Reese (Ed.), *Advances in child development and behavior* (Vol. 21, pp. 297-340). San Diego, CA: Academic Press.

Pomonis, A. (1990). The Spitak (Armenia, USSR) earthquake: Residential building typology and seismic behavior. *Disasters, 14*, 89-114.

Pynoos, R. S., & Eth, S. (1984). The child as witness to homicide. *Journal of Social Issues, 40*(2), 87-108.

Pynoos, R. S., Goenjian, A. K., Tashjian, M., et al. (1993). Posttraumatic stress reactions in children after the 1988 Armenian earthquake. *British Journal of Psychiatry, 163*, 239-247.

Saylor, S. F., Swenson, C. C., & Powell, K. (1992). Hurricane Hugo blows down the broccoli: Preschoolers' post-disaster play and adjustment. *Child Psychiatry and Human Development, 22*, 139-147.

Scheeringa, M. S., Zeanah, C. H., Drell, M. J., & Larrieu, J. A. (1995). Two approaches to the diagnosis of post-traumatic stress disorder in infancy and early childhood. *Journal of the American Academy of Child and Adolescent Psychiatry, 34*, 191-200.

Sheingold, K., & Tenney, Y. J. (1982). Memory for a salient childhood event. In U. Neisser (Ed.), *Memory observed* (pp. 201-212). New York: Freeman.

Skriptchenko-Gregorian, V. G., Azarian, A. G., & DeMaria, M. B. (1996). Colors of disaster: The psychology of the "black sun." *The Arts in Psychotherapy, 23*(1), 1-14.

Sugar, M. (1992). Toddlers' traumatic memories. *Infant Mental Health Journal, 13*, 245-251.

Terr, L. C. (1988). What happens to early memories of trauma? A study of twenty children under age five at the time of documented traumatic events. *Journal of the American Academy of Child and Adolescent Psychiatry, 27*, 96-104.

Terr, L. C. (1990). *Too scared to cry: Psychic trauma in childhood.* New York: Harper & Row.

Terr, L. C. (1994). *Unchained memories: True stories of traumatic memories lost and found.* New York: Basic Books.

Usher, J. N., & Neisser, U. (1993). Childhood amnesia and the beginnings of memory for four early life events.

Journal of Experimental Psychology: General, 122, 155-165.

Verluise, P. (1995). *Armenia in crisis: The 1988 earthquake.* Detroit, MI: Wayne State University Press.

Watts, J. (1989, November 5). Armenia speaks. *Observer Magazine,* pp. 49-58.

Williams, L. M. (1994a). Recall of childhood trauma: A prospective study of women's memories of child sexual abuse. *Journal of Consulting and Clinical Psychology, 62,* 1167-1176.

Williams, L. M. (1994b). What does it mean to forget child sexual abuse? A reply to Loftus, Garry, and Feldman (1994). *Journal of Consulting and Clinical Psychology, 62,* 1182-1186.

Winograd, E., & Killinger, W. A., Jr. (1983). Relating age at encoding in early childhood to adult recall. *Journal of Experimental Psychology: General, 112,* 413-422.

Wyrwicka, W. (1972). *The mechanism of conditioned behavior.* Springfield, IL: Charles C Thomas.

24

Stability and Fluctuation of Veterans' Reports of Combat Exposure

Barbara L. Niles
Elana Newman
Brigette A. Erwin
Lisa M. Fisher
Danny G. Kaloupek
Terence M. Keane

The stability of memories of traumatic childhood events has been closely examined in recent years due to the controversy over "false memories" (e.g., Bowers & Farvolden, 1996a, 1996b; Loftus, 1993; Pennebaker & Memon, 1996; Pope, 1996). Surprisingly, this controversy has not spurred similarly close scrutiny of memories of traumatic events experienced in adulthood, despite the fact that the long-term stability of such memories has not been established.

Stability of Retrospective Report

Most of the existing trauma literature reflects the implicit assumption that reports of stressors are stable over time. As Roemer, Litz, Orsillo, Ehlich, and Friedman (1996) note, the combat trauma literature in particular appears to assume that retrospective reports of exposure are objective, accurate, and reliable recollections of past events. This assumption may be unfounded, however, as evidence begins to accumulate that reports of exposure to stressful or traumatic events are not stable and reliable over the months and years immediately following the trauma exposure (McFarlane, 1988; Roemer et al., 1996; Schwarz, Kowalski, & McNally, 1993).

In an investigation of firefighters exposed to a bushfire disaster in Australia, McFarlane (1988) examined firefighters' descriptions of the traumatic events at 4 and 11 months posttrauma. He found that a subset of individuals changed their reports of certain aspects of traumatic events over the 7-month interim. During this time, there was a significant falloff in the reporting of physical injury for those who reported no substantial psychological distress. In contrast, participants who reported substantial psychological distress had consistent reports of the physical injuries that took place during the fire.

Schwarz et al. (1993) also explored differences in retrospective reports at two time points following a disaster. In their study of 12 school personnel who were exposed to a school shooting, participants were asked to report on aspects of the traumatic event (i.e., emotional reactions, sense of life threat, and sensory experiences) at 6 and at 18 months following the incident. All of the participants changed some aspect of their recall at 18 months. Enlargement in report of the traumatic event (i.e., more emotional reactions, a greater sense of life threat, and more sensory experiences) was associated with symptoms of posttraumatic stress disorder (PTSD). Conversely, diminishment was associated with lessening of anxiety and increase in self-confidence.

Roemer and colleagues (1996) obtained frequency estimates of exposure to war-zone stressors at two time points from American soldiers who had served in the peacekeeping mission in Somalia. Overall, there was a significant increase in participants' frequency reports from initial (within a year of returning) to follow-up assessments (an average of 21 months later). Increase in frequency reports was associated with severity of reported PTSD symptomatology.

These three studies illustrate that substantial changes in retrospective recall are not uncommon among adults who experience traumatic events. They also show that reports of trauma exposure are not entirely reliable over a period of months or years after the trauma exposure. Further, they suggest that diminishment in report of severity of trauma exposure is related to absence of psychological distress and that enlargement is associated with the presence of psychological symptoms.

PTSD and Dose-Response Theory

☐ Posttraumatic stress disorder, first codified in the third edition of the *Diagnostic and Statistical Manual of Mental Disorders* (*DSM-III;* American Psychiatric Association, 1980), has been identified as one of the most common sequelae of exposure to trauma. Many of the empirical studies on the psychological aftermath of trauma exposure have examined the nature and extent of the exposure (Criterion A for PTSD diagnosis) and the subsequent severity of the symptoms of psychological, social, and biological impairment (Criteria B, C, and D) in traumatized populations (e.g., Kulka et al., 1990; Yule & Williams, 1990). PTSD researchers have supported the notion of a "dose-response" relationship—that is, greater exposure to traumatic events leads to greater dysfunction following exposure (e.g., Fairbank, Schlenger, Caddell, & Woods, 1994; Green, 1990; Kaylor, King, & King, 1987; Kulka et al., 1990; March, 1993).

Dose-response theory presumes both that reports of trauma exposure are constant and that the magnitude of trauma exposure influences response. However, as noted above, report of dose can change substantially over time, and enlargement in report of dose is associated with more psychological symptomatology. Thus, contrary to previous assumptions, it appears that current psychological symptoms may influence the report of dose.

Trauma Exposure and Criterion A

☐ In the area of combat-related stress disorders, exposure to potential traumatic events has most commonly been measured by the Combat Exposure Scale (CES; Kaylor et al., 1987; Keane et al., 1989; Kulka et al., 1990), a retrospective set of self-ratings. The CES was the instrument chosen to assess dose in the National Vietnam Veterans Readjustment Study (NVVRS; Kulka et al., 1990), the most comprehensive and rigorous investigation of psychological adjustment in war veterans to date. Literature generated from this large-scale project has provided the foundation for the dose-response theory that is now commonly endorsed by researchers and clinicians in the field of PTSD. Thus, the CES has been instrumental in the development of this theory.

Measures of trauma exposure, such as the CES, overlap with but have important differences from the identification of a traumatic event necessary to fulfill Criterion A for *DSM-IV* PTSD diagnosis (American Psychiatric Association, 1994). The conditions that must be met for an event to qualify for PTSD Criterion A include confrontation with death or threat to physical integrity accompanied by fear, horror, or helplessness. These conditions do not require a specific amount or intensity of exposure. Thus, a salient traumatic event is identified but not quantified for PTSD Criterion A. In most studies of PTSD symptoms, Criterion A has been ascertained by interview in a relatively unstructured way; substantial qualitative judgment is required in determining whether an event is of sufficient magnitude to qualify for Criterion A. Reliability of Criterion A assessment has rarely been examined.

The study reported in this chapter examined long-term reliability of reports of traumatic military events decades after military service. We compared CES scores at two evaluation points separated by at least 4 years in treatment-seeking Vietnam theater veterans who experienced chronic PTSD subsequent to military service in early adulthood. In addition, we compared descriptive features of the most salient traumatic military events reported (Criterion A) at these two times to investigate the stability of these reports. Finally, we considered measures of PTSD symptomatology at both time points in relation to CES scores to evaluate the dose-response relationship.

Method

Population

Participants were 38 male Vietnam theater veterans who were given comprehensive clinical assessments for PTSD between 1986 and 1990 (Time 1) and who agreed to take part in a follow-up research study in 1994 or 1995 (Time 2). The mean time span between Times 1 and 2 was 6.59 years (range 4.42 to 10 years).

Demographic and Military Service Descriptors

Mean age of participants at Time 1 was 39.7 years; 81% were Caucasian and 19% were African American. At Time 1, 31.6% were married, 23.7% were never married, 21.1% were divorced, and 7.9% were unmarried and living with a partner. Also at Time 1, 39.5% were employed full-time, 2.6% were employed part-time, 2.6% were students, and 52.6% were unemployed. Mean annual income of participants at Time 1 was \$14,838 ($SD = 9,263$). Mean number of jobs between discharge from the military and Time 1 was 15.3 ($SD = 21.9$).

Mean number of months the participants spent in the Vietnam theater was 13.7 ($SD = 3.9$). The majority of the participants (60.5%) had served in the Army; 31.6% had served in the Marine Corps, 5.3% in the Air Force, and 2.6% in the Navy.

Measures and Procedures

Time 1

Between 1986 and 1990, 111 treatment-seeking Vietnam veterans took part in extensive clinical assessment for PTSD lasting 8 to 10 hours. As part of that process, each completed a clinical interview to determine *DSM-III-R* PTSD (American Psychiatric Association, 1987), the Combat Exposure Scale (Keane et al., 1989), and the Mississippi Scale for Combat-Related PTSD (M-PTSD). The CES is a 7-item, self-report measure of combat-related stressors experienced by combatants. Keane and colleagues (1989) found this measure to have high internal consistency (alpha = .85) and high test-retest reliability over a 1-week period ($r = .97, p < .0001$). The M-PTSD is a 35-item scale that reflects severity of PTSD symptoms. Respondents rate 35 symptoms on 5-point Likert-type scales. This instrument has also been found to have high internal consistency (alpha = .94) and high test-retest reliability over a 1-week period ($r = .97$, $p < .0001$; Keane, Caddell, & Taylor, 1988). In the course of the clinical interview, veterans were asked to describe combat experiences that continue to bother them. These events were noted in a clinical assessment report and used to determine Criterion A at Time 1 for the current study.

Time 2

A follow-up study was conducted in 1994 and 1995 to examine the course of PTSD symptomatology. The research team attempted to contact and recruit all 111 veterans assessed at Time 1. A total of 38 veterans (34.3%) completed the follow-up protocol; of the remainder, 19 (17.1%) declined to participate, 14 (12.6%) were identified as deceased, 2 (1.8%) were housed in controlled environments (prison or inpatient program) and unable to participate, 14 (12.6%) were reached but failed to appear for the evaluation, and 24 (21.6%) could not be located despite extensive efforts, including the use of a national locator service. Of the 38 participants, 30 were interviewed in person at the clinic where the original interviews took place. The other 8 had moved away from the area but agreed to be interviewed over the telephone and to complete self-report measures that were sent to them in the mail.

Chi-square statistics and t tests were utilized to compare the 38 participants and the 73 individuals who did not participate in follow-up in terms of demographic and military variables and scores on psychometric measures. No significant differences were found between these two groups in demographic variables (ethnicity, marital status, employment status, income, number of jobs postmilitary), military characteristics (number of months in Vietnam theater, branch of service), or scores on psychometric instruments (CES and M-PTSD).

The protocol at Time 2 included the Clinician Administered PTSD Scale for *DSM-III-R* diagnosis (CAPS; Blake et al., 1990), the CES, and the M-PTSD. Using a systematic series of questions, participants were asked to describe the salient stressful military event or events that continue to bother them. The clinician recorded

these responses and used them to determine whether Criterion A was established for the CAPS PTSD diagnosis.

Telephone participants were given an abbreviated version of this protocol. They did not complete the CAPS or the interview about salient stressful military events; instead, they completed a shorter standardized clinical interview for PTSD, the PTSD module of the Structured Clinical Interview for Diagnosis (Spitzer, Williams, Gibbons, & First, 1990).

Results

PTSD Symptomatology

At Time 1, 31 of the 38 (81.6%) participants met *DSM-III-R* diagnostic criteria for PTSD; at Time 2, 29 of the 38 participants (76.3%) met diagnostic criteria. The mean M-PTSD scores were 123.6 ($SD = 20.0$) at Time 1 and 120.9 ($SD = 26.9$) at Time 2. These were well above the 107 cutoff for PTSD suggested by Keane et al. (1988).

Combat Exposure Scale

A total of 29 participants completed the CES at both Times 1 and 2. The correlation between CES scores on each occasion was substantial and significant ($r = .67$, $p < .001$). The mean CES score was 29.06 ($SD = 7.77$) at Time 1 and 29.34 ($SD = 9.80$) at Time 2. These mean scores fall into the "moderate to heavy" range for this scale.

Although 22 (76%) of the participants' scores on the CES were within one standard deviation or 8 points of their original score, examination of the individual scores illustrated substantial change for a few participants. For 5 participants (17%), CES scores increased 8 or more points (range +8 to +19). For 2 participants (7%), the scores decreased more than 8 points (range −11 to −17).

Verbal Reports of Criterion A

There were 30 participants interviewed at both Times 1 and 2 for Criterion A, and 82% (23 participants) reported identical Criterion A events at both Times 1 and 2.

Of the 5 participants who reported nonidentical traumatic stressors, none reported new recall for previously forgotten events; 4 reported combat events on both occasions, but different events were considered most salient. At Time 2, all 4 of these participants reported that they could recall the events identified at Time 1; they described that the events related at Time 1 continued to bother them, but that other events were currently more prominent for them. These participants noted various reasons for the change: reflecting on and talking about the incidents changed their thinking about them, reminders or triggers in current life influenced current salience, and differences in interviewers across occasions led to differential disclosures.

The remaining participant had reported combat events at Time 1 but changed to a noncombat military event (not previously reported) at Time 2. This individual described that therapy between Times 1 and 2 helped him to understand the impact of childhood abuse experiences on his subsequent functioning. As a result, the traumatic military event he found most salient at Time 2 was not a combat experience, but an event he linked to his childhood abuse. He reported that he was severely humiliated by some of his fellow soldiers for masturbating in the shower. This participant described that the combat events detailed at Time 1 continued to bother him, but not as much as the noncombat shower incident he detailed at Time 2.

CES and M-PTSD

No correlation or association was found between changes in CES and changes in M-PTSD ($r = -.01$, $p = .76$).

Discussion

PTSD Symptomatology

More than 75% of the Vietnam theater veterans seeking treatment for PTSD in this sample were diagnosed with PTSD at each assessment point. In addition, M-PTSD scores indicate that most had clinically significant symptoms of

PTSD. By contrast, the NVVRS, an epidemiological study including treatment-seeking and non-treatment-seeking veterans, found that the majority of Vietnam theater veterans have had few readjustment problems; in the NVVRS only 26.1% of all male Vietnam theater veterans had clinically significant symptoms of PTSD (Kulka et al., 1990). Thus, the current sample likely represents a restricted range of Vietnam theater veterans with significant PTSD symptoms. Although this sample may be representative of treatment-seeking veterans with PTSD, caution must be exercised in generalizing the results from this small, extreme sample to non-treatment-seeking samples.

Combat Exposure Scale

The CES scores remained stable over a 6-year span, despite the potential influence of several hypothesized factors that might cause variability in reporting over time. These factors include (a) poor recall for events that took place years prior to assessment under conditions of stress; (b) enhanced recall of past events due to therapy, reflection, or discussion with others; (c) deliberate or unintentional distorting in response to demand characteristics of the situation; and (d) variability due to random factors such as fatigue or misinterpretation of questions. Thus, the stability of this measure over several years is noteworthy.

When the scores are examined individually, however, dramatic changes can be seen for some participants. These findings suggest that mean scores and correlations, which indicate few differences for the whole sample between Times 1 and 2, may not be adequate to characterize the changes for all individuals.

Verbal Reports of Criterion A

The verbal reports of Criterion A also illustrate marked stability. In more than 80% of the cases, the events described at Time 1 to establish Criterion A for diagnosis were the same as those described several years later. For 5 individuals, Criterion A did change. None of these 5 forgot the events first reported, nor did they have new recall of events, but the relative prominence of military events changed. In 4 of the 5 cases, the events described at Times 1 and 2 were similar; they were combat incidents at both times. In one case, however, the event described at Time 2 was quite different and had not been reported at Time 1. These cases suggest that relative salience of traumatic events may change over time for some individuals, and in some cases the changes can be marked.

CES and M-PTSD

The lack of a significant correlation between changes in CES and M-PTSD suggests that there is no common factor that influences both report of trauma exposure and symptoms of PTSD in this sample. These results are not consistent with the findings of Schwarz et al. (1993) or those of Roemer et al. (1996), showing enlargement in reports of trauma exposure to be associated with symptoms of PTSD. The participants in the current study were seeking treatment for PTSD at Time 1, however, whereas the participants in the Schwarz et al. and Roemer et al. studies were not seeking treatment. Because the base rate of PTSD is so high in the current sample, an association between changes in report of Criterion A and changes in PTSD symptoms may be undetectable.

Limitations

□ This study has some limitations with respect to sampling, measurement, and method that should be recognized. The relatively small number of participants reduces the statistical power of the study, although the focus on within-subject effects mitigates this issue somewhat. And even though the sample is grossly comparable to the full patient cohort from which it was drawn, there may have been some selection bias on variables not measured in this study. Replication will help resolve this concern.

In terms of measurement, this study used the CES to quantify exposure to potentially traumatic events in a war zone. The CES is narrowly focused on traditional combat roles and duties, and may fail to capture other aspects of trau-

matic exposure that are currently considered important in the assessment of Criterion A. Subjective appraisal of fear or horror, for example, is not included in this measure. Reports about these elements of trauma exposure might be more likely to change over time given their subjective nature. Thus, measures of trauma that are consistent with the *DSM-IV* Criterion A might show more variability over time.

In terms of method, the aims for evaluation differed at the two assessment points. The initial evaluations were made for clinical purposes, with no plan for subsequent follow-up. The Time 2 evaluations were implemented for research and program evaluation purposes, and participation was solicited. As a result, participants' comfort levels, alliance with interviewers, and trust regarding confidentiality of information—all of which likely affected willingness to report openly and accurately—may have differed across the two evaluations.

Conclusion

□ Reports of dose of trauma exposure (as measured by the CES) and reports of most salient traumatic military events (identified as Criterion A) were generally consistent over time in this study. However, there were some dramatic revisions in these reports at Time 2 for some individuals. Thus, although reports of trauma exposure may be stable over time for most people, there exists a subset of individuals whose reports can change markedly. The substantial heterogeneity of this sample was not conveyed by considering the data in aggregated form; examination of changes in report of trauma for individuals is recommended.

The results of the current study, considered along with previous findings on the fluctuation in reports of exposure to trauma (McFarlane, 1988; Roemer et al., 1996; Schwarz et al., 1993), suggest that clinicians and researchers should not assume that reports of trauma exposure are stable. The findings of the current study were not consistent with recent investigations using non-treatment-seeking populations that found associations between PTSD symptoms and enlargement in reports of trauma exposure

(Roemer et al., 1996; Schwarz et al., 1993). However, the treatment-seeking sample in this study was too small and the range too restricted to detect such an association adequately. Further research is needed to identify the factors that influence changes in reports of trauma exposure and to identify the individuals who are likely to be influenced by these factors.

References

American Psychiatric Association. (1980). *Diagnostic and statistical manual of mental disorders* (3rd ed.). Washington, DC: Author.

American Psychiatric Association. (1987). *Diagnostic and statistical manual of mental disorders* (3rd ed., rev.). Washington, DC: Author.

American Psychiatric Association. (1994). *Diagnostic and statistical manual of mental disorders* (4th ed.). Washington, DC: Author.

Blake, D. D., Weathers, F. W., Nagy, L. M., Kaloupek, D. G., Klauminzer, G., Charney, D. S., & Keane, T. M. (1990). A clinician rating scale for assessing current and lifetime PTSD: The CAPS-1. *Behavior Therapist, 13,* 187-188.

Bowers, K. S., & Farvolden, P. (1996a). Revisiting a century-old Freudian slip: From suggestion disavowed to the truth repressed. *Psychological Bulletin, 119,* 355-380.

Bowers, K. S., & Farvolden, P. (1996b). The search for the canonical experience: Reply to Pennebaker and Memon (1996). *Psychological Bulletin, 119,* 386-389.

Fairbank, J. A., Schlenger, W. E., Caddell, J. M., & Woods, M. G. (1994). Posttraumatic stress disorder. In P. B. Sutker & H. E. Adams (Eds.), *Comprehensive handbook of psychopathology* (2nd ed., pp. 145-165). New York: Plenum.

Green, B. L. (1990). Defining trauma: Terminology and generic stressor dimensions. *Journal of Applied Social Psychology, 20,* 1632-1642.

Kaylor, J. A., King, D. W., & King, L. A. (1987). Psychological effects of military service in Vietnam: A meta-analysis. *Psychological Bulletin, 102,* 257-271.

Keane, T. M., Caddell, J. M., & Taylor, K. L. (1988). Mississippi Scale for Combat-Related Posttraumatic Stress Disorder: Three studies in reliability and validity. *Journal of Consulting and Clinical Psychology, 56,* 85-90.

Keane, T. M., Fairbank, J. A., Caddell, J. M., Zimering, R. T., Taylor, K. L., & Mora, C. A. (1989). Clinical evaluation of a measure to assess combat exposure. *Psychological Assessment, 1,* 53-55.

Kulka, R. A., Schlenger, W. E., Fairbank, J. A., Hough, R. L., Jordan, B. K., Marmar, C. R., & Weiss, D. S. (1990). *Trauma and the Vietnam War generation.* New York: Brunner/Mazel.

Loftus, E. F. (1993). The reality of repressed memories. *American Psychologist, 48,* 518-537.

March, J. S. (1993). What constitutes a stressor? The "Criterion A" issue. In J. R. T. Davidson & E. B. Foa (Eds.), *Posttraumatic stress disorder: DSM-IV and beyond* (pp. 37-54). Washington, DC: American Psychiatric Press.

McFarlane, A. C. (1988). The longitudinal course of posttraumatic morbidity. *Journal of Nervous and Mental Disease, 176,* 30-39.

Pennebaker, J. W., & Memon, A. (1996). Recovered memories in context: Thoughts and elaborations on Bowers and Farvolden (1996). *Psychological Bulletin, 119,* 381-385.

Pope, K. S. (1996). Memory, abuse, and science: Questioning claims about the false memory syndrome epidemic. *American Psychologist, 51,* 957-974.

Roemer, L., Litz, B. T., Orsillo, S. M., Ehlich, P. J., & Friedman, M. J. (1996). *Increases in retrospective accounts of war-zone exposure over time: The role of PTSD symptom severity.* Manuscript submitted for publication.

Schwarz, E. D., Kowalski, J. M., & McNally, R. J. (1993). Malignant memories: Post-traumatic changes in memory in adults after a school shooting. *Journal of Traumatic Stress, 6,* 545-553.

Spitzer, R. L., Williams, J. B., Gibbons, M., & First, M. B. (1990). *Structured clinical interview for DSM-III-R: Patient edition (SCID–P, Version 1.0).* Washington, DC: American Psychiatric Press.

Yule, W., & Williams, R. (1990). Posttraumatic stress reactions in children. *Journal of Traumatic Stress, 3,* 279-295.

25

True Lies, False Truths, and Naturalistic Raw Data

Applying Clinical Research Findings to the False Memory Debate

Richard P. Kluft

In recent years, the mental health professions have been rocked by strident, vituperative, politicized, and highly divisive debates over the reality of accounts of abuse reported by patients in psychotherapy. The veracity of reports based on recollections made after years without conscious memory of the events in question has come under particular scrutiny (Loftus, 1993), and has been subjected to especially vigorous attacks (e.g., Loftus & Ketcham, 1994; Ofshe & Watters, 1994). Skeptical authorities have derided the reality of dissociative identity disorder (DID), or multiple personality disorder, as a mental disorder (Fahey, 1988; McHugh, 1993; Merskey, 1992; Piper, 1994; Simpson, 1995). Allegations made by DID patients, most of whose memories of traumatiza-

tion emerge in the course of treatment, have been challenged as largely unconfirmed and/or iatrogenic (Frankel, 1992; Piper, 1994; Simpson, 1995).

Interestingly, the skeptical literature has taken little notice of a number of reports that confirm that DID patients indeed have been abused, some of which are listed in Table 25.1. These studies demonstrate that DID/DDNOS (dissociative disorder not otherwise specified) patients generally have suffered true abuse and/or genuinely overwhelming experiences. However, they do not correlate apparent memories reported in psychotherapy with external corroborations. A patient who has suffered genuine trauma may offer accounts in treatment that differ from the traumas that have been

AUTHOR'S NOTE: This chapter was originally presented as a paper at Trauma and Memory: An International Research Conference, in Durham, New Hampshire, July 27, 1996. It is based on and contains materials also published in Kluft (1995a, 1997).

Table 25.1 Documentation of Abuse in Histories of DID/DDNOS Patients

Study	Findings
Bliss (1984)	documented abuse in 8/9 adult patients (89%)
Fagan and McMahon (1984)	documented abuse in 4/4 children (100%)
Kluft (1984a)	documented abuse in 5/5 children (100%)
Coons and Milstein (1986)	documented abuse in 17/20 adults (85%)
Hornstein and Putnam (1992)	documented abuse in 61/66 children/adolescents (95%)
Coons (1994)	documented abuse in 20/21 children/adolescents (95%)

documented (for a related observation, see Williams, 1994), or may refer to incidents that either cannot be assessed for accuracy or may actually be disproved.

I recently explored the possibility of confirming or disconfirming always available and retrieved memories of mistreatment by DID patients, examining naturalistic clinical material without introducing unduly intrusive or invasive interventions that could alter the process of the therapy (Kluft, 1995a, 1997). I hoped to demonstrate whether amnesia for documentable trauma and the recovery of accurate memories were naturalistically occurring clinical phenomena.

The first hypothesis of this study was that a review of clinical records would reveal instances in which once-unavailable memories recovered in therapy could be confirmed. The second hypothesis was that a review of clinical records would reveal instances in which allegations made and/or memories recovered in therapy could be disconfirmed. However, these hypotheses were transparently disingenuous from the first, because I was not blind to the data I would study, having acquired it myself.

It may be more useful to formulate a major goal of the study in terms of the so-called recovered memory debate. Its premise as a debate resolution might be stated as follows: Resolved, there is no demonstrable instance in which accurate once-unavailable memories have been recovered. If the affirmative is proven, there is no such thing as recovering an accurate but once-unavailable memory. If the negative is proven, such a phenomenon exists. One instance of the recovery of an accurate memory formerly absent from conscious recollection proves the negative.

Method

☐ For this study, I reviewed the records of a series of DID patients I treated in therapy during a 30-day period in 1995 for instances of the confirmation and disconfirmation of allegations of abuse.

Subjects

DID is a complex chronic dissociative psychopathology characterized primarily by lesions of memory and identity. DID patients are characterized by high hypnotizability (Frischholz, Lipman, Braun, & Sachs, 1992). The criteria stated in the *Diagnostic and Statistical Manual of Mental Disorders,* fourth edition (*DSM-IV*), are as follows:

1. The presence of two or more distinct identities or personality states (each with its own relatively enduring pattern of perceiving, relating to, and thinking about the environment and self).

2. At least two of these identities or personality states recurrently take control of the person's behavior.

3. Inability to recall important personal information that is too extensive to be explained by ordinary forgetfulness.

4. The disturbance is not due to the direct physiological effects of a substance . . . or a general medical condition. (American Psychiatric Association, 1994, p. 487)

To be included in the study, patients had to have fulfilled these criteria for the DID diagnosis at some point while under my observation, and had to be in ongoing psychotherapy with me. Of the 43 DID patients whom I saw over the study period, 34 (79%) qualified. Of those who qualified, 32 (94%) were female and 2 (6%) were male; 1 female was African American, and 1 was Asian American. Their average age (for 32/34 patients) was 44.4 years (range 19-70). They had been in treatment with me for an average of 5.5 years (range 3 months to 19 years). At the time of the study, 6 were integrated, 4 were nearly integrated, and 4 had ceased to show overt DID behavior, but they continued to have alters. The remaining 20 patients fulfilled *DSM-IV* criteria at the time of the study. Most had additional diagnoses not relevant to the purposes of this study. The majority were being seen in one to four sessions per week. One patient was hospitalized throughout the study, and one died of an intercurrent cardiac event. The modal patient in the study was an outpatient in her mid-40s seen slightly less than twice a week, and a "treatment veteran."

Procedures

After observing and reporting on the variety of accurate and inaccurate memories recounted by DID patients in the 1970s (Kluft, 1984b), I routinely collected and flagged events in which patients' memories were either confirmed or disconfirmed. This effort facilitated a review of the charts for such events. To classify an event as confirmed, I required the following: (a) the witnessing of the event to be acknowledged to myself, to the patient, or to another medical, mental health, or legal professional by the witness, or to be detailed in the witness's diary or correspondence; and/or (b) the oral or written confession of the alleged perpetrator; and/or (c) legal documentation of the relevant data. The account by the witness or perpetrator, or in the documentation, had to be sufficiently detailed for me to be confident that the same event had been reported by the patient and the confirmatory source, or had to be an acknowledgment of

a specific circumstance. Although I accepted my patients' accounts of confirmations and confessions, on many occasions I was witness either to confirmations or confessions by alleged perpetrators. I also received telephone calls and letters from witnesses. I did not accept "confirmation by inference" in this study; that is, a patient's averring that "my sister remembers he did it to her, so my memories must be right" was not tabulated as a confirmation. When sources disagreed, I did not score a confirmation. Disconfirmations were treated similarly.

I selected these criteria to reflect the realities of clinical practice and to protect the frame of the therapy. In deciding to score sibling confirmations only when all relevant siblings agreed, I accepted the possibility of underreporting actual abuse. By restricting the study to charted materials, I accepted a degree of systematic underreportage; at times I had acceded to patients' requests that I not record certain information, such as their discovery of confirmatory pornographic films, tapes, or photographs. Naturally, I declined to review such materials myself, in deference to prioritizing the boundaries of the therapy and the emotional needs of my patients. Internal indices of confirmation, which may be suitable for clinical use (e.g., Alpert, 1995a), were neither tabulated nor considered.

I did not consider allegations that seemed unlikely or implausible to be disconfirmed a priori. They had to be disproved. I accepted the possibility that this decision might result in a systematic bias toward underreporting inaccurate recollections. Examples of unlikely or implausible events include abuses reported from prior lives and extraterrestrial abductions. Recanting was not considered a disconfirmation unless it was corroborated by sources other than the alleged perpetrators. Denials by alleged perpetrators were not considered disconfirmations unless accompanied by testimony from other witnesses to the alleged circumstances.

Finally, no incident first called to a patient's attention and later recalled by that patient was included in the study. My rationale was that an apparent memory recovered under such circum-

Table 25.2 Sources of Confirmation of Abuse Allegations for 19 DID Patients

	Total	Always Recalled	Recovered in Therapy
Confirmation by a sibling who witnessed abuse[a]	12	4	8
Confirmation by one parent of abuse by the other parent	5	3	2
Confession by abusive parent (deathbed or serious illness)	4	1	3
Confession by abusive parent (other circumstances)	3	1	2
Confirmation by police/court records	3	2	1
Confirmation to author by abusive therapist	2	1	1
Confirmation by a childhood neighbor of witnessed abuse	1		1
Confession by abusive sibling (during terminal illness)	1		1
Confession by abusive sibling (other circumstances)	1		1
Confirmation by relative (neither parent nor sibling)	1		1
Confirmation by friend who witnessed and interrupted abuse attempt	1		1
Totals	34	12	22

SOURCE: Reprinted with permission in a corrected form from Kluft (1995a, p. 255). Copyright 1995 by Dissociative Disorders Research Publications, Ltd.

a. For three patients, siblings confirmed both material always recalled and material recovered in therapy; one report is unclassified because the dissociative handling of the incident involved depersonalization and derealization, but not frank amnesia.

stances would be subject to the criticism that it was in fact an instigated imagined product misperceived as a memory.

Findings

☐ Among the 34 charts, I discovered 34 instances of memories of abuse for which there was corroboration. There were 3 instances in which there was corroboration that alleged abuse did not take place. A total of 19 of my DID patients, 56% of the series, had instances of confirmed abuse, averaging 1.8 instances apiece. Of the 19, 10 (53%) had always recalled the abuses that were confirmed; 13 of the 19 (68%) obtained documentation of events that had been retrieved during their treatment with me. Among the 34 charts, 4 patients (11.7%) had confirmations of both always-recalled and recently retrieved memories. Of the 34 corroborated memories, 22 (65%) were so-called recovered memories. Interestingly, 11 of the 13 patients (85%) with confirmed recovered memories had recovered their confirmed memories in interventions facilitated by hypnosis. In fact, 20 of the 22 corroborated recovered memories (91%) had been retrieved with the help of hypnosis. One patient's recovered mem-

ory occurred during free association in psychodynamic psychotherapy; the last occurred during eye movement desensitization and reprocessing treatment (Shapiro, 1995).

The sources of the confirmations of mistreatment are presented in Table 25.2. Clearly, several patients had multiple sources of confirmation. Furthermore, a single entry of sibling verification often represented many confirmations from within the siblingship. For example, one patient had eight siblings, all of whom confirmed instances of the patient's abuse, and three of whom—in addition to the patient's mother—made their confirmations directly to me in a family meeting. Also, an allegation of extrafamilial abuse was confirmed by police and medical reports. The confirmed abuses involved physical and sexual abuse, usually occurring within the family of origin.

Three patients (9%) had instances in which allegations could be conclusively disproved. Of this series, 13 (38%) alleged memories of having suffered satanic ritual abuse. One such allegation was disproved, because certain unique factors in the report had particular referents that were amenable to rechecking with the patient's school records (see Table 25.3). In this series, there were no allegations of alien abductions, prior lives, or similar phenomena that inspire

Table 25.3 Confirmations and Disconfirmations in an Illustrative Case of DID—A Professional Woman in Her 40s

Alleged Abuse	Source of Confirmation or Disconfirmation
Father-daughter incest (general)	Three sisters, one brother, and mother were aware of incest; father confessed and apologized while terminally ill.
Father-daughter incest (specific incidents)	Three sisters, one brother, and mother recall walking in on specific episodes; patient recovered the memories in hypnosis and asked family members for confirmation.
Incest rape by brother	Confession by brother dying of cancer confirmed memory recovered under hypnosis.
Abuse by physician mentor	No data.
Satanic ritual abuse	School records demonstrate patient was not at location of alleged abuse.

knee-jerk skepticism in many scholars. Of the three disconfirmations, one was an incident of alleged satanic ritual abuse, one involved an alleged assault with satanic ritual abuse connections, and one was an incident of alleged incest rape.

Table 25.3 illustrates the corroboration patterns in an illustrative case in which both confirmation and disconfirmation were documented. Confirmations occurred in a wide variety of fashions (see Table 25.2). For example, when one woman returned to her home to pay a visit to her terminally ill father, he asked her forgiveness for his incestuous use of her. The sister of a woman who alleged father-daughter incest informed me in a family therapy session that she had frequently come upon her father having intercourse with the patient. A brother who had raped his sister called me to confirm his sister's account when he was terminally ill.

Disconfirmations were established through the use of documents placing the patient far from the scene of an alleged satanic abuse in one case, and through the testimony to both me and the patient of numerous witnesses trusted by the patient in another. In the third, the wounds allegedly inflicted on the patient by an assailant were determined to be self-inflicted by a forensic pathologist I had called (with the patient's consent) to examine her.

Several incidents of recanting were encountered; all recantations were rescinded. Some patients recanted and rescinded several times. I did not attempt to quantify recanter phenomena because many such incidents were too equivocal, too inconsistent across personalities, or too transient to study.

Although I did not precisely tabulate the length of time that patients had been in treatment before corroborations occurred, I note that only one occurred within the first 2 years of treatment with me, and most occurred when the patient was well on the way to recovery. In that single episode the patient had been in therapy for more than 16 years before entering treatment with me.

Discussion

□ The vast majority of the memories of alleged abuse reported by DID patients during their assessments and their psychotherapies are neither confirmed nor disconfirmed. The 34 confirmed incidents and the 3 disconfirmed episodes constitute a small fraction of the abuse recollections reported by this cohort of patients. Many DID patients in treatment have been abused, and often their abuse can be documented (Bliss, 1984; Bowman, Blix, & Coons, 1985; Coons, 1994; Coons & Milstein, 1986; Fagan & McMahon, 1984; Hornstein & Putnam, 1992; Kluft, 1984a). This study extends these findings. It demonstrates that whereas confirmable traumas are often retained in available memory, many genuine traumas are not. Amnesia for genuine trauma is a demonstrable clinical phenomenon. Further, it demonstrates that in some instances such amnesia can be lifted in the course of treatment without undue distortion occurring in the process. It disconfirms the often-voiced caution that information retrieved with the help of hypnosis is invariably contaminated and/or unreliable, but does not in any way suggest that pseudomemories will not be encountered.

The hypotheses that both confirmations and disconfirmations of abuse recollections by DID patients would be discovered have been proven. The debate format proposition—Resolved, there is no demonstrable instance in which accurate once-unavailable memories have been recovered—has been refuted. Furthermore, many of the instances that might be cited in the refutation fulfill the stringent tests for demonstrating recovered memory proposed by False Memory Syndrome Foundation sympathizers Pope and Hudson (1995).

These findings do not support either an extreme credulous or an extreme skeptical position on the recovery of memories of trauma. They demonstrate that there are no grounds on which to discount a priori the observations of clinicians who maintain that repressed/dissociated memories of trauma and their recovery and confirmation in clinical settings are commonplace. Nor do they offer grounds on which to dispute the relevance of laboratory studies on the potential distortion of memory for clinical practice. Although they have often gone uncited and apparently unheard, there has been a small but important group of scholars who have tried from the first to acknowledge the complexity of this situation and who refuse to be stampeded into a premature disambiguation of this most complex and important area of study (e.g., Alpert, 1995b; Brown, 1995a, 1995b; Hammond et al., 1995; Kluft, 1984b, 1995b; Nash, 1994; Schooler, 1994; Spiegel & Scheflin, 1994; van der Kolk, 1995; van der Kolk & Fisler, 1995). It is their stance that the current findings support. Traumatic memory and traumatic amnesia remain frontier areas in the mental health sciences. We have yet to ap-

preciate their nature, master their mysteries, or answer the profound questions that they raise. At times, I wonder if we have even begun to ask the right questions.

When a patient has one or more memories confirmed, this does not allow the inference that all other memories produced by that patient are accurate. Nor does the disproving of one allegation allow the inference that the remainder of the patient's allegations may be dismissed summarily. Table 25.3 illustrates the coexistence of accurate, inaccurate, and indeterminate allegations in a single patient. To demonstrate this crucial point further, one patient whose alleged primary abuser was tried, convicted, and jailed later made an incest allegation that was disproved by the testimony of several witnesses.

The major findings of this study may be summarized as follows:

1. DID patients' abuse experiences can be documented in many instances.
2. Once-unavailable memories of trauma retrieved in psychotherapy of DID patients can be documented in many instances.
3. Accurate recovered memories of abuse can be documented in clinical DID populations.
4. Confabulated memories of abuse can be documented in clinical DID populations.
5. Memories of abuse retrieved from DID patients during hypnosis can be documented as accurate in many instances.
6. The proposition that recovered memories of childhood abuse are invariably inaccurate and can be discounted a priori is refuted.
7. The proposition that recovered memories of childhood abuse are invariably accurate and can be accorded credibility a priori is refuted.
8. Most memories of abuse reported by DID patients are neither confirmed nor denied in the course of their therapies.

Reflections and Further Observations on the Confirmations and Disconfirmations

☐ Many who advocate a skeptical view toward the possibility of the recovery of accurate repressed or dissociated memories currently advise that practitioners make efforts to confirm allegations of abuse before proceeding with therapy. In this connection, it is useful to recall that, with one exception, a woman in her second year of treatment with me but in her 18th year of psychotherapy, no confirmations had occurred in these patients' first 2 years of psychotherapy. In many instances, siblings who initially had denied that the patient could have been abused later admitted they had lied, usually to protect family unity, and in one instance, to safeguard an anticipated inheritance. Not infrequently, it was the death or incapacitation of an abusive parent that made siblings willing to speak up more forthrightly. Virtually all sibling confirmations occurred in cases where patients had been in treatment for quite a while, during which the health and circumstances of their alleged abusers changed substantially. Some siblings came forward when they appreciated their siblings were improving in connection with dealing with the past, while they, in their disavowal of what they knew, were becoming increasingly symptomatic. It is extremely naive to assume that deeply shameful family secrets will be yielded up so readily to a therapist hoping to confirm or disconfirm allegations of abuse prior to beginning psychotherapy.

When one parent confirms the other's abusiveness, it is essential to ask whether this might be pseudoconfirmation, possibly emerging in the context of domestic discord, where false accusations are an increasingly common weapon. In this series there were no such circumstances. All five spousal confirmations were further confirmed by the confession of the alleged perpetrator in four cases and by sibling confirmation in the fifth. Four of these confirmations came from wives about their deceased or dying husbands. The fifth was made by the husband of an abusive mother, only after the mother had admitted to abusing their daughter in a family therapy session conducted by myself and a social worker.

I found it significant that the confessions by abusers were almost invariably made by males of the Roman Catholic faith who literally feared going to hell unless they made amends. One abusive mother made her confession on her deathbed. Three mothers confessed to inflicting physical abuse upon study patients. I was present for two of these confessions; the third was made by a mother who confessed to her daughter as she "worked" a 12-step program. Two abusive therapists made confessions to me directly. In one unique case, a friend of a patient returned with the patient to the patient's parents' home on an errand. The patient entered the house first. When her friend followed her a minute or two later, she found the patient on her knees before her partially disrobed father, who was trying to induce her to perform a sexual act. The patient was amnestic for this event for several weeks. Increasing distress without apparent cause had led me to use exploratory hypnosis to uncover its etiology. The patient's friend (who initially had told me only that "something bad" had happened and did not inform her friend of what she had witnessed) later described to me in detail the event I had retrieved from the patient, who, in her mid-40s, was still using dissociation to handle difficult events and experiencing considerable revictimization (Kluft, 1990).

Improbable Events

☐ In this series, there were no allegations of alien abductions, prior lives, or similar phenomena, which inspire knee-jerk skepticism in many scholars. However, 13 patients (38%) alleged memories of having suffered satanic ritual abuse. One such allegation was disproved, because certain unique factors in the report had particular referents that were amenable to rechecking with the patient's school records (see Table 25.3). The rest remained of uncertain veracity. In some instances, legal authorities had become involved with these patients and investigated some of their allegations, in each case with inconclusive results.

Recanting

☐ As noted above, I did not consider recanting as disconfirmation, because a recantation has no more or less credibility than an initial allegation. In the study, neither was accorded standing without external corroboration. Apart from instances in which patients shared their fluctuating degree of self-doubt about their autobiographical memories and others inferred recanting from what actually were expressions of uncertainty, almost every instance of recanting encountered in this series occurred under circumstances of profound interpersonal persuasive influence fulfilling criteria for interrogatory suggestibility (see discussions of interrogatory suggestibility in Brown, 1995a, 1995b), and was contaminated for that reason. Furthermore, every episode of recanting was followed by at least one cycle of renewed insistence on the allegation's veracity. Cycles of allegation and recantation were not uncommon, and I hypothesize that some instances of this phenomenon are related to the cycles of intrusive and restrictive phenomena so familiar in the study of posttraumatic states (American Psychiatric Association, 1994).

The recanting observed in this series was usually not a naturalistic phenomenon. No recanters remained in a recanting stance at the time of the study. In only one case did I attempt to influence a recanter. I reminded her that she was recanting episodes corroborated by others, and I asked her to explore her thoughts about this curious circumstance. In all other instances, I took a nonjudgmental and noninterventive stance, allowing the process of psychotherapy to address the patient's changing understanding of his or her circumstances.

Cautions

☐ Cautions against generalizing from this study are in order. Although this study makes several observations that are relevant to hotly debated issues and controversies, it has certain limitations and does not address some issues of concern. This was a study on DID patients. The distinction between amnesias associated with dissociation and those linked with repression is regarded as inconsequential by investigators who do not find it useful to distinguish between these mechanisms. Yet there are those who con-

sider the difference to be of crucial importance. Investigators in this latter category might be concerned that the study addressed amnesia per se in DID patients, but did not specify or explore its mechanism. It is not certain how thoroughly findings in DID patients can be applied to the wider range of trauma victims.

Although many confirmations were made to me, or were in official documentation of some form, most were made to the patients, whose accounts of the confirmations were accepted at face value. In every instance of sibling confirmation, I was given permission to talk to the sibling, but I chose not to do so, as this would violate the frame of therapy. At times, siblings called or wrote me at their own or the patient's insistence, which I permitted with the patient's consent and release, or they spoke up in family therapy sessions.

I appreciate that the events most crucial to this study were those in which persons other than the patients made direct confessions to me, or where the corroboration was found in legal documents. However, I elected not to isolate those materials because I wanted the study to reflect the realities of clinical practice. Elsewhere (Kluft, 1998) I have given more details of these instances. In short, 50% of the confirmed retrieved memories were confirmed by me.

Likewise, independent assessments of the confirmations would have been preferable, but this is not realistic in private practice, especially with a patient population that poorly tolerates nontherapeutic interventions. I chose an approach that neither challenged my patients' veracity (unless clinical evidence suggested I should) nor distorted their treatments in the service of research. It will be useful to follow this study with one that employs a far more demanding protocol.

It is my hope that neither confirmatory bias (Baron, Beattie, & Hershey, 1988) nor motivated skepticism (Ditto & Lopez, 1992) played a major role in this study. I did not set out to prove or disprove either polarized position in the debate over recovered memory. I let the charts speak for themselves. My study almost certainly underreports the degree to which alleged abuses can be confirmed and disconfirmed.

Remarks on the Nature of Traumatic Memory

☐ There is much current interest in the nature of traumatic memory and in studying whether traumatic memory differs from more routine recollection. Unfortunately for the exploration of this issue, the current study relied on data that had been collected prior to modern conceptualizations of the nature of traumatic memory. Van der Kolk (1995) and van der Kolk and Fisler (1995) have argued persuasively that much traumatic memory is initially fragmentary, with affective and somatic/sensory elements. My records rarely documented the steps in which traumatic memories emerged, and did not always indicate the forms in which traumatic memories were first expressed.

I cannot offer systematic observations on whether my patients recalled vague bits that were augmented as therapy continued and that combined with additional aspects that are clearly reconstructive as therapy brought once-dissociated implicit memory to the level of explicit memory. My own recollection of sessions years in the past is a dubious resource. However, my records included many small samples of verbatim notes taken as patients told their stories. The verbatim materials include instances in which memories emerged in a fragmentary, piecemeal way and were reassembled over time, and instances in which the memories emerged in a full narrative form from the first session. Instances of both types of recall were found among the confirmed recovered memories. Elsewhere, I have explained why I think both types of memory can be recovered in clinical populations, arguing that there is an inherent logic in conceptualizing *traumatic memories or memory systems,* rather than traumatic memory (Kluft, 1997).

Hypnosis

☐ Of the confirmed retrieved memories in this study, 91% had been accessed with hypnosis. This was an unanticipated finding, but I was not surprised that this proved to be the case. Con-fabulation can occur with hypnosis; it is appropriate that its use in legal settings be carefully scrutinized. Unfortunately, in the heated, often oversimplified atmosphere of the false memory debate, this has been misrepresented, so that what is possible has been described as if it were likely, even inevitable. The relationship of hypnosis and memory is a most complicated area of study. Most laboratory studies of memory distortion, with or without hypnosis, lack general ecological validity in the clinical situation (Kluft, 1997), but may, in certain instances, illuminate the mechanism of a variety of clinical mishaps and therefore be relevant to bear in mind (Brown, 1995a, 1995b).

Most critics of hypnosis have not appreciated that hypnosis is a facilitator of therapy, not a treatment in and of itself (Frischholz & Spiegel, 1983). McConkey's (1992) analysis of the literature of hypnosis and memory distortion has demonstrated that, given the hypnotizability of the subject and the demand characteristics of the situation, inducing formal hypnosis does not add to the likelihood of memory distortion. The problematic factors are the nature of the interpersonal influence that is being applied and the vulnerability to suggestion of the subject. The crucial considerations, to the thoughtful student of the problem, are what the hypnosis is being used to facilitate and with whom it is being used. Generic condemnations of the use of hypnosis with trauma victims represent overgeneralization to the point of irrationality. Some uses are problematic and deserve condemnation; others are probably safe with most patients.

Let me illustrate this point with three hypothetical scenarios in which hypnosis is used to explore a period for which the patient has apparent amnesia, and during which the therapist wonders if abuse might have occurred (derived from Kluft, 1997). In the first, trance is induced and the patient is requested to return to the time in question and respond to inquiries such as the following: "Were you being hurt?" "You see someone—is it your father?" "Is he wearing any clothing?" I think we can all agree that this approach is provocative and suggestive, and thus might promote confabulation.

In a second hypothetical vignette, trance is induced and the patient is requested to return to the time in question and the following type of inquiries are made: "What do you observe?" "Can you identify the person you noticed?" "Does anything more strike your attention?" In contrast with the previous scenario, we might concur that these inquiries are open-ended and permissive, and thus relatively unlikely to promote confabulation.

In a third situation, the patient expects to find an abuse memory on the basis of previously known trauma, the notions of a friend or relative, the media, the professional literature, the tenor of the therapy to date, a recent dream, or some other influence. In this instance, no matter how circumspect and cautious the clinician, the self-suggestion inherent in the patient's own expectations may exert pressure toward confabulation despite the therapist's most scrupulous efforts to avoid such an outcome.

The essential point here is that the culprits are interpersonal influence and the expectations that it creates. Hypnosis is a virtually innocent bystander, and it has received a tremendous amount of undeserved bad press.

I employ hypnosis in the service of an approach to therapy that is psychoanalytically informed and sensitive, on an ongoing basis, to the risk of undue suggestion. I train my patients to report the influences in their current lives that bear on what we discuss in therapy, much as I elicit day residue when I attempt to explore the meaning of dreams. My use of hypnosis directed toward the specific goal of recovering memory is fairly infrequent. Given these considerations, I am not surprised that much of what is retrieved with the use of hypnosis in my daily practice proves valuable.

Conclusion

☐ The findings of this study indicate that it is essential to move beyond the polemics that have clouded the study of memory in the traumatized. Both clinicians and researchers are in possession of data and approaches to understanding that can enrich one another. The clini-

cian should not condescend to the researcher, nor should the researcher treat the clinician with contempt. The disregard of data and/or ideas is unscientific in the extreme. Those who dismiss relevant ideas and data to which they are not sympathetic will be remembered by history as fanatics and fools.

References

Alpert, J. L. (1995a). Criteria: Signposts toward the sexual abuse hypothesis. In J. L. Alpert (Ed.), *Sexual abuse recalled: Treating trauma in the era of the recovered memory debate* (pp. 363-396). Northvale, NJ: Jason Aronson.

Alpert, J. L. (Ed.). (1995b). *Sexual abuse recalled: Treating trauma in the era of the recovered memory debate.* Northvale, NJ: Jason Aronson.

American Psychiatric Association. (1994). *Diagnostic and statistical manual of mental disorders* (4th ed.). Washington, DC: Author.

Baron, J., Beattie, J., & Hershey, J. D. (1988). Heuristics and biases in diagnostic reasoning: Congruence, information, and certainty. *Organizational Behavior and Human Decision Processes, 42,* 88-110.

Bliss, E. L. (1984). Spontaneous self-hypnosis in multiple personality disorder. *Psychiatric Clinics of North America, 7,* 135-148.

Bowman, E. S., Blix, S., & Coons, P. M. (1985). Multiple personality in adolescence: Relationship to incestual experience. *Journal of the American Academy of Child and Adolescent Psychiatry, 24,* 109-114.

Brown, D. (1995a). Pseudomemories, the standard of science, and the standard of care in trauma treatment. *American Journal of Clinical Hypnosis, 37,* 1-24.

Brown, D. (1995b). Sources of suggestion and their applicability to psychotherapy. In J. L. Alpert (Ed.), *Sexual abuse recalled: Treating trauma in the era of the recovered memory debate* (pp. 61-100). Northvale, NJ: Jason Aronson.

Coons, P. M. (1994). Confirmation of childhood abuse in childhood and adolescent cases of multiple personality disorder and dissociative disorder not otherwise specified. *Journal of Nervous and Mental Disease, 182,* 461-464.

Coons, P. M., & Milstein, V. (1986). Psychosexual disturbances in multiple personality: Characteristics, etiology, and treatment. *Journal of Clinical Psychiatry, 47,* 106-110.

Ditto, P. H., & Lopez, D. F. (1992). Motivated skepticism: Use of differential decision criteria for preferred and non-preferred conclusions. *Journal of Personality and Social Psychology, 63,* 568-584.

Fagan, J., & McMahon, P. P. (1984). Incipient multiple personality in children: Four cases. *Journal of Nervous and Mental Disease, 172,* 26-36.

Fahey, T. A. (1988). The diagnosis of multiple personality disorder: A critical review. *British Journal of Psychiatry, 153,* 597-606.

Frankel, F. H. (1992). Adult reconstruction of childhood events in the multiple personality disorder literature. *American Journal of Psychiatry, 149,* 954-958.

Frischholz, E. J., Lipman, L. S., Braun, B. G., & Sachs, R. G. (1992). Psychopathology, hypnotizability, and dissociation. *American Journal of Psychiatry, 149,* 1521-1525.

Frischholz, E. J., & Spiegel, D. (1983). Hypnosis is not therapy. *Bulletin of the British Society of Clinical and Experimental Hypnosis, 6,* 3-8.

Hammond, D. C., Garver, R. B., Mutter, C. B., Crasilneck, H. B., Frischholz, E., Gravitz, M. A., Hibler, N. S., Olson, J., Scheflin, A., Spiegel, H., & Wester, W. (1995). *Clinical hypnosis and memory: Guidelines for clinicians and for forensic hypnosis.* Chicago: American Society of Clinical Hypnosis Press.

Hornstein, N. L., & Putnam, F. W. (1992). Clinical phenomenology of child and adolescent multiple personality disorder. *Journal of the American Academy of Child and Adolescent Psychiatry, 31,* 1055-1077.

Kluft, R. P. (1984a). Multiple personality in childhood. *Psychiatric Clinics of North America, 7,* 121-134.

Kluft, R. P. (1984b). Treatment of multiple personality disorder. *Psychiatric Clinics of North America, 7,* 9-29.

Kluft, R. P. (1990). Dissociation and subsequent vulnerability: A preliminary study. *Dissociation, 3,* 167-173.

Kluft, R. P. (1995a). The confirmation and disconfirmation of memories of abuse in dissociative identity disorder patients: A naturalistic clinical study. *Dissociation, 8,* 253-258.

Kluft, R. P. (1995b). Current controversies surrounding multiple personality disorder. In L. Cohen, J. Berzoff, & M. Elin (Eds.), *Dissociative identity disorder* (pp. 347-377). Northvale, NJ: Jason Aronson.

Kluft, R. P. (1997). The argument for the reality of the delayed recall of trauma. In P. S. Appelbaum, L. Uyehara, & M. Elin (Eds.), *Trauma and memory: Clinical and legal issues* (pp. 25-57). New York: Oxford University Press.

Kluft, R. P. (1998). Reflections on the traumatic memories of dissociative identity disorder patients. In S. J. Lynn & K. M. McConkey (Eds.), *Truth in memory* (pp. 304-322). New York: Guilford.

Loftus, E. F. (1993). The reality of repressed memories. *American Psychologist, 48,* 518-537.

Loftus, E. F., & Ketcham, K. (1994). *The myth of repressed memory: False memories and allegations of sexual abuse.* New York: St. Martin's.

McConkey, K. M. (1992). The effects of hypnotic procedures on remembering: The experimental findings and their implications for forensic hypnosis. In E. Fromm & M. R. Nash (Eds.), *Contemporary hypnosis research* (pp. 405-426). New York: Guilford.

McHugh, P. R. (1993). Multiple personality disorder. *Harvard Mental Health Letter, 10*(3), 4-6.

Merskey, H. (1992). The manufacture of personalities. *British Journal of Psychiatry, 160,* 327-340.

Nash, M. R. (1994). Memory distortion and sexual trauma: The problem of false negatives and false positives. *International Journal of Clinical and Experimental Hypnosis, 42,* 346-362.

Ofshe, R. J., & Watters, E. (1994). *Making monsters: False memory, psychotherapy, and sexual hysteria.* New York: Scribner's.

Piper, A., Jr. (1994). Multiple personality disorder: A critical review. *British Journal of Psychiatry, 164,* 600-612.

Pope, H. G., & Hudson, J. I. (1995). Can individuals "repress" memories of childhood sexual abuse? An examination of the evidence. *Psychiatric Annals, 25,* 715-719.

Schooler, J. W. (1994). Seeking the core: The issues and evidence surrounding recovered accounts of sexual trauma. *Consciousness and Cognition, 3,* 452-469.

Shapiro, F. (1995). *Eye movement desensitization and reprocessing: Basic principles, protocols, and procedures.* New York: Guilford.

Simpson, M. A. (1995). Gullible's travels, or the importance of being multiple. In L. Cohen, J. Berzoff, & M. Elin (Eds.), *Dissociative identity disorder* (pp. 87-134). Northvale, NJ: Jason Aronson.

Spiegel, D., & Scheflin, A. W. (1994). Dissociated or fabricated: Psychiatric aspects of repressed memory in criminal and civil cases. *International Journal of Clinical and Experimental Hypnosis, 42,* 411-432.

van der Kolk, B. A. (1995). The body, memory, and the psychobiology of trauma. In J. L. Alpert (Ed.), *Sexual abuse recalled: Treating trauma in the era of the recovered memory debate* (pp. 29-60). Northvale, NJ: Jason Aronson.

van der Kolk, B. A., & Fisler, R. (1995). Dissociation and the fragmentary nature of traumatic memories: Overview and exploratory study. *Journal of Traumatic Stress, 8,* 505-525.

Williams, L. M. (1994). Recall of childhood trauma: A prospective study of women's memories of sexual abuse. *Journal of Consulting and Clinical Psychology, 62,* 1167-1176.

26

The Sociopolitical Context of the Delayed Memory Debate

Connie M. Kristiansen
Carolyn Gareau
Jennifer Mittleholt
Nancy H. DeCourville
Wendy E. Hovdestad

During the past 5 years, there has been much scientific and social debate about the validity of adults' recovered memories of childhood abuse. Some people believe that about 5% of adults' recovered memories are false, an estimate based on the findings of a field study of the incidence of false memories (Hovdestad & Kristiansen, in press), the incidence of the false reporting of other crimes (Torrey, 1991), and the percentage of children's allegations found to be false (Everson & Boat, 1989; Jones & McGraw, 1987). Others, however, argue that such recovered memories frequently, even typically, constitute part of "false memory syndrome" (FMS), whereby adults develop pseudomemories of child abuse in response to the iatrogenic suggestions of therapists, self-help books, and other

authoritative sources (Loftus & Ketcham, 1994; Ofshe & Watters, 1993, 1994; Tyroler, 1996). Such divergent estimates of the likelihood of false memories are clearly perplexing, particularly when they come from social scientists who claim to have critically examined the relevant research literature. These disparate perspectives may, however, be reconciled by experimental findings that "people are less skeptical consumers of desirable than undesirable information" (Ditto & Lopez, 1992, p. 568). In view of this, the research reported in this chapter was designed to examine the social, psychological, and political underpinnings of people's beliefs about recovered memories.

One social psychological factor that may underlie people's beliefs about the validity of

AUTHORS' NOTE: We extend our thanks to Victoria Banyard, Jan Heney, and Linda Williams for their helpful comments on an earlier version of this chapter.

recovered memories is their need to believe that the world is a just place, where people get what they deserve and therefore deserve what they get (Lerner, 1980). In this regard, many studies have found that people will hold innocent victims of rape and partner abuse responsible for their fate in order to defend their belief in a just world and related beliefs regarding their own invulnerability to negative life events (Janoff-Bulman, 1992; Kristiansen & Giulietti, 1990). Perhaps, as Alice Miller (1983) argues, "the scorn we as a society heap on all victims originates in our defensive rejection of the unacknowledged helplessness and suffering of our childhood. Hence, victim-blame stems from childhood cruelty" (quoted in Rose, 1991, p. 44). Indeed, "victims [themselves] frequently tend to assume responsibility for the abuse, thereby restoring an illusion of control; alternatively, they may redefine and minimize the event, thereby protecting a view of the world as just and orderly" (Rieker & Carmen, 1986, p. 362). Thus, the social denial of recovered memories of child abuse may occur because people, both victims and nonvictims alike, simply cannot cope with the injustice of child abuse and its implications for their own sense of security (Herman, 1992; Herman, Perry, & van der Kolk, 1989; McFarlane & van der Kolk, 1996; Olafson, Corwin, & Summit, 1993).

Given that the majority of incest survivors are women and most perpetrators are men (Berliner & Elliott, 1996), people's beliefs about the validity of recovered memories may also be tied to their attitudes toward women (Enns, McNeilly, Corkery, & Gilbert, 1995). This is a bone of contention for FMS proponents, who claim that "the policy question lies in the mine field of political correctness. Sexual assault, particularly of children, has become starkly political in recent years. . . . In the recovered memory movement the formation of FMS is classified as merely part of the backlash against women and children" (Ofshe & Watters, 1993, p. 5). Nonetheless, people with positive attitudes toward women's equality have been found to be more sympathetic toward women who have experienced rape or partner abuse (Kristiansen & Giulietti, 1990). Similarly, in a simu-

lated jury study, Gabora, Spanos, and Joab (1993) observed that jurors with less favorable attitudes toward women held more erroneous beliefs about incest and were more likely to derogate a child victim of incest.

Going beyond attitudes toward women and just world beliefs, a more encompassing personality characteristic frequently implicated in violence toward women and children is authoritarianism. Walker, Rowe, and Quinsey (1993), for example, report that "men admitting both past sexual aggression and future likelihood of forcing sex or raping were more authoritarian than their counterparts admitting only past sexual aggression or future likelihood of forcing sex or raping, who were in turn more authoritarian than men indicating neither past nor potential future sexual aggression" (p. 1040). Miller (1983) claims that the authoritarian

ideology supporting adult power over children . . . is contained in religion, law, and conventional child-rearing practices. . . . These principles include: (a) blind obedience to authority as represented by the parents and other (usually) male authority figures (i.e., God); (b) the endorsement of coercion, including humiliation and physical abuse, in order to achieve this end; (c) glorification of the aggressor (parent, priest, dictator) who enacts the oppression; and (d) the tenet that such abuse is for the child's own good. (cited in Rose, 1991, pp. 43-44)

Supporting Miller's contention that authoritarianism underlies child abuse, many of the women in Westerlund's (1992) sample of 43 incest survivors described the perpetrator as "generally respected in the community as a man who adequately provided for his family, embraced traditional values and conventional attitudes about sex, practiced religion as often as not, and seemingly functioned appropriately for the most part on a social basis. Within the home, this same man was authoritarian, unpredictable, and as often given to physical violence as not" (p. 45).

The potential role of authoritarianism in beliefs about recovered memories also follows from findings that authoritarians tend to believe in a just world (Janoff-Bulman, 1992; Rubin & Peplau, 1975) and express negative attitudes toward feminists (Duncan, Peterson, & Winter, 1997; Haddock & Zanna, 1994), and that attitudes toward women mediate the relation between authoritarianism and sexual aggression (Walker et al., 1993). Further, that authoritarians claim that feminists violate traditionally cherished values (Haddock & Zanna, 1994) is in line with Faludi's (1991) journalistic exposé of the New Right's attempt to appeal to socially sanctioned values to justify opposition to policies designed to enhance women's equality, such as the Equal Rights Amendment. In this regard, Faludi writes that the New Right's "Orwellian wordplay served to conceal their anger at women's rising independence. This was a fruitful marketing tool, as they would gain more sympathy from the press and draw more followers from the public if they marched under the banner of traditional family values" (p. 238). Reading the FMS Foundation's (1993) mission statement reveals that, like the New Right, members of this organization also appeal to socially shared values to justify their beliefs about recovered memories. For example, the mission statement expresses concern with "the consequences of false allegations where whole families are split apart" and says the foundation will provide access to legal counsel "to alleviate or remedy damages done by such accusations," thereby drawing traditional values such as family security and law and order into the debate. If Faludi's backlash hypothesis applies in the present context, however, it is likely that authoritarians' beliefs about recovered memories are more strongly tied to their attitudes toward women than they are to these values. Indeed, given Miller's (1983) contention that abuse involves the exploitation of children for the satisfaction of an adult's own needs for power, admiration, and acceptance, one would expect people's beliefs about recovered memories to vary positively with their orientation toward narcissistic values and negatively with the priority they assign to social values.

Finally, because authoritarians are typically right-wing conservatives (Altemeyer, 1988), people's political orientations may also underlie their stances in the recovered memory controversy. To the contrary, however, Olafson et al.

(1993) point out that "information about the prevalence and impact of sexual abuse may constitute unwelcome news on all shades of the political spectrum. Political conservatives, who are traditionally defenders of the family, can hardly be expected to applaud an apparent challenge to paternal authority. Liberals caution against the possible undermining of the civil liberties of adults and the dangers of state intrusion into the private sphere" (p. 19).

In an attempt to understand the sociopolitical basis of the FMS debate, we designed two studies to examine the extent to which the just world, backlash, and narcissism hypotheses account for people's beliefs regarding adults' recovered memories of child abuse. In the first study, these hypotheses were tested using data provided by a sample of university students. The second study consisted of a conceptual replication that was conducted to examine the generalizability of the findings to the general public.

Study 1

Method

In return for bonus course credit, 187 students in an introductory psychology course (93 males, 90 females, and 4 of unspecified gender; mean age = 24.3 years, SD = 6.72 years) completed a "Social Issues Survey." [1]

Predictor variables. The questionnaire package included Spence, Helmreich, and Stapp's (1973) Attitudes toward Women Scale (AWS), on which students used 4-point scales to rate their agreement with 25 items assessing their attitudes toward the equality of women. An example statement from this scale reads: "Swearing and obscenity are more repulsive in the speech of a woman than that of a man." The package also contained Altemeyer's (1988) Right-Wing Authoritarianism (RWA) scale, on which students used 9-point scales to rate their agreement with 30 items, such as "Obedience and respect for authority are the most important virtues children should learn."

A 3-item measure of Belief in a Just World (BJW)—derived from a factor analysis of Rubin and Peplau's (1975) scale (Lydon, Ellard, & Lerner, 1984)—was embedded within the RWA scale. These items asked the extent to which participants believed "People who meet with misfortune often have brought it on themselves"; "By and large, people deserve what they get"; and "Basically, the world is a just place."

Participants also completed a modified version of Rokeach's (1967) Terminal Value Survey, on which they ranked the importance of 18 values as "guiding principles in their lives." The modification consisted of replacing the value "a comfortable life" with "law and order (maintaining order in society)" and redefining the value "salvation (saved, eternal life)" as "spirituality (your spiritual/religious practices)." To allow parametric analyses, we transformed these value ranks into Z scores corresponding to a division of the normal curve into 18 equal areas (Hays, 1967), and we also added a constant so that all scores would be positive. As a result, value importance scores ranged from a low of 0.04 to a high of 3.96.

In addition to the above, the students completed Berger, Knutson, Mehm, and Perkins's (1988) Physical Punishment Questionnaire, which asked whether they had childhood experience with eight forms of physical punishment other than spanking (e.g., being hit with an object, punched, locked in a closet, injured), and Finkelhor, Hotaling, Lewis, and Smith's (1990) sexual abuse items, which asked whether they had experienced any of four types of self-defined sexual abuse prior to age 16 (touching, grabbing, or kissing; exhibitionism/photography; oral or anal sex; attempted intercourse). The students also indicated their political orientations along a left- to right-wing continuum (New Democratic, Liberal, Conservative, Reform) and rated their interest in politics using a 5-point scale ranging from *no interest at all* to *very interested.*

Criterion variables. After completing the measures of the predictor variables, participants used 9-point scales to rate their agreement with a series of items concerning child abuse. Most of these items ($n = 26$) were derived from the literature of the FMS Foundation (n.d.) and its proponents (e.g., Tavris, 1993). These "FMS beliefs" assessed the extent to which students believed that people could develop false memories from therapists' suggestions or after reading a book about incest, and whether people are making up stories of abuse to gain sympathy or as excuses for other psychological problems (e.g., "An adult who claims they were sexually abused on the basis of their recently recovered memories is probably wrong if they have lots of other severe psychological problems"). Six items assessed students' "legal beliefs" regarding the admissibility of recovered memories as evidence in court and the need for corroborating witnesses (e.g., "On the basis of their recovered memories, adults should be able to charge their abusers with sexual assault"), and 17 items, some of which were taken from Gabora et al. (1993), measured participants' "incest beliefs" more generally (e.g., "Children secretly want to have sexual relationships with their parents").

Upon completing the questionnaire package, the students were debriefed in a class lecture on child abuse and the recovered memory controversy.

Results

Preliminary Analyses

The initial analyses examined the reliability of the predictor and criterion scales, their descriptive statistics, and the correlations within and between the predictor and criterion variables.

Predictor variables. Item analyses revealed that the predictor scales were internally consistent (AWS $\alpha = .86$; RWA $\alpha = .89$; BJW $\alpha = .51$). Scale scores were therefore formed by calculating the mean, resulting in higher scores reflecting more of the characteristic in question.

The descriptive statistics for the predictor variables, presented in Table 26.1, indicated that

Table 26.1 Descriptive Statistics for Predictor and Criterion Variables in Studies 1 and 2

Variable	Study 1 (Students)			Study 2 (Public)		
	Potential Range	M	SD	Potential Range	M	SD
RWA	1-9	4.32	1.19	1-7	3.91	0.88
BJW	1-9	4.47	1.74	1-7	3.49	1.47
AWS	1-4	3.41	0.41	1-4	3.44	0.52
Family security	0.04-3.96	2.33	0.84	0.00-3.60	2.58	0.88
Law and order	0.04-3.96	1.42	0.73	0.00-3.60	1.53	0.73
Political party	1-4	2.18	0.85	1-4	2.42	0.94
Political interest	1-5	2.69	1.16	1-5	2.62	1.08
FMS beliefs	1-9	3.90	1.22	1-7	2.89	1.07
Legal beliefs	1-9	3.90	1.49	1-7	2.67	1.01
Incest beliefs	1-9	2.70	1.10	1-7	2.16	0.78
Battering beliefs	—	—	—	1-7	2.38	0.87
PMS beliefs	—	—	—	1-7	3.02	0.87

NOTE: Given missing data, Ns in Study 1 vary from 159 for political party and 179 to 187 for the remaining variables. In Study 2, Ns were 163 for political party and 182 to 187 for the other variables.

this sample had moderate RWA and BJW scores and favorable attitudes toward women's equality. This sample was, on average, right-wing liberal and slightly to moderately interested in politics. These participants also reported experiencing an average of 1.20 ($SD = 1.63$) of the eight types of physical abuse, with being hit with objects reported most frequently (36.8%) and requiring medical services for injuries least frequently (1.2%). When experience with sexual abuse was dichotomized, 35.2% of the sample reported experiencing at least one of the four types of abuse, with inappropriate touching, grabbing, or kissing disclosed most often (30.8%) and oral sex or sodomy least often (7.7%).

As displayed in Table 26.2, the correlations among the predictor variables indicated that students who were more authoritarian more strongly believed that the world is just, expressed less favorable attitudes toward women, and gave more priority to the values of family security and law and order. Students with more positive attitudes toward women were less likely to believe that the world is just, placed less value on law and order, were older, and were more often female than male. In addition, participants who had experienced sexual abuse were more likely to be female than male ($r = .35, p < .001$), were older ($r = .26, p < .001$), and

expressed slightly more positive attitudes toward women's equality ($r = .15, p < .05$). None of the predictor variables was related to participants' experience of physical abuse ($rs = -.03$ to .10, *ns*).

Criterion variables. Because the measures of the three criterion variables were internally consistent (FMS beliefs $\alpha = .92$; legal beliefs $\alpha = .70$; incest beliefs $\alpha = .82$), scale scores were based on the mean of participants' responses. Hence, higher scores reflected stronger endorsement of the arguments against the validity of recovered memories, the need for more stringent legal evidence in court, and more erroneous beliefs about incest. As shown in Table 26.1, the descriptive statistics revealed that these students were slightly opposed to the FMS arguments, required at least some substantiation of recovered memories in legal cases, and were somewhat misinformed about incest. Further, as displayed in Table 26.3, participants' scores on the measures of these three criterion beliefs were substantially interrelated ($rs = .55$ to .71).

Main Analyses

The primary analyses first examined the correlates of participants' FMS, legal, and incest

Table 26.2   Correlations Among Predictor Variables in Studies 1 and 2

Predictor Variable	1	2	3	4	5	6	7	8	9
1. Gender		-.07	-.11	-.23**	.33***	.00	-.27***	-.06	-.05
2. Age	.13		.15*	-.10	-.06	.24***	.16*	-.17*	.25***
3. RWA	-.00	-.06		.10	-.32***	.10	.23***	.25***	-.05
4. BJW	-.14	-.10	.25***		-.16*	-.09	.05	.18*	-.07
5. AWS	.27***	.22**	-.48***	-.28***		.06	-.40***	-.21*	.10
6. Family security	-.07	.08	.19**	-.02	-.13		.03	-.08	.15*
7. Law and order	-.03	-.03	.28***	.05	-.24***	.13		.11	.08
8. Political party	-.09	-.08	.13	.06	.04	-.07	-.03		-.08
9. Political interest	-.05	.02	-.10	-.12	.10	-.16*	-.01	.02	

NOTE: Numbers below the diagonal refer to Study 1; numbers above the diagonal refer to Study 2. Given missing data, Ns in Study 1 vary from 159 for political party and 179 to 187 for the remaining variables. In Study 2 Ns were 163 for political party and 182 to 187 for the others.
$*p < .05$; $**p < .01$; $***p < .001$ (two-tailed).

beliefs. Regression analyses and causal modeling were then used to test the just world, backlash, and narcissism hypotheses regarding the impacts of authoritarianism, just world beliefs, attitudes toward women, and values on beliefs about recovered memories and incest.

Belief correlates. Pearson correlations, shown in Table 26.4, indicated that participants who were male rather than female, younger, more authoritarian, more opposed to women's equality, and believed more strongly in a just world were more likely to endorse FMS, required more stringent legal evidence, and had more erroneous beliefs about incest. Identifying with more conservative political parties and not having experienced childhood sexual abuse ($r = -.18$, $p < .05$) were also associated with greater endorsement of FMS.

The just world and backlash hypotheses. Structural equation modeling was used to assess the suggestion that authoritarians' appeals to values are simply rhetorical justifications of beliefs that are actually based on their opposition to women's independence and their need to maintain the illusion that the world is just. These analyses were carried out using EQS software (Bentler, 1989) and maximum likelihood estimation procedures. This approach, which tested all the relevant equations simultaneously, provided indices of the fit of the model to the data, significance tests for all the path coefficients, and information

about the amount of variance explained by the model. Figure 26.1 illustrates the significant paths that resulted from this analysis, and the goodness-of-fit indices indicated that this model successfully captured the underlying data ($\chi^2[3] = 7.99$, $p = .048$; Normed Fit Index = .983; Comparative Fit Index = .989).

Going from left to right in Figure 26.1, we can see that, as hypothesized, students with higher RWA scores believed more in a just world ($\beta = .251$, $R^2 = .063$, $Z = 3.52$, $p < .001$), expressed less favorable attitudes toward women ($\beta = -.476$, $R^2 = .226$, $Z = -7.34$, $p < .001$), and gave greater priority to the values of law and order ($\beta = .274$, $R^2 = .075$, $Z = -3.86$, $p < .001$) and family security ($\beta = .191$, $R^2 = .036$, $Z = 2.64$, $p < .01$).

The middle set of variables in Figure 26.1 illustrates that, consistent with the just world hypothesis, students with higher BJW scores more strongly endorsed FMS ($\beta = .248$, $Z = 3.98$, $p < .001$), required stronger legal evidence ($\beta = .174$, $Z = 2.46$, $p < .05$), and were more misinformed about incest ($\beta = .302$, $Z = 5.35$, $p < .001$). Following Faludi's (1991) backlash hypothesis, participants' AWS scores were closely tied to their beliefs. Students with more positive attitudes toward women were less likely to believe in FMS ($\beta = -.398$, $Z = -5.80$, $p < .001$), required less stringent legal evidence ($\beta = -.357$, $Z = -4.59$, $p < .001$), and had fewer erroneous incest beliefs ($\beta = -.494$, $Z = -7.94$, $p < .001$). Further, while the value of family security was independent of students' legal ($\beta =$

Table 26.3 Correlations Among Criterion Beliefs in Studies 1 and 2

Belief	FMS	Legal	Incest	Battering	PMS
FMS		.75***	.70***	.64***	.65***
Legal	.68***		.64***	.56***	.62***
Incest	.71***	.55***		.70***	.57***
Battering	—	—	—		

NOTE: Numbers below the diagonal refer to Study 1; numbers above the diagonal refer to Study 2. Given missing data, Ns in Studies 1 and 2 vary from 182 to 187.

***$p < .001$ (two-tailed).

Table 26.4 Correlations Between Predictor and Criterion Variables in Studies 1 and 2

	Criterion Variable							
	FMS Beliefs		Legal Beliefs		Incest Beliefs		Battering Beliefs	PMS Beliefs
Predictor Variable	Study 1	Study 2	Study 1	Study 2	Study 1	Study 2	Study 2 Only	Study 2 Only
Gender	−.28***	−.45***	−.24***	−.30***	−.22**	−.35***	−.37***	−.45***
Age	−.27***	−.01	−.26***	−.04	−.24***	−.07	−.09	−.02
RWA	.36***	.10	.07	.04	.40***	.19**	.15*	.22**
BJW	.38***	.39***	.23***	.29***	.45***	.44***	.29***	.37***
AWS	−.52***	−.48***	−.34***	−.46***	−.61***	−.44***	−.53***	−.54***
Family security	−.04	−.08	−.04	−.13	.05	−.12	−.12	−.06
Law and order	.13	.30***	.02	.21**	.14	.15*	.22**	.18*
Political party	.19*	.12	.09	.00	−.02	.13	.12	.15
Political interest	−.04	−.16*	.00	−.13	−.04	−.04	−.02	−.13

NOTE: Given missing data, Ns in Study 1 vary from 159 for political party and 179 to 187 for the remaining variables. In Study 2, Ns were 163 for political party and 182 to 187 for the others.

*$p < .05$; **$p < .01$; ***$p < .001$ (two-tailed).

−.071, $Z = -1.03$, ns) and incest beliefs ($\beta = -.030$, $Z = -0.55$, ns), resulting in these paths being deleted from the model, students' valuation of family security was related to their FMS beliefs ($\beta = -.138$, $Z = -2.25$, $p < .05$). Contrary to the FMS Foundation's (1993) expressed concern with maintaining family unity, however, students who assigned more priority to family security were less rather than more likely to endorse FMS.[2] Finally, because students' valuation of law and order was independent of their beliefs (FMS $\beta = .014$, $Z = 0.23$, ns; Legal $\beta = -.021$, $Z = -0.29$, ns; Incest $\beta = -.008$, $Z = -0.14$, ns), these paths were removed from the model. Taken together, these mediating variables accounted for 33.2%, 13.1%, and 44.9% of the variance in students' FMS, legal, and incest beliefs, respectively.

Finally, Figure 26.1 shows that the residual variances of the FMS, legal, and incest belief scores were correlated ($rs = .46$ to $.64$, $ps < .001$, two-tailed). This shared "error" variance may stem from common method variance or from common causal antecedents that were not specified in the model.

The narcissism hypothesis. Given Miller's (1983) contention that narcissism underlies child abuse, we conducted forward stepwise regression analyses to examine whether students' beliefs about FMS and incest were tied to self-centered rather than interpersonal values. The regression of FMS beliefs onto students' 18 value scores revealed that students were more likely to challenge the validity of recovered memories if they allocated more

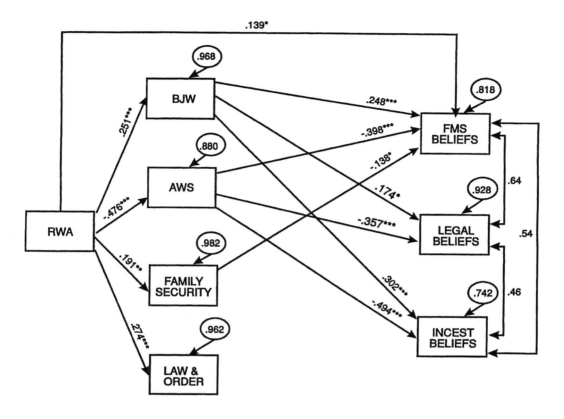

Figure 26.1. Standardized Path Coefficients and Residual Variances for the Model Testing the Just World and Backlash Hypotheses

*p < .05, ** p < .01, *** p < .001.

priority to pleasure (β = .269, R^2 change = .101, $F[1, 182]$ = 20.54, $p < .001$) and law and order (β = .164, R^2 change = .023, $F[1, 181]$ = 4.75, $p < .05$),[3] and less priority to equality (β = −.167, R^2 change = .025, $F[1, 180]$ = 5.24, $p < .05$), values that together explained 14.9% of the variance in FMS beliefs, $F(3, 180)$ = 10.52, $p < .001$. Only the value pleasure made a significant contribution to the equation predicting legal beliefs, whereby students who allocated more priority to pleasure required stronger legal evidence (β = .250, R^2 change = .063, $F[1, 182]$ = 12.16, $p < .001$). Finally, more erroneous incest beliefs were expressed by students who gave more priority to pleasure (β = .274, R^2 change = .074, $F[1, 182]$ = 14.45,

$p < .001$) and national security (β = .194, R^2 change = .046, $F[1, 181]$ = 9.38, $p < .01$), and less priority to inner harmony (β = −.153, R^2 change = .022, $F[1, 180]$ = 4.64, $p < .05$), R^2 = .141, $F(3, 180)$ = 9.88, $p < .001$.

Political orientation. Hierarchical regression analyses were used to examine the relation between students' political orientations and their beliefs. In these analyses, participants' political party preferences and political interest scores were entered simultaneously on the first step, and their interaction was entered on the second step. None of these terms was able to account for a significant portion of the variance in students' FMS, legal, or incest beliefs.

Discussion

The results of this study are entirely in keeping with the just world, backlash, and narcissism hypotheses. In line with the suggestion that people deny the validity of recovered memories because they cannot cope with the injustice of child abuse (Herman, 1992; Herman et al., 1989; McFarlane & van der Kolk, 1996; Olafson et al., 1993), students' assumptive beliefs about a just world mediated the relation between their authoritarianism and their FMS and incest beliefs. Similarly, consistent with findings that authoritarians have negative attitudes toward women in general (Walker et al., 1993) and feminists in particular (Duncan et al., 1997; Haddock & Zanna, 1994), as well as the observation that attitudes toward women mediate the relation between authoritarianism and sexual aggression (Walker et al., 1993), students' attitudes toward women mediated the relation between their authoritarianism and their beliefs about recovered memories and child abuse. Further, unlike the FMS Foundation's (1993) claim that its concern for family security and law and order motivates its skepticism toward recovered memories, these values were largely independent of students' beliefs about recovered memories and incest. Taken together, then, these findings support Faludi's (1991) hypothesis that the New Right uses values rhetorically to justify attitudes that are really based on opposition to women's equality and independence. Finally, the finding that students' beliefs were positively tied to the importance they assigned to self-centered values such as pleasure, and negatively related to socially oriented values such as equality, is consistent with Miller's (1983) claim that narcissistic self-interest underlies people's reactions to child abuse.

Students' own experiences with physical and sexual abuse played a minimal role in their beliefs. Indeed, students' experience of physical abuse was entirely independent of their beliefs, and students' experience of sexual abuse was correlated only with their FMS beliefs, and even this correlation was negligible. Further, given that authoritarianism was unrelated to students' political orientations, and that students' political orientations generally failed to account for

their beliefs, it is unlikely that it was the political conservatism of authoritarianism that was responsible for students' beliefs. In this regard, one might speculate that it is authoritarians' submissiveness to authority, aggressiveness against weaker people, and conventionalism (Altemeyer, 1988), rather than their politics, that underlies their beliefs about recovered memories and child abuse.

Finally, it is interesting to note that students' FMS, legal, and incest beliefs were substantially interrelated. This finding was unexpected as these beliefs could, theoretically, be independent. That is, whereas some people might believe that recovered memories are often false, there was no reason to expect that they would also endorse erroneous beliefs regarding incest more generally. Given the observed correlations, however, it appears that people who endorse FMS tend to harbor misconceptions of child abuse, misconceptions not unlike Freud's recantation that (as one FMS belief item puts it) "children secretly want to have sexual relationships with their parents." These relations are clearly problematic given Briere, Henschel, and Smiljanich's (1992) finding that students who believed that "many children would enjoy sex with an adult" also condoned sexual aggression against women and admitted that they would be willing to abuse children sexually if they knew they would not be detected.

Although these findings are consistent with the contention that people's beliefs about recovered memories and child abuse are tied to sociopolitical rather than purely scientific factors (Herman et al., 1989; Ofshe & Watters, 1993), their generalizability merits consideration. In some ways, this sample is similar to others. For example, the prevalence of physical abuse was like that reported by Berger et al. (1988) in their student and public samples, and the finding that 35.2% of these students reported experiences of child sexual abuse is consistent with the prevalence rates observed in other studies (Berliner & Elliott, 1996). Despite these similarities, we examined the generalizability of these findings in a second study. In Study 2 we also examined whether the just world, backlash, and narcissism hypotheses could account for people's opinions regarding other issues relevant to women.

Study 2

Method

Participants were 187 members of the general public who, when approached by a male researcher in one of three Ottawa, Ontario, launderettes, agreed to participate in a "Social Opinions Survey" (87 females, 99 males, and 1 person of unspecified gender; mean age = 35.6, *SD* = 13.8 years). These locations were chosen so that the people recruited would have sufficient time to complete the 30- to 40-minute questionnaire package; further, the launderettes were located in parts of the city of varying socioeconomic status.

Predictor variables. After giving their informed consent, participants completed a questionnaire package that included a reduced 10-item version of the Attitudes toward Women Scale that was derived from the items that had the largest item-total correlations in Study 1. Participants also used 7-point scales to rate their agreement with 10 items from Altemeyer's (1988) Right-Wing Authoritarianism scale that were representative of the three dimensions underlying RWA, namely, submission, aggression, and conventionalism (Haddock & Zanna, 1994). As in Study 1, Lydon et al.'s (1984) 3-item Belief in a Just World scale was embedded within the RWA scale.

Participants were also presented with a modified version of Rokeach's (1967) Terminal Value Survey on which they ranked the importance of 14 rather than 18 values. The values of mature love, self-respect, true friendship, and wisdom—values that in Study 1 exhibited the least variability and were unrelated to students' FMS, legal, and incest beliefs—were deleted to reduce task demands. To allow parametric analyses, we transformed these ranks into *Z* scores (Hays, 1967) and added a constant, resulting in value importance scores ranging from a low of 0.00 to a high of 3.60.

Finally, participants answered questions regarding their age, gender, marital status, income, education, political orientation, and political interest.

Criterion variables. After completing the measures of the predictor variables, which appeared in random order, participants used 7-point bipolar scales to indicate their endorsement of five criterion variables. As in Study 1, three of these criteria involved people's FMS, legal, and incest beliefs as assessed by the 15, 6, and 15 items, respectively, that displayed the highest item-total correlations in Study 1.[4]

To evaluate whether the hypotheses applied to issues regarding women more generally, we had respondents use 7-point scales to rate their beliefs regarding two issues known to be related to attitudes toward women (e.g., Caplan, 1992, 1995; Kristiansen & Giulietti, 1990), namely, battered women and premenstrual syndrome (PMS). We assessed participants' beliefs about battered women using 14 items derived from Walker (1979) and the Ontario Women's Directorate's (1991) documentation of myths about battered women (e.g., "Women who stay in abusive relationships obviously like to be beaten."). We measured participants' PMS beliefs using 20 items taken from Moos (1968) and Brooks-Gunn and Ruble (1980) (e.g., "Many women are unsuitable for top management positions because, for a few days each month, they simply can't function at their best.").

After completing the questionnaire package, participants were debriefed, given a list of social support services, and invited to contact the researchers for additional information.

Results

Preliminary Analyses

Sample characteristics. On average, participants' reported family incomes ranged from $45,000 to $65,000 per annum. In regard to education, 14.0% of participants had an elementary education, 26.3% had completed high school, 21.0% had trade or college certificates, 24.7% had some university education, and 14.0% had more than a bachelor's degree. Most respondents were single (45.2%) or cohabiting (40.8%), and 14.0% were separated, divorced, or widowed. Finally, and as shown by the descriptive statistics in Table 26.1, the sample consisted largely of conservative liberals who were somewhat interested in politics.

Predictor variables. Item analyses revealed that the measures of RWA ($\alpha = .66$) and AWS ($\alpha = .84$) were internally homogeneous. For the BJW scale, however, deleting the item that read "Basically the world is a just place" enhanced consistency ($\alpha = .70$), perhaps because respondents misconstrued the term *just*. Scale scores were determined by the mean, resulting in higher scores reflecting more of the characteristic in question. As shown in Table 26.1, this sample scored near the midpoint of the RWA scale, was slightly disinclined to believe that the world is just, and had favorable AWS scores. They also regarded family security as moderately important in their lives, whereas they regarded law and order as slightly important, $t(185) = 12.75$, $p < .001$.

Pearson correlations between respondents' demographic characteristics and the predictor variables revealed that people who were more educated had lower BJW scores ($r = -.16$, $p < .05$), gave more priority to the values of family security ($r = .15$, $p < .05$) and law and order ($r = .17$, $p < .05$), and were more interested in politics ($r = .32$, $p < .001$). Respondents with higher family incomes expressed slightly more favorable attitudes toward women ($r = .18$, $p < .05$), allocated more priority to family security ($r = .22$, $p < .01$), and were somewhat more interested in politics ($r = .16$, $p < .05$). People who were older were also more interested in politics ($r = .25$, $p < .001$). In addition, and as displayed in Table 26.2, people who were more authoritarian held less favorable attitudes toward women's equality, assigned greater priority to the value of law and order, and were politically more conservative. Participants who believed more strongly that the world is just endorsed less positive attitudes toward women, were more conservative, and were likely to be male rather than female, whereas respondents with more favorable attitudes toward women were likely to be female rather than male, were less concerned with law and order, and were less conservative. Finally, people with more interest

in politics were slightly more likely to value family security.

Criterion variables. Because item analyses indicated that the criterion measures were internally consistent, scores were derived from the mean of participants' responses (FMS beliefs $\alpha = .90$; legal beliefs $\alpha = .64$; incest beliefs $\alpha = .76$; battering beliefs $\alpha = .80$; PMS beliefs $\alpha = .87$). Descriptive statistics, shown in Table 26.1, indicated that these participants were somewhat anti-FMS, required moderate legal evidence for abuse allegations based on recovered memories, and were at least slightly misinformed about incest, battered women, and PMS. As shown in Table 26.3, respondents' scores on the five criterion beliefs were interrelated, with correlations ranging from .56 to .75.

As displayed in Table 26.4, correlations between the demographic variables and the criterion measures indicated that, relative to men, women were more opposed to FMS, required less stringent legal evidence, and were less misinformed about incest, battered women, and PMS, and those with more interest in politics were slightly more opposed to FMS. In addition, respondents with greater incomes required less legal evidence ($r = -.21$, $p < .01$) and were less likely to endorse myths about battered women ($r = -.17$, $p < .05$), whereas those with more education were better informed about incest generally ($r = -.16$, $p < .05$).

Main Analyses

Belief correlates. Pearson correlations, shown in Table 26.4, revealed that participants who were older and those who more strongly believed that the world is just, expressed less favorable attitudes toward women, or gave more priority to law and order agreed more strongly with each of the five criterion beliefs. In addition, people with higher RWA scores were more misinformed about incest, battered women, and PMS, and respondents with more interest in politics were slightly more opposed to the notion of FMS and required less legal evidence. Participants' political orientations

Table 26.5 Results of Path Analysis From RWA, Showing Tests of Standardized Path Coefficients (βs), Residuals, and Variance Explained by the Predictors in Study 2 ($N = 182$)

Path	Variable	β	Z	Residual	R^2
RWA to	BJW	.133	1.81†	.991	.018
	AWS	−.283	−3.97***	.959	.080
	Law and order	.201	2.77**	.980	.040

† $p = .07$; ** $p < .01$; *** $p < .001$.

and their valuation of family security were independent of all five criterion beliefs.

The backlash and just world hypotheses. As in Study 1, we used structural equation modeling to examine the just world and backlash hypotheses. Because respondents' valuation of family security was independent of both the other predictors and the five criterion beliefs, this variable was deleted from the model. The goodness-of-fit indices indicated that this trimmed model captured the underlying data reasonably well ($\chi^2[3] = 24.18$, $p < .001$; Normed Fit Index = .967; Comparative Fit Index = .970).

Table 26.5 shows that respondents with higher RWA scores believed marginally more in a just world, expressed less favorable attitudes toward women, and assigned more importance to law and order. As in Study 1, AWS accounted for the majority (8.0%) of the explained variance in authoritarianism. Table 26.6 presents the results of the tests of the significance of the paths from the model's mediating variables to respondents' five beliefs. Following the just world hypothesis, the more people believed in a just world, the more they endorsed FMS, the more legal evidence they required, and the more erroneous their beliefs about incest, battered women, and PMS. In line with the backlash hypothesis, respondents with less favorable attitudes toward women were more likely to believe in FMS, required more substantiation in recovered memory cases, and were more misinformed about incest, battered women, and PMS. Participants' valuation of law and order, however, was related to their beliefs regarding only one of the five issues, namely, FMS.

Finally, the model accounted for 24.5% to 38.2% of the variation in respondents' belief

scores and was equally able to account for participants' opinions about childhood sexual abuse and other issues relevant to women, namely, battering and PMS.

The narcissism hypothesis. As in Study 1, regression analyses indicated that participants' beliefs were positively associated with self-centered values and negatively related to other-oriented values. The regression of respondents' FMS beliefs onto their 14 value scores revealed that people who endorsed FMS gave more priority to law and order ($\beta = .306$, R^2 change = .085, $t[179] = 4.59$, $p < .001$) and an exciting life ($\beta = .270$, R^2 change = .073, $t[179] = 4.05$, $p < .001$), and less priority to a world of beauty ($\beta = −.221$, R^2 change = .039, $t[179] = −3.32$, $p < .01$), $R^2 = .206$, $F(3, 179) = 15.52$, $p < .001$. Participants who required more stringent legal evidence in recovered memory cases regarded law and order ($\beta = .214$, R^2 change = .041, $t[180] = 3.00$, $p < .01$) and an exciting life ($\beta = .208$, R^2 change = .043, $t[180] = 2.91$, $p < .01$) as more important values, $R^2 = .084$, $F(2, 180) = 8.22$, $p < .001$. Finally, more erroneous incest beliefs were expressed by participants who gave more priority to an exciting life ($\beta = .263$, R^2 change = .059, $t[179] = 3.75$, $p < .001$) and national security ($\beta = .171$, R^2 change = .048, $t[179] = 2.32$, $p < .05$), and less priority to a world of beauty ($\beta = −.168$, R^2 change = .026, $t[179] = −2.30$, $p < .05$), $R^2 = .133$, $F(3, 179) = 9.14$, $p < .001$.

Regression analyses indicated that participants' beliefs regarding battered women and PMS were also positively tied to their valuation of personal rather than social values. People who more strongly endorsed myths about battered women assigned greater priority to an

Table 26.6 Results of Path Analysis, Showing Tests of Standardized Path Coefficients (βs), Residuals, and Variance Explained by the Predictors in Study 2

	FMS Beliefs		Legal Beliefs		Incest Beliefs		Battering Beliefs		PMS Beliefs	
Variable	β	Z	β	Z	β	Z	β	Z	β	Z
BJW	.316	5.13***	.216	3.32***	.337	5.43***	.191	3.06**	.265	4.50***
AWS	−.451	−7.08***	−.459	−6.81***	−.409	−6.38***	−.513	−7.94***	−.531	−8.72***
Law and order	.157	2.52**	.061	0.93	−.008	−0.12	.027	0.43	−.015	−0.26
RWA	−.078	−1.19	−.124	−1.79*	.063	0.96	−.016	−0.24	.051	0.82
Residual	.822		.869		.828		.834		.786	
R^2	.324		.245		.314		.304		.382	

*$p < .05$; **$p < .01$; ***$p < .001$ (two-tailed).

exciting life ($\beta = .284$, R^2 change = .073, $t[180] = 4.06$, $p < .001$) and law and order ($\beta = .229$, R^2 change = .052, $t[180] = 3.28$, $p < .01$), $R^2 = .125$, $F(2, 180) = 12.90$, $p < .001$. Similarly, the less participants valued equality ($\beta = -.259$, R^2 change = .053, $t[179] = -3.61$, $p < .001$), inner harmony ($\beta = -.161$, R^2 change = .027, $t[179] = -2.24$, $p < .05$), and a world of beauty ($\beta = -.151$, R^2 change = .023, $t[179] = -2.13$, $p < .05$), the more they endorsed negative beliefs about PMS, $R^2 = .102$, $F(3, 179) = 6.78$, $p < .001$.

Political orientation. As observed in Study 1, neither participants' political orientations nor their political interest scores, nor the interaction between these variables, were able to account for respondents' scores on the five criterion beliefs.

Discussion

The findings derived from this sample of the general pubic replicated both the descriptive statistics and the tests of the hypotheses observed in the student sample. Like the student sample, this public sample was, on average, composed of right-wing liberals who were somewhat authoritarian, who believed that the world is somewhat just, and who expressed favorable attitudes toward women's equality. Both samples were also somewhat opposed to the notion of FMS, agreed that there should be at least some corroborative evidence for recovered memories, and were somewhat misinformed about incest. The outcomes of the re-

gression analyses and causal modeling were largely the same in both studies, and supported the just world, backlash, and narcissism hypotheses regarding the sociopolitical factors underlying people's beliefs about recovered memories. Finally, in both studies, people's political orientations were independent of their beliefs about recovered memories, legal issues, and incest more generally, beliefs that were interrelated. Given these similarities, it seems unlikely that these findings are peculiar to the samples that were investigated.

Consistent with the notion that FMS is a sociopolitical "women's issue" (Enns et al., 1995; Ofshe & Watters, 1993, 1994), the more the members of the public sample believed in FMS, the more they endorsed other derogatory myths about women, including statements that read "Women who stay in abusive relationships obviously like to be beaten" and "Many women are unsuitable for top management positions because, for a few days each month, they simply can't function at their best." Indeed, the public sample's endorsement of myths about battered women and premenstrual syndrome were tied to the same factors as their beliefs about recovered memories and incest, namely, their need to defend the illusion that the world is just, their authoritarian opposition to women's equality, and their orientation toward narcissistic values. Given that the participants' authoritarian opposition to women's equality was as strong a predictor of their beliefs about recovered memories and incest as it was of their beliefs about battered women and PMS, it seems that the delayed memory debate is as much a woman's issue as these other issues. These findings, therefore, contradict FMS advocates such as Loftus and Ketcham (1994), who assert that this debate is not "about the hard-won gains of the women's movement. It is a debate about memory, not ideology" (p. 213). Moreover, that participants' valuation of family security was independent of their attitudes toward women and their beliefs about recovered memories detracts from the claims of FMS proponents that feminists are using recovered memories "in their fight against the cornerstone of society—the traditional family of origin" (Tyroler, 1996, p. 72; see also Ofshe & Watters, 1993, 1994).

General Discussion

☐ That people's beliefs about the validity of recovered memories are strongly tied to autocratic misogyny, social denial, and narcissistic self-interest has important implications for all those involved in the recovered memory controversy. If people's beliefs about the validity of recovered memories are rooted primarily in ideology rather than science, the debate's adverse effects on survivors are unjustifiable and unconscionable. For example, this sociopolitical debate is retraumatizing women with recovered memories, having a detrimental effect on their therapy, and causing some survivors to doubt their memories and remain silent (Allard, Kristiansen, & Hovdestad, in press). The delayed memory debate has also restricted the resources available to survivors because some therapists have become reluctant to help survivors for fear of "allegations of unscientific conduct, faulty techniques, implantation of memories, and unethical behavior" (Quirk & DePrince, 1995, p. 259; see also Maingot, 1996). Further, survivors are being detrimentally affected by the debate in the courts, where, like rape myths, the notion of false memories is being used to challenge both their credibility and their rights to the confidentiality of their therapy records (Kelly, Kristiansen, & Haslip, 1997; Kristiansen, Haslip, & Kelly, 1997; Torrey, 1991).

Given the harmful impact of the debate on survivors, its ideological basis suggests that researchers should stop playing what philoso-

phers of science call the "god-trick," claiming that—like god—they can see everything from absolutely nowhere (Haraway, 1988). Rather than pretending that the recovered memory debate is uniquely impervious to ideology, perhaps we would get a bit closer to the truths of women's lived realities if we acknowledged the role of patriarchal politics and personal fears and factored them into our thoughts. As philosopher of science Sandra Harding (1987) puts it, "Introducing this 'subjective' element into the analysis in fact increases the objectivity of the research and decreases the 'objectivism' which hides this kind of evidence from the public" (p. 9).

Alleged perpetrators may be tempted to use the present findings to argue that people who acknowledge the injustice of child abuse or support women's equality are overzealous in their acceptance of recovered memories. However, given the long-standing social, legal, and psychiatric devaluation of women (Caplan, 1992, 1995; Torrey, 1991; van der Kolk, Weisaeth, & van der Hart, 1996), discriminatory biases against women who have experienced childhood abuse are likely a greater concern. Such biases are perhaps most apparent in clinicians' neglect of child abuse. Current epidemiological estimates, for example, suggest that there may be at least 2 and maybe as many as 135 women in therapy whose abuse goes undetected for each woman given a false diagnosis of child abuse (Fish, 1996).

The negative consequences of the debate notwithstanding, the debate has the potential to increase professionals' awareness of gender issues (e.g., Brown & Ballou, 1992; Caplan, 1992, 1995), including gender biases in the attribution of stigmatizing personality disorders to women who have experienced childhood abuse (Brown, 1992; Herman, 1992) and gender biases in procedural and substantive justice (Kelly et al., 1997). Thus, to the extent that the delayed memory controversy encourages therapists of all ideological persuasions to provide good therapy and the judiciary to provide due process, the debate may be beneficial. However, people's stereotypes of women operate unconsciously and affect their decisions without their awareness (Banaji & Hardin, 1996). As Faludi

(1991) notes, "The backlash is not a conspiracy, with a council dispatching agents from some central control room, nor are people who serve its ends often aware of their role; some even consider themselves feminists" (pp. xx-xxii). Any beneficial effects this debate could have, therefore, seem unlikely unless efforts are made to enhance people's attitudes toward women, reduce their exaggerated perceptions of the threat posed by women's equality (Duncan et al., 1997), and make them aware of the consequences of their beliefs about recovered memories. As Herman et al. (1989) observe, "There seems to be something special about data on childhood abuse that demands this extraordinary standard of proof. We suspect, in fact, that no amount of evidence, clinical or legal, will ever finally put the credibility question to rest" (p. 1359).

Finally, because the notion of false memories is premised on the traditional stereotype of women as gullible, conforming, passive, narcissistic, and masochistic (Enns et al., 1995), the delayed memory debate has the potential to have a more general adverse effect on women, because it perpetuates negative stereotypes of women. Together with the present findings, this suggests that the delayed memory debate promotes the patriarchal oppression of women and that therefore it is indeed a women's issue.

Notes

1. All of the research described in this chapter was approved by the Carleton University Psychology Department Ethics Committee, using the ethical guidelines of the American and Canadian Psychological Associations.

2. The indices of model fit were slightly improved when the value law and order was removed from the model.

3. One might expect that the relation between the values of law and order and family security might be positive among high authoritarians and negative among low authoritarians. Contrary to this, hierarchical regression analyses showed that RWA scores did not moderate the relation between these values and participants' FMS, legal, or incest beliefs. Regression analyses also showed that gender did not moderate any of the findings reported in this chapter.

4. Although the value of law and order was not a significant predictor of students' beliefs in the structural equation model, it was occasionally a significant predictor when students' beliefs were regressed onto their values. This likely occurred because we calculated the structural equations si-

multaneously, after removing any shared variance among the model's predictor variables.

5. When 25 members of the FMS Foundation professional advisory board completed the FMS belief scale (Harrington, 1996), their scores were, on average, higher than those of the members of this public sample. This ability of the FMS belief scale to discriminate between known groups provides some evidence for its construct validity.

References

Allard, C. B., Kristiansen, C. M., & Hovdestad, W. E. (in press). The retraumatizing impact of the recovered memory debate on adult survivors of child sexual abuse. *Journal of Interpersonal Violence.*

Altemeyer, B. (1988). *Enemies of freedom.* San Francisco: Jossey-Bass.

Banaji, M. R., & Hardin, C. D. (1996). Automatic stereotyping. *Psychological Science, 7,* 136-141.

Bentler, P. M. (1989). *EQS: Structural equation program manual.* Los Angeles: BMDP Statistical Software.

Berger, A., Knutson, J., Mehm, J., & Perkins, K. (1988). The self-report of punitive childhood experiences of young adults and adolescents. *Child Abuse and Neglect, 12,* 251-262.

Berliner, L., & Elliott, D. M. (1996). Sexual abuse of children. In J. Briere, L. Berliner, J. A. Bulkley, C. Jenny, & T. Reid (Eds.), *The APSAC handbook on child maltreatment* (pp. 51-71). Thousand Oaks, CA: Sage.

Briere, J., Henschel, D., & Smiljanich, K. (1992). Attitudes toward sexual abuse: Sex differences and construct validity. *Journal of Research in Personality, 26,* 398-406.

Brooks-Gunn, J., & Ruble, D. N. (1980). The Menstrual Attitude Questionnaire. *Psychosomatic Medicine, 42,* 503-511.

Brown, L. S. (1992). A feminist critique of personality disorders. In L. S. Brown & M. Ballou (Eds.), *Personality and psychopathology: Feminist reappraisals* (pp. 206-228). New York: Guilford.

Brown, L. S., & Ballou, M. (Eds.). (1992). *Personality and psychopathology: Feminist reappraisals.* New York: Guilford.

Caplan, P. J. (1992). Gender issues in the diagnosis of mental disorder. *Women and Therapy, 12,* 71-82.

Caplan, P. J. (1995). *They say you're crazy: How the world's most powerful psychiatrists decide who's normal.* Reading, MA: Addison-Wesley.

Ditto, P. H., & Lopez, D. F. (1992). Motivated skepticism: Use of differential decision criteria for preferred and nonpreferred conclusions. *Journal of Personality and Social Psychology, 63,* 568-584.

Duncan, L. E., Peterson, B. E., & Winter, D. G. (1997). Authoritarianism and gender roles: Toward a psychological analysis of hegemonic relationships. *Personality and Social Psychology Bulletin, 23,* 41-49.

Enns, C. Z., McNeilly, C. L., Corkery, J. M., & Gilbert, M. S. (1995). The debate about delayed memories of child sexual abuse: A feminist perspective. *Counseling Psychologist, 23,* 181-279.

Everson, M. D., & Boat, B. W. (1989). False allegations of sexual abuse by children and adolescents. *Journal of the American Academy of Child and Adolescent Psychiatry, 28,* 230-235.

Faludi, S. (1991). *Backlash: The undeclared war against American women.* Garden City, NY: Anchor.

Finkelhor, D., Hotaling, G. T., Lewis, I., & Smith, C. (1990). Sexual abuse in a national survey of adult men and women: Prevalence, characteristics and risk factors. *Child Abuse & Neglect, 14,* 19-28.

Fish, V. (1996). *The delayed memory controversy in an epidemiological framework.* Manuscript in preparation.

FMS Foundation. (1993, August). *FMS Foundation mission statement.* Philadelphia: Author.

FMS Foundation. (n.d.). *The false memory syndrome phenomenon.* Philadelphia: Author.

Gabora, N. J., Spanos, N. P., & Joab, A. (1993). The effects of complainant age and expert psychological testimony in a simulated child sexual abuse trial. *Law and Human Behavior, 17,* 103-119.

Haddock, G., & Zanna, M. P. (1994). Preferring "housewives" to "feminists": Categorization and the favorability of attitudes to women. *Psychology of Women Quarterly, 18,* 25-52.

Haraway, D. J. (1988). Situated knowledges: The science question in feminism and the privilege of partial perspective. *Feminist Studies, 14,* 575-599.

Harding, S. (1987). *Feminism and methodology.* Bloomington: Indiana University Press.

Harrington, E. R. (1996, June). *Attitudes of the False Memory Syndrome Foundation scientific and professional advisory board.* Paper presented at the NATO Advanced Study Institute "Recollections of Trauma: Scientific Research and Clinical Practice," Port de Bourgenay, France.

Hays, W. L. (1967). *Quantification in psychology.* Belmont, CA: Brooks/Cole.

Herman, J. L. (1992). *Trauma and recovery: The aftermath of violence—from domestic abuse to political terror.* New York: Basic Books.

Herman, J. L., Perry, J. C., & van der Kolk, B. A. (1989). Dr. Herman and associates reply [Letter to the editor]. *American Journal of Psychiatry, 146,* 1358-1359.

Hovdestad, W. E., & Kristiansen, C. M. (1996). A field study of "False Memory Syndrome": Construct validity and incidence. *Journal of Psychiatry and Law, 24,* 299-338.

Janoff-Bulman, R. (1992). *Shattered assumptions: Towards a new psychology of trauma.* New York: Free Press.

Jones, D. P. H., & McGraw, J. M. (1987). Reliable and fictitious accounts of sexual abuse of children. *Journal of Interpersonal Violence, 2,* 27-45.

Kelly, K. D., Kristiansen, C. M., & Haslip, S. J. (1997). *Gender bias, rape myths, and the use of "false memory syndrome" in the courts.* Manuscript submitted for publication.

Kristiansen, C. M., & Giulietti, R. (1990). Perceptions of wife abuse: Effects of gender, attitudes toward women,

and just-world beliefs among college students. *Psychology of Women Quarterly, 14,* 177-189.

Kristiansen, C. M., Haslip, S. J., & Kelly, K. D. (1997). Scientific and judicial illusions of objectivity in the recovered memory debate. *Feminism and Psychology, 7,* 39-45.

Lerner, M. J. (1980). *The belief in a just world.* New York: Plenum.

Loftus, E. F., & Ketcham, K. (1994). *The myth of repressed memory: False memories and allegations of sexual abuse.* New York: St. Martin's.

Lydon, J. E., Ellard, J., & Lerner, M. J. (1984). [Factor structure of justice orientations]. Unpublished raw data, University of Waterloo, ON.

Maingot, S. (1996, July). *The impact of false memory syndrome on the practice and experiences of therapy related to incest and sexual abuse.* Paper presented at Trauma and Memory: An International Research Conference, Durham, NH.

McFarlane, A. C., & van der Kolk, B. A. (1996). Trauma and its challenge to society. In B. A. van der Kolk, A. C. McFarlane, & L. Weisaeth (Eds.), *Traumatic stress: The effects of overwhelming experience on mind, body, and society* (pp. 24-46). New York: Guilford.

Miller, A. (1983). *For your own good: Hidden cruelty in child-rearing and the roots of violence.* New York: Farrar, Straus & Giroux.

Moos, R. H. (1968). The development of a menstrual distress questionnaire. *Psychosomatic Medicine, 30,* 853-862.

Ofshe, R. J., & Watters, E. (1993). Making monsters. *Society, 30,* 4-16.

Ofshe, R. J., & Watters, E. (1994). *Making monsters: False memory, psychotherapy, and sexual hysteria.* New York: Scribner's.

Olafson, E., Corwin, D., & Summit, R. (1993). Modern history of child sexual abuse awareness: Cycles of discovery and suppression. *Child Abuse & Neglect, 17,* 7-25.

Ontario Women's Directorate. (1991). *Wife assault: Dispelling the myths.* Ottawa: Author.

Quirk, S. A., & DePrince, A. P. (1995). Backlash legislation targeting psychotherapists. *Journal of Psychohistory, 22,* 257-264.

Rieker, P. P., & Carmen, E. (1986). The victim-to-patient process: The disconfirmation and transformation of abuse. *American Journal of Orthopsychiatry, 56,* 360-370.

Rokeach, M. (1967). *Value survey.* Sunnyvale, CA: Halgren Tests.

Rose, S. (1991). The contribution of Alice Miller to feminist therapy and theory. *Women and Therapy, 11,* 41-53.

Rubin, Z., & Peplau, L. A. (1975). Who believes in a just world? *Journal of Social Issues, 31,* 65-89.

Spence, J. T., Helmreich, R., & Stapp, J. (1973). A short version of the Attitudes toward Women Scale (AWS). *Bulletin of the Psychonomic Society, 2,* 219-220.

Tavris, C. (1993, January 3). Beware the incest-survivor machine. *New York Times Book Review,* pp. 1, 16-17.

Torrey, M. (1991). When will we be believed? Rape myths and the idea of a fair trial in rape prosecutions. *University of California at Davis Law Review, 24,* 1013-1071.

Tyroler, P. M. (1996). The recovered memory movement: A female perspective. *Issues in Child Abuse Allegations, 8,* 72-78.

van der Kolk, B. A., Weisaeth, L., & van der Hart, O. (1996). History of trauma in psychiatry. In B. A. van der Kolk, A. C. McFarlane, & L. Weisaeth (Eds.), *Traumatic stress: The effects of overwhelming experience on mind, body, and society* (pp. 47-74). New York: Guilford.

Walker, L. E. A. (1979). *The battered woman.* New York: Harper & Row.

Walker, W. D., Rowe, R. C., & Quinsey, V. L. (1993). Authoritarianism and sexual aggression. *Journal of Personality and Social Psychology, 65,* 1036-1045.

Westerlund, E. (1992). *Women's sexuality after childhood incest.* New York: W. W. Norton.

Index

About the Editors

Linda M. Williams, Ph.D., is Director of Research at the Stone Center, Wellesley Centers for Women, at Wellesley College, Wellesley, Massachusetts, and is Research Associate Professor at the Family Research Laboratory, University of New Hampshire, Durham. A sociologist who received her doctorate from the University of Pennsylvania in 1979, she has conducted research on family violence and sexual assault for 25 years. She has authored three books and many articles on sexual abuse, including *Nursery Crimes: Sexual Abuse in Day Care* (1988) and *The Aftermath of Rape* (1979). She has directed research on family violence sex offenders and the consequences of child abuse. She is principal investigator on grants from the National Center on Child Abuse and Neglect and the U.S. Department of the Navy. She has directed research funded by the National Institute of Mental Health, the U.S. Justice Department, and private foundations. In 1995-1996, she served as President of the American Professional Society on the Abuse of Children.

Victoria L. Banyard, Ph.D., is Assistant Professor in the Psychology Department at the University of New Hampshire. She earned her doctorate in clinical psychology from the University of Michigan and has worked as a postdoctoral fellow at the Family Research Laboratory at the University of New Hampshire. Her research interests center on the long-term consequences of traumatic stress, and she has done work on family coping with homelessness and adjustment of adult survivors of child sexual abuse.

About the Contributors

Mary W. Armsworth, Ed.D., is Associate Professor in the Department of Educational Psychology at the University of Houston, Texas, where she teaches in the Counseling Psychology Program. She received her doctorate from the University of Cincinnati. She has developed a research and teaching specialty in the effects of trauma on human development, and authored and has taught a doctoral seminar on the psychology of trauma and victimization for the past 13 years, with an emphasis on using theory to guide interventions with various traumatized populations. She has conducted research projects examining adult attachment patterns in mother-child dyads, the role of trauma in ego development, disclosure dilemmas in abuse cases, self-mutilation and dissociative defenses related to early trauma, and intergenerational aspects of trauma related to parenting. She currently serves as Cochair of the Intergenerational Aspects of Trauma special interest group of the International Society for Traumatic Stress Studies. She has conducted many training seminars and workshops for practitioners who work with traumatized children and adults and is a frequent media speaker and consultant in the area of coping with trauma and loss. She maintains a part-time private practice as a licensed psychologist specializing in clinical work with individuals who have experienced psychologically traumatic events.

Anait G. Azarian, Ph.D., BCETS, is a Clinical Psychologist at Bradley Hospital and a Visiting Professor of Child Development at Brown University. She is a board certified expert in traumatic stress, American Academy of Experts in Traumatic Stress. In 1989, she helped found and direct the Children's Psychotherapy Center in Armenia. The multifaceted treatment of children with PTSD symptoms that she developed has been disseminated internationally through her articles, documentary films, and presentations and workshops in Europe and the United States.

Andrew Baum, Ph.D., received his B.S. in psychology from the University of Pittsburgh in 1970 and his doctoral degree from the State University of New York at Stony Brook in 1974. He is currently director of Behavioral Medicine and Oncology in the University of Pittsburgh Cancer Institute, and Professor of Psychiatry and Psychology at the University of Pittsburgh. He has studied chronic stress and long-term consequences of traumatic or persistent stressors since 1972 and has focused specifically on mental health and psychological and physical symptoms of disasters and motor vehicle accidents. He also studies the effects of stress on immune system activity and psychosocial and biobehavioral aspects of cancer.

Iris Bell, M.D., is Associate Professor of Psychiatry and Psychology at the University of Arizona and the Tucson Veterans Administration Medical Center. Her research interests focus on physiological responses to environmental stressors.

Lucy Berliner, M.S.W., is the Research Director for Harborview Center for Sexual Assault and Traumatic Stress, and Clinical Associate Professor at the University of Washington School of Social Work. Her professional activities include clinical practice with child and adult trauma victims, research on the impact of trauma and the effectiveness of clinical and societal interventions, and participation in local and national social policy initiatives to promote the interests of trauma victims. She has produced numerous journal articles, book chapters, and edited books on these topics, and currently serves on the editorial boards of the *Journal of Interpersonal Violence, Child Abuse & Neglect, Child Maltreatment,* and *Sexual Abuse: A Journal of Research and Treatment.*

J. Douglas Bremner, M.D., is Director of the Yale Psychiatric Institute Trauma Assessment Unit, a research clinic for women with sexual abuse-related PTSD, and Assistant Professor of Diagnostic Radiology and Psychiatry at Yale University School of Medicine. He is also a Research Associate-Staff Nuclear Medicine Physician at the Yale/VA PET Center, and a VA Career Awardee performing imaging research with PET and MRI in PTSD. His current research uses brain-imaging and neuroendocrine measures.

Timothy D. Brewerton, M.D., is currently Professor of Psychiatry and Behavioral Sciences, and Director of the Eating Disorders Program, at the Institute of Psychiatry, Medical University of South Carolina, in Charleston. He also serves

as Medical Consultant at the National Crime Victims Research and Treatment Center at MUSC. He earned his medical degree from Tulane University School of Medicine, New Orleans, and has held postgraduate fellowships at the National Institute of Mental Health (1984-1987) and at MUSC in child and adolescent psychiatry (1994-1996). He is board certified in adult psychiatry as well as child and adolescent psychiatry. He has published and lectured widely on various aspects of eating and eating-related disorders, most recently focusing on the role of victimization in the etiology and maintenance of eating disorders. He serves on the board of directors of the American Academy of Clinical Psychiatrists and the editorial boards of the *Annals of Clinical Psychiatry* and *Eating Disorders: The Journal of Treatment and Prevention,* and is also a referee for many more scientific journals in psychiatry. His honors include listings in *The Best Doctors in America,* South and Southeast region; *Who's Who in Medicine and Healthcare;* and *Who's Who in Science and Engineering.*

John Briere, Ph.D., is Associate Professor in the Departments of Psychiatry and Psychology at the University of Southern California School of Medicine, and a Clinical Psychologist in the Division of Emergency Psychiatry of L.A. County-USC Medical Center. He is also a fellow of the American Psychological Association and a member of the board of directors of the International Society for Traumatic Stress Studies and the Advisory Board of the American Professional Society on the Abuse of Children. He is the author of many research papers, chapters, and books in the areas of child abuse, psychological trauma, and interpersonal violence. His recent books include *Psychological Assessment of Adult Posttraumatic States* (1997), *Therapy for Adults Molested as Children: Beyond Survival* (second edition, 1996), and *Child Abuse Trauma: Theory and Treatment of the Lasting Effects* (1992). He is also coeditor of *The APSAC Handbook on Child Maltreatment* (1996) and author of two standardized psychological tests: the *Trauma Symptom Inventory* and the *Trauma Symptom Checklist for Children.* He provides consultation on clinical and forensic issues to various groups and agencies, and is a frequent workshop presenter.

Gordon A. Bush, Ph.D., is a clinical psychologist in private practice in Houston, Texas. His areas of specialization include both long- and short-term psychotherapy with adults and adolescents on both individual and family bases. He is interested in working with disturbances in personality and attachment arising from traumatic experiences that have occurred during adulthood as well as in early development. He received his doctorate from Ohio State University in 1988 and completed an internship at the Baylor College of Medicine and a postdoctoral fellowship at the University of Texas Mental Sciences Institute, both of which are in Houston. In addition to his private practice, he is an adjunct clinical faculty member at Baylor.

Jon R. Conte, Ph.D., is currently a Professor in the School of Social Work at the University of Washington, where he teaches courses on various aspects of clinical social work, interpersonal violence, and adult psychopathology. He is editor of the *Journal of Interpersonal Violence* and serves on the editorial boards of the *Journal of Child Sexual Abuse* and *Child Abuse & Neglect.* A past president of the American Professional Society on the Abuse of Children, he is currently on the Board of Councillors of the International Society for the Prevention of Child Abuse and Neglect. He maintains a private practice in Bellevue, Washington, where he works with individual children, teens, and adults, and in forensic mental health.

Juanita V. Copley, Ph.D., is an Associate Professor at the University of Houston. She holds an appointment in the Curriculum and Instruction Department and is the Program Chair of the early childhood area. Her research interests involve the cognitive development of young children, especially in the area of mathematics, inclusion programs, and effective staff development. She is an author in the 1998 national mathematics series MathCentral, editor of the 1999 National Council of Teachers of Mathematics volume *Mathematics in the Early Years,* and author and coauthor of numerous

journal articles concerning the teaching of mathematics. She has presented at the international and national levels, most notably in Indonesia, where she helped develop the primary mathematics program for that country.

Bonnie S. Dansky, Ph.D., is Assistant Professor of Psychology and staff psychologist at the National Crime Victims Research and Treatment Center and the Center for Drug and Alcohol Programs in the Department of Psychiatry and Behavioral Sciences of the Medical University of South Carolina in Charleston.

Suzanne L. Davis is a doctoral candidate in social psychology at the University of Illinois at Chicago. She received her B.A. from Purdue University (1992) and her M.A. from the University of Illinois at Chicago (1995). She has conducted research on children's eyewitness testimony, jurors' perceptions of child abuse allegations, and clinicians' and laypersons' perceptions of recovered memory allegations. Her research has been funded by Sigma Xi, the American Psychological Foundation, the American Psychology-Law Society, and the Society for the Psychological Study of Social Issues. She is a member of the student section of the *Law and Human Behavior* editorial board.

Nancy H. DeCourville, Ph.D., is Associate Professor of Psychology at Brock University in St. Catherine's, Ontario, where she teaches courses in the psychology of women, research design, and statistics, and is conducting research on employment and underemployment among young adults.

Joyce Sese Dorado, Ph.D., is a clinical psychologist whose work focuses on the intersection between psychology and law as it pertains to women and children who are victims of violence. She earned her doctoral degree from the University of Michigan. Formerly a graduate research fellow for the National Center on Child Abuse and Neglect, she is interested in integrating her research and clinical work to help make the forensic investigation and judicial processes more sensitive to the needs of women and children and to provide training and consultation to professionals in the legal system involved in cases of violence against women and children.

Robert C. Drugan, Ph.D., is Associate Professor of Psychology at the University of New Hampshire. He has also served as an Assistant Professor of Psychology at Brown University and as a postdoctoral fellow in the Clinical Neuroscience Branch of the National Institute of Mental Health. He earned his doctoral degree from the University of Colorado, Boulder. His research examines the neurochemical and behavioral correlates of stress and coping. His work is especially concerned with the alterations in the benzodiazepine/GABA receptor complex in the brain, which may be an important site in determining stress vulnerability versus stress resilience. He has been the recipient of an Alfred P. Sloan Research Fellowship and has published more than 50 scientific articles and chapters in the field of behavioral neuropharmacology.

Mitchell L. Eisen is Assistant Professor of Psychology at the California State University, Los Angeles. He received his Ph.D. from the University of Miami and his M.A. from the University of Chicago. Prior to his current appointment, he served as Director of Research for the Under the Rainbow Program at Mt. Sinai Hospital in Chicago, where he also worked as a clinical psychologist specializing in the assessment and treatment of maltreated and otherwise traumatized children.

Brigette A. Erwin, B.A., contributed to the chapter she coauthored for this volume while working as a research technician at the National Center for PTSD. She is currently enrolled in a psychology doctoral program at Temple University in Philadelphia.

Kathryn M. Feltey, Ph.D., is Associate Professor of Sociology and Director of Women's Studies at the University of Akron. Her research focuses on the life experiences of homeless women and on women who have been both victims and perpetrators of violence in family relationships. Recently, she has been conducting focus group research on citizen participation at

the local community level. She teaches courses in family violence, social inequality, and deviant behavior.

Aurelio José Figueredo, Ph.D., is Associate Professor of Psychology at the University of Arizona, where he is also Director of the new graduate program in ethology and evolutionary psychology.

Lisa M. Fisher, Ph.D., is Associate Director of Clinical Services at the Behavioral Sciences Division of the National Center for PTSD. She served as a collaborator in the research presented in her chapter in this volume, following up veterans with PTSD at the Boston Veterans Administration Medical Center.

Corinne E. Frantz, Ph.D., is in full-time private practice in Springfield, New Jersey, specializing in neuropsychological evaluation of children and adults, psychotherapeutic treatment of brain-injured patients, and psychoanalytic psychotherapy. She has been a contributing faculty member in the Graduate School of Applied and Professional Psychology for the past 16 years, teaching a course on introduction to neuropsychology. She has held numerous adjunct faculty positions at various universities, including Adelphi University, Seton Hall University, and the University of Houston, where she has assisted students with their dissertations. For many years, she was Program Director of the Neuropsychiatric Evaluation Unit and Director of Neuropsychology at Fair Oaks Hospital in Summit, New Jersey. She has given presentations in the field of neuropsychology, and has published in the fields of neuropsychology and projective assessment.

Carolyn Gareau recently received an honors B.A. in psychology and is currently negotiating reality beyond the academy.

Gail S. Goodman, Ph.D., is Professor of Psychology at the University of California, Davis. She has served on the faculties of the University of Denver and the State University of New York at Buffalo. The recipient of numerous grants and awards, she publishes widely and has been the president of two divisions of the American Psychological Association (Division 41/American Psychology-Law Society, and Division 37/ Child, Youth, and Family Services). She received her Ph.D. in developmental psychology from the University of California, Los Angeles, in 1977. Her research focuses on memory development, children's eyewitness memory, and child abuse.

Mary R. Harvey, Ph.D., is a clinical and community psychologist, Assistant Clinical Professor of Psychology in the Department of Psychiatry at Harvard Medical School, and the founding Director of the Cambridge Hospital Victims of Violence program. She is coauthor, with Mary Koss, of *The Rape Victim: Clinical and Community Interventions* (1991).

Wendy E. Hovdestad, M.A., is a doctoral candidate in the Department of Psychology at Carleton University. Her research interests are in the areas of women's resilience and coping with child abuse, and the delayed memory debate.

Ira E. Hyman, Jr., received his B.A. from Duke University and his Ph.D. in cognitive and developmental psychology from Emory University. He is Associate Professor at Western Washington University in Bellingham, Washington. He conducts research on human memory, and his recent work has focused on false childhood memories, memory for phobia onset, autobiographical memory, and remembering in differing social contexts. He teaches courses in human cognition, research design, and statistics.

Danny G. Kaloupek, Ph.D., is Deputy Director of the Behavioral Sciences Division of the National Center for PTSD. He served as a collaborator in the research presented in his chapter in this volume, following up veterans with PTSD at the Boston Veterans Administration Medical Center.

Terence M. Keane, Ph.D., is Director of the Behavioral Sciences Division of the National Center for PTSD. He served as a collaborator in the research presented in his chapter in this volume,

following up veterans with PTSD at the Boston Veterans Administration Medical Center.

Dean G. Kilpatrick, Ph.D., is Professor of Psychology at the Medical University of South Carolina and Director of the National Crime Victims Research and Treatment Center in the Department of Psychiatry and Behavioral Sciences at MUSC.

Erica E. Kleinknecht received her B.A. and M.S. in general psychology from Western Washington University. She is currently working toward a Ph.D. in developmental psychology at the University of Arkansas. Her research has focused on autobiographical memory and memory for phobia onset. Currently, she is concerned with preschoolers' cognitive development in two areas: the cognitive skills necessary for developing autobiographical memories and the ability to make appropriate inductive inferences from human social categories and novel object categories.

Richard P. Kluft, M.D., is Clinical Professor of Psychiatry at Temple University School of Medicine and practices psychiatry and psychoanalysis in Bala Cynwyd, Pennsylvania. He is founding editor in chief of *Dissociation* and advisory editor of the *American Journal of Clinical Hypnosis*. His edited books include *Childhood Antecedents of Multiple Personality, Treatment of Victims of Sexual Abuse,* and *Incest-Related Syndromes of Adult Psychopathology*. He has served as President of the International Society for the Study of Dissociation and of the American Society of Clinical Hypnosis. He has received awards for his work from several scientific societies.

Mary P. Koss, Ph.D., is Professor of Public Health, Psychiatry, and Psychology in the Arizona Prevention Center at the University of Arizona College of Medicine in Tucson. She is the co-chair of the APA Task Force on Violence Against Women, which in 1994 published *No Safe Haven: Male Violence Against Women at Home at Work and in the Community,* winner of the Washington Educational Press award for the outstanding book on a social concern in 1994.

Dr. Koss is on the national faculty of the Women's Veteran's Health Programs. She has served on the National Research Council Panel on Violence Against Women. Her national study of college students' experiences with sexual aggression and victimization was the subject of the book *I Never Called it Rape: The Ms. Guide to Recognizing, Surviving, and Fighting Date and Acquaintance Rape,* published in its second edition in 1994. She is co-author of the book *The Rape Victim: Clinical and Community Interventions,* and is Associate Editor of *Violence and Victims,* as well as a member of the editorial boards of several journals. She is a recipient of a Research Scientist Development Award from the National Institute of Mental Health.

Wilma Koutstaal received her Ph.D. in psychology from Harvard University in 1996. Her interests in experimental cognitive psychology have focused on factors that affect the accessibility and accuracy of memory, including the effects of intentional or "directed" forgetting, postevent review or "retrieval practice," and memory errors due to normal aging. She has also published papers on the history of automatic writing, statistical methods, ethics and memory, and aesthetics. She is currently a postdoctoral fellow in the Department of Psychology at Harvard University.

Connie M. Kristiansen, Ph.D., is Associate Professor of Psychology at Carleton University in Ottawa, Ontario, Canada, where she teaches courses on family violence, the psychology of women, and research design and statistics. Her current research concerns violence toward women and children, and the nature of traumatic memory.

Lewis P. Lipsitt, Ph.D., is Professor Emeritus of Psychology, Medical Science, and Human Development at Brown University. He is a recipient of the Nicholas Hobbs Award from the APA (1990) and the Lifetime Achievement Mentor Award from AAAS (1994), and has served as President of the Eastern Psychological Association (1994), as the APA's Executive Director for Science, and as Founding Director of

Brown's Child Study Center (1967-1991). Founding coeditor of *Advances in Child Development and Behavior* and founding editor of *Infant Behavior and Development,* he is currently coeditor of *Advances in Infancy Research* and the *Brown University Child & Adolescents Behavior Letter.*

Judy L. Martin, Ph.D., is a Lecturer in Behavioral Science at the Otago Medical School in Dunedin, New Zealand. She has been involved since 1988 with the Otago Women's Health Survey, a large community study on the prevalence and impact of child sexual abuse in adult women. Her research focuses on the methodology of retrospective research on abuse.

Madelyn Miller, C.S.W., A.C.S.W., is Adjunct Assistant Professor at Shirley M. Ehrenkranz School of Social Work, New York University, where she teaches a clinical practice course on treatment with adult survivors of childhood sexual abuse. She is also a psychotherapist in private practice, specializing in individual and group treatment with adult survivors of incest trauma, and provides clinical supervision, training, and consultation to colleagues working broadly with trauma survivors. She offers workshops, seminars, and presentations on treatment and the treatment relationship in the context of trauma and dissociative adaptations. She gives attention in her work to attachment and loss issues, developmental considerations, and understanding adults' childhood experience of trauma. Her writings include a focus on the complex intersection of gender, sociocultural context, and trauma. Her curriculum development for academic, institute, and continuing education settings incorporates her concern for the experience and process of the student of traumatic stress studies as much as it reflects her concern for the clinician's experience of vicarious traumatization. She is an active member of the Curriculum and Education Committee of the International Society of Traumatic Stress Studies, and is committed to the development of trauma curricula for professional schools, postmaster's and postdoctoral education, and intra/interdisciplinary exchange and study.

Thomas W. Miller, Ph.D., A.B.P.P., is Professor in the Department of Psychiatry, University of Kentucky College of Medicine, and the Department of Psychology at Murray State University. He is a diplomate of the American Board of Professional Psychology in clinical psychology and a fellow of the APA. He is widely published in professional journals and is an editor of the Stress & Health monograph series. His main area of research is the impact of stressful life events on children, adolescents, and adults.

Jennifer Mittleholt recently received an honors B.A. in psychology and is currently negotiating reality beyond the academy.

Eleanor M. Morris, B.A., is a researcher in the Department of Psychological Medicine at the University of Otago, New Zealand. She coordinates the Otago Women's Health Survey Study of Child Sexual Abuse. Her professional background includes extensive experience in social policy.

Elana Newman, Ph.D., collaborated in the research reported in her coauthored chapter in this volume while she was a postdoctoral fellow at the Behavioral Sciences Division of the National Center for PTSD. She is currently an Assistant Professor in the Department of Psychology at the University of Tulsa in Oklahoma.

Barbara L. Niles, Ph.D., is a staff psychologist in the Behavioral Sciences Division of the National Center for PTSD at the Boston Veterans Administration Medical Center and an Instructor in the Department of Psychiatry at Tufts University School of Medicine. She received her Ph.D. in clinical psychology from Rutgers, the State University of New Jersey, in 1993. The emphasis of her clinical work and research has been in the area of combat-related posttraumatic stress disorder in veterans. Her recent work has been focused on the longitudinal course of this often chronic disorder.

Pallavi Nishith, Ph.D., is Assistant Research Professor of Psychology in the Center for Trauma Recovery at the University of Missouri at St. Louis. She is a project director on a National Institute of Mental Health-funded grant looking at treatment outcome processes in female sexual assault victims diagnosed with posttraumatic stress disorder. She is also assisting with the implementation of an NIMH-funded research study looking at the etiology of PTSD in victims of domestic violence. She received her B.A. and M.A. from the University of Lucknow, India, in 1986, and her Ph.D. from Washington State University in 1993. She completed her internship at the Eastern Pennsylvania Psychiatric Institute, Medical College of Pennsylvania, and then proceeded to complete her postdoctoral fellowship at the Department of Psychiatry, University of Pennsylvania. During her training, she received advanced research and clinical training in the assessment and treatment of adult victims of sexual assault. Her current research and clinical interests include assessment and treatment of victims of sexual assault, etiological factors related to the development of posttraumatic stress disorder, the role of dissociative processes and substance use in the maintenance of PTSD, and the impact of PTSD symptomatology on sleep and memory functioning. She has published and presented a number of papers in the area of sexual assault and PTSD.

Kenneth A. Norman is a doctoral student in the Cognition, Brain, and Behavior Program in the Harvard University Psychology Department. He received his bachelor's degree in symbolic systems from Stanford University in 1993. His research involves using computational modeling and testing of normal elderly, young adults, and memory-impaired stroke patients to investigate how different brain structures (e.g., the hippocampus, prefrontal cortex) implement different facets of episodic memory.

Patrick M. O'Neil, Ph.D., is Professor of Psychology and Director of the Weight Management Center in the Department of Psychiatry and Behavioral Sciences of the Medical University of South Carolina in Charleston.

Laura K. Palmer, Ph.D., is a licensed psychologist and Assistant Professor in the Counseling Psychology Program at Seton Hall University. She received her Ph.D. from the University of Houston in 1995 with a major in counseling psychology. She completed an internship at Children's Hospital/Judge Baker Children's Center in Boston, followed by a 1-year fellowship in pediatric neuropsychology at Children's Specialized Hospital in Mountainside, New Jersey. She most recently completed a 1-year postdoctoral fellowship in neuropsychology at the Epilepsy Center of the Hospital for Joint Disease of the New York University Medical School. She currently holds a clinical affiliation with the Children's Hospital of New Jersey. She has worked in the field of pediatric mental health services since 1980, and her many years of direct service with children who have experienced various forms of emotional and physical trauma have fostered her research activities in the investigation of emotional and neurocognitive sequelae of psychological trauma. She has presented nationally and internationally on her research. She also has a long-standing commitment to training and supervision of students.

Katherine Perrott is a graduate in anthropology and has carried out qualitative research in aboriginal issues and in child sexual abuse in Australia and New Zealand, respectively. She is currently involved in initiatives in aboriginal land rights and permaculture in Australia.

Craig C. Piers, Ph.D., is Assistant Director of Admissions and a staff psychologist at the Austen Riggs Center in Stockbridge, Massachusetts. He is also in private practice in Stockbridge. He received his doctorate in clinical psychology from the Graduate Faculty, New School for Social Research, in New York City. He completed predoctoral training at Dartmouth Medical School and a postdoctoral fellowship at the Erik H. Erikson Institute for Education and Research at the Austen Riggs Center.

Jianjian Qin received his M.A. in experimental psychology from East China Normal University, and he is currently an advanced doctoral student in cognitive psychology at the University of California, Davis. His research interests include adults' and children's eyewitness memory, suggestibility, and false event memory.

Patricia A. Resick, Ph.D., received her doctorate in clinical psychology from the University of Georgia in 1976. She joined the faculty of the University of Missouri at St. Louis in 1981. She is currently Professor of Psychology and Director of the Center for Trauma Recovery. She has received grants from the National Institute of Mental Health and the National Institute of Justice to conduct several research projects, two of which address variables affecting recovery from rape or domestic violence; a third project involves conducting a treatment trial of cognitive processing therapy for rape victims with PTSD. She has published one book and 70 scientific articles and book chapters. She has served on the board of the Association for the Advancement of Behavior Therapy and is now on the board of the International Society for Traumatic Stress Studies. She works actively with community agencies in St. Louis that assist victims of crime. In 1988, she was the recipient of an award from the National Association of Victim Assistance for outstanding research contributions to the victims assistance field. In 1995, she received the Chancellor's Award for Excellence in Research from the University of Missouri at St. Louis.

Sarah E. Romans, M.D., is Professor and Head of the Department of Psychological Medicine, Dunedin Clinical School of Medicine, University of Otago, and a New Zealand-born and -trained psychiatrist. Her research interests are in the general fields of women's mental health and mood disorders. As a social psychiatrist, she has considered and written about social networks, abuse experiences (particularly child sexual abuse), and demographic factors such as parenthood and employment, exploring each of these topics within the context of their effects on women's vulnerability to depression and anxiety. She is a founder and codirector of a clinic for people with bipolar affective disorder, which provides a resource for a number of social and genetic studies of this baffling condition. She is currently working on projects to assess the relationship between physical assault and symptoms of unknown etiology in general practice, the knowledge and skills of general practitioners in recognition of psychiatric disorders, the neuroendocrinological consequences of significant child sexual abuse in women, and the use of telepsychiatry in modern psychiatric practice. She teaches both undergraduate- and postgraduate-level courses in general psychiatry topics, women's psychological issues, mood disorders, professional relationships, psychotherapies, and behavioral science topics. She is currently involved in the development of new community teaching opportunities for future medical education.

Daniel L. Schacter received his Ph.D. from the University of Toronto in 1981. He remained at Toronto for the next 6 years, as Director of the Unit for Memory Disorders and Assistant Professor of Psychology. In 1987, he moved to the University of Arizona as an Associate Professor, and was promoted to Professor in 1989. He accepted a position as Professor of Psychology at Harvard University in 1991, and became Department Chair in 1995. His research has focused on psychological and biological aspects of human memory and amnesia, with a particular emphasis on the distinction between implicit and explicit memory and, more recently, on brain mechanisms of memory distortion. He has received the Distinguished Award for an Early Career Contribution to Psychology from the American Psychological Association and the Troland Research Award from the National Academy of Sciences. He has written two books, edited four volumes, and published more than 150 scientific articles and chapters. Much of his work is summarized in his recent book, *Searching for Memory: The Brain, the Mind, and the Past* (1996), which was selected by the *New York Times Book Review* as a Notable Book of the Year for 1996.

Jonathan W. Schooler is Associate Professor of Psychology at the University of Pittsburgh and a Research Scientist at the University of Pittsburgh's Learning Research and Development Center. He received his B.A. from Hamilton college and his M.S. and Ph.D. from the University of Washington. His research interests span many areas of cognition, as well as social and clinical psychology. One of his long-standing interests is understanding the mechanisms that lead to memory distortions in naturalistic settings, including examining the impact of postevent suggestion on event memories and assessing the disruptive consequences of verbalizing nonverbal memories. Recently, he has applied this interest to evaluating the accuracies and inaccuracies of discovered memories of abuse. His other interests include creativity, problem solving, decision making, and the relationship between language and thought. He has been an author on more than 50 publications and recently coauthored a book titled *Scientific Approaches to Consciousness*. He serves on the editorial board of *Memory and Cognition* and *Consciousness and Cognition* and is an associate editor of *Cognitive Technology*.

Tonya Y. Schooler, Ph.D., received her B.S. in psychology from the University of Washington in 1987 and her doctoral degree from the University of Pittsburgh in 1994. She is currently a Research Principal at the University of Pittsburgh Cancer Institute. Her research interests include cognitive aspects of traumatic experience, including the role of cued and uncued intrusive thoughts in maintaining chronic stress. Her ongoing projects include investigation into petrochemical workers' "flashbulb" memories of workplace explosions.

Judith A. Sheiman is Assistant Professor at Kutztown University in Kutztown, Pennsylvania. She received her Ph.D. in clinical psychology from Purdue University and her J.D. from Boston University Law School. Her research interests include sexual abuse and trauma survivors, especially the area of memories, and psychology and the legal system.

Vitali G. Skriptchenko-Gregorian, Ph.D., is a Visiting Professor of Child Development at Brown University Center for the Study of Human Development. In 1989, he cofounded the Children's Psychotherapy Center in Armenia. His professional interests encompass issues in psychology, medicine, education, artificial intelligence, and engineering.

Paul Swank, Ph.D., is a Professor in the Educational Psychology Department at the University of Houston. He teaches courses in quantitative methods, research design, and psychometric scaling, with particular emphasis on linear models, mixed models for repeated measures, and structural equation modeling and the application of these approaches to research in the behavioral, social, and biomedical sciences. As a consulting statistician and co-principal investigator on numerous projects, both federally funded and otherwise, he has published extensively in the professional literature.

Melinda Tharan is a research specialist in the Arizona Prevention Center at the University of Arizona College of Medicine in Tucson.

Shannon Tromp earned her Ph.D. in clinical psychology from the University of Arizona.

Mary H. Uhlmansiek has a B.A. in psychology from the University of Missouri at St. Louis. She was working as a Research Assistant on the NIMH project "Cognitive Processes in PTSD: Treatment" (awarded to Dr. Patricia A. Resick) during the time the study she and her coauthors report on in this volume was implemented. Currently, she is employed as a Research Assistant and Database Manager at the St. Louis Metropolitan Police Department.

Susan Warner is a graduate student in the Sociology Program at the University of Akron in Akron, Ohio. Her research interests center on women who have recovered memories of childhood incest and the controversy surrounding

this topic in the professional community. Her master's thesis was on the influence of childhood socialization on adolescent social behavior. Her recent work includes research on women in transitional housing programs and evaluation of a sexual abuse educational program in a public school system.

Terri L. Weaver, Ph.D., is Assistant Research Professor of Psychology in the Center for Trauma Recovery at the University of Missouri at St. Louis. She is currently assisting with the implementation of two NIMH-funded research studies targeting assessment and treatment of acute rape victims. Recently, she received a subcontract from the U.S. Air Force to conduct a meta-analytic review on the domestic violence literature, which she completed in December 1996. She received her B.S. from the University of Florida in 1985 and her Ph.D. from Virginia Polytechnic Institute and State University in 1994. She completed an NIMH-funded predoctoral and postdoctoral fellowship at the National Crime Victims Research and Treatment Center at the Medical University of South Carolina, where she received advanced research and clinical training in the assessment and treatment of victims of interpersonal violence. She has worked in the field of interpersonal violence for 7 years, beginning with clinical work within shelters for battered women. Currently, her research and clinical interests include assessment and treatment of victims of domestic violence, etiological factors related to the development of posttraumatic stress disorder, factors related to multiple victimization, and crime victims program and policy development. She has served as an ad hoc reviewer for a number of professional journals and has published and presented many papers in the area of interpersonal violence.